8414

CALIFORNIA CRIMINAL LAW
AND PROCEDURE

The West Legal Studies Series

Your options keep growing with West Legal Studies

Each year our list continues to offer you more options for every area of the law to meet your course or on-the-job reference requirements. We now have over 140 titles from which to choose in the following areas:

Administrative Law	Family Law
Alternative Dispute Resolution	Federal Taxation
Bankruptcy	Intellectual Property
Business Organizations/Corporations	Introduction to Law
Civil Litigation and Procedure	Introduction to Paralegalism
CLA Exam Preparation	Law Office Management
Client Accounting	Law Office Procedures
Computer in the Law Office	Legal Research, Writing, and Analysis
Constitutional Law	Legal Terminology
Contract Law	Paralegal Employment
Criminal Law and Procedure	Real Estate Law
Document Preparation	Reference Materials
Environmental Law	Torts and Personal Injury Law
Ethics	Will, Trusts, and Estate Administration

You will find unparalleled, practical support

Each text is augmented by instructor and student supplements to ensure the best learning experience possible. We also offer custom publishing and other benefits such as West's Student Achievement Award. In addition, our sales representatives are ready to provide you with dependable service.

We want to hear from you

Our best contributions for improving the quality of our books and instructional materials is feedback from the people who use them. If you have a question, concern, or observation about any of our materials, or you have a product proposal or manuscript, we want to hear from you. Please contact your local representative or write us at the following address:

West Legal Studies, 3 Columbia Circle, P.O. Box 15015, Albany, NY 12212-5015

For additional information point your browser at
www.westlegalstudies.com

West Legal Studies
an imprint of Delmar Publishers

an International Thomson Publishing company I(T)P®

CALIFORNIA CRIMINAL LAW AND PROCEDURE

William D. Raymond, Jr.
Daniel E. Hall

WEST LEGAL STUDIES

an International Thomson Publishing company I(T)P®

Albany • Bonn • Boston • Cincinnati • Detroit • London • Madrid
Melbourne • Mexico City • Minneapolis/St. Paul • New York • Pacific Grove
Paris • San Francisco • Singapore • Tokyo • Toronto • Washington

NOTICE TO THE READER

Delmar Staff:

Publisher: Susan Simpfenderfer
Acquisitions Editor: Joan Gill
Developmental Editor: Rhonda Dearborn

Production Manager: Wendy Troeger
Production Editor: Laurie A. Boyce
Marketing Manager: Katherine Hans

COPYRIGHT © 1999
By West Legal Studies
an imprint of Delmar Publishers
a division of International Thomson Publishing

The ITP logo is a trademark under license.

Printed in Canada

For more information, contact:

Delmar Publishers
3 Columbia Circle, Box 15015
Albany, New York 12212-5015

International Thomson Publishing Europe
Berkshire House
168-173 High Holborn
London WC1V 7AA
United Kingdom

Nelson ITP, Australia
102 Dodds Street
South Melbourne
Victoria, 3205 Australia

Nelson Canada
1120 Birchmont Road
Scarborough, Ontario
M1K 5G4, Canada

International Thomson Publishing France
Tour Maine-Montparnasse
33 Avenue du Maine
75755 Paris Cedex 15, France

International Thomson Editores
Seneca 53
Colonia Polanco
11560 Mexico D. F. Mexico

International Thomson Publishing GmbH
Königswinterer Strasse 418
53227 Bonn
Germany

International Thomson Publishing Asia
60 Albert Street
#15-01 Albert Complex
Singapore 189969

International Thomson Publishing Japan
Hirakawa-cho Kyowa Building, 3F
2-2-1 Hirakawa-cho, Chiyoda-ku,
Tokyo 102, Japan

ITE Spain/Paraninfo
Calle Magallanes, 25
28015-Madrid, Espana

8 9 10 XXX 06

Library of Congress Cataloging-in-Publication Data

Raymond, William D.
    California criminal law and procedure / William D. Raymond, Jr.,
  Daniel E. Hall.
      p.   cm.
    Includes bibliographical references and index.
    ISBN 0-8273-7940-4
           riminal law—California. 2. Criminal procedure—California.
       tants—United States—Handbooks, manuals, etc.
       l (Daniel E.) II. Title.
      39 1998
     21   98-8348
                                          CIP

CONTENTS

PART II
CRIMINAL PROCEDURE

≡ CHAPTER 17   Trial   410

≡ CHAPTER 18   Judgment and Sentencing   434

≡ CHAPTER 19   Postconviction Remedies   461

≡ Appendices

PREFACE

This text was written to meet the need for a state–law-specific text on the subjects of California criminal law and procedure. Although there is a vast body of literature on federal criminal law and procedure, most activity in these fields is in the state courts, applying state law. Texts of general applicability explaining legal principles common to the various states are useful, but California students studying criminal law and procedure, whether for use in their future careers or simply to learn about the legal environment in which they live, will be better served by a text on California law than by a text of general applicability.

California Criminal Law and Procedure is an adaptation of the second edition of Daniel Hall's very fine work, *Criminal Law and Procedure,* and generally follows the structure of that text. Mr. Hall's material has been retained to the extent that it is applicable to the California legal system. Subjects in Mr. Hall's work that have California-specific counterparts have been rewritten.

This text was written principally for students in paralegal training programs. It contains sufficient depth of information to be used as a text in undergraduate college courses, police academy programs, and other programs at a similar academic level. Because of its depth of coverage, the text is able to reveal California criminal law and procedure in sufficient detail to impart to the student a true understanding of these subjects.

Criminal law and criminal procedure are treated in separate parts of the text. Part I, which comprises Chapters 1 through 11, addresses the subject of substantive criminal law. Chapters 1 and 2 present introductory material on the California and federal legal systems and on the subjects of criminal law and procedure. The materials in these chapters may be omitted if students are already familiar with the structure of the legal system and sources of law. Detailed material on the subject of substantive criminal law is contained in Chapters 3 through 11 and includes: the mental and physical components of crimes (Chapter 3), homicide (Chapter 4), other crimes against the person (Chapter 5), crimes against property (Chapter 6), crimes against public morality and public order (Chapter 7), crimes against the administration of government and against the environment (Chapter 8), parties to crimes and inchoate offenses (Chapter 9), defenses to crimes (Chapter 10), and constitutional limits on the power of government to define and prosecute offenses (Chapter 11).

Part II of the text, consisting of Chapters 12 through 19, addresses the subject of California criminal procedure, and is subdivided into the following chapters: introduction to California criminal procedure and discussion of participants in the criminal process (Chapter 12); the constitutional aspects of criminal procedure (Chapter 13); searches, seizures, and arrests (Chapter 14); interrogation and other law enforcement practices (Chapter 15); the pretrial process (Chapter 16); trial (Chapter 17); judgment and sentencing (Chapter 18); and postconviction remedies (Chapter 19).

California Criminal Law and Procedure contains many case excerpts, primarily from the California appellate courts and the United States Supreme Court. These decisions bring the real matter of the law to the student first-hand, illustrating and amplifying the textual discussions. Students should note, however, that these are heavily edited excerpts; in most instances, citations and footnotes have been omitted for improved utility and comprehensibility. Full citations to the cases from which the excerpts were drawn are given for those wishing to pursue further research.

All statements of California law are fully cited to applicable primary or secondary legal authority, such as statutory law, case law, and the major treatises on California criminal law and procedure. In addition, each text is accompanied by a compact disk containing the entire 1998 California Penal Code and pertinent excerpts from the Business and Professions Code, the Code of Civil Procedure, the Health and Safety Code, the Vehicle Code, the Welfare and Institutions Code, and the California Rules of Court. Through these features, the text provides the student not only with a discussion of California criminal law and procedure, but also with direct exposure to the primary and secondary legal authority underlying the principles discussed.

The extensive citation of legal authority should make the text a valuable research tool, permitting the student to pursue further research by going to the cited sources, both in the academic setting and later while pursuing a legal career. Students should be reminded, however, that any legal material can become outdated; in a nonacademic setting, the most current law should always be consulted.

Several techniques have been employed in the text to reinforce the instructional material presented. Principal among these are the use of hypothetical fact situations to illustrate legal points being made, the inclusion of excerpts from California judicial decisions, and the inclusion at the end of each chapter of a series of review questions and review problems designed to reinforce the main points discussed in the chapter. The Sidebar format used in Daniel Hall's text is continued to provide statistical and other information pertinent to the topics discussed.

Appendices containing the first ten Amendments to the United States Constitution and the Preamble and Article I of the California Constitution are included at the end of the text. The appendices are current as of 1998. An extensive glossary of the terms defined in the text and a comprehensive subject index are included as well.

The text is accompanied by an *Instructor's Guide,* which contains complete answers to the review questions and review problems at the end of the chapters, as well as an extensive and usable test bank.

The author wishes to extend his gratitude to the reviewers whose insightful comments were of great help in revision of the initial manuscript, as well as to all on the Delmar staff who were responsible for seeing this text through to completion.

It is hoped that *California Criminal Law and Procedure* will be a textbook of manageable length and acceptable cost that is sufficiently adaptable that it can be used in a variety of academic programs.

List of Reviewers for *California Criminal Law and Procedure*

Marilyn Garber
California State University Dominguez Hills

Pamela Kleinkauf
San Diego State University

Brian McCully
Fresno City College

Michael T. Quane
De Anza College

Dennis Reid
Cal State Hayward

Richard Shaffran
UCLA Extension Business and Management

Credits and Acknowledgements

24–25, 46, 47, 68, 100, 104, 122–123, 143, 144, 161, 170–171, 189, 225, 239, 241, 249, 302, 306, 307, 320, 327, 329, 330, 339, 341, 350, 386, 400, 411, 421, 427, 428, 436, 448, 450, 462, 475 Reprinted with permission of West Group from Witkin and Epstein, *California Criminal Law, Second Edition.*

117, 118, 133, 135, 139, 142, 143, 144, 146, 147, 150, 167, 168, 171–172, 173, 183–184, 186, 208, 234, 235, 236, 238, 248 CALJIC, Reprinted with permission from West Group.

272 Reprinted with permission of West Group from Witkin, *Summary of California Law, Ninth Edition.*

284–285 Reprinted with permission from the California Peace Officers Association.

285 Reprinted with permission from International Association of Chiefs of Police.

287 Reprinted with permission from the California District Attorney's Association.

291, 473 Reprinted with permission from California Continuing Education of the Bar (CEB).

295 Reprinted with permission from National Association of Legal Assistants, Code of Ethics.

How to Use the Appendix on CD-ROM with This Book

1998 Compact California Penal Code

- There are numerous references made to the 1998 Compact edition of the California Penal Code throughout this text.

- This icon will alert you to full text readings of the applicable sections on the CD-ROM.

- Use the hotlinks in the Table of Contents on the CD-ROM to quickly access specific sections.

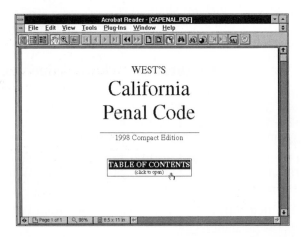

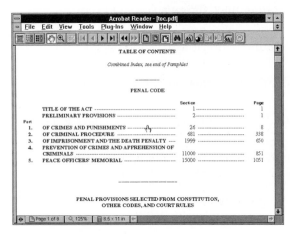

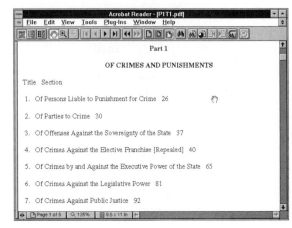

TABLE OF CASES

PART I

CRIMINAL LAW

CHAPTER 1

Introduction to the Legal Systems of the United States and the State of California

OUTLINE

§ 1.1 Federalism

Before one can undertake learning California criminal law and criminal procedure, a basic understanding of the legal system of the United States and the state of California is necessary. This can be a complex task, as criminal law and procedure are significantly influenced by federal and state constitutional law, the common law, and statutory law at both the federal and state levels. It will be easier to understand how these areas of law affect criminal law if we first explore the basic structure of American government.

The United States is divided into two sovereign forms of government—the government of the United States and the governments of the many states. This division of power is commonly known as **federalism**. It is also common to refer to this division as the vertical division of power, as the national government rests above the state governments in hierarchy. The framers of the Constitution of the United States established these two levels of government in an attempt to prevent the centralization of power, that is, too much power being vested in one group. The belief that "absolute power corrupts absolutely" was the catalyst for the division of governmental power.

SIDEBAR

At trial, a *sidebar* is a meeting between the judge and the attorneys, at the judge's bench, outside the hearing of the jury. Sidebars are used to discuss issues that the jury is not permitted to hear. In this text, sidebars will appear periodically. These features contain information relevant to the subject being studied.

In theory, the national government, commonly referred to as the *federal government,* and the state governments each possess authority over citizens, as well as over particular policy areas, free from the interference of the other government (dual sovereignty).

Determining what powers belong to the national government, as opposed to the states, is not always an easy task. The framers of the Constitution intended to establish a limited national government. That is, most governmental powers were to reside in the states, with the national government being limited to the powers expressly delegated to it in the federal Constitution. This principle is found in the Tenth Amendment, which reads, "The powers not delegated to the United States by the Constitution, nor prohibited by it to the States, are reserved to the States respectively, or to the people."

What powers are delegated to the United States by the Constitution? There are several, including, but not limited to the power:

1. To coin money, punish counterfeiters, and fix standards of weights and measures.
2. To establish a post office and post roads.
3. To promote the arts.
4. To punish piracy and other crimes on the high seas.
5. To declare war and raise armies.
6. To conduct diplomacy and foreign affairs.
7. To regulate interstate and foreign commerce.
8. To make laws necessary and proper for carrying into execution other powers expressly granted in the Constitution.

The last two of these powers—the regulation of interstate commerce and the making of all necessary and proper laws—have proven to be significant sources of federal power. Also important is the Supremacy Clause of Article VI, which provides that

> This Constitution, and the Laws of the United States which shall be made in Pursuance thereof; and all Treaties made, or which shall be made, under the Authority of the United States, shall be the supreme Law of the Land; and the Judges in every State shall be bound thereby, any Thing in the Constitution or Laws of any State to the Contrary notwithstanding.

Simply stated, the Supremacy Clause declares national law, if valid, to be a higher form of law than state law. Of course, if the national government attempts to regulate an area belonging to the states, its law is invalid and the state law is controlling. But if the national government possesses **jurisdiction** and a state enacts a conflicting law, the state law is invalid. This is not a common issue in criminal law, because state and federal laws rarely conflict; rather, they are more likely to be parallel or complementary.

The jurisdiction of the federal government and state governments—that is, the power of the federal and state governments—to enact laws addressing particular subjects may be exclusive or concurrent. The term **exclusive jurisdiction** means that the government concerned, federal or state, has the exclusive authority to legislate with respect to a given subject. If the federal government has exclusive jurisdiction to legislate with respect to a particular subject, the states have no power to legislate with respect to that subject. Conversely, if the state governments have exclusive jurisdiction over a particular subject, the federal government may not legislate with respect to it.

Many crimes fall within the **concurrent jurisdiction** of the federal and state governments. This means that both the federal and state governments have the power to proscribe and punish the same acts. Crimes falling within the concurrent jurisdiction of the federal and state governments are those that have elements bringing them within the legislative jurisdiction of each level of government.

An example of a crime falling within the concurrent jurisdiction of the federal and state governments is robbery of a federally insured banking institution. A state may enact laws making it a crime to rob a bank located in the state. The federal government may enact laws making it a crime to rob a bank in which the deposits are insured by the Federal Deposit Insurance Corporation. An individual robbing such a bank would be committing offenses under both state and federal law, and could be prosecuted in the courts of the state, the federal courts, or both. It is not a violation of double jeopardy (discussed in Chapter 11) for an individual to be tried and punished by both federal and state governments, even for the same act.

Keep in mind that the United States Constitution is the highest form of law in the land. It is the national constitution that establishes the structure of our government. You will learn later the various duties of the judicial branch of government. One duty is the interpretation (determining what written law means) of statutes and constitutions. The highest court in the United States is the United States Supreme Court; as such, that Court is the final word on what powers are exclusively federal or state, or concurrently held.

The sphere of federal government power in criminal law has increased dramatically in this century. Largely through use of the federal government's constitutional power to regulate interstate commerce, the United States Congress has enacted a number of criminal laws proscribing as federal crimes certain types of conduct that previously had been within the exclusive legislative jurisdiction of the states. Each of these statutes defines the crime involved in terms of the federal commerce power. For example, the Lindbergh Law, at 18 U.S.C. § 1201, makes kidnapping a federal crime if interstate transportation of the victim occurs. The federal Civil Rights Act of 1964, which is a major piece of federal antidiscrimination legislation, is premised on Congress's power to regulate interstate commerce. The Act prescribes criminal and civil penalties for discriminatory practices in places of public accommodation on the basis of race, color, religion, or national origin, if the place of public accommodation uses products that have moved in interstate commerce or otherwise affects interstate commerce.

Through its use of the federal interstate commerce power to define crimes, Congress has enabled the federal government to regulate activities that would otherwise be considered purely intrastate in character and, thus, within the exclusive jurisdiction of the states. The use of the commerce power has significantly expanded the scope of federal criminal law and has added to the list of crimes falling within the concurrent jurisdiction of the federal and state governments.

Regardless of the expansion of federal jurisdiction, most crimes continue to fall within the exclusive jurisdiction of the states. This is because one of the responsibilities of the states is to regulate for the health and safety of its citizens. This is known as the **police power**. Most murders, rapes, and thefts are state-law crimes.

Note that local governments have not been mentioned so far. This is because the Constitution does not recognize the existence of local governments. However, state constitutions and laws establish local forms of government, such as counties, cities, and districts. These local entities are often empowered by state law with limited authority to create criminal law. These laws are usually in the form of ordinances. (Ordinances are discussed in Chapter 2.) For example, the California Constitution, at art. XI, § 7, provides that, "[a] county or city may make and enforce within its limits all local police, sanitary, and other ordinances and regulations not in conflict with general laws."

The result of this division of power is that the states (as well as other jurisdictions, such as the District of Columbia), the federal government, and local governments each have a separate set of criminal laws.

§ 1.2 Separation of Powers

Another principle of governmental structure is known as **separation of powers**. This is the division of governmental power into three branches, the executive, legislative, and judicial, making a horizontal division of power, just as federalism is the vertical division. (See Figure 1-1.) Each branch is delegated certain functions that the other two may not encroach upon. At the federal level, the executive branch consists of the president of the United States, the president's staff, and the various administrative agencies that the president oversees. Generally, it is the duty of the executive branch to carry out programs established through congressional legislation and to otherwise enforce the laws of the national government. In criminal law, the executive branch investigates alleged violations of the law, gathers the evidence necessary to prove that a violation has occurred, and brings violators before the judicial branch for disposition. The president does this through the various federal law enforcement and administrative agencies.

The legislative branch consists of the United States Congress, which creates the laws of the United States. Congressionally created laws are known as **statutes**. Finally, the judicial branch is composed of the various federal courts of the

FIGURE 1-1
Division of governmental power

	LEGISLATIVE BRANCH	EXECUTIVE BRANCH	JUDICIAL BRANCH
The Government of the United States (Federal Government)	United States Congress	President of the United States	Federal courts
State Governments	State legislatures	Governors	State courts

land. That branch is charged with the adjudication of cases involving civil disputes and alleged violations of the criminal laws. A more comprehensive discussion of the judicial branch follows later in this chapter.

In a further attempt to diffuse governmental power, the framers designed a system of checks and balances that prevents any one branch from exclusively controlling a function. Several checks can be found in the Constitution.

For example, Congress is responsible for making the law. This function is checked by the president, who may veto legislation. The president is then checked by Congress, which may override a veto with a two-thirds majority. The president is responsible for conducting foreign affairs and making treaties, and is the Commander-in-Chief of the military. Congress, however, must approve treaties and declare war, and it appropriates funding for and establishes the rules that regulate the military.

Through the power of judicial review, the judiciary may invalidate actions of the president or Congress that violate the Constitution. In contrast, the political branches select federal judges through the nomination (president) and confirmation (Senate) process. Unpopular judicial decisions may be changed either by statute, if the issue is one of statutory interpretation, or by constitutional amendment, if the issue is one of constitutional interpretation.

The United States Constitution does not establish three branches of government for the many states (the United States Constitution only designs the structure of the federal government). All state constitutions are, however, modeled after the federal constitution, albeit in varying forms. The result is a two-tiered system with each tier split into three parts. The California state government, for example, is structured in a manner similar, although not identical, to the federal government, and is composed of executive, legislative, and judicial branches.

The executive branch is headed by the governor, who is the chief executive officer of the state. As in the federal government, the function of the executive branch of the California state government is to administer and enforce state law.

The legislative branch of the California state government, the California State Legislature, is divided into two houses: the Senate and the Assembly. Legislators are elected by district, one member per district. The California Constitution provides for forty Senate districts and eighty Assembly districts. Legislative enactments are called statutes, as they are in the federal government.

The judicial branch of the California state government consists of a multi-tiered court system. The California court system is discussed in greater detail later in this chapter.

The California Constitution provides a system of checks and balances similar to that found in the federal government. The governor is empowered to veto legislation. The legislature may, however, override the governor's veto by a two-thirds vote of both houses. The legislature has statutory influence over the funding, organization, and procedures used by administrative agencies of the executive branch. Also, the legislature has the power to impeach elected officials accused of misconduct in office. The courts, through the power of judicial review, may invalidate actions of the governor, state agencies, or the legislature which violate the federal or state constitutions.

The legislatures are responsible for defining what acts are criminal, what process must be used to assure that a wrongdoer answers for an act, and what punishment should be imposed for the act.

It is the duty of the executive branch to enforce and implement the laws created by the legislature, as well as to enforce the orders of courts. For example, if a state legislature prohibits the sale of alcohol on Sundays, it is the duty of the appropriate state law enforcement agencies, such as the police or alcohol, firearm, and tobacco agents, to investigate suspected violations and take whatever lawful action is necessary to bring violators to justice. Law enforcement, in the criminal law context, is accomplished through law enforcement agencies and prosecutorial agencies. At the federal level, there are many law enforcement agencies. The Federal Bureau of Investigation, Drug Enforcement Administration, United States Marshal Service, and Department of the Treasury are only a few.

In California, the chief law enforcement officer is the attorney general, who heads the state Department of Justice. California has numerous law enforcement agencies, at the state, county, and local levels. Among these agencies are the California Highway Patrol, county sheriffs, local police departments, specialized police forces such as the University of California and California State University police departments, the Department of Fish and Game, Bay Area Rapid Transit (BART) police, park rangers, and numerous governmental agencies the members of which are designated "peace officers" in the California Penal Code.

These and other enforcement agencies are responsible for investigating criminal conduct and for gathering evidence to prove that a criminal violation has occurred. When the law enforcement agency has completed its investigation, the case is turned over to a prosecutor. The prosecutor is the attorney responsible for representing the people. The prosecutor files the formal criminal charge, or conducts a grand jury, and then sees the prosecution through to completion. In the federal system, the prosecutor is called a United States Attorney. In the California system, prosecutors are usually known as district attorneys.

Finally, the judicial branch is charged with the adjudication of criminal cases. The courts become involved after the executive branch has arrested or accused an individual of a crime. This is explored further in the next section of this chapter. Lawyers, legal assistants, and law enforcement officials are likely to have significant contacts with state and federal courts; therefore, it is important to understand the structure of the court system.

§ 1.3 The Structure of the Court System

Within the federal and state judiciaries, a hierarchy of courts exists. All state court systems, as well as the federal court system, have at least two types of courts, trial courts and appellate courts. However, each state is free to structure its judiciary in any manner; hence, significant variation is found in the different court systems.

Trial courts are what most people envision when they think of courts. Trial courts are where a case begins, where witnesses are heard and evidence is presented, often to a jury as well as to a judge. In the federal system, trial courts are known as United States District Courts. The United States is divided up into ninety-four judicial districts, using state boundaries to establish district limits.

Each state constitutes at least one district, although larger states are divided into several districts. For example, Kansas has only one district, and the federal trial court located in Kansas is known as the United States District Court for the District of Kansas. California, in contrast, is made up of four districts, the Northern, Eastern, Central, and Southern Districts of California.

State trial courts are known by various names, such as district, superior, county, and circuit courts. Despite variations in name, these courts are very similar.

In California, there are two types of trial courts: superior courts and municipal courts. Both types of trial courts are state, as opposed to county, courts, although they are physically located within specific counties. The principal trial court in each county is the **superior court**. The correct full title for a superior court is "Superior Court of the State of California for the County of [name of county]." This title reflects the fact that the superior court is a state court, but sits in a particular county. The superior court is a court of general jurisdiction, which means that it is empowered to adjudicate all types of cases, civil and criminal, except as otherwise provided by law. For example, the superior court is precluded by law from adjudicating civil cases in which the amount in controversy is less than $25,000, because such cases are within the exclusive jurisdiction of the municipal court. Similarly, the superior court may not conduct bankruptcy proceedings, because bankruptcy is within the exclusive jurisdiction of the federal courts.

In the area of criminal law, superior courts are responsible for hearing all felony cases. Misdemeanor and infraction cases are within the jurisdiction of the municipal courts. Felonies are the most serious crimes; misdemeanors are crimes that are less serious than felonies, and infractions are the least serious offenses. Section 17 of the California Penal Code defines a **felony** as a crime that is punishable by death or by imprisonment in the state prison. Every other crime is a **misdemeanor**, except offenses that are classified by statute as **infractions**. Misdemeanors are usually punishable by confinement to the county jail and fines. Infractions are not punishable by imprisonment. Conviction of an infraction usually results in imposition of a fine or a sentence to perform community service.

Municipal courts are sometimes referred to as **inferior courts**. The correct full title for a municipal court is "Municipal Court of the State of California for the County of [name of county]." Municipal courts are courts of limited jurisdiction. This means that they may hear only the types of cases specified by law. Municipal courts, for example, are limited to adjudicating civil actions involving amounts in controversy up to $25,000. If a lawsuit involves an amount greater than $25,000, it must be heard in the superior court. Other restrictions on the jurisdiction of the municipal courts have to do with subject matter. Municipal courts may not, for example, hear matters involving family law or probate. In the area of criminal law, municipal courts do not try felony cases. They try all misdemeanors and infractions. They also conduct preliminary hearings in felony cases.

Appellate courts review the decisions and actions of trial courts (or lower appellate courts, as discussed later) for error. These courts do not conduct trials, but review the record from the trial court and examine it for mistakes, known as trial court error. Usually, appellate courts will hear argument from the attorneys involved in the case under review, but witnesses are not heard nor other evidence submitted. After the appellate court has reviewed the record and examined it for error, the court renders an opinion. An appellate court can reverse, affirm, or remand the lower court decision. To *reverse* is to determine that the court below has rendered a wrong decision and to change that decision. When an appellate court *affirms* a lower court, it is approving the decision made and leaving it unchanged.

In some cases an appellate court will remand the case to the lower court. A *remand* is an order that the case be returned to the lower court and that some action be taken by the judge when the case is returned. Often this will involve conducting a new trial. For example, if an appellate court decides that a judge took an action that prevented a criminal defendant from having a fair trial, and the defendant was convicted, an appellate court may reverse the conviction and remand the case to the trial court for a new trial with instructions that the judge not act in a similar manner.

In the federal system and many states, there are two levels of appellate courts, an intermediate and highest level. The intermediate level courts in the federal system are the United States Courts of Appeal.[1] There are eleven judicial circuits in the United States, with one court of appeal in each circuit. Additionally, there is a court of appeal for Washington, D.C. and for the Federal Circuit. Therefore, there are thirteen United States Courts of Appeal in total (see Figure 1-2). Appeals from the district courts are taken to the circuit courts. The highest court in the country is the United States Supreme Court. Appeals from the circuit courts are taken to the Supreme Court. Also, appeals of federal issues from state supreme courts are taken to the United States Supreme Court.

California has a multi-tiered appellate court system. Appeals from the superior courts are heard by the **California Courts of Appeal**. The state is divided geographically into six court of appeal districts, numbered First through Sixth (see Figure 1-3). One court of appeal sits in each district, although the court may have a number of separate locations within its district (which are called *divisions*). The divisions of each court of appeal are numbered. For example, an appeal might be heard by the Court of Appeal for the Second Judicial District, Division 5. Division 5 would be located in a municipality within the geographical jurisdiction of the Court of Appeal for the Second Judicial District. The other divisions would be located in other municipalities within the court's geographical jurisdiction.

Frequently, one party to an appeal remains dissatisfied after determination of the appeal by the court of appeal. In such a case, the party may wish to appeal to the next, and highest, level of the California appellate court system, the **California Supreme Court**. The California Supreme Court consists of six associate justices and a chief justice. Four justices must concur in a judgment. Determinations by the California Supreme Court are the final word in a case in the California court system unless the case involves a question of federal law, in which event further appeal to the United States Supreme Court may be possible.

In both the federal and California judicial systems, a first appeal is an appeal of right. That means that one has a right to appeal, and the appellate court is required to hear the case. However, second appeals are not appeals of right. To have a case heard by the United States Supreme Court, the person appealing must seek **certiorari**, an order from the Supreme Court to the lower court requiring the record to be transmitted to the higher court for review. When certiorari

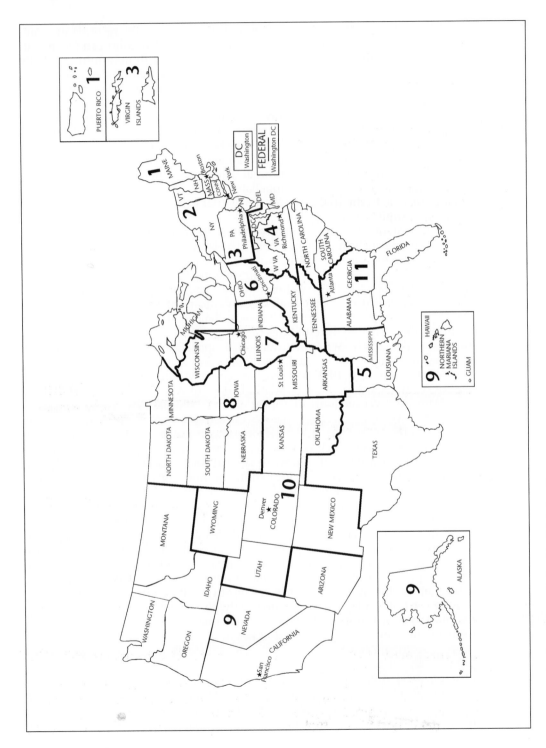

FIGURE 1-2   The thirteen federal judicial circuits

FIGURE 1-3 The six California court of appeal districts

is granted, the United States Supreme Court will hear the appeal, and when certiorari is denied it will not.

Certiorari is granted in only a small number of cases. In recent years, for example, the United States Supreme Court has granted certiorari in approximately 3 percent of the cases appealed. In the California judicial system, review by the supreme court is requested by means of a **petition for review**. Technically, the California Supreme Court grants or denies "review" rather than "certiorari," although, as a practical matter, the procedures are similar. Like the United States Supreme Court, the California Supreme Court grants review in only a small fraction of the cases appealed. In both the federal and California systems, the supreme courts weigh a number of factors when determining whether to grant certiorari or review. Generally, certiorari or review is limited to cases in which an issue of widespread public importance is involved or cases involving issues upon which the lower appellate courts have reached conflicting decisions or interpretations of the law. In the latter situation, a determination of the issue by the supreme court is necessary to assure uniformity in the law within the system over which the supreme court presides. For example, if the California Courts of Appeal for the First, Third, and Fifth Districts have rendered decisions stating that the rear driver in a rear-end traffic collision is presumed to be negligent, and the courts of appeal for the remaining districts have rendered decisions stating that there is no such presumption, an inconsistency exists in the law of California on this subject. A decision by the California Supreme Court will settle the issue and will provide a uniform rule of law throughout the state; once the California Supreme Court has ruled on an issue, all courts in the state are bound to follow the ruling.

Recall that California has inferior courts: the municipal courts. Appeals from the municipal courts are not directed initially to the California courts of appeal. Instead, appeals from decisions of the municipal courts are heard by the appellate divisions of the superior courts. When sitting as an appellate court, the superior court uses a panel of three superior court judges. The judges hear and determine the appeal in a manner similar to that utilized by the courts of appeal. There is generally no right of further appeal to the courts of appeal, although a superior court may, on its own initiative, send a matter to the court of appeal by a process known as *certification* when necessary to secure uniformity of decision or to settle important questions of law.

Figure 1-4 is a basic diagram of the federal and California court systems. The appellate routes are indicated by lines drawn from one court to another. Later in this book you will learn how the appeals process works and how the federal and California systems interact in criminal law. Note where this diagram is located so that you may refer to it later.

§ 1.4 The Duties and Powers of the Judicial Branch

Of the three branches of government, attorneys and paralegals have the most interaction with the judicial branch. For that reason, we single out the judicial branch for a more extensive examination of its functions.

First, it must be emphasized that all courts—local, state, and federal—are bound by the United States Constitution. The effect of this is that all courts have a duty to apply federal constitutional law. This is important in criminal law because it allows defendants to assert their United States constitutional claims and defenses in state court, where most criminal cases are heard. Of course, defendants may also assert applicable state defenses as well.

FIGURE 1-4
State and federal
court structures

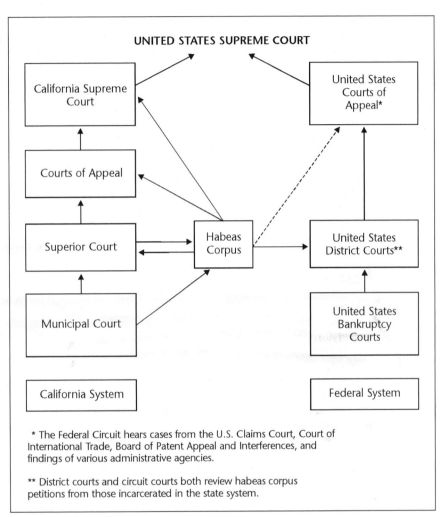

As previously stated, the judicial branch is charged with the adjudication of cases involving civil disputes and violations of the criminal laws. The courts accomplish these functions by acting as the conduit for dispute resolution. The courts are the place where civil and criminal disputes are resolved, if the parties cannot reach a resolution themselves. In an effort to resolve disputes, courts must apply the laws of the land. To apply the law, judges must **interpret** the legislation and constitutions at the federal and state levels. To *interpret* means to read the law in an attempt to understand its meaning. This nation's courts are the final word in declaring the meaning of written law. If a court interprets a statute's meaning contrary to the intent of a legislature, then the legislature may later rewrite the statute to make its intent more clear. This has the effect of reversing the judicial interpretation of the statute. The process is much more difficult if a legislature desires to change a judicial interpretation of a constitution.

At the national level, for example, the Constitution has been amended twenty-six times. The amendment process is found in Article V of the Constitution and requires not only action by the federal legislature but also action by the states. To amend a constitution is a more cumbersome and time-consuming endeavor than amending legislation.

The judicial branch is independent from the other two branches of government. Often people think of the courts as enforcers of the law. Though this is true in a sense, it is untrue in that the judicial branch does not work with the executive branch in an attempt to achieve criminal convictions. It is the duty of the courts of this nation to remain neutral and apply the laws in a fair and impartial manner.

The need for an independent judiciary is most important when considering the power of **judicial review**. Judicial review is a power held by the judicial branch, which permits it to review the actions of the executive and legislative branches and of the states and declare acts that are in violation of the Constitution void.

The landmark case dealing with judicial review is *Marbury v. Madison,* 1 Cranch 137, 2 L. Ed. 60 (1803). Chief Justice Marshall wrote the opinion for the Court and determined that, although the Constitution does not contain explicit language providing for the power of judicial review, Article III of the Constitution implicitly endows the power in the judiciary. It is now well established that courts possess the authority to review the actions of the executive and legislative branches and to declare any law, command, or other action void if such violates the United States Constitution. The power is held by both state and federal courts. Any state or federal law that violates the United States Constitution may be struck down by either federal or state courts. Of course, state laws that violate state constitutions may be stricken for the same reason.

The power to invalidate statutes is rarely used, for two reasons. First, the judiciary is aware of how awesome the power is, and this causes courts to be reluctant to use it. Second, many rules of statutory constructions exist, which have the effect of preserving legislation. For example, if two possible interpretations of a statute are possible, one that violates the Constitution and one that does not, one rule of statutory construction requires that the statute be construed so that it is consistent with the Constitution. Although rarely done, statutes are occasionally determined invalid.

§ 1.5 Comparing Civil Law and Criminal Law

The difference between civil law and criminal law appears obvious, and great differences do exist. Yet, most students are surprised at the similarities that can be found.

The source of most of the dissimilarities between criminal law and civil law is the differing objectives of the two. The purpose of criminal law is twofold. First, it is intended to prevent behavior that society has determined to be undesirable. A second purpose of criminal law is to punish those who commit the acts deemed undesirable by society. Arguably, there is only one purpose, to prevent antisocial behavior. Under this theory, punishment is only used as a tool to achieve the primary goal of preventing antisocial behavior. In any event, prevention and punishment are essential reasons why we have criminal law and a criminal justice system.

In contrast, civil law has as its primary purpose the resolution of disputes and the compensation of those injured by someone else's behavior. It is argued that the real purpose of civil law is the same as that of criminal law. By allowing lawsuits against individuals who have behaved in a manner not consistent with society's rules, civil law actually acts to prevent undesirable behavior. However, prevention of bad behavior may be more the consequence of civil law than the purpose. To understand this you must know something about civil law.

Many definitions of civil law exist. The *American Heritage Dictionary of the English Language* (1980) defines it as "The body of law dealing with the rights of private citizens." *Black's Law Dictionary,* Sixth Edition (1990) defines civil law as "Laws concerned with civil or private rights and remedies, as contrasted with criminal laws." This author prefers a negative definition similar to the latter, such as, all law except that which is criminal law. Whatever definition you accept, many areas of law fall under the umbrella of civil law. Two of the largest categories of civil law are contract law and tort law.

Contract law is a branch of civil law that deals with agreements between two or more parties. You probably have already entered into a contract. Apartment leases, credit card agreements, and book-of-the-month club agreements are all contracts. To have a **contract**, two or more people must agree to behave in a specific manner. Generally, there must be mutuality of consideration for such an agreement to be enforceable. That is, all the parties must both acquire a benefit and suffer a detriment. For example, when you agree to lease an apartment, you gain the use of the apartment during the lease period and your landlord loses the right to use the property. The flip side is that the landlord gets your money, in the form of rent, and you lose the value of that rent. You promise to pay rent at a specified time, and the landlord promises to give you the use of the premises during the rental period. In contract law, the duties and obligations of the parties are created by the parties themselves and appear in the form of a contract. If you violate your obligation to your landlord under the contract (i.e., you move out earlier than the contract allows), you have committed a civil wrong called a breach of contract. The landlord may sue you for your breach and receive **damages**, which are monetary compensation for loss.

Tort law is a branch of civil law that is concerned with civil wrongs, but not contract actions. We have all seen television ads for personal injury attorneys. These attorneys are practicing in the tort law area. A civil wrong, other than a breach of contract, is known as a **tort.** In contract law, the duty owed another party is created by the parties through their agreement. In tort law, the duty is imposed by the law. For example, at a party you are struck and injured by a beer bottle heaved by an intoxicated partier: a tort has been committed. The partier is known as a *tortfeasor,* which is the term used to describe one who commits a tort. Yet, why does that partier owe you a duty to not strike you with a flying beer bottle? You have not entered into a contract with the partier whereby he has promised not to harm you in this manner. The answer is that the law imposes the duty to act with caution when it is possible to injure another or cause injury to another's property. This duty is imposed upon all people at all times. The law requires that we all act reasonably when conducting our lives.

When a person fails to act reasonably and unintentionally injures another, that person is responsible for a **negligent** tort. Automobile accidents and medical malpractice are examples of negligent torts. When a person injures another intentionally, an **intentional** tort has occurred. Many intentional torts are also crimes, and this is an area where civil law and criminal law have much in common. If at that fraternity party you make a partier angry, and as a result he intentionally strikes you with the bottle, then he has committed both a crime and an intentional tort. Although criminal law may impose a jail sentence (or other punitive measures), tort law normally seeks only to compensate you for your injury. So, if you suffered $1,000 in medical bills to repair your broken nose, you would be entitled to that amount, but the partier cannot be sentenced to jail or otherwise be punished within the civil tort action. A separate criminal charge would have to be filed by the government.

The final type of tort is the **strict liability** tort. In these situations liability exists even though the tortfeasor acted with extreme caution and did not intend to cause harm. An example of a strict liability tort is blasting. Whenever a mining or demolition company engages in blasting, it is liable for any injuries or damages it causes to property, even if the company exercises extreme caution.

Damages that are awarded (won) in a lawsuit to compensate a party for actual loss are **compensatory damages**. Compensatory damages do just what the name states—compensate the injured party. However, another type of damages exists, **punitive damages**. Punitive damages are awarded in civil suits and are intended to prevent undesirable behavior by punishing those who commit outrageous acts. Punitive damages are often requested by plaintiffs in lawsuits, but are rarely awarded. They are virtually never awarded in contract cases. In tort cases, punitive damages are generally awarded only in cases of intentional, as opposed to negligent, torts. Do not worry if the idea of punitive damages confuses you because it appears to be a criminal law concept. They are penal in nature and many lawyers argue that punitives should not be allowed because a person can end up punished twice, once when convicted and sentenced by a criminal court and again by a civil court if punitives are awarded. Yet, punitive damages have been upheld in most instances by the United States Supreme Court. A note of caution: Do not get the concept of punitive damages mixed up with restitution or fines, which are discussed in the chapter on sentencing.

Finally, a few other differences between criminal law and civil law should be mentioned. First, in civil law the person who brings the lawsuit (the plaintiff) is the person who was injured. For example, you go to the grocery store to do your shopping and request the assistance of a checkout person who recently was divorced from a spouse who looks very much like you. The checker immediately becomes enraged and vents all of his anger for his ex-wife on you by striking you with a box of cereal, which he was checking. He has committed a possible assault and battery in both tort law (these are intentional torts) and criminal law. However, in tort law you must sue the checker yourself to recover any losses you suffer.

This is not true in criminal law. The government, whether national, state, or local, is always the party that files criminal charges. Often you will hear people say that they have filed criminal charges against someone. This is not true. What they have usually done is file a complaint; the government determines whether criminal charges are to be filed. This is because a violation of criminal law is characterized as an attack on the citizens of a state (or the federal government), and, as such, a violation of public, not private, law. Because it is public, the decision to file, or not file, is made by a public official, the prosecutor. So, in our example, you have to contact either the police or your local prosecutor to have a criminal action brought against the checker. Civil cases are entitled Citizen v. Citizen; in criminal law, it is Government (i.e., State of Montana) v. Citizen. In some jurisdictions criminal actions are brought under the name of the people. This is done in California, where criminal cases are entitled The People of the State of California v. Citizen.

There is no difference between a criminal action brought in the name of the state and a criminal action brought in the name of the people of a state. All prosecutions at the national level are brought by the United States of America. Note that governments may become involved in civil disputes. For example, if the state of California enters into a contract with a person, and a dispute concerning that contract arises, the suit will either be Citizen v. California or California v. Citizen.

SIDEBAR

About Case Names, Titles and Captions

Cases filed with courts are given a case title, also known as a case name. The title consists of the parties to the action. In civil cases the title is citizen v. citizen, for example, Joe Smith v. Anna Smith. In criminal actions in California courts, the title is "The People" v. citizen; for example, The People v. Joe Smith.

Cases also have captions. The caption appears at the top of the title page of all documents filed with a court and includes the case name, the court name, the case number, and the name of the document being filed with the court. The illustration in Figure 1-5 is an example of a caption.

FIGURE 1-5

Simple caption—criminal case and civil case

```
              SUPERIOR COURT OF THE STATE OF CALIFORNIA
                      FOR THE COUNTY OF GOLDEN

    THE PEOPLE,                  )
                 Plaintiff,      )    CASE NO. _____
                                 )
          v.                     )    COMPLAINT
                                 )
    JOE SMITH,                   )
                 Defendant       )

    ─────────────────────────────────────────────────

              SUPERIOR COURT OF THE STATE OF CALIFORNIA
                      FOR THE COUNTY OF GOLDEN

    JOE SMITH,                   )
                 Plaintiff,      )    CASE NO. _____
                                 )
          v.                     )    COMPLAINT
                                 )
    ANNA SMITH,                  )
                 Defendant       )
```

The two fields also differ in what is required to have a successful case. In civil law, one must usually show actual injury or loss in order to secure an award of compensatory damages in a lawsuit. For example, a tort victim who suffers no actual injury to his or her person, property, or other interests will, with certain limited exceptions specified in tort law, receive only nominal damages. *Nominal damages* is the name given to the token sum—sometimes as little as one dollar—awarded to a plaintiff who proves that a tort was committed against him or her, but cannot establish that he or she suffered any actual injury as a result. If, in our example, the box of cereal missed your head and you suffered no injury, you could sue the checker for the tort of assault, but would likely receive only an award of nominal damages from the court. In a criminal prosecution for the same assault, however, the checker would potentially be liable for the full penalty provided by law for the crime of assault. This is because the purpose of criminal law is to prevent this type of conduct, not to compensate for actual injuries.

To turn this around, there are many instances in which a person's negligence could be the basis for a civil cause of action, but not a criminal action. If a person accidently strikes another during a game of golf with a golf ball, causing injury, the injured party may sue for the concussion received, but no purpose would be served by prosecuting the individual who hit the ball. No deterrent effect is achieved, as there was no intent to cause the injury. In most cases, society has made the determination (through its criminal laws) that a greater amount of culpability should be required for criminal liability than for civil. Criminal law is usually more concerned with the immorality of an act than is tort law. This is consistent with the goals of the two disciplines, as it is easier to prevent intentional acts than accidental ones. These concepts are discussed later in the chapter on mens rea.

Key Terms

appellate court A court to which a party to a civil lawsuit or criminal proceeding may appeal the decision of a lower court.

California Courts of Appeal The intermediate-level appellate courts in the California judicial system. California is divided geographically into six appellate districts, with one court of appeal sitting in each district.

California Supreme Court The highest court in the California judicial system.

certiorari An order issued by the United States Supreme Court to a lower court directing the lower court to transmit the record of a case so that it may be reviewed by the Supreme Court.

compensatory damages A monetary sum, awarded to a plaintiff in a civil lawsuit, which is intended to compensate the plaintiff for monetary losses suffered because of the wrong complained of in the lawsuit.

concurrent jurisdiction Authority possessed by more than one government to legislate with respect to certain subjects, or the authority of more than one type of court to adjudicate certain types of cases.

contract An agreement between two or more persons which is enforceable in a court of law because it is supported by consideration and is not violative of law or public policy.

damages The monetary recovery awarded to a successful plaintiff in a civil lawsuit.

exclusive jurisdiction The authority of a government to legislate with respect to certain subjects to the exclusion of other governments, or the authority of a court to adjudicate certain types of cases to the exclusion of other courts.

federalism The governmental structure established by the United States Constitution, consisting of a central or federal government possessing limited powers and state governments possessing all powers not reserved exclusively to the federal government.

felony In California, a crime punishable by death or by imprisonment in the state prison.

inferior court In jurisdictions having more than one level of trial court, the lower level trial court. Usually a court of limited subject matter jurisdiction. In California, the municipal court is an inferior court.

infraction The least serious form of criminal offense in California. Infractions are not punishable by imprisonment. They are usually punished by imposition of a fine or a sentence to community service.

intentional Purposefully done.

interpret To determine or explain the meaning of.

judicial review The power of the judiciary to review actions of the legislative and executive branches and to declare acts that are in violation of the constitution void.

jurisdiction The power to act with respect to a particular subject. The jurisdiction of a legislature is the power to legislate with respect to particular subjects. The jurisdiction of a court is the power to adjudicate particular types of cases.

misdemeanor Any crime that is less serious than a felony and more serious than an infraction. Misdemeanors are usually punishable by imprisonment in the county jail and/or a fine.

municipal court The inferior trial court in the California judicial system. The municipal court is a court of limited jurisdiction (it can hear only those types of cases specifically authorized by law). For example, the municipal court may hear civil cases involving amounts in controversy of not more than $25,000. In criminal cases, the jurisdiction of the municipal court is limited to misdemeanor and infraction cases.

negligence The failure of a person to act with the same degree of care that a reasonable person would exercise in the same or similar circumstances.

petition for review A petition filed by an appellant with the California Supreme Court requesting that the court review the decision of a lower appellate court. The California Supreme Court may grant or deny the petition as a matter of discretion.

police power The power of a government to enact laws to protect the health, safety, and welfare of its citizens.

punitive damages A monetary sum awarded to a successful plaintiff in a civil lawsuit over and above compensatory damages; designed to punish the defendant for the wrong done. Punitive damages are usually awarded only in tort cases in which the defendant intentionally committed the wrong complained of by the plaintiff.

separation of powers A division of power within a government and an allocation of specific powers to designated branches of the government. Thus, the legislative branch is given exclusive power to enact laws, the executive branch is given exclusive power to administer and enforce the law, and the judicial branch is given exclusive power to hear and determine cases and controversies.

statutes Laws enacted by the United States Congress and state legislatures.

strict liability Liability without fault.

superior court The principal trial court in the California judicial system. The superior court is a court of general jurisdiction (it can hear all types of cases except as otherwise provided by law). There is one superior court in each California county. There may be several branches of the court within the county.

tort A civil wrong involving a breach of duty imposed by law, in contrast to a breach of duty under a contract.

trial court The level of court in which civil lawsuits and criminal cases are initially adjudicated based on the presentation of evidence and the determination of the case by a judge or jury.

Review Questions

1. What is the primary duty of the executive branch of government in criminal law? The legislative branch? The judicial branch?

2. Define jurisdiction, as that term applies to the legislature; define it as it applies to the courts. Differentiate between a court of general jurisdiction and a court of limited jurisdiction.

3. What are the two types of trial courts in the California judicial system?

4. What are the goals of criminal law? Civil law?

5. Who may file a civil suit? A criminal prosecution? How are these different?

6. What are compensatory damages? Punitive damages?

7. What are nominal damages?

8. Should punitive damages be permitted in civil lawsuits? Explain your position.

9. Describe the appellate court system in California.

Review Problems

1. In 1973 the United States Supreme Court handed down the famous case of *Roe v. Wade,* 410 U.S. 113 (1973), wherein the Court determined that the decision to have an abortion is a private decision that is protected from government intervention, in some circumstances, by the United States Constitution. Suppose that a state legislature passes legislation (a state statute) that attempts to reverse the *Roe* decision by prohibiting all abortions in that state. Which is controlling in that state, the statute or the decision of the United States Supreme Court? Explain your answer.

2. Same facts as in problem 1, except the state supreme court has determined that the state constitution protects the life of fetuses from abortion, except when the life of the mother is endangered. Which is controlling when a mother seeks to have an abortion and her life is not endangered to any greater amount than the average pregnancy, the state constitutional provision protecting fetuses or the decision of the United States Supreme Court? Explain your answer.

3. Assume that the United States Supreme Court has previously determined that regulation of traffic on county roads is a power reserved exclusively for the states. In reaction to this opinion, the United States Congress enacts a statute providing that the regulation of county roads will be within power of the United States Congress from that date forward. Your law office represents a client who is charged with violating the federal statute that prohibits driving on all roads while intoxicated. Do you have a defense? If so, explain.

4. What would be the proper California courts in which to bring the following civil or criminal actions?
    a. A civil suit for breach of contract in which the plaintiff is claiming damages of $15,000.
    b. A criminal prosecution for spray-painting graffiti on a highway overpass (a misdemeanor).
    c. A proceeding for dissolution of marriage.
    d. A civil suit for personal injury in which the plaintiff is claiming damages of $100,000.
    e. A criminal prosecution for armed robbery (a felony).

Notes

1 28 U.S.C. § 41 *et seq.*

CHAPTER 2

Introduction to Criminal Law

OUTLINE

§ 2.1   The Distinction Between Criminal Law and Criminal Procedure

In all areas of legal study, a distinction is made between substance and procedure. Substantive law defines rights and obligations. Procedural law establishes the methods used to enforce legal rights and obligations. The substance of tort law tells you what a tort is and what damages an injured party is entitled to recover from a lawsuit. Substantive contract law defines what a contract is, tells us whether it must be in writing to be enforceable, who must sign it, what the penalty for breach is, and other such information. The field of civil procedure sets rules for how to bring the substance of the law before a court for resolution of a claim. To decide that a client has an injury that can be compensated under the law is a substantive decision. The question then becomes how this injured client gets the compensation to which he or she is entitled. This is the procedural question. Procedural law tells you how to file a lawsuit, where to file, when to file, and how to prosecute the claim. Such is the case for criminal law and procedure.

Criminal law, as a field of law, defines what constitutes a crime. It establishes what conduct is prohibited and what punishment can be imposed for violating its mandates. Criminal law establishes what degree of intent is required for criminal liability. In addition, criminal law sets out the defenses to criminal charges that may be asserted. Alibi, insanity, and the like are defenses and fall under the umbrella of criminal law.

Criminal procedure puts substantive criminal law into action. It is concerned with the procedures used to bring criminals to justice, beginning with police investigation and continuing throughout the process of administering justice. When and under what conditions may a person be arrested? How and where must the criminal charge be filed? When can the police conduct a search?

How does the accused assert a defense? How long can a person be held in custody by the police without charges being filed? How long after charges are filed does the accused have to wait before a trial is held? These are all examples of questions that criminal procedure deals with. Do not worry if you cannot always distinguish between a procedural question and a substantive one. There is considerable overlap between the two concepts.

The first half of this text is devoted to criminal law and the latter half to criminal procedure. In the remainder of the book, the phrase "criminal law" is used often. This, in most cases, refers to general criminal law, including both substantive criminal law and criminal procedure.

§ 2.2 The Purposes of Punishing Criminal Law Violators

You have already learned that the general goal of criminal law is to prevent behavior determined by society to be undesirable. The criminal justice system uses punishment as a prevention tool. Many theories support punishing criminal law violators. Although some people focus on one theory and use it as the basis for punishment, a more accurate approach, in this author's opinion, is to recognize that many theories have merit and that when a legislature establishes the range of punishment applicable to a particular crime, many theories are involved in motivating individual legislators. It is unlikely that every member of a legislature will be motivated by the same objective. It is also unlikely that an individual legislator will be motivated by one theory only. Rather, all of the following objectives influence legislative decision making to some degree.

Specific Deterrence

Specific deterrence seeks to **deter** individuals already convicted of crimes from committing crimes in the future. It is a negative reward theory. By punishing Mr. X for today's crime, we teach him that he will be disciplined for future criminal behavior. The arrest and conviction of an individual show that individual that society has the capability to detect crime and is willing to punish those who commit crimes.

General Deterrence

General deterrence attempts to deter all members of society from engaging in criminal activity. In theory, when the public observes Mr. X being punished for his actions, the public is deterred from behaving similarly for fear of the same punishment. Of course, individuals will react differently to the knowledge of Mr. X's punishment. Individuals weigh the risk of being caught and the level of punishment against the benefit of committing the crime. All people do this at one time or another. Have you ever intentionally run a stoplight? Jaywalked? If so, you have made the decision to violate the law. Neither crime involves a severe penalty. That fact, in addition to the likelihood of not being discovered by law enforcement agents, probably affected your decision. Presumably, if conviction of either crime was punished by incarceration (time in jail), then the deterrent effect would be greater. Would you be as likely to jaywalk if you knew that you could spend time in jail for such an act? Some people would; others would not. It is safe to assume, however, that as the punishment increases, so does compliance. However, one author observed that it is not as effective to increase the punishment as it is to increase the likelihood of being punished.[1] It is unknown how much either of these factors influences behavior, but it is generally accepted that they both do.

Incapacitation

Incapacitation, also referred to as restraint, is the third purpose of criminal punishment. Incapacitation does not seek to deter criminal conduct by influencing people's choices, but prevents criminal conduct by restraining those who have committed crimes. Criminals who are restrained in jail or prison, or in the extreme, executed, are incapable of causing harm to the general public. This theory is often the rationale for long-term imprisonment of individuals who are believed to be beyond rehabilitation. It is also promoted by those who lack faith in rehabilitation and feel that all criminals should be removed from society to prevent the chance of repetition.

Rehabilitation

Rehabilitation is another purpose of punishing criminals. The theory of rehabilitation is that if the criminal is subjected to educational and vocational programs, treatment and counseling, and other measures, it is possible to alter the individual's behavior to conform to societal norms. Another author noted that:

> To the extent that crime is caused by elements of the offender's personality, educational defects, lack of work skills, and the like, we should be able to prevent him from committing more crimes by training, medical and psychiatric help, and guidance into law-abiding patterns of behavior. Strictly speaking, rehabilitation is not "punishment," but help to the offender. However, since this kind of help is frequently provided while the subject is in prison or at large on probation or parole under a sentence that carries some condemnation and some restriction of freedom, it is customary to list rehabilitation as one of the objects of a sentence in a criminal case.[2]

The concept of rehabilitation has come under considerable scrutiny in recent years, and the success of rehabilitative programs is questionable.

Retribution

Retribution, or societal vengeance, is the fifth purpose. Simply put, punishment through the criminal justice system is society's method of avenging a wrong. The idea that one who commits a wrong must be punished is an old one. The Old Testament speaks of an "eye for an eye." However, many people question the place of retribution in contemporary society. Is retribution consistent with American values? Jewish or Christian values? The question is actually moot, as there are few instances in which retribution stands alone as a reason for punishing someone who did not comply with the law. In most instances society's desire for revenge can be satisfied while fulfilling one of the other purposes of punishment, such as incapacitation.

It has also been asserted that public retribution prevents private retribution.[3] That is, when the victim (or anyone who might avenge a victim) of a crime knows that the offender has been punished, the victim's need to seek revenge is lessened or removed. Therefore, punishing those who harm others has the effect of promoting social order by preventing undesirable conduct by victims of crimes. Retribution in such instances has a deterrent effect, as victims of crimes are less likely to seek revenge. This is a good example of how the various purposes discussed are interrelated.

The California View

In a 1992 decision, the California Supreme Court succinctly stated the fundamental objective of criminal law in the state of California as follows:

> The object of the criminal law is to deter the individual from committing acts that injure society by harming others, their property, or the public welfare, and to express society's condemnation of such acts by punishing them.[4]

The Supreme Court's statement incorporates many of the sociological and philosophical concepts previously addressed. California Rule of Court 410, which guides criminal courts in determining appropriate sentences for persons convicted of crimes, provides more detail:

Rule 410. General objectives in sentencing

General objectives in sentencing include:
(a) Protecting society.
(b) Punishing the defendant.
(c) Encouraging the defendant to lead a law-abiding life in the future and deterring him from future offenses.
(d) Deterring others from criminal conduct by demonstrating its consequences.
(e) Preventing the defendant from committing new crimes by isolating him for the period of incarceration.
(f) Securing restitution for the victims of crime.
(g) Achieving uniformity in sentencing.

Public perception of the purposes of the criminal justice system and the perceived faithfulness of the courts in adhering to those purposes when deciding cases is not always in harmony with the views of the courts themselves. Witkin and Epstein, in their authoritative treatise, *California Criminal Law* (2d ed.), note the continuous tension in the criminal law between protection of the rights of persons accused of crime and protection of the general public from criminal acts. There has been a perception on the part of some members of the public that the judicial system is soft on criminals, that it tends to emphasize the rights of criminal defendants at the expense of the right of the public to be protected from crime. This tendency is not unique to California, and has been criticized by some jurists, including Justices of the United States Supreme Court.[5]

California, in recent years, has periodically experienced upsurges of public opinion opposed to perceived liberal tendencies of courts in emphasizing the rights of criminal defendants and seemingly disregarding the interest of the general citizenry to be protected from criminal acts. These upsurges of public opinion have been effectuated through the initiative process. By way of example, Proposition 8, an initiative measure amending the California Constitution and several statutes, was adopted in the June 1982 primary election. The principal changes in California criminal law made by Proposition 8 included: (1) imposition of restrictions on plea bargaining (discussed in Chapter 16); (2) abolition of the defense of diminished capacity (discussed in Chapter 10); (3) restoration of the *M'Naghten* test of insanity (discussed in Chapter 10); and (4) adoption of new provisions on sentencing and the sentencing process (discussed in Chapter 18).[6]

A more recent example of use of the initiative process to bring about changes in California criminal law by the electorate is the so-called "three strikes and you're out" law. Proposition 184, adopted in the November 6, 1994, general election, amended California criminal law to require that a person convicted of a felony who has one prior conviction for a serious or violent felony receive twice the prison term otherwise required under law for the new conviction; a person convicted of a felony who has two prior convictions for serious or violent felonies receives a mandatory sentence of life imprisonment with the minimum term being the greater of (1) three times the term otherwise required under law for the new felony conviction, (2) twenty-five years, or (3) the term determined by the court for the new conviction. Proposition 184 was added to the California Penal Code as § 1170.12. Similar provisions had previously been adopted by the legislature by legislation enacted on March 7, 1994, and are found in § 667 of the Penal Code. The "three strikes and you're out" law is discussed more fully in Chapter 18. The initiative process is discussed in the next section of this chapter.

§ 2.3 Sources of Criminal Law

Criminal law is actually a body of many laws emanating from many sources. Today most American criminal law is a product of legislative enactment. That has not always been so. Further, administrative regulations now make up a much larger percentage of the criminal law than in the past. It is vital to successful legal research that you understand the sources of criminal law. As you read this section, you will begin to see why an understanding of the functions of the three branches of government is important to an understanding of all criminal law.

The Common Law

The oldest form of criminal law in the United States is the **common law**. The common law was developed in England and brought to the United States by the English colonists.

The common law, as it exists in this country, is of English origin. Founded on ancient local rules and customs and in feudal times, it began to evolve in the King's courts and was eventually molded into the viable principles through which it continues to operate. The common law migrated to this continent with the first English colonists, who claimed the system as their birthright; it continued in full force in the 13 original colonies until the American Revolution, at which time it was adopted by each of the states as well as the national government of the new nation.[7]

But what exactly is this common law? Simply stated, the common law is judge-made law. It is law that has been developed by the judges of both England and the United States. To comprehend how common law developed, you must understand the concepts of precedence and **stare decisis.** When a court renders a legal decision, that decision becomes binding on itself and its inferior courts, whenever the same issue arises again in the future. The decision of the court is known as a **precedent.** The principle that inferior courts will comply with that decision when the issue is raised in the future is known as "stare decisis et non quieta movera" (a Latin phrase meaning "stand by precedents and do not disturb settled points"). The Supreme Court of California expressed its view of stare decisis:

> It is, of course, a fundamental jurisprudential policy that prior applicable precedent usually must be followed even though the case, if considered anew, might be decided differently by the current justices. This policy, known as the doctrine of stare decisis, "is based on the assumption that certainty, predictability and stability in the law are the major objectives of the legal system, i.e., that parties should be able to regulate their conduct and enter into relationships with reasonable assurance of the governing rules of law."[8]

The common law is fluid and dynamic, changing to meet societal values and expectations. As one court has stated:

> The inherent capacity of the common law for growth and change is its most significant feature. Its development has been determined by the social needs of the community which it serves. It is constantly expanding and developing in keeping with advancing civilization and the new conditions and progress of society, and adapting itself to the gradual change of trade, commerce, arts, inventions, and the needs of the country.[9]

What happened historically is that courts defined crimes, as there was usually no legislative enactment that determined what acts should be criminal. As time passed, established "common-law crimes" developed. First the courts determined what acts should be criminal, and then the specifics of each crime developed; that is, what exactly had to be proved to establish guilt, what defenses were available, and what punishment was appropriate for conviction. Although there is great similarity in the common law of the many jurisdictions, differences exist because judicial decisions of one state are not binding precedents on other states and because customs and practices vary among communities. However, courts may look outside their jurisdictions for opinions to guide them in their decision making if no court in their jurisdiction has addressed the issue under consideration. Each state, as a separate and sovereign entity, has the power to decide whether to adopt the common law, in whole or in part, or to reject it.

Initially, the thirteen original states all adopted the common law. Most did so through their state constitutions. Today, only Louisiana has not adopted the common law in some form. However, for reasons you will learn later, approximately half of the states, including California, no longer recognize common-law crimes.[10] Even in those states, though, the civil common law and portions of the criminal common law (e.g., defenses to criminal charges) continue in force. Most states have expressly adopted the common law either by statute or constitutional authority. Many states adopted only parts of the common law.

California has expressly adopted the common law by statute. The legislature refers to common law as "unwritten law." Code of Civil Procedure § 1899 provides:

> Unwritten law is the law not promulgated and recorded ... but which is, nevertheless, observed and administered in the courts of the country. It has no certain repository, but is collected from the reports of the decisions of the courts, and the treatises of learned men.

California Civil Code § 22.2 provides that the common law of England is the rule of decision of the courts of the state of California, "so far as it is not repugnant to or inconsistent with the Constitution of the United States, or the Constitution or laws of this State." This particular statutory provision is interesting given the historical background of the state. Prior to the annexation of California by the United States in 1848, California was part of Mexico, and was governed by the law of Mexico. Mexican law was a derivative of the law of Spain, which is a civil-law country. Civil law in the present context means a legal system which, unlike the legal systems of common-law countries, does not recognize decisions of the courts as a source of law. There is no body of common law in civil-law legal systems. Before April 13, 1850, the date of adoption of the predecessor statute to Civil Code § 22.2, the civil law prevailed in California. From and after April 13, 1850, and except as modified or changed by statute, the rules of the common law, as distinguished from the rules of the civil law or Mexican law, form the basis of the state's jurisprudence. The California courts have interpreted Civil Code § 22.2 as adopting not only the common law of England, but the decisions of American courts as well. The courts have also held that the common law adopted by Civil Code § 22.2 includes legal principles developed by the courts after, as well as before, enactment of the statute.[11]

Finally, be aware that legislative enactments (i.e., statutes) are superior to the common law. This means that the legislature can change particular common-law principles or even abolish the common law as the law of the state. Although it has the power to do so, the California legislature has not abolished the common law in California, as can be seen from the previous discussion of Civil Code § 22.2. In 1872, however, the legislature enacted Penal Code § 6, which abolished common-law crimes in California. Since that time, only acts proscribed by statute or local enactments, such as ordinances, are punishable as crimes. Accordingly, there are no common-law crimes in California.

The Principle of Legality

Although the issue has been settled in California by Penal Code § 6, the question of whether common-law crimes should continue to exist continues to be a subject of debate in some states. Those who favor permitting common-law crimes claim that it permits courts to "fill in the gaps" left by the legislatures when those bodies either fail to foresee all potential crimes or simply forget to include a crime that was foreseen. You should question whether the judicial branch should be actively second-guessing or cleaning house for the legislative branch. There appears to be a separation of powers issue when the judicial branch begins to behave in such a manner. However, few people want intentionally dangerous or disruptive behavior not to be criminalized.

Those who oppose a common law of crimes point to the concept embodied in the phrase "nullum crimen sine lege," which means, "there is no crime if there is no statute." Similarly, "nulla poena sine lege" has come to mean that "there shall be no punishment if there is no statute." These concepts, when considered in concert, insist that the criminal law must be written, that the written law must exist at the time that the accused committed the act in question, and that criminal laws be more precise than civil laws.[12] This is the *principle of legality.*

The legality principle is founded on the belief that all people are entitled to know, prior to committing an act, that an act is criminal and that punishment could result from such behavior. This is commonly referred to as *notice.* The idea is sensible, as it appears to be a rule consistent with general notions of fairness and justice. Does it appear fair to you to hold an individual criminally accountable for committing an act that he or she could not have known was prohibited? The legality principle remedies the notice problem by requiring that written law be the basis of criminal liability, not unwritten common law. Understand that the law imposes a duty on all people to be aware of written law; thus, all people are presumed to be aware of criminal prohibitions. The *Keeler* case discusses the legality principle.

Note the concern expressed by the California Supreme Court in *Keeler* that it not venture into the province of the legislature to define crimes and fix penalties. This concern reflects the separation of powers established in the California Constitution. Note also the court's reference to its authority to interpret statutes, but its declination to use that authority to rewrite Penal Code § 187, stating that the rewriting of the statute is the function of the legislature. As an interesting aside, the legislature lost no time in responding to the *Keeler* decision. In 1970, the same year in which the court rendered its decision, the legislature amended Penal Code § 187 by adding the words "or a fetus" to the definition of murder. Penal Code § 187(a) now reads: "Murder is the unlawful killing of a human being, or a fetus, with malice aforethought." Murder and its elements are discussed in detail in Chapter 4. Finally, note also the court's reference to the common law in determining the presumed meaning of the term *human being* intended by the legislature when it enacted the statute in 1850. This is an example of the continued relevance of the common law to modern criminal law.

In *Keeler,* the court observed that prior notice of legal proscriptions on conduct is required by "ordinary notions of fair play" and that no warning or notice was given to Keeler that his act could be defined as murder. As the court noted,

KEELER v. SUPERIOR COURT
Supreme Court of California
2 Cal.3d 619, 470 P.2d 617 (1970)

In this proceeding for writ of prohibition we are called upon to decide whether an unborn viable fetus is a "human being" within the meaning of the California statute defining murder. We conclude that the legislature did not intend such a meaning, and that for us to construe the statute to the contrary and apply it to this petitioner would exceed our judicial power and deny petitioner due process of law.

The evidence received at the preliminary examination may be summarized as follows: Petitioner and Teresa Keeler obtained an interlocutory decree of divorce on September 27, 1968. They had been married for sixteen years. Unknown to petitioner, Mrs. Keeler was then pregnant by one Ernest Vogt, whom she had met earlier that summer. She subsequently began living with Vogt in Stockton, but concealed the fact from petitioner. Petitioner was given custody of their two daughters, aged 12 and 13 years, and under the decree Mrs. Keeler had the right to take the girls on alternate weekends.

On February 23, 1969, Mrs. Keeler was driving on a narrow mountain road in Amador County after delivering the girls to their home. She met petitioner driving in the opposite direction; he blocked the road with his car, and she pulled over to the side. He walked to her vehicle and began speaking to her. He seemed calm, and she rolled down her window to hear him. He said, "I hear you're pregnant. If you are you had better stay away from the girls and from here." She did not reply, and he opened the car door; as she later testified, "He assisted me out of the car... [I]t wasn't rough at this time." Petitioner then looked at her abdomen and became "extremely upset." He said, "You sure are. I'm going to stomp it out of you." He pushed her against the car, shoved his knee into her abdomen, and struck her in the face with several blows. She fainted, and when she regained consciousness petitioner had departed.

Mrs. Keeler drove back to Stockton, and the police and medical assistance were summoned. She had suffered substantial facial injuries, as well as extensive bruising of the abdominal wall. A Caesarian section was performed, and the fetus was examined in utero. Its head was found to be severely fractured, and it was delivered stillborn. The pathologist gave as his opinion that the cause of death was skull fracture with consequent cerebral hemorrhaging, that death would be immediate, and that the injury could have been the result of force applied to the mother's abdomen. There was no air in the fetus' lungs, and the umbilical cord was intact. ...

The evidence was in conflict as to the estimated age of the fetus; the expert testimony on the point, however, concluded "with reasonable medical certainty" that the fetus had developed to the stage of viability, i.e., that in the event of premature birth on the date in question it would have had a 75 percent to 96 percent chance of survival.

An information was filed charging petitioner, in count I, with committing the crime of murder. ...

Penal Code section 187 provides: "Murder is the unlawful killing of a human being, with malice aforethought." The dispositive question is whether the fetus which petitioner is accused of killing was, on February 23, 1969, a "human being" within the meaning of the statute. If it was not, petitioner cannot be charged with its "murder".

* * *

We conclude that in declaring murder to be the unlawful and malicious killing of a "human being" the Legislature of 1850 intended that term to have the settled common law meaning of a person who had been born alive, and did not intend the act of feticide—as distinguished from abortion—to be an offense under the laws of California.

* * *

The People urge, however that the sciences of obstetrics and pediatrics have greatly progressed since 1872, to the point where with proper medical care a normally developed fetus prematurely born ... is "viable" ... since an unborn but viable fetus is now fully capable of independent life .... But we cannot join in the conclusion sought to be deduced: we cannot hold this petitioner to answer for murder by reason of his alleged act of killing an unborn—even though viable—fetus. To such a charge there are two insuperable obstacles, one "jurisdictional" and the other constitutional.

Penal Code section 6 declares in relevant part that "No act or omission" accomplished after the code has taken effect "is criminal or punishable, except as prescribed by this code ... ." This section embodies a fundamental principle of our tripartite form of government, i.e., that subject to the constitutional prohibition against cruel and unusual punishment, the power to define crimes and fix penalties is vested exclusively in the legislative branch. Stated differently, there are no common law crimes in California. ... In order that a public offense be committed, some statute, ordinance or regulation prior in time to the commission of the act, must denounce it.

* * *

Applying these rules to the case at bar, we would undoubtedly act in excess of the judicial power if we were to adopt the People's proposed construction of section 187. As we have shown, the Legislature has defined the crime of murder in California to apply only to the unlawful and malicious killing of one who has been born alive. We recognize that the killing of an unborn but viable fetus may be deemed by some to be an offense of similar nature and gravity; but as Chief Justice Marshall warned long ago, "It would be dangerous, indeed, to carry the principle, that a case which is within the reason or mischief of a statute, is within its provisions, so far as to punish a crime not enumerated in the statute, because it is of equal atrocity, or of kindred character, with those which are enumerated." ... Whether to thus extend liability for murder in California is a determination solely within the province of the Legislature. For a court to simply declare, by judicial fiat, that the time has now come to prosecute under section 187 one who kills an unborn but viable fetus would indeed be to rewrite the statute under the guise of construing it. ... to make it "a judicial function" ... "raises very serious questions concerning the principle of separation of powers."

The second obstacle to the proposed judicial enlargement of section 187 is the guarantee of due process of law. ...

The first essential of due process is fair warning of the act which is made punishable as a crime. "That the terms of a penal statute creating a new offense must be sufficiently explicit to inform those who are subject to it what conduct on their part will render them liable to its penalties, is a well-recognized requirement, consonant alike with ordinary notions of fair play and the settled rules of law."

this requirement is embodied in the **Due Process Clauses** of the United States Constitution and the constitutions of the many states. Due process, in both civil and criminal law, requires that individuals be put on notice of impending government action, be given an opportunity to be heard and to present evidence, and often the right to a jury trial. Due process is founded upon principles of fair play and justice. However, the United States Supreme Court has determined that states may, under some circumstances, use the common law to define criminal conduct. The court in *Keeler* based its decision on the California Constitution's Due Process Clause. You should remember that the California Supreme Court is the final word on California law, and *Keeler* teaches you that the California Constitution provides more protection than the United States Constitution in this regard. Still, the United States Constitution places limits on the use of the common law by the states to create crimes. This is done primarily through the Due Process Clause and the provision prohibiting ex post facto laws. You will learn more about the Due Process and Ex Post Facto clauses later in this book when we examine defenses to criminal charges. If states, such as California in the *Keeler* case, want to increase a defendant's rights beyond what the United States Constitution protects, they may through their own statutes or constitutions.

Other Uses of the Common Law

Despite the fact that California has abandoned the use of the common law to create crimes, the common law continues to have great significance in the state's criminal law.

First, many statutes mirror the common law in language. That is, in enacting those statutes, the legislature simply codified the common law's criminal prohibitions. Hence, when a question arises as to whether a particular act of a defendant is intended to fall under the intent of a criminal prohibition, the case law handed down prior to codification of the common law may continue to be helpful. The result is that the crime remains the same, but the source of the prohibition has changed. It is also possible for the legislature to change only part of a common-law definition and leave the remainder the same. If so, prior case law may be helpful when considering the unaltered portion of the definition.

Second, the legislature occasionally enacts a criminal prohibition without establishing the potential penalty for violation. In such cases, courts often look to the penalties applied to similar common-law crimes for guidance.

Third, a body of common law has grown around the statutorily defined crimes. This body of common law has to do with the function of the courts to interpret the meaning of statutes. Thus, although one looks to the language of statutes to initially determine what acts constitute crimes, one must also examine the body of judicial decisions interpreting the meaning of those statutes if one is to have a complete picture of the law on the subject being examined.

Fourth, in addition to defining crimes, the common law defined defenses to crimes. What defenses could be raised, as well as how and when, were determined by the common law. To the extent the legislature has not changed the common law in this area, it remains a part of California law.

Finally, a large part of the criminal law deals with the rights of persons accused or suspected of crimes under the United States and California Constitutions. These rights, although stated succinctly in the constitutions themselves, have been expounded upon at great length by the courts at the federal and state levels.

SIDEBAR

Understanding Case Citations

Many of the legal principles discussed in this text are established or illustrated by the written decisions of appellate courts. These decisions are compiled in collections of books known as *case reporters* or *reports*. A specific appellate court decision may be found by a citation to the volume number of the reporter in which the decision is found and the page number on which it begins. The name of the case and the year in which the decision was rendered are also included in the citation. In a citation to a decision of a federal court of appeals, the circuit is also cited. The following are fictitious citations illustrating the citation formats used in this text.

United States Supreme Court Decisions

United States v. Smith, 466 U.S. 872 (1983)
United States v. Smith, 92 S. Ct. 2432 (1983)

These citations refer to the decision of the United States Supreme Court in the case of *United States v. Smith.* The first citation is to the official *United States Reports,* abbreviated "U.S." The second citation is to the same decision found in another reporter, the *Supreme Court Reporter,* published by West Publishing Company. In both citations, the initial number is the volume number of the reporter in which the decision appears. The second number is the page number on which the decision begins. Thus, the *Smith* decision (fictitiously) would be found in volume 466 of the *United States Reports,* beginning at page 872. It would also be found in volume number 92 of the *Supreme Court Reporter,* beginning at page 2432. The year of the Court's decision is indicated in parentheses.

United States Courts of Appeals Decisions

United States v. Jones, 24 F.3d 632 (9th Cir. 1991)

Decisions of the United States Courts of Appeals are collected in the *Federal Reporter.* Because of the number of decisions rendered by the federal courts of appeals over the years, the *Federal Reporter* is now in its third series. The example citation is to volume 24 of the *Federal Reporter, Third Series,* abbreviated as "F.3d" Were the decision in volume 24 of the *Federal Reporter, Second Series,* it would be abbreviated "24 F.2d," or, if in the *First Series,* "24 F." The decision in the fictitious citation begins on page 632. The circuit in which the decision was rendered is indicated for the decisions of the United States Courts of Appeals; in our example, the Ninth Circuit. The year of the decision is also indicated.

United States District Court Decisions

United States v. Black, 822 F. Supp. 56 (C.D. Cal. 1992)

Although the United States District Courts are not appellate courts, some of their decisions are reported in a reporter known as the *Federal Supplement,* abbreviated "F. Supp." The example citation is to the case of *United States v. Black,* reported in volume 822 of the *Federal Supplement,* beginning at page 56. The specific United States District Court rendering the decision is indicated in parentheses; in this case, the United States District Court for the Central District of California. The year of the decision is also indicated.

California Supreme Court Decisions

People v. Smith (1987) 36 Cal.3d 542

Other than differing placement of the year of a decision, the citation format used in this text for California court decisions is basically similar to that used for federal court decisions: volume number of the reporter, followed by the abbreviated name of the reporter, followed by the page number on which the decision begins. The official reporter for California Supreme Court decisions is entitled *California Reports.* The reporter is presently in its fourth series. The sample citation is to volume 36 of the third series, page 542. A citation to volume 36 of the first series would read "36 Cal.," to the second series "36 Cal.2d," and to the fourth series "36 Cal.4th."

California Court of Appeal Decisions

People v. Jones (1991) 226 Cal.App.3d 769

The official reporter for decisions of the California Courts of Appeal is entitled *California Appellate Reports,* abbreviated "Cal.App." As with *California Reports* for the California Supreme Court, *California Appellate Reports* is in its fourth series. The sample citation is to volume 226 of the third series, page 769. A citation to volume 226 of the first series would read "226 Cal.App.," to the second series "226 Cal.App.2d," and to the fourth series "226 Cal.App.4th."

Decisions of Appellate Departments of the Superior Courts

People v. Black (1988) 204 Cal.App.3d Supp. 17

Appeals from the municipal and justice courts are taken to the appellate department of the appropriate superior court. The appellate department of a superior court consists of a panel of three superior court judges. Decisions rendered by the appellate departments of the superior courts are sometimes published. If published, they are printed in the "Supplement" portions of the *California Appellate Reports.* The Supplements appear at the ends of the volumes of the *California Appellate Reports* and are separately paginated. The sample case would be found in the Supplement portion of volume 204 of the *California Appellate Reports, Third Series,* beginning at page 17 of the Supplement.

Statutory Law

As you have already learned, the legislative branch is responsible for the creation of law. You have also learned that legislatures possess the authority to modify, abolish, or adopt the common law, in whole or in part. During the nineteenth century, the codification of criminal law began. This effectively displaced the role of the judiciary in defining crimes. Today, nearly all criminal law is found in criminal codes.

Although the power of the legislative branch to declare behavior criminal is significant, there are limits. The constitutions of the United States and of the many states contain limits on such state and federal authority. For example, the first amendment to the federal Constitution prohibits government from punishing an individual for exercising choice of religion. If a legislature does enact law that violates a constitutional provision, it is the duty of the judicial branch to declare the law void. This is the power of judicial review, previously discussed in Chapter 1. For now, you need only understand that legislatures do not have unlimited authority to create criminal law. Individual (civil) rights limit legislative power to make conduct criminal, and the judicial branch acts to protect individuals from unconstitutional legislation.

As discussed previously, acts are made criminal in California by statutes enacted by the legislature and by enactments of subordinate entities, such as municipalities. The substantive crimes covered in later chapters are principally those defined by the state legislature, that is, by statute. California statutory law, like federal statutory law and the statutory law of other states, has been codified. Each year, the legislature enacts statutes governing a vast array of subjects. These statutes are compiled in roughly chronological order in the *California Statutes*. There is no attempt in the *California Statutes* to arrange the statutory enactments by subject matter. There is also no attempt to provide up-to-date statutory language in the *California Statutes*. For example, the legislature may enact a statute in 1995 which amends part of a statute enacted in 1970. The only way to read the amended version of the statute using the *California Statutes* is to open the volumes containing the 1970 statute and the 1995 amendment and then painstakingly read both together, mentally substituting the amended language where appropriate.

Codification is a process whereby statutes are grouped by subject matter into **codes**. California statutes have been divided into numerous codes. The principal codes in which statutes defining crimes are to be found include the Penal Code, the Health and Safety Code, and the Vehicle Code. Numerous other codes, however, provide criminal sanctions for violation of certain of their provisions. The Business and Professions Code, for example, makes violation of many of its provisions, such as professional licensing requirements and its regulatory provisions applicable to construction contractors (to name but a few), misdemeanors. The Welfare and Institutions Code contains statutes that establish procedures for dealing with juvenile offenders. As can be seen from the titles of these California Codes, each Code is given a name descriptive of the subject matter it covers.

The two principal sources of codified California statutes are *Deering's California Codes Annotated* and *West's Annotated California Codes*. One or the other of these resources will be found in virtually any law library in California. Both the

Deering's and West's Codes contain all the volumes of the various California Codes, arranged by title in alphabetical order. A Code may consist of one or several volumes, depending on the number of statutes contained within it. You may have noted that each of the code compilations has the word "annotated" in its name. The word *annotated* means that the Codes contain material in addition to the text of the statutes. After each statutory provision in an annotated Code are references to the legislative history of the statute; judicial decisions interpreting or otherwise applying the statute, if any; cross-references to related Code provisions; and references to secondary materials, such as legal encyclopedias and law review articles, discussing the subject matter covered by the statute. In modern terminology, annotated Codes are user-friendly, in the sense that they greatly facilitate research of statutory law and the cases and secondary materials that apply or interpret that law. Annotated Codes provide another valuable service, as well. They are updated annually, and each statutory provision in a current edition of an annotated Code incorporates all prior changes in the language of that provision. This means that a researcher reading a current Code will be able to read statutes in their current form, that is, as statutory language into which all prior amendments have been incorporated.

SIDEBAR

Understanding Statutory Citations

Numerous statutes are cited in this text. Standard citation format is used. The following examples illustrate the manner in which statutes are cited.

Federal Statutes

18 U.S.C. § 224

Federal statutes are codified in the *United States Code,* abbreviated "U.S.C." They are grouped by subject matter into "titles," which are numbered. The *United States Code* contains fifty titles. Each title contains numerous statutory provisions, each of which is assigned a section number. Most criminal provisions of the *United States Code* appear in Title 18. The sample citation is to section 224 of Title 18 of the *United States Code.*

California Statutes

Penal Code § 187
Vehicle Code § 1285

California statutes are codified into separate Codes by subject matter. Unlike the single *United States Code* for federal statutes, which is subdivided into subject-matter titles, there are numerous separate California Codes, each bearing the name of the subject matter contained within the Code. Examples of California Codes cited in this text include the Penal Code, the Health and Safety Code, the Business and Professions Code, the Vehicle Code, and the Code of Civil Procedure. There are many other California Codes in addition to these. Each Code contains numerous statutory provisions, each of which is assigned a section number. The sample citations are to section 187 of the Penal Code and section 1285 of the Vehicle Code.

Ordinances

The written laws of political entities below the state level are called **ordinances.** The California Constitution, art. XI, § 7, provides that "[a] county or city may make and enforce within its limits all local, police, sanitary, and other ordinances and regulations not in conflict with general laws." Ordinances typically regulate such matters as traffic, zoning, construction, health standards for businesses, and numerous other activities appropriate for local regulation. Local ordinances cannot replace state law in the same field, but may validly supplement existing state law.

Some ordinances are of a penal character. Such ordinances constitute an additional part of the criminal law of California. Violations of penal ordinances are generally misdemeanors or infractions and are prosecuted in the same courts and in the same manner as criminal violations of state law.

Initiative and Referendum

California is one of a number of states in which the people may enact and annul laws by means of the initiative and referendum processes. The **initiative** is a procedure whereby voters may adopt laws, both at the state and local level, and amendments to the California Constitution, as part of the electoral process. A proposed statute, ordinance, or constitutional amendment is drafted by a citizen or group of citizens. Petitions proposing adoption of the initiative are then circulated throughout the state. If a sufficient number of registered voters sign the petitions, the initiative measure is placed on a statewide ballot for approval or rejection by the voters at the next election. An initiative becomes law if approved by a majority of the voters who vote on it. As discussed earlier in this chapter, the initiative procedure has been used by the electorate with some frequency in recent years to amend the constitution or enact statutes to correct perceived deficiencies in the state's criminal law and procedure.

The **referendum** gives voters the power to place a measure passed by the legislature on a statewide ballot for voter approval. The legislative enactment is temporarily suspended pending a decision by the voters. The referendum process has not been used by the electorate with the same frequency as the initiative process and has not been used at all with respect to penal statutes.[13]

Administrative Law

It is likely that at some time in your life you have had to deal with an administrative agency. Agencies are governmental units, federal, state, and local, that administer the affairs of the government. Although often lumped together, there are actually two types of agencies, social welfare and regulatory. The two names reflect the purposes behind each type. Social welfare agencies put into effect government programs. For example, in California, the Health and Welfare Agency administers state and federal programs for health care, social services, public assistance, job training, and rehabilitation. In contrast, state medical licensing boards are regulatory, because their duty is to oversee and regulate the practice of medicine in the various states. Regulatory and social welfare agencies usually receive their power from the legislative branch. In California, however, some agencies receive their authority directly from the constitution or by direct enactment of the people under the power of initiative.

Because legislatures do not possess the time or the expertise to write precise statutes, they often enact a statute that is very general and in that statute grant one or more administrative agencies the authority to make more precise laws.

These statutes are frequently referred to as *enabling acts* or *enabling statutes*. Just as legislative enactments are known as statutes (or codes), administrative laws are known as **regulations** or rules. The extent to which a legislature may delegate its law-making authority has been a continuing source of debate. It is argued that legislatures may not grant such an important legislative function to agencies. This is believed to be a violation of the principle of separation of powers, because agencies usually fall under the control of the executive branch, and the legislative branch is not permitted to delegate its powers to the executive branch, or vice versa.

Finding Administrative Regulations

Federal administrative regulations are found in the Code of Federal Regulations (C.F.R.). New rules that have not yet been added to the C.F.R. may be found in the *Federal Register*. In California, regulations of administrative agencies are contained in the California Code of Regulations (Cal. Code Regs.), which can be found in most law libraries.

Despite this, the United States Supreme Court has determined that agencies may create regulations that have the effect of law, including criminal prohibitions. The Court's opinion on how much authority may be given administrative agencies has undergone a few changes over the years. In 1911 the United States Supreme Court handed down the opinion in the *Grimaud* case.

Grimaud is the law at the federal level today. Federal agencies may be delegated penal rulemaking authority. However, the United States Supreme Court has said that although Congress may delegate to an agency the authority to make criminal laws, it may not delegate the responsibility of establishing penalties to an agency, with the possible exception of small fines. Congress must either set the precise penalty or set a range from which an agency can further determine the appropriate penalty.

Note the distinction drawn by the Court in the *Grimaud* case between the power to legislate, which cannot be delegated to an administrative agency, and the power to "fill up the details" of existing legislation, which can be delegated. California law is similar to federal law in this regard. In California, an administrative agency may be delegated the authority to enact rules and regulations to promote the purposes of an enabling statute if the statute declares the legislature's policy and purpose and provides standards for the exercise of the delegated power. An enabling statute may not, however, delegate to an agency the power to adopt rules and regulations that abridge, enlarge, extend, or modify the enabling statute. In addition, any penal sanction for violation of an administrative agency regulation must be established by the legislature, not the agency. The legislature may, however, empower an agency to adopt regulations; may provide in the enabling statute that violation of such regulations will be a criminal offense of a specified nature, such as a misdemeanor; and may specify the penalty to which a violator may be subjected. In other words, an administrative agency may not declare that a violation of its regulations is a crime, but the legislature may do so and leave to the agency the actual writing and promulgation of its regulations. Administrative agency regulations that meet the foregoing criteria have the force and effect of law in California.[14]

UNITED STATES v. GRIMAUD
United States Supreme Court
220 U.S. 506 (1911)

The defendants were indicted for grazing sheep on the Sierra Forest Reserve without having obtained the permission required by the regulations adopted by the Secretary of Agriculture. They demurred on the ground that the Forest Reserve Act of 1891 was unconstitutional, in so far as it delegated to the Secretary of Agriculture power to make rules and regulations and made a violation thereof a penal offense.

* * *

From the various acts relating to the establishment and management of forest reservations it appears that they were intended "to improve and protect the forest and to secure favorable conditions to water flows." ... It was also declared that the Secretary "may make such rules and regulations and establish such service as will insure the objects of such reservation, namely, to regulate their occupancy and use to prevent the forests thereon from destruction; *and any violation of the provisions of this act or such* rules and regulations shall be punished," as is provided in [the statute].

Under these acts, therefore, any use of the reservations for grazing or other lawful purpose was required to be subject to the rules and regulations established by the Secretary of Agriculture. To pasture sheep and cattle on the reservation, at will and without restraint, might interfere seriously with the accomplishment of the purposes for which they were established. But a limited and regulated use for pasturage might not be inconsistent with the object sought to be attained by the statute. The determination of such questions, however, was a matter of administrative detail. What might be harmless in one forest might be harmful to another. What might be injurious at one stage of timber growth, or at one season of the year, might not be so at another.

In the nature of things it was impracticable for Congress to provide general regulations for these various and varying details of management. Each reservation had its peculiar and special features; and in authorizing the Secretary of Agriculture to meet these local conditions Congress was merely conferring administrative functions upon an agent, and not delegating to him legislative power.

* * *

It must be admitted that it is difficult to define the line which separates legislative power to make laws, from administrative authority to make regulations. This difficulty has often been recognized [as] referred to by Chief Justice Marshall ... : "It will not be contended that Congress can delegate to the courts, or to any other tribunals, powers which are strictly and exclusively legislative. But Congress may certainly delegate to others, powers which the legislature may rightfully exercise itself." What were these non-legislative powers which Congress could exercise but which might also be delegated to others was not determined, for he said: "The line has not been exactly drawn which separates those important subjects, which *must* be entirely regulated by the legislature itself, from those of less interest, in which a general provision may be made, and power given to those who are to act under such general provisions to fill up the details."

From the beginning of the Government various acts have been passed conferring upon the executive officers power to make rules and regulations — not for the government of their departments, but for administering the laws which did govern. None of these statutes could confer legislative power. But when Congress had legislated and indicated its will, it could give to those who were to act under such general provisions "power to fill up the details" by the establishment of administrative rules and regulations, the violation of which could be punished by fine or imprisonment fixed by Congress, or by penalties fixed by Congress or measured by the injury done.

* * *

It is true that there is no act of Congress which, in express terms, declares that it shall be unlawful to graze sheep on a forest reserve. But the statutes, from which we have quoted, declare, that the privilege of using reserves for "all proper and lawful purposes" is subject to the proviso that the person shall comply "with the rules and regulations covering such forest reservation." The same act makes it an offense to violate those regulations.

* * *

The Secretary of Agriculture could not make rules and regulations for any and every purpose. As to those here involved, they all regulate matters clearly indicated and authorized by Congress.

Court Rules

Just as administrative agencies need the authority to fill in the gaps of legislation, because statutes do not spell out every detail of an agency's regulatory responsibilities, so do courts. The United States Congress and all of the state legislatures have enacted some form of statute establishing general rules of civil and criminal procedure. In California, for example, these statutory provisions are found principally in the Code of Civil Procedure and the Penal Code. However, to fill in the gaps left by legislatures, courts adopt **court rules,** which also govern civil and criminal court proceedings. Court rules deal with procedural matters, which can range from relatively routine topics such as caption formats for court documents and filing deadlines to weightier matters such as the criteria to be considered and the procedures to be followed by courts in determining sentences to be imposed on persons convicted of crimes.[15] Even seemingly routine court rules are important, as failure to follow them may be harmful or even fatal to a party's case.

Court rules may not conflict with legislative mandates. If a rule does conflict with a statute, the statute is controlling. One exception to this rule may be when the statute is unconstitutional and the rule is a viable alternative, but discussion of that issue is best left to a course on constitutional law and judicial process.

In California, court rules are promulgated at both the state and local levels. The state-level rules are entitled the *California Rules of Court.* The California Rules of Court are promulgated by the Judicial Council, which is established by art. VI, § 6, of the California Constitution. The Judicial Council consists of the chief justice and one other judge of the supreme court, three judges of courts of appeal, five judges of superior courts, five judges of municipal courts, four members of the state bar, and one member of each house of the legislature. The California Rules of Court are uniformly applicable in courts throughout the state. At the local level, individual courts may adopt rules that refine or add detail to the procedural matters covered by the California Rules of Court or impose local requirements not addressed in the California Rules of Court.

The Model Penal Code

The **Model Penal Code** is one of the uniform and model acts developed by the American Law Institute, which is a private organization. These acts are drafted by individuals expert in the subject areas covered, but do not become law unless adopted by state legislatures. The Model Penal Code was adopted by the American Law Institute in 1962. The intent of the drafters was to draft a consistent, thoughtful code that could be adopted by states as their statutory criminal law. According to one source, by 1985 thirty-four states had "enacted widespread criminal-law revision and codification based on its provisions; fifteen hundred courts had cited its provisions and referred to its commentary."[16] Although California has not adopted the Model Penal Code, California courts occasionally refer to it, or its accompanying commentary, when addressing novel issues of California law.

Constitutional Law

Finally, constitutional law is included in this list of sources of criminal law, not because it defines what conduct is criminal, but because of its significant impact on criminal law generally. In particular, the United States Constitution, primarily through the **Bill of Rights**, and the California Constitution through its provisions protecting the rights of persons suspected or accused of crimes, are responsible for establishing many of the rules governing criminal procedure. This has been especially true in the past few decades. You will become more aware of why this is true as you learn more about criminal law and procedure. Pay close attention to the dates of the cases included in this text; it is likely that many were handed down in your lifetime, a significant number of them during the last two decades.

Although it is common to associate the study of constitutional law with the study of the United States Constitution, it is important to remember California has its own constitution with its own body of case law interpreting its meaning. Even though the dominant source for defending civil liberties has been the United States Constitution, the California Constitution has played an important role in protecting the rights of those suspected or accused of crimes. Remember, the United States Constitution is the highest form of law, and the states may not decrease the individual protections secured by it. States may, however, increase **civil liberties** through state law. As you will see when you study the portions of this text dealing with criminal procedure, the California Constitution and the judicial decisions applying and interpreting it, in many instances, provide greater protections to criminal suspects and defendants than does the United States Constitution.

SOURCES OF CRIMINAL LAW

Source	Comment
CONSTITUTIONS	The United States and every state have a constitution. The United States Constitution is the supreme law of the land.

Source	Comment
STATUTES	The written law created by legislatures, frequently compiled by subject matter into codes. State statutes may not conflict with either their own constitution or the federal constitution. State statutes are also invalid if they conflict with other federal law, and the federal government has concurrent jurisdiction with the states. Statutes of the United States are invalid if they conflict with the United States Constitution or if they attempt to regulate matters outside federal jurisdiction. Legislatures may change statutes at will.

Source	Comment
COMMON LAW	Law which evolved as courts, through judicial opinions, recognized customs and practices. Legislatures may alter, amend, or abolish the common law at will. In criminal law, the common law has been responsible for the creation of crimes and for establishing defenses to crimes. Many states, including California, have abolished common-law crimes.

Source	Comment
REGULATIONS	Created by administrative agencies under a grant of authority from a legislative body. Regulations must be consistent with statutes and constitutions and may not exceed the legislative grant of power. The power to make rules and regulations is granted to fill in the gaps left by legislatures when drafting statutes.

Source	Comment
ORDINANCES	Written law of local bodies, such as city councils. Must be consistent with all higher forms of law.

Source	Comment
INITIATIVE	Direct action by voters in California to amend the California Constitution or to adopt or amend a California statute.

Source	Comment
MODEL PENAL CODE	Written under the direction of the American Law Institute. It was drafted by experts in criminal law to be presented to the states for adoption. It is not law until a state has adopted it, in whole or part. More than half the states have adopted at least part of the Model Penal Code. California has not adopted the Model Penal Code.

Source	Comment
COURT RULES	Rules created by courts to manage their cases. Court rules are procedural and commonly establish deadlines, lengths of filings, etc. Court rules may not conflict with statutes or constitutions.

Key Terms

Bill of Rights   The first ten amendments to the United States Constitution; establishes certain fundamental rights of the citizenry.

civil liberties   Freedoms granted to the people by the constitutions of the United States and the states.

code   A compilation of statutes, usually arranged by subject matter.

codification   The process of organizing the enacted statutes of a government into one or more codes.

common law   The body of law created by judicial decisions and contained in the text of those decisions, rather than in statutes or other legislative enactments.

court rules   Rules of procedure for the courts promulgated on both a statewide basis (California Rules of Court) and by individual courts (local rules).

criminal law   The field of law that defines crimes, specifies the punishments for crimes, and specifies defenses to crimes.

criminal procedure   The field of law that establishes principles governing the procedures used in the investigation and prosecution of criminal offenses.

deter   To influence another to refrain from acting.

Due Process Clauses   The provision appearing in the Fifth and Fourteenth Amendments to the United States Constitution and in the California constitution that a person may not be deprived of life, liberty, or property without due process of law.

initiative   A procedure in California whereby the electorate may directly enact laws and amend the California Constitution.

Model Penal Code   One of the uniform and model acts developed by the American Law

Institute; does not constitute law unless enacted by a state legislature. California has not adopted the Model Penal Code.

ordinances Written laws of a political entity below the state level, such as a county or city.

precedent A legal principle developed or followed by an appellate court when deciding an issue that will be followed in future cases involving the same issue.

referendum A procedure in California whereby the electorate may annul or approve legislation enacted by the legislature.

regulations Legislative enactments of administrative agencies.

rules of court Rules promulgated both at the state level and by individual courts establishing court procedures.

stare decisis An attribute of appellate court decisions in common-law legal systems which requires that the legal principles developed by an appellate court are to be followed by the same court and lower courts within its jurisdiction in later cases.

Review Questions

1. What are civil liberties? Give two examples of civil liberties that are protected by the Constitution of the United States.

2. What is the common law? How do the concepts of stare decisis and precedent relate to the common law?

3. The common law is different in every state. Why?

4. What does the Latin phrase "nullum crimen sine lege" translate to? Explain the significance of that phrase.

5. Explain how the common law can violate the principle of legality.

6. State three uses the common law has in criminal law in jurisdictions that do not permit common-law creation of crimes.

7. Has the common law always been the rule of decision in the courts of California? Explain.

8. What is the source of most criminal law today? Where does that law come from?

9. What does *codification* mean when applied to statutes? Briefly explain the advantages of using an annotated code when researching statutory law.

10. What is an ordinance?

11. Explain how the voters can change law in California using the initiative process.

12. What is a court rule?

13. Place the following sources of law in order of authority, beginning with the highest form of law and ending with the lowest. Notice that both state and federal sources of law are included: United States Code, state constitutions, federal administrative regulations, ordinances, United States Constitution, state administrative regulations, state statutes.

Review Problems

1. In theory, people can increase their "freedom" by establishing a government and relinquishing freedoms (civil liberties) to that government. Explain why this paradox is true.

2. List the various purposes for punishing criminal law violators.

   3–6. Using your answers from question 2, determine if the goals of punishment can be achieved if prosecution is sought for the following acts:

3. John, having always wanted a guitar, stole one from a fellow student's room while that student was out.

4. Jack suffers from a physical disease of the mind that causes him to have violent episodes. Jack has no way of knowing when the episodes will occur. However, the disease is controllable with medication. Despite this, Jack often does not take the medicine, as he finds the injections painful and inconvenient. One day, when he had not taken the

medicine, Jack had an episode and struck Mike, causing him personal injury.

5. Same facts as in question 4, except there is no treatment or medication that can control Jack's behavior. He was diagnosed as having the disease years prior to striking Mike and has caused such an injury before during a similar violent episode.

6. Unknown to Kevin, he is an epileptic. One day while he was driving his automobile, he suffered his first seizure. The seizure caused him to lose control of his car and strike a pedestrian, inflicting a fatal injury.

Notes

[1] *See* E. Puttkammer, *Administration of Criminal Law* 16–17 (1953).

[2] Schwartz & Goldstein, *Police Guidance Manuals* (University of Virginia Press, 1968), Manual No. 3, at 21–32, reprinted in *Cases, Materials, and Problems on the Advocacy and Administration of Criminal Justice* 173 by Harold Norris (unpublished manuscript available in the Detroit College of Law library).

[3] *See* Note, 78 *Colum. L. Rev.* 1249, 1247–59 (1978); LaFave & Scott, *Criminal Law* 26 (Hornbook Series, West, 1986).

[4] *People v. Roberts* (1992) 2 Cal.4th 271, 316, 826 P.2d 274, 6 Cal.Rptr.2d 276.

[5] 1 Witkin & Epstein, *California Criminal Law* § 2 (2d ed., Bancroft-Whitney, 1988).

[6] 1 Witkin & Epstein, *supra* note 5, § 7.

[7] 15A Am. Jur. 2d *Common Law* 6 (1976).

[8] *People v. Latimer* (1993) 5 Cal.4th 1203, 1212–13 (citation omitted).

[9] *Rodriquez v. Bethlehem Steel Corp.* (1974) 12 Cal.3d 382, 394, quoting 15A Am. Jur. 2d, *supra* note 7.

[10] T. Gardner, *Criminal Law: Principles and Cases* (4th ed., West, 1989).

[11] *See* 58 Cal. Jur. 3d *Statutes* 4 (1980).

[12] P. Robinson, *Fundamentals of Criminal Law* (Little, Brown, 1988).

[13] League of Women Voters of California, *Guide to California Government,* 13th ed. (1986).

[14] 2 Cal. Jur. 3d *Administrative Law* §§ 64–65 (1973).

[15] *See, e.g.,* California Rule of Court 401 *et seq.,* "Sentencing Rules for the Superior Courts."

[16] J. Samaha, *Criminal Law* (3d ed., West, 1990).

CHAPTER 3

The Two Essential Elements

§ 3.1   Mens Rea

Nearly every crime consists of two essential elements: the mental and the physical. Stated another way, most crimes require a physical act accompanied by a criminal mental state. If either of these elements is missing, a crime has not been committed. This requirement has been codified in California and is found in § 20 of the Penal Code:

In every crime or public offense there must exist a union, or joint operation of act and intent, or criminal negligence.

This chapter begins by addressing the mental component of crimes and concludes by examining the physical component.

It is common to distinguish between acts that are intentional and those that occur accidentally. Everyone has had an experience where they have caused injury to another person or another person's property accidentally. The fact that the injury was accidental and not intended often leads to a statement such as, "I'm sorry, I didn't mean to hurt you." In these situations people often feel a social obligation to pay for any injuries they have caused, or to assist the injured party in other ways, but probably do not expect to be punished criminally. As the late Supreme Court Justice Holmes stated, "Even a dog distinguishes between being stumbled over and being kicked." As this statement implies, to make such a distinction between accidental and intentional acts that injure others appears to be natural and consistent with common notions of fairness. The criminal law often models this theory; that is, people are often held accountable for intentional behavior and not for accidental, even though the consequences may be the same.

43

However, this is not always so. Under some circumstances accidental behavior (negligent or reckless) may be the basis of criminal liability.

Mens rea is the mental part, the state of mind required to be criminally liable. It is often defined as "a guilty mind" or possessing a criminal intent. It is best defined as the state of mind required to be criminally liable for a certain act. It is sometimes the case that no intent whatsoever is required to be guilty of a crime, although most criminal laws require intent of some degree before criminal liability attaches to an act.

Mens rea is an important concept in criminal law. It is also a confusing one. This is in large part because of the inconsistency and lack of uniformity between criminal statutes and judicial decisions. One author found seventy-nine words and phrases in the United States Criminal Code used to describe mens rea.[1] The California Supreme Court recognized the difficulty of the concept of mens rea in the following passage:

> The primordial concept of *mens rea,* the guilty mind, expresses the principle that it is not conduct alone but conduct accompanied by certain specific mental states which concerns, or should concern, the law. In a broad sense the concept may be said to relate to such important doctrines as justification, excuse, mistake, necessity and mental capacity, but in the final analysis it means simply that there must be a "joint operation of act and intent," as expressed in section 20 of the Penal Code, to constitute the commission of a criminal offense. The statutory law, however, furnishes no assistance to the courts beyond that, and the casebooks are filled to overflowing with the courts' struggles to determine just what state of mind should be considered relevant in particular contexts.[2]

Mens Rea and the Common Law

One principle under the common law was that there should be no crime if there was no act accompanied by a guilty mind. The Latin phrase that states this principle is "actus non facit reum nisi mens sit rea." Today, under some statutes, no intent is required to be guilty of a crime. Despite this, the principle that "only conscious wrongdoing constitutes crime is deeply rooted in our legal system and remains the rule, rather than the exception."[3]

Many terms have been used to describe a guilty mind. Malicious, mischievous, purposeful, unlawful, intentional, with specific intent, knowing, fraudulent, with an evil purpose, careless, willful, negligent and reckless are examples of terms and phrases used to describe the mental state required to prove guilt.

General and Specific Intent

A principal distinction in criminal law between mental states necessary to convict someone of a crime is the distinction between general intent and specific intent. The courts, when assessing the guilt or innocence of an accused, frequently address this question: Is the crime charged a general-intent crime or a specific-intent crime? General intent is the intentional performance of an act that the law declares criminal, without the additional intent to cause a particular result. A general-intent crime is a crime committed by the mere performance of the prohibited act. The actor need not intend that a specific consequence result from the commission of the act.

Consider, for example, a statute that makes it a crime to vandalize (i.e., damage, destroy, or deface) private property. This is a general-intent crime because all a person has to do to commit the crime is to perform the prohibited act—damaging, destroying, or defacing private property. There is no requirement that the person intend to achieve some further criminal result by his or her act. If a person intentionally spray-paints graffiti on the property of another, he or she has committed the crime of vandalism. Another example of a general-intent crime would be target shooting in one's back yard in violation of a local ordinance prohibiting the discharge of a firearm within the city limits. As with the vandalism offense, the city ordinance is violated by the mere discharge of the firearm. The ordinance does not require that the actor entertain an intent to achieve a further criminal result (such as battery or murder) by the discharge of the weapon. Intentional firing of the weapon is sufficient.

It should be remembered that the term *general intent* includes the word *intent*. This means that the prohibited act must be intentionally performed. In the two examples just given, the vandal must intentionally spray-paint the property of another person, and the shooter must intentionally discharge a firearm. There is generally no requirement, however, that the person intend to violate the law. One is presumed to know the law, and if he or she intentionally commits an act that the law has made a crime, he or she has done enough to be guilty of a general-intent crime, regardless of his or her knowledge that the act is prohibited.

The term *specific intent* means the intent to cause a particular result. The intentional commission of an unlawful act (general intent) coupled with the intent to achieve a particular criminal result constitutes specific intent. A statute defining a specific-intent crime generally makes it a criminal offense to commit a specified act with the intent to achieve a specified result. Consider, for example, Penal Code § 220:

> Every person who assaults another with intent to commit mayhem, rape, sodomy, oral copulation, or any violation of Section 264.1, 288, or 289 is punishable by imprisonment in the state prison for two, four, or six years.

Section 220 defines a specific-intent crime. It prohibits an act (assault), but mere commission of the act does not in itself violate this particular statute (assault is a crime under another provision of the Penal Code). To constitute a violation of § 220, the assault must be coupled with an intent to achieve a further criminal result (mayhem, rape, etc.).

The significance of the distinction between general-intent crimes and specific-intent crimes has to do mainly with the quantum of proof required to convict the defendant. If the defendant is charged with a general-intent crime, the prosecution must prove only that the defendant intentionally committed the act in question. If the defendant is charged with a specific-intent crime, the prosecution must not only prove that the act was intentionally committed, but also that the defendant entertained an intent to achieve the further unlawful result specified in the statute defining the crime. It should be apparent that it is generally simpler to convict a defendant of a general-intent crime than of a specific-intent crime.

A common way to determine whether a crime is a general-intent crime or a specific-intent crime is to examine the language of the statute defining the crime. For example, it is clear from the language of Penal Code § 220 that the offense prescribed is a specific-intent crime. Contrast the language of § 220 with that of § 281(a) defining the offense of bigamy:

> Every person having a husband or wife living, who marries any other person, except in the cases specified in Section 282, is guilty of bigamy.

In the case of § 281(a), intentional commission of the prohibited act—marrying another while being already married—is sufficient to constitute the offense. Section 281(a) does not require that one who marries, while being already married to another, do so with the intent to achieve some additional unlawful purpose. Accordingly, § 281(a) defines a general-intent crime. All one need do to commit the crime is to marry while being already married to another.

The law does not always fall into neat categorizations, and it is not always possible to determine whether a crime is a specific-intent or general-intent crime simply by examining the statute prescribing the crime. In such cases, courts may look to the common law or the **legislative history** of the statute to determine its meaning.

Other Mental States

Some California penal statutes define crimes in terms of mental states other than general or specific intent. Some mental states used in certain sections of the Penal Code and other codes defining crimes include willfulness, knowledge, recklessness, malice, and negligence. With the exception of negligence and strict liability offenses, general intent is always an element of crimes requiring a mental state, because it is necessary that the defendant have intentionally committed the act prohibited by the statute.

The term **willfully** is defined in Penal Code § 7(1):

> The word "willfully," when applied to the intent with which an act is done or omitted, implies simply a purpose or willingness to commit the act, or make the omission referred to. It does not require any intent to violate the law, or to injure another, or to acquire any advantage.

On its face, § 7(1) appears to define *willfulness* as a mental state synonymous with general intent, and the courts have so held in many cases. In other cases, however, particularly those involving crimes traditionally requiring a more culpable mental state than general intent, the courts have interpreted the term *willful* as requiring knowledge of the unlawfulness of the act, or at least criminal negligence on the part of the defendant.[4]

Knowingly is defined in Penal Code § 7(5):

> The word "knowingly" imports only a knowledge that the facts exist which bring the act or omission within the provisions of this code. It does not require any knowledge of the unlawfulness of such act or omission.

Note that § 7(5) is explicit that, in a crime requiring that the defendant "knowingly" commit a prohibited act, the defendant need only know that he or she is committing the act. He or she need not know that the act is prohibited by law or that it is a crime. The courts frequently interpret "knowing" offenses as general-intent crimes. Thus, in one case in which the defendant was convicted for "knowing possession of an unregistered firearm," the court held that the only knowledge required on the defendant's part was that of the character of the object possessed. In other words, the defendant, to be guilty of the crime, need only have known that he was in possession of an unregistered firearm. He did not have to know that such possession was unlawful.[5]

A number of California penal statutes make it a crime to commit a specified act **recklessly.** Unlike *willfully* and *knowingly, recklessly* is not defined in § 7 of the Penal Code, the general definitional section. It is defined in certain statutes defining offenses involving recklessness. For example, Penal Code § 452 provides that a person is guilty of unlawfully causing a fire when he or she recklessly sets fire to, burns, or causes to be burned any structure, forest land, or property. *Recklessly* for purposes of this offense is defined in Penal Code § 450(f), as follows:

> "Recklessly" means a person is aware of and consciously disregards a substantial and unjustifiable risk that his or her act will set fire to, burn, or cause to burn a structure, forest land, or property. The risk shall be of such a nature and degree that disregard thereof constitutes a gross deviation from the standard of conduct that a reasonable person would observe in the situation.

Although § 450(f) defines *recklessly* in the context of burning, the definition has been used by courts in cases involving other crimes, without the reference to burning.

Malice has more than one meaning in California criminal law. It is generally defined in the definitional section of the Penal Code, at § 7(4):

> The words "malice" and "maliciously" import a wish to vex, annoy, or injure another person, or an intent to do a wrongful act, established either by proof or presumption of law.

As framed by the statutory definition, malice consists of actual ill will or intent to injure another or to do a wrongful act. The courts, however, have found malice in the absence of these factors. Witkin and Epstein state that the element of malice in most criminal statutes is satisfied by the intentional doing of a wrongful act without justification, excuse, or mitigating circumstances.[6] Yet another definition of *malice* is found in Penal Code § 188, which defines the term in the context of the **"malice aforethought"** element of the crime of murder. The concept of malice aforethought is further explored in Chapter 4.

Negligence is generally not a basis for criminal liability. Negligent acts are normally redressed in the civil courts. Some crimes are, however, defined in terms of negligence. Involuntary manslaughter is an example. Penal Code § 7(2) provides as follows:

> The words "neglect," "negligence," "negligent," and "negligently" import a want of such attention to the nature or probable consequences of the act or omission as a prudent man ordinarily bestows in acting in his own concerns.

The foregoing definition is very similar to the definition of negligence in civil tort law. Despite this similarity, the courts have required a greater degree of negligence for criminal liability than for civil liability, particularly in homicide cases. According to the California Supreme Court:

> The negligence must be aggravated, culpable, gross, or reckless, that is, the conduct of the accused must be such a departure from what would be the conduct of an ordinarily prudent or careful man under the same circumstances as to be incompatible with a proper regard for human life or an indifference to consequences.[7]

As stated earlier, the language of a penal statute does not always indicate with clarity whether an offense is a general- or specific-intent crime. In the case of *People v. Glover,* the Court of Appeal for the Second District, Division Five, analyzed Penal Code § 451(b), arson of an inhabited structure, in an effort to make this determination.

Note the court's discussion of the mental states prescribed by § 451, "willfully and maliciously," and their relation to the general- and specific-intent mental states. It was the inclusion of "willfully and maliciously" in § 451, together with the convoluted history of the statute (largely omitted from this case excerpt), that rendered uncertain the type of intent required for the crime.

Note also the court's disagreement, in *People v. Glover,* with the decision of another appellate court in *In re Stonewall F.,* a 1989 decision, indicating an inconsistency among the appellate courts on the question of whether arson of an inhabited structure is a general-intent or specific-intent crime. Resolution of such inconsistencies is a function of the California Supreme Court. Ms. Glover petitioned the supreme court for review of the appellate court's decision, but the petition was denied. One justice was of the opinion that the petition should be granted.

PEOPLE v. JOAN GLOVER
233 Cal.App.3d 1476; 285 Cal.Rptr. 362
[Sept. 1991]

TURNER, P.J.

Defendant Joan Glover appeals from a judgment of conviction for arson of an inhabited structure. On appeal, defendant contends that the evidence was insufficient to support her conviction of arson of an inhabited structure because defendant did not act with the requisite specific intent to set fire to an inhabited dwelling rather than her personal property and there was instructional error. We find that no prejudicial error has occurred and, as a result, the judgment is affirmed.

On April 17, 1987, defendant lived in apartment 25 at 1170 Murchison Street in Pomona. Previously, in September of 1986, defendant had told her former husband that "she got some insurance and that she was gonna burn her apartment up because she needed some money." Defendant met with several persons including Albert Dukes (Dukes) and asked him to start a fire with kerosene in her apartment. She never stated why she wanted the fire started. Dukes stated that defendant wanted two other residents of the apartment building out of the building at the time the fire was started.

In compliance with her instructions, Dukes started the fire by pouring kerosene over furniture which was placed in the middle of defendant's living room. He poured kerosene "all over the floor and left a trace to the back door." He then dropped a burning paper bag "onto the trace of kerosene" and the fire ignited. He fled the scene of the incident.

Shortly thereafter, Pomona firefighters arrived at defendant's apartment. An arson investigation indicated that the fire had been intentionally set within a six-square-foot area in the living room of the apartment. A petroleum product was used to start the fire according to an arson investigator, and the carpet had burned down to the concrete through the carpet pad. Cupboards in the kitchen had been burned. When the fire ignited, the arson investigator stated that there had been a low-level explosion. In the upstairs area of the apartment, there had been smoke damage or residue. Both Dukes and the fire investigator identified words that had been spray painted in the upstairs area of the apartment in an effort to make the fire look as though it was "gang related." After the fire, defendant applied for fire insurance proceeds and ultimately received an insurance settlement as a result of the fire.

* * *

Defendant contends that the evidence is insufficient to support a conviction for arson of an inhabited dwelling because it is necessary that a defendant possess a specific intent to set fire to the structure. Relying upon the decision of *In re Stonewall F.* (1989) 208 Cal.App.3d 1054, 1066 [256 Cal.Rptr. 578], defendant argues that an essential element of the crime was the existence on defendant's part of a specific intent to set fire to the structure. Because we believe that *Stonewall F.* does not correctly state California law and, in any event, there was substantial evidence of a specific intent, we affirm.

First, we believe that arson remains a general intent crime. No doubt, the Court of Appeal in the decision of *In re Stonewall F.*, ... held that arson of an inhabited structure within the meaning of section 451, subdivision (b) was a specific intent crime.

* * *

Since 1899, despite the substantial changes in the arson provisions of the Penal Code, the California Supreme Court has only commented in dicta concerning the issue of whether there is a requirement that a specific intent exist before the crime of arson may be committed. For example, in *People v. Ashley* (1954) 42 Cal.2d 246, 264, fn. 4 [267 P.2d 271], the Supreme Court noted that arson was not a specific intent crime. This discussion in *Ashley* did not focus upon any particular section of the Penal Code. On the other hand, in *People v. Nichols* (1970) 3 Cal.3d 150, 165 [89 Cal.Rptr. 721, 474 P.2d 673], the Supreme Court stated in dicta that arson was a general intent offense.

Prior to the decision of *In re Stonewall F.*, the Courts of Appeal in this state have consistently held that there is no requirement of a specific intent in an arson prosecution. ... Other jurisdictions have without exception concluded that there is no specific intent requirement in order to commit the crime of arson unless an arson statute requires the existence of a particular intention.

* * *

In evaluating whether a crime under California law requires a specific or general intent, the California Supreme Court has held that unless the crime defines a specific intent, the offense is a general intent crime. In *People v. Hood* (1969) 1 Cal.3d 444, 456–457 [82 Cal.Rptr. 618, 462 P.2d 370], the California Supreme Court held: "When the definition of a crime consists of only the description of a particular act, without reference to intent to do a further act or achieve a future consequence, we ask whether the defendant intended to do the proscribed act. This intention is deemed to be a general criminal intent. When the definition refers to defendant's intent to do some further act or achieve some additional consequence, the crime is deemed to be one of specific intent."

Section 451 requires that the act be done "willfully and maliciously" but does not indicate that any particular intent such as the intent to burn an inhabited structure is to exist. In order to act willfully, there is no requirement a defendant act with a specific intent. ... Furthermore, a defendant who acts maliciously need not possess a specific intent. ... Section 450, subdivision (e) defines "maliciously" in terms of the arson statutes as "a wish to vex, defraud, annoy, or injure another person, or an intent to do a wrongful act ... ." Section 450, subdivision (e) does not define the term "maliciously" as requiring an intent to burn an "inhabited structure, forest land, or property" as that language appears in section 451, subdivision (b), the statute under which defendant was convicted. The definition of "maliciously" in section 450, subdivision (e) which applies to arson prosecutions, is the same language appearing in section 7, subdivision 4. No court has ever interpreted section 7, subdivision 4 to require the presence of a specific intent as an element of a crime. Section 451, subdivision (b) which defines the particular punishment range to be imposed against a person who causes an inhabited structure or inhabited property to burn does not require any specific intent. Accordingly, because the statute under which defendant was convicted does not require a specific intent and the general rule of law throughout this country is that no specific intent is required absent language in an arson statute which requires the existence of a specific intent, we respectfully disagree with our colleagues' decision in the case of *In re Stonewall F.*

However, even if there was a requirement of a specific intent, there was substantial evidence to support the jury's verdict. Defendant's former husband spoke with her in September 1986 before the fire. According to her former husband, defendant said that "she got some insurance and that she was gonna burn her apartment up because she needed some money." Defendant told Dukes she wanted him and several others to start a fire by pushing "all" of her furniture to the middle of the floor. She gave Dukes "two jugs" of kerosene she obtained from her car. The "jugs" of kerosene were poured into a metal bowl while defendant was still in the apartment. The jugs were emptied into the metal bowl in the upstairs portion of the apartment. She instructed Dukes to insure that "Harold and Dicey" were out of the apartment building when the fire was started. Dukes, who was acting on defendant's instruction, poured the kerosene "all over the floor"

and created a "trace" or path of the flammable liquid all the way to the back door of the apartment. When the kerosene provided by defendant ignited, Dukes and his accomplice were blown from the apartment through an open door by the force of the sudden ignition. This certainly constituted sufficient evidence of a specific intent to do more than simply burn personal property as asserted by defendant. Coupled with her statement to her former husband that she was "gonna burn her apartment up," the manner in which she directed that the fire be started so that it was inevitable that there would be a burning throughout the apartment constituted substantial evidence of a specific intent to burn the inhabited apartment building.

* * *

The judgment is affirmed.

Finally, you should have observed the court's reliance on the treatment of arson statutes by the courts of other states. Reference to the decisions of other jurisdictions is a common practice of appellate courts when the law of the jurisdictions in which they sit does not resolve the issue before them.

Malum in Se and Malum Prohibitum

Often crimes are characterized as either **malum in se** or **malum prohibitum**. If a crime is inherently evil, it is malum in se. If a crime is not evil in itself, but is only criminal because declared so by a legislature, then it is malum prohibitum. Murder, rape, arson, and mayhem are examples of crimes that are malum in se. Failure to file your quarterly tax report or to get the proper building permit are both crimes malum prohibitum.

The distinction between malum in se and malum prohibitum is used throughout criminal law, but the importance of the distinction is in how it affects intent. Crimes malum in se are treated as requiring an evil intent, and crimes malum prohibitum are not. Some crimes may be both malum in se and malum prohibitum, depending upon the degree of violation. For example, speeding "a little over the limit may be malum prohibitum, but speeding at high speed malum in se."[8] Whether an act is malum prohibitum or malum in se often determines what crime may be charged. This usually revolves around the issue of foreseeability of harm. In the preceding example, speeding slightly over the limit is not likely to cause another's death, whereas racing through a city thirty miles over the speed limit can foreseeably cause a fatal accident. If while driving four miles over the speed limit the defendant strikes and kills a pedestrian who walks into the driver's path from behind another car, the act is likely to be determined malum prohibitum, and no resulting manslaughter charge will follow.

However, the same may not be true if the driver is traveling thirty miles over the speed limit at the time the accident occurs.

Transferred Intent

Whenever a person intends a harm, but because of bad aim or other cause the intended harm befalls another, the intent is transferred from the intended victim to the unintended victim. This is the doctrine of **transferred intent**. If John Defendant observes a neighbor burning the American flag and in anger shoots at him, missing him but killing William, the doctrine of transferred intent permits prosecution of Defendant as if he intended to kill William.

There are limits on the doctrine of transferred intent. First, the harm that actually results must be similar to the intended harm. If the harms are substantially different, then the intent does not transfer. For example, if A throws a baseball at B's window, hoping to break it, and the ball instead hits C in the head and kills him, it cannot be said that the intent to break the window transfers to C and that A can be punished for intentionally killing C. A may be criminally liable for a lesser crime, such as involuntary manslaughter, depending upon the amount of negligence involved, but he is not responsible for intentionally causing C's death.

A second limitation on the doctrine is that the transfer cannot increase the defendant's liability. Another way of stating this is that any defenses the defendant has against the intended victim are transferred to the unintended victim. For example, A shoots at B in self-defense, but hits C, inflicting a fatal wound. Because A had a valid defense if B had been killed by the shot, then A also has a defense as to C. In this case A has committed no crime.

In California, the doctrine of transferred intent is applied only to the crimes of homicide, assault, and battery. Thus, for example, the doctrine would not be applied in a case in which a defendant intended to steal or destroy the property of A but mistakenly stole or destroyed the property of B. However, the defendant will not escape criminal liability in such a situation, because theft or destruction of the property of another is a crime regardless of the defendant's knowledge of the identity of the owner of the property.

Strict Liability

At the beginning of this chapter it was noted that some acts are criminal although no mens rea accompanies the prohibited act. These crimes are proven simply by showing that the act was committed, and no particular mental state has to be proved at all. This is **strict liability**, or liability without fault, and is an exception to the requirement of Penal Code § 20 that there be both an evil mind and an evil act to have a crime. The term *strict liability* also has a tort meaning. Do not confuse criminal liability without fault with tort strict liability. However, for convenience, the phrase "strict liability" is used in this text.

In California, strict liability crimes are commonly referred to as "regulatory offenses" or "public welfare" offenses. This terminology reflects the fact that these crimes are established by the legislature and local governments for the protection of the health, safety, and welfare of the public. Regulatory offenses have been described by commentators as not true crimes, in the sense that they do not involve inherently evil acts (i.e., acts malum in se), but rather involve acts or omissions that have been declared criminal for the protection of the public welfare (i.e., acts malum prohibitum). Witkin and Epstein, quoting another leading authority, note that a rough classification of strict liability offenses includes: (1) illegal sales of intoxicating liquor, (2) sales of impure or adulterated food or drugs, (3) sales of misbranded articles, (4) criminal nuisances, (5) violations of traffic regulations, (6) violations of motor vehicle laws, and (7) violations of general police regulations, passed for the safety, health, or well-being of the community.[9]

In *People v. Dillard,* the Court of Appeal for the First Appellate District, Division Four, discussed the rationale behind strict liability offenses. As the decision illustrates, strict liability can negate the requirement for mental states other than intent, such as knowledge.

In the *Dillard* opinion, the court used the term *scienter,* which has not yet been discussed in this chapter. **Scienter** is defined in *Ballentine's Law Dictionary* as:

> Knowledge, particularly guilty knowledge; i.e., knowledge a person has that, as a matter of law, will result in her liability or guilt. Example: knowledge on the part of a person making a fraudulent representation that the representation is false.

In many cases, strict liability laws deal with potential, rather than actual, harms. For example, a murder statute can be applied only after someone has been murdered. However, many strict liability offenses deal with violations and no harm. For example, running a stoplight, speeding, or failing to have adequate fire extinguishers in your business may or may not result in an injury. Regardless

---

PEOPLE v. MOSES DILLARD, JR.
154 Cal.App.3d 261; 201 Cal.Rptr. 136
[Apr. 1984]

PANELLI, J.—A jury found Moses Dillard, Jr., guilty of the misdemeanor offense of carrying a loaded firearm on his person in a public place, in violation of Penal Code section 12031, subdivision (a). On appeal from the judgment of conviction, the appellate department of the superior court affirmed. On application of the parties, the court certified the case for transfer to this court. The question presented is whether knowledge that the firearm is loaded is an element of the offense of carrying a loaded firearm in a public place. We hold that such knowledge is not an element of the offense and affirm the judgment.

In the early morning hours of June 1, 1981, Oakland Police Officer Luis Torres observed appellant riding a bicycle on the 1300 block of 100th Avenue in Oakland. Appellant was carrying what appeared to be a rifle case. Torres activated the lights on his patrol car and asked appellant to stop. Appellant complied. In response to the officer's request, he placed the rifle case on the ground, stepped away from it, and stood by the patrol car.

Officer Torres unzipped the rifle case and lifted out the rifle. The rifle, a 30.30 Winchester, had one round of ammunition inside the chamber and six additional rounds inside the cylinder. Seven more rounds were loose in the case.

Appellant testified that the rifle belonged to him and that he had picked it up from his stepfather's house about three hours before he was stopped. He did not open the carrying case between the time he picked up the weapon and his stop by Torres.

Relying on *People v. Harrison* (1969) 1 Cal.App.3d 115, 120 [81 Cal.Rptr. 396], the court ruled inadmissible as irrelevant evidence tending to show that appellant was unaware that the rifle was loaded. The court rejected defense counsel's offer of proof, outside the presence of the jury, that appellant's stepfather had taken the rifle hunting, that appellant had loaned it to him for this purpose on several prior occasions, that his stepfather had never before returned the rifle to appellant loaded, and that on the day of the offense appellant had acted in reliance on his stepfather's past conduct. Over defense objection, the court instructed the jury that knowledge that the weapon is loaded is not an element of the offense of violating Penal Code section 12031, subdivision (a). The court refused appellant's requested instructions concerning joint operation of act and intent, the meaning of "knowingly," and ignorance or mistake of fact.

Penal Code section 12031, subdivision (a) provides in pertinent part: "Except as provided in subdivision (b), (c), or (d) [not here applicable], every person who carries a loaded firearm on his or her person or in a vehicle while in any public place or on any public street ... is guilty of a misdemeanor." In *People v. Harrison,* the court in dictum stated that the section "does not require knowledge that the gun was loaded, as the statute prohibits the carrying of a loaded firearm and does not specify knowledge it is loaded as an element of the crime." Appellant argues that to construe section 12031 as not requiring knowledge that the weapon is loaded violates his due process right to present a defense, and violates the basic principle of common law, expressed in section 20, that to constitute a crime there must be a union of act and wrongful intent.

In *United States v. Balint* (1922) 258 U.S. 250, the Supreme Court stated: "While the general rule at common law was that the *scienter* was a necessary element in the indictment and proof of every crime, and this was followed in regard to statutory crimes even where the statutory definition did not in terms include it, there has been a modification of this view in respect to prosecutions under statutes the purpose of which would be obstructed by such a requirement. It is a question of legislative intent to be construed by the court." ...

In California the common law concept of scienter, or mens rea is codified in section 20. "So basic is this requirement [of a union of act and wrongful intent] that it is an invariable element of every crime unless excluded expressly or by necessary implication." Nevertheless, notwithstanding the admonition of section 20 and the common law tradition upon which it is based, the courts, albeit with some reluctance, have recognized that certain kinds of regulatory offenses enacted for the protection of the public health and safety are punishable despite the absence of culpability or criminal intent in the accepted sense. "Although criminal sanctions

are relied upon, the primary purpose of the statutes is regulation rather than punishment or correction. The offenses are not crimes in the orthodox sense, and wrongful intent is not required in the interest of enforcement." As the Supreme Court stated in *Morissette v. United States,* [342 U.S. 246 (1952)]: "Many of these offenses are not in the nature of positive aggressions or invasions, with which the common law so often dealt, but are in the nature of neglect where the law requires care, or inaction where it imposes a duty. Many violations of such regulations result in no direct or immediate injury to person or property but merely create the danger or probability of it which the law seeks to minimize. ... In this respect, whatever the intent of the violator, the injury is the same, and the consequences are injurious or not according to fortuity. Hence, legislation applicable to such offenses, as a matter of policy, does not specify intent as a necessary element. *The accused, if he does not will the violation, usually is in a position to prevent it with no more care than society might reasonably expect and no more exertion than it might reasonably exact from one who assumed his responsibilities.* ... Under such considerations, courts have turned to construing statutes and regulations which make no mention of intent as dispensing with it and holding that the guilty act alone makes out the crime" ... (italics added).

With these principles in mind, we consider whether it was the legislative intent to exclude knowledge that the weapon is loaded as an element of the offense of carrying a loaded weapon in a public place. Section 12031 was enacted in 1967 as one of a series of statutes directed to prohibiting the carrying of loaded weapons in specified public places. Other provisions of the 1967 act prohibited the carrying of a loaded weapon into the State Capitol, the office of any legislator or constitutional officers, or on the grounds of any public school, and prohibited carrying a loaded weapon within the Governor's Mansion or on its grounds. The act was declared an urgency statute "necessary for the immediate preservation of the public peace, health or safety." As facts constituting such necessity, the Legislature cited the danger to the peace and safety of the people of this state from the increased incidence of organized groups or individuals publicly arming themselves, and the inadequacy of existing laws to protect the people from "either the use of such weapons or from violent incidents arising from the mere presence of such armed individuals in public places."

In light of this clear expression of legislative concern for the public safety as against the presence of armed individuals in public places, we conclude that section 12031, subdivision (a), by necessary implication excludes knowledge or criminal intent as an element of the offense. ... The carrying of a loaded weapon in a public place, we believe, falls within the class of cases involving " 'acts that are so destructive of the social order, or where the ability of the state to establish the element of criminal intent would be so extremely difficult if not impossible of proof, that in the interest of justice the legislature has provided that the doing of the act constitutes a crime, regardless of knowledge or criminal intent on the part of the defendant. In these cases it is the duty of the defendant to know what the facts are that involved or resulted from his acts of conduct.' " Section 12031, subdivision (a), is, in our view, a quintessential public welfare statute which embraces a legislative judgment that in the interest of the larger good, the burden of acting at hazard is placed upon a person who, albeit innocent of criminal intent, is in a position to avert the public danger.

* * *

Appellant was presumed to know that it is unlawful to carry a loaded firearm in a public place. To avoid the sanction of the law, appellant need only to have taken care to make certain that the weapon he carried was in fact unloaded—"no more care than society might reasonably expect and no more exertion than it might reasonably exact from one who assumed his responsibilities."

* * *

The judgment is affirmed.

of whether harm results, you are liable for the offense. This is considered regulatory because the purpose is to induce compliance with the law, rather than to punish for caused harm. Increased compliance is a result of an awareness by people that violation alone means liability; hence, they are more cautious and less likely to engage in the prohibited conduct. Of course, this argument can be made to justify making all crimes strict liability. The idea of not requiring any intent for acts to be criminal is contrary to American values of fairness and justice, and the California courts have been reluctant to view any "true" crime (i.e., any malum in se crime), as a strict liability offense.

The United States Supreme Court, for example, has upheld strict liability statutes in most instances.[10] Despite this recognition of strict liability offenses by the judiciary, the courts will not hesitate to infer a mens rea requirement in a statute that is silent on the necessity of a mental element if the offense has traditionally required proof of criminal intent or some other mental state. Such was the situation in the *Morissette* case. In *Morissette*, the defendant entered federal property, a military bombing range, and collected spent bomb casings which had been on the site for years. The casings were exposed to the weather and were rusting when the defendant removed them. The defendant was charged with converting (stealing) the casings. The defendant was convicted at the trial level, but the United States Supreme Court reversed that conviction.

Strict Liability and Statutory Construction

The problem addressed by the Supreme Court in *Morissette* occurs often: What is the mens rea requirement when a statute does not provide for such? That decision depends on many factors. First, the legislative history of the statute may indicate whether the crime was intended to have a mens rea requirement or not. The statements of members of legislatures while debating the law (before it became law and was a bill), reports of legislative committees of Congress, and

MORISSETTE v. UNITED STATES
342 U.S. 246 (1952)

The contention that an injury can amount to a crime only when inflicted by intention is no provincial or transient notion. It is universal and persistent in mature systems of law as belief in freedom of the human will and a consequent ability and duty of the normal individual to choose between good and evil. A relation between some mental element and punishment for a harmful act is almost as instinctive as the child's familiar exculpatory "But I didn't mean to," and has afforded the rational basis for a tardy and unfinished substitution of deterrence and reformation in place of retaliation and vengeance as the motivation for public prosecution. ...

Crime, as a compound concept, generally constituted only from concurrence of an evil-meaning mind with an evil-doing hand, was congenial to an intense individualism and took deep and early root in American soil. As the states codified the common law of crimes, even if their enactments were silent on the subject, their courts assumed that the omission did not signify disapproval of the principle but merely recognized that intent was so inherent in the idea of the offense that it required no statutory definition.

However, [some crimes fall into a] category of another character, with very different antecedents and origins. The crimes there involved depend on no mental element but consist only of forbidden acts or omissions. ... The industrial revolution multiplied the number of workmen exposed to injury from increasingly powerful and complex mechanisms, driven by freshly discovered sources of energy, requiring higher precautions by employers.

Traffic of velocities, volumes and varieties unheard of came to subject the wayfarer to intolerable casualty risks if the owners and drivers were not to observe new cares and uniformities of conduct. Congestion of cities and crowding of quarters called for health and welfare regulations undreamed of in simpler times. Wide distribution of goods became an instrument of wide distribution of harm when those who dispersed food, drink, drugs, and even securities, did not comply with reasonable standards of quality, integrity, disclosure and care. Such dangers have engendered increasingly numerous and detailed regulations which heighten the duties of those in control of particular industries, trades, properties, or activities that affect public health, safety or welfare.

... Many violations of such regulations result in no direct or immediate injury to person or property but merely create the danger or probability of injury which the law seeks to minimize.

* * *

Stealing, larceny, and its variants and equivalents, were among the earliest offenses known to the law that existed before legislation [common law]. ... State courts of last resort, on whom fall the heaviest burden of interpreting criminal law in this country, have consistently retained the requirement of intent in larceny-type offenses. If any state has deviated, the exception has neither been called to our attention nor disclosed by our research.

We hold that the mere omission from [the conversion statute] of any mention of intent will not be construed as eliminating that element from the crimes denounced.

other related materials may indicate whether the legislature intended a mens rea requirement. Second, courts look to whether the crime existed under the common law. If so, the mens rea used under the common law may be adopted by the court. Other factors include the seriousness of the harm to the public; mens rea standards for other related crimes; the punishment imposed upon conviction; the burden that would be placed on the prosecution if mens rea were required; and rules of statutory construction.

Generally, the greater the potential harm to the public and the more difficult it is for prosecution to prove mens rea, the more likely a court is to find that strict liability is to be imposed.[11] The amount of penalty can also play a role. The greater the penalty, the more likely that some intent will be read into the statute. Also, courts will look to other related statutes for guidance. If a state legislature has consistently required proof of intent for all crimes of larceny and theft, then if a new statute is enacted dealing with a particular theft (i.e., theft of computer information), and that law does not specify the mental state that must be proven, then the court will fill in the missing element with intent.

The approach of the California courts has been repeated verbatim in numerous cases:

> The doctrine codified in Penal Code Section 20, that in every crime there must exist a union, or joint operation, of act and intent is so basic that it is an invariable element of every crime unless excluded expressly or by necessary implication.[12]

Applying this principle, the California courts interpret every criminal statute as requiring criminal intent unless the statutory language excludes the requirement "expressly or by necessary implication."

In *People v. Johnson,* the Court of Appeal for the First Appellate District, Division One, applied the foregoing standard and rejected the government's argument that the crimes in question were strict liability crimes. In *Johnson,* the defendant, David Earl Johnson, and Twila Rickley had lived together, unmarried, from 1972 to 1980. They had two children during that period. After the couple separated in 1980, Johnson maintained contact with the children, including periods when they resided in his home.

PEOPLE v. DAVID EARL JOHNSON
151 Cal.App.3d 1021; 199 Cal.Rptr. 231
[Feb. 1984]

NEWSOM, J.—

* * *

On September 6, 1981, respondent [Johnson] visited the children, ostensibly to bring them school clothes. Twila agreed he could take the children out for ice cream before dinner. Respondent left with the children at 6 P.M., promising to return them for dinner an hour later. When neither respondent nor the children returned, Twila contacted the Guerneville police, but was told nothing could be done without a court order.

Twila attempted to contact respondent by calling and visiting [Johnson's] parents' residence, but did not discover the whereabouts of the children until September 7, when she received a phone call from respondent warning that if she wanted to see her children again she should agree to give him custody. He also said she would be hearing from his lawyer.

On September 15, 1981, a few days after the children had disappeared, an order to show cause, including a temporary custody order giving custody to Twila, was filed. An investigator for Twila's attorney made numerous unsuccessful efforts to locate and serve defendant.

Twila tried to find the children by visiting Santa Cruz, Sunol and Los Angeles. She glimpsed them twice: once in a pickup truck with respondent and his present wife, and another time in the yard of respondent's in-laws. Not knowing what to do, she returned to Santa Rosa and from there contacted respondent. She did not see the children again until April 6, 1982, in a children's facility in Norman, Oklahoma.

On August 4, 1982, respondent filed a cross-complaint for custody, visitation and support, requesting joint legal custody of the children, with physical custody in him.

On August 13, 1982, respondent was charged with two counts of child abduction and two counts of false imprisonment. The charges were dismissed pursuant to respondent's section 995 motion, based upon the trial court's finding that respondent had a right to custody of the children. The People have appealed.

Penal Code section 278 criminalizes the taking, concealing or detaining of a child by one "not having a right of custody." Respondent's defense was that his right to custody of the children was at the time of the alleged crimes ... coequal with that of their mother. Civil Code section 197 provides that the father of a minor child is "equally entitled to the custody, services and earnings" of the child "*if presumed to be the father* under subdivision (a) of Section 7004." (Italics added.) The People content that respondent does not qualify as a person "presumed to be the father under subdivision (a) of Section 7004," and thus had no right to custody of the children when he took them from their mother.

The Uniform Parentage Act (hereinafter Act) sets forth, in subdivision (a)(4) of section 7004 of the Civil Code, rebuttable presumptions which apply where the identity of the "natural father" of a child is at issue. As pertinent here, it provides that "A man is presumed to be the natural father of a child if ... [h]e receives the child into his home and openly holds out the child as his natural child."

It is undisputed that respondent received the children into his home, which he shared with Twila, and in all respects treated them as his own.

* * *

The Act—including section 7004—was plainly intended to establish and promote the rights of putative fathers, and to remove obstacles to the maintenance of parental relations for the benefit of "illegitimate" children. ... [I]t grants equal custodial rights to anyone "presumed to be a father under section 7004." ... Finally, respondent is concededly the natural father of the children, and resorting to section 7004 to establish paternity is therefore superfluous. ... We accordingly conclude that for purposes of section 197, respondent is a presumptive father with equal right to custody of the children ... .

* * *

The People ... argue that section 278 is a "strict liability crime," making respondent's ignorance of the trial court's order irrelevant to the charge. ...

Penal Code sections 278 and 278.5 defined specific intent crimes: Section 278 provided that abduction of the child must be "with intent to detain or conceal such child from a parent"; section 278.5 similarly states that violation of a child custody decree is criminal if the child is detained or concealed "with the intent to deprive the other person of such right to custody or visitation" ... . [I]n the case at bench, respondent was acting under a belief—mistaken or not—that he had never been deprived of his custodial right to the children. The *fact* of the custody order ... was unknown to him.

His mistaken belief negates not only the requisite intent to deprive Twila of custody, but also discloses his lack of awareness that his conduct was proscribed by section 278.

Penal Code section 26 provides that a person does not commit a crime when the act was committed under a mistake of fact "which disproves any criminal intent." Section 20 adds: "In every crime or public offense there must exist a union, or joint operation of act and intent, or criminal negligence." ... " 'So basic is this requirement [of a union of act and wrongful intent] that it is an invariable element of every crime unless excluded expressly or by necessary implication.' " ...

Recent appellate decisions manifest a refusal to impose criminal sanctions absent a showing of intent. In *People v. Hernandez* (1964) 61 Cal.2d 529, for example, the court found it a defense to the charge of statutory rape that the defendant had honestly and reasonably believed the prosecutrix was over 18 years of age. Similarly, in *People v. Mayberry* [(1975)] 15 Cal.3d 143, the court considered defendant's mistaken belief of consent to be a valid defense to charges of forcible rape and kidnaping, explaining: "If a defendant entertains a reasonable and bona fide belief that a prosecutrix voluntarily consented to accompany him and to engage in sexual intercourse, it is apparent he does not possess the wrongful intent that is a prerequisite under Penal Code section 20 to a conviction of kidnaping or rape by means of force or threat."

Even more closely in point here is *People v. Vogel,* 46 Cal.2d 798, where defendant's reasonable but erroneous belief that his first wife had divorced him negated the criminal intent necessary to support a conviction for bigamy. Noting that the intent requirement of section 20 was not excluded expressly or by necessary implication, the court declared: "Nor would it be reasonable to hold that a person is guilty of bigamy who remarries in good faith in reliance on a judgment of divorce or annulment that is subsequently found not to be the 'judgment of a competent court' " ... .

In the case at bench, respondent was unaware of the *existence* of a court order, which negates the specific intent required to establish the crime.

The false imprisonment charge suffers from the same infirmity, and falls with the kidnaping charge. We conclude that all counts were properly dismissed.

The judgment is affirmed.

Vicarious Liability

The term **vicarious liability** refers to situations in which one person is held accountable for the actions of another. Under vicarious liability, there is no requirement of mens rea, and additionally there is no requirement for an act, at least not by the defendant. The person who is liable for the actions of another need not act, encourage another to act, or intend any harm at all. As is true with vicarious liability in tort law, this situation is most common between employers and employees.

Unlike vicarious liability in tort law, however, vicarious criminal liability of an employer for the acts of an employee does not apply to all crimes. The California courts have held that vicarious criminal liability will be imposed only for strict liability offenses, because those offenses do not require criminal intent. With respect to crimes requiring criminal intent, an employer is not liable unless it is a party to the crime, that is, he or she aids or abets the employee in the commission of the crime or orders the employee to commit the crime.

Employers may be liable for the actions of their employees when strict liability criminal laws relating to the operation of the business are violated. For example, the owner of a business may be prosecuted for failure to comply with product safety regulations, even though that was a duty delegated to an employee and the owner had no knowledge that the products manufactured were substandard. In *People v. Travers* (1975) 52 Cal.App.3d 111, a service station owner was convicted for sale of mislabeled motor oil, despite the fact that the offense was actually committed by his employee and the owner neither knew of nor condoned the employee's actions. Vicarious liability is also imposed on those who market food and drugs.[13] This is because of the significant public welfare interest in the quality of these products.

Corporate Liability

Corporate liability is a form of vicarious liability. Under the common law, corporations could not be convicted of crimes. However, this is no longer the law.

Corporations can be held criminally accountable for the acts of their employees and agents. The agent must be working within the scope of his or her employment for the company to be liable. If an employee of Burger King strikes an enemy while on break in the parking lot of the store, the company is not criminally liable for battery. However, if officers of a corporation send employees into a workplace knowing that it is dangerous and represent to the employees that it is safe, the company may be liable for battery to the employee, or even manslaughter if death results.

Obviously, corporations cannot be incarcerated, so fines are usually imposed. In some instances, **injunctions** may be imposed. Finally, note that corporate liability does not free the agent from criminal liability. In most cases the agent or employee remains criminally liable for his or her act.

In contrast to the situation with corporations, California law does not regard a partnership as an entity for the purposes of criminal liability. As a result, a partnership may not be convicted of a crime. The individual partner who committed the crime may, of course, be convicted.

Proving Mens Rea

At trial the prosecution has the burden of establishing that the defendant possessed the required mental state when the act was committed. In most cases defendants do not admit to committing the acts in question. Even when defendants do admit to committing some acts, they commonly deny intent. For crimes that require intent, admission of the act is not enough to sustain a conviction. The question is, how does a prosecutor gain a conviction for a crime that requires a showing of intent when the defendant denies possessing the required intent? The answer is by using **inferences**. An *inference* is a conclusion that a judge or jury is permitted to make after considering the facts of a case.

Penal Code § 21(a) states: "The intent or intention is manifested by the circumstances connected with the offense." This statutory language refers to the fact that a defendant's intent is established by means of **circumstantial evidence**. A defendant cannot be compelled to testify against himself. Additionally, even if a defendant were to testify, he could be expected to deny entertaining the criminal intent necessary for a conviction. Under Penal Code § 21(a), the defendant's intent may be inferred from an evaluation of the circumstances attending the commission of the defendant's act.

Imagine that a man walks up to another man and strikes him in the head with a hammer, using great force in his swing. The wound is fatal, and the attacker is charged with first-degree murder. Assume for the purposes of this example that to sustain a first-degree murder charge in this jurisdiction, it must be shown that the man intended to cause the victim's death. The defendant disavows such intent, admitting only that he intended to hit and injure the victim. In such a case the jury would be permitted to infer the defendant's intent to kill the victim from the circumstances connected with the offense. In other words, the jury could reasonably conclude from the defendant's actions that he did intend to kill the victim, despite the defendant's denial of such intent.

A **presumption** is a conclusion that must be made by a judge or jury. Most people have heard of the presumption of innocence in criminal law. This presumption is a rebuttable presumption. Rebuttable presumptions are conclusions that must be made by a judge or jury, unless disproven by the facts. Hence, defendants are innocent until proven guilty. *Irrebuttable presumptions,* also called *conclusive presumptions,* are conclusions that must be made by the judge or jury and cannot be disproved. Regardless of what the evidence shows, an irrebuttable presumption stands as a fact.

Presumptions have their use in criminal prosecutions. However, the criminal intent, general or specific, of a defendant may not be presumed, because such a presumption would be inconsistent with the presumption that the defendant is innocent until proven guilty, as well as with the prosecution's duty to prove every element of the offense. Intent must be proven like any other element of the charged offense. Remember, however, that intent may be proven through the use of inferences based upon the conduct of the defendant.

Motive

The reason a person commits a crime is **motive**. More particularly, the reason that leads a person to a desired result or particular action is motive.

Motive is different from mens rea. Motive leads to mens rea. Motive is concerned with why people act. Mens rea, in contrast, is concerned with whether a person intended to act. For example, greed is a motive for many acts. A bank robber's motive for robbing a bank is greed (or even, possibly, the challenge). The robber's mens rea is neither greed nor the emotional thrill resulting from the risk; rather, it is the intent to take money using force or threat. Said another way, the robber's mens rea (intent) is used to satisfy his or her motive (greed).

Motive is not an element of crimes. Therefore, prosecutors do not have to prove motive to be successful in a prosecution. Proof of motive is, however, admissible in a criminal case because it is relevant to the question of whether the accused committed the offense. If the prosecution can establish that the accused had a motive to commit the crime, the prosecution's case against the defendant is strengthened because the existence of motive makes it plausible that the defendant committed the charged act and entertained the requisite criminal intent. The prosecution might be able to obtain a conviction without proof of motive, but introducing evidence that the defendant had a motive to commit the offense increases the chances of a conviction. In many crimes, the motive will be apparent. Greed is easily understood and is imputed by juries to accused thieves. In other crimes, such as murder, there may be no apparent motive. Was the murder motivated by greed (e.g., to gain an inheritance), or by passion (e.g., in revenge for infidelity), or some other emotion?

A bad motive does not make an otherwise lawful act criminal. Conversely, a good motive does not excuse the commission of a crime. The issue is simply whether the prosecution has proven, beyond a reasonable doubt, that all the elements of the crime were committed.

Motive plays a role at sentencing. A good motive may justify a mitigation of sentence, whereas a bad motive may act in the reverse.

In some instances, a good motive may prevent charges from being filed at all. Police and prosecutors do not pursue some cases, even though a crime has been committed, when a person acted with good intentions. Conversely, law enforcement officials may pursue a case more passionately if the defendant acted from an evil motive.

§ 3.2   Actus Reus

Earlier in this chapter you learned the Latin phrase "actus non facit reum nisi mens sit rea." The phrase expresses the common-law requirement that two essential elements must be present to have a crime: a guilty mind and a guilty act. This requirement is reflected in Penal Code § 20, cited earlier in this chapter: "In every crime or public offense there must exist a union, or joint operation of act and intent, or criminal negligence."

Actus reus is the physical part of a crime; it is the act prohibited by the statute that defines the crime. For example, Penal Code § 187 defines murder as "the unlawful killing of a human being with malice aforethought." The actus reus element of murder is the unlawful killing of a human being. The mens rea element is malice aforethought. To establish the existence of the actus reus element in a murder case, the prosecution must prove that the defendant unlawfully killed a human being. In most cases, proving that the defendant killed the victim is a relatively straightforward process. In some cases, however, issues of voluntariness or causation can cloud the picture.

Normally, the act prohibited by a criminal statute involves some type of physical movement on the part of the defendant. There are, however, other types of acts that can constitute the basis for criminal liability in certain situations. These types of acts are discussed later in this chapter.

Voluntariness

To be held criminally liable for one's actions, those actions must be voluntary. To be voluntary, an act must occur as a result of the actor's conscious choice. The person accused must have acted freely, or no liability attaches. Under California law, a person who commits an act without being conscious of it is not criminally liable for the act. This is the defense of unconsciousness. A person is "unconscious" for this purpose if he or she is unaware of committing the act as a result of a cause that is not voluntarily induced. Examples of "unconsciousness" that have appeared in California cases include sleepwalking, delirium from fever or drugs, and lack of awareness resulting from a blow on the head.[14] The Model Penal Code reflects the same principles, and specifically lists the following as being involuntary:

1. reflexes and convulsions;
2. bodily movements during unconsciousness or sleep;
3. conduct during hypnosis or resulting from hypnotic suggestion; and
4. other movements that are not a product of the effort or determination of the actor.[15]

Do not confuse the concepts of mens rea and actus reus. All that is required to have an act is a choice by the defendant to act. No evil intent is required to have an act; that is a question of mens rea. Say that Jim chooses to swing his arm. As a result he hits Tom. What intent is required to prove battery and whether Jim possessed that intent are questions of mens rea. For actus reus, all that need be known is whether Jim voluntarily chose to swing his arm. His swing would be involuntary if Bill grabbed Jim's arm and moved it, causing it to strike Tom.

In the case excerpt from *People v. Freeman*, the Court of Appeal for the Second Appellate District, Division Two, reversed the appellant's conviction because the trial court erroneously instructed the jury on the effect of the defendant's possible unconsciousness.

Note that, in the *Freeman* case, the issue did not revolve only around the defendant's unconsciousness at the time of the automobile collision. The principal error perceived by the appellate court was the failure of the trial court to instruct the jury that it could consider the possible effect of the defendant's oncoming state of unconsciousness on his culpability for deciding to drive. In the view of the appellate court, the trial court should have instructed the jury that it could acquit the defendant if it found that the epileptic attack had clouded the defendant's judgment at the time he made the decision to drive the automobile.

PEOPLE v. JAMES A. FREEMAN
61 Cal.App.2d 110
[Oct. 1943]

MOORE, P.J.—This appeal is from the order denying defendant's motion for a new trial and from the final judgment of conviction for violating section 500 of the Vehicle Code by the commission of negligent homicide.

The grounds for appeal are (1) the insufficiency of the evidence to support the verdict and (2) errors committed by the court in the refusal of certain instructions and the giving of others.

At the times herein mentioned the defendant resided in the city of Pasadena where he was engaged in the mercantile business. He had a branch store in the neighboring city of Alhambra which was operated by one Ruben Pfieffer. The latter's residence was in the adjacent city of San Gabriel. About one o'clock in the afternoon of January 24, 1943, defendant drove from Pasadena to the home of Mr. Pfieffer. He remained three hours during which he felt ill and drank two highballs of Seven-up and whiskey. About 4:30 o'clock P.M. he started to drive back home. His return was by way of the intersection of Winston Avenue and California Street which is about four miles from the Pfieffer place. During the last 700 or 800 feet before arriving at the intersection he drove at a speed in excess of 60 miles per hour. Upon entering the intersection, his car collided with another driven by Mrs. Clark and in which Miss Della Heath was riding. As a result of the collision Miss Heath was killed and Mrs. Clark severely injured. Details will appear hereafter in the instruction under attack.

The charging part of the information was that defendant willfully drove an automobile with reckless disregard of and willful indifference to the safety of others, thereby injuring Miss Heath who died on the same day as the proximate result of her injuries suffered on that occasion. The sole defense to the accusation was that the defendant was unconscious from the moment he entered his car at the Pfieffer home until after the accident when he stood upon a nearby lawn. His testimony was in support of that defense. Promptly after the accident, defendant was given a sobriety test at the Huntington Memorial Hospital and pronounced sober. The defense is based upon section 26, subdivision 5 of the Penal Code which reads as follows:

"All persons are capable of committing crimes except those belonging to the following classes: ...

FIVE. Persons who committed the act charged without being conscious thereof."

Stated in other words: No person can be guilty of a crime who is not conscious at the time of doing the act charged.

In order to violate section 500 of the Vehicle Code a motorist must drive his automobile with reckless disregard of or willful indifference to the safety of others, which is the equivalent of "the intentional doing of an act with wanton and reckless disregard of its possible results." It is the same as willful misconduct which implies at least the intention of doing an act either with knowledge that serious injury is a probable result or the intention of doing an act with a wanton and reckless disregard of its probable result.

* * *

In answer to a comprehensive hypothetical question four physicians testified that at the time of the collision of his automobile with that of Mrs. Clark defendant was, at the time and in the course of his drive from the [Pfieffers'], unconscious; also, that his spells of unconsciousness and his frequently recurring violent headaches were due to epilepsy from which appellant had suffered many attacks since he was nine years of age and had been unconscious at the time of each attack until one that occurred about six years prior to the collision.

* * *

Predicated upon the evidence admitted the court read the following instruction to the jury:

* * *

"It is the testimony of the experts & the defendant that he was unconscious at the time of the accident.

"Under the circumstances above related and all the other evidence in the case it is for you, the jury, to determine the following questions.

"1. Was the defendant, knowing he was subject to the attacks of unconsciousness as disclosed by all the evidence, and being in the condition the evidence shows he was at his friend's house,—was he guilty of a reckless disregard of the safety of others in undertaking to drive his automobile along the public highways and as I have just defined 'reckless disregard' for you.

"2. Did he know or have reason to know of facts which would lead a reasonable man to realize that such conduct on his part would create an unreasonable risk of bodily harm to others and would also involve a high degree of probability that substantial harm would result to others?

"If you answer these questions in the affirmative then you will find the defendant guilty as charged in the information and this in spite of the fact that he was unconscious at the time of the accident, if you so find.

"On the other hand, if you find that the defendant was unconscious at the time of the accident, and you answer the two questions I have just propounded in the negative, then you must find the defendant not guilty unless you shall also find that the unconsciousness was proximately caused by his voluntary use of intoxicants, for intoxication."

In order fairly to evaluate the meaning of the language of the foregoing instruction, we turn to a consideration of the physical and nervous condition from which defendant suffered according to the proof. Basing their opinions upon his recitals of his experience, the four experts testified that on the occasion of his accident defendant was suffering a loss of consciousness and that it was due to epilepsy. "Epilepsy is defined as the falling sickness; a chronic apyretic nervous affection, characterized by seizures of loss of consciousness, with tonic or clonic convulsions." "It is a chronic nervous affection characterized by sudden losses of consciousness." "It is a disease of the brain which occurs in paroxysms with uncertain intervals between; ... the attack is characterized by loss of consciousness, sudden falling down, distortion of the eyes and face ... and by muscular spasms."

* * *

In view of the behavior of the victim of epilepsy as defined by the foregoing authorities, and in the light of the expert proof of defendant's condition, we now turn to a consideration of the above instruction.

The instruction is assumptive and arbitrary. It assumes that, before leaving Pfieffer's, defendant had a present consciousness of his past sufferings, and that he had the normal powers of his will. It should have left for the jury's determination what the evidence disclosed the condition of defendant to be while at the Pfieffer home. It assumes that, throughout the three hours of his visit, his mind was clear, that his vision was unclouded, that he knew and comprehended the meaning of his current sensations, and that he was capable of appraising his contemplated effort to drive his car upon the highways. ... [I]t was for the jury to determine whether defendant, while he was visiting the Pfieffer home and at

the time of his departure therefrom, had the power of an ordinarily prudent man to conceive, and estimate the significance of, his undertaking the drive back to Pasadena. If he was unconscious at the end of a four mile drive, the jury had to determine whether the transition from a state of normal consciousness to that of unconsciousness was sudden; whether it occurred on the highway prior to the collision or whether it had taken place at some time during his visit with Mr. Pfieffer and as a result of an epileptic attack. If the defendant was on the verge of losing consciousness from epilepsy before commencing his homeward journey it is probable that he might before starting already have lost the power to envisage the consequences to others of his undertaking. And what is of even greater importance, in order for him to be guilty of driving with a reckless disregard of, or with a willful indifference to, the safety of others, before leaving the Pfieffer home, he must have had the power to will to drive or not to drive; that is, to direct the execution of a clearly conceived plan. When a human being loses consciousness as the result of a diseased condition of his nervous system there is no distinct line over which the mind leaps from the sunlit fields of clear consciousness to the dark canyons of unconsciousness. Surely, there must be, in the case of the epileptic, a period of penumbra when the will is in a state of total or partial paralysis. Under proper guidance the jury should have been permitted to determine whether defendant was suffering a state of clouded understanding or of obstructed will as a result of his epilepsy prior to his departure from the Pfieffer home.

The instruction told the jury that if they should find that the defendant was guilty of a reckless disregard of the safety of others in undertaking to make the drive and if they should find that he knew facts which would lead a reasonable man to realize that such a drive would involve a high degree of probability that substantial harm would result to others, *they should find him guilty as charged in spite of the fact that they might find he was unconscious at the time of the accident.* Such is absolutely contrary to the statute which declares one not guilty if at the time he commits a criminal act he is not conscious thereof.

No principle of criminal jurisprudence was ever more zealously guarded than that a person is guiltless if at the time of his commission of an act defined as criminal he has no knowledge of his deed. "It is a sacred principle of criminal jurisprudence that the intention to commit the crime is of the essence of the crime, and to hold that a man shall be held criminally responsible for an offense of the commission of which he was ignorant at the time would be intolerable tyranny." (*Duncan v. State,* 26 Tenn. (7 Humph. 148) 118, 120.) In *State v. Lewis,* 136 Mo. 84, the defendant having pleaded unconsciousness at the time she shot the deceased, the jury was instructed to acquit her if they believed from any cause she was so nearly unconscious as not to know what she was doing. In *People v. Sameniego* it was declared that where the evidence shows the conscious mind of the accused ceased to operate and his actions were "controlled by the subconscious or subjective mind" the jury should be instructed as to the legal effect of such unconsciousness. A person who cannot comprehend the nature and quality of his act is not responsible therefor. An act done in the absence of the will is not any more the behavior of the actor than is an act done contrary to his will.

The attorney general contends that in order for defendant to prove his unconsciousness at the time of the accident it was incumbent upon him to plead insanity. Such is not the law. The fact that at Pfieffer's house defendant made such statements as "I think I can make it home," which in the case of a normal mental condition would indicate the possession of a clear understanding, did not necessarily signify such ability. Whether he clearly recognized his probable, early collapse was itself a fact for the jury's determination. If they had determined that he was unconscious at the intersection and that such state of being had wholly, or to a material extent, overtaken him before leaving on his fatal drive, the instruction should have authorized his acquittal. …

The judgment and the order are reversed.

The *Cogdon* case excerpt is included because it reflects California legal principles and because it presents a clear case of unconsciousness. In the case, a woman was acquitted of murdering her daughter because it was determined that her acts were not voluntary.

Thoughts and Statements as Acts

Thoughts alone are not acts that can be made criminal. People may think evil thoughts, but if there is no act furthering such a thought, there is no crime.

Generally, people are also free to speak. The First Amendment to the United States Constitution protects freedom of speech. When the First Amendment applies, speech may not be made criminal. There are, however, limits to First Amendment protection of speech. Inciting riots, treason, solicitation, conspiracy, and causing imminent harm to others are examples of speech that may be prohibited.

Personal Status as an Act

Generally, a person's status cannot be declared criminal. Illness, financial status, race, sex, and religion are examples of human conditions. Some conditions are directly related to illegal behavior. For example, being addicted to illegal narcotics is a condition that cannot be punished. This is because status is generally believed not to be an act. However, using and selling prohibited narcotics are acts and may be punished.

In *Robinson v. California*, 370 U.S. 660 (1962), the United States Supreme Court was called upon to review a California statute that made it a crime "either

KING v. COGDON
Supreme Court of Victoria (1950)[16]

Mrs. Cogdon was charged with the murder of her only child, a daughter called Pat, aged 19. Pat had for some time been receiving psychiatric treatment for a relatively minor neurotic condition of which, in her psychiatrist's opinion, she was now cured. Despite this, Mrs. Cogdon continued to worry unduly about her. Describing the relationship between Pat and her mother, Mr. Cogdon testified: "I don't think a mother could have thought any more of her daughter. I think she absolutely adored her." On the conscious level, there was no doubt [of] Mrs. Cogdon's deep attachment to her daughter.

To the charge of murdering Pat, Mrs. Cogdon pleaded not guilty. Her story, though somewhat bizarre, was not seriously challenged by the Crown, and led to her acquittal. She told how on the night before her daughter's death she had dreamt that their house was full of spiders and that these spiders were crawling all over Pat. In her sleep, Mrs. Cogdon left the bed she shared with her husband, went into Pat's room and awakened to find herself violently brushing at Pat's face, presumably to remove the spiders. This woke Pat. Mrs. Cogdon told her she was just tucking her in. At the trial, she testified that she still believed, as she had been told, that the occupants of a nearby house bred spiders as a hobby, preparing nests for them behind the pictures on their walls. It was these spiders that in her dreams had invaded their home and attacked Pat. There had also been a previous dream in which ghosts had sat at the end of Mrs. Cogdon's bed and she had said to them, "Well, you have come to take Pattie." It does not seem fanciful to accept the psychological explanation of these spiders and ghosts as the projections of Mrs. Cogdon's subconscious hostility towards her daughter; a hostility which was itself rooted in Mrs. Cogdon's own early life and marital relationship.

The morning after the spider dream she told her doctor of it. He gave her a sedative and, because of the dream and certain previous difficulties she had reported, discussed the possibility of psychiatric treatment. That evening Mrs. Cogdon suggested to her husband that he attend his lodge meeting, and asked Pat to come with her to the cinema. After he had gone Pat looked through the paper, not unusually found no tolerable programme, and said that as she was going out the next evening she thought she would rather go to bed early. Later while Pat was having a bath preparatory to retiring, Mrs. Cogdon went into her room, put a hot water bottle in the bed, turned back the bedclothes, and placed a glass of hot milk beside the bed ready for Pat. She then went to bed herself. There was some desultory conversation between them about the war in Korea, and just before she put out her light Pat called out to her mother, "Mum, don't be so silly worrying about the war, it's not on our front step yet."

Mrs. Cogdon went to sleep. She dreamt that "the war was all around the house," that the soldiers were in Pat's room, and that one soldier was on the bed attacking Pat. This is all of the dream that she could later recapture. Her first "waking" memory was of running from Pat's room, out of the house to the home of her sister who lived next door. When her sister opened the front door Mrs. Cogdon fell into her arms crying, "I think I've hurt Pattie."

In fact Mrs. Cogdon had, in her somnambulistic state, left her bed, fetched an axe from the woodheap, entered Pat's room, and struck her two accurate forceful blows on the head with the blade of the axe, thus killing her.

* * *

At all events the jury believed Mrs. Cogdon's story ... [Mrs. Cogdon] was acquitted because the act of killing itself was not, in law, regarded as her act at all. ...

to use narcotics, or to be addicted to the use of narcotics." The Court reversed Robinson's conviction and in the opinion stated:

> This statute, therefore, is not one which punishes a person for the use of narcotics, for their purchase, sale or possession, or for antisocial or disorderly behavior resulting from their administration. It is not a law which even purports to provide or require medical treatment. Rather, we deal with a statute which makes the "status" of narcotic addiction a criminal offense,

for which the offender may be prosecuted "at any time before he reforms." California has said that a person can be continuously guilty of this offense, whether or not he has ever used or possessed any narcotics within the state, and whether or not he has been guilty of any antisocial behavior there.

It is unlikely that any State at this moment in history would attempt to make it a criminal offense for a person to be mentally ill, or a leper, or to be afflicted with a venereal disease. A State might determine that the general health and welfare require that the victims of these and other human afflictions be dealt with by compulsory treatment, involving quarantine, confinement, or sequestration. But, in the light of contemporary human knowledge, a law which made a criminal offense of such a disease would doubtless be universally thought of to be an infliction of cruel and unusual punishment in violation of the Eighth and Fourteenth Amendments. ...

We cannot but consider the statute before us as of the same category. ... We hold that a state law which imprisons a person thus afflicted as a criminal, even though he has never touched any narcotic drug within the State or been guilty of any irregular behavior there, inflicts a cruel and unusual punishment in violation of the Fourteenth Amendment. ...

Possession as an Act

Possession of certain items, such as narcotics, burglary tools, or dangerous weapons, may be made criminal. Possession is not, strictly speaking, an act. Possession does not involve an active body movement; rather, possession is a passive state of being. Even so, most possession laws have been upheld.

California law recognizes two types of possession: actual possession and constructive possession. *California Jury Instruction-Criminal* (referred to in California as "CALJIC") number 1.24 defines *possession* as follows:

There are two kinds of possession: actual possession and constructive possession.

Actual possession requires that a person knowingly exercise direct physical control over a thing.

Constructive possession does not require actual possession but does require that a person knowingly exercise control or the right to control a thing, either directly or through another person or persons.

One person may have possession alone, or two or more persons together may share actual or constructive possession.

SIDEBAR

The *California Jury Instructions-Criminal,* commonly referred to as "CALJIC," is a publication containing jury instructions for use in criminal cases. The function of jury instructions is to inform the jury of the law applicable to the facts of the case the jury is deliberating. Jury instructions are discussed in Chapter 17. The jury instructions contained in CALJIC are prepared under the direction of the Los Angeles Superior Court with the assistance of specially qualified members of the bar. CALJIC is not an official form book, but the instructions contained in CALJIC are widely accepted and extensively used by the California courts.

Actual possession exists when an object is on one's person. **Constructive possession** exists when the object is not on one's person, but is within one's "dominion and control." An object is within a person's dominion and control if it is readily accessible to that person. Courts have found constructive possession in numerous fact situations. For example, defendants have been convicted of possession of illegal drugs when the drugs were found in automobiles they were operating. In these cases, the illegal drugs were not on the persons of the defendants, but were located in areas under the defendants' dominion and control— the interiors of their automobiles. In one case, a defendant was found to have been in possession of illegal narcotics when police officers found the narcotics in the kitchen of an apartment in which the defendant was sleeping, there was no other person in the apartment, and the defendant had access to the narcotics. *Hacker v. Superior Court* (1968) 268 Cal.App.2d 387.

A question that frequently arises in possession cases is whether the defendant must knowingly be in possession and, if so, the type of knowledge required to constitute the offense. Virtually all possession offenses require that the defendant be aware of the fact of possession. For example, if Sue secretly places a bag containing marijuana in Mary's purse, and Mary is unaware of its presence, she does not have knowledge of the fact of possession and has not committed a criminal offense. Now, change the facts and assume that Mary knows Sue has placed a bag containing a brown vegetable-like substance in Mary's purse. Must Mary also know that the substance is an illegal drug in order to be guilty of the offense of unlawful possession of a controlled substance, or need she only know of the fact of possession without knowing the nature of the thing possessed? In the case of possession of a controlled substance, California law requires knowledge on the part of the defendant both of the fact of possession (i.e., of the presence of the item) and of the nature of the thing possessed (i.e., that it is a controlled substance). Accordingly, if Mary knew of the presence of the bag in her purse, but did not know it contained a controlled substance, she would not be guilty of the crime of possession of a controlled substance. If she knew both of the presence of the bag and the fact that it contained a controlled substance, Mary would be guilty of the crime.

Although all possession statutes, or the judicial interpretations of such statutes, require knowledge of possession, not all require that the defendant know the illegal nature of the thing possessed. For example, possession of illegal weapons is treated differently by the law than possession of illegal narcotics. A possible explanation for the difference is that the nature of weapons is fairly obvious, whereas the nature of narcotics is not. A lay person may be unable to determine by observing a substance whether it is an illegal drug or a perfectly lawful medication. In contrast, most people recognize a weapon when they see one. The Dangerous Weapons Control Law, found at Penal Code § 12000 and following sections, prohibits the possession of a number of weapons specified in § 12020. Offenses under the Dangerous Weapons Control Law, like all possession offenses, require that the defendant know of the fact of possession, i.e., the defendant must know he is in possession of the weapon in question. Unlike narcotics possession offenses, however, a defendant in possession of an illegal weapon need not know that the weapon possessed is one prohibited by law. Knowledge of possession, alone, is sufficient to constitute the offense.

Finally, the law recognizes a concept known as **joint possession.** Joint possession exists when two or more persons are regarded as being in possession of the same thing. In cases of joint possession, there may be only one prohibited thing, but two or more persons may be convicted of being in possession of it. Joint possession is analogous to constructive possession by more than one person. Thus, persons jointly occupying premises where controlled substances are found may be held to be in joint possession of the controlled substances. With respect to each person, however, the knowledge requirements discussed in the preceding paragraphs must be established. Joint occupancy of premises, alone, is not sufficient to establish possession as a matter of law.

Omissions as Acts

Generally, only acts are prohibited by criminal law. However, in some situations people have a duty to act, and failure to act is criminal. An **omission** is a failure to act when required to do so by law. The duty to act may be imposed by statute or by common law.

Duty Imposed by Statute

First, criminal statutes may impose a duty to act. For example, in California, one has a statutory duty to report information to governmental agencies in certain situations. Among these situations are the obligation of taxpayers to file annual state income tax returns, the obligation of health care practitioners to report wounds or other physical injuries inflicted by means of a firearm or as a result of assaultive or abusive conduct, and the obligation of persons involved in motor vehicle or boating accidents to make specified reports. Another duty imposed by statute is the duty of a manufacturer of dangerous products to warn of the dangers of the products, by appropriate labeling or otherwise. Yet another statutory duty is the duty of an automobile driver, operator of a boat, or hunter who accidentally injures another person to stop and render aid. Other duties imposed by statute include duties imposed on owners and operators of businesses to take certain actions for the health and safety of employees and members of the public, and the duty of parents to support and protect their children. Failure of a person to act in compliance with these statutorily imposed duties constitutes a criminal offense.[17]

Duty Imposed by Common Law

The issue of whether a person has a duty to act under the common law generally arises in cases involving the existence or lack of a duty to protect another person from harm. It is often the case that a person who may have a moral duty to act does not have a legal duty to act. In most instances, people do not have a legal duty to assist one another in times of need. It would not be criminal, for example, for a beachgoer who is an excellent swimmer to watch another drown.

In certain situations, the common law imposes a duty on a person to protect another from harm. In such situations, the person having the duty may be criminally liable if he or she willfully or negligently permits harm to come to the person to whom the duty is owed. The duty to protect another from harm may be imposed simply by virtue of the relationship between the two persons, such as the parent-child relationship. In a recent decision that raised constitutional issues regarding free exercise of religion, the California Supreme Court upheld the involuntary manslaughter conviction of the parents of a child who died from lack of medical care because the parents attempted to treat the child by prayer alone.[18] The duty to protect another from harm may also arise as the result of voluntary assumption of the duty. Such assumption may occur gratuitously or by contract. A common example of contractual assumption of a duty to protect another from harm is the agreement of a home for the elderly to care for persons placed in the home. If one of the home's charges dies as a result of criminal neglect, the person or persons responsible may be prosecuted for manslaughter.

Causation

Some acts are criminal even though the prohibited result does not occur. For example, it is a crime to lie when testifying in court (the crime of perjury). Assume that the purpose of the lie is to deceive the jury and change the outcome of the case. Even if no juror, or anyone else for that matter, believes the lie, and the purpose is not achieved, it is a crime. Causation is not an issue in such crimes.

The same holds true in attempt cases. An *attempt* is an unsuccessful effort to commit a crime. Because the effort is unsuccessful, there is no cause-and-effect relationship between the defendant's act and the attempted result. Possession offenses are yet another example of offenses not involving cause-and-effect relationships.

Any crime involving an act or omission and an effect resulting from the act or omission requires a causal link between the act or omission of the defendant and the criminal result. In California, causation issues have arisen most frequently in homicide cases. In such cases, the inquiry is: was the defendant's act the cause of the victim's death? At first glance, it might seem that this question should be easy to answer. In fact, analysis of causation can be relatively complex, as will be seen from the following discussion.

First, the law recognizes two forms of causation: *cause in fact* and *proximate cause,* also termed *legal cause.* Both forms of causation must exist for the defendant to be guilty of the crime charged. **Cause in fact** is pure causation, unaffected by legal or policy considerations. An act is the cause in fact of a result if the act was the actual cause, or one of the actual causes, of the result. If Mark aims a pistol at Joe and pulls the trigger, killing Joe, Mark's pulling of the trigger is the cause in fact of Joe's death. There are two generally recognized tests for determining whether an act is the cause in fact, or one of the causes in fact, of a criminal result. The first test is known as the *but-for test,* which may be stated as follows: A defendant's act will be considered the cause in fact of a particular result if it is established that "but for" the act by the defendant, the result would not have occurred. In the Mark and Joe situation, Mark's pulling of the trigger will be considered the cause in fact of Joe's death if it is concluded that "but for" the pulling of the trigger by Mark, Joe would not have died. Phrased another way, the but-for test is met if it is concluded that, had Mark not pulled the trigger, Joe would not have died. It is clear that the but-for test is met in the Mark-Joe situation. Mark's pulling of the trigger is the cause in fact of Joe's death.

The second test used to determine whether the act of a defendant was the cause in fact of a particular result is known as the *substantial factor test.* This test is employed in situations in which more than one act or occurrence contributed to the resulting harm to the victim. For example, A and B may be engaged in a gunfight. C is caught in the crossfire and is struck by bullets fired by both A and B. Assuming that the wound inflicted by either bullet would have been fatal, the shooting by both A and B will be considered the cause in fact of C's death, because the shooting by each defendant was a substantial factor in the causal chain of events leading to C's death. The effect of application of the substantial factor test is that neither A nor B can successfully claim that his firing of his weapon was not the cause in fact of C's death because C would have died anyway (from the wound inflicted by the other shooter). To the contrary, the law holds both A and B accountable by regarding the act of each as a cause in fact of C's death.

If a defendant's act is determined not to be the cause in fact of a criminal result, the causation inquiry need go no further. A defendant cannot be held criminally liable for a result that he or she did not cause. If, however, the defendant's act is determined to be the cause in fact of the criminal result, the causation analysis continues, the next question being: Was the defendant's conduct the proximate (or legal) cause of the criminal result? **Proximate cause** can be a confusing concept because it is not an independent type of causation. Rather, proximate or legal cause is a legal principle that, under certain circumstances, limits the criminal liability of a defendant whose act is the cause in fact of the injury to the victim. Under the concept of proximate cause, there are situations in which a defendant will not be criminally liable for the harm resulting from his or her conduct. It has been said that every act, like a pebble dropped into water, produces effects out to infinity. The act is the cause in fact, or a cause in fact, of each of those effects. The concept of proximate cause limits the liability of a defendant for any effects that are remote or unforeseeable.

Consider, for example, hot-tempered Herb. Herb is in Sam's garage discussing a problem with Sam. An argument ensues and becomes heated. Herb grabs a wrench and hurls it at Sam. Fortunately, Sam sees the wrench coming and ducks, avoiding it. The wrench strikes the fuse box in Sam's garage, causing a short-circuit and a power failure in Sam's house. Herb stomps out of Sam's garage and returns home. Sam calls the power company, which dispatches a repair crew to Sam's home. While en route, the driver of the repair truck negligently runs a red light and collides with an automobile driven by Mildred. Mildred is killed in the accident. The force of the collision causes a piece of the repair truck to strike and puncture a gasoline pump at a nearby service station. The pump explodes and the service station is destroyed by fire. Several persons are severely burned in the fire. If Herb had not thrown the wrench, none of the foregoing events would have occurred. In terms of the but-for test, but for Herb's throwing of the wrench, Mildred would not have died, the service station would not have been destroyed by fire, and the persons would not have been burned. Herb's act was a cause in fact of all of the foregoing harms. Should Herb be considered to have murdered Mildred? Is he guilty of arson (i.e., burning down the service station)? What about battery (i.e., the burning of the victims in the service station)? These questions call into play the proximate cause concept. Under this concept, Herb's act, though a cause in fact of the various harms, will not be considered the cause for purposes of criminal liability unless it is also the proximate or legal cause of the harms. The proximate cause analysis generally poses the following inquiry: Given that Herb's throwing of the wrench was a cause in fact of the resulting harms, will the law refuse to hold him criminally liable because the harms were too remote or unforeseeable?

Two approaches are generally used to evaluate proximate cause. The first of these is the *foreseeability test,* which asks: Is the harm that ultimately results from the defendant's act a type of harm that would have been reasonably foreseeable to a person in the defendant's position at the time the defendant committed the act? If the answer is yes, the defendant's act will be considered the proximate cause of the harm to the victim. If the answer is no, the defendant's act will not be considered the proximate cause of the harm to the victim, despite the fact that the act is the cause in fact of the harm. What is the answer in Herb's case? At the time Herb threw the wrench at Sam, was it reasonably foreseeable that the act would ultimately contribute to a traffic fatality, destruction of a service station by fire, and burning of persons in the service station? Note that the question is one of reasonable foreseeability, not one of any possibility, however remote. The inquiry is not "is it possible that such-and-such a result could occur," which would encompass a broad range of unforeseeable results; rather, we ask "is it reasonably foreseeable that the result would occur?" As one eminent jurist said, "reasonable minds may differ." It would seem fairly clear, however, that the extreme results in Herb's case were not reasonably foreseeable at the time Herb threw the wrench. Accordingly, under the foreseeability test, Herb's throwing of the wrench at Sam would not be considered the proximate cause of Mildred's death, the destruction of the service station, or the burning of the persons in the service station, and Herb would not be criminally liable for those results.

Contrast Herb's situation with the following scenario. Philip attacks Matthew with a knife and clearly intends to kill Matthew. Matthew flees and is pursued by Philip. In a state of panic, Matthew runs into a busy street without looking and is struck and killed by a truck. Is Philip's act of assaulting Matthew with intent to kill the proximate cause of Matthew's death? Using the foreseeability test, the question becomes: At the time Philip was pursuing Matthew, was it reasonably foreseeable that Matthew would unwittingly expose himself to danger in his efforts to flee the attack? Again, although reasonable minds may differ, the answer to this question appears to be yes. Philip's attack would therefore be the proximate cause of Matthew's death, and Philip could be prosecuted for homicide, rather than assault.

One situation in which a defendant's act will be considered the proximate cause of an unforeseeable result is the situation in which the victim of the crime suffers unforeseeable harm because of a preexisting condition. This concept is informally known as the "take your victim as you find him" principle. For example, in one California case, the defendants robbed an individual who, unknown to the defendants, had a history of heart disease. The victim was so frightened that he died of shock approximately twenty minutes after the robbery, and the defendants were convicted of murder as well as of the robbery. *People v. Stamp* (1969) 2 Cal.App.3d 203. Another example might involve a hemophiliac who is stabbed by the defendant. If the wound would be nonfatal to most persons, but is fatal to the hemophiliac, the defendant's act will be considered the proximate cause of the victim's death.

The second approach to proximate cause employs the concept of intervening causes. Using this approach, the question is: After the defendant committed the act, did another cause intervene in the chain of events and directly cause the harm to the victim? The law distinguishes between dependent intervening causes and independent intervening causes. A *dependent intervening cause* is one that is a normal result of the defendant's act. The Philip-Matthew scenario is an example of a dependent intervening cause. Philip did not force Matthew to place himself in front of the oncoming truck. Matthew placed himself in front of the truck by fleeing from Philip. The immediate cause of Matthew's death was Matthew's own act, rather than Philip's knife attack. Matthew's act was an intervening cause that broke the chain of causation initiated by Philip's attack and produced death in a manner not intended by Philip. Panic-stricken flight is, however, a normal result of a deadly attack such as that perpetrated by Philip on Matthew. Matthew's exposure of himself to danger by fleeing into the street was, therefore, a dependent intervening cause of his death. A dependent intervening cause does not supersede the defendant's original act as the proximate cause of the harm to the victim. Therefore, the fact that Matthew, by his own act, placed himself in front of the truck will not supersede Philip's attack as the proximate cause of Matthew's death.

An *independent intervening cause* is a cause that intervenes in the chain of causation initiated by the defendant's original act which is not a normal result of the defendant's act. For example, in the Philip-Matthew scenario, assume that Matthew, rather than running into the street, flees on the sidewalk and, while fleeing, is struck and killed by lightning. Matthew would not have been where he was if Philip had not attacked him, and it can be said that Matthew would not have been struck by the lightning had it not been for the attack. This, however, is a but-for cause in fact analysis. Under such analysis, there is no question that Philip's attack was a cause in fact of Matthew's death. There was, however, another cause in fact of Matthew's death, an intervening cause: the bolt of lightning. The issue in the proximate cause analysis is, given that there were two succeeding causes in fact of Matthew's death, was the second cause (the lightning strike) a normal result of the knife attack by Philip? If the answer is no, as it undoubtedly is, the fatal lightning strike was an independent intervening cause of Matthew's death. As such, the lightning strike will, as a matter of law, be considered to have superseded Philip's attack as the cause of Matthew's death, and Philip will not be criminally liable for the death despite the fact that Philip's attack was a cause in fact of Matthew's death.

Contrast this scenario with Matthew's fleeing into a busy street without due regard for his own safety, which would be considered a normal result of Philip's attack and would not supersede Philip's attack as the cause of the death. Remember also that, although Philip would not be criminally liable for Matthew's death in the lightning-strike situation, he could be prosecuted for other crimes associated with the attack, such as assault with a deadly weapon or attempted murder.

Let us now observe how the courts apply these principles in actual practice. In the *Armitage* case, the defendant claimed that his reckless operation of a boat was not the proximate cause of the victim's death, because the victim's own acts contributed to his death. Unfortunately for the defendant, the appellate court was not persuaded.

PEOPLE v. DAVID JAMES ARMITAGE
194 Cal.App.3d 405; 239 Cal.Rptr. 515
[Aug. 1987]

SPARKS, J.—On a drunken escapade on the Sacramento River in the middle of a spring night, defendant David James Armitage flipped his boat over and caused his companion to drown. As a result of this accident, defendant was convicted of the felony of drunk boating causing death in violation of former Harbors and Navigation Code section 655, subdivision (c).

* * *

On the evening of May 18, 1985, defendant and his friend, Peter Maskovich, were drinking in a bar in the riverside community of Freeport. They were observed leaving the bar around midnight. In the early morning hours defendant and Maskovich wound up racing defendant's boat on the Sacramento River while both of them were intoxicated. ...

James Snook lives near the Sacramento River in Clarksburg. Some time around 3 A.M. defendant came to his door. Defendant was soaking wet and appeared quite intoxicated. He reported that he had flipped his boat over in the river and had lost his buddy. He said that at first he and his buddy had been hanging on to the overturned boat, but that his buddy swam for shore and he did not know whether he had made it. As it turned out, Maskovich did not make it; he drowned in the river.

Mr. Snook notified the authorities of the accident. Deputy Beddingfield arrived and spent some time with defendant in attempting to locate the scene of the accident or the victim. Eventually Deputy Beddingfield took defendant to the sheriff's boat shed to meet with officers who normally work on the river. At the shed they were met by Deputy Snyder. Deputy Snyder attempted to question defendant about the accident and defendant stated that he had been operating the boat at a high rate of speed and zig-zagging until it capsized. Defendant also stated that he told the victim to hang on to the boat but his friend ignored his warning and started swimming for the shore. As he talked to defendant, the officer formed the opinion that he was intoxicated. Deputy Snyder then arrested defendant and informed him of his rights. Defendant waived his right to remain silent and repeated his statement.

* * *

Defendant ... contends his actions were not the proximate cause of the death of the victim. In order to be guilty of felony drunk boating the defendant's act or omission must be the proximate cause of the ensuing injury or death. Defendant asserts that after his boat flipped over he and the victim were holding on to it and the victim, against his advice, decided to abandon the boat and try to swim to shore. According to defendant the victim's fatally reckless decision should exonerate him from criminal responsibility for his death.

We reject defendant's contention. The question whether defendant's acts or omissions criminally caused the victim's death is to be determined according to the ordinary principles governing proximate causation. Proximate cause of death has traditionally been defined in criminal cases as "a cause which, in natural and continuous sequence, produces the death, and without which the death would not have occurred." Thus, as Witkin notes, "[p]roximate cause is clearly established where the act is directly connected with the resulting injury, with no intervening force operating."

Defendant claims that the victim's attempt to swim ashore, whether characterized as an intervening or a superseding cause, constituted a break in the natural and continuous sequence arising from the unlawful operation of the boat. The claim cannot hold water. It has long been the rule in criminal prosecutions that the contributory negligence of the victim is not a defense. In order to exonerate a defendant the victim's conduct must not only be a cause of his injury, it must be a superseding cause. "A defendant may be criminally liable for a result directly caused by his act even if there is another contributing cause. If an intervening cause is a normal and reasonably foreseeable result of defendant's original act the intervening act is 'dependent' and not a superseding cause, and will not relieve defendant of liability." [Moreover,] "[a]n obvious illustration of a dependent cause is the victim's attempt to escape from a deadly attack or other danger in which he is placed by the defendant's wrongful act." Thus, it is only an unforeseeable intervening cause, an extraordinary and abnormal occurrence, which rises to the level of an exonerating, superseding cause. Consequently, in criminal law a victim's predictable effort to escape a peril created by the defendant is not considered a superseding cause of the ensuing injury or death. As leading commentators have explained it, an unreflective act in response to a peril created by defendant will not break a causal connection. In such a case, the actor has a choice, but his act is nonetheless unconsidered. "When defendant's conduct causes panic an act done under the influence of panic or extreme fear will not negative causal connection unless the reaction is wholly abnormal."

Here defendant, through his misconduct, placed the intoxicated victim in the middle of a dangerous river in the early morning hours clinging to an overturned boat. The fact that the panic-stricken victim recklessly abandoned the boat and tried to swim ashore was not a wholly abnormal reaction to the perceived peril of drowning. Just as "[d]etached reflection cannot be demanded in the presence of an uplifted knife," neither can caution be required of a drowning man. Having placed the inebriated victim in peril, defendant cannot obtain exoneration by claiming the victim should have reacted differently or more prudently. In sum, the evidence establishes that defendant's acts and omissions were the proximate cause of the victim's death.

* * *

The judgment is affirmed.

Judicial decisions holding that the defendant's actions were not the proximate cause of the victim's death are relatively few. In *People v. Hebert,* the court reversed the defendant's conviction of involuntary manslaughter because the trial court failed to properly instruct the jury on proximate cause. Implicit in the court's decision is its recognition that the defendant's actions may not have been the proximate cause of the victim's death.

PEOPLE v. HENRY HEBERT
228 Cal.App.2d 514 [Jul. 1964]

SHINN, P.J.—Henry Hebert was charged with the murder of Charles Swallow, pleaded not guilty, and after a trial by jury was convicted of involuntary manslaughter, a lesser included offense. ...

Defendant was a patron in a Venice bar, drinking beer but not intoxicated, when the victim entered at about 11 P.M. According to all the witnesses who testified on the subject, Swallow appeared to be either drunk or ill; the barmaid refused him service. He sat on a stool near defendant and an argument arose between them. It was established that defendant, while standing, hit Swallow in the face with his fist while Swallow was sitting on a bar stool, and that the assault was without sufficient provocation. When hit, the victim was knocked to the floor. ... No one actually saw Swallow fall, but several witnesses heard him fall. There was sufficient evidence to prove that the victim was knocked off the bar stool by the force of defendant's blows and that his head hit the wooden barroom floor with what one witness described as a loud "thud."

Officers arrived about 10 minutes later. Swallow was lying on the floor on his back, but apparently conscious. Officers assisted him to a sitting position and thought he was not seriously injured, but was intoxicated. They partly carried, partly dragged him to a patrol car and took him to the police station for booking for being intoxicated in a public place. Thelma McCord, the barmaid, testified that the two officers dragged Swallow from the place where he lay on the floor to the sidewalk; one officer lifted Swallow by holding onto his belt in the rear; the other lifted at his head; Swallow's feet were dragging; at the sidewalk the officers dropped him on his face; the drop was 12 to 14 inches; he was perfectly limp. The two officers testified that they partly carried, partly dragged Swallow to the sidewalk, sat him down in a sitting position and then laid him gently on his back; they did not drop him.

The officers arrived at the station with the victim about 35 minutes after the altercation. According to the officers, during the booking procedure and just after Swallow was searched and as he was standing with his hands high against a wall, he was observed to fall over backwards with his arms at his sides and "completely rigid as though a plank were falling"; his buttocks hit the floor first and then the back of his head; his head bounced about 6 inches off the floor and fell back, striking the floor a second time. The floor was concrete with an asphalt tile covering. Immediately after hitting the floor he started bleeding from one ear and within a few seconds from both ears. He was removed to a hospital where he died that morning.

The determinative question on the trial was whether defendant's act of striking decedent and knocking him to the floor was a proximate cause of death.

* * *

The evidence of the several injuries, the blow to the face, the fall in the barroom, the incident on the sidewalk and the fall in the police station presented the critical question as to the proximate cause of the death.

Upon this issue the primary factual question was whether the injuries received in the barroom would have resulted in death. Defendant was responsible for all the injuries inflicted in the barroom and if the jury had found those injuries to have been so severe as to have resulted in death the fact that other injuries were suffered later would have been immaterial. ...

It is of common knowledge that a blow which causes a broken nose does not ordinarily cause death. The picture of deceased taken at the police station merely showed him lying on his back with his head on the floor. ... If it was doubted that the first injuries would have produced a fatal result and that death would have resulted despite the injuries received in the police station, the question necessarily arose whether defendant was responsible for the consequences of the later fall. It was, therefore, vitally important that the jury be adequately and correctly instructed on the doctrine of proximate cause.

The court instructed that in order to find the defendant guilty of either murder or involuntary manslaughter the jury must find that the injury inflicted by defendant was a proximate cause of the death and that "The proximate cause of an injury is that cause which, in natural and continuous sequence, unbroken by any efficient intervening cause, produces the injury, and without which the result would not have occurred. It is the efficient cause—the one that necessarily sets in operation the factors that accomplish the injury."

The court also instructed as follows: "You are instructed that to be a legal cause of death, a defendant's act must be its proximate cause not merely its possible cause. A defendant's act may be considered the proximate cause of the death of another though it is not the immediate cause, if it is the ultimate cause. But where there is a supervening cause the defendant's act cannot be considered a proximate cause. The fact, if it be a fact, that the deceased or some other person or persons were guilty of negligence, which was a contributory cause of the death involved in the case, is not deemed to be a supervening cause and is no defense to a criminal charge if the defendant's own conduct was a proximate cause of the death." We are of the opinion that these instructions were wholly inadequate.

It has been the practice for many years to instruct in the language of the first quoted instruction, but we do not believe it was a satisfactory or sufficient instruction to give in the present case where the question of proximate cause was an intricate and difficult one to be resolved by the jury. We do not say the instruction misstates the law, but only that in the present case it was unclear and confusing as a statement of the doctrine of proximate cause. ...

As stated by Prosser, [*Law of Torts* 266 (2d ed.)]: "The defendant ordinarily will not be relieved of liability by an intervening cause which could reasonably have been foreseen, nor by one which is a normal incident of the risk created. The defendant will ordinarily be relieved of liability by an unforeseeable and abnormal intervening cause which produces a result which could not have been foreseen."

There have been many attempts to phrase an all-purpose definition of proximate cause, but we think that in ordinary circumstances all the definitions have had their roots in the doctrine of foreseeability. We think the jury should have been instructed in clear and simple language as to the measure of the responsibility of defendant for the acts which caused Swallow's death. He was responsible not only for the injuries inflicted in the barroom, but for any later injuries to Swallow that were reasonably foreseeable, and which he would not have sustained if in a normal condition. The issue here was clear-cut and vital and should have been submitted to the jury upon the test of foreseeability. Instead of being submitted in this simple form, the issue was confused by the use in the first instruction of the terms "natural and continuous sequence," "efficient intervening cause" and "necessarily sets in operation the factors that accomplish the result." And in the second quoted instruction, we find "superseding cause" added. The jury was given no definition of "efficient intervening cause" or "supervening cause." These are vague and confusing terms, at best, and the jury should not have been left to guess at their meaning and their application to the facts. ...

We cannot doubt that in an effort to understand the full purport of the instructions the minds of the jurors would have been distracted from the question of foreseeability of future injury. They were told to look for an "efficient intervening cause" or a "supervening cause" as if it made no difference whether after-occurring causes were reasonably foreseeable. The fall in the police station, judged from appearances, was extremely serious, as evidenced by the bleeding from both ears. The jury could well have believed that except for that fall death would not have occurred. Of course, the question was not whether that particular event might occur, but whether any serious injury was likely to occur be-

cause of Swallow's condition. Defendant had a duty to anticipate the common and ordinary consequences of his act, and these he was responsible for. They could be said to be the direct consequences. But the fall in the police station could have been found to be an extraordinary and abnormal occurrence, not reasonably foreseeable as a result of the first injuries. The failure of the court to instruct that defendant would have been responsible for the consequences of the injuries received after Swallow was taken from the barroom only if further injury was reasonably to be anticipated, and the giving of instructions that enabled the jury to hold him responsible for later injuries even if the same were not reasonably foreseeable was prejudicial and reversible error.

The judgment is reversed.

The "Three Year and a Day Rule"

At common law, a person could not be charged with murder if the victim did not die within one year and one day after the act took place. The rule was one of causation. It was developed to prevent a conviction for murder at a time in history when medical science was not precise enough to determine the actual cause of a person's death. If a person lived for more than a year and a day after being injured by a defendant's acts and then died, it was assumed that medical science could not pinpoint the exact cause of death and that to hold the defendant liable would be unjust. It is questionable, in light of the advances in medicine, whether the rule should continue to exist;[19] it has been abolished in many states. In California, the time duration has been increased. According to Penal Code § 194: To make the killing either murder or manslaughter, it is requisite that the party die within three years and a day after the stroke received or the cause of death administered.

§ 3.3   Concurrence

In this chapter you have learned that there are two primary components of crimes, the mental and the physical. Although a showing of mens rea is not required for every crime, there must be a showing of some act or omission for all crimes.

For crimes that have both a mental and a physical element, an additional requirement of concurrence must be proved. *Concurrence* is the joining of mens rea and the act. Recall the words of Penal Code § 20, quoted earlier in this chapter: "In every crime or public offense there must exist a union, or joint operation of act and intent, or criminal negligence."

The mens rea must be the reason that the act was taken. Stated another way, the mental state must occur first and set into motion the act. For example, Doug hates Andy and desires to see him dead. Because of this feeling, Doug waits for Andy to leave the house one night and runs him down with a car. In such a case, Doug's mens rea set into motion the act that caused Andy's death. Now imagine that Doug accidentally kills Andy in an auto accident. After the accident Doug exclaims his happiness over Andy's demise. In this case, the mens rea did not set in motion the act that killed Andy, and thus there was no concurrence.

The mere fact that the mental state happens before the act does not mean that there is concurrence. There must be a connection between the intent and the act; the mens rea must set the act into motion. So if Doug forms the desire to kill Andy today, but takes no action to further the desire, he cannot be charged with murder a year later when he accidentally shoots Andy while hunting.

§ 3.4 A Suggested Analytical Approach

It may be generally stated that if a person commits an act prohibited by law with the requisite mental state (except in the case of a strict liability crime), he or she has committed the crime denounced by the statute. As should be clear from the materials in this chapter, however, the foregoing statement can be deceptively simple. For example, the inquiry, "Did the defendant commit the prohibited act?," may, in a given case, require not only a determination of the precise act committed by the defendant, but also an evaluation of the voluntariness of the defendant's conduct, and/or a resolution of causation issues. This total picture of the defendant's act is the actus reus element of the charged offense. Analysis of the mental element of the crime charged, mens rea, requires a determination of the mental state prescribed by law for the crime in question. As discussed earlier in this chapter, criminal mental states can include general intent, specific intent, willfulness, knowledge, recklessness, malice, and negligence. One must look either to the statute prescribing the crime, or to judicial interpretations of the statute, to ascertain the mental state associated with the specific crime being considered.

The question "Did the defendant commit the crime with which he or she is charged?" is best answered using a structured mental process. The decision model at Figure 3-1 is a suggested method for conducting this evaluation. To use the decision model, first determine the crime with which the defendant is to be charged. Next, determine the actus reus of the offense, i.e., the act prohibited by the penal statute. The top half of the decision model will assist you in evaluating whether the defendant committed the prohibited act, as a matter of law. The answer will be clearly yes (indicated by a "Y"), clearly no ("N"), or uncertain ("?") if there are voluntariness or causation issues. If there are voluntariness or causation issues, follow the steps in the decision model to evaluate them. The outcome of the evaluative process in the top half of the model will be a determination either that actus reus is established (i.e., the defendant did commit the prohibited act) or that it is not. In the latter event, the defendant did not commit the charged offense.

If you determine that the defendant did commit the prohibited act, go to the bottom half of the decision model to evaluate the mens rea element of the offense. If the offense is a strict liability crime, no mental state is required, and you can determine that the defendant committed the offense without further analysis. If the offense requires a mental state, determine what that mental state is from the language of the penal statute or judicial decisions interpreting it. Next ask whether the defendant possessed the requisite mental state. If yes, the defendant has committed the charged offense. If no, he or she has not committed the offense.

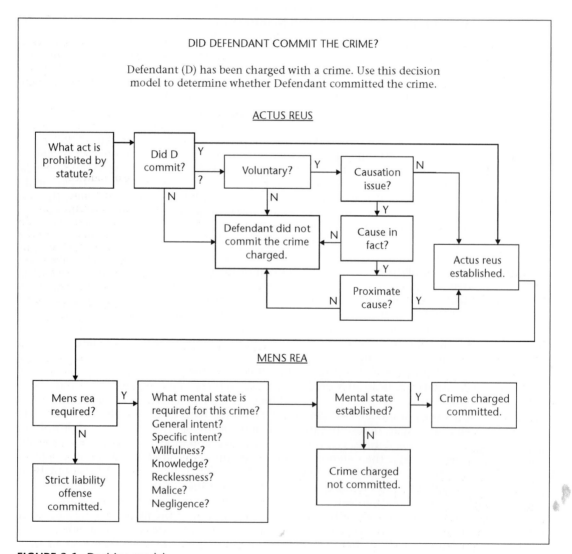

FIGURE 3-1   Decision model

Use the decision model to evaluate the hot-tempered Herb and Phillip-Matthew scenarios presented in the causation section of this chapter, as well as other hypothetical situations. Remember that, if you determine that the defendant did not commit the charged offense, he or she may have committed another offense, frequently a lesser included offense of the charged offense. Remember also that the decision model does not take into account the possibility that the defendant may have a defense to the charged offense. Defenses are discussed in Chapter 10.

Key Terms

actual possession Actual physical possession of a thing, i.e., when it is on one's person.

actus reus An act or omission which, when joined with a criminal mental state, constitutes a crime.

cause in fact An occurrence (cause) that produces a result (effect). An act or omission by a defendant is the cause in fact of the criminal result if it can be said that, but for the act or omission, the criminal result would not have occurred, or if the act or omission was a substantial factor in producing the criminal result.

circumstantial evidence Facts and circumstances from which a jury or judge may reason and reach conclusions in a case.

constructive possession Possession deemed by the law to exist when one does not have actual physical possession of a thing, but exercises dominion and control over it.

corporate liability The liability of a corporation for criminal offenses committed by persons acting on its behalf.

inference A conclusion that may be drawn by the finder of fact from the evidence presented at trial.

injunction A court order that a person or entity refrain from a specified act or course of conduct.

joint possession Simultaneous possession of one thing by two or more persons.

knowingly In California criminal law, a mental state involving knowledge on the part of the actor of the facts surrounding his or her act or omission which make the act or omission a crime. The actor need only know the facts; he or she need not know that they constitute a crime.

legislative history Records of legislative proceedings from which the intent of the legislature in enacting a statute may be determined that provide a basis for determining the legislative intent underlying a statute.

malice In California criminal law, other than for the crime of murder, means a mental state that imports a wish to vex, annoy, or injure another person, or an intent to do a wrongful act. (See definition of *malice aforethought* for the malice element of the crime of murder.)

malice aforethought The mental state required for the crime of murder. Malice aforethought may be express or implied. It is express when the killer manifests a deliberate intention unlawfully to take away the life of a fellow creature. It is implied when no considerable provocation appears, or when the circumstances attending the killing show an abandoned and malignant heart.

malum in se A crime involving an act that is inherently evil, such as murder, rape, arson, or mayhem.

malum prohibitum A crime involving an act or omission that is not inherently evil but has been declared criminal by a legislative enactment. Malum prohibitum crimes frequently involve acts that are prohibited (or failures to perform acts that are required) for reasons of public health, welfare, or safety.

mens rea A criminal mental state; a state of mind which, when joined with an act or omission prohibited by law, results in the commission of a crime.

motive The reason for a person's act.

negligence In California criminal law, a mental state involving a want of such attention to the nature or probable consequences of an act or omission as a prudent person ordinarily bestows in acting in his or her own concerns. To constitute the basis for criminal liability, negligence must generally be aggravated, culpable, gross, or reckless, that is, the conduct of the actor must be such a departure from what would be the conduct of an ordinarily prudent or careful person under the same circumstances as to be incompatible with a proper regard for human life or to signal an indifference to consequences.

omission A failure to act or to do what is required by law.

presumption A rule of law that accords probative value to certain facts in evidence or mandates a specific inference as to the existence of a fact; a conclusion that must be drawn. May be rebuttable or irrebuttable.

proximate cause The legal principle that limits the criminal liability of a person for remote or unforeseeable results of his or her acts or omissions, and holds the person accountable only for foreseeable results not produced by independent causes.

recklessly In California criminal law, a mental state in which a person is aware of and consciously disregards a substantial and unjustifi-able risk that his or her act will cause harm to another person or property. The risk must be of such a nature and degree that disregard thereof constitutes a gross deviation from the standard of conduct that a reasonable person would observe in the situation.

scienter Knowledge that the act one is committing is legally or morally wrong.

strict liability Liability imposed regardless of fault, intent, or negligence; absolute liability.

transferred intent A legal principle which holds that when one acts intending to harm a specific person, but instead harms another person, the actor will be deemed to have intended to harm the person actually injured.

vicarious liability Criminal liability imposed on a person for an act or omission of another person.

willfully In California criminal law, a mental state that implies simply a purpose or willingness to commit the act or to make the omission referred to. It does not require any intent to violate the law, or to injure another, or to acquire any advantage.

Review Questions

1. In criminal law, causation is broken down into two forms. Name and briefly describe each.

2. Can a person be prosecuted for failing to save a stranger from danger? Why or why not?

3. What is concurrence?

4. What is an omission?

5. The Model Penal Code recognizes four types of mens rea. Name and briefly describe each.

6. Name and briefly describe the mental states recognized by California criminal law.

7. What is the meaning of the term *transferred intent*?

8. Which of the two essential elements discussed in this chapter is unnecessary in a strict liability crime?

9. What is vicarious liability?

10. What is the difference between an inference and a presumption?

11. Is it true, in a criminal trial, that the specific intent of the accused may be presumed from the fact that he committed an unlawful act? Why or why not?

12. Can corporations be guilty of crimes? Can partnerships?

13. Distinguish mens rea from motive. Is proof of motive allowed in a criminal trial?

14. Where should one normally look to determine the actus reus of a particular crime?

15. What is the difference between actual and constructive possession?

16. Do all possession offenses require the same type of knowledge on the part of the defendant? Briefly explain.

CHAPTER 3 THE TWO ESSENTIAL ELEMENTS **81**

Review Problems

1–6. Many prisoners in the state and federal correctional systems are held at minimum-security "farms." Only inmates considered not to be dangerous are housed at these facilities because of the minimal security. In fact, in many cases it is possible for inmates to simply walk off. Of course, most do not leave the premises, because to do so results in an increased sentence (either due to a conviction for escape or a decrease in "good time") and a likelihood that the sentence will be spent in prison rather than the more desirable farm. Despite this, prisoners of these facilities do escape. What follows are two fictitious statutes and several different fact situations involving a fictitious inmate, Spike Vincelli. For each fact situation, discuss whether Spike has committed the crime defined by either statute. Use the decision model in Figure 3-1 to aid in your analysis.

> Statute I:
>   It shall be unlawful for any person committed to any correctional facility to escape from that facility. Escape is defined as passing beyond the borders of a facility with an intent to never return or being lawfully beyond the borders of the facility and not returning when required to do so with an intent to never return. Violation of this statute constitutes a felony.

> Statute II:
>   It shall be unlawful for any person committed to any correctional facility to leave the premises of the facility. Leaving is defined as passing over the boundary lines of the facility. Violation of this statute constitutes a misdemeanor.

1. On June 21, Spike Vincelli received a telephone call from a hospital informing him that his mother had been involved in a serious accident. That evening Spike left to see his mother, intending to return in the morning.

2. On June 21, Spike Vincelli had his first epileptic seizure. The seizure caused Spike to fall outside the boundary line surrounding the facility.

3. On June 21, Spike Vincelli decided that he was bored with living on the farm. That night he walked off the premises and fled for a friend's house 300 miles away, intending never to return.

4. On June 21, Spike Vincelli became involved in a fight with Ben Ichabod. In a fit of rage, Ben picked Spike up and threw him over the fence surrounding the farm. Spike was caught outside the fence by a guard before he had an opportunity to return.

5. In early April, Spike Vincelli decided that he was going to escape. He developed a plan that called for him to leave in July and meet his brother, who was passing through the area. As part of the plan, Ben Ichabod, a fellow inmate, was enlisted to pick Spike up off the ground and throw him over the fence that surrounded the facility. However, Ben, who is not very bright, threw Spike over the fence on June 21.

6. On June 21, Spike Vincelli became involved in a fight with Ben Ichabod. Ben, in a fit of rage, picked Spike up and threw him over the fence surrounding the facility. While outside the fence Spike became overcome with a sense of freedom and ran from the facility.

7. Fred failed to show up for a date he had made with Penni. Penni, who was angered by Fred's actions, decided to vent her anger by cutting the tires of Fred's automobile. However, Penni did not know what make of automobile Fred drove and mistakenly cut the tires of a car owned by Fred's neighbor, Stacey. Penni is now charged with the "purposeful destruction of personal property." Penni claims that her act was not purposeful because she did not intend to cut the tires of Stacey's car. Discuss this defense.

8. William, an experienced canoeist, was hired by a Boy Scout troop to supervise a canoe trip. While on the trip two boys fell out of their canoe and began to drown. William watched as the boys drowned. Is William criminally liable for the deaths?

9. Sherri, who was near bankruptcy, decided to burn her house down and make an insurance claim for the loss. Sherri started the fire, which spread to a neighbor's house located twenty feet from Sherri's home. Unknown to Sherri, her neighbor was storing massive quantities of dynamite in the home. The fire at the neighbor's house spread to the room where the explosives were being stored, and the resulting explosion caused such vibrations that

a construction worker one block away fell off a ladder and subsequently died from the fall. Sherri is charged with arson and murder. She has pled guilty to arson, but maintains that she is not liable for the death of the worker. Is she correct?

10. The following statute was enacted by State Legislature:

    It shall be unlawful for any person to be a pedophile. Pedophilia is defined as a condition where a person over the age of seventeen years possesses a sexual desire for a person under the age of eight years.

    While attending a group therapy session, Jane admitted that she had sexual interest in boys under eight years of age. A member of the group contacted the local police and reported Jane's statement. Jane was subsequently arrested and charged with violating the quoted statute. Discuss her defenses, if any.

11. Ashley, Amy, and Karen are roommates in college. They occupy a four-bedroom apartment, and all share in the bills and household duties. One weekend a friend of Karen's, Janice, came to visit. Janice arrived on Thursday and was scheduled to stay until Monday. She stayed in the extra bedroom. On Thursday evening Ashley discovered, while she was watching Janice unpack, that Janice had a significant amount of cocaine in one suitcase. Later that night, Ashley discussed this discovery with Karen, who stated, "I'm sure she does—why does it matter to you?" Ashley immediately confronted Janice and told her that she would have to remove the cocaine from the premises or Ashley would call the police. Janice picked up the suitcase, carried it to her car, and placed it in the trunk. The next morning, when Karen learned what Ashley had done, she encouraged Janice to bring the suitcase back into the apartment.

    On Sunday morning the police arrived with a warrant to search the apartment. The search uncovered the suitcase in the extra bedroom. Later, at the police station, the suitcase was opened and the drugs were discovered. All four women were charged with possession. Are Amy, Ashley, or Karen guilty of possession?

12. In some nations, vicarious criminal liability is much broader than in the United States. For example, parents may be vicariously liable for the criminal acts of their children until the children reach adulthood. Should such laws be adopted in the United States? Explain your answer.

Notes

[1] J. Goldstein et al., *Criminal Law: Theory and Process* (Free Press, 1974).

[2] *People v. Hernandez* (1964) 61 Cal.2d 529, 39 Cal.Rptr. 361, 393.

[3] 21 Am. Jur. 2d *Criminal Law* 129 (1981).

[4] 1 Witkin & Epstein, *California Criminal Law* § 103 (2 ed. Bancroft-Whitney, 1988).

[5] *Galvan v. Superior Court* (1969) 70 Cal.2d 851, 868.

[6] 1 Witkin & Epstein, *supra* note 4, § 107.

[7] *People v. Penny* (1955) 44 Cal.2d 861, 879.

[8] LaFave & Scott, *Criminal Law* 34 (West, 1980).

[9] 1 Witkin & Epstein, *supra* note 4, § 110.

[10] *See Lambert v. California*, 355 U.S. 225 (1957), in which the United States Supreme Court found that a strict liability statute was violative of the due process clause of the United States Constitution.

[11] LaFave & Scott *supra* note 8, at 244–45.

[12] *See, e.g., McKinney's California Digest,* "Criminal Law," § 8 (Bancroft-Whitney, 1996).

[13] *See United States v. Dotterweich,* 320 U.S. 277 (1943).

[14] 20 Cal. Jur. 3d *Criminal Law* § 2249 (1985).

[15] Model Penal Code § 2.01.

[16] From N. Morris, "Somnambulistic Homicide: Ghosts, Spiders, and North Koreans," 5 *Res Judicata* 29 (1951).

[17] 1 Witkin & Epstein, *supra* note 4, § 116.

[18] *Walker v. Superior Court* (1988) 47 Cal.3d 112.

[19] A. Loewy, *Criminal Law,* 55 (2d ed., West, 1987).

CHAPTER 4

Crimes Against the Person: Part I

§ 4.1   Studying Crimes

In the next five chapters you will learn about many crimes. It would be impossible to include a discussion of all crimes. What follows is a discussion of the major crimes recognized in California. The crimes have been categorized as crimes against the person, crimes against property, and crimes against the public. Although it is common to make these distinctions, do not become involved with understanding why these classifications have been made, as they are used only for organizational purposes. In a sense, all crimes are offenses against the public. That is why the public prosecutes crimes and private individuals may not. Also, any offense "against property" is actually injuring a person, not the property. A stolen television set does not long to be returned to its rightful owner. However, the rightful owner does feel wronged and desires the return of the stolen item. In a sense the classifications are often accurate in that they describe the focus of the criminal conduct. The focus of a thief's act is property; hence, a crime against property. The focus of a rapist's attack is a human; hence, a crime against a person.

Every crime has certain integral components which can be found in the statute defining the crime or in decisional law applying or interpreting the statute. Each component of a crime is an **element** of that crime. At trial, every element of a crime must be proven beyond a reasonable doubt by the prosecution. If any element is not proven beyond a reasonable doubt, the accused must be found not guilty. The rule requires that each element be proved individually. That is, if a crime consists of six elements, and a jury is convinced that five have been proven, but cannot say that the sixth has been proven beyond a reasonable doubt, then there must be a not-guilty verdict. This is true even if the jury was solidly convinced that all the other elements were true and generally believed that the defendant committed the crime. Later you will learn more about the "beyond a reasonable doubt" standard.

Finally, you may notice that, often, if one crime has been proven, all the elements of a related lesser crime can also be proved. The lesser crime is frequently referred to as a *lesser included offense*. For example, if a defendant is convicted of murdering someone with a hammer, he has also committed a battery of the victim. In such circumstances, the lesser offense merges into the greater offense. This is the **merger** doctrine. Under this doctrine, both crimes may be charged, but if the defendant is convicted of the more serious crime the lesser is absorbed by the greater, and the defendant is not punished for both. If acquitted of the greater charge, the defendant may be convicted of the lesser.

The remainder of this chapter examines the crime of homicide in its varying forms and the vast body of law that has developed around offenses involving unlawful killing of human beings. Chapter 5 deals with other crimes against the person, including assault and battery, mayhem, sex crimes, kidnapping, false imprisonment, stalking, and civil rights and hate crimes.

SIDEBAR

Crime and Delinquency in California

The California Department of Justice compiles statistics relating to California crimes and publishes the results in an annual publication entitled *Crime and Delinquency in California*. At the time of this writing, the most recent edition is the 1995 edition. *Crime and Delinquency in California* contains a wealth of statistical information relating to crime rates, arrest rates, felony arrest dispositions, corrections, and criminal justice expenditures and personnel. Statistical information from *Crime and Delinquency in California* will be presented in sidebar material in this and later chapters.

One means of monitoring crime trends in California is the California Crime Index (CCI) compiled by the Office of the Attorney General each year. The CCI for the current year and all prior years is included in *Crime and Delinquency in California*. The CCI measures the frequency of occurrence of a composite of crimes consisting of certain "violent crimes" and "property crimes." Violent crimes included in the CCI are homicide (excluding involuntary manslaughter), forcible rape, robbery, and aggravated assault. Property crimes included in the CCI are burglary and motor vehicle theft. The CCI measures the frequency of occurrence of the composite of crimes, of the categories "violent crimes" and "property crimes," and of each individual type of crime included in the CCI per 100,000 persons in the California population. CCI statistics are available for years 1952 through 1995.

The overall CCI rate for 1995 was 2,929.0 per 100,000 population, which means that, statistically, one out of every 33 persons in California was victimized by one of the CCI crimes during 1995. The overall CCI rate in 1952 was 898.1 per 100,000 population, reflecting a 226.1 percent increase in the rate of CCI crimes between 1952 and 1995.

The CCI rate for violent crimes (homicide, forcible rape, robbery, and aggravated assault) for 1995 was 951.2 per 100,000 population. In 1952, the rate was 153.1 per 100,000. The 1995 rate represents a 521.3 percent increase over the 1952 rate.

The CCI rate for property crimes (burglary and motor vehicle theft) for 1995 was 1,977.8 per 100,000 population. In 1952, the rate was 745 per 100,000, reflecting a 165.5 percent increase in the rate of these property offenses between 1952 and 1995.

The CCI peaked in 1980 at 3,922.1 per 100,000. The peak was caused by the peak in CCI property crimes the same year at 3,035.3 per 100,000. Violent crimes peaked in 1992 with a rate of 1,103.9 per 100,000.

Theft –
& 400 < petty
is 400 < petty

In 1952, the violent crime rate accounted for 17 percent of the CCI, with the property crime rate accounting for 83 percent. In 1995, the violent crime rate had increased to 32.5 percent of the CCI, with the property crime rate decreasing to 67.5 percent.

Source: Crime and Delinquency in California, 1995, California Department of Justice, Division of Law Enforcement.

§ 4.2 Homicide

Homicide is the killing of one human being by another. Not all homicides are crimes. It is possible to cause another person's death accidentally, that is, accompanied by no mens rea, which gives rise to no criminal liability.

Criminal homicide occurs when a person takes another's life in a manner proscribed by law. The law proscribes more than intentional killings. Under California law, reckless and criminally negligent homicides may be punished.

The mens rea part of homicide is important. The determination of what mens rea was possessed by the defendant (actually, what mens rea can be proven by the prosecution) will usually determine what crime may be punished. At common law, various forms of murder were developed. This is where we begin.

Homicide and the Common Law

defense against lethal force
may be lethal.

Initially, at common law, all murders were punished equally: the murderer was executed.[1] Over time, judges realized that the rule was harsh, and the belief that not all homicides should be punished equally developed. As a result, homicides were divided into murder and manslaughter. Manslaughter was punished by incarceration, not death.

Murder, at common law, was defined as: (1) The unlawful killing of a (2) human being with (3) malice aforethought. It was the requirement of malice aforethought that distinguished murder from manslaughter. Although malice aforethought was defined differently among the states, the following types of homicide became recognized as murder under the common law:

1. When the defendant intended to cause the death of the victim.
2. When the defendant intended to cause serious bodily harm, and death resulted.
3. When the defendant created an unreasonably high risk of death that caused the victim's death. This was known as "depraved-heart murder."
4. When the doctrine of felony-murder was applicable.

All criminal homicides that did not constitute murder were treated as manslaughter. Today, California, like most other jurisdictions, further divides murder into degrees, first and second, and defines three types of manslaughter: voluntary, involuntary, and vehicular. These are the five basic types of criminal homicide in California. Two other types, felony-murder and misdemeanor-manslaughter, are also recognized.

Murder

The crime of murder is defined by Penal Code § 187(a) as follows:

> Murder is the unlawful killing of a human being, or a fetus, with malice aforethought.

Recall from Chapter 2 that the provisions of Penal Code § 187, relating to the killing of a fetus, were added by the legislature in response to the decision of the California Supreme Court in *Keeler v. Superior Court* (1970) 2 Cal.3d 619. Feticide constitutes only a very small part of the subject of murder, and we wish to direct our attention to the crime generally. Accordingly, for purposes of the following discussion, we will use the following definition of murder: "the unlawful killing of a human being ... with malice aforethought." From this statutory language, it is clear that the elements of the crime of murder are: (1) the killing of a human being, (2) which is unlawful, (3) with malice aforethought.

Killing of a Human Being   The focal point of the crime of murder is, of course, the killing of a human being. There is not much room for debate on what constitutes a human being. The concept of killing may, however, raise issues. The question of whether the defendant killed the victim can be difficult to answer if there are causation or voluntariness questions. Recall, for example, the Philip-Matthew scenario presented in the discussion of causation in Chapter 3. Causation issues are numerous in criminal law and arise most frequently in homicide cases. In such cases, legal analysis will be required to determine the answer to the seemingly simple question: Did the defendant kill the victim?

 Killing Must Be Unlawful   In addition to requiring that the defendant kill a human being, Penal Code § 187(a) requires that the killing be unlawful. This requirement reflects the fact that not all killings are unlawful. Penal Code §§ 195 through 198 address the subjects of excusable and justifiable homicide. A killing is unlawful only if it is not excusable or justifiable under those sections. A killing is excusable when it is accidental and not the result of criminal negligence (see Penal Code § 195(1)). An example of an excusable homicide would be a hunting accident in which one hunter is killed by another hunter and the hunter committing the killing is not negligent. Justifiable homicide includes lawful killings by law enforcement officers (see Penal Code § 196) and killings by private citizens under certain circumstances, such as resisting the commission of a dangerous felony (see Penal Code §§ 197 and 198.5).

Malice Aforethought   Questions regarding whether the defendant killed the victim or whether the killing was excusable or justifiable go to the actus reus element of murder: the unlawful killing of a human being. The mens rea element of murder is **malice aforethought**.

  Malice aforethought is a mental state that applies only to murder and is to be distinguished from the general malice mental state defined in Penal Code § 7(4) (discussed in Chapter 3). The Penal Code recognizes two types of malice aforethought: express and implied (see Penal Code § 188).

Malice aforethought is express when the perpetrator manifests a specific intent to kill. There are certain exceptions to this principle. For example, one may *[handwritten margin note: Can kill someone else to defend another person, not but only during survival (justifiable homicide)]*

manifest a specific intent to kill in a situation constituting justifiable homicide. In such a case, the actor's mental state will not constitute malice aforethought. Also, if the actor kills another intentionally in the heat of passion, his or her mental state may or may not constitute malice aforethought, depending on the nature of the provocation that induced his or her emotional outrage. Adequate provocation negates malice aforethought and reduces the killing from murder to voluntary manslaughter. Thus, it may be said that a specific intent to kill constitutes malice aforethought in the absence of circumstances constituting justifiable homicide or provocation adequate to reduce the killing to voluntary manslaughter.

Malice aforethought will be implied under Penal Code § 188 in two situations. First, when a person, although not outwardly manifesting a specific intent to kill, kills another without "a considerable provocation," such person will be deemed to have acted with malice aforethought. In other words, if a person kills another person, and there is no evidence that the killing was the result of extreme provocation, the law concludes that the actor possessed malice aforethought. As previously noted, the presence or absence of adequate provocation distinguishes murder from voluntary manslaughter. Malice aforethought will also be implied when the circumstances attending the killing show an "abandoned and malignant heart." This phrase has its origins in the common law. It can be defined in a number of ways, but essentially means that the actor acted in callous disregard of a serious threat to human life created by his or her conduct, and a person died as a result.

Malice aforethought does not require actual hatred or ill will on the part of the actor toward the victim. Consider, for example, the contract killer who does not know the victim and has no feeling toward the victim one way or the other. Nor need malice arise before commission of the act of killing. The word *aforethought* is a relic of the past and has no practical significance today. The malice need only exist at the time of the killing.

Degrees of Murder

California law prescribes two degrees of murder: murder in the first degree and murder in the second degree. It is important not to be confused by the division of the crime of murder into degrees. Both first- and second-degree murder are murder. In other words, both constitute the unlawful killing of a human being, or a fetus, with malice aforethought. But the law recognizes that some types of murder are particularly heinous, and categorizes these types of murder as murder in the first degree. The practical significance of this distinction, from the perspective of the defendant, is the potential sentence. First-degree murder is punishable by death, imprisonment in the state prison for life without the possibility of parole, or imprisonment in the state prison for a term of twenty-five years to life. Second-degree murder is punishable by imprisonment in the state prison for a term of fifteen years to life, with certain exceptions (see Penal Code § 190). The practical significance to the prosecution of the distinction between first- and second-degree murder is the additional elements the prosecution must prove to establish murder in the first degree. These elements are discussed in following paragraphs. Even greater burdens are placed on the prosecution if the death penalty is sought—a *capital case*. The procedure for obtaining the death penalty is discussed in Chapter 18.

First-Degree Murder   First-degree murder is defined by Penal Code § 189, which prescribes three categories of first-degree murder: (a) murder by specified means; (b) other willful, deliberate, and premeditated murder; and (c) murder committed in the perpetration of or attempt to perpetrate certain enumerated felonies, which is termed felony-murder.

The first category of first-degree murder under § 189, murder by specified means, includes murder perpetrated by means of a destructive device or explosive, knowing use of ammunition designed primarily to penetrate metal or armor, poison, lying in wait, or torture.

The second category—willful, deliberate, and premeditated murder—reflects the traditional definition of first-degree murder. You will recall from Chapter 3 that *willfully* is defined in Penal Code § 7(1), which states that the term "implies simply a purpose or willingness to commit the act, or make the omission referred to." Accordingly, if one purposefully kills another, he or she has acted willfully. This, however, is not enough to make the killing first-degree murder. The killing must also be deliberate and premeditated.

The terms *deliberate* and *premeditated* are not defined in the Penal Code. The courts have addressed these concepts on numerous occasions, although they tend to speak in terms of **premeditation** and **deliberation** rather than in the statutory terms *deliberate* and *premeditated*. The California Supreme Court, in the leading case of *People v. Anderson* (1968) 70 Cal.2d 15, 26, indicated that premeditation and deliberation involve a "pre-existing reflection" and "careful thought and weighing of considerations" rather than "mere unconsidered or rash impulse hastily executed." *Premeditation* is the "pre-existing reflection" referred to by the court, and *deliberation* is the "careful thought and weighing of considerations." Combining the definition of murder in Penal Code § 187 with the "willful, deliberate, and premeditated" criteria specified in § 189, an unlawful killing of a human being or a fetus with malice aforethought (murder), committed purposefully and after preexisting reflection and careful thought and weighing of considerations, constitutes first-degree murder. This relatively straightforward definition of first-degree murder must, however, be read in light of the consistent holdings of the courts that the preexisting reflection and careful thought and weighing of considerations (i.e., premeditation and deliberation) can occur in a very brief span of time, even the instant before the act of killing. They need not occur over a prolonged period. They must, however, exist sufficiently to distinguish the killing from a "mere unconsidered or rash impulse hastily executed," which would constitute second-degree murder.

As can be seen from the foregoing, the distinction between first- and second-degree murder can be a fine one and difficult to apply in close situations. In the *Anderson* case, the supreme court set forth analytical standards to be applied when determining whether a murder is of the first or second degree. The court delineated three categories of evidence sufficient to sustain a finding of premeditation and deliberation: (1) facts about how and what the defendant did prior to the actual killing which show that the defendant was engaged in activity directed toward, and explicable as intended to result in, the killing (planning activity); (2) facts about the defendant's prior relationship with and/or conduct toward the victim from which the jury could reasonably infer a motive to kill the victim (motive); and (3) facts about the nature of the killing from which the jury could infer that the manner of killing was so particular and exacting that the defendant must have intentionally killed according to a preconceived design to take the victim's life in a particular way (exacting manner of killing). To establish premeditation and deliberation sufficient to constitute first-degree murder, the court requires at least (1) strong evidence of planning activity, or (2) evidence of motive in conjunction with evidence either of planning activity or an exacting manner of killing.

The *Pensinger* case excerpt illustrates use of the *Anderson* factors by the California Supreme Court to determine whether the defendant committed a deliberate and premeditated murder. The case is a particularly disturbing one, involving the murder of a five-month-old child under circumstances involving torture and possible sexual abuse. The defendant, Pensinger, met a woman named Vicki in a bar. Vicki had two children, a five-year-old boy and a five-month-old girl. A short time later, Vicki and the children rode with the defendant in his truck. When Vicki left the truck for a moment, the defendant drove off with the children. He traveled to a remote area, where he told the boy to get out of the truck. The boy complied. The defendant then took the baby to a dump where he tortured and killed her, and then mutilated the body. Pensinger was convicted of first-degree murder and sentenced to death. Review by the California Supreme Court is automatic in such cases. The defendant argued to the court that there was insufficient evidence to support his conviction of willful, premeditated, and deliberate murder. The supreme court's application of the *Anderson* factors is set out in the excerpt.

PEOPLE v. BRETT PATRICK PENSINGER
52 Cal.3d 1210; 278 Cal.Rptr. 640; 805 P.2d 899
[Feb. 1991]

We conclude that there was sufficient evidence of premeditation to support a verdict on that theory. We have found three categories of evidence which are sufficient to sustain a finding of premeditated, deliberate murder: evidence of planning, motive or of an exacting manner of killing. Evidence in only one of these categories most often is insufficient; we require either very strong evidence of planning, or some evidence of motive in conjunction with planning or a deliberate manner of killing.

Here, there was considerable evidence of planning. There was evidence that defendant introduced himself under an alias, that he drove off with two children, taking advantage of their mother's temporary absence, that he drove out of town for at least half an hour, that he dropped off the child who was old enough to be able to hinder him in any way or identify him and testify to his acts, that he then drove in the dark along unlighted dirt roads to an abandoned dump, the sign for which was invisible until a vehicle had already made the turn and that

he then broke the infant's arm, dashed her head against the rocks and stepped on her. There was evidence that at some point he also sexually abused the body. It can be inferred from the location and poor markings for the dump that petitioner was familiar with it before he abducted the children and planned to use it for its isolation.

Cases indicate that the total vulnerability of the victim and the evidence of a previously selected remote spot for the killing do suggest planning. This, combined with the evidence that defendant selected the more helpless of his victims and abandoned the one who might resist him in any way or testify as to his acts, provides substantial evidence of a planned killing, "the most important prong of the *Anderson* test."

There is also some evidence of motive. The district attorney argued that defendant was motivated by an incomprehensible need for revenge over the theft of his rifle. Respondent points to evidence of defendant's conduct before the killing which suggested that defendant killed the child in order to have sexual intercourse with her. Although either motivation was totally unreasonable, this is true of any senseless killing, but the incomprehensibility of the motive does not mean that the jury could not reasonably infer that the defendant entertained and acted on it.

As for the final *Anderson* category, the evidence of the manner of the killing, brutality alone cannot show premeditation; a brutal killing is as consistent with a killing in the heat of passion as with a premeditated killing. However, it must be remembered that the victim was five months old, and so could not walk, or presumably crawl. There can be no question of any struggle, and the fact that there is substantial evidence that defendant took the child from the truck, removed her from her infant carrier and took her in his arms to the place of her destruc-

tion, supports an inference that the killing was preconceived. We recognize that a cold and calculating decision to kill can be arrived at very quickly; we do not measure the necessary reflection solely by its duration.

We are satisfied that the jury could find beyond a reasonable doubt from substantial evidence that defendant committed a deliberate and premeditated murder.

* * *

We affirm the judgment and the penalty imposed by the superior court.

It should be noted that the specified types of first-degree murder stated in Penal Code § 189 all involve willfulness, premeditation, and deliberation. Consider, for example, murder by poisoning. Such murder involves a purposeful killing (willfulness). Poisoning, by its very nature, involves preparatory activities such as obtaining the poison and employing it in such a manner that it will enter the victim's body. Planning of this nature is the first *Anderson* factor. One who poisons another frequently has a prior relationship with the victim from which may be inferred a motive to kill the victim (the second *Anderson* factor). Also, poisoning reflects a preconceived design to kill the victim (the third *Anderson* factor). Consequently, murder by poisoning frequently involves all three *Anderson* factors, or may involve strong evidence of planning activity, or may involve evidence of motive in conjunction with planning activity or an exacting manner of killing. Any of these combinations of the *Anderson* factors supports a finding of premeditation and deliberation. The same analysis holds true for the other types of first-degree murder enumerated in § 189.

Second-Degree Murder   Second-degree murder is defined in § 189 as follows: "All other kinds of murders are of the second degree." Accordingly, if a killing constitutes murder under Penal Code § 187, and is not first-degree murder under § 189, it is second-degree murder. Put another way, second-degree murder is murder which is not one of the types specifically enumerated in § 189; is not another form of "willful, deliberate, and premeditated" murder; and is not first-degree felony-murder. The absence of any one of the three factors—willfulness, premeditation, or deliberation—will convert the murder from first to second degree. Using the language of the California Supreme Court in *Anderson*, the absence of one or more of these factors will tend to indicate that the killing was more an "unconsidered or rash impulse hastily executed," rather than the result of a "pre-existing reflection" and "careful thought and weighing of considerations."

Consider the case of Mark, the extremely possessive boyfriend. Jill, whom Mark has been dating, is tired of and somewhat frightened by Mark's possessiveness, so she informs Mark that the relationship is terminated. Mark, in a threatening manner, tells Jill that she is making a "big mistake," and that "if I can't have you, nobody can." The next day, Mark goes to a sporting goods store and buys a hunting knife. He then proceeds to Jill's house and kills her with the knife. This incident would constitute first-degree murder because it was a willful, deliberate, and premeditated killing. It was purposeful (willful). There is strong evidence of planning for the murder (purchase of the knife) (first *Anderson* factor); the prior relationship of the parties supports an inference that Mark had a motive to kill Jill (second *Anderson* factor); and the manner of the killing shows a preconceived design to kill Jill (third *Anderson* factor).

Contrast the preceding situation with the following. Jill tells Mark the relationship is over. Mark becomes extremely upset and pleads with Jill not to end the relationship, stating that he "can't live without her." Jill refuses to reconsider and also tells Mark there is another person in whom she has become interested. The thought of Jill directing her affections to another person is more than Mark can bear and, acting on an impulse, Mark picks up a large rock and strikes Jill in the head, killing her. This killing would constitute second-degree murder because the elements of premeditation and deliberation are lacking. There is no evidence of planning activities (first *Anderson* factor). There *is* evidence of the parties' relationship sufficient to give rise to an inference that Mark had a motive to kill Jill (second *Anderson* factor). However, this factor, standing alone, does not establish the existence of premeditation and deliberation. Finally, the nature of the killing does not indicate a preconceived design to kill Jill (third *Anderson* factor.)

An examination of the types of murder constituting first-degree murder under Penal Code § 189 reveals that first-degree murder invariably involves a specific intent to kill. In contrast, second-degree murder, may, but need not, involve a specific intent to kill. This characteristic of second-degree murder is reflected in California Jury Instruction—Criminal (CALJIC) 8.31:

> Murder of the second degree is [also] the unlawful killing of a human being when:
> 1. The killing resulted from an intentional act,
> 2. The natural consequences of the act are dangerous to human life, and
> 3. The act was deliberately performed with knowledge of the danger to, and with conscious disregard for, human life.
>
> When the killing is the direct result of such an act, it is not necessary to establish that the defendant intended that his act would result in the death of a human being.

The mental state described by CALJIC 8.31 is the form of implied malice specified in Penal Code § 188 as a killing "with an abandoned and malignant heart." It is a killing that results from an act done with callous disregard for the extreme danger to human life caused by the actor's conduct.

SIDEBAR

Crime and Delinquency in California

During 1995, California experienced 3,530 reported homicides, which equated to 11.0 homicide victims per 100,000 population. In 1995, homicide accounted for 1.2 percent of the California Crime Index violent crimes.

Of the 3,530 homicides reported in California in 1995, the type of weapon was known in 3,501 cases. Firearms accounted for 74.0% (2,590), knives or cutting instruments 11.6%

(405), blunt objects 4.5% (156), personal weapons such as hands, feet, etc., 4.7% (165), and other weapons 5.3% (185).
Source: Crime and Delinquency in California, 1995, California Department of Justice, Division of Law Enforcement.

Felony-Murder

It sometimes happens that, during the commission of a felony, the offender or an accomplice causes the death of another person. The killing may be intentional or unintentional. The **felony-murder doctrine** was developed at common law to deal with this situation. The essence of the felony-murder doctrine is that the defendant and his accomplices will be liable for murder if a death results from their commission of a felony. This is so even if the defendant and his accomplices did not intend to kill anyone. The law holds persons criminally responsible for deaths resulting from felonious situations that they have instigated.

Felony-murder always involves an underlying felony, that is, the felony the offender or offenders were in the process of committing when the death occurred. Consider, for example, Max and Bert, who enter a convenience store late at night and hold it up. Both Max and Bert are armed. The convenience store clerk readily hands over all the cash in the cash register. Max is heading for the door when he hears a gunshot. He turns and sees that Bert has shot and killed the clerk. Max had no intention to kill anyone as part of the robbery. Unfortunately for Max, under the felony-murder doctrine, he will be chargeable with murder, probably first-degree murder. Bert will, of course, be chargeable with murder with or without invoking the felony-murder doctrine, although he could also be charged with murder under a felony-murder theory. The underlying felony in this situation is robbery. The felony-murder doctrine is applicable because a death resulted from the felonious situation created by the robbers.

 Felony-murder, like other types of murder, may be of the first or second degree. The analytical approach to the two is different, so they are discussed separately here.

First-Degree Felony-Murder   First-degree felony-murder is defined by statute. Penal Code § 189 provides, in pertinent part, that: "All murder ... which is committed in the perpetration of, or attempt to perpetrate, arson, rape, carjacking, robbery, burglary, mayhem, kidnapping, train wrecking, or any act punishable under Section 286 [sodomy], 288 [lewd acts with child], 288a [oral copulation], or 289 [penetration by foreign object] ... is murder of the first degree" (bracketed language added).

The underlying felonies that will support a charge of first-degree felony-murder are specified in § 189. Despite the use of the term *murder* in the initial portion of the statute, the California courts have held that first-degree felony-murder does not require malice aforethought or premeditation. The view of the courts is that the statutory definition of first-degree felony-murder does not include those mental states. The only intent required for first-degree felony-murder is the specific intent to commit the underlying felony. Thus, in the preceding convenience store example, because Max entertained the specific intent to rob the store, he could be convicted of first-degree felony-murder for the death of the clerk, despite the fact that he had no desire or intent to kill the clerk.

Why is Max chargeable with murder when it was Bert who actually killed the clerk? The answer lies in the concept of vicarious liability, discussed in Chapter 3, and in the mutual responsibility of principals to a crime, which is discussed in Chapter 9. For present purposes, it is sufficient to state that all the persons participating directly in the underlying felony will be chargeable with felony-murder if a death results from the felonious situation they have created, even if the killing is done by only one of them.

For the doctrine of felony-murder to apply, there must be a connection between the underlying felony and the death. The commission of the felony need not be the cause of the death, but the felony and the death must be parts of what has been referred to as a "continuous transaction." Thus, the death must occur during the commission of the felony and must bear some relationship to the felony. Consider again the convenience store robbery involving Max and Bert. Let us assume that, at the time of the robbery, a customer in the store is so frightened by the robbery that she suffers a fatal heart attack. The felony-murder doctrine would apply in this situation, and Max and Bert would be guilty of first-degree murder. Assume now that the customer is hard of hearing and is unaware that the robbery is in progress. She suffers a fatal heart attack during the robbery, but it has no relationship to the robbery. In this situation, the offenders would not be chargeable with felony-murder for the customer's death. As may be apparent from the first scenario (in which the customer dies because she is frightened by the robbery), there is no requirement under the felony-murder doctrine that the death be foreseeable or that the person who dies have been the intended victim of the underlying felony. Unforeseeable deaths of persons such as innocent bystanders are chargeable under the felony-murder doctrine.

The requirement that the underlying felony and the death be parts of a continuous transaction can raise questions in certain situations, such as "When did commission of the felony begin?" and "When did it end?" If the killing occurs before the commission of the underlying felony, the felony-murder doctrine does not apply. For example, assume Sharon shoots and kills Lisa, and then decides to rob her. The felony-murder doctrine would not apply to this situation because the underlying felony, robbery, did not commence until after the killing. One may be wondering at this point why such analysis matters. Is not Sharon, after all, chargeable with murder regardless of the felony-murder doctrine? Yes. But the murder committed by Sharon may have been only second-degree murder, depending on the facts of the case. Remember that the present discussion is about first-degree felony-murder. If Sharon's killing of Lisa occurred during the commission of the robbery, it would constitute first-degree murder under Penal Code § 189 despite the fact that the murder, if the robbery were not considered, might only be second-degree murder. What is more, if Sharon's killing of Lisa could be brought within the felony-murder doctrine, the prosecution would not have to prove malice aforethought or premeditation because, as previously noted, the courts have held that first-degree felony-murder does not require malice or premeditation.

A question more common than "When did the underlying felony begin" is "When did the underlying felony end?" This question frequently arises in escape/pursuit situations, i.e., situations in which the offender is fleeing the crime scene and is being pursued by police. In such situations, the rule has developed that the underlying felony ceases when the offender reaches a place of temporary safety. Thus, if Frank commits robbery and flees the scene in his automobile with the police in hot pursuit, any killing that occurs during the pursuit (of a police officer, of another motorist or a pedestrian) is first-degree felony murder. If, in contrast, Frank flees the scene of the robbery, is not pursued, and reaches his home, his killing of a police officer who comes to his home later to investigate is not felony-murder because the underlying felony, the robbery, has ceased. As with the Sharon–Lisa scenario, the significance of the cessation of the underlying felony in Frank's case is that if the circumstances of Frank's killing of the police officer make the killing second-degree murder, the felony-murder doctrine is not available to the prosecution to upgrade the offense to first-degree murder, and the prosecution will have to prove that Frank killed with malice aforethought.

The case of *People v. Morlock* illustrates the application of the felony-murder doctrine to a death occurring during the commission of a burglary. Although the killing, standing alone, probably would not have constituted first-degree murder, it became first-degree murder under the felony-murder doctrine, resulting in a sentence of death for the defendant.

PEOPLE v. EUGENE AUGUSTINE MORLOCK
46 Cal.2d 141; 292 P.2d 897 (1956)

CARTER, J.—This is an automatic appeal from a judgment of the Superior Court of San Diego County imposing the death penalty.

Defendant Eugene Augustine Morlock was charged with the murder of one Annie Morales … . He pleaded not guilty and not guilty by reason of insanity … . After trial by jury he was found guilty as charged and sane at the time of the commission of the offenses. A motion for a new trial was made and denied and a judgment imposing the death penalty was rendered.

There is little or no dispute as to the facts. On May 11, 1955, Gus Pico, George Piepa, Frank Cuervas, defendant's uncle, and Annie Morales were drinking together in a two-room dwelling on the Rincon Indian Reservation. At approximately 7 o'clock in the evening, defendant in the company of Lindy Parcel (a codefendant) broke down the door of the house with a fence post defendant had picked up outside and which he used as a battering ram. He then asked Piepa for a drink while still holding the post in a threatening manner. Piepa informed him there was nothing to drink, whereupon defendant struck Piepa with his fists knocking him to the floor. The record disclosed that defendant was 6 feet 4 inches tall and weighed over 200 pounds. Annie Morales, the common-law wife of Piepa, came through the opening from the next room and may have started to attack the defendant. He thereupon struck her in the face with his fists knocking her to the floor where he then kicked her three or four times in the face with his steel-toed boots. He left her lying on her back on the floor of the bedroom where she fell and went back into the kitchen where he struck Piepa with the flat side of an axe he had found in the house and then kicked him. Parcel took the axe away from him, but defendant found a broken bread knife with which he proceeded to cut Piepa. The knife was taken from him by Parcel. … Parcel testified that before entering the house defendant said he was going to "clobber" Piepa because Piepa had beaten his uncle.

* * *

The People argue that defendant was guilty of first degree murder in that the death of Annie Morales occurred in the commission of … burglary … . Defendant contends that the evidence is insufficient to establish that the murder occurred in the perpetration of … burglary … .

Section 459 of the Penal Code provides that "Every person who enters any house, room … with intent to commit grand or petit larceny or *any felony* is guilty of burglary."

* * *

The fence post involved here measured 4 feet 11 inches in length, was 4 inches by 4 inches square and weighed 10 pounds, and therefore comes well within the definition of a "deadly weapon." ... Defendant contends that if this was a burglary, the crime was complete upon the entry; that Annie Morales was, therefore, not killed in the perpetration of burglary but was killed in the perpetration of an assault upon Piepa. Defendant's contentions are without merit. The statute provides that all murder which is committed in the perpetration of or attempt to perpetrate burglary is murder of the first degree. As we have heretofore pointed out burglary is committed when a person enters any house "with intent to commit ... any felony" and that section 245 of the Penal Code provides that a person is guilty of a felony when he commits an assault upon the person of another with a deadly weapon "or by any means of force likely to produce great bodily injury." It may justifiably be inferred from the evidence here that defendant entered the house of Piepa with intent to assault him with the fence post with which he had armed himself prior to the entry and that such fence post was a deadly weapon within the meaning of the term. ... Defendant's argument is, apparently, that he did not intend to assault Annie Morales when he entered the house ... . It is immaterial to the guilt of defendant that Annie Morales was the one killed rather than Piepa whom he intended to assault. We said in *People v. Coefield,* 37 Cal.2d 865, 868, that a killing is murder of the first degree by force of section 189 of the Penal Code, regardless of whether it was intentional or accidental.

We conclude, therefore, that the evidence was more than sufficient to sustain the judgment of conviction on the theory that the killing was perpetrated in the commission of burglary.

* * *

The judgment and order denying a new trial are affirmed.

Second-Degree Felony-Murder   **Second-degree felony-murder** is a killing that occurs during the commission of a felony which is not one of the felonies enumerated in Penal Code § 189. Unlike first-degree felony-murder, second-degree felony-murder is not defined by statute. As a result, the courts have held that second-degree felony-murder requires all the elements of murder, particularly malice aforethought. The malice aforethought element of second-degree felony-murder is the sort of implied malice described in Penal Code § 188 by the words: "when the circumstances attending the killing show an abandoned and malignant heart." What this language means is that the actors have consciously created a situation that is inherently dangerous to human life. This callous disregard for the risk to human life caused by the actors' conduct constitutes implied malice aforethought. If one of the actors causes the death of another person, principles of vicarious liability and the law regarding shared responsibility of principals to crime impute the act to all the offenders. Thus, all are responsible for the killing of the victim, and by virtue of participating in a situation in which they have put human life at risk, all will be considered to possess the mental state of malice aforethought. These are the elements of second-degree murder.

Not all underlying felonies will support a conviction of second-degree felony-murder. The courts have limited the underlying felonies to those that are inherently dangerous to human life. This limitation makes sense for more than policy reasons. If an underlying felony is not inherently dangerous to human life, it may be difficult or impossible to establish implied malice aforethought on the part of the perpetrators. If malice cannot be established, a murder conviction is impossible. In *People v. Patterson* (1989) 49 Cal.3d 615, the California Supreme

Court held that a felony is "inherently dangerous to human life" when there is a high probability that its commission will result in death.

An important limitation on the felony-murder doctrine in California is that the doctrine applies only to killings committed by the persons committing the underlying felony. This principle leaves unanswered an important question: What is the criminal liability of the felons if a killing occurs during the felony as the result of the acts of a third person, such as the victim of the underlying felony or a police officer? Judicial decisions have developed a body of law to deal with such situations.

Liability for Deaths Caused by Acts of Third Persons   Consider the following situation. Alexander, Julius, and Nero attempt to rape Patricia at gunpoint. Patricia, however, is an off-duty police officer. She pulls her service revolver out of her purse and fires, killing Alexander. A gun battle ensues between Julius and Nero, on the one hand, and Patricia on the other. During the battle, a round fired by Patricia strikes an innocent bystander who is also killed. What is the criminal liability, if any, of Julius and Nero for the deaths of Alexander and the innocent bystander?

The felony-murder doctrine does not apply to this situation because, in California, the courts have limited the doctrine to situations in which the felons, or one of them, directly kills someone. The courts approach cases in which a victim or police officer kills during the commission of a felony by first evaluating the situation created by the felony to determine whether it supports a finding of implied malice aforethought on the part of the perpetrators. Creation by the perpetrators of a situation posing a high probability of death, with wanton disregard for human life, constitutes implied malice aforethought—but malice aforethought, standing alone, does not constitute murder. The perpetrators must also have caused the death. The courts have held that when the perpetrators, with a conscious disregard for human life, intentionally commit an act that is likely to result in the death of a person, and their victim or a police officer kills in reasonable response to such act, the perpetrators' actions constitute both the cause in fact and proximate cause of the resulting death. Under these principles, the perpetrators may be convicted of murder for a killing by a third person.

Manslaughter

Manslaughter is a less culpable form of homicide than murder. It is defined in Penal Code § 192 as "the unlawful killing of a human being without malice." Like murder, manslaughter involves the unlawful killing of a human being. As discussed in the consideration of murder, an unlawful killing is one that is not excusable or justifiable. There is no difference between the crimes of murder and manslaughter in this regard. Unlike murder, manslaughter does not include the unlawful killing of a fetus. Recall that the courts have been unwilling to interpret the term *human being* as including a fetus, absent specific statutory language to that effect, and the words "or a fetus" have not been added to Penal Code § 192 as they have to Penal Code § 187. The principal distinction between murder and manslaughter has to do with the mental states required for the two crimes. Murder requires malice aforethought, whereas manslaughter does not.

Because manslaughter is a killing without malice aforethought, it is considered less culpable than murder and is punished less severely. Manslaughter does, however, carry heavy penalties because it involves the unlawful killing of a human being.

Penal Code § 192 defines three types of manslaughter: voluntary manslaughter, involuntary manslaughter, and vehicular manslaughter.

Voluntary Manslaughter

Heat of passion

Voluntary manslaughter is defined in Penal Code § 192(a) as the unlawful killing of a human being without malice, "upon a sudden quarrel or heat of passion." Voluntary manslaughter is an intentional killing, but the element of malice is negated by the circumstances described in the statute with the words "upon a sudden quarrel or heat of passion." Voluntary manslaughter is a provoked killing, i.e., it invariably involves a situation in which the actor has been provoked by the victim. This element of provocation is the critical distinction between voluntary manslaughter and second-degree murder. Recall that malice aforethought will be implied under Penal Code § 188 if there is "no considerable provocation" for the killing. The element of implied malice makes the killing murder. If, however, the killing is the result of adequate provocation, the killing is reduced from murder to voluntary manslaughter. What, then, is adequate provocation?

Provocation is adequate to reduce a killing from murder to voluntary manslaughter if it is so serious as to cause a reasonable person to kill. If a defendant argues that a killing was voluntary manslaughter rather than murder, the question is: Would the circumstances that provoked the defendant to kill have provoked a reasonable person to kill? If so, sufficient provocation exists to reduce the crime to voluntary manslaughter. Sufficient provocation has been found in cases in which the defendant was the victim of a violent or painful assault and struck back at the assailant, killing him or her. The killing of a family member is considered adequate provocation to reduce the killing of the killer by another family member to voluntary manslaughter. The discovery of a spouse's adultery, particularly catching the spouse in the act of adultery, has been held to constitute adequate provocation to reduce a killing of the spouse or his or her paramour to voluntary manslaughter. Some cases have held that insulting words may sometimes constitute sufficient provocation to reduce a killing from murder to manslaughter, although this is a departure from the common law rule that words alone are never sufficient provocation, and probably cannot be stated as a general principle.

Sufficiency of provocation is not the only consideration in determining whether a killing is murder or voluntary manslaughter. The killing must be in the "heat of passion." For purposes of voluntary manslaughter, a person kills in the heat of passion when, as a result of a provocation, he or she acts emotionally rather than rationally. Remember that the provocation must be sufficient to cause the same reaction in a reasonable person. If a person resorts to deadly violence under circumstances that would not provoke the same response in a reasonable person, the killing will be murder rather than manslaughter. The reasonable person standard is an objective standard, and is applied in each case by the trier of fact, i.e., the jury or, in a bench trial, by the judge alone.

To be considered "in the heat of passion," a killing must occur soon enough after the provoking incident to be the product of an emotional response, rather than a rational act. The actor must still be under the overpowering influence of the provocation when he or she kills the victim. If sufficient time elapses for a reasonable person's passions to cool, a subsequent killing will not be considered to be in the heat of passion, and will thus be murder, not manslaughter. Indicia of cooling of the passions include such circumstances as lapse of time, rational activity on the part of the actor, or acts indicating rational preparation for the killing.

In the excerpt from *People v. Berry,* the California Supreme Court held that, under the facts of the case, the trial court should have instructed the jury on the voluntary manslaughter concepts of provocation and heat of passion, and held further that the trial court's failure to do so constituted reversible error. The court noted that provocation by the victim, culminating in a killing of the victim in the heat of passion, may occur over a prolonged period. The facts of the case, as recited by the court, may be summarized as follows: Berry married Rachel Pessah, a twenty-year-old woman from Israel, on May 27, 1974. Three days later, Rachel went to Israel by herself, returning on July 13, 1974. Rachel announced to Berry that while in Israel, she had fallen in love with another

---

PEOPLE v. ALBERT JOSEPH BERRY
18 Cal.3d 509; 134 Cal.Rptr. 415, 556 P.2d 777 (1976)

Dr. Martin Blinder, a physician and psychiatrist, called by the defense, testified that Rachel was a depressed, suicidally inclined girl and that this suicidal impulse led her to involve herself ever more deeply in a dangerous situation with defendant. She did this by sexually arousing him and taunting him into jealous rages in an unconscious desire to provoke him into killing her and thus consummating her desire for suicide. Throughout the period commencing with her return from Israel until her death, that is from July 13 to July 26, Rachel continually provoked defendant with sexual taunts and incitements, alternating acceptance and rejection of him. This conduct was accompanied by repeated references to her involvement with another man; it led defendant to choke her on two occasions, until finally she achieved her unconscious desire and was strangled. Dr. Blinder testified that as a result of this cumulative series of provocations, defendant at the time he fatally strangled Rachel, was in a state of uncontrollable rage, completely under the sway of passion.

We first take up defendant's claim that on the basis of the foregoing evidence he was entitled to an instruction on voluntary manslaughter as defined by

statute which is "the unlawful killing of a human being, without malice ... upon a sudden quarrel or heat of passion." In *People v. Valentine* (1946) 28 Cal.2d 121, this court, in an extensive review of the law of manslaughter, specifically approved the following quotation from *People v. Logan* (1917) 175 Cal. 45, 48–49 as a correct statement of the law: "In the present condition of our law *it is left to the jurors* to say whether or not the facts and circumstances in evidence are sufficient to lead them to believe that the defendant did, or to create a reasonable doubt in their minds as to whether or not he did, commit his offense under a heat of passion. The jury is further to be admonished and advised by the court that this heat of passion must be such a passion as would naturally be aroused in the mind of an ordinarily reasonable person under the given facts and circumstances, and that, consequently, no defendant may set up his own standard of conduct and justify or excuse himself because in fact his passions were aroused, unless further the jury believe that the facts and circumstances were sufficient to arouse the passions of the ordinarily reasonable man. ... For the fundamental of the inquiry is whether or not the defendant's reason was, at the time of his act, so disturbed or obscured by some passion—not necessarily fear and never, of course, the passion for revenge—to such an extent as would render ordinary men of average disposition liable to act rashly or without due deliberation and reflection, and from this passion rather than from judgment."

We further held in *Valentine* that there is no specific type of provocation required by section 192 and that verbal provocation may be sufficient. In *People v. Borchers* (1958) 50 Cal.2d 321, 329 in the course of explaining the phrase "heat of passion" used in the statute defining manslaughter we pointed out that "passion" need not mean "rage" or "anger" but may be any "[v]iolent, intense, high-wrought or enthusiastic emotion" and concluded there "that defendant was aroused to a heat of 'passion' by a series of events over a considerable period of time. ..." Accordingly we there declared that evidence of admissions of infidelity by the defendant's paramour, taunts directed to him and other conduct, "supports a finding that defendant killed in wild desperation induced by [the woman's] long continued provocatory conduct." We find this reasoning persuasive in the case now before us. Defendant's testimony chronicles a two-week period of provocatory conduct by his wife Rachel that could arouse a passion of jealousy, pain and sexual rage in an ordinary man of average disposition such as to cause him to act rashly from this passion. It is significant that both defendant and Dr. Blinder testified that the former was in the heat of passion under an uncontrollable rage when he killed Rachel.

The Attorney General contends that the killing could not have been done in the heat of passion because there was a cooling period, defendant having waited in the apartment for 20 hours. However, the long course of provocatory conduct, which had resulted in intermittent outbreaks of rage under specific provocation in the past, reached its final culmination in the apartment when Rachel began screaming. Both defendant and Dr. Blinder testified that defendant killed in a state of uncontrollable rage, of passion, and there is ample evidence in the record to support the conclusion that this passion was the result of the long course of provocatory conduct by Rachel, just as the killing emerged from such conduct in *Borchers*.

* * *

[The] court did commit error in refusing to instruct on voluntary manslaughter based on sudden quarrel or heat of passion. Defendant contends that this constitutes prejudicial error which compels reversal of the judgment as to the murder count. ... Since this theory ... constituted defendant's entire defense to the first count, we have no difficulty concluding that the failure to give such instruction was prejudicial error ... and requires us to reverse the conviction of murder of the first degree.

man, one Yako; had enjoyed his sexual favors; that Yako was coming to this country to claim her; and that she wanted a divorce. During the next two weeks, Rachel alternately taunted Berry with her involvement with Yako and indicated her desire to remain with Berry. One minute she would declare her love for Berry and engage in sexual activity with him, and the next minute state that she loved Yako and was saving herself for him. Berry moved out of the couple's apartment on July 22. On July 25, Berry returned to the apartment to talk to Rachel, but she was out. He spent the night in the apartment. Rachel returned at approximately 11 A.M. on July 26. Upon seeing Berry there, Rachel said, "I suppose you have come here to kill me." Berry responded, "yes," changed his response to "no," and then again to "yes" and finally stated "I have really come to talk to you." Rachel began screaming. Berry grabbed her by the shoulder and tried to stop her screaming. Rachel continued. They struggled, and finally Berry strangled Rachel with a telephone cord, killing her. The court's analysis of the foregoing facts appears in the excerpt.

There is another form of voluntary manslaughter, sometimes referred to as **imperfect self-defense.** This type of voluntary manslaughter involves a killing resulting from an honest but unreasonable belief that use of deadly force in self-defense is necessitated by the circumstances. For example, Sue is walking on a dark street late at night when she is approached by a man who asks her what time it is. Fearing robbery or rape, Sue pulls a pistol out of her purse and kills the man. In fact, no conduct by the man indicated that he intended to rob or rape Sue. Accordingly, Sue cannot escape criminal liability for the homicide. If, however, her belief that she was in danger was honest, although unreasonable, the element of malice is negated and the homicide is reduced from murder to voluntary manslaughter.

Voluntary manslaughter is a felony, punishable by imprisonment in the state prison for three, six, or eleven years. (See Penal Code § 193(a).) Chapter 18 discusses sentencing under statutes that prescribe two or more possible prison terms.

Involuntary Manslaughter

Involuntary manslaughter is the lowest—that is, the least culpable—form of criminal homicide. It is defined in Penal Code § 192(b) as the unlawful killing of a human being without malice

> in the commission of an unlawful act, not amounting to a felony; or in the commission of a lawful act which might produce death, in an unlawful manner, or without due caution and circumspection.

Section 192(b) does not apply to deaths resulting from the driving of a vehicle. Such deaths are covered by § 192(c), which delineates the crime of vehicular manslaughter.

The first part of the statutory definition of involuntary manslaughter is the manslaughter counterpart of felony-murder. The crime is known as **misdemeanor-manslaughter.** The doctrine is more narrowly applied than the felony-murder doctrine, largely because many misdemeanors involve low levels of culpability, and some involve no culpability at all (strict liability offenses). Because many misdemeanors are relatively low-level crimes, the courts have, through statutory interpretation, placed limits on the misdemeanor-manslaughter rule enunciated in § 192(b).[2] One such limitation is the court-imposed requirement that there be a causal connection between the commission of the misdemeanor and the death. In the words of one court, the death "must be the probable consequence naturally flowing from the commission of the unlawful act."[3] A second limitation placed on the misdemeanor-manslaughter rule by the courts is that the underlying misdemeanor be committed with criminal intent. This requirement rules out strict liability offenses as the basis for application of the rule (unless they are committed with criminal intent). Finally, the courts require that the misdemeanor be one that is inherently dangerous to human life. This is the same requirement imposed by the courts for second-degree felony-murder.

To summarize, a death occurring during the commission of a misdemeanor will result in liability for involuntary manslaughter only if the misdemeanor is one inherently dangerous to human life, it is committed with criminal intent, and there is a causal connection between the commission of the misdemeanor and the death.

Misdemeanor-manslaughter is not the only form of involuntary manslaughter. The language of Penal Code § 192(b) also includes negligent homicides. Thus, one who commits a negligent act that results in the death of another has committed involuntary manslaughter. As discussed in Chapter 3, the type of negligence required to support a homicide conviction is greater than that required for imposition of civil liability. In a civil suit, negligence is established by producing evidence that the defendant failed to use the degree of care that a reasonable person would have used in the same or similar circumstances. This standard is sometimes called *simple negligence*. In a criminal case, the degree of negligence must be more culpable than that embodied in the civil standard. In the words of one court:

> The negligence must be aggravated, culpable, gross, or reckless, that is, the conduct of the accused must be such a departure from what would be the conduct of an ordinarily prudent or careful man under the same circumstances as to be incompatible with a proper regard for human life, or, in other words, a disregard of human life or an indifference to consequences.[4]

Death resulting from the negligent handling of firearms has been a frequent basis for involuntary manslaughter convictions. For example, if one negligently points a loaded weapon at another and the weapon accidentally discharges, killing the person, the actor has committed involuntary manslaughter. Remember that the negligence must be of the criminal, not the civil, type. The accidental discharge of a weapon being carried in a public place with a round in the chamber has also supported convictions for involuntary manslaughter. In one particularly tragic case, the defendant was practicing his "fast draw." He drew the weapon and pointed it at his four-year-old niece. The weapon accidentally discharged, killing the child. The defendant was convicted of involuntary manslaughter and the conviction was affirmed on appeal. The court held that despite the defendant's belief that the weapon was not loaded, he acted with criminal negligence in drawing and pointing the gun at the child.[5]

Defendants have been convicted of involuntary manslaughter for acts other than those involving weapons. They have also been convicted in cases involving negligent omissions. Recall the discussion in Chapter 3 about criminal liability for failure to act if one has a duty to act. Parental neglect resulting in death of a child, if the neglect amounts to criminal, rather than simple, negligence, is an example of an omission to act that will constitute involuntary manslaughter. Also, one such as a nursing home operator, who contracts to care for a helpless person, may be held criminally liable for death of a resident caused by criminal neglect on the part of the operator.

Involuntary manslaughter is a felony punishable by imprisonment in the state prison for two, three, or four years (see Penal Code § 193(b)).

Vehicular Manslaughter

The third type of manslaughter specified in Penal Code § 192 is **vehicular manslaughter**. Vehicular manslaughter is defined in § 192(c) as the unlawful killing of a human being without malice under the following circumstances:

Section 192(c)(1)—The operation of a motor vehicle with gross negligence resulting in the death of a human being.

Section 192(c)(2)—The operation of a motor vehicle with simple negligence resulting in the death of a human being.

Section 192(c)(3)—The operation of a motor vehicle with simple negligence while under the influence of alcohol or drugs resulting in the death of a human being.

Not surprisingly, the penalties for the various forms of vehicular manslaughter differ. Conviction of vehicular manslaughter under § 192(c)(1) (gross negligence) carries a possible sentence of imprisonment in the county jail for not more than one year or by imprisonment in the state prison for two, four, or six years. Conviction under § 192(c)(2) (simple negligence) is punishable by imprisonment in the county jail for not more than one year. Conviction under § 192(c)(3) (simple negligence under the influence of alcohol or drugs) is punishable by imprisonment in the county jail for not more than one year or by imprisonment in the state prison for sixteen months or two or four years.[6]

Gross negligence, as used in § 192(c)(1), means something similar to recklessness. Gross negligence is defined in CALJIC No. 8.92 as "the failure to exercise any care, or the exercise of so little care that you [the jury] are justified in believing that the person whose conduct is involved was wholly indifferent to the consequences of his conduct and to the welfare of others." For example, continuing to drive at excessive speed despite the requests of passengers that the driver slow down has been held to evidence gross negligence.[7]

In contrast to the criminal negligence required to constitute involuntary manslaughter under Penal Code § 192(b), the degree of negligence required to support a conviction of vehicular manslaughter under §§ 192(c)(2) and 192(c)(3) is simple negligence, i.e., the failure to exercise that degree of care that a reasonable person would exercise in the same or similar circumstances. There is no requirement that the negligence be "aggravated, gross, or reckless," as in the case of involuntary manslaughter.

Penal Code § 191.5, which became effective in 1992, defines the crime of **gross vehicular manslaughter while intoxicated**. This crime is the gross negligence counterpart of the form of vehicular manslaughter defined in Penal Code § 192(c)(3), which imposes criminal liability for a killing committed while operating a vehicle under the influence of alcohol or drugs, with simple negligence. Gross vehicular manslaughter requires gross negligence and, not surprisingly, the penalties for the crime are greater than for vehicular manslaughter under § 192(c)(3). Gross vehicular manslaughter while intoxicated is punishable by imprisonment in the state prison for four, six, or ten years. The crime of gross vehicular manslaughter while intoxicated also applies to operation of a vessel, such as a boat, with gross negligence while intoxicated.

Death inflicted by means of a motor vehicle can be murder rather than manslaughter. For example, if a person uses a motor vehicle as a weapon in an attempt to run down and kill another person, malice aforethought will be either express or implied under § 188, and the attack, if successful, will constitute murder. Death caused by operation of a motor vehicle can also be murder if the elements of implied malice are present. For example, death caused by the operation of a motor vehicle can constitute murder if the facts of the case exhibit wantonness and a conscious disregard for life. Thus, one who operates a motor vehicle in an extremely reckless manner resulting in the death of a human being may be charged with murder rather than with vehicular manslaughter.

Life, Death, and Homicide

The actus reus of murder and manslaughter is the unlawful killing of a human being or a fetus (in the case of murder). Determining when life begins and ends can be a problem in criminal law.

Penal Code § 187 does not specifically address the question of when life begins. Rather, it makes the killing of a fetus murder, with certain exceptions. The question therefore is not so much when life begins, but when does an unborn child become a fetus. The California Supreme Court, in the 1994 decision of *People v. Davis*, 7 Cal.4th 797, held that an unborn child can be a fetus within the meaning of Penal Code § 187 as early as seven or eight weeks after fertilization. The court adopted a medical definition and stated that "[generally] ... a fetus is defined as the 'unborn offspring in the postembryonic period, after major structures have been outlined.' " The court indicated that it is up to the trier of fact (the jury, or the judge in a case without a jury) to determine whether an unborn child has achieved that state in a given case. If the jury finds that the defendant unlawfully killed an unborn child that had achieved the legal status of fetus, the defendant may be convicted of murder.

At the other end of the spectrum is death. Medical advances have made the determination of when death occurs more complex than it was only years ago. For a long time, a person was considered dead when there was no heartbeat and no breathing. Today, artificial means can be used to sustain both heart action and respiration. That being so, should one be free of criminal homicide in cases where the victim is being kept "alive" by artificial means and there is no reasonable hope of recovery?

California, reflecting the trend in many states, has adopted a dual definition of death. The definition is found in Health and Safety Code § 7180, which states:

> An individual who has sustained either (1) irreversible cessation of circulatory and respiratory functions, or (2) irreversible cessation of all functions of the entire brain, including the brain stem, is dead.

The second type of death described in the statute, termed "brain death," can occur even when the victim's heartbeat and respiration are being artificially sustained.

Suicide

Successful suicide was a crime under the common law of England. The property owned by the one who committed suicide was forfeited to (taken by) the Crown. In early American common law attempted suicide was a crime, usually punished as a misdemeanor. Today suicide is not treated as a crime. However, it is possible to restrain and examine individuals who have attempted to commit suicide under civil psychiatric commitment laws.

It continues to be criminal to encourage or aid another to commit suicide. Penal Code § 401 states that "Every person who deliberately aids, or advises, or encourages another person to commit suicide, is guilty of a felony." Aiding, advising, or encouraging another to commit suicide is to be distinguished from active involvement in the killing of the suicide victim. In the latter situation, the defendant can be charged with murder.

§ 4.3 Corpus Delicti

Corpus delicti is a Latin phrase that translates as "the body of the crime." The prosecution must establish the corpus delicti independently of any admissions or confessions of the defendant made prior to the trial. In essence, the significance of the concept of corpus delicti is that the prosecution must establish that the crime has occurred before introducing into evidence any confessions or admissions made by the defendant. The purpose of this rule is to protect defendants from being prosecuted for crimes that have not actually been committed.

Witkin and Epstein describe corpus delicti as having two components: (1) the fact of the injury, loss, or harm, and (2) the existence of a criminal agency as its cause.[8] In a homicide case, for example, producing evidence that a person has been killed is not sufficient to establish the corpus delicti of the crime of murder or manslaughter. The prosecution must also establish that the person died as the result of a criminal act. Wounds on the body of the victim, eyewitness testimony, and circumstantial evidence are all means that can be used to establish that death was the result of a criminal act. Once the prosecution has established the corpus delicti of the crime, the confessions or admissions of the defendant, if any, may be introduced into evidence to establish that the defendant is the person who committed the crime.

Key Terms

corpus delicti The "body of the crime," which consists of two factors: (1) injury, loss, or harm, and (2) a criminal act or omission as its cause. In a criminal trial, the prosecution must establish the corpus delicti—i.e., that a crime occurred—independently of any admissions or confessions of the defendant made prior to the trial.

deliberation As an element of the crime of first-degree murder, means careful thought and weighing of considerations.

element An essential component of a crime.

felony-murder doctrine The legal doctrine that an unintended or accidental killing caused by the perpetrator of a felony during the commission of the felony is murder. Felony murder may be of the first or second degree.

first-degree felony-murder A killing that occurs during the commission of those felonies specified in Penal Code § 189.

gross vehicular manslaughter while intoxicated The killing of a human being as the result of operation of a motor vehicle or a vessel with gross negligence while intoxicated.

imperfect self-defense A killing resulting from an honest but unreasonable belief that use of deadly force in self-defense is necessitated by the circumstances. Imperfect self-defense is a form of voluntary manslaughter.

involuntary manslaughter The unlawful killing of a human being without malice as a result of criminal negligence, or during the commission of certain misdemeanors.

malice aforethought The mens rea of the offense of murder. According to Penal Code § 188, malice aforethought may be express or implied. It is express when the killer manifests a deliberate intent to kill. It is implied when no considerable provocation appears or when the circumstances attending the killing show an abandoned and malignant heart.

manslaughter The unlawful killing of a human being without malice aforethought.

merger of offenses The doctrine that when a lesser offense is a component of a more serious offense, and the defendant is convicted of the more serious offense, the lesser is absorbed by the greater, and the defendant is not punished for both.

misdemeanor-manslaughter The legal doctrine that an unintended or accidental killing caused

by the perpetrator of a misdemeanor during commission of the misdemeanor is manslaughter if: the misdemeanor is one inherently dangerous to human life, it is committed with criminal intent, and there is a causal connection between the commission of the misdemeanor and the death.

premeditation As an element of the crime of first-degree murder, means preexisting reflection.

second-degree felony-murder A killing that occurs during the commission of a felony not

enumerated in Penal Code § 189. The felony must be inherently dangerous to human life.

vehicular manslaughter The killing of a human being resulting from the operation of a motor vehicle in one of the following circumstances: (1) with gross negligence; (2) with simple negligence; (3) with simple negligence while under the influence of alcohol or drugs.

voluntary manslaughter The unlawful killing of a human being without malice, upon a sudden quarrel or heat of passion.

Review Questions

1. Why is there no crime of fetal manslaughter in California?

2. Explain some of the distinctions between first- and second-degree murder.

3. What is felony-murder?

4. Explain some of the distinctions between first- and second-degree felony-murder.

5. What is the difference between murder and manslaughter?

Review Problems

1. On May 5, Mark and Sam, who had been neighbors for three years, argued over Sam's construction of a ditch that diverted water onto Mark's property. Mark told Sam to stop construction of the ditch or he would "pay with his life." The following day, Mark and Sam met again in Sam's garage. Within minutes, Mark became very angry and struck Sam in the leg with an axe he found in Sam's garage. After striking Sam, Mark panicked and ran home. Sam attempted to reach a telephone to call for help, but the wound proved fatal. Mark has been charged with first-degree murder. He claims that he had no intent to kill Sam; rather, he only intended to hit him on the leg with the dull, flat side of the axe in an effort to scare Sam. Discuss the facts and explain what crimes could be proved and why.

2. On July 1, 1990, Jeff shot Megan during a bank robbery. Megan remained on life-support systems until September 4, 1991. At that time, the systems were disconnected and Megan ceased breathing. On June 15, 1991, Megan's physician declared her brain dead. It was not until September 4, 1991, that Megan's family decided to stop the life-support system. Jeff is charged with murder. Discuss any defenses he may have.

3. Bonnie and Clyde hold up a bank. One of the tellers sets off a silent alarm, and the police soon arrive. To avoid capture, Bonnie holds a gun to the head of one of the bank customers and threatens to kill him. A police officer aims carefully at Bonnie and fires his revolver, but hits and kills the customer. Assume that the shooting by the police officer would be deemed a reasonable response to the life-threatening situation created by Bonnie. Bonnie and Clyde are captured and are tried for murder of the customer. Can Bonnie be convicted of the murder? Can Clyde? Can either or both of them be convicted under the felony-murder doctrine? If not, what legal principles can be applied to convict one or both of them of murder?

4. Fred is awakened at 3 A.M. by a noise in the downstairs part of his house. He takes a pistol from his closet and goes downstairs to investigate. As he rounds a corner, he is surprised by the shadowy figure of an adult male. There are no adult males living in the house other than Fred. Fred immediately fires at the figure, killing him. Investigation later reveals that the deceased was wanted by the police for several burglaries in the community, and that he entered the house by forcibly opening a

sliding glass door. Considering that Fred did not confront the individual and ask the purpose of his presence in the house before shooting him, has Fred committed a criminal homicide? You should read Penal Code § 198.5 before answering this question.

5. Mike has lost a bitter child custody dispute in his dissolution of marriage proceeding. Enraged and distraught, he leaves the courthouse and walks to his car, where he removes a loaded pistol from the glove compartment. He returns to the courthouse, walks up to his spouse and her attorney, and shoots them, killing them both. Apply the *Anderson* factors to determine whether the killing is first- or second-degree murder (assume it is not voluntary manslaughter).

6. Joe is a window washer. He is standing on a suspended platform washing the thirty-fifth-floor windows of a skyscraper when he accidentally, but carelessly, kicks a bucket of water. The bucket falls from the platform and strikes a pedestrian on the sidewalk below, killing the pedestrian. Is Joe guilty of a criminal homicide? If so, of which type of homicide is he guilty?

Notes

[1] A. Loewy, *Criminal Law* (2d ed., West 1987).

[2] 1 Witkin & Epstein, *California Criminal Law* § 518 (2d ed., Bancroft-Whitney 1988).

[3] *People v. Kerrick* (1927) 86 Cal.App. 542, 548.

[4] *People v. Penny* (1955) 44 Cal.2d 861, 879.

[5] *People v. Walls* (1966) 239 Cal.App.2d 543, 546.

[6] Penal Code § 193.

[7] *People v. Hansen* (1992) 10 Cal.App.4th 1065, 1076.

[8] 1 Witkin & Epstein, *supra* note 2, at § 136.

CHAPTER 5

Crimes Against the Person: Part II

OUTLINE

Introduction

Chapter 4 examined the many forms of criminal homicide recognized by California law. This chapter addresses other crimes against the person. Included are discussions of assault and battery, mayhem, sex crimes, kidnapping and false imprisonment, stalking, and civil rights and hate crimes. Numerous other crimes against the person are defined by California law, but space does not permit coverage of them. There are also variants of the crimes discussed in this chapter, which again cannot be covered because of space. Mastery of the subjects discussed in Chapters 4 and 5 will, however, provide a satisfactory comprehension of the major subjects addressed by California law in the area of crimes against the person.

§ 5.1 Assault and Battery

Generally

Assault and **battery** are two different crimes, although they often occur together. Battery is defined in Penal Code § 242 as "any willful and unlawful use of force or violence upon the person of another." As mentioned previously in this

107

text, *willful* means purposefully committed. *Unlawful* means that the use of force or violence is not either privileged (e.g., reasonable discipline by a parent) or consented to by the victim (e.g., engaging in a contact sport). Judicial decisions have rendered the terms "force or violence" somewhat meaningless. Any touching, however slight, if not privileged or consented to, constitutes a battery. The touching need not cause injury or pain.

Battery is a general-intent crime. This means that a person commits a battery by intentionally touching another person, if the touching is not privileged or consented to. It is unnecessary to establish that the actor intended to achieve some particular result by the touching. If Mike kisses Joan without her consent, Mike has committed a battery upon Joan. Note that Joan has suffered no pain or physical injury. Mike's act constitutes a battery nevertheless.

Although a battery technically need not cause harm to another person, those most frequently prosecuted are ones in which pain or harm has been inflicted—those in which force or violence in the traditional sense have been used against the victim. Typical batteries include striking with the fist, kicking, tripping, pushing, spitting, and other harmful or offensive touchings. A battery may be committed by a direct touching of the victim's person with the actor's body, such as striking the victim with a fist. Battery may also be committed with an object which the assailant is holding, such a crowbar, hammer, or baseball bat. In such a case, the object is considered an extension of the assailant's body. There have been cases in which battery has been committed with an automobile, i.e., the assailant used the automobile as a weapon and intentionally struck the victim with it. Also, many battery cases involve the striking of a victim by an object thrown or otherwise projected at the victim. Thus, striking a victim with a knife which the assailant has thrown or a bullet which the assailant has fired constitutes battery. In short, any intentional striking of another by a part of the assailant's body or an object set in motion by the assailant constitutes battery unless the striking is privileged or consented to by the victim.

Assault is defined in Penal Code § 240 as "an unlawful attempt, coupled with a present ability, to commit a violent injury on the person of another." As with battery, the word *violent* has been disregarded by the courts. Assault is, in effect, an attempt to commit a battery. If Joe attempts to strike Bob with his fist and misses, Joe has committed an assault against Bob. Similarly, if Virginia throws a knife or fires a gun at Rebecca and misses, Virginia has committed an assault against Rebecca.

Historically, there has been some inconsistency in the judicial decisions regarding whether assault is a general- or specific-intent crime. In the 1994 decision of *People v. Colantuono,* 7 Cal.4th 206, the California Supreme Court resolved the issue by definitively holding that assault is a general-intent crime.

If an assault is successful, it results in the striking of another person, which is a battery. It is said that every battery includes an assault. If one successfully commits a battery, he or she can be charged with either assault, or battery, or both. The defendant may, however, be convicted of and punished for only one of the crimes.

Section 240 of the Penal Code defines *assault* as an attempt, *coupled with a present ability,* to commit a battery. The present ability requirement means that, to be guilty of assault, the actor must have the actual ability to commit the battery being attempted. Present ability has most frequently arisen as an issue in cases involving an attempt to shoot a person with a weapon that is not loaded. The courts have held that present ability is absent in such cases, thereby rendering the defendant not guilty of assault. The courts have distinguished the unloaded weapon situation from the situation in which the weapon is loaded but jams. In such cases, the defendant has been held to have present ability to commit the attempted battery—the reasoning being that the defendant potentially can quickly unjam the gun. Also, present ability is not negated by actions taken by the victim to protect himself. For example, a robber who attempts to shoot a person standing behind a bulletproof window would be considered to have present ability because he has the ability to fire the weapon at the victim. The fact that the intended victim has taken actions to protect himself from the attempted battery has no bearing on whether the defendant has the present ability to discharge the weapon in his direction.

The statutory definition of assault as an attempted battery has not been entirely acceptable to the courts. Consider, for example, the situation in which Steve points a loaded gun at Barbara and orders her to do something he does not have the legal right to order her to do. If assault is viewed strictly as an attempted battery, Steve will not be liable for assault unless he attempts to shoot Barbara. The courts have, however, held that this situation constitutes an assault.

Simple Assault and Battery

The crimes of assault and battery have many gradations, which depend on factors such as the amount of force employed or whether the assault or battery is committed in an effort to perpetrate a dangerous felony. Assault and battery that do not involve the use of force likely to produce death or great bodily injury are called *simple assault* and *simple battery*. These offenses are misdemeanors. Simple assault is punishable by a fine not exceeding $1,000, by imprisonment in the county jail for not more than six months, or both. (See Penal Code § 241(a).) Simple battery is punishable by a fine not exceeding $2,000, by imprisonment in the county jail for not more than six months, or both. (See Penal Code § 243(a).)

The penalties for assault and battery are increased if the crimes are committed against specified categories of persons, such as a peace officer, firefighter, emergency medical technician, or process server when in the performance of his or her duties. To be guilty of the more serious offense, the actor must know or reasonably should know the official status of the victim and that the victim is engaged in the performance of his or her duties. If such a person actually suffers physical injury as a result of a battery, the crime is elevated to a felony-misdemeanor. A **felony-misdemeanor** is a crime that may be charged and prosecuted either as a felony or as a misdemeanor, in the discretion of the district attorney. A felony-misdemeanor is identifiable by the way in which the statute defining the crime specifies the potential sentence. In such a statute, the possible sentence is expressed in the alternative as a specified period of time in the county jail (misdemeanor) or a greater period of time in the state prison (felony). Section 243(c), the section that addresses battery against an official resulting in actual injury, is typical, stating that the offense "is punishable by imprisonment in a county jail for a period of not more than one year, or by a fine of not more than two thousand dollars ($2,000), or by imprisonment in the state prison for

16 months, or two or three years." The term *felony-misdemeanor* is used frequently in the discussion of the remaining substantive crimes in this text.

Aggravated Assault and Battery

Many forms of aggravated assault and battery are proscribed by the Penal Code. Space constraints do not permit complete coverage of all of them, but some of the more significant types are discussed to illustrate the broad applicability of these crimes. These forms of assault and battery are generally termed *aggravated* because they are more serious than simple assault or battery.

Penal Code § 220 makes it a felony to assault another person with the intent to commit mayhem, rape, sodomy, oral copulation, acting in concert to commit rape or other specified sex crimes, lewd acts with a child under age fourteen, or penetration of genital or anal openings with foreign objects by means of force or violence. The crime is a specific-intent crime, i.e., the assault must be accompanied by the intent to accomplish the specified felony. A violation of § 220 is punishable by imprisonment in the state prison for two, four, or six years.

Penal Code § 245 defines the offense of assault with a deadly weapon or force likely to produce great bodily injury. The many subsections of § 245 address assaults with a firearm, assaults with a deadly weapon or instrument other than a firearm or any means of force likely to produce great bodily injury, assaults with a machine gun or semiautomatic firearm, and assaults by the foregoing means against specified persons such as peace officers and firefighters while in the performance of their duties. Assault with a firearm, a deadly weapon or instrument other than a firearm, or by means of force likely to produce great bodily injury is a felony-misdemeanor, except when perpetrated against one of the specified categories of official engaged in the performance of his or her duties, in which case it is a felony. Assault with a semiautomatic weapon or machine gun is a felony in every case.

Penal Code § 243(d) sets out the offense of battery resulting in serious bodily injury. *Serious bodily injury* is defined in § 243(f)(5) as "a serious impairment of physical condition, including, but not limited to, the following: loss of consciousness; concussion; bone fracture; protracted loss or impairment of function of any bodily member or organ; a wound requiring extensive suturing; and serious disfigurement." Some of the specified types of injuries overlap with the crime of mayhem, which is discussed in the next section. Battery resulting in serious bodily injury is a felony-misdemeanor, punishable by imprisonment in a county jail for not more than one year or imprisonment in the state prison for two, three, or four years.

SIDEBAR

Crime and Delinquency in California

186,337 aggravated assaults were reported in California in 1995. For reporting purposes, *aggravated assault* means "the unlawful attack or attempted attack by one person upon another for the purpose of inflicting severe or aggravated bodily injury." This type of assault is usually accomplished by the use of a weapon or by means likely to produce death or great bodily harm. The California Crime Index (CCI) rate for aggravated assaults was 581.2 per 100,000 population. Aggravated assaults accounted for 61.1 percent of the CCI violent crimes in 1995.

Of the 186,337 aggravated assaults reported in California in 1995, firearms were involved in 19.7% (36,760), knives or cutting instruments in 12.8% (23,810), other dangerous weapons in 28.6% (53,211), and personal weapons (hands, feet, etc.) in 38.9% (72,556).

Source: Crime and Delinquency in California, 1995, California Department of Justice, Division of Law Enforcement.

Penal Code § 243.4 defines the crime of sexual battery. The crime involves unconsented-to touchings of intimate parts of the body for the purpose of sexual arousal, sexual gratification, or sexual abuse. The touching may be done by the perpetrator, or may involve a touching of the perpetrator by the victim. Most offenses under § 243.4 are felony-misdemeanors. The statute provides increased penalties if the perpetrator is an employer and the victim is his or her employee.

§ 5.2 Mayhem

Mayhem is an aggravated form of battery, committed with malice, that results in maiming or disfigurement of the victim. (See Penal Code § 203.) Maiming includes dismemberment and infliction of disability. Thus, one who unlawfully and maliciously causes the loss to another of a member of his or her body, or impairs the use of the member to the point of disability, or disfigures another, commits mayhem. The disability and disfigurement forms of mayhem contemplate permanent disability and disfigurement. The permanence of the disability or disfigurement is, however, determined without regard to whether they can, with medical treatment, be remedied. In other words, if a disability or disfigurement would be permanent without medical treatment, the fact that modern medicine might be able to remedy the condition is not a defense to the crime of mayhem. This principle has had particular applicability in disfigurement cases because of the advances made in the field of cosmetic surgery.

Mayhem is a general-intent crime. This means that the perpetrator need not intend to dismember or permanently disable or disfigure the victim. All that is required is that the perpetrator intentionally commit battery on the victim. Mayhem has a second mental element: the element of malice. The malice required for mayhem is the type defined in Penal Code § 7(4), namely, "a wish to vex, annoy, or injure another person, or an intent to do a wrongful act." Combining the general intent and malice requirements for mayhem, there must be an intentional battery committed with a wish to injure the victim. If the battery results in dismemberment or permanent disability or disfigurement, the perpetrator has committed mayhem.

Mayhem is a felony punishable by imprisonment in the state prison for two, four, or eight years. (See Penal Code § 204.)

In 1987, the legislature enacted § 205 of the Penal Code establishing the crime of **aggravated mayhem**. The offense is committed by one who intentionally causes permanent disability or disfigurement of another person or deprives a person of a limb, organ, or member of his or her body. Unlike simple mayhem, aggravated mayhem is a specific-intent crime. The perpetrator must specifically intend to dismember or permanently disable or disfigure the victim. Aggravated mayhem is a felony punishable by imprisonment in the state prison for life with the possibility of parole.

§ 5.3   Torture

The crime of **torture** is defined in Penal Code § 206 as the infliction of great bodily injury with the intent to cause cruel or extreme pain and suffering for the purpose of revenge, extortion, persuasion, or for any sadistic purpose. For purposes of the offense, *great bodily injury* means a significant or substantial physical injury. (See Penal Code § 12022.7(e).)

Two mental states are required for the crime of torture. First, the great bodily injury must be inflicted with the intent to cause cruel or extreme pain and suffering. The statute is specific, however, that the crime does not require proof that the victim actually suffered pain; the perpetrator's intent to inflict pain is sufficient. Second, the perpetrator must have acted for the purpose of revenge, extortion, persuasion, or for any sadistic purpose. Note that the statute does not require a specific intent to inflict great bodily injury. Rather, it requires a specific intent to inflict cruel or extreme pain and suffering. Great bodily injury must occur for the crime of torture to exist, but it need not have been specifically intended by the perpetrator.

§ 5.4   Sex Crimes

This section deals with crimes that involve sex. Keep in mind that crimes such as assault and battery may be sexually motivated. For example, if a man touches a woman's breast, he has committed a battery (provided that the touching was unwelcome).

The phrase *sex crimes* actually encompasses a variety of sexually motivated crimes. Rape, sodomy, incest, and sexually motivated batteries and murders are included. Obscenity, prostitution, abortion, distribution of child pornography, and public nudity are examples of other sex-related offenses.

Rape

Rape is defined in Penal Code § 261. It may be generally described as sexual intercourse with a person not the spouse of the perpetrator committed without such person's legally effective consent. The language of § 261 is gender-neutral, raising the possibility that rape may be committed by a female. However, no reported California case has addressed this issue.

The act of sexual intercourse sufficient to constitute rape has been defined by statute (see Penal Code § 263) and judicial decisions as something other than the normal meaning of the term. Vaginal penetration of a female is not required; any penetration of the female genitalia is sufficient. Also, completion of the act of intercourse (i.e., by ejaculation of the male) is not required. The unlawful penetration is sufficient.

The crime of rape under Penal Code § 261 may be committed only against a person who is not the spouse of the perpetrator. Section 262 defines the separate crime of spousal rape, which is discussed later.

The essential element of rape, other than sexual intercourse, is the lack of consent of the person with whom the perpetrator has intercourse. *Consent* is defined as "positive cooperation in act or attitude pursuant to an exercise of free will." The person must "act freely and voluntarily and have knowledge of the nature of the act or transaction involved."[1] Penal Code § 261 enumerates a number of circumstances that constitute lack of consent. Sexual intercourse committed under these circumstances is rape. They include the following situations:

1. The victim is incapable, because of a mental disorder or developmental or physical disability, of giving legal consent, and this is known or reasonably should be known to the perpetrator.

2. The act is accomplished against a person's will by means of force, violence, duress, menace, or fear of immediate and unlawful bodily injury to the person or another. Consent in this type of rape is vitiated by intimidation of the victim. Prior to amendment of § 261 in 1980, lack of consent in this form of rape required actual resistance by the victim. Resistance can, of course, increase the risk of great bodily harm or even death, and it has come to be recognized that the fact that one submits to sexual intercourse imposed by means of force, violence, duress, menace, or fear of immediate and unlawful bodily injury does not mean that one has consented to the act. One may submit to protect one's life or physical well-being, and such submission will not constitute consent.

3. The victim is prevented from resisting by any intoxicating or anesthetic substance, or any controlled substance, and this condition is known, or reasonably should be known, by the perpetrator.

4. The victim is unconscious of the nature of the act being perpetrated, and this fact is known to the perpetrator. "Unconscious of the nature of the act" has a number of meanings. One meaning is that the victim is unconscious or asleep. *Unconscious* can also mean that the victim is not aware that the act is occurring. An example of the latter type of unconsciousness is found in the case of *People v. Ogunmola* (1987) 193 Cal.App.3d 274. In that case, the defendant, a gynecologist, under the pretense of examining his patients, engaged in sexual intercourse with them. The patients were unaware of the nature of the defendant's acts until penetration had occurred, at which point the crime of rape was completed.

5. The victim submits to sexual intercourse under the belief that the person committing the act is the victim's spouse, and this belief is induced by any artifice, pretense, or concealment practiced by the perpetrator, with intent to induce the belief.

6. The act of sexual intercourse is accomplished against the victim's will by threatening to retaliate in the future against the victim or another person, and there is a reasonable possibility that the perpetrator will carry out the threat.

7. The act is accomplished against the victim's will by threatening to use the authority of a public official to incarcerate, arrest, or deport the victim or another, and the victim has a reasonable belief that the perpetrator is a public official.

Rape is a general-intent crime. The crime is committed if one intentionally engages in sexual intercourse without the consent of the other person. There is no requirement that the perpetrator intend to achieve some further purpose by engaging in the act (which would make rape a specific-intent crime).

Rape is punishable by imprisonment in the state prison for a period of three, six, or eight years. (See Penal Code § 264).

In *People v. Iniguez,* the California Supreme Court reviewed a rape case involving sexual intercourse accomplished against the victim's will by means of force, violence, duress, menace, or fear of immediate and unlawful bodily injury. At the time of the offense, the crime was set forth in Penal Code § 261(2), and the court makes reference to that section in its opinion. In the opinion, the court gives great weight to the amendment of § 261 in 1980 to eliminate the requirement that the victim actively resist the perpetrator's attack. The facts of the case may be briefly summarized as follows: Mercy P. spent the night before her wedding at the house of her friend, Sandra S. While Mercy was sleeping, Sandra's fiancé (the defendant), naked, approached her from behind, removed her pants,

---

PEOPLE v. HECTOR GUILLERMO INIGUEZ
7 Cal.4th 847; 30 Cal.Rptr.2d 258;
872 P.2d 1183 [May 1994]

Prior to 1980, section 261, subdivisions 2 and 3 "defined rape as an act of sexual intercourse under circumstances where the person resists, but where 'resistance is overcome by force or violence' or where 'a person is prevented from resisting by threats of great and immediate bodily harm, accompanied by apparent power of execution … .' " (*People v. Barnes* (1986) 42 Cal.3d 284, 292 [228 Cal.Rptr. 228, 721 P.2d 110]). Under the former law, a person was required to either resist or be prevented from resisting because of threats.

Section 261 was amended … to eliminate both the resistance requirement and the requirement that the threat of immediate bodily harm be accompanied by an apparent power to inflict the harm. …

In discussing the significance of the 1980 amendments in *Barnes,* we noted that "studies have demonstrated that while some women respond to sexual assault with active resistance, others 'freeze,' " and "become helpless from panic and numbing fear."

* * *

The deletion of the resistance language from section 261 by the 1980 amendments thus effected a change in the purpose of evidence of fear of immediate and unlawful injury. Prior to 1980, evidence of fear was directly linked to resistance; the prosecution was required to demonstrate that a person's *resistance* had been overcome by force, or that a person was prevented from resisting by threats of great and immediate bodily harm. … As a result of the amendments, evidence of fear is now directly linked to the overbearing of a victim's will; the prosecution is required to demonstrate that the act of sexual intercourse was accomplished against the person's *will* by means of force, violence, or fear of immediate and unlawful bodily injury.

* * *

[T]he element of fear of immediate and unlawful bodily injury has two components, one subjective and one objective. The subjective component asks whether a victim genuinely entertained a fear of immediate and unlawful bodily injury sufficient to induce her to submit to sexual intercourse against her will. …

In addition, the prosecution must satisfy the objective component, which asks whether the victim's fear was reasonable under the circumstances, or, if unreasonable, whether the perpetrator knew of the victim's subjective fear and took advantage of it. ...

Applying these principles, we conclude that the evidence that the sexual intercourse was accomplished against Mercy's will by means of fear of immediate and unlawful bodily injury was sufficient to support the verdict in this case. First, there was substantial evidence that Mercy genuinely feared immediate and unlawful bodily injury. Mercy testified that she froze because she was afraid, and the investigating police officer testified that she told him she did not move because she feared defendant would do something violent.

* * *

In addition, immediately after the attack, Mercy was so distraught her friend Pam could barely understand her. Mercy hid in the bushes outside the house waiting for Pam to pick her up because she was terrified defendant would find her ... .

Second, there was substantial evidence that Mercy's fear of immediate and unlawful bodily injury was reasonable. ... Defendant, who weighed twice as much as Mercy, accosted her while she slept in the home of a close friend, thus violating the victim's enhanced level of security and privacy. (Cf. *People v. Jackson* (1992) 6 Cal.App.4th 1185, 1190 [8 Cal.Rptr.2d 239] ["A person inside a private residence, whether it be their own or that of an acquaintance, feels a sense of privacy and security not felt when outside or in a semipublic structure. ... providing the [attacker] with the advantages of shock and surprise which may incapacitate the victim(s)."].)

Defendant, who was naked, then removed Mercy's pants, fondled her buttocks, and inserted his penis into her vagina for approximately one minute, without warning, without her consent, and without a reasonable belief of consent. Any man or woman awakening to find himself or herself in this situation could reasonably react with fear of immediate and unlawful bodily injury. Sudden, unconsented-to groping, disrobing, and ensuing sexual intercourse while one appears to lie sleeping is an appalling and intolerable invasion of one's personal autonomy that, in and of itself, would reasonably cause one to react with fear. ...

The Court of Appeal's suggestion that Mercy could have stopped the sexual assault by screaming and thus eliciting Sandra S.'s help, disregards both the Legislature's 1980 elimination of the resistance requirement and our express language in *Barnes* upholding that amendment. (*Barnes, supra*, 42 Cal.3d at p. 302.) ... (See *People v. Bermudez, supra*, 157 Cal.App.3d at p. 624 ["The law has outgrown the resistance concept; a person demanding sexual favors can no longer rely on a position of strength which draws no physical or verbal protest."]; Estrich, Real Rape (1987) p. 69.) There is no requirement that the victim say "I am afraid, please stop," when it is the defendant who has created the circumstances that have so paralyzed the victim in fear and thereby submission. (See *People v. Bermudez, supra*, 157 Cal.App.3d at p. 622 [a criminal invasion of sexual privacy does not become a nonrape merely because the victim is too fearful or hesitant to say, "I guess you know I don't want you to do this."].) Moreover, it is sheer speculation that Mercy's assailant would have responded to screams by desisting the attack, and not by causing her further injury or death.

The jury could reasonably have concluded that under the totality of the circumstances, this scenario, instigated and choreographed by defendant, created a situation in which Mercy genuinely and reasonably responded with fear of immediate and unlawful bodily injury, and that such fear allowed him to accomplish sexual intercourse with Mercy against her will. ...

The judgment of the Court of Appeal is reversed, and the case is remanded to that court for further proceedings consistent with this opinion.

---

fondled her buttocks, inserted his penis inside her vagina, and ejaculated. The entire incident lasted only a few minutes. The defendant then returned to the bedroom. Mercy did not actively resist the attack. She later told police that she panicked and froze. She was afraid that if she said or did anything, the defendant might become violent. Mercy became distraught after the incident. She called a friend, Pam, to come to the house and pick her up. She then left the house and hid in the bushes outside for fear the defendant would look for her.

The defendant was apprehended and admitted what he had done. He was tried and convicted of rape and was sentenced to the state prison for six years. However, on appeal, the court of appeal reversed the conviction, concluding that there was insufficient evidence that the act of sexual intercourse was accomplished by means of force or fear of immediate bodily injury. The supreme court granted the attorney general's petition for review.

Crime and Delinquency in California

10,550 forcible rapes were reported in California during 1995. The number includes actual rapes (8,646) and attempted rapes (1,904). The California Crime Index (CCI) rate for forcible rape in 1995 was 32.9 per 100,000 population, generally, and 63.8 per 100,000 female population. Forcible rapes accounted for 3.5% of the CCI violent crimes reported in 1995. Reported forcible rapes declined steadily from 1991 to 1995: 12,942 were reported in 1991; 12,751 in 1992; 11,754 in 1993; and 10,960 in 1994. In 1952, 1,941 forcible rapes were reported in California, which represented a rate of 16.7 per 100,000 general population (female population rate not reported).

Source: Crime and Delinquency in California, 1995, California Department of Justice, Division of Law Enforcement.

Spousal Rape

Can one commit the crime of rape against one's spouse? In California, the answer is yes. Penal Code § 262 provides that sexual intercourse with one's spouse is rape if the act is performed without the consent of the spouse. Circumstances constituting lack of consent under § 262 are the same as those enumerated in the rape statute, § 261, with the exception of two categories: lack of legal capacity to consent because of a mental disorder or physical or mental disability, and lack of consent because the offender is impersonating the victim's spouse. A prosecution for **spousal rape** may not occur unless the victim spouse reports the offense to medical personnel, a member of the clergy, an attorney, a shelter representative, a counselor, a judicial officer, a rape crisis agency, a prosecuting agency, a law enforcement officer, or a firefighter within one year after the date of the violation. The one-year reporting requirement does not apply if the victim's allegation of the offense is corroborated by independent evidence that would otherwise be admissible during trial.

Like rape under § 261, spousal rape is a general-intent crime punishable by imprisonment in the state prison for a period of three, six, or eight years.

Unlawful Sexual Intercourse

Unlawful sexual intercourse is the name given in California to the crime commonly known as "statutory rape." The crime is proscribed by Penal Code § 261.5 and consists of an act of sexual intercourse with a person under the age of eighteen. Unlike the forms of rape proscribed by § 261, consent is not an issue in an unlawful sexual intercourse case. Because the person with whom the perpetrator has sexual relations is under the age of majority, such person's consent to the act is deemed legally ineffective. Thus, a girl under the age of eighteen may be a willing participant in an act of sexual intercourse, and may even instigate it, but these facts do not constitute defenses for the perpetrator. Unlike some states, however, California does recognize one defense to unlawful sexual intercourse: a reasonable and good faith belief that the female was eighteen years of age or older. The rationale behind this rule is that if the defendant has a reasonable and good faith belief that the female is eighteen or older, he lacks criminal intent.[2]

Prior to amendment of § 261.5 in 1993, the statute specifically proscribed sexual intercourse with a "female" under the age of eighteen. Under the statute as then written, a female over eighteen having sex with a male under age eighteen did not commit the offense of unlawful sexual intercourse. The statute has now been rewritten in gender-neutral terms, but it is unclear whether this means that females can commit the crime of unlawful sexual intercourse. CALJIC 10.40, the jury instruction on unlawful sexual intercourse, continues to speak in terms of sexual intercourse with a "female" under the age of eighteen. The one-sided nature of this crime has been challenged in the United States Supreme Court as a denial of equal protection of the law to males. The Supreme Court upheld the statute in question, reasoning that one of the goals of statutory rape statutes is the prevention of teenage pregnancy. Because females can be impregnated, states have a legitimate interest in prosecuting males who have sex with females who are under the age of consent.[3] Using this analysis, a state may prosecute males only, as females cannot impregnate young men or women. However, many acts by adult females (or adult males with young males) may be prosecuted under other laws, such as child molestation statutes.

The punishment prescribed by § 261.5 for unlawful sexual intercourse depends on the age difference between the perpetrator and the minor. If the minor is not more than three years older or younger than the perpetrator, the offense is a misdemeanor. Note that the perpetrator may be younger than the minor, which means that the perpetrator may be a minor, also. Thus, if a boy of fourteen has sex with a girl of seventeen, the boy, but not the girl, is guilty of unlawful sexual intercourse, assuming the amended statutory language does not make females liable for the crime. If the minor is more than three years younger than the perpetrator, the offense is a felony-misdemeanor, and the perpetrator may be sentenced to the county jail for up to one year or the state prison for an unspecified period. If the perpetrator is over the age of twenty-one and the minor is under the age of sixteen, the offense is a felony-misdemeanor, and the perpetrator may be sentenced to the county jail for up to one year or the state prison for two, three, or four years.

Sodomy

Sodomy is defined in Penal Code § 286 as sexual conduct consisting of contact between the penis of one person and the anus of another person. Any sexual penetration, however slight, is sufficient to complete the crime of sodomy. Sodomy was formerly referred to in the Penal Code as the "infamous crime against nature." It was also referred to as "buggery."

Under the current version of § 286, sodomy between consenting adults is not a crime. Virtually all other forms of sodomy are criminal. The severity of the punishment prescribed for sodomy depends on the circumstances of the case.

The punishment for sodomy committed on a minor varies, depending on the age of the minor and the age difference between the minor and the perpetrator. The younger the minor, and the greater the age difference between the perpetrator and the minor, the greater the penalty. For example, sodomy committed on a minor under the age of fourteen, and more than ten years younger than the perpetrator, is punishable by imprisonment in the state prison for three, six, or eight years. Sodomy committed under circumstances in which an act of sexual intercourse would constitute rape under § 261 (by means of force or violence, upon an intoxicated person who is unable to resist, upon a person who is unable to understand the nature of the act, upon an unconscious person, etc.) is severely punished. Punishment is specified for each circumstance enumerated in the statute. The most common punishment is imprisonment in the state prison for three, six, or eight years.

Oral Copulation

Oral copulation is prohibited by Penal Code § 288a. The statute defines it as "the act of copulating the mouth of one person with the sexual organ or anus of another person." *Copulating* means any contact, however slight. Thus, one who places his or her mouth on the sexual organ or anus of another commits oral copulation. Similarly, placing one's sexual organ on the mouth of another person, or requiring the other person to place his or her mouth on the perpetrator's sexual organ, constitutes oral copulation. Penetration of the mouth or anus is not required.[4]

The prohibition against oral copulation in § 288a is structured like the proscription against sodomy in § 286. Thus, oral copulation between consenting adults is not a crime. Oral copulation committed with a minor, or under circumstances that would constitute rape if the act were sexual intercourse, is punished as acts of sodomy would be under corresponding circumstances.

Penetration of Genital or Anal Openings by Foreign or Unknown Objects

Under Penal Code § 289, a person is guilty of a crime who "causes the penetration, however slight, of the genital or anal openings of any person or causes another person to so penetrate the defendant's or another person's genital or anal openings for the purpose of sexual arousal, gratification, or abuse by any foreign object, substance, instrument, or device, or by any unknown object … ." As used in § 289, the phrase "foreign object, substance, instrument, or device" does not include a sexual organ, but does include any other part of the body. "Unknown object" means any foreign object, substance, instrument, or device, or any part of the body, including a penis, when it is not known whether penetration was by a penis or by a foreign object, substance, instrument, or device, or by any other part of the body.

Section 289 is structured like the statutory prohibitions against sodomy and oral copulation. The acts described in the statute, if committed by consenting adults, are not crimes. They are crimes if committed on minors or under circumstances that would constitute rape if the act were sexual intercourse. The penalties prescribed in § 289 are the same as those prescribed for sodomy and oral copulation, in most instances being imprisonment in the state prison for three, six, or eight years.

AIDS and Sex Offenses

Penal Code § 12022.85 provides a sentence enhancement of three years for a person who commits rape, unlawful sexual intercourse, spousal rape, sodomy, or oral copulation with knowledge that he or she has autoimmune deficiency syndrome (AIDS) or that he or she carries antibodies to the human immuno-deficiency virus at the time of commission of the offense.

Rape Shield Laws

So-called **rape shield laws** were enacted in many states during the 1970s and 1980s in an effort to protect rape victims from harassment by defense attorneys at trial. Before such laws existed, defense attorneys often would use evidence of a victim's prior sexual conduct to infer that the victim had consented to the act. It is thought that the humiliation of the rape itself, matched with this treatment at trial, accounted for the nonreporting of many rapes.

California has two shield provisions, both found in the Evidence Code. Section 782 of the Evidence Code permits introduction of evidence of the sexual conduct of the victim for purposes of attacking the credibility of the victim as a witness in prosecutions for rape, sodomy, lewd acts with a child, oral copulation, penetration by foreign or unknown objects, and certain other sex offenses. Such evidence may not be admitted, however, unless the defendant makes a written motion accompanied by an affidavit stating the relevance of the evidence in attacking the credibility of the victim. The judge must evaluate the affidavit and make a determination as to whether the affidavit demonstrates that the evidence is relevant. If the judge determines that the affidavit is sufficient, a hearing is held out of the presence of the jury at which the complaining witness (the victim) is questioned about her (or his) sexual conduct. At the conclusion of the hearing, the judge determines whether any questioning of the complaining witness regarding sexual conduct will be permitted in the presence of the jury.

The second shield provision is Evidence Code § 1103(c). Under that section, in a prosecution for a specified sex offense (including most, but not all of those specified in § 782), opinion evidence, reputation evidence, and evidence of the complaining witness's sexual conduct are not admissible by the defendant to prove consent by the complaining witness. This proscription does not apply to evidence of the complaining witness's prior sexual conduct with the defendant. Section 1103(c) does not make inadmissible any evidence that is admissible under § 782 to attack the credibility of the complaining witness.

Incest

Sexual intercourse between related persons is the crime of **incest**. (See Penal Code § 285.) For purposes of § 285, *related persons* are persons who are prohibited by law from marrying. These include parents and children, ancestors and descendants of every degree, brothers and sisters of the half or whole blood, and uncles and nieces or aunts and nephews. The crime is committed whether or not both parties consent. If one of the parties does not consent, the additional crime of rape will have been committed. Also, if one of the parties is a minor, child molestation laws will have been violated. Although the decisional law is not entirely consistent on this point, lack of knowledge of the relationship appears to be a defense. Thus, if Paul and Amy, brother and sister, were separated as babies and raised separately, and meet each other as adults, they will not be guilty of incest if they engage in sexual intercourse without knowledge of their biological relationship.

Sex Offenses Against Children

It is perhaps an unfortunate commentary on our society that minors are frequently the victims of sexual offenses. The statutory provisions defining rape, sodomy, oral copulation, and penetration by foreign or unknown objects contain subsections criminalizing such acts when committed on minors. In addition to the provisions of these statutes criminalizing sex acts on minors, California has a number of other statutes specifically aimed at protecting children from sexual abuse and exploitation.

Lewd or Lascivious Acts with a Child under Age Fourteen

Penal Code § 288 defines the offense of **lewd or lascivious acts with a child under age fourteen**. The operative language is as follows:

> Any person who willfully and lewdly commits any lewd or lascivious act, including any of the acts constituting other crimes provided for in Part 1, upon or with the body, or any part or member thereof, of a child who is under the age of 14 years, with the intent of arousing, appealing to, or gratifying the lust, passions, or sexual desires of that person or the child, is guilty of a felony ... .

The reference in the statutory language to "Part 1" is to other sex crimes such as rape, sodomy, oral copulation, and penetration by foreign or unknown objects. A lewd or lascivious act can include any touching, fondling, rubbing, or feeling of a part of the child's body, even through his or her clothing. The offense proscribed by § 288 is a specific-intent crime. The perpetrator must touch the child with the intent of arousing, appealing to, or gratifying the lust or passions or sexual desires of the perpetrator or the child. If the perpetrator possesses this intent, any touching of a child, even a touching that is not of an objectively sexual nature, violates the statute. The consent of the child to the act is not a defense. The penalty for violating § 288 is imprisonment in the state prison for three, six, or eight years.

Continuous Sexual Abuse of a Child

Section 288.5 of the Penal Code defines the crime of **continuous sexual abuse of a child**. The crime is committed by a person who either resides in the same home with a child under the age of fourteen or has recurring access to the child, and who over a period of not less than three months engages in three or more acts of substantial sexual conduct with the child or three or more acts of lewd or lascivious conduct under § 288. *Substantial sexual conduct* is defined in Penal Code § 1203.066(b), and means "penetration of the vagina or rectum of either the victim or the offender by the penis of the other or by any foreign object, oral copulation, or masturbation of either the victim or the offender." The offense is punishable by imprisonment in the state prison for a term of six, twelve, or sixteen years.

Seduction of Minors

Penal Code § 288.2 prohibits **seduction of minors**. The statute provides that any person who distributes or exhibits "any harmful matter" to a minor visually or over the telephone, "with the intent of arousing, appealing to, or gratifying the lust or passions or sexual desires of that person or the minor, with the intent, or for the purpose of seducing the minor, is guilty of a public offense, punishable by imprisonment in the state prison or county jail." The crime contains a double mens rea requirement. First, the perpetrator must intend to sexually arouse, etc., himself or herself or the minor. Second, the perpetrator must intend to seduce the minor or have the purpose of seducing the minor. "Harmful matter" is defined in Penal Code § 313 and essentially means obscene matter.

Aggravated Sexual Assault of a Child

Penal Code § 269, added by the legislature in 1994, defines the crime of **aggravated sexual assault of a child**. Aggravated sexual assault consists of any of the following acts, accomplished by means of force, violence, or fear, committed upon a child under the age of fourteen by a person who is ten or more years older than the child: rape, sodomy, oral copulation, and penetration of genital or anal openings by foreign or unknown objects. Any person committing one of these acts is guilty of a felony punishable by imprisonment in the state prison for fifteen years to life.

Sexual Exploitation of a Child

Penal Code § 311.3 proscribes the **sexual exploitation of a child**. A person is guilty of the crime of sexual exploitation of a child when he or she knowingly develops, duplicates, prints, or exchanges any film, photograph, videotape, negative, or slide in which a person under the age of eighteen years is shown engaged in an act of sexual conduct. *Sexual conduct* as defined in the statute includes a wide variety of sex acts. A first offense under § 311.3 is a misdemeanor, punishable by a fine of not more than $2,000, imprisonment in the county jail for not more than one year, or both. Second and subsequent offenses are felonies.

Employment of Minor to Perform Sexual Acts

Penal Code § 311.4(b) makes it a felony to employ a minor in the preparation of visual media or in a live performance involving sexual conduct by the minor. If the preparation of the visual media or the live performance is done for commercial purposes, the offense is a felony punishable in the state prison for three, six, or eight years.

§ 5.5 Kidnapping

Kidnapping is a felony and carries a harsh penalty. Additionally, if the kidnapping takes the victim across state lines, the crime is a violation of the Federal Kidnapping Act.[5] The federal government, usually the Federal Bureau of Investigation, may become involved in any kidnapping twenty-four hours after the victim has been seized, by virtue of the Federal Kidnapping Act, which creates a presumption that the victim has been transported across state lines after that period of time.[6]

The California Penal Code defines three types of kidnapping: simple kidnapping; kidnapping for ransom, reward, extortion, or robbery; and kidnapping during commission of a carjacking.

Simple Kidnapping

Simple kidnapping is defined in Penal Code § 207. There are several types of simple kidnapping. For example, § 207(a) defines the offense of kidnapping accomplished by force or by other means of instilling fear. Section 207(b) defines the offense of kidnapping of a child under the age of fourteen, for purposes of committing lewd acts, accomplished by means of persuasion, enticement, or deception. Subsections (c) and (d) of § 207 define other forms of simple kidnapping.

Restraint of Liberty

All types of kidnapping require a restraint of liberty of the victim. In a kidnapping under § 207(a), the restraint is accomplished by means of force or fear. In a kidnapping under § 207(b), the restraint is accomplished by means of persuasion or trickery. Kidnapping under § 207(a) may be perpetrated against an adult or a child, whereas that under § 207(b) may be perpetrated only against a child under the age of fourteen.

In the case of a forcible kidnapping (i.e., a kidnapping under § 207(a)), the initial abduction need not be forcible if subsequent restraint is applied. Thus, if one voluntarily accompanies another, and later is forcibly prevented from leaving the other's presence, a kidnapping occurs at the time the person's liberty is forcibly restrained—assuming the element of asportation (discussed in the next paragraph) is present. In one case, for example, the victim voluntarily entered an automobile in which the defendant was a passenger. Instead of being driven home, as she expected, she was taken elsewhere, and was forcibly restrained and raped. The defendant's conviction for kidnapping was upheld on appeal, despite the fact that the victim initially entered the automobile voluntarily.[7]

Asportation

An essential element of all kidnappings is asportation. *Asportation* means a carrying away of the victim. To constitute asportation, the movement of the victim must be more than slight or trivial, that is, it must be substantial. The decisional law on the amount of movement necessary to meet the asportation requirement of kidnapping is not entirely clear. One must look to the decided cases in an attempt to perceive a trend or trends in this area. Thus, in one case, the forcing of the victim at gunpoint to walk a quarter of a mile was held to constitute asportation. In another case, the victim was dragged from the front to the rear of a laundromat before she was sexually assaulted. The court held that the movement was insufficient to constitute asportation. Moving of a victim ninety feet from the victim's car to a river, when the car was in the victim's immediate presence at all times, was held insufficient to constitute asportation. Again, the forcible movement of a victim from the garage of her home, through the hall, kitchen, dining room, and into the den, was held insufficient. In contrast, the movement of two women more than 840 feet on a major street of a large city at nighttime was held sufficient to constitute asportation.[8]

One basis for holding certain movements insufficient to constitute asportation is the court-made rule that movement which is merely incidental to the commission of another crime does not constitute asportation for the purposes of kidnapping. If the perpetrator of a crime forces the victim to move, the movement must exceed the amount of movement necessary for commission of the crime if the defendant is to be chargeable with kidnapping in addition to the other crime. For example, if a defendant forces his victim to move from the front door of her apartment into the bedroom for the purpose of raping her, the movement is incidental to the crime of rape and will not support an additional charge of kidnapping. Contrast this situation with the situation in which the defendant forces the victim into his car and drives around aimlessly for a distance of ten miles, with a gun pointed at the victim's head, before stopping and raping her. In this case, the trier of fact would be justified in finding that the movement was more than necessary to commit the crime of rape, and the defendant could be convicted both of rape and kidnapping.

Simple kidnapping is a general-intent crime. In other words, the act of kidnapping must be intentional, but need not be accompanied by an intent to achieve some further purpose.

Simple kidnapping is punishable by imprisonment in the state prison for three, five, or eight years. If the victim is under fourteen years of age, the punishment is imprisonment in the state prison for five, eight, or eleven years. If the victim is kidnapped with the intent to commit rape, oral copulation, sodomy, or rape by instrument, it is punishable by imprisonment in the state prison for five, eight, or eleven years.

As previously stated, the element of asportation has been problematic for the courts. The requirement that the movement of the victim be "substantial" is ambiguous, as the excerpt from *People v. Daniels* illustrates. In *Daniels,* the defendant entered the victim's home looking for one Terrel Oliver. When he did not find Oliver there, he grabbed the victim by her hair, at gunpoint, and forced her into his automobile, stating, "Come on, bitch, we are going to find him." The defendant's accomplice drove the automobile while the defendant kept the gun pointed at the victim. They drove approximately two blocks to a liquor store, but did not find Oliver there. They then drove back to the victim's house, but the defendant did not permit the victim to leave the automobile. They then drove to the home of Oliver's mother approximately one-half block away. At that time, the police arrived and arrested the defendant and the driver. The jury had difficulty determining whether the movement involved in this case was

PEOPLE v. DEREK LINDSAY DANIELS
18 Cal.App.4th 1046; 22 Cal.Rptr.2d 877
[Sept. 1993]

The trial court instructed the jury that kidnapping requires moving another person by force or threat, without consent, and "the movement of such other person was for a substantial distance, that is, a distance more than slight or trivial."

Shortly after commencing their deliberations the jury made this written request of the trial court: "[N]eed clarification on what is substantial distance, that is, a distance more than slight or trivial."

In response, the trial court instructed the jury as follows: "You are to apply the ordinary and common meaning to those words, 'substantial,' 'slight,' and the word 'trivial.' Use the common ordinary meaning that one uses in life with regards to those words, and then determine if the distance involved in this car that is where Ms. Moncrief, Melynda Moncrief, the distance that she went from the house to the liquor store, to the other location, returned to the house, and the location of the arrest was slight or trivial or substantial. It is for you the jury to make that determination.

"You have to consider the total distance of the movement of that automobile."

The jury then requested a dictionary. The record does not disclose whether they were provided one.

If they were, it did not help. The next day they sent to the trial court this message: "It appears we have a hang-up with some people of the jury who interpret kidnapping as taking a person a [ ] few miles in order for him (the defendant) to be charged with kidnapping. We need a clarification on what constitutes kidnapping. Does the distance the victim is taken (miles) and the nature of the route have any bearing on a person being kidnapped? It seems we are hung up on the interpretation of the word kidnapping."

Over appellant's objection, the trial court then stated to the jury: "I am going to instruct the jury [a]s a matter of law, 500 feet is substantial ... . When I say substantial, I mean for the crime of kidnapping."

Appellant contends this last instruction constitutes prejudicial error because it removed from the jury's determination an element of the offense. Appellant is correct.

Apposite is our recent decision in *People v. Reyes Martinez* (1993) 14 Cal.App.4th 1412. There the kidnapping victim was driven 3 blocks or about 1,200 to 1,500 feet. The trial court instructed the jury: " 'If you find from the facts that the victim in this case was forcibly moved a distance of 500 feet or more, then this movement is sufficiently substantial to sustain a kidnapping conviction.' " We held this instruction equivalent to a mandatory presumption and reversed the kidnapping conviction.

The instant instruction is even more compelling. It flatly stated that "... as a matter of law 500 feet is [a] substantial [distance]." Clearly, it was this peremptory instruction which eliminated jury uncertainty and triggered a guilty verdict.

As we explained in *People v. Reyes Martinez,* movement of the victim for a substantial distance is a kidnapping element. Being an element, the *jury* must decide (beyond a reasonable doubt) whether it has been proved. ...

Our Supreme Court has stated: "In many criminal cases, the prosecution's evidence will establish an element of the charged offense 'as a matter of law.' Similarly, in many instances, the accused will not seriously dispute a particular element of the offense. ... However, neither of these sometime realities of trial practice justifies the giving of an instruction which takes an element from the jury and decides it adversely to the accused. Such an instruction confuses the roles of the judge and jury."

In the event of a retrial, we offer the following guidance to the trial court should it be asked by the jury to clarify the definition of "substantial."

The jury may be told: "The law does not provide an exact measure of 'substantial distance.' The issue is one of fact for you to decide, not one of law for the court to decide. Based upon the facts you determine from the evidence, you may decide the distance was substantial or that it was not substantial."

... The kidnapping conviction ... is reversed. The case is remanded to the superior court with directions to enter a conviction of felony false imprisonment, a lesser included offense of kidnapping, if the prosecution consents to forego retrying appellant for kidnapping; or, in the alternative to set the kidnapping charge for retrial if the prosecutor does not so consent.

substantial, and sought guidance from the judge; thereafter they found the defendant guilty of kidnapping. Unfortunately, the guidance provided by the judge was erroneous, as is discussed in the appellate court's decision.

The court of appeal in *Daniels* crafted a suggested jury instruction on the concept of substantial distance as applied to the amount of movement of a victim necessary to constitute asportation. Does the court's suggested instruction resolve the dilemma faced by the jury in *Daniels*, or is it likely to be faced by juries in future kidnapping cases?

Aggravated Kidnapping

Penal Code §§ 209 and 209.5 define the following forms of **aggravated kidnapping**: kidnapping for ransom, reward, extortion, or robbery (§ 209); and kidnapping during commission of a carjacking (§ 209.5). Kidnapping for ransom, reward, or extortion, because of the statutory history, does not require asportation of the victim. Kidnapping for robbery and kidnapping during the commission of a carjacking do require asportation. Aggravated kidnapping is severely punished. Kidnapping for ransom, reward, or extortion is punishable by imprisonment in the state prison for life without the possibility of parole if the victim suffers death or serious bodily harm, or is intentionally confined in a manner that exposes the victim to a substantial likelihood of death. In other cases, kidnapping for ransom, reward, or extortion is punishable by imprisonment in the state prison for life with the possibility of parole. Kidnapping for robbery is punishable by imprisonment in the state prison for life with the possibility of parole, as is kidnapping during commission of a carjacking.

Parental Kidnapping

Parental kidnapping has received considerable public attention in recent years and has become the subject of both federal and California legislation. The California statute is found at Penal Code § 278.5, which provides that any person, including a parent, who takes or conceals a child and maliciously deprives another person (the other parent) of custody or visitation rights is guilty of a felony-misdemeanor. Note that the taking or concealment must be done maliciously. *Maliciously,* as we have seen in the discussion of other crimes, is defined in § 7(4) of the Penal Code as importing a wish to vex, annoy, or injure another person, or an intent to do a wrongful act. The taking or concealing of a child by one parent is not an offense under § 278.5 if that parent has a good faith and reasonable belief that the child, if left with the other parent, will suffer immediate bodily injury or emotional harm. In such a case, the parent taking or concealing the child must make a report to the district attorney within ten days. The report must include the name of the parent, the address and telephone number of the parent and the child, and the reason the child was taken or concealed from the other parent. The parent must also commence a custody proceeding in court within thirty days. (See Penal Code § 278.7.)

Penal Code § 278 proscribes the crime of **child stealing**. It applies to a person who has no right to custody of a child who maliciously takes, detains, conceals, or entices away any minor child with intent to detain or conceal the child from a person, guardian, or public agency having lawful charge of the child. The crime is a felony-misdemeanor. A parent who has been deprived of custody by a court order is within the scope of § 278 rather than § 278.5.

§ 5.6   False Imprisonment

False imprisonment is essentially kidnapping less the element of asportation. Because of this, false imprisonment is a lesser included offense of kidnapping. In other words, if a defendant is charged with kidnapping, and the prosecution establishes all the elements of kidnapping except asportation, the defendant can be convicted of false imprisonment.

False imprisonment is defined in Penal Code § 236 as follows: "False imprisonment is the unlawful violation of the personal liberty of another." The essence of the crime is an unlawful confinement of another. *Confinement* may be defined as the deprivation of another's freedom of movement. It may occur in many ways, including locking a person in a room or closet, detaining a person in a room without authority, refusing to allow a person to leave a moving vehicle when the person requests to do so, or forcing a person to go from one place to another, when the movement does not amount to asportation. An example of the last situation would be a bank robbery in which the perpetrators order everyone in the bank to move to a particular location within the bank. Such movement would not constitute asportation sufficient to make the offense kidnapping, but would constitute confinement for purposes of false imprisonment. Naturally, for confinement to constitute the crime of false imprisonment, it must be unlawful. Confinement is unlawful if it is accomplished against the will of the victim and without legal authority.

False imprisonment is a general-intent crime. Intentional deprivation of the liberty of another is all the intent required. There is no requirement that the perpetrator intend to achieve some further criminal result by effecting the false imprisonment.

False imprisonment is a misdemeanor punishable by a fine not exceeding $1,000, imprisonment in the county jail for not more than one year, or both. If, however, the confinement of the victim is effected by violence, menace, fraud, or deceit, the crime is a felony punishable by imprisonment in the state prison.

§ 5.7   Stalking

In recent years, **stalking** has been the subject of considerable media, public, and legislative attention. Public awareness of stalking increased when prominent public figures who were the victims of stalkers, including politicians, actors, and law enforcement officials, began to speak out.

Stalking posed unique problems to law enforcement officials, prosecutors, and judges. Before 1990, no state had a law specifically aimed at combatting stalking. Therefore, preexisting criminal laws, such as assault, battery, and threats, as well as the use of restraining orders, were relied upon in dealing with stalkers. But these laws proved ineffective. Often there is no assault, battery, or provable threat until the victim has been injured or murdered.

In response to the growing public interest in stalking, California enacted the nation's first stalking law in 1990. By 1993, another forty-six states had enacted similar laws.[9]

California's stalking statute is found at Penal Code § 646.9. Under that section, a person commits the crime of stalking if he or she: (1) willfully, maliciously, and repeatedly follows or harasses another person, and (2) makes a credible threat, (3) with the intent to place that person in reasonable fear for his or her safety or the safety of his or her immediate family.

The term *harasses* as used in the statute means a knowing and willful course of conduct directed at a specific person that seriously alarms, annoys, torments, or terrorizes the person, and that serves no legitimate purpose. The course of conduct must be such as would cause a reasonable person to suffer substantial emotional distress, and must actually cause substantial emotional distress to the person who is the target of the stalker. The term *credible threat* means a verbal or written threat or a threat implied by a pattern of conduct, or a combination of the foregoing, made with the intent and the apparent ability to carry out the threat, so as to cause the person who is the target of the threat to reasonably fear for his or her safety or the safety of his or her immediate family.

The crime of stalking is a felony-misdemeanor. The department of corrections, county sheriff, or director of the local department of corrections is required to give fifteen days' prior notice of the impending release of a convicted stalker to the victim, a family member of the victim, or a witness to the offense.

§ 5.8 Civil Rights and Hate Crimes

The federal and state governments have enacted laws criminalizing acts that encroach upon an individual's civil liberties. It is a crime against the United States for two or more persons to conspire to injure, oppress, threaten, or intimidate a person for exercising a federally secured right.[10]

In addition, any person acting pursuant to state law or authority (under color of law) who deprives a person of a federally secured right because of alienage, race, or color is guilty of a federal civil rights crime.[11] Because of the color of law requirement, defendants are usually state or local officials. It was under this statute that the police officers who beat Rodney King in Los Angeles were tried and convicted in federal court. In addition to criminal remedies, victims may seek civil remedies under a separate civil rights statute.[12] States have similar civil rights laws. For example, California Penal Code § 422.6 makes it a misdemeanor for a person, whether or not acting under color of law, by means of force or threat of force, to willfully injure, intimidate, interfere with, oppress, or threaten any other person in the free exercise or enjoyment of any right or privilege secured to him or her by the Constitutions or laws of California or the United States because of the other person's race, color, religion, ancestry, national origin, disability, gender, or sexual orientation. The section also makes it an offense to damage, deface, or destroy another person's property for such purposes. Section

422.7 provides an enhanced sentence for persons committing other crimes when the crimes are motivated by the factors set out in § 422.6.

So-called "hate crimes" laws have become popular in recent years. By 1993, forty-nine states had enacted hate crimes statutes.[13] California Penal Code § 422.75, for example, provides that a person who commits a felony or attempts to commit a felony because of the victim's race, color, religion, nationality, country of origin, ancestry, disability, or sexual orientation shall receive an additional term of one, two, or three years in the state prison, at the court's discretion. Other hate crimes are discussed in connection with the offense of terrorizing, in Chapter 7.

Hate crimes laws have been attacked on First Amendment grounds as violating a person's right to expression. Clearly, a statute that makes a person's beliefs, and the expression of those beliefs, criminal is unconstitutional. But the United States Supreme Court has upheld statutes that enhance sentences when otherwise prohibited acts are taken because of a prejudicial motive. For example, a state cannot make it illegal to hate a particular ethnic group. Further, with few exceptions (e.g., fighting words), the state may not regulate a person's First Amendment right to express hatred of a particular group. But if the person's beliefs motivate a criminal act, such as a trespass or battery, then the sentence for that crime may be enhanced.

Key Terms

aggravated kidnapping Kidnapping for ransom, reward, extortion, or robbery, and kidnapping during commission of a carjacking.

aggravated mayhem The malicious and intentional maiming or permanent disfiguring of another.

aggravated sexual assault of a child The commission upon a child under the age of fourteen, and at least ten years younger than the perpetrator, of rape, sodomy, oral copulation, or penetration of genital or anal openings, accomplished by means of force, violence, or fear.

assault An unlawful attempt, coupled with a present ability, to commit a violent injury on the person of another.

battery Any willful and unlawful use of force or violence upon the person of another.

child stealing The malicious taking, detaining, concealing, or enticing away of a minor child by a person having no right to custody of the child, with the intent to detain or conceal the child from a person, guardian, or public agency having lawful charge of the child.

continuous sexual abuse of a child Three or more sex acts with a child under the age of fourteen committed by a person who resides

with the child or who has recurring access to the child over a period of three months or more.

employment of minor to perform sexual acts Employment of a minor in the preparation of visual media or a live performance involving sexual conduct by the minor.

false imprisonment The unlawful violation of the personal liberty of another.

felony-misdemeanor A crime that may be charged either as a felony or as a misdemeanor, in the discretion of the district attorney.

hate crime A crime motivated by the victim's race, color, religion, ancestry, national origin, disability, gender, or sexual orientation.

incest Sexual intercourse between related persons who are prohibited by law from marrying.

kidnapping The unlawful restraint of the liberty of another person, coupled with asportation, or a carrying away, of the person which is more than slight or trivial and which is not merely incidental to the commission of another offense.

lewd or lascivious act with a child A touching of any part of the body of a child under the age of fourteen with the specific intent to sexually arouse either the perpetrator or the child.

mayhem The crime of maiming or permanently disfiguring another.

oral copulation As a criminal offense, the act of copulating the mouth of one person with the sexual organ or anus of another person.

parental kidnapping The taking or concealing of a child by a parent with the malicious intent to deprive the other parent of the right to custody or visitation.

rape Sexual intercourse with a person not the spouse of the perpetrator committed without such person's legally effective consent.

rape shield laws Provisions of the California Evidence Code that limit the admissibility at a sex crime trial of evidence of the victim's past sexual conduct, or opinion or reputation evidence concerning the victim's sexual habits, for the purpose of attacking the victim's credibility or establishing that the victim consented to the sexual act constituting the offense.

seduction of minor Distributing or exhibiting obscene matter to a minor with the dual intent of sexually arousing the perpetrator or the minor and of seducing the minor.

sexual exploitation of a child The creation or exchanging of any photograph or other visual media depicting a child under the age of eighteen engaged in an act of sexual conduct.

simple kidnapping Kidnapping without the specific intent to commit enumerated crimes necessary to make the offense aggravated kidnapping.

sodomy As a criminal offense, sexual conduct consisting of contact between the penis of one person and the anus of another person. Formerly referred to as "the infamous crime against nature" and "buggery."

spousal rape Sexual intercourse with one's spouse committed without the spouse's legally effective consent.

stalking The willful, malicious, and repeated following or harassing of another accompanied by a credible threat with the intent to place the person in reasonable fear for his or her safety or the safety of his or her immediate family.

torture The crime of infliction of great bodily injury with the intent to cause cruel or extreme pain and suffering for the purpose of revenge, extortion, persuasion, or for any sadistic purpose.

unlawful sexual intercourse An act of sexual intercourse with a minor who is not the spouse of the perpetrator; called *statutory rape* in some jurisdictions.

Review Questions

1. What is the difference between an assault and a battery?

2. Describe at least two types of aggravated assault or battery.

3. What is the principal distinction between mayhem and aggravated mayhem?

4. What are the two mental states required for the crime of torture?

5. Describe three of the situations specified in Penal Code § 261 as vitiating consent to sexual intercourse, thereby making the act the crime of rape.

6. What is another name for the crime of unlawful sexual intercourse? Does California recog-

nize any defense to the crime? If so, describe the defense.

7. What act constitutes the crime of sodomy? Of oral copulation? Are these acts crimes if committed by consenting adults?

8. If a man has sexual intercourse with his sixteen-year-old granddaughter, what crimes has he committed?

9. What are the three types of kidnapping specified in the Penal Code?

10. What is the primary distinction between false imprisonment and kidnapping?

Review Problems

1. Penelope and Brenda had been enemies for years. One evening Penelope discovered that Brenda had attempted on many occasions to "pick up" Penelope's boyfriend. Penelope told a friend that she was "going to fix Brenda once and for all—that she was going to mess

her face up bad." That evening Penelope waited for Brenda outside of her home and attacked her with a knife. Penelope slashed her in the face four times and cut off one ear. Brenda reported the event to the police, who have turned it over to the county prosecutor's office. As the office legal assistant, you have been assigned the task of determining what crime can be charged.

2. One evening after a play Tracy was approached by a woman who pointed a pistol at her and ordered her to "give me all your money and jewelry." Tracy removed her jewels and handed them over, but told the robber that her money was in her purse, which was in the trunk of her car. The robber asked her where her car was parked, and Tracy pointed to a car thirty feet away. Tracy was then ordered to go to the automobile, remove the purse, and give it to the robber. She complied, and the woman ran off. The thief was eventually captured and tried for aggravated robbery and kidnapping. She was convicted of both and has appealed the kidnapping conviction. What do you think her argument would be to reverse the kidnapping conviction?

3. Mark is babysitting his nine-year-old nephew. Unfortunately, Mark is a pedophile. He puts a sexually explicit video portraying homosexual sex acts on the videocassette player for the purpose of arousing himself and the boy, intending to engage in sex acts with the boy. Mark also holds the boy's hand for the purpose of sexually arousing himself and the boy. The boy tells Mark to stop and then goes outside to play. What crimes has Mark committed?

4. Samantha has been the victim of continuous sexual harassment by the president of the company where she works. Having had enough of it, she borrows her boyfriend's pistol and waits in the parking lot at the end of the business day. When the president drives by in his car, she fires three rounds at the windshield, directly in front of the president.

Unknown to Samantha, the president's car is armored and the glass is bulletproof. As a result, Samantha's rounds bounce harmlessly off the windshield. Samantha is charged with assault with a deadly weapon. She defends on the ground that, because the windshield was bulletproof, she lacked the present ability to complete the attempted battery. Will this defense be successful?

5. Barbara, a seventeen-year-old girl, makes sexual advances toward Paul, a fourteen-year-old boy. Paul initially resists, but Barbara persists and, ultimately, the two engage in sexual intercourse. Under California law, who can be charged with the crime of unlawful sexual intercourse?

6. Bob and Elizabeth are involved in a child custody dispute as part of their dissolution of marriage proceeding. They have been married for ten years. To enhance her chances of winning custody of the children, Elizabeth visits the district attorney's office and files a complaint accusing Bob of raping her three years earlier. Assuming the charge is true, but there is no evidence of the rape other than Elizabeth's testimony, can Bob be convicted of spousal rape? Why or why not?

7. Maxine has broken up with her overly possessive boyfriend, Matt. Matt calls her on the telephone at all hours of the day and night. Sometimes he makes threats such as "I'm gonna hurt you, baby." Other times, he says nothing and hangs up. Matt also follows Maxine. For example, on more than one occasion Matt has followed Maxine's car with his car and has attempted to run her off the road. Matt frequently sits in his parked car outside Maxine's house, just staring at the house. Maxine has found notes in her mailbox which say "It won't be much longer now." Maxine is completely terrorized by Matt's conduct. Other than attempting to run Maxine off the road with his car, has Matt committed any crime?

Notes

1 Penal Code § 261.6.

2 *See* CALJIC 10.67.

3 *Michael M. v. Superior Court,* 450 U.S. 464 (1981).

4 *See* CALJIC 10.10.

5 18 U.S.C. § 1201.

6 18 U.S.C. § 1201(b).

7 *People v. Trawick* (1947) 78 Cal.App.2d 604.

8 1 Witkin & Epstein, *California Criminal Law*
§ 536 (2d ed., Bancroft-Whitney 1988).

9 Karen Brooks, "The New Stalking Laws: Are
They Adequate to End Violence?," 14 *Hamline
J. Pub. L. & Pol'y* 259 (1993).

10 18 U.S.C. § 241.

11 18 U.S.C. § 242.

12 42 U.S.C. § 1983.

13 *People v. Superior Court* (1993) 15 Cal.App.4th
1593, 1599.

CHAPTER 6

Crimes Against Property and Habitation

Introduction

In this chapter, the focus shifts from crimes against the person, covered in Chapters 4 and 5, to crimes against property. As mentioned at the beginning of Chapter 4, the phrase "crime against property" is something of a misnomer. All crimes are really against persons, but for purposes of academic organization, those directed at the physical person of another are termed "crimes against persons," whereas those directed at the property of another are termed "crimes against property." The victim in a crime against property is, of course, not the property, but the person who owns or has the right to possess the property destroyed, damaged, or stolen.

§ 6.1   Arson

At common law, **arson** was defined very narrowly. It was the (1) malicious (2) burning of a (3) dwelling house of (4) another. This definition was so narrowly construed that an owner could burn her own property with an intent to defraud her insurer and not be guilty of arson, because she did not burn the dwelling of another.[1] In addition, the structure burned had to be a *dwelling*, which was defined as a structure inhabited by people. This definition did include outhouses and the area directly around the home (*curtilage*), so long as the area was used frequently by people. However, the burning of businesses and other structures was not arson.

The California arson statutes are found at Penal Code §§ 450 through 457.1. Penal Code § 451 defines the crime of arson as follows:

> A person is guilty of arson when he or she willfully and maliciously sets fire to or burns or causes to be burned or who aids, counsels, or procures the burning of, any structure, forest land, or property.

Elements   To establish the crime of arson, the following elements must be proved: (1) a person set fire to, burned, or caused to be burned, a structure, forest land, or property; and (2) the fire was willfully and maliciously set.[2] Section 450 defines the terms *structure, forest land,* and *property. Structure* means any building, or commercial or public tent, bridge, tunnel, or powerplant. *Forest land* means any brush-covered land, cut-over land, forest, grasslands, or woods. *Property* means any real or personal property other than a structure or forest land.

The definition of the crime of arson in § 451 and the definitions of the terms *structure, forest land,* and *property* in § 450 greatly expand the scope of the crime from its common-law definition. Also, the current arson statutes make no distinction as to the ownership of the property burned. Thus, one who burns his or her own property may be guilty of arson. The arson statutes recognize a qualified exception to this principle: one who burns or causes to be burned his or her own personal property has not committed arson unless there is an intent to defraud (e.g., fraud on an insurance carrier) or there is injury to another person or another person's structure, forest land, or property.

Burning   The crime of arson requires a burning. Generally, burning has been viewed by the courts as involving destruction by fire of any part, however small, of the property in question. Charring of any part of the property will constitute burning. In contrast, blackening from smoke does not constitute burning.

Mens Rea   The words "willfully and maliciously" in § 451 describe the mens rea of arson. *Willfully* is defined in Penal Code § 7(1) and, essentially, means "purposefully." *Maliciously* is defined, for purposes of the crime of arson, in § 450(e) as importing "a wish to vex, defraud, annoy, or injure another person, or an intent to do a wrongful act, established either by proof or presumption of law." Although one court of appeal appears to have held that arson is a specific-intent crime, other courts, and the weight of authority, hold that arson is a general-intent crime. Thus, if one intentionally burns a structure, forest land, or other property (no intent to achieve a further result is required), purposefully, and with malice, one has the requisite mental state, and has committed arson.

Punishment   All crimes of arson are felonies, punishable by imprisonment in the state prison. The prescribed punishment varies depending on the relative severity of the type of arson committed. Arson of a structure, other than an inhabited structure, or forest land is punishable by imprisonment for two, four, or six years. Arson of an inhabited structure or inhabited property is punishable by imprisonment for three, five, or eight years. *Inhabited* is defined in § 450 as meaning "currently being used for dwelling purposes, whether occupied or not." Thus, if Lindsay burns down the house of a neighboring family while the family is away on vacation, she has committed arson of an inhabited structure, rather than simply arson of a structure. Arson that causes great bodily injury is punishable by imprisonment for five, seven, or nine years. Arson of property is punishable by imprisonment for sixteen months, two, or three years. Remember that this final type of arson does not apply to the burning of one's own personal property unless there is an intent to defraud or there is injury to another person or another person's structure, forest land, or property.

Crime and Delinquency in California

Arson is not included in the California Crime Index (CCI), but arson statistics are included in *Crime and Delinquency in California,* published by the California Department of Justice. In 1995, 17,105 arsons were reported in California; 34.0% (5,813) of the offenses involved structural properties, with an estimated total structural property damage of $117,895,000. Mobile properties accounted for 27.3% of arsons in 1995, with a total damage figure of $20,343,000. Other forms of property, such as crops, timber, fences, and signs, accounted for 38.7% of all arsons in 1995, with a total property damage of $42,034,000. The total estimated value of all arson damage in California in 1995 was $180,272,000.

Source: Crime and Delinquency in California, 1995, California Department of Justice, Division of Law Enforcement.

Aggravated Arson

Penal Code § 451.5 defines the crime of **aggravated arson**. Aggravated arson is arson committed "willfully, maliciously, deliberately, with premeditation, and with the intent to cause" personal injury, property damage under circumstances likely to produce personal injury, or damage to one or more structures or inhabited dwellings, if the defendant has been convicted of arson within the past ten years, or the fire causes property damage in excess of $5 million, or the fire causes damage to or destruction of five or more inhabited structures. The mens rea element of aggravated arson differs from that for arson by virtue of the additional elements of premeditation and deliberation, as well as the intent requirement that makes aggravated arson a specific-intent crime. Aggravated arson is punishable by imprisonment in the state prison for ten years to life.

Unlawfully Causing a Fire

Penal Code § 452 prescribes the crime of unlawfully causing a fire. According to the statute: "A person is guilty of unlawfully causing a fire when he recklessly sets fire to or burns or causes to be burned, any structure, forest land or property." Unlawfully causing a fire is thus distinguished from arson by the mens rea element. If one burns intentionally, purposefully, and with malice, he or she commits arson. If one burns recklessly, he or she commits the crime of unlawfully causing a fire. If Landon builds a campfire on a dry grassy hillside during windy conditions, and a brush fire results, Landon may have acted recklessly and, if so, will be guilty of unlawfully causing a fire. Unlawfully causing a fire is a felony-misdemeanor.

§ 6.2 Burglary

At common law, **burglary** was narrowly defined as a crime against the habitation. The offense required that the structure be a dwelling, that the defendant have broken in, and that the offense have occurred at night.

The crime of burglary has been greatly expanded by California statutory law. Penal Code § 459 provides:

> Every person who enters any house, room, apartment, ... shop, ... barn, ... other building, ... locked or sealed cargo container, ... house car, ... vehicle ... when the doors are locked, ... aircraft, ... or mine ... with intent to commit grand or petit larceny or any felony is guilty of burglary.

The statute enumerates a number of other enclosed places, generally structures or vehicles, which have been omitted here for the sake of brevity. (See Penal Code § 459).

Elements   The elements of the crime of burglary are: (1) entry of a building or other enclosed place described in Penal Code § 459; (2) with the specific intent to commit larceny or any felony.[3]

Building   There is a considerable amount of decisional law regarding what constitutes a building for purposes of burglary. The legal principle which has emerged is that a building must have four walls and a roof. Thus, breaking into a bin that has three walls and a roof does not constitute burglary. In the *In re Amber S.* case, the defendant, a minor, was found by the juvenile court to have committed burglary. The court of appeal disagreed because the "open pole barn" which the defendant entered was not a type of structure included within the scope of Penal Code § 459.

Entry   The common-law crime of burglary required that the defendant break in to a structure. Breaking in meant gaining entry by forcible or fraudulent means. Breaking in is no longer required under the burglary statute. Entry without a break-in, such as through an open door, is sufficient. Entry may occur in a number of ways. Physical entry of the defendant's entire body, such as by walking into a structure, constitutes entry. Entry of only part of the defendant's body also constitutes entry for the purposes of burglary. If, for example, Melvin reaches through an open window of a house for the purpose of stealing a wallet from the top of a dresser, Melvin has committed an "entry" within the meaning of § 459. Entry may also be accomplished through the use of an instrument, without actual entry of any part of the offender's body. In the preceding example, if Melvin had extended a fishing rod through the window to steal the occupant's car keys, Melvin would have entered through the instrumentality of the fishing rod. In one case, the court of appeal held that insertion of a stolen automatic teller machine card into a bank automatic teller machine constituted an entry into the bank sufficient to support a charge of burglary.[4]

To constitute burglary, an entry must be unlawful, i.e., without the consent of the person entitled to possession of the place entered. Entries without permission and entries achieved by fraudulent representations are considered to be without consent.

In re AMBER S.
33 Cal.App.4th 185; 39 Cal.Rptr.2d 672
[Mar. 1995]

KING, J.—In this case we hold that an "open pole barn" without walls is not a building within the scope of California's burglary statute.

Amber S. and an accomplice were caught in the act of stealing some 30 bales of hay from a structure described by the owner as an "open pole barn." The structure was open on all sides, consisting of a roof and overhang held up by poles. Amber was charged with burglary, and a referee found the allegation to be true. The referee adjudged Amber a ward of the court and placed her on probation.

Amber correctly contends the structure at issue is not within the scope of Penal Code section 459, which applies to "any house, room, apartment, tenement, shop, warehouse, store, mill, barn, stable, outhouse or other building" and certain enumerated nonbuildings not relevant here. It has long been the rule that a "building" within the meaning of California's burglary statute "is any structure which has walls on all sides and is covered by a roof." The walls can take various forms and need not reach the roof, but they must "act as a significant barrier to entrance without cutting or breaking." "The proper question is whether the nature of a structure's composition is such that a reasonable person would expect some protection from unauthorized intrusions." The open pole barn described by the owner in the present case does not meet this test, for lack of any walls whatsoever. There was no significant barrier to entrance, no protection from unauthorized intrusions.

The Attorney General argues Penal Code section 459 encompasses this structure because it is a "barn," which is specifically enumerated in the statute. But the list of structures in which "barn" appears ends with the phrase "or *other* building." Thus, the statute treats a barn as a type of building, making it subject to the requirement of walls.

Everyday knowledge is consistent with the applicable law here. We have all heard that it is pointless to close the barn door after the horse has gotten out. But if there are no walls, there is no barn door, and the horse is free to leave anytime. This venerable aphorism is not just a metaphor, but tells us something practical about barns: they must have walls and a door to keep the horse in. If there are no walls, there is no barn.

We conclude this structure is not within the scope of the burglary statute. Amber might have committed a theft or trespass offense, but she did not commit burglary. She was charged with the wrong offense.

The judgment is reversed.

The time of entry no longer has any bearing on the offense of burglary. Unlike the common law, the California burglary statute does not specify that the entry must be at night. Burglary may be committed at any time.

Intent to Commit Theft or Felony An unconsented-to entry of a structure or vehicle of the type enumerated in Penal Code § 459 constitutes a burglary if it is committed with the intent to commit grand or petit larceny, or any felony. Burglary is, therefore, a specific-intent crime. Note that burglary is not limited to entry for the purpose of committing theft. An unlawful entry for the purpose of committing any felony constitutes burglary, as well.

The crime of burglary is committed at the time of the unlawful entry coupled with the specific intent to commit the intended crime, i.e., theft or any felony. Completion of the intended crime is not material to the offense of burglary, and the defendant may be convicted of burglary regardless of whether he or she was successful in accomplishing the other crime. Thus, if one unlawfully enters a home with the intent to commit rape or murder, and is thwarted in the attempted commission of the rape or murder, the person is chargeable with the crime of burglary.

Crime and Delinquency in California

In 1995, 332,726 burglaries and attempted burglaries were reported in California. The California Crime Index (CCI) rate for burglaries was 1,103.5 per 100,000 population. Burglaries accounted for 55.8% of the CCI property crimes in 1995. CCI property crimes are limited to burglary and motor vehicle theft. Robbery is included in the CCI, but is listed as a violent crime. Arson and theft crimes are also included in the CCI, but are not listed in the property crimes category.

Burglaries of residential structures constituted 62.2% of all reported burglaries in 1995; burglaries of nonresidential structures accounted for 37.8%. CCI reports that 30.6% of reported burglaries occurred at night, 35.8% occurred during the day, and 33.5% occurred at unknown times. (Note that the total percentage may not add up to 100 because of independent rounding.)

Source: Crime and Delinquency in California, 1995, California Department of Justice, Division of Law Enforcement.

Degrees of Burglary and Punishment Penal Code § 460 divides burglary into first and second degree. First-degree burglary is burglary of an inhabited building, vessel, floating home, or trailer coach. As in the arson statutes, *inhabited* means "currently being used for dwelling purposes, whether occupied or not." Burglary in the first degree is a felony punishable by imprisonment in the state prison for two, four, or six years. All burglaries that are not of the first degree are of the second degree. Second degree burglary is a felony-misdemeanor.

Looting Penal Code § 463 defines the offense of **looting** as second-degree burglary committed during a state of emergency resulting from an earthquake, fire, flood, riot, or other natural or manmade disaster. Looting is a felony-misdemeanor, except when it involves theft of a firearm, in which case it is a felony.

§ 6.3 Theft Crimes

Introduction to Theft Crimes

There are many types of theft. It is theft to take a pack of gum from a grocery store and not pay for it; for a lawyer to take a client's trust fund and spend it on personal items; for a bank officer to use a computer to make a paper transfer of funds from a patron's account to the officer's with an intent to later withdraw the money and abscond; and to hold a gun on a person and demand that property and money be surrendered. However, they are all fundamentally different crimes.

Some thefts are more violative of the person, such as robbery, and others are more violative of a trust relationship, such as an attorney absconding with a client's money. The crimes also differ in the methods by which they are committed. A robbery involves an unlawful taking. Embezzlement, however, involves a lawful taking with a subsequent unlawful conversion.

Larceny was the first theft crime. It was created by judges as part of the common law. The elements of larceny were very narrow and did not cover most thefts. Larceny began as one crime, but developed into many different crimes. This was not a fluid, orderly development, for two reasons. First, when larceny was first created, well over 600 years ago, the purpose of making larceny criminal was more to prevent breaches of the peace (fights over possession of property) than to protect ownership of property. Larceny did not prohibit fraudulent takings of another's property. The theory was that an embezzlement or other theft by trick was less likely to result in an altercation (breach of the peace) between the owner and the thief, because the owner would not be aware of the theft until after it was completed. Using this theory, many courts were reluctant to expand the scope of larceny. Second, at early common law, larceny was punishable by death. For this reason, some judges were reluctant to expand its reach.[5]

Eventually, two other theft crimes were created, embezzlement and false pretenses. Despite the creation of these crimes, many theft acts continued to go unpunished because they fell into the cracks that separated the elements of the three common-law theft crimes. Some courts attempted to remedy this problem by broadening the definitions of the three crimes. However, computers, electronic banking, and other technological advances have led to new methods of stealing money and property, posing problems not anticipated by the judges who created the common-law theft crimes. Some states have changed their definitions of larceny, false pretenses, and embezzlement to be more contemporary. Other states have simply abandoned the common-law crimes and have enacted consolidated theft statutes.

The differences among the crimes of larceny, embezzlement, and false pretenses sometimes led to a defendant's being charged with one when he or she had actually committed another. In such cases, the defendant would be acquitted when, in fact, a theft crime—albeit one different from the one charged— had been committed. Or, if the defendant were convicted, the conviction would be reversed on appeal. In an effort to remedy the difficulties caused by the technical distinctions among the three common-law theft crimes, California, in 1927, amended Penal Code § 484 to transform it into a **consolidated theft statute**. Section 484 includes the elements of larceny, embezzlement, and false pretenses, and consolidates all of these crimes into the generic crime of "theft." One who violates § 484 is guilty of theft, whether the form of theft be larceny, embezzlement, or false pretenses. This consolidation avoids the problems experienced in the past with mischarging defendants, thereby resulting in acquittal at trial or reversal of a conviction on appeal.

Section 484(a) states, in pertinent part:

> Every person who shall feloniously steal, take, carry, lead, or drive away the personal property of another [larceny], or who shall fraudulently appropriate property which has been entrusted to him [embezzlement], or who shall knowingly and designedly, by any false or fraudulent representation or pretense, defraud any other person of money, labor or real or personal property [false pretenses] … is guilty of theft.

This consolidated theft statute simplifies the charging of defendants because, for charging purposes, it is immaterial whether the crime charged is larceny, embezzlement, or false pretenses. All can simply be charged as theft. At trial, however, the prosecution is still required to prove the elements of one of the three offenses. Therefore, the common-law definitions of the three crimes and the decisional law with respect to them remain relevant.

Theft is divided into two degrees: grand theft and petty theft. The degree of a particular theft depends on factors such as the value or type of property taken by the perpetrator. *Grand theft* is defined generally as theft of property of a value exceeding $400 (see Penal Code § 487(a)). The dollar threshold is lowered for specified types of property (see Penal Code §§ 487, 487a, 487b, 487d, 487e, and 487g).

Petty theft is defined as any theft that is not grand theft (see Penal Code § 488).

Penal Code §§ 489 and 490 prescribe the punishment for theft. Grand theft involving the theft of a firearm is a felony punishable in the state prison for sixteen months, two years, or three years. Other forms of grand theft are felony-misdemeanors. Petty theft is a misdemeanor punishable by a fine of not more than $1,000, by imprisonment in the county jail not exceeding six months, or both.

The consolidated theft statute covers only the three common-law crimes of larceny, embezzlement, and false pretenses. Many other types of theft crimes are defined in the Penal Code. Most of these crimes were not offenses under the common law, but have been created by statute to address specific situations.

As previously mentioned, although a defendant may be charged with theft without concern as to which of the three theft offenses he or she has committed, the prosecution, at trial, must prove the commission of at least one of the offenses. An understanding of the elements of larceny, embezzlement, and false pretenses is therefore essential in prosecutions under the consolidated theft statute.

Larceny

Larceny is the first theft crime defined in § 484(a) of the Penal Code. The operative language is: "Every person who shall feloniously steal, take, carry, lead, or drive away the personal property of another ... is guilty of theft."

Elements   To establish the crime of larceny, the following elements must be proved: (1) A taking of personal property of some value belonging to another; (2) a specific intent to deprive the other person permanently of the property; and (3) a carrying away of the property by obtaining possession and control for some period of time and by some movement of the property.[6]

Trespassory Taking   Larceny involves a trespassory taking of property from one who is in possession of the property. As such, larceny is a crime against possession, rather than ownership, although the possession of the property and ownership of the property frequently reside in the same person. A trespassory taking is a taking that violates the victim's possession, that is, a taking without the victim's consent. A taking without the victim's consent may occur in several ways. The taking may occur by stealth, such as the stealing of a person's property when the person is absent. The taking may occur by force, such as the force used in a purse snatching. If, however, more force is used than is necessary to take the property, the crime becomes robbery.

A final method of taking without the consent of the victim is the use of trickery. This form of larceny is called *larceny by trick*. For example, if Martha causes Judith to turn over a sum of money to her by falsely representing that she will invest the money for Judith when, in fact, she really intends to appropriate the money to herself, Martha has committed a taking without Judith's consent. This is true despite the fact that Judith turned the money over to Martha voluntarily. Martha's fraud is considered to have nullified Judith's consent to the taking of the money.

Personal Property   The crime of larceny applies only to the taking of personal property. *Personal property* is generally anything that is not land or something permanently affixed to land, such as a building, fence, or tree. This common-law limitation of the crime to personal property has been changed by statute in one regard: Penal Code § 495 declares that the severance and taking of any fixture or part of realty constitutes larceny, if the other elements of the crime are present.

Both tangible and intangible personal property may be the subject of larceny. *Tangible personal property* is generally any physical object other than a document that is merely evidence of a right or entitlement. *Intangible personal property* is a document that evidences the holder's right or entitlement to something else. Examples include a deed, which evidences the holder's ownership of real property; a stock certificate, which evidences the holder's ownership of corporate stock; and a promissory note, which evidences the holder's right to the funds represented by the note.

Value   The item stolen must have some value, but even slight value is sufficient to support a charge of larceny. For example, in one case, the court indicated in **dictum** that an empty cigarette carton might have enough value to support a conviction for larceny.[7]

Possession   As previously stated, larceny is a crime against possession. The crime involves the taking of property from the person in possession. That person is usually the owner of the property, but need not be. If Rachel steals a mink coat from the coat room of a restaurant, she has violated the possession of the restaurant and has committed a taking within the meaning of Penal Code § 484(a). The law also recognizes a concept known as *constructive possession*. Constructive possession addresses the legal difficulty that arises in a situation in which the owner, or person entitled to possession, delivers an item to another for a limited purpose, and the recipient then decides to steal the item. Under the constructive possession principle, the recipient is considered to have custody rather than possession, and possession is deemed to continue in the owner or person entitled to possession. If the recipient steals the item, he or she is deemed to have taken it from the person having possession, i.e., the person who delivered custody of the item to him or her; this constitutes a taking for purposes of § 484(a). The constructive possession principle is most often applied in employer-employee situations, but can be applied in any situation in which the taker has only custody, rather than legal possession. An example would be the patron of a store who picks up an item of merchandise to examine it and then decides to steal it. The merchandise, although in the hand of the perpetrator before the decision to steal is made, is considered to remain in the possession of the store, and the wrongful taking of the merchandise constitutes a taking from the store, supporting a charge of larceny.

Asportation   Just as the "stealing" of a person requires asportation, or a carrying away, to constitute kidnapping, the stealing of property requires asportation to constitute larceny. Asportation for larceny purposes requires that the property be severed from the possession of the one in possession and that the property be moved. Unlike the requirement under the kidnapping laws that the movement of the victim be substantial, asportation for larceny purposes occurs if the property is moved only slightly. Thus, in one case, a thief removed a purse from the owner's automobile but was seen and immediately dropped the purse between the automobile and another automobile, a movement of only a few feet. This movement of the property was held to constitute sufficient asportation to support a conviction for larceny.[8]

Intent to Steal   The mens rea for the crime of larceny is the specific intent to steal. This means a specific intent to permanently deprive another of the possession of the property taken. The word *feloniously* in the statutory definition of larceny in Penal Code § 484(a) refers to this intent requirement. Note that the perpetrator must intend to *permanently* deprive the possessor of the property for the taking to constitute larceny. Thus, one who takes the property of another without consent, intending to return it at a later time, does not commit larceny. Also, specific intent to steal may be negated when the perpetrator has a mistaken but good faith belief that the property is his or her own, or that he or she otherwise has a legal right to possession of the property.

Remember that the offense of larceny is charged as theft under the consolidated theft statute. The elements of larceny and related legal principles just discussed are pertinent to prosecution of the offense because, as previously stated, the prosecution must prove the elements of one of the three offenses under Penal Code § 484 to obtain a conviction for the crime of theft under the statute.

Crime in the United States

The United States Department of Justice includes shoplifting, pocket-picking, purse-snatching, thefts from automobiles, thefts of motor vehicles, and all other thefts of personal property, which occur without the use of force, as larceny for the purpose of the Uniform Crime Reporting Program. That program shows that there were nearly 8 million reported larcenies in the United States in 1993. That is one larceny every four seconds. Larceny accounted for 55% of all crimes in 1992.

Source: Uniform Crime Reports, United States Department of Justice, Federal Bureau of Investigation, *1993 & 1994.*

Embezzlement

The definition of larceny left a large gap that permitted people in some circumstances to steal from others. That gap was caused by requiring a trespassory taking of the property. For various reasons, people entrust money and property to others. The intent is not to transfer ownership (title), only possession. A depositor of a bank gives possession of money to the bank; a client may give an attorney money to hold in a trust account; a stockbroker may keep an account with a client-investor's money in it. In all of these situations the money is taken lawfully; there is no trespassory taking. So, what happens if the person entrusted with the money *converts* (steals) it after taking lawful possession? At the early common law, it was not a crime. However, the thief could have been sued for recovery of the stolen money.

This theory was carried to an extreme in a case in which a bank teller converted money handed to him by a depositor to himself, by placing the money in his own pocket. It was held that there was no larceny, because the teller acquired the money lawfully. The court also determined that there was no larceny under the theory of constructive possession, because the employer (bank) never had possession of the money. If the teller had put the money in the drawer and then taken it, the bank would have had constructive possession, and he would have committed larceny. The result was that the teller was guilty of no crime.[9] Unsatisfied with this situation, the English Parliament created a new crime: embezzlement.

In California, the crime of embezzlement was initially defined in § 503 of the Penal Code. Although this statutory provision has not been repealed, embezzlement is now generally prosecuted as theft under Penal Code § 484, the consolidated theft statute. The operative words of § 484(a) which add embezzlement to the statute are: "Every person ... who shall fraudulently appropriate property which has been entrusted to him ... is guilty of theft."

Elements   The elements of the crime of embezzlement are: (1) A relationship of trust and confidence between two persons; (2) the acceptance by one of the persons, pursuant to the relationship, of money or property entrusted to him or her by the other person; (3) the appropriation or conversion of the property to his or her own use or purpose by the person to whom the property was entrusted; and (4) specific intent on the part of the person to whom the property was entrusted to deprive the other person of the property.[10]

Entrustment   For the wrongful taking of the property of another to constitute embezzlement, the property must have been entrusted to the offender by the owner or person entitled to possession. *Entrustment* means that possession of the property is delivered pursuant to a relationship of trust and confidence. Such a relationship may be found in many situations. The examples given previously (the delivery of funds to a banker, attorney for deposit in a trust account, or a stockbroker for deposit in the client's account) involve relationships of trust and confidence. Another example of entrustment would be delivery of funds by an employer to the company bookkeeper.

Property Subject to Embezzlement   Both real and personal property are subject to being embezzled. This attribute of the crime distinguishes it from larceny, which is limited to theft of personal property and real property that has been severed from the land. If, for example, the trustee under a deed of trust fraudulently records documents creating the appearance of foreclosure on the real property subject to the deed of trust, and ultimately conveys the property to himself, he has committed embezzlement if he acted with the requisite mental state. The trustee, under the same circumstances, could not be convicted of larceny of the real property.

Appropriation with Fraudulent Intent   To constitute the crime of embezzlement, the appropriation of property by a person to whom it has been entrusted must be with "fraudulent intent." Fraudulent intent is the mens rea element of embezzlement. It is the intent to deprive the owner, or person entitled to possession, of the property. Although some states appear to hold differently, in California the intent to deprive temporarily is sufficient. Thus, if the company bookkeeper is experiencing personal financial difficulties and appropriates some of the employer's funds, with the intent to return them at a later date, the bookkeeper possesses fraudulent intent and has committed the crime of embezzlement. This attribute of the mens rea element of embezzlement constitutes another distinction between the crimes of embezzlement and larceny, the latter of which requires an intent to permanently deprive the owner or possessor of the property.

As previously stated, embezzlement is generally charged and prosecuted as the offense of theft, under Penal Code § 484. The defendant, if convicted, will be convicted of grand or petty theft.

False Pretenses

Larceny is a crime against possession. Under the common law, if one obtained ownership, as opposed to mere possession, of another's property by means of trickery and deception, there was no crime because larceny was limited to the obtaining of possession. Thus, if one fraudulently induced another to transfer ownership of property to him, a criminal offense was not committed. The crime of false pretenses was created to address this situation.

The crime of **false pretenses** was originally prescribed by Penal Code §§ 532 and 532a. These statutes are still included in the Penal Code but, to the extent they may conflict with the false pretenses provisions of the consolidated theft statute at Penal Code § 484, they are superseded by the latter statute.[11] The operative language of § 484 defining the crime of false pretenses is as follows:

> Every person ... who shall knowingly and designedly, by any false or fraudulent representation or pretense, defraud any other person of money, labor or real or personal property, or who causes or procures others to report falsely of his wealth or mercantile character and by thus imposing upon any person, obtains credit and thereby fraudulently gets or obtains possession of money, or property or obtains the labor or service of another ... is guilty of theft.

Elements   To establish the crime of false pretenses, the following elements must be proved: (1) A false representation; (2) made with specific intent to defraud; (3) belief of and reliance upon the false representation by the person to whom made; (4) the materiality of the false representation; and (5) the person to whom the false representation was made parted with his or her money or property intending to transfer ownership thereof.[12]

False Representation   Generally, a false representation, to support a charge of false pretenses, must be one of a present or past fact. Some examples of such representations include: false representation of ownership interests in property, or kind, quality, or condition of property, to prospective buyers or investors; false representations to a prospective buyer as to the profitability of a business; and false representations of credit or financial condition for the purpose of obtaining credit.[13]

False representations of opinion are generally not criminal. The puffing involved in advertising of products is an example. Predictions of future events, such as representations of future "facts," are speculative and do not constitute criminal false representations. For example, predictions of the future performance of an investment will not serve as the basis for a false pretenses prosecution if the predictions turn out to be incorrect. An exception to this general rule is a false promise made without intention to perform. One who deliberately makes a false promise to another for the purpose of inducing the other to transfer money or property to him makes a criminal false representation.

Specific Intent to Defraud   To be guilty of false pretenses, the perpetrator must possess the specific intent to defraud the victim at the time the false representation is made. *Defraud* in this context means to cause the victim to transfer ownership of his or her property by means of a deliberate falsehood or deception. California judicial decisions have also held that a false statement made recklessly—that is, without information that would justify a reasonable belief in the truth of the statement—satisfies the specific-intent requirement for false pretenses.

Reliance on the Representation/Materiality   One who makes a false representation to another is not guilty of false pretenses unless the victim relies on the representation in deciding to transfer his or her property to the perpetrator. Additionally, the false representation must be *material*, i.e., it must be sufficiently significant that it motivates the victim's decision to part with the property. Combining the reliance and materiality requirements, the false representation must have induced the victim to part with his or her property.

There is no requirement that the reliance of the victim on the false representation be reasonable. Thus, one who makes a preposterous representation to an unusually gullible person, who parts with his or her property in reliance on it, commits the crime of false pretenses, even if it can be shown that a reasonable person would not have believed the representation.

Parting with Property   This element of the offense requires little explanation. It is met if the victim, as a result of the false representation, parts with his or her property with the intent to transfer ownership. Recall that the transfer of ownership is what distinguishes the crime of false pretenses from larceny by trick, which involves only the transfer of possession.

Conviction and Punishment   As with larceny and embezzlement, the crime of false pretenses is generally charged as theft under Penal Code § 484, and a defendant convicted of the crime will be convicted of grand or petty theft.

Fraudulent Check

One who writes or transfers a check to another, with knowledge that insufficient funds exist in the account to cover the check, commits the offense of **fraudulent check** if he or she possesses the intent to fraudulently cause a person to part with money or property in reliance on the check. (See Penal Code § 476a). The offense is committed at the time the check is written and signed, or used (i.e., delivered to the intended recipient.)[14] It is not necessary that the recipient attempt to cash the check, or that the check be presented to the perpetrator's bank and dishonored. It is also not necessary that the recipient suffer any loss as a result of the fraudulent check. The mere writing or use of the check by the perpetrator constitutes the crime.

The offense of fraudulent check is similar to false pretenses. The only distinction between the two is that false pretenses requires actual transfer of ownership to the perpetrator, whereas fraudulent check is committed at the time of writing or using of the check, regardless of whether any property is ultimately transferred to the perpetrator. If property is transferred to one who commits the offense of fraudulent check, he or she may be prosecuted for theft (false pretenses).

Forgery

Another crime related to fraud is **forgery**. Forgery involves the making of a false document with intent to defraud. The basic forgery statute in California is Penal Code § 470.

Section 470 contains a long recitation of documents the falsification of which constitutes forgery. The common characteristic of the documents listed in the statute is that they are all instruments having legal significance; in other words, they are writings that, if genuine, would create a legal right or obligation. The falsification of documents that do not have legal significance does not constitute the crime of forgery. For example, the falsification of a deed or a promissory note constitutes forgery because these documents, if genuine, have legal significance. The falsification of a personal letter generally would not constitute forgery unless, under some unusual circumstance, the falsified letter purported to create some legal right or obligation.

Section 470 proscribes several types of forgery. A person is guilty of forgery if he or she, with intent to defraud:

1. Signs the name of another real or fictitious person knowing that he or she has no authority to do so.
2. Makes a false document or alters a genuine document to make it false.
3. Counterfeits or forges the seal or handwriting of another.
4. Alters, corrupts, or falsifies any will, codicil, conveyance, or other instrument the record of which constitutes evidence, or any record of any judgment of a court or the return of any officer to any process of a court.

Technically, forgery involves the falsification of documents. Penal Code § 470 also describes the act of *uttering*, which involves the use of a falsified document to defraud another person. Under the statute, a person commits uttering if he or she: (1) utters, publishes, passes, or attempts to pass, as true and genuine, any of the categories of false documents enumerated in the statute, (2) knowing the same to be false, altered, forged, or counterfeited, and (3) with the intent to prejudice, damage, or defraud any person.

Forgery (and uttering) is a felony-misdemeanor, punishable by imprisonment in the state prison for an unspecified period, or in the county jail for not more than one year. (See Penal Code § 473).

Receiving Stolen Property

Not only is it a crime to steal another's property, it is also a crime to receive property that one knows is stolen. The offense of **receiving stolen property** is defined by Penal Code § 496.

Elements   Section 496 actually describes two crimes: (1) buying or receiving stolen property, and (2) concealing, selling, withholding, or aiding in concealing, selling, or withholding stolen property. The elements of the first offense are: (1) buying or receiving stolen property, (2) with actual knowledge that the property is stolen. The elements of the second offense are: (1) concealing, selling, or withholding, or aiding in concealing, selling, or withholding, stolen property, (2) with actual knowledge that the property is stolen.[15]

The primary distinction between these two offenses has to do with receipt of the stolen property. The first offense requires receipt, whereas the second does not. The principal focus of the offense of receiving stolen property is the "fence," a person who buys stolen goods and resells them for a profit. A fence acts as the retailer of stolen property, with the thieves acting as suppliers.

Stolen Property   Stolen property for purposes of § 496 includes property taken by any kind of theft, including larceny, robbery, burglary, embezzlement, and false pretenses.

Receiving   Receiving stolen property, which is required for the "buying or receiving" offense, includes both personal and constructive receipt. *Personal* receipt means actual receipt by the perpetrator resulting in personal possession of the stolen property. *Constructive receipt* means that the offender does not acquire personal possession, but exercises dominion and control over the property. An example of constructive receipt would be delivery of the goods to a storage facility rented by the offender.

Concealing, Selling, or Withholding   The second offense described in § 496 prohibits the concealing, selling, or withholding, or aiding in concealing, selling, or withholding, of stolen property from the owner. This offense does not require possession by the offender. If, for example, Joe arranges a sale of stolen property by facilitating negotiations between the thief and the buyer, Joe has committed an offense under this portion of § 496(a).

Knowledge   Actual knowledge that the goods are stolen is required for both offenses prescribed by § 496. It is not sufficient that a reasonable person might realize that the goods are stolen. The defendant must actually know they are stolen. The statute makes special provision for swap meet vendors and other persons whose principal business is dealing in or collecting used or secondhand merchandise or personal property. If such persons buy or receive stolen property under circumstances that should cause them to make reasonable inquiry to determine that the person from whom the goods are bought or received has the legal right to sell or deliver the property, they are presumed to know that the property is stolen if they fail to make the reasonable inquiry. This provision is, however, the exception rather than the rule. All other persons must have actual knowledge of the stolen nature of the property in order to violate the statute.

Intent   The offenses detailed in § 496 are general-intent crimes. Thus, if one buys, receives, conceals, sells, or withholds, or aids in concealing, selling, or withholding stolen property, knowing it is stolen, he or she violates the statute, without more. No intent to achieve a further criminal purpose is required.

Punishment   Both types of offenses under § 496 are felony-misdemeanors, punishable by imprisonment in the state prison for an unspecified sentence or in a county jail for not more than one year.

Robbery

Robbery is essentially larceny accomplished by means of an assault. The offense is defined in Penal Code § 211, as follows:

> Robbery is the felonious taking of personal property in the possession of another, from his person or immediate presence, and against his will, accomplished by means of force or fear.

Elements   To establish the offense of robbery, the following elements must be proved: (1) possession of property by a person, (2) taking of the property from the person or from the person's immediate presence, (3) the taking is against the will of the person, (4) the taking is accomplished by force or fear, and (5) the property is taken with the specific intent to permanently deprive the person of the property.[16]

Possession of Property   As in larceny, the item taken must be personal property or real property severed from the realty. The property must have intrinsic value, but the amount of value is not material. "Some" value is sufficient, and a pack of cigarettes has been held to have sufficient value to support a charge of robbery.[17] The property must be in the possession of the person from whom it is taken. Usually, this requirement provides no difficulty. Recall from the discussion of larceny, however, the concept of constructive possession, in which a person, such as an employee, may have custody of an item without having legal possession of it. In such cases, possession is considered to continue in the original possessor, such as the employer. The concept of constructive possession is not applied to the offense of robbery. The result is that the crime of robbery may be committed against anyone who has actual possession of the property taken, whether that possession would constitute legal possession or only custody in a larceny situation.

Taking from Person or Person's Immediate Presence   A *taking from the person of another* means a taking from the person's body (such as an item the person is holding in her hand) or the clothing being worn by the person (e.g., from a pocket in the person's clothing). A *taking from a person's immediate presence* has been held to mean from any place within the perception of the person's senses, i.e., any place within the person's senses of sight, hearing, or smell.

Taking Against the Will of the Victim   Robbery, like larceny, involves a trespassory taking, i.e., a taking in violation of the victim's possession without the victim's consent. Also, as in larceny, there must be asportation, or a carrying away of the property. Recall from the discussion of larceny that asportation involves severing the property from the possessor together with a movement of the property. Slight movement is sufficient. For example, if a robber, standing two feet from the victim, forces the victim to hand her wallet to the robber, the movement of the wallet, although only two feet, plus the severing of the wallet from the possession of the victim, would constitute asportation.

Accomplished by Means of Force or Fear   This is the element of robbery that distinguishes it from larceny. A theft from a person or the person's immediate presence, accomplished without the use of force or fear, is larceny from the person. If accomplished with the use of force or fear, it is robbery.

Although extreme force is sometimes used to perpetrate a robbery, the force required to make a theft robbery need not be extreme. All that is required is that more force be employed than is necessary to take possession of the property. Thus, as was stated in the discussion of larceny, if Joe, the purse snatcher, quickly and easily plucks a purse from the hands of an unresisting victim, he has used only the amount of force necessary to take possession of the purse, and has committed larceny from the person. If the victim detects Joe and holds onto the purse, leading to a scuffle, Joe has used more force than is necessary to merely take possession of the purse, and has committed robbery.

Fear, for purposes of robbery, is defined in Penal Code § 212 as: (1) the fear of an unlawful injury to the person or property of the person robbed, or of any relative of his or member of his family; or (2) the fear of an immediate and unlawful injury to the person or property of anyone in the company of the person robbed at the time of the robbery. The fear of the victim need not be extreme. It is sufficient if it motivates the victim to comply with the robber's demands. In other words, sufficient fear exists if the victim hands over his or her property in order to avoid the harm threatened by the robber, although the victim may not experience feelings of terror.

Specific Intent to Permanently Deprive the Possessor of the Property   As in larceny, the use of the term *feloniously* in § 211 means that the taking must be with the specific intent to permanently deprive the victim of the property. Also as in larceny, this specific intent may be negated when the perpetrator has a good faith, though mistaken, belief that he or she has a right to possession or ownership of the property.

SIDEBAR

Crime and Delinquency in California

There were 104,581 robberies reported in California in 1995. Of these, 58.8% (61,506) were armed robberies and 41.2% (43,076) were strong-arm robberies. Firearms were involved in 65.5% of armed robberies (40,308), knives or cutting instruments in 21.0% (12,937), and other dangerous weapons in 13.4% (8,261). Highway robbery (streets, parks, parking lots, etc.) accounted for 52.6% of all robberies (55,035), commercial robbery 21.3% (22,284), residential robbery 7.8% (8,137), bank robbery 2.3% (2,360), and robberies in other locations (churches, schools, trains, etc.) 16.0% (16,765). The California Crime Index rate for robberies in 1995 was 326.2 per 100,000 population, down from 348.9 in 1994 and 398.0 in 1993.

Source: Crime and Delinquency in California, 1995, California Department of Justice, Division of Law Enforcement.

Degrees of Robbery and Punishment   Robbery is defined by Penal Code § 212.5 as being of the first or second degree. First-degree robbery includes the robbery of the operator of, or passenger in, a public conveyance, such as a bus or taxicab, and robberies occurring in an inhabited dwelling house, inhabited vessel, inhabited floating home or trailer coach, or the inhabited portion of any other building. A 1994 change to § 212.5 adds robbery of a person using an automated teller machine to the forms of robbery constituting first-degree robbery. All other types of robbery are of the second degree.

Punishment for robbery is prescribed by Penal Code § 213. Most forms of first-degree robbery are punishable by imprisonment in the state prison for three, four, or six years. Second-degree robbery is punishable by imprisonment in the state prison for two, three, or five years.

Carjacking

The offense of carjacking is included in the chapter of the Penal Code dealing with robbery. It is defined in § 215. A comparison of §§ 211 and 215 will reveal that the language of the two statutes is practically parallel. Thus, for all practical purposes, carjacking is a form of robbery in which the property taken is a motor vehicle. There is one distinction between the two statutes, however, which has to do with the mens rea element. Robbery requires a specific intent to permanently deprive the victim of the property taken. Carjacking is committed by a taking accompanied by a specific intent to either permanently or temporarily deprive the victim of the property. Thus, if by means of force or fear, David takes Joanne's car from her possession for the purpose of taking it on a joyride, David commits the crime of carjacking, even if he intends to return the car to Joanne. This situation is to be distinguished from the situation in which David takes the car when it is unoccupied and goes for a joyride. In the latter situation, David would not be guilty of carjacking, because he did not take the car from the possession of another, but would violate the joyriding statute, Vehicle Code § 10851.

Carjacking is a felony, punishable by imprisonment in the state prison for three, five, or nine years.

Extortion

Extortion is commonly known as *blackmail*. It is similar to robbery in the sense that the victim is caused to part with his or her property by means of a threat. Robbery, however, involves a threat of immediate harm, whereas extortion involves a threat of future harm. Also, the types of harm that may be threatened are broader for extortion than for robbery. At common law, extortion applied only against public officials. Today, extortion is much broader, and can be committed by any person.

Elements   Extortion is defined in Penal Code § 518. The elements of extortion are: (1) the obtaining of property from another; (2) with the consent of the other; (3) with the specific intent to induce the other to consent to the obtaining of his or her property; (4) the consent is involuntary and is induced by the wrongful use of force or fear.[18]

Obtaining of Property   To commit extortion, the perpetrator must obtain property, which can include money, from the victim. No distinction is made in the statute between real and personal property. The taking of either may be the subject of extortion.

Consent of the Victim   The requirement that the victim consent to the taking is one of the differences between extortion and robbery. Consent, for purposes of extortion is, however, not voluntarily given. Rather, it is consent given to avoid a harm threatened by the perpetrator.

Specific Intent   The perpetrator must threaten the victim with the specific intent of inducing the victim to consent to the taking of the victim's property.

Consent Induced by Wrongful Use of Force or Fear   The threat involved in extortion is described in the statute as the wrongful use of force or fear. In actuality, extortion by wrongful use of force is uncommon, because such an act normally would constitute robbery. Most crimes of extortion are committed through the wrongful use of fear. Penal Code § 519 specifies four types of threats that may constitute the fear element of extortion. They are:

1. A threat to do an unlawful injury to the person or property of the person threatened or of a third person.
2. A threat to accuse an individual, or any relative of his, or member of his family, of any crime. Although citizens are encouraged to report crimes to the authorities, one is not permitted to use the fact that another has committed a crime to wrongfully exact money (or property) from that person.
3. A threat to expose or to impute to another person any "deformity, disgrace, or crime."
4. A threat to expose any secret affecting the victim. The secret must concern a factual matter and must affect the victim in a way so unfavorable to her reputation or other interest that the threatened exposure would be likely to induce her to pay out money or property to avoid the exposure.[19]

Causation   The fear employed by the perpetrator must be the controlling cause of the paying of money or property by the victim. In other words, it must be such that the victim would not have paid the money or property if the fear had not been employed by the perpetrator.

Punishment   Extortion is a felony, punishable by imprisonment in the state prison for two, three, or four years.

The question of whether a defendant has committed robbery or extortion can sometimes be difficult to answer. In *People v. Torres,* the court was faced with the task of determining which of the two crimes the defendant had attempted to commit. The court's analysis sheds some light on the distinction between the crimes.

PEOPLE v. FREDDY MORENO TORRES
33 Cal.App.4th 37; 39 Cal.Rptr.2d 103
[Mar. 1995]

JOHNSON, J.—Defendant appeals from the judgment following his conviction of one count of first degree murder with robbery as a special circumstance and two counts of attempted robbery. Defendant argues his convictions should be reversed because, as to each victim, he committed at most the crime of attempted extortion, not attempted robbery ... .

Defendant was a "rent" collector for the 18th Street gang in Los Angeles. His duty was to collect payments, referred to by the gang as "rent," from drug dealers in the gang's territory for the privilege of doing business there. As we describe more fully below, one night defendant's rent collecting activities went too far and he shot and killed Jose Argueta, one of the drug dealers from whom he was attempting to collect rent. The same night, defendant also attempted to obtain money at gunpoint from Jose Gonzales, who was not a drug dealer, but simply a passerby on his way to his car.

* * *

Whether Argueta was killed in the course of an attempted robbery or an attempted extortion was a crucial issue in this case. A killing in the course of an attempted robbery would constitute a special circumstance and would also support a first degree felony-murder verdict, a killing in the course of an attempted extortion would not support either.

* * *

Robbery is defined as "the felonious taking of personal property in the possession of another, from his person or immediate presence, and against his will, accomplished by means of force or fear. (Pen. Code, § 211.) Extortion is defined in relevant part as "the obtaining of property from another, with his consent, . . . induced by a wrongful use of force or fear . . . ." (Pen. Code, § 518.)

"The crime of extortion is related to and sometimes difficult to distinguish from the crime of robbery." (*People v. Hesslink* (1985) 167 Cal.App.3d 781, 790 [213 Cal.Rptr. 465].) Both crimes have their roots in the common law crime of larceny. Both crimes share the element of an acquisition by means of force or fear. One distinction between robbery and extortion frequently noted by courts and commentators is that in robbery property is taken from another by force or fear "against his will" while in extortion property is taken from another by force or fear "with his consent."[6] [FN6: The paradox of a taking which is both consensual *and* the result of force or fear has been the subject of numerous court decisions and commentaries. ...] The two crimes, however, have other distinctions. Robbery requires a "felonious taking" which means a specific intent to permanently deprive the victim of the property. (*People v. Ford* (1964) 60 Cal.2d 772, 792 [36 Cal.Rptr. 620, 388 P.2d 892].) Robbery also requires the property be taken from the victim's "person or immediate presence." (Pen. Code, § 211.) Extortion does not require proof of either of these elements. (*People v. Peck* (1919) 43 Cal.App. 638, 645 [185 P. 88] [defendant convicted of extortion even though the property was to be returned to the victim]; (*People v. Cadman* (1881) 57 Cal. 562, 563 [threat to expose victim to disgrace unless he dropped an appeal constituted intent to extort property]; *People v. Hopkins* (1951) 105 Cal.App.2d 708, 709 [233 P.2d 948] [based on defendant's threats, victim went to bank, withdrew money, and gave it to defendant].) Extortion does, however, require the specific intent of inducing the victim to consent to part with his or her property. (*People v. Hesslink, supra,* 167 Cal.App.3d at p. 789.)

* * *

In the afternoon of March 21st, defendant approached Argueta as he was getting into a car with some friends and asked him for money. Argueta responded he had no money and told defendant,

"You come back later , 'cause I'm leaving." Defendant said, "You are not giving me any money then? Well, if you are not giving me any money you will see." Defendant did not attempt to prevent Argueta from leaving.

Later that evening, defendant approached a group of men standing on a street corner. Defendant told the men he was collecting money for the 18th Street gang. Angry words were exchanged. Defendant forced the men up against a wall and began hitting one of the men with a gun.

While this confrontation was taking place, Jose Gonzales walked by on the way to move his car. Defendant pointed his gun at Gonzales and ordered him up against the wall with the other men. Gonzales testified, "[Defendant] asked me about money" and he replied he had no money. Defendant then asked Gonzales what he was doing there to which Gonzales responded he was going to move his car. Defendant ran his hands over Gonzales's pockets but did not put them inside Gonzales's pockets. Gonzales was then told by defendant to stay there against the wall.

At this point, Argueta approached the street corner where defendant, Gonzales and the other men were standing. Defendant stopped Argueta and asked him, "Where is the money?" Argueta denied having any money and told defendant, "It is late. Come back, [I] will give you some." Defendant, still holding a gun, began pushing Argueta. Defendant told Argueta this was "not a game" and that he wanted the money "now." Defendant then grabbed Argueta by the hair and put his gun to Argueta's head. Defendant told Argueta, "Just give me [the money] now or I put your brains out." Argueta replied, "Go ahead if you want." Defendant then shot Argueta in the head at point-blank range and fled.

The evidence described above satisfies all the elements of an attempted robbery of Argueta and Gonzales.

There can be no doubt defendant intended to permanently deprive Argueta and Gonzales of their property.

The intent to take property from Argueta's person is shown by the fact that, unlike their confrontation earlier in the day, this time defendant did not accept Argueta's statement he would give the defendant money later. Defendant told Argueta he was not playing games and to give him the money "now" or "I [blow] your brains out." To emphasize his point defendant grabbed Argueta by the hair and placed a gun to his head.[7] [FN 7: A distinction traditionally drawn between robbery and extortion is that a person commits robbery when he threatens immediate harm to the victim whereas he commits extortion when he threatens future harm to the victim. … Here, defendant threatened Argueta with immediate harm in contrast to the incident earlier in the day in which he threatened Argueta with future harm, telling him if he did not pay money to defendant, "[Y]ou will see."] This evidence also establishes defendant's intent to take Argueta's money by force or fear against his will. At the same time, this evidence negates the specific intent to obtain Argueta's money through consent, a necessary element of extortion.

The intent to take property from Gonzales's person is demonstrated by the fact defendant stopped Gonzales at gunpoint and indicated he wanted money from Gonzales. When Gonzales stated he had no money defendant patted Gonzales's pockets while continuing to train his gun on Gonzales, thereby demonstrating an intent to take Gonzales's money through force against his will rather than with his consent induced by fear. … Here, the evidence supported a finding on all the elements of robbery and negated a necessary element of extortion. Therefore, we do not believe the jury could reasonably have reached any other conclusion than defendant's acts constituted attempted robbery of Argueta and Gonzales.

The judgment is affirmed.

Destruction of Property

Every year a significant amount of financial loss results from the destruction of property. Arson accounts for much of this total, but not all. Most, if not all, states have statutes making the destruction of another's property criminal. In California, damage to or destruction of the property of another is the crime of **vandalism**. More precisely, vandalism is defined in Penal Code § 594 as the malicious defacement with graffiti or other inscribed material, damage to, or destruction of the real or personal property of another.

To constitute the crime of vandalism, the defacement, damage, or destruction must be committed maliciously. The severity of the punishment depends on the amount of defacement, damage, or destruction done. If the amount is $5,000 or more, the offense is a felony-misdemeanor. If the amount is less than $5,000, the offense is a misdemeanor. In all cases, a person convicted of vandalism may be punished by imposition of both a fine and imprisonment. Additionally, § 594 provides that, upon conviction of a person for defacing property with graffiti or other inscribed materials, the court may, at the victim's option, and in addition to imposition of the regular sentence for the offense, order the perpetrator to clean up, repair, or replace the damaged property. The statute provides that if the offender is a minor, and the sentence includes a fine the minor is incapable of paying, the parent of the minor is liable for the fine. The court may waive payment of part or all of the fine by the parent upon a finding of good cause.

Vandalism is but one of a long list of crimes defined in Title 14 of Part 1 of the Penal Code. These crimes are all included under the generic name "malicious mischief." Some of the malicious mischief offenses deal with property, such as the vandalism just mentioned, and various types of trespass to land. Many other malicious mischief offenses involve cruelty to animals. Other malicious mischief offenses deal with a host of differing antisocial acts.

Computer Crimes

Computer-related crimes cost U.S. businesses $3.5 billion yearly, and that figure does not include unreported crimes.[20] Moreover, the number of computer-related crimes is rapidly growing.

In 1987, the California legislature enacted § 502 of the Penal Code, which covers a number of computer crimes. The legislature stated its explicit recognition that the proliferation of computer technology has resulted in a concomitant proliferation of computer crime. The legislature further stated its finding that protection of the integrity of all types and forms of lawfully created computers, computer systems, and computer data is vital to the protection of the privacy of individuals, as well as to the well-being of financial institutions, business concerns, governmental agencies, and others.

Section 502 makes numerous acts criminal offenses. A representative sampling includes:

1. Knowingly accessing and without permission altering, damaging, destroying, or otherwise using any data, computer, computer system, or computer network in order to either devise or execute any scheme or artifice to defraud, deceive, or extort, or to wrongfully control or obtain money, property, or data.

2. Knowingly stealing or making use of data in a computer, computer system, or computer network.

3. Knowingly and without permission using computer services.

4. Knowingly altering or destroying computer software or programs.

5. Knowingly introducing a "contaminant" (i.e., a so-called computer virus) into a computer, computer system, or computer network.

Penalties are specified for each described offense. Some are felonies and others are misdemeanors.

In *People v. Gentry,* the defendant was convicted under § 502 for "improving" his clients' credit histories by gaining unauthorized access to the databases of credit reporting services and creating false files for the clients.

The private sector expends considerable resources in the prevention and detection of computer crimes. Law enforcement agencies have been forced to hire investigators and consultants with computer expertise to effectively investigate claims and educate the public in preventing computer crimes. As computer use and dependence increase, so will computer crimes.

On the other side, computer technology has advanced law enforcement in some respects. The National Crime Information Center (NCIC) is used by law enforcement agencies nationwide in the reporting and detection of wanted persons. Computers are used to organize and manage case files. Graphics programs are used to recreate crimes and to project a fugitive's appearance after donning a disguise or after having aged. These are but a few of the uses computers play in law enforcement.

PEOPLE v. LELAS CHARLES GENTRY
234 Cal.App.3d 131; 285 Cal.Rptr. 591
[Sept. 1991]

SILLS, P. J.—In this modern computer age, creative entrepreneurs are carving out large fortunes by providing new and unique services to the untrained public. Lelas Charles Gentry was just such an entrepreneur, advertising his services in the field of credit history improvement to individuals who found themselves floundering in a financial morass. Unfortunately, rather than throwing them a lifeline, he merely offered them a rope and anchor.

Gentry was convicted of three counts of illegal computer access ... .

Gentry was convicted based on the transcript of a preliminary hearing received into evidence without objection. At that preliminary hearing, three witnesses, each representing a different credit reporting company (TRW, CBI and Trans Union), testified about the nature of their businesses and the security measures taken to restrict access to their computer database of credit files. Each testified Gentry was not authorized "to access" their files. ...

Gloria D. Manchester testified she contacted Gentry in 1987 to assist her with improving her credit rating and gave him her Social Security number. She wanted a business loan but her credit history was

"very negative." She was not sure what, if anything, could be done, but she did want to ascertain whether *something* could be done to improve her credit rating. She had heard Gentry speak at a business club luncheon on improving credit records and decided to contact him. Gentry took her to lunch where he told her he could "clean up" her credit report. She did not understand the process and he did not explain it. He simply told her he had many different ways to improve her credit rating. She paid him about $1,000.

At their next meeting, Gentry gave her some credit applications and detailed instructions on how to apply for certain credit opportunities. He told her, in essence, to commit fraud: to state she had been married to a recently deceased man; to say her name was Dolores G. Manchester instead of Gloria D. Manchester; and to assert a Social Security number that differed from her own by one digit. He also instructed her to tell the Department of Motor Vehicles that she had lost her driver's license, and wanted a replacement in her "correct" name of Dolores G. Manchester.

Along with the credit applications, he gave her some documents which he said were new, clean credit reports from Trans Union, CBI and TRW under the name "Dolores Manchester." Each report reflected no credit history and made no reference to the bankruptcy and collection problems listed on her true credit report.

Manchester was quite upset by these instructions and refused to comply with them. She had never given Gentry permission to enter information into these data bureaus and particularly not false information. She put the whole package in a drawer and never used it, even though she had paid him a fee of nearly $1,000.

[The court's recitation of similar services provided by Gentry to two other persons is omitted.]

* * *

Gentry was convicted of "intentionally [gaining access to a] ... computer system ... for the purpose of (1) devising or executing [a] scheme or artifice to defraud ... or (2) obtaining ... services with false or fraudulent intent, ..." (Pen. Code, § 502, subd. (b) [as it read in 1987].) Gentry contends the prosecution failed to prove any intention on his part to defraud. ...

CALJIC No. 15.26 defines "intent to defraud" as "an intent to deceive another person for the purpose of gaining some material advantage over that person or to induce that person to part with prop-

erty or to alter that person's position to [his] [her][its] injury or risk, and to accomplish that purpose by some false statement, false representation of fact, wrongful concealment or suppression of truth, or by any other artifice or act designed to deceive." Here, Gentry gained access to the confidential files of TRW, CBI, and Trans Union without their permission or knowledge. Upon gaining access, he deliberately entered false information, such as the false names and numbers, which he knew would result in the subscribers to these companies' services extending credit to individuals they would otherwise refuse. Gentry's scheme was exactly the kind of manipulation of computer data files the statute was designed to prohibit.[8] [FN 8: One of the legislative purposes of Penal Code section 502 was "to deter and punish ... browsers and hackers—outsiders who break into a computer system to obtain or alter the information contained there. ..." (*Mahru v. Superior Court* (1987) 191 Cal.App.3d 545, 549 [237 Cal.Rptr. 298].)]

* * *

The judgment is affirmed.

Key Terms

aggravated arson Arson committed willfully, maliciously, deliberately, with premeditation, and with the intent to cause personal injury, property damage under circumstances likely to produce personal injury, or damage to one or more structures or inhabited dwellings, if the defendant has been convicted of arson within the past ten years, or the fire causes property damage in excess of $5,000,000, or the fire causes damage to or destruction of five or more inhabited structures.

arson The offense committed by one who willfully and maliciously sets fire to, burns, or causes to be burned, or who aids, counsels, or procures the burning of, any structure, forest land, or property.

burglary Entry of a building or other enclosed place described in Penal Code § 459 with the specific intent to commit larceny or any felony.

carjacking The felonious taking of a motor vehicle in the possession of another, from his or her person or immediate presence, or from the person or immediate presence of a passenger of the motor vehicle, against his or her will and with the intent to either permanently or temporarily deprive the person in possession of the motor vehicle of his or her possession, accomplished by means of force or fear.

consolidated theft statute Penal Code § 484, which defines the crime of theft as any stealing involving the elements of larceny, embezzlement, or false pretenses.

dictum (pl. dicta) Comments in the decision of an appellate court about principles of law which are not part of the legal basis of the court's opinion.

embezzlement The fraudulent appropriation of property by a person to whom it has been entrusted.

extortion The crime committed by the obtaining of property from another, with his or her involuntary consent, or the obtaining of an official act of a public officer, induced by a wrongful use of force or fear, or under color of official right.

false pretenses The use of false representations of fact for the purpose of inducing another to transfer ownership of money or property, with the result that the person defrauded transfers ownership of the money or property.

forgery The falsification of a document having legal significance or the uttering (use) of such a falsified document with intent to defraud.

fraudulent check The crime of writing or transferring a check to another with knowledge that insufficient funds exist in the account to cover the check, accompanied by the intent to fraudulently cause a person to part with money or property in reliance on the check.

larceny A taking of personal property of some value belonging to another, without the consent of the owner or person entitled to possession, with a specific intent to permanently deprive the owner, or person entitled to possession, of the property.

looting Second-degree burglary committed during a state of emergency resulting from an earthquake, fire, flood, riot, or other natural or manmade disaster.

receiving stolen property The crime committed by one who buys or receives stolen property, or conceals, sells, withholds, or aids in concealing, selling, or withholding stolen property, with actual knowledge that the property is stolen.

robbery The felonious taking of personal property in the possession of another, from his or her person or immediate presence, and against his or her will, accomplished by means of force or fear.

unlawfully causing a fire The offense committed by one who recklessly sets fire to, burns, or causes to be burned any structure, forest land, or property. The offense is less serious than arson, which involves willful and malicious burning.

vandalism The crime committed by one who maliciously defaces, with graffiti or other inscribed material, damages, or destroys the property of another.

Review Questions

1. Explain the concept of "burning" as used in the crime of arson.

2. What is the difference between the crime of unlawfully causing a fire and arson?

3. Define the crime of burglary.

4. What is the crime of looting?

5. What is a consolidated theft statute?

6. What is the principal difference between the mens rea for larceny and the mens rea for embezzlement?

7. In the crime of issuing a fraudulent check, does it matter whether the victim cashes the check? Why or why not?

8. Forgery and uttering, though involving different types of acts, are both classified as forgery under Penal Code § 470. What is the difference between forgery and uttering?

9. Is the following statement true or false? A person is guilty of receiving stolen property if he or she receives stolen property and he or she knows, or reasonably should know, that the property is stolen.

10. Why do you think the concept of constructive possession is inapplicable to the crime of robbery? Explain your answer.

11. How many degrees of robbery are there? What degree of robbery is robbery of a person using an automated teller machine at a bank?

12. Describe some of the differences between extortion and robbery.

13. What is the crime of vandalism?

14. Describe some of the acts that constitute computer crimes under Penal Code § 502.

Review Problems

1. Arson is quite different today than it was at common law. What are the major differences?

2. Burglary is quite different today than it was at common law. What are the major differences?

3. Doug and Sherri are an elderly couple who are retired and residing in California. Both have suffered substantial physical deterioration, including vision loss and poor memory. Ned, who had coveted their 1962 Corvette for years, told the couple that they should trust him with their financial affairs, including giving him title to their vehicle. He told the two that he would drive them to the places they needed to go, but falsely stated that state law required that his name appear on the title of the car, as he would be the sole driver. Doug and Sherri complied with his request, believing that his statement concerning California law was correct.

   Subsequently, the couple created a trust account and named Ned as trustee. The purpose of the account was to provide Ned with a general fund from which he was to pay the household bills. Ned withdrew all the money and placed it into his personal account. When this occurred, the couple contacted Ned, who claimed to know nothing about the incident. Sherri contacted the local prosecutor, who conducted an investigation. Through that investigation, it was discovered that Ned held title to the Corvette.

   You work for the prosecutor. Your assignment is to determine what crimes have been committed, if any. If theft has been committed, specify the type or types.

4. Gary and Paige were friends until they discovered that they shared an interest in Tracy. After Paige won her affection, Gary became enraged and took a key and ran it down the side of Paige's car. He then poured gasoline over the car and set it on fire. Gary has been arrested. What crimes should be charged?

5. Kevin was walking down the sidewalk that passed in front of Sean's home. As he passed Sean's house, he looked in a front window and noticed a carton of soft drinks sitting in the kitchen. As he was thirsty, Kevin broke the front window and crawled into Sean's house. Once inside, he poured himself a glass of cola and sat down at the dining room table. While seated at the table, he picked up a ring with a value in excess of $1,000, and put it into his pocket. When he finished his drink, he placed the empty glass in the sink and left. He later sold the ring and bought a stereo with the proceeds. What crimes have been committed?

6. Brogan has an affair with Janice, who is married. After Janice ends the affair, Brogan threatens to tell Janice's husband about their sexual involvement unless Janice pays Brogan $5,000. Janice complies. What crime has been committed?

7. Penni is working the night shift at a local convenience store when Craig and Guido come in. Craig states to Penni, "Give us all the money in the register and we will not hurt you. Give us any trouble and we will knock the #?!@ out of you!" Penni complied. What crime has been committed?

8. Melinda is purchasing a car. She writes a personal check for $2,000 and gives it to the salesperson as a down payment. Melinda has more than $2,000 in her account, but she also has checks outstanding which, when combined with the down payment check, exceed the balance of her account. The salesperson calls the merchant's verification service at Melinda's bank and is informed that Melinda's balance is sufficient to cover the check. The salesperson accepts the check as a down payment on the car. Melinda signs financing papers for the balance due on the car. The transaction is completed and Melinda drives the car home.
   a. What, if any, offenses has Melinda committed?
   b. Assume that Melinda's paycheck is paid by her employer by direct deposit to her bank account on the first day of each month. Melinda buys the car and writes the check on May 1. Melinda assumes that her paycheck will be deposited in her account that day. When her paycheck is added to her current balance, there will be sufficient funds in the account to cover the down payment check plus all other outstanding checks. Unknown to Melinda, her employer, through an administrative error, has failed to deposit her May 1 paycheck.

When Melinda writes and delivers the check to the salesperson, does she commit a criminal offense? Explain your answer.

9. Marvin has a counterfeit copy of the seal of the Los Angeles County Superior Court made. He then uses the seal to create false abstracts of judgment. (An *abstract of judgment* is a document issued by a court stating that a judgment has been entered against a defendant and specifying the terms of the judgment.) Marvin researches real estate listings for Los Angeles County and then creates abstracts to falsely reflect that he has obtained judgments against the sellers named in the listings. Marvin records the fake abstracts with the Los Angeles County Recorder's Office. His intent is to require the escrow companies involved in the sales transactions to pay him the amounts of the fake judgments out of the sales proceeds of the homes, as the escrow companies would normally do in the case of valid judgments. Assuming he is successful and actually receives funds, what crime or crimes has Marvin committed?

10. Beth acts as an intermediary between her friend, Larry, and a local fence. Larry is in possession of a quantity of artwork he has stolen, and is negotiating with the fence, through Beth, regarding possible purchase of the artwork from Larry. Beth knows the property is stolen and finds her participation in this transaction distasteful, but continues to participate because of her friendship with Larry. Finally, a deal is closed and Larry sells the artwork to the fence. Beth has at no time been in possession of the stolen artwork. What crime, if any, has Beth committed?

Notes

1 5 Am. Jur. 2d Arson 2 (1962).

2 CALJIC No. 14.81.

3 CALJIC No. 14.50.

4 *People v. Ravenscroft* (1988) 198 Cal.App.3d 639.

5 A. Loewy, *Criminal Law* (2d ed., West 1987).

6 CALJIC No. 14.02.

7 *People v. Franco* (1970) 4 Cal.App.3d 535, 542.

8 *People v. Quiel* (1945) 68 Cal.App.2d 674, 679.

9 *Bazeley's Case*, 2 East P.C. 571 (Cr. Cas. Res. 1799); *see* LaFave & Scott, *Criminal Law* § 8.1 (West, 1986).

10 CALJIC No. 14.07.

11 2 Witkin & Epstein, *California Criminal Law* § 602 (2d ed., Bancroft-Whitney, 1988).

12 *See* CALJIC No. 14.10.

13 2 Witkin & Epstein, *supra* note 11, at § 607.

14 CALJIC No. 15.23 and No. 15.25.

15 CALJIC No. 14.65.

16 CALJIC No. 9.40

17 *People v. Simmons* (1946) 28 Cal.2d 699, 705.

18 CALJIC No. 14.70.

19 CALJIC No. 14.75. *See also* 2 Witkin & Epstein, *supra* note 11, at § 651.

20 "Trespassers Will Be Prosecuted: Computer Crime in the 1990's," 12 *Computer L.J.* 61, 62 (1993).

CHAPTER 7

Crimes Against the Public: Part I

OUTLINE

§ 7.1   Defining a "Crime Against the Public"

Chapters 4, 5, and 6 were concerned with crimes that victimize particular individuals or entities, such as corporations and other business organizations. This chapter and Chapter 8 examine crimes that victimize society generally, rather than individual victims. These are crimes involving the public welfare, social order, and society's morals. Because they do not have individual victims, these crimes are sometimes referred to as "victimless" crimes. Some critics call for an end to victimless crimes. In spite of this, many victimless crimes exist and are likely to continue to be prohibited.

Some of the crimes discussed here and in Chapter 8 bear directly upon the administration of government and justice. Others are based upon moral determinations. For example, contempt of court is a crime against the public, and the premise of its prohibition is the theory that if society punishes offenders, others will comply with court orders, and the administration of justice will be enhanced. Prostitution is an example of a crime that is prohibited more for moral reasons than any other.

The crimes included in this chapter have been divided into two subsections: crimes against public morality and crimes against the public order. The crimes discussed in Chapter 8 are divided into two additional subsections: crimes against the administration of government and crimes against the environment.

§ 7.2   Crimes Against Public Morality

Prostitution and Related Offenses

Prostitution is prohibited in every state except Nevada, where each county is given authority to determine whether to make it criminal.

Prostitution, Solicitation, and Agreeing to Engage in Prostitution

In California, **prostitution** is prohibited by Penal Code § 647(b). The statute defines three offenses: (1) engaging in an act of prostitution, (2) soliciting an act of prostitution, and (3) agreeing to engage in an act of prostitution. *Prostitution* is defined by § 647(b) as "any lewd act between persons for money or other consideration." By use of the phrase "any lewd act" the statute proscribes more than just sexual intercourse. Any type of sexual act can be the subject of prostitution. In addition, the consideration for the act can be something other than money. Any type of compensation, if rendered in payment for sex, will support a charge of prostitution.

One **solicits prostitution** when one offers to buy or sell sexual services. A person agrees to engage in an act of prostitution when he or she manifests acceptance of an offer or solicitation to engage in the act. To be guilty of **agreeing to engage in prostitution**, the agreeing party must do so with the specific intent to engage in the act. In addition, to constitute a criminal offense under § 647(b), an agreement to engage in an act of prostitution must be accompanied by an additional act in furtherance of an act of prostitution. An example of such an additional act would be the payment or acceptance of money or other consideration in furtherance of the agreement.

Prostitution, solicitation of prostitution, and agreeing to engage in prostitution are misdemeanors.

Pimping

The crime of **pimping** is committed by a person who, knowing that another person is a prostitute, derives economic benefit from acts of prostitution committed by that other person. An example of pimping would be making money by soliciting customers for one or more prostitutes. Pimping is prohibited by Penal Code § 266h, and is a felony punishable by imprisonment in the state prison for three, four, or six years. If the person engaged in prostitution is under the age of sixteen years, pimping is punishable for a term of three, six, or eight years.

Pandering

Pandering is the offense of causing another person to become a prostitute. Pandering is defined in Penal Code § 266i. The means used to cause another person to become a prostitute may include promises, threats, force, violence, fraud, or other device or scheme. As with the offense of pimping, pandering is a felony punishable by imprisonment in the state prison for three, four, or six years. If the person who becomes a prostitute as a result of pandering activities is under the age of sixteen years, pandering is punishable for a term of three, six, or eight years.

Deviate Sexual Conduct

Many states continue to criminalize deviate sexual conduct, even between consenting adults. Deviate sexual conduct under the penal laws of such states commonly includes fellatio, cunnilingus, anal sex, and homosexual activity. The constitutionality of laws prohibiting such conduct, even within the privacy of the home, has been upheld by the United States Supreme Court. In its 1986 decision in *Bowers v. Hardwick,* 478 U.S. 186, the Supreme Court upheld the conviction of an adult male for engaging in consensual sodomy with another adult male in his home under the Georgia penal statute criminalizing sodomy.

 The California statutes addressing so-called deviate sexual conduct are the statutes prohibiting sodomy (see Penal Code § 286) and oral copulation (see Penal Code § 288a). Before revision of these provisions in 1975, sodomy and oral copulation between consenting adults was a crime. Since the revision of the statutory provisions, such acts are not criminal. Nonconsensual sodomy and oral copulation, and such acts with minors, whether consensual or not, continue to be crimes under §§ 286 and 288a.

Indecent Exposure and Lewdness

Indecent exposure is prohibited by Penal Code § 314. The offense is committed by one who willfully and lewdly exposes his or her private parts in a public place, or by one who procures, counsels, or assists another person to do so. The mens rea element of the offense requires that the act be done "willfully and lewdly." *Willfully,* as has been discussed elsewhere in this text, means purposefully, that is, the actor intentionally exposes himself or herself. *Lewdly* has been held by judicial decision to mean that one entertains a specific intent to "direct public attention to his or her genitals for purposes of sexual arousal, gratification, or affront."[1] If one exposes himself or herself in public without such specific intent, one does not commit the offense of indecent exposure. Examples of exposure that would not violate the statute are nude sunbathing on an isolated beach and nude modeling for an art class, assuming the actor does not possess the proscribed specific intent.

The exposing of one's private parts in public is considered a form of expression. Freedom of expression is a right guaranteed by the First Amendment to the United States Constitution, and attempts by the state to proscribe or regulate such conduct raises a tension between the right of the individual to express himself or herself and the interest of the state in maintaining public order. The United States Supreme Court addressed this problem in its 1991 decision in *Barnes v. Glen Theatre,* 501 U.S. 560. In that case, two bars and the dancers employed by the bars challenged an Indiana statute prohibiting complete nudity in public places. The Supreme Court upheld the constitutionality of the Indiana statute on the grounds that the statute furthered a legitimate state interest in protecting societal order and morality, and that the restriction on freedom of expression caused by the statute was incidental and no greater than necessary to further the legitimate governmental interest.[2]

Obscenity

> Congress shall make no law respecting the establishment of religion, or prohibiting the free exercise thereof; *or abridging the freedom of speech,* or of the press; or the right of the people peaceably to assemble, and to petition the Government for a redress of grievances.

This is the First Amendment to the United States Constitution. The italicized language guarantees that the right of individual expression will be free from interference by the federal government. The Fourteenth Amendment to the United States Constitution imposes this guarantee on state governments as well. Obscenity is a form of expression, and regulation of obscenity by the state involves a tension between the freedom of expression guaranteed to individuals by the First Amendment and the interest of the government in maintaining societal order and morality. Regulation of obscenity is primarily within the jurisdiction of state governments in the exercise of their general police power (i.e., their power to regulate for the health, welfare, and safety of their citizens). As a result of its constitutional implications, however, the subject of obscenity has been addressed in numerous United States Supreme Court cases involving challenges to state obscenity statutes, and the law in this area has been developed predominantly by that court.

Not all indecencies may be criminalized. It is important that the First Amendment be flexible and tolerant of new ideas and methods of expression. Simply because the majority of citizens would not see value in a form of expression does not mean it has no value. This is not to say that there is no limit on the freedom of expression. When considering sexually oriented expression, that line is drawn when the expression becomes obscene.

Obscenity has proven to be an elusive concept for the Supreme Court. Through a series of decisions, from 1957 to the present, the Court has attempted to define *obscenity*. The famous quotation from Justice Potter Stewart ("I shall not today attempt further to define [obscenity]; and perhaps I could never succeed in intelligibly doing so. But I know it when I see it."—*Jacobellis v. Ohio*, 378 U.S. 184 [1964]) is a testament to the difficulty in defining such a concept. It also reflects what many people believe: that they may not be able to define obscenity, but they recognize it when they see it.

In *Roth v. United States,* 354 U.S. 476 (1957), it was held that obscenity is not protected by the First Amendment because it lacks redeeming social importance. The Court then established a test for determining whether something was obscene, and, as such, not protected by the First Amendment. That test was "whether to the average person, applying contemporary community standards, the dominant theme of the material taken as a whole appeals to prurient interest." In addition, the material had to be "utterly without redeeming social value." Simply because "literature is dismally unpleasant, uncouth, and tawdry is not enough to make it "obscene."[3]

In 1973 the Supreme Court reexamined the *Roth* obscenity test in *Miller v. California*, 413 U.S. 15 (1973). In *Miller* the Court rejected the requirement that the material be "utterly without redeeming social value," and lowered the standard to lacking "serious literary, artistic, political, or scientific value." The test under *Miller* has three parts:

1. The average person, applying contemporary community standards, would find that the work, taken as a whole, appeals to the prurient interest and

2. the work must depict or describe, in a patently offensive manner, sexual conduct specifically defined by the applicable state law, and

3. the work, when taken as a whole, must lack serious literary, artistic, political, or scientific value.

The *Miller* test makes it easier for states to regulate sexual materials. An "average person" has been equated with a reasonable person, as used in tort law.[4] The material must appeal to "prurient interest." Materials that have a tendency to excite a lustful, "shameful or morbid interest in nudity, sex or excretion" meet the prurient interest element.[5] The Court gave examples in *Miller* of "patently offensive" materials that included depictions or descriptions of "ultimate sex acts, normal or perverted, actual or simulated … of masturbation, excretory functions, and lewd exhibition of the genitals."

One place where the power of government to regulate sexually explicit materials is lessened is in homes. In many respects, the law reflects the attitude that a "man's home is his castle" and deserves special protection. Thus, the United States Supreme Court struck down the conviction of a man for possession of obscene materials in his home.[6]

States have substantially more power to regulate obscenity when minors are involved. The Court has held that all child pornography is unprotected because of the special interest in preventing exploitation of children.[7] Similarly, governments may prohibit the distribution and sale of erotic materials to minors, even if such materials are not obscene.[8] Also, in *Osborne v. Ohio,* 494 U.S. 103 (1990), the Supreme Court held that a person may be convicted for possession of child pornography in the home. This is an exception to the general rule that a person may possess obscene material in the home.

California law has kept pace with the development of obscenity law by the United States Supreme Court and reflects the current status of the law as established by the decisions of that Court. Section 311(a) of the Penal Code adopts the definition of **obscene matter** enunciated by the United States Supreme Court in *Miller v. California.*

Matter, in the context of "obscene matter," is broadly defined in § 311(b) to mean "any book, magazine, newspaper, video recording, or other printed or written material or any picture, drawing, photograph, motion picture, or other pictorial representation or any statue or other figure, or any recording, transcription, or mechanical, chemical, or electrical reproduction or any other articles, equipment, machines, or materials." *Matter* is further defined by the same section to include "live or recorded telephone messages when transmitted, disseminated, or distributed as part of a commercial transaction."

The Penal Code prohibits a number of activities associated with obscene matter. It may be best first to mention what the Penal Code does *not* prohibit. In keeping with the principle developed by the United States Supreme Court, private possession of obscene matter is not a crime. Again, in keeping with decisions of the Supreme Court, an exception to this principle is recognized for possession of child pornography, which is criminalized. (See Penal Code § 311.11.) With the exception of the crime of possession of child pornography, the obscenity statutes are aimed primarily at the production, distribution, and exhibition of obscene matter. (See Penal Code §§ 311.1, 311.2, 311.3, 311.4, and 311.10.)

The Penal Code also prohibits *obscene live conduct,* defined in § 311(g) as "any physical human body activity, whether performed or engaged in alone or with other persons, including but not limited to singing, speaking, dancing, acting, simulating, pantomiming, taken as a whole, which to the average person, applying contemporary statewide standards [appeals] to the prurient interest and is conduct which, taken as a whole, depicts or describes in a patently offensive way sexual conduct and which, taken as a whole, lacks serious literary, artistic, political, or scientific value." Under Penal Code § 311.6, any person who knowingly engages or participates in, manages, produces, sponsors, presents, or exhibits obscene live conduct to or before another person in any place open to the public or exposed to public view is guilty of a misdemeanor.

Finally, the Penal Code prohibits the distribution or exhibition of "harmful matter" to minors. *Harmful matter* is defined in § 313(a) as "matter, taken as a whole, which to the average person, applying contemporary statewide standards, appeals to the prurient interest, and is matter which, taken as a whole, depicts or describes in a patently offensive way sexual conduct and which, taken as a whole, lacks serious literary, artistic, political, or scientific value *for minors*" (emphasis added). Implicit in this definition is a recognition that material that may not be obscene matter for adults may constitute obscene matter for minors. Distribution or exhibition of harmful matter to minors is a misdemeanor on the first offense. An exception is found at § 313.1(e), which requires video shops to place video recordings containing harmful matter in sections labeled "adults only," and provides that a violation constitutes an infraction punishable by a fine not to exceed $100.

We have all heard the term "obscene language." The *Perlman* case illustrates that colloquial usages of the term *obscenity* and its legal definition may not be one and the same.

You may notice that the court in *Perlman* applied a definition of obscenity different from that discussed in this text. The reason for the difference is that the *Miller v. California* definition of obscenity was not added to the Penal Code until 1988. *Perlman,* decided in 1971, relied on the Penal Code definition of obscenity, which was based on the United States Supreme Court's 1957 decision in *Roth v. United States,* discussed previously. The *Perlman* decision illustrates the fact that words having sexual meaning, when used in a nonsexual way, may be offensive, but do not constitute obscenity.

§ 7.3 Crimes Against the Public Order

Introduction

Crimes against the public order are crimes that involve breaches of the peace. The phrase *breaches of the peace* refers to all crimes that involve disturbing the tranquility or order of society. Making breaches of the peace criminal has

In re RICHARD PERLMAN
18 Cal.App.3d 178, 95 Cal.Rptr. 599 (1971)

On May 8, 1970, while driving on Interstate Highway 5 in Tehama County, petitioner displayed, in open view on the rear of his automobile, a sign or poster two feet long and eight inches high, white in color with blue lettering reading "Fuck War."

He was cited by a state traffic officer for violation of Penal Code section 311.2, subdivision (a) (exhibiting "obscene matter" to others). Convicted thereof by the justice court sitting without a jury, he was sentenced to 30 days in jail. After serving approximately two weeks of that sentence, he was released on bail pending appeal.

The judgment was affirmed in an unpublished opinion by the superior court, which denied certification to this court. On petitioner's application to this court for a writ of habeas corpus, we issued an order to show cause, stayed further proceedings in the justice court, and ordered that petitioner remain free on bail pending our further order.

It is unnecessary for us to elaborate upon petitioner's claim that his display of the sign was protected by the First Amendment of the United States Constitution, since we find obvious merit in his alternative contention that the record is wholly devoid of evidence to support his conviction.

"Obscene matter" within the scope of section 311.2, subdivision (a), "means matter, taken as a whole, the predominant appeal of which to the average person, applying contemporary standards, is to prurient interest, i.e., *a shameful or morbid interest in nudity, sex, or excretion;* and is matter which taken as a whole goes substantially beyond customary limits of candor in description or representation of such matters; and is matter which taken as a whole is *utterly without redeeming social importance.*" (Pen. Code, § 311, subd. (a).) (Italics added.)

Assuming that petitioner's use of the words "Fuck War" went "substantially beyond customary limits of candor," by no stretch of the imagination can his statement be considered to have related to matters of "nudity, sex, or excretion. ..." Petitioner's automobile sign obviously was not advocating sexual intercourse with war. In a similar case, the United States Supreme Court recently said that "Whatever else may be necessary to give rise to the States' ... power to prohibit obscene expression, such expression must be, in some significant way, erotic." (*Cohen v. California* (1971) 403 U.S. 15, 20 [29 L. Ed. 2d 284, 291, 91 S. Ct. 1980] (holding, inter alia, that the words "Fuck the Draft" were not obscene).) Taken in conjunction with the word "War," the word "Fuck" was totally devoid of any sexual connotation and can only be deemed to have been employed in its alternative sense as an expression of decisive rejection by the person using it (equivalent to "To Hell With War"), or as an indication of his extreme dismay, anger, or aversion.

Nor could it reasonably be said that the poster was "utterly without redeeming social importance." To the contrary, in its condemnation of war, petitioner's language—whatever its bad taste—might reasonably be deemed a condemnation of what some view as mankind's greatest "obscenity."

The writ is granted with directions to the justice court to vacate the judgment of conviction and enter a judgment of acquittal.

its roots in early English common law. In England, breaches of the peace by individuals were criminal, as were breaches by groups.

Three groups of breaches were recognized; all were punished as misdemeanors. If three or more people met with an intention of causing a disturbance, they committed the common-law offense of unlawful assembly. If the group took some action in an attempt to breach the peace, they were guilty of rout; if they were successful, the crime was riot.

California continues to proscribe the offenses of unlawful assembly, rout, and riot, as well as a number of other offenses involving breach of the peace, in Part 1, Title 11, of the Penal Code, entitled "Of Crimes Against the Public Peace."

Unlawful Assembly, Riot, and Rout

Unlawful Assembly

Under Penal Code § 407, whenever two or more persons assemble together to do an unlawful act, or to do a lawful act in a violent, boisterous, or tumultuous manner, they commit the offense of **unlawful assembly**. The First Amendment to the United States Constitution, quoted in the discussion of obscenity, guarantees to the people the right of peaceable assembly. This right is applicable to the states through the Fourteenth Amendment. Because of the potential conflict between the proscriptions of § 407 and the constitutional freedom of assembly, the courts have limited the situations in which the statute applies to "tumultuous disturbances" by persons having "no legal object for their acts," and deporting themselves in such a way as to cause "terror, alarm, and consternation" in others.[9]

Riot

The offense of **riot** is defined in Penal Code § 404 as "any use of force or violence, disturbing the public peace, or any threat to use force or violence, if accompanied by immediate power of execution, by two or more persons acting together, and without authority of law." The requirement that two or more persons act "together" does not imply an agreement or understanding between or among the persons. All that is required is that the persons commit or threaten to commit acts of force or violence at the same time and place, and as part of the same incident. Unlawful acts by a mob would be an example of the crime of riot.

Rout

The offense of **rout** is defined in Penal Code § 406 as follows: "Whenever two or more persons, assembled and acting together, make any attempt or advance toward the commission of an act which would be a riot if actually committed, such assembly is a rout." As thus defined, rout is essentially an attempted riot. If an assembled mob marches on Jeremy's house, intending to burn it, and desists because of the presence of law enforcement officers, the participants have committed the offense of rout.

Punishment

Penal Code § 408 provides that every person who participates in any rout or unlawful assembly is guilty of a misdemeanor. Section 405 provides that a person who participates in a riot is punishable by a fine not exceeding $1,000, by imprisonment in the county jail not exceeding one year, or both.

Incitement to Riot

Penal Code § 404.6 defines the crime of **incitement to riot**. Under that section, every person who, with intent to cause a riot, urges a riot, or urges others to commit acts of force or violence, or burning or destroying of property, commits the offense of incitement to riot if the time, place, and circumstances are such as to produce a clear and present and immediate danger that the acts urged will be committed. As so defined, incitement to riot is a specific-intent crime.[10] Incitement to riot involves speech or expression, and thus any attempt by the government to regulate it raises issues under the First Amendment to the United States Constitution. The inclusion of the requirement that the circumstances be such as to produce a clear, present, and immediate danger that the acts urged will be committed is designed to keep the statute within the confines of the First Amendment. Under decisions of the United States Supreme Court, speech that creates a "clear and present danger" of imminent unlawful activity may be regulated.[11] Hence, merely advocating unlawful conduct in the abstract is protected. Advocating future unlawful conduct is also protected, as it poses no imminent threat.

Disturbing the Peace

Disturbing the peace is another crime falling with the group of offenses under Part 1, Title 11, of the Penal Code ("Of Crimes Against the Public Peace"). Although the offense is not presently called "disturbing the peace," acts traditionally constituting the offense are proscribed by Penal Code § 415. Under § 415, the following acts are punishable by imprisonment in the county jail for a period of not more than 90 days, a fine of not more than $400, or both such imprisonment and fine: (1) unlawfully fighting in a public place or challenging another person in a public place to fight; (2) maliciously and willfully disturbing another person by loud and unreasonable noise; and (3) using offensive words in a public place that are inherently likely to provoke an immediate violent reaction.

The first of the offenses, commonly known as **affray**, requires that the fighting be in a public place. A *public place* is defined as "any place which is open to common or general use, participation and enjoyment by members of the public."[12] The fight must be mutual; that is, an attack by one person resulting in acts of self-defense by the victim does not constitute an affray in violation of § 415(1). (The attack would, however, constitute assault or battery, if unjustified.)

The second offense prescribed by § 415 involves the mens rea elements of malice and willfulness. (See Penal Code § 7.) The phrase "loud and unreasonable noise" is not generally defined, but presumably could include any kind of noise. If, however, the noise constitutes a form of speech, First Amendment considerations come into play. These considerations are dealt with in CALJIC No. 16.261, which explains that, in the context of speech, "loud and unreasonable noise" means "loud shouting and cheering where there is a clear and present danger of its giving rise to immediate violence or where such loud shouting and cheering is not intended as a means of communication to inform or persuade but is used as a guise to disrupt lawful endeavors."

The third offense under § 415, use of offensive words in a public place, also involves speech, and, in keeping with the requirements of the First Amendment, is tempered by the requirement that the words be likely to "provoke an immediate violent reaction." CALJIC No. 16.261 explains that the speech prohibited by the statute is speech that constitutes a clear and present danger of provoking others to immediate violence. This is the so-called **fighting words** doctrine. The

To decibls goint is a ticket

offense is a general-intent crime, because all one need do is intentionally utter the offensive words. There is no requirement that the speaker intend that a violent reaction will result.[13]

In *In re Alejandro G.*, the issue was whether the fighting words doctrine should be applied differently when offensive words are directed to a police officer than when they are directed to an ordinary citizen. The defendant's contention was that a police officer is required by his or her duty, and is trained, to exercise restraint, thereby diminishing the likelihood that words that might incite violence in an ordinary citizen would have the same effect on a police officer.

Certain statutory provisions prohibit disturbing the peace of certain gatherings of people. For example, Penal Code § 415.5 criminalizes disturbing the peace of a school, community college, or university. Disturbing the peace of an assemblage of persons gathered for religious worship is a misdemeanor under § 302. Penal Code § 402, a catch-all provision, makes it a misdemeanor for any person, without lawful authority, to willfully disturb or break up any assembly or meeting that is not unlawful in its character.

In re ALEJANDRO G.
37 Cal.App. 4th 44; 43 Cal.Rptr.2d 471
[July 1995]

The juvenile court found that Alejandro G. committed two counts of assault with a firearm, one against Darrick Freeman and one against Tony Campbell (Pen. Code, § 245, subd. (a)(2)), discharged a firearm at an unoccupied motor vehicle (§ 247, subd. (b)), and, in a separate incident, used words in a public place that were inherently likely to provoke an immediate violent reaction. (§ 415, subd. (3).) The court committed Alejandro to the California Youth Authority for a maximum period of 11 years and 7 months.

* * *

On-duty and uniformed San Diego Police Officer James Stevens contacted Alejandro and his uncle, Christopher Parraz, in front of a residence on Altadena Avenue in San Diego. The contact resulted in Officer Steven's arresting Parraz.

As Stevens was handcuffing Parraz, Alejandro said, "You ain't taking my uncle, mother fucker." Stevens ignored Alejandro and continued handcuffing Parraz. Alejandro then said, "Hey, punk ass mother fucker, take off that gun and badge, and I'll kick your ass." Stevens again ignored Alejandro and finished handcuffing Parraz. At that point, Alejandro said, "Come on. Come on, me and you. Come on, man, me and you." Stevens then walked over to

Alejandro and said, "Are you challenging me to a fight?" Alejandro responded, "Fuck yes," at which point Stevens arrested him for challenging him to fight. ...

Pursuant to section 415, subdivision (3), it is a misdemeanor to use "offensive words in a public place which are inherently likely to provoke an immediate violent reaction."

Alejandro argues that the obscene language and challenge to fight he directed to Officer Stevens were not likely, as a matter of law, to incite a violent reaction because Officer Stevens was required by his duties as a police officer to refuse Alejandro's challenge to fight. The People urge the requirements of section 415, subdivision (3) have been satisfied because the issue is Alejandro's conduct, not Officer Stevens's reaction.

Section 415, subdivision (3) codifies the "fighting words" exception to the right of free speech under the First Amendment of the United States Constitution. "Fighting words" are " 'those which by their very utterance inflict injury or tend to incite an immediate breach of the peace. ... [S]uch utterances are no essential part of any exposition of ideas, and are of such slight social value as a step to truth that any benefit that may be derived from them is clearly outweighed by the social interest in order and morality.' "

Whether offensive words uttered in a public place are inherently likely to provoke an immediate violent reaction must be decided on a case-by-case basis. "[T]he mere use of a vulgar, profane, indecorous, scurrilous, opprobrious epithet cannot alone be grounds for prosecution ... . [¶] The context in which the words are used must be considered, and there must be a showing that the words were uttered in a provocative manner, so that there was a clear and present danger violence would erupt."

The words uttered by Alejandro to Officer Stevens would constitute "fighting words" in violation of section 415, subdivision (3) if addressed with hostility to an average citizen. The issue we must decide is whether the court reasonably concluded that Alejandro's words were inherently likely to provoke an immediate violent reaction under the particular circumstances surrounding their utterance, including the fact they were addressed to a police officer.

* * *

We are unaware of any reported California case addressing the applicability of section 415, subdivision (3) to offensive language uttered to an on-duty police officer.

* * *

We reject the contention that "fighting words" uttered to a police officer cannot, as a matter of law, constitute a violation of section 415, subdivision (3) because a police officer is required to exercise a higher degree of restraint than the average citizen in reacting to verbal abuse. However, we also reject the People's suggestion that courts should look solely to the content of the words without regard to the fact they were uttered to a police officer. In determining whether section 415 subdivision (3) was violated, courts must consider the totality of the circumstances, including the status of the addressee. That the addressee was a police officer trained and obliged to exercise a higher degree of restraint than the average citizen is merely one factor to be considered along with the other circumstances.

Turning to the present case, we conclude the court's true finding on the section 415, subdivision (3) count is substantially supported by the evidence. First, it is significant that Alejandro expressly challenged Officer Stevens to fight, thereby posing a real threat of violence, as opposed to addressing language to Stevens which was merely vulgar, insulting and/or annoying. Second, Stevens testified he felt personally threatened by Alejandro and "felt that based upon his verbal assaults that it could turn into physical assault."

* * *

[T]he evidence in the present case shows that Alejandro made threats of actual violence which caused the police officer to whom they were directed to feel personally threatened. Viewing that evidence in the light most favorable to the judgment, we conclude the court could reasonably have found that Alejandro's words to Officer Stevens, under the circumstances, were offensive words inherently likely to provoke an immediate violent reaction within the meaning of section 415, subdivision (3).

The judgment is affirmed.

Threats and Terrorizing

Another form of conduct that violates public order is threats and terrorizing. **Threats** are criminalized by Penal Code § 422. A threat constitutes a criminal offense if it is a threat to commit a crime that will result in death or great bodily injury to another person, accompanied by the specific intent that the statement is to be taken as a threat, even if there is no intent of actually carrying it out. Also, the threat must be so unequivocal, unconditional, immediate, and specific as to convey to the person threatened a gravity of purpose and an immediate prospect of execution of the threat, and thereby cause the person reasonably to be in sustained fear for his or her own safety or for the safety of his or her immediate family. The offense is a felony-misdemeanor. By way of example, in *People v. Brooks* (1994) 26 Cal.App.4th 142, the defendant was convicted of a violation of § 422 for threatening to kill a witness to a robbery if she testified against the defendant's fellow gang members.

Terrorizing, which bears a conceptual similarity to threats, is prohibited by §§ 11410 through 11414 of the Penal Code. The offense of terrorizing is more narrowly defined, however, than the offense of threats, and is generally aimed at hate-related activities. For example, in § 11410, the legislature states its finding and declaration that "it is the right of every person regardless of race, color, creed, religion or national origin, to be secure and protected from fear, intimidation, and physical harm caused by the activities of violent groups and individuals." *Terrorize* is defined to mean to cause a person of ordinary emotions and sensibilities to fear for personal safety. The offense of terrorizing includes such acts as: (1) the placing of a mark or object, such as a Nazi swastika, or burning or desecration of a cross on the property of another for the purpose of terrorizing the owner or occupant (see Penal Code § 11411); (2) causing or attempting to cause a person to refrain from exercising his or her religion by means of a threat (see Penal Code § 11412); and (3) the destruction or attempted destruction of certain types of facilities by means of explosive device or arson for the purpose of terrorizing another (see Penal Code § 11413). The types of facilities protected by § 11413 are: health care facilities, places of worship, places at which counseling or education for or against abortion take place, bookstores, libraries, courthouses, the home or office of a judicial officer, and offices of county probation department personnel. Also protected is any private property if the property is targeted because of the race, color, religion, ancestry, national origin, disability, gender, or sexual orientation of the owner or occupant. Violation of § 11411 is a felony-misdemeanor. Violation of § 11412 or § 11413 is a felony.

Vagrancy and Panhandling

Vagrancy, as a criminal law issue, has received considerable attention. At common law, a *vagrant* was one who wandered from place to place with no means of support except the charity of others. At one time, in early English law, vagrancy applied to disorderly persons, rogues (dishonest wanderers), and vagabonds (homeless persons with no means of support).

Beginning in the 1880s, it was common in the United States for statutes to prohibit a wide range of behavior as vagrancy. These statutes were drafted broadly to allow law enforcement officers considerable discretion in their enforcement. This discretion was used to control the "undesirables" of society. Many statutes made the status of being homeless, a gambler, and a drug addict a crime.

Today, states may not make personal status, such as drug addiction or alcoholism, a crime. The United States Supreme Court has held that doing so violates the Eighth Amendment's prohibition on cruel and unusual punishment.[14] California's former vagrancy statute was Penal Code § 647. Section 647 criminalized certain statuses or conditions, such as being a beggar, a lewd and dissolute person, a prostitute, or a loiterer.[15] In 1961, the legislature repealed § 647, and enacted a new section defining the crime of **disorderly conduct**. Many of the offenses covered by the former version of the statute are retained in the revised statute, but are expressed in terms of acts rather than statuses or conditions. Disorderly conduct offenses may take a number of forms, and may roughly grouped in the following categories: (1) offenses of sexual misconduct;

(2) loitering, begging, and trespassing; (3) public intoxication; and (4) molesting or loitering about children.[16] Disorderly conduct offenses are misdemeanors.

A number of offenses fall under the first disorderly conduct category, offenses of sexual misconduct. Prostitution was discussed earlier in this chapter (see Penal Code § 647(b)). Another offense in this category is engaging in lewd or dissolute conduct in a public place (see Penal Code § 647(a)). CALJIC No. 16.400 explains that *lewd or dissolute conduct* means conduct that involves the touching of the genitals, buttocks, or female breast. Other sexual misconduct offenses include loitering about a toilet open to the public for the purpose of engaging in or soliciting any lewd or lascivious or unlawful act (see Penal Code § 647(d)), and observing a person through a hole, or by means of a periscope, binoculars, or television camera in a restroom, changing room, or other area in which the occupant has a reasonable expectation of privacy (see Penal Code § 647(k)).

The second category of disorderly conduct offenses includes loitering, begging, and trespassing. *Loitering* generally means to delay or linger without a lawful purpose and for the purpose of committing a crime as opportunity may be discovered. One who loiters on the private property of another commits an offense under § 647(h). One who, while loitering, prowling, or wandering upon the private property of another, "peeks in the door or window of any inhabited building or structure located thereon, without visible or lawful business with the owner or occupant thereof," commits a misdemeanor under § 647(i). Section 647(c) provides that a person is guilty of a misdemeanor "who accosts other persons in any public place or in any place open to the public for the purpose of begging or soliciting alms." To violate this provision, the person must "accost" another person for the purpose of begging or soliciting alms. The term *accost* is not defined in the Penal Code or CALJIC instructions, but the word's common dictionary definition is "to approach and speak to." One does not violate § 647(c) who solicits alms passively, i.e., who does not solicit by approaching and speaking to other persons.

A third category of disorderly conduct is **public intoxication**. Under § 647(f), a person is guilty of a misdemeanor if he or she is found in any public place under the influence of intoxicating liquor or any drug in such a condition that he or she is unable to exercise care for his or her own safety or the safety of others or, by reason of his or her being under the influence of the foregoing substances, interferes with or obstructs or prevents the free use of any street, sidewalk, or other public way.

The fourth category of disorderly conduct is molesting or loitering about children. Penal Code § 647.6 makes it an offense to annoy or molest a child under the age of eighteen. The focus of the statute is the child molester, and its purpose is to protect children from sex offenders.[17] CALJIC No. 16.440, which defines the offense, is explanatory. *Annoying or molesting* means conduct "which would unhesitatingly disturb or irritate a normal person," when "motivated by an unnatural or abnormal sexual interest in the child victim." The instruction states further that, to constitute the offense, it is not necessary that the acts or conduct actually disturb or irritate the child, or that the body of the child actually be touched. The offense is distinguishable from the felony proscribed by § 288 (lewd and lascivious acts upon the body of a child under the age of fourteen) by the facts that it may be committed upon a victim up to age seventeen and that the body of the child need not be touched. An example of the offense is found in *People v. Thompson* (1988) 206 Cal.App.3d 459, in which the defendant, in his automobile, repeatedly drove past a twelve-year-old girl who was riding her bicycle to school, stared and gestured at her, drove more slowly while approaching and beside her, and stopped his car along her route so that she had to pass him. The child was greatly disturbed by the incident.

The offense of loitering about children is prescribed in Penal Code § 653g, and is committed by one who loiters about any school or public place at or near which children attend or normally congregate. As with other loitering offenses, *loiter* in the context of § 653g means "to delay, linger, or idle about any such school or public place without a lawful purpose for being present for the purpose and with the intent of committing some criminal act as opportunity may be discovered."[18]

Drug and Alcohol Crimes

Introduction

Crimes that involve the use or sale of narcotics and alcohol may be classified in many ways. In one sense, such activity offends many people in society and appears to be an offense against the public morality. Whenever a pimp uses a young woman's drug addiction to induce her to become involved in prostitution, it appears to be a crime against an individual.

Drug and alcohol crimes are included in this section because of their impact on the order of society. Alcohol-related driving accidents are the cause of many fatalities. Drug addiction often is the cause of other crimes, such as theft, assaults, and prostitution. Police report that a number of domestic problems are caused by alcohol and drugs and that much of the violence directed toward law-enforcement officers is drug-related. Large cities have experienced a virtual drug boom, which has led to increased assaults, batteries, and drug-related homicides. Many addicts, desperate for a "fix," steal for drug money.

Drug and alcohol use are also expensive. Corporate America has recently awakened to the expenses associated with employee drug use. Employees who use drugs have high absenteeism and low productivity. Decreased performance caused by drug use can be costly, in both human and dollar terms. This is true especially in positions that require great concentration or pose risks to others, such as that of commercial pilots. In addition to business expenses, the high cost of rehabilitation can disable a family financially, and the price of drug-abuse detection and prosecution is high.

Alcohol Crimes

Although alcohol is considered a drug, the law treats alcohol differently than it does other drugs. Alcohol may be legally possessed, consumed, and sold, subject only to a few restrictions. Other types of drugs are significantly restricted. Their sale, possession, and consumption are limited to specific instances, such as for medical use. The federal government, as well as every state, has statutes that spell out what drugs are regulated.

There are many alcohol-related crimes. One such crime is being drunk in a public place, mentioned in the preceding section on disorderly conduct.

The purchase and sale of alcoholic beverages are regulated primarily by the Business and Professions Code. The Business and Professions Code prescribes criminal penalties for violation of certain of its provisions. Prominent among these are the provisions governing sale of alcoholic beverages to underage persons. Under Business and Professions Code § 25658, it is a misdemeanor for any person to sell, furnish, or give any alcoholic beverage to any person under the age of twenty-one years. A person under age twenty-one is guilty of a misdemeanor if he or she purchases alcoholic beverages or consumes any alcoholic beverages in any on-sale premises (Business and Professions Code § 25658(b)); if he or she presents or possesses false evidence of age (§ 25661); if he or she possesses an alcoholic beverage on a street or public place or place open to the public, except in making a legal delivery (§ 25662); and if he or she remains in licensed premises without lawful business therein (§ 25665).[19]

An alcohol-related offense receiving considerable public attention today is operation of a motor vehicle while under the influence of alcohol. There are actually a number of such offenses, and they are found principally in the Vehicle Code. The Vehicle Code prescribes both misdemeanor and felony drunk driving offenses. These offenses include operation of vehicles while under the influence of alcohol, drugs, or a combination of alcohol and drugs.

Vehicle Code § 23152(a) provides that it is unlawful for any person who is under the influence of any alcoholic beverage or drug, or under the combined influence of any alcoholic beverage and drug, to drive a vehicle. Section 23152(b) provides that it is unlawful for any person who has 0.08 percent or more, by weight, of alcohol in his or her blood to drive a vehicle. The first offense is committed regardless of the blood alcohol level of the vehicle operator, if the operator is "under the influence." A person is under the influence of alcohol or drugs, or a combination of the two, when, as a result of ingestion of alcohol or drugs, his or her physical or mental abilities are impaired to such a degree that he or she no longer has the ability to drive a vehicle with the caution characteristic of a sober person of ordinary prudence, under the same or similar circumstances.[20] The offense is generally proven by evidence of the manner in which the person operated the vehicle (e.g., crossing the center line, weaving) and by the results of field sobriety tests administered to the person at the time of apprehension.

The second offense, driving a vehicle with a blood alcohol level of 0.08 percent or more, applies only to intoxication by alcohol. Unlike the **driving under the influence** offense, the offense under § 23152(b) does not require proof that the operator was under the influence of alcohol, i.e., that he or she was unable to operate the vehicle safely. The statute is violated simply by operating the vehicle while having the prescribed blood alcohol level.

In the *Lewis* case, an interesting anomaly occurred. The defendant was charged with drunk driving under both §§ 23152(a) (driving under the influence) and 23152(b) (driving a vehicle with a blood alcohol level of 0.08 percent or more). The jury found the defendant guilty under § 23152(b), but was unable to agree on the charge under § 23152(a). The defendant, presumably feeling it was unfair to be convicted based on a mechanical measurement of blood alcohol content when there was apparently insufficient evidence that he was actually operating his vehicle in an impaired condition, appealed the conviction challenging the validity of § 23152(b) as a standard for determining when one is operating a vehicle while under the influence of alcohol. In its opinion, the appellate court discusses the relationship between the offenses proscribed by §§ 23152(a) and 23152(b).

Note that at the time of the *Lewis* decision (1983), the blood alcohol level specified in § 23152(b) was 0.10 percent. The statute has since been modified to set the prohibited blood alcohol level at 0.08 percent. Note also that, in upholding the validity of § 23152(b), the court in *Lewis* relied largely on its perception that the scientific community is in virtually unanimous agreement that anyone with a blood alcohol content of 0.10 percent is under the influence.

PEOPLE v. EDWARD FRED LEWIS
148 Cal.App.3d 614; 196 Cal.Rptr. 161
[Oct. 1983]

We are asked to consider the constitutionality of Vehicle Code section 23152, subdivision (b), driving with a blood alcohol level of .10 percent or more. ...

When Lewis was arrested, section 23152, subdivision (b) provided, "It is unlawful for any person who has 0.10 percent or more, by weight, of alcohol in his or her blood to drive a vehicle upon a highway or upon other than a highway in areas which are open to the general public. ..." Lewis was convicted under this section on evidence of blood alcohol breath tests of .13 and .14; the jury was unable to agree on the companion charge of driving under the influence of alcohol (Veh. Code, § 23152, subd. (a)).

* * *

The burden the (b) section places on the drinking motorist is new in this state in the sense that it uses precise numbers to define a long recognized social evil. However, in light of the now virtually unanimous scientific opinion that all persons are under the influence at .10 for purposes of the traditional offense of driving under the influence described by the (a) section, the new law does not seem to us to create the dramatic hardship its detractors proclaim. If a person is under the influence, he or she should not drive at *any* blood alcohol level (Veh. Code, § 23152, subd. (a)). A person who is *not* under the influence does not have a blood alcohol level at .10 or above, according to the experts. ...

In other words, in cases at .10 and above, the statutes can be viewed as proscriptions of the same conduct with different elements of proof. As our facts illustrate, the (b) section may be the easier to prove in a given case, perhaps in most cases, but a violator has no cause to complain on that score. Regulation of the drinking driver is not rooted in the Bill of Rights, the Magna Carta, or the tablets of Moses. The Legislature is free to address the matter in various, and varying, ways.

* * *

Does the (b) section create an impermissible conclusive or irrebuttable presumption? Although we have frankly acknowledged the (a) and (b) sections do proscribe the same conduct when the blood alcohol level is .10 or higher (assuming the scientific lore is accurate), this is not the same as saying the (b) section is merely the (a) section in disguise—with conclusive presumption grafted on. The problems of proof will differ with each offense and so will the jury's verdict on occasion, as this case illustrates. The (b) section requires no evidence of impairment; the (a) section does. They are clearly different offenses. Nothing precludes the Legislature from proscribing the same general conduct in different and overlapping ways, although there can be but one punishment imposed. (Pen. Code, § 654.) And nothing prevents the defendant from challenging the test result under the new law; it is not presumed to be correct or to reflect the actual blood alcohol level at the time of driving.

* * *

Judgment affirmed.

Thus, according to the court, although §§ 23152(a) and (b) prescribe separate offenses, they are both intended to prohibit the same unlawful conduct: operating a motor vehicle while under the influence.

Vehicle Code § 23152(c) provides that it is unlawful for any person who is addicted to the use of any drug to drive a vehicle. *Addicted* means more than that one is accustomed and habituated to the use of drugs. It means that the person is so physically dependent on drugs that his or her body undergoes an abstinence syndrome or withdrawal illness on a sudden cessation of use, so as to make the person a potential danger on the highway.[21]

All of the foregoing offenses are misdemeanors. Punishment for a first offense includes imprisonment in the county jail, a fine, suspension of the offender's driving privilege for six months or restriction of the driving privilege for ninety days, and participation in an approved alcohol or drug education and counseling program. The Vehicle Code provides increasingly severe penalties for second and subsequent misdemeanor drunk driving offenses.

Felony drunk driving is prescribed by Vehicle Code § 23153. The offense is committed by driving under the influence or driving with a blood alcohol content of 0.08 percent or more, the same as in the misdemeanor drunk driving offenses prescribed by §§ 23152(a) and (b), and concurrently doing any act forbidden by law or neglecting any duty imposed by law in driving the vehicle which proximately causes bodily injury to another person. Conviction of a first violation of § 23153 is punishable by imprisonment in the state prison or county jail, a fine, suspension of the operator's license for a period of one year, and participation in an alcohol or drug education and counseling program. If more than one person is injured or killed as a result of the offender's felony drunk driving, a sentence enhancement of one year in the state prison is to be imposed for each additional victim unless the court finds that the enhancement should not be imposed because of mitigating circumstances. As with misdemeanor drunk driving, the Vehicle Code provides increasingly severe penalties for second and subsequent felony drunk driving offenses.

Finally, recall from Chapter 4 that one who kills another while operating a vehicle under the influence of alcohol or drugs may be guilty of vehicular manslaughter or gross vehicular manslaughter, depending on the degree of negligence (simple or gross) with which the offender is operating the vehicle.

Drug Crimes

Unlike alcohol, possession of other drugs is a crime. Every state and the federal government have enacted some variation of the Uniform Controlled Substance Act, a model act (similar to the Model Penal Code) drafted by the Commissioners on Uniform Laws. California adopted the Uniform Controlled Substances Act, with amendments, in 1972. The provisions of that Act are found in several of the California codes, but the most significant appear in Division 10 of the Health and Safety Code, beginning with § 11000. Division 10 is known as the California Uniform Controlled Substances Act, and is referred to here as the "Act." The Act divides drugs into five categories, or schedules, numbered I through V. The lower the number of the schedule on which a drug appears, the less the drug's social utility or legal acceptability, i.e., the more harmful it is. For example, Schedule I includes controlled substances that have a high potential for abuse and have no accepted medical use. Schedule V covers controlled substances that have low potential for abuse and are currently accepted for medical use, but which may lead to limited physical dependence if abused.[22] Under § 11007, the term *controlled substance* means a drug that is listed on one of the five schedules. Sections 11054 through 11058 of the Health and Safety Code contain Schedules I through V, respectively, and identify each drug on each schedule.

Prior to adoption of the Act and its schedules, California divided drugs into two categories: "narcotics" and "restricted dangerous drugs." The drugs falling into these two categories are the same as those appearing on the schedules under the Act, but there is crossover; that is, certain drugs appearing on a particular schedule may be narcotics, whereas others on the same schedule may be restricted dangerous drugs. California has retained the "narcotic" and "restricted dangerous drug" (frequently referred to as "non-narcotic drug" or "not a narcotic drug") designations, in addition to adopting the schedules in the Act. The former designations are used primarily in the provisions prescribing offenses. For example, Health and Safety Code § 11350 makes possession of a narcotic drug an offense by specifying the narcotic drugs that appear on each schedule.

There are a number of types of crimes involving controlled substances. These include, but are not limited to, simple possession; possession for sale; use; sale or distribution; drug paraphernalia offenses; and production.

Simple Possession   The offense of simple possession of a controlled substance involves possession for personal use. (The concept of possession as an act was previously considered in Chapter 3.) Recall that, to be guilty of possession of a controlled substance, one must know both the fact of possession and the nature of the thing possessed. Drug possession offenses require that the drug be possessed in a usable quantity and form. Issues as to usable quantity have arisen in cases in which defendants had possessed drug paraphernalia containing only residue of controlled substances. The courts have held that residue is not a usable quantity of a controlled substance, i.e., it does not contain enough of the drug to produce the drug's effect in a person. As to form, the controlled substance must be in a form to be used as a controlled substance. In one case, the defendant possessed a jar containing marijuana immersed in alcohol, which he used to treat his rheumatism. The court held that marijuana in this form is not usable as a narcotic and thus the defendant could not be convicted of possession of a controlled substance.[23]

Possession of controlled substances constituting narcotics is a felony or felony-misdemeanor, depending on the drug possessed. Possession of controlled substances constituting restricted dangerous drugs is a felony-misdemeanor or a misdemeanor, also depending on the drug possessed. Marijuana, and a few other drugs, are accorded special treatment. For example, Health and Safety Code § 11357 provides that possession of 28.5 grams or less (approximately one ounce) of marijuana, other than concentrated cannabis, is a misdemeanor punishable by a fine of not more than $100. Possession of more than 28.5 grams of marijuana, other than concentrated cannabis, is a misdemeanor punishable by imprisonment in the county jail for not more than six months, by a fine of not more than $500, or both. Possession of concentrated cannabis is a felony-misdemeanor.

Possession for Sale   Simple possession is a general-intent crime, i.e., the defendant need only intentionally possess the controlled substance. Intent to achieve some further unlawful purpose is not required. Possession for sale involves the same elements as simple possession, except that possession for sale is a specific-intent crime—the specific intent being the intent to sell the controlled substance. Not surprisingly, possession for sale is punished more severely than simple possession. Under Health and Safety Code § 11351, possession for sale of a narcotic drug is a felony punishable by imprisonment in the state prison for two, three, or four years. Section 11378 provides that possession for sale of a non-narcotic drug, i.e., a restricted dangerous drug, is a felony punishable in the state prison, without specifying the term of years of incarceration. Section 11359 specifies the same punishment (imprisonment in the state prison without specifying the term of years) for the offense of possession for sale of marijuana.

Use   Health and Safety Code § 11550 makes it a crime to use or be under the influence of specified narcotic and non-narcotic drugs. Not all narcotic and non-narcotic drugs are included within the proscription of the section. Under the statute, using or being under the influence of the specified drugs is a crime "except when administered by or under the direction of a person licensed by the state to dispense, prescribe, or administer controlled substances." A person convicted of using or being under the influence of one of the specified drugs is guilty of a misdemeanor and must be sentenced to at least ninety days, but not more than one year, in the county jail. Section 11550(c) authorizes the court, when it would be in the interest of justice to do so, to permit a person convicted of violating § 11550 to complete a licensed drug rehabilitation program in lieu of part or all of the imprisonment in the county jail. Note that, although the use of many drugs is not criminalized, use of any drug involves possession, which is a crime.

Sale or distribution   The phrase "sale or distribution" covers a number of prohibited activities. Health and Safety Code § 11352(a), for example, provides that:

> every person who transports, imports into this state, sells, furnishes, administers, or gives away, or offers to transport, import into this state, sell, furnish, administer, or give away, or attempts to import into this state or transport any [narcotic drug], unless upon written prescription ... shall be punished by imprisonment in the state prison for three, four, or five years.

Section 11379(a) contains similar provisions for restricted dangerous drugs, except that the prescribed term of imprisonment is two, three, or four years. Section 11360(a) provides for imprisonment for two, three, or four years for identically described acts involving marijuana.

Dealings with Minors   Health and Safety Code § 11353 prohibits any person eighteen years of age or over from "soliciting, inducing, encouraging, or intimidating" a minor to commit a drug offense involving a narcotic drug, to employ a minor to transport or sell a narcotic drug, or to provide a narcotic drug to a minor. The offense is a felony, punishable by imprisonment in the state prison for three, six, or nine years. Section 11380 is similar to § 11353, but applies to restricted dangerous drugs.

Drug Paraphernalia Offenses   The term *drug paraphernalia* covers a wide range of items, and is defined in § 11014.5 of the Health and Safety Code:

> "Drug paraphernalia" means all equipment, products and materials of any kind which are designed for use or marketed for use, in planting, propagating, cultivating, growing, harvesting, manufacturing, compounding, converting, producing, processing, preparing, testing, analyzing, packaging, repackaging, storing, containing, concealing, injecting, ingesting, inhaling, or otherwise introducing into the human body a controlled substance … .

The remainder of § 11014.5 lists numerous specific examples of drug paraphernalia, such as kits for growing plants that are controlled substances, hypodermic syringes, smoking devices, and many others. Section 11364.7 provides that it is a misdemeanor for a person to deliver, furnish, or transfer, or to possess or manufacture with the intent to deliver, furnish, or transfer, drug paraphernalia, if the person knows or reasonably should know that it will be used in the commission of any of the acts described in the quoted portion of § 11014.5. Section 11364 makes it unlawful to possess an opium pipe or any device used for unlawfully injecting or smoking certain specified controlled substances. The offense is punishable by a fine.

Production Offenses   Production offenses involve activities such as cultivating, harvesting, processing, and manufacturing controlled substances. Cultivation and harvesting apply to the growing of plants from which controlled substances may be produced. Such plants include marijuana, peyote, and mushrooms containing hallucinogenic substances. Cultivation and harvesting of marijuana is a felony, whereas cultivation and harvesting of peyote and mushrooms is a felony-misdemeanor.[24] The defendant must have knowledge of the existence of the plant and of its character as containing a controlled substance. If, for example, a person had marijuana plants growing in her back yard, but did not realize what they were, she would not commit the offense of cultivating marijuana.

The term *processing* is not defined in the Health and Safety Code, but generally means converting a controlled substance into usable form. For example, in *People v. Tierce* (1985) 165 Cal.App.3d 256, the court held that removal of the leaves from the stems of marijuana plants so that they could be smoked constituted processing.

The offense of manufacturing a controlled substance is defined in Health and Safety Code § 11379.6. Under that section:

> every person who manufactures, compounds, converts, produces, derives, processes, or prepares, either directly or indirectly by chemical extraction or independently by means of chemical synthesis, any controlled substance … shall be punished by imprisonment in the state prison for three, five, or seven years and by a fine not exceeding fifty thousand dollars ($50,000).

Under § 11379.6, a person who offers to perform one of the enumerated acts may be punished by imprisonment in the state prison for three, four, or five years.

Key Terms

affray The offense committed by a person who unlawfully fights in a public place or challenges another person to fight in a public place.

agreeing to engage in prostitution The crime involving agreement to engage in an act of prostitution accompanied by an act in furtherance of an act of prostitution, such as the payment or receipt of money.

disorderly conduct A general category of misdemeanor offenses involving: (1) offenses of sexual misconduct; (2) loitering, begging, and trespassing; (3) public intoxication; and (4) molesting or loitering about children.

disturbing the peace A description of a group of offenses involving: (1) unlawfully fighting in a public place or challenging another person to fight in a public place; (2) maliciously and willfully disturbing another person by loud and unreasonable noise; and (3) using offensive words in a public place which are inherently likely to provoke an immediate violent reaction.

driving under the influence The offense committed by driving a vehicle while under the influence of any alcoholic beverage or drug or the combined influence of any alcoholic beverage or drug. A person is under the influence when, as a result of ingestion of alcohol or drugs, his or her physical or mental abilities are impaired to such a degree that he or she no longer has the ability to drive a vehicle with the caution characteristic of a sober person of ordinary prudence, under the same or similar circumstances. This offense is to be contrasted with the offense of driving a vehicle with a blood alcohol level of 0.08 percent or more, which does not require evidence that the person's ability to operate the vehicle was actually impaired. The latter offense is committed by having the requisite blood alcohol level, without regard to actual impairment.

fighting words Speech that is not protected by the First Amendment because it creates a clear and present danger of provoking others to immediate violence.

incitement to riot The offense committed by a person who, with intent to cause a riot, urges a riot, or urges others to commit acts of force or violence, or burning or destroying of property, if the time, place, and circumstances are such as to produce a clear and present and immediate danger that the acts urged will be committed.

indecent exposure The willful and lewd exposure of one's person or private parts in the presence of other persons, or the procuring, counseling, or assisting of another person to do so.

obscene matter As defined in Penal Code § 311, matter, taken as a whole, which to the average person, applying contemporary statewide standards, appeals to the prurient interest, and is matter which, taken as a whole, depicts or describes in a patently offensive way sexual conduct; and which, taken as a whole, lacks serious literary, artistic, political, or scientific value.

pandering The crime of causing another person to become a prostitute.

pimping The crime of knowingly deriving economic benefit from acts of prostitution committed by another person.

prostitution Any lewd act between persons for money or other consideration.

public intoxication The offense committed by one who is found in any public place under the influence of intoxicating liquor, any drug, controlled substance, toluene, or any combination of the foregoing, in such a condition that he or she is unable to exercise care for his or her own safety or the safety of others, or who, by reason of his or her being under the influence of any of the foregoing substances, interferes with or obstructs or prevents the free use of any street, sidewalk, or other public way.

riot The crime involving any use of force or violence, disturbing the public peace, or any threat to use force or violence, if accompanied by immediate power of execution, by two or more persons acting together, and without authority of law.

rout The offense committed whenever two or more persons, assembled and acting together, make any attempt or advance toward the commission of an act which would be a riot if actually committed.

solicitation of prostitution The crime committed by one who offers to buy or sell sexual services.

terrorizing A group of criminal offenses directed at persons because of race, religion, or other protected classification, which involve acts that would place reasonable persons in fear for their personal safety.

threat A criminal offense involving the making of a threat to commit a crime that will result in death or great bodily injury under circumstances that cause the person threatened to reasonably

be in sustained fear for his or her safety or the safety of his or her immediate family.

unlawful assembly The crime committed when two or more persons assemble together to do an unlawful act, or to do a lawful act in a violent, boisterous, or tumultuous manner.

Review Questions

1. Andy approaches Roberta, who is standing on a street corner, and offers her $50 for sex. Roberta, an undercover vice officer, arrests Andy. What crime should he be charged with? Assume that, rather than immediately arresting Andy, Roberta agrees to have sex for $50 and, arrests him after Andy hands her the $50. Roberta does not really intend to have sex with Andy. Has Roberta committed a crime? If so, what crime?

2. John secures business for several prostitutes and receives a commission on their earnings. Fred makes money by inducing runaway teenage girls to enter houses of prostitution. What crime is John committing? What crime is Fred committing?

3. Under the current view of the United States Supreme Court, is there a constitutional right to engage in homosexual conduct between mature, consenting adults?

   Is it a crime in California for adult homosexuals to engage in consensual sodomy or oral copulation?

4. When may a state regulate material that is thought to be sexually repulsive? What constitutional provision hinders governments from regulating such expression?

5. Does California law prohibit the private possession of obscene matter? Does it prohibit

the private possession of child pornography? Does California law prohibit the production, distribution, or exhibition of obscene matter?

6. Briefly describe the three offenses of unlawful assembly, riot, and rout.

7. What are *fighting words*? Are they protected by the First Amendment? Does any provision of the Penal Code criminalize fighting words?

8. Penal Code § 11411 makes it an offense to "terrorize" another person by the commission of certain specified acts. What does *terrorize* mean?

9. What are the four categories of offenses under Penal Code § 647, the disorderly conduct statute?

10. Clarence, who is nineteen years old, visits a liquor store and purchases a bottle of whiskey. The proprietor of the store does not request identification to determine Clarence's age. Who has committed a criminal offense in this situation?

11. Explain the relationship between the five schedules of drugs contained in the California Uniform Controlled Substances Act and the terms *narcotics* and *restricted dangerous drugs*.

12. Several types of drug offenses are discussed in this chapter. What are they?

Review Problems

1. The Happy Valley nudist colony is located in a remote mountain area. Its residents believe that nudism is healthful, both physically and emotionally, and wear no clothing while within the colony. Their unclothed way of life is not sexually motivated. Are these persons guilty of indecent exposure? Why or why not?

2. Martin purchases photographs depicting a ten-year-old boy and girl engaging in sexual conduct and keeps them in his home. Has Martin committed an offense? If so, what offense?

3. Milford is on trial for the kidnap and murder of a young boy. The jury finds him guilty of both offenses, but the judge, believing the

evidence insufficient, disregards the verdict and enters a judgment acquitting Milford of both charges. The local citizenry is in an uproar over the judge's action and a group of approximately 100 persons gathers outside the courthouse to protest. Caldwell, who is something of a firebrand, begins addressing the crowd and working them into a frenzy of anger. Then Caldwell shouts, "Let's show that judicial jerk that he can't live in this community if he's going to make it unsafe for our children. Let's go to his house right now and burn it to the ground!" Upon hearing these words, the crowd begins moving toward the judge's house. They are intercepted by the police and dispersed before they can carry out their intent to burn down the judge's house. The police release everyone except Caldwell, whom they charge with a crime. With what crime do you think they charge him?

4. A group of gang members captures a member of a rival gang and refuse to release him. They form a circle around him and then the gang leader pulls out a knife and says to the captive, "I'm going to cut your ears off." In fact, the leader does not intend to cut off the captive's ears, but wants the captive to believe he is serious. The captive does believe that the gang leader is serious and begins pleading for mercy. This amuses the gang members immensely, whereupon they release the captive. Disregarding the false imprisonment committed by the gang, what offenses has the gang leader committed?

5. Greg and Alex are both homeless and destitute. Greg sits on the sidewalk outside a shopping center with a sign that says "Homeless and destitute. Please help." Greg accepts money from persons who read the sign and want to give money to him. Alex is more aggressive than Greg. He approaches cars stopped at red lights and asks the drivers for money. If a driver refuses, Alex frequently argues with the driver in an attempt to make the driver to change his or her mind. If Alex is still unsuccessful, he usually insults the driver before moving on to another car. Are Greg's and Alex's begging techniques lawful?

6. Steve goes to a local playground and sits on a bench watching the children play. Eventually, he goes over to an eight-year-old girl who is playing by herself and attempts to strike up a conversation with her. His hope is to befriend her and, if opportunity permits, commit a sex offense with her. The girl rebuffs Steve's advances, telling him she is not allowed to talk to strangers. Steve falsely claims he is not a stranger because he knows the girl's parents. This causes the girl to be more friendly, and she begins talking to Steve. Steve then tells her that there is something really interesting in a nearby wooded area and tries to persuade her to go there with him. At that point, the girl's mother arrives on the scene and Steve rapidly departs. Despite Steve's unlawful intent, he did not at any time touch the girl. Has he committed an offense? If so, what offense?

7. Distinguish between the offense of driving a motor vehicle while under the influence of alcohol or drugs and the offense of driving a motor vehicle with a blood alcohol level of 0.08 percent or more.

8. Veronica is visiting her friend Jessica. The hour is late and Jessica suggests that Veronica spend the night. Veronica agrees and sleeps on the couch in the living room. Unknown to Veronica, Jessica is a drug dealer and keeps bags of cocaine under the couch cushions. Veronica notices a lumpiness under the cushions, removes them, and finds the bags of cocaine. Being somewhat innocent, Veronica does not realize or suspect that the bags contain illegal drugs. She even picks up a bag and examines it. Then she goes to sleep. Has Veronica committed the offense of unlawful possession of a controlled substance? Why or why not?

9. During a routine traffic stop, a police officer notices what appears to be an opium pipe lying on the passenger seat of George's car. George is alone in the car. On further examination, the pipe appears to contain opium residue. Assuming that the residue in the pipe is opium, with what offense or offenses can George be charged?

10. Paul owns a parcel of land in the countryside. He grows a crop of marijuana on the land. In a building located on the property, Paul processes the marijuana plants into usable marijuana. He also has a laboratory in the building in which he manufactures heroin. Paul sells the marijuana and heroin to drug dealers. What offenses is Paul committing?

Notes

1 *In re Smith* (1972) 7 Cal.3d 362, 366.

2 2 Witkin & Epstein, California Criminal Law, § 802 (2d ed., Bancroft-Whitney, 1988).

3 *Manual Enterprises, Inc. v. Day,* 370 U.S. 478 (1962) (opinion by Justice Harlan).

4 50 Am. Jur. 2d, *Lewdness, Indecency, etc.,* § 7 (1970).

5 *See Roth v. United States,* 354 U.S. 476, 487 n.20 (1957).

6 *Stanley v. Georgia,* 394 U.S. 557 (1969).

7 *See New York v. Ferber,* 458 U.S. 747 (1982).

8 *See* Penal Code § 313.1.

9 *People v. Kerrick* (1927) 86 Cal.App. 542, 551–52, quoted in 2 Witkin & Epstein, *supra* note 2, at § 889.

10 *See* CALJIC No. 16.230.

11 *See, e.g., Brandenburg v. Ohio,* 395 U.S. 444 (1969).

12 CALJIC No. 16.431.

13 CALJIC No. 16.262.

14 See Chapter 3 on personal status as an act.

15 2 Witkin & Epstein, *supra* note 2, at § 865.

16 *Id.,* at § 866.

17 2 Witkin & Epstein, *supra* note 2, § 876.

18 CALJIC No. 16.450.

19 *See* 2 Witkin & Epstein, *supra* note 2, at §§ 966–968.

20 CALJIC No. 16.831.

21 *People v. O'Neil* (1965) 62 Cal.2d 748, 755.

22 2 Witkin & Epstein, *supra* note 2, at § 976.

23 *People v. Vargas* (1973) 36 Cal.App.3d 499.

24 *See Health & Safety Code* §§ 11358, 11363, and 11390.

CHAPTER 8

Crimes Against the Public: Part II

Introduction

In addition to crimes against public morality and crimes against public order, crimes against the public include crimes against the administration of government and crimes against the environment. These categories of crimes are discussed in this chapter.

§ 8.1   Crimes Against the Administration of Government

Perjury

At common law, the crime of **perjury** was limited to false testimony under oath in a judicial proceeding. Under modern statutory law, perjury can be committed in other proceedings as well. Perjury is defined in Penal Code § 118. The section describes two types of perjury offenses: (1) lying under oath in a proceeding in which oaths are administered, and (2) lying in a statement made under penalty of perjury.

Elements   The elements of the offense of perjury are: (1) the making of a statement under oath or penalty of perjury; (2) in a case in which an oath may be administered or a situation in which a statement may be made under penalty of

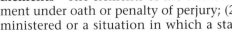

perjury; (3) willfully stating as true matter that is false; (4) knowledge that the statement is false; (5) materiality of the statement; and (6) specific intent to make the false statement under oath or penalty of perjury.[1]

Statement Under Oath or Penalty of Perjury   A statement is made under oath when the person making the statement swears, affirms, or solemnly declares that the statement is true before a person authorized by law to administer oaths. A statement is made under penalty of perjury when it is in writing and contains at the end a declaration to the following effect: "I declare under penalty of perjury under the laws of the State of California that the foregoing is true and correct."

Case in Which Oath May Be Administered or Situation in Which Statement May Be Made Under Penalty of Perjury   One may be convicted of perjury only if the false statement is made in a matter or proceeding in which statements under oath or penalty of perjury are required or authorized by law. For example, testimony at trial must be under oath, affirmation, or solemn declaration that the witness will testify truthfully. Written testimony submitted to a court in support of a motion must be by declaration under penalty of perjury or by affidavit (sworn written statement). In civil lawsuits, certain pleadings must be *verified*, that is, the truth of the facts alleged in the pleadings must be attested to by affidavit or declaration under penalty of perjury.

Willfully Stating as True Matter That Is False   The term *willfully* (as discussed elsewhere in this text) is defined at Penal Code § 7(1), and essentially means "purposefully." Thus, one who purposefully states as true a matter that is false commits this element of the offense. The matter may be one of fact or opinion.

Knowledge That Statement Is False   To be guilty of perjury, a person must both make a false statement and know that it is false. A false statement made on the good faith but mistaken belief that it is true is not a basis for a charge of perjury. Under Penal Code § 125, however, an unqualified statement of that which one does not know to be true is equivalent to a statement of that which one knows to be false.

Materiality of Statement   For an untruth to constitute a basis for perjury, it must be material. A false statement is material if it could affect the outcome of the proceedings. For example, if Jennifer, an eighteen-year-old witness in an automobile accident case, lies and says that she is seventeen years old, the false statement is probably not material because it is unlikely to have any effect on the outcome of the proceedings. If, however, Jennifer is the complaining witness in a statutory rape case, the lie would be material because one of the elements the prosecution must prove is that the victim is under the age of eighteen. In the second situation, Jennifer's false statement could constitute perjury.

Specific Intent   The specific intent necessary for perjury is different from the specific intent required for other specific-intent crimes. Usually, *specific intent* is defined as the intent to achieve a further unlawful purpose by the commission of the underlying unlawful act. The specific intent for perjury is the intent to testify or declare falsely under oath. Thus, from a mens rea standpoint, one commits perjury when he or she makes a statement under oath which he or she knows is false with the specific intent to make a false statement under oath.

Punishment   Penal Code § 126 provides that perjury is a felony punishable by imprisonment in the state prison for two, three, or four years.

Prosecutions for perjury are relatively uncommon. Truth is a complete defense to a charge of perjury. What is truthful, however, is not always easy to determine, and in most questionable cases prosecutors choose not to pursue the matter.

Subornation and Solicitation of Perjury

An offense related to perjury is **subornation of perjury**. Penal Code § 127 provides that: "[e]very person who willfully procures another person to commit perjury is guilty of subornation of perjury, and is punishable in the same manner as he would be if personally guilty of the perjury so procured." To be guilty of subornation of perjury, the defendant's design must be successful—the suborned witness must actually testify and commit perjury. The offense has a dual knowledge element. The defendant must know that the testimony the witness will give is false. The defendant must also know that the witness knows the testimony to be given is false because, unless the witness knows his or her testimony is false, he or she does not commit perjury. If the witness does not knowingly perjure himself or herself, the defendant has not committed the offense of subornation of perjury, despite the fact that he or she may have procured false testimony.

Penal Code § 653f defines a number of solicitation offenses, including **solicitation of perjury**. One who, with the intent that perjury be committed, solicits another to commit perjury is guilty of the offense of solicitation of perjury. If the witness actually commits perjury, the solicitor becomes guilty of subornation of perjury. If, however, the witness does not commit the solicited perjury, the solicitor remains guilty of the crime of solicitation of perjury. Solicitation of perjury is a felony-misdemeanor.

Bribery

As is true of perjury, **bribery** was a crime at English common law. Actually, bribery was initially a violation of biblical law, because it was wrong to attempt to influence judges, who were considered to be God's earthly representatives. Eventually, the crime was recognized by the courts of England.

Today, bribery is a statutory crime in the states and in the United States. In California, the crime of bribery is prescribed in a number of provisions of the Penal Code. The multiplicity of the statutory provisions is the result of the specificity of the Penal Code in defining the various categories of persons who may be bribed.

Bribery is committed by giving, offering to give, requesting, receiving, or agreeing to receive a bribe. Note that both the giving or offering of a bribe, and the requesting, receiving, or agreeing to receive a bribe, constitute bribery. Thus, in a case in which a bribe is offered and accepted, both parties commit the offense of bribery. If a bribe is offered, but not accepted, the offeror commits bribery. If a bribe is requested but not given, the requester commits bribery.

Persons who may be bribed, and the applicable statutory or other provisions, include: executive and ministerial officers of the government at the state and local levels (see Penal Code §§ 67, 67.5, and 68); members of the state legislature (see California Constitution, art. IV, § 15; Penal Code, §§ 85 and 86); judicial officers and jurors (see Penal Code §§ 92 and 93); witnesses (see Penal Code §§ 137(a) and 138); participants or officials in sporting events (see Penal Code §§ 337b through 337e); officers of financial institutions to influence the procuring of a loan or credit (see Penal Code §§ 639 and 639a); parents to influence them to consent to adoption of their child (see Penal Code § 273); and employees to influence them to reveal their employers' trade secrets (see Penal Code § 499c(c)).

Elements   The elements of the offense of bribery are: (1) a person gave, offered, requested, received, or agreed to receive a bribe; (2) the person to whom the bribe was given or offered, or the person requesting, receiving, or agreeing to receive the bribe, was one of the persons described in the bribery statutes; and (3) the person giving or offering the bribe, or the person requesting, receiving, or agreeing to receive the bribe, possessed the specific intent that the recipient would be corruptly influenced as to some act to be performed in his or her official or public capacity.[2]

Giving, Offering, Requesting, Receiving, or Agreeing to Receive a Bribe   A *bribe* is anything of value or advantage, or a promise of future value or advantage, asked for, given, or accepted, with a corrupt intent to influence a person in the discharge of his or her official or public duty (see Penal Code § 7(6)). The thing of value or advantage can be any form of benefit to the intended recipient, including money, property, or services. Also, the benefit can be realized by the recipient immediately or promised to be given in the future.

Intended Recipient Is One of the Persons Described in the Bribery Statutes
This element requires little elaboration. Refer to the previous enumeration of the bribery statutes. One attempting to corruptly influence a person not within the scope of one of the bribery statutes, and one not within the scope of the bribery statutes who seeks to be corruptly influenced, does not commit the offense of bribery.

Specific Intent to Corruptly Influence the Intended Recipient in His or Her Official Capacity   The word *corruptly* means that the bribe giver or receiver must specifically intend, by means of the bribe, to secure some benefit to himself or herself, or to another person, to which he, she, or the other person is not lawfully entitled. The specific-intent element also requires that the bribe giver or receiver intend that the receiver will be influenced in the performance of his or her official or public duty. If the intent is to influence the receiver to perform an act that is not within the scope of his or her official or public duty, the offense of bribery has not been committed.

Punishment   Each of the bribery statutes prescribes the punishment for violation of its provisions. Most forms of bribery constitute felonies. Bribery of a public official, if the bribe is accepted by the public official, also results in loss of public office and prohibition from holding office in the future.

The *Brigham* case involves the requesting and receiving of a bribe by a drivers' license examiner in Los Angeles. The defendant, Frank Brigham, was an examiner for illiterate license applicants. As such, he administered an oral examination and driving test to the applicants and, if they passed, issued them their drivers' licenses. Brigham was convicted under Penal Code § 68. At trial, the principal witness for the prosecution was Dock Berry, the person who paid the bribe to Brigham. Brigham requested that the jury be given jury instructions on accomplice testimony, which would have caused the jury to view Berry's testimony with distrust. Brigham's theory was that the offense of bribery requires an agreement between the bribe giver and receiver that, in consideration of the bribe, the bribe receiver's actions will be influenced. If such an agreement existed, argued Brigham, Berry must have been his accomplice. As will be seen, the appellate court did not agree. An interesting point illustrated by the case is the apparent value of a dollar in 1945, as compared to the value of a dollar today.

PEOPLE v. FRANK BRIGHAM
72 Cal.App.2d 1 [Dec. 1945]

This is an appeal from the judgment following a verdict of guilty.

Defendant was charged by information with the violation of section 68 of the Penal Code. The information alleged the offense substantially in the language of the statute. The evidence established that defendant was employed by the California Department of Motor Vehicles as Drivers' License Examiner at Los Angeles. ... The evidence further reveals that Dock Berry applied for a driver's license. ... After the oral examination he took an eye test, which he passed all right. Defendant then got the license and told him to get his car for a driving test. ... After driving, in the next block from the Motor Vehicle Department defendant told him to 'draw to the curb and stop' and then asked him what the license was worth to him and he replied 'a lot' because he had 'just paid a ticket' for not having one. That defendant told him he would let him have this license for $10.00. Witness told defendant he didn't have $10.00, but would go back to his wife and see what she had. Defendant then told him to drive around on the next block when he got out and told him to come back around three. He then drove around and picked up his wife, who gave him $5.00 and drove back where he left defendant and gave him the $5.00 telling defendant that he would bring him the other five the next evening; that defendant told

him 'You be god damn sure you bring it' .... That same evening he drove down Central Avenue until he saw the highway patrolmen, showed them the license, and then went home. The next morning the policemen came to his home. He went with them to Newton Street Police Station and they gave him five $1.00 bills. He went back to the Motor Vehicle Department and found defendant in his office .... Defendant went out and told him to wait. When defendant came back Berry told him he had brought him the money and he gave him the five one dollar bills."

* * *

It is contended by appellant that the court erred in refusing to instruct the jury on the subject of accomplice.

* * *

The evidence falls far short of establishing or even suggesting the so-called *agreement* contended for by appellant. But, appellant's argument, in effect, goes further; it assumes that, in order to complete the offense defined by section 68 of the Penal Code, there must be proof of an *"agreement."* And, that an *agreement* of necessity would constitute Berry the accomplice of the defendant.

* * *

Section 68 of the Penal Code, the violation of which appellant was adjudged guilty, is concerned with the bribe seeking executive or ministerial officer, employee of the state, county or city, etc. There is nothing in the language, when analyzed, to suggest any intention to include the victim as an offender. Here the culprit is the bribe seeker. And, the crime is complete when the individual described in the section "asks, receives, or agrees to receive any bribe." No action on the part of the victim, such as payment, delivery or otherwise, is necessary to complete the offense.

* * *

It may be conceivable that in some situations, under the provisions of either sections 67 or 68, the bribe seeker could be the accomplice of the bribe giver or vice versa but, by reason of the evidence in the within action, no such problem is presented. The crime was complete when defendant, in substance and effect, sought the bribe. There is nothing in the evidence to suggest that Dock Berry aided or abetted the defendant in seeking the bribe. Dock Berry, therefore, was not an accomplice; hence the instructions on that subject were properly refused.

* * *

For the foregoing reasons the judgment is affirmed

Commercial Bribery

Most of the bribery offenses mentioned in this section involve public officials or persons performing a public duty, such as jurors and witnesses. Penal Code § 641.3, added in 1989, establishes the offense of **commercial bribery**. The offense involves the bribery of an employee to use his or her position to benefit the bribe giver or some other person, accompanied by the specific intent to injure or defraud the employee's employer, the employer of the person giving the bribe, or a competitor of either employer. As with other forms of bribery, the offense may be committed by the employee, by the person offering the bribe, or both. The offense of commercial bribery is a misdemeanor, punishable by imprisonment in the county jail for not more than one year if the amount of the bribe is $1,000 or less. If the amount of the bribe is more than $1,000, the offense is a felony-misdemeanor, punishable by imprisonment in the county jail, or in the state prison for sixteen months, or two or three years. Section 641.3 does not apply in a situation in which the amount of money or monetary worth of the thing of value is $100 or less.

Tax Crimes

We have all heard the quip, "In life, only two things are certain, death and taxes." Tax revenues are the lifeblood of government. In the United States, people are taxed at the federal level, state level, and local level. These taxes come in many forms, including income tax, gift and estate tax, sales tax, and excise taxes. Tax laws apply to individuals, estates, and business entities.

All taxing authorities have statutes that impose both civil and criminal penalties for violation of tax laws. Many tax-related crimes are prescribed at both the federal and state levels. Crimes involving federal taxes are defined in the Internal Revenue Code, which is found in Title 26 of the United States Code. Crimes involving California taxes are defined principally in the California Revenue and Taxation Code, although some tax crimes are also found in the Penal Code. The focus in this section is on California tax laws.

Personal Income Taxes   The Revenue and Taxation Code prescribes a number of criminal offenses associated with the California personal income tax. Section 19701 provides that the following acts are misdemeanors: (1) failing to file a tax return; (2) failing to file required information; (3) filing a false tax return or information; (4) aiding, abetting, encouraging, or counseling another person to commit the foregoing offenses; and (5) willfully failing to pay any required tax or estimated tax on time. The offenses prescribed in § 19701 have been held to be strict liability crimes, that is, no criminal intent on the part of the offender is required.[3]

Under Revenue and Taxation Code § 19705, the following acts are felonies: (1) willfully making and signing a false tax return under penalty of perjury; (2) willfully aiding and abetting another in the preparation of a false tax return or tax-related document; (3) forging a false tax-related document; (4) removing or concealing goods or property with the intent to evade payment of income tax; and (5) destroying or falsifying records, or making false statements, in connection with a compromise tax agreement.

Revenue and Taxation Code § 19706 provides that it is a felony-misdemeanor to willfully fail to file a tax return or supply information with the intent to evade tax, or to make a false tax return with the intent to evade tax. A violation of § 19706 is punishable by imprisonment in the county jail for a period not to exceed one year, or imprisonment in the state prison, or by a fine of up to $20,000, or both such fine and imprisonment.

In the *Pedersen* case, defendant Wayne Pedersen was convicted of embezzlement and signing a false income tax return with intent to evade payment of taxes. In discussing the latter offense, the appellate court refers to Revenue and Taxation Code § 19406, the predecessor statute to § 19706. In *Pedersen,* the defendant managed a golf and country club owned by a corporation. The corporation was, in turn, owned by a limited partnership, of which the defendant was a limited partner. Pedersen used his position as manager of the golf and country club to withdraw approximately $40,000 from the corporation and partnership bank accounts for his personal use. He was convicted of embezzlement for this conduct. On appeal, he challenged his embezzlement conviction on the theory that, as a partner, he was a part owner of the funds and could not be convicted of stealing from himself. The court rejected Pedersen's argument. Pedersen's conviction under then Revenue and Taxation Code § 19406 was for failing to report and pay tax on the embezzled funds. The court rejected Pedersen's challenge of that conviction as well. Pedersen's conviction on the tax charge illustrates the fact that illegal income is taxable. More than one criminal has cleverly avoided prosecution for criminal activities, only to find herself being prosecuted for failing to pay tax on the income generated by such activities.

Employers are required to withhold income tax from the pay of employees and pay the withheld tax to the California Employment Development Department. A willful failure by an employer to do so constitutes a felony under Revenue and Taxation Code § 19708. A nonwillful failure to withhold or pay over withheld tax is a misdemeanor under § 19709.

Other sections of the Revenue and Taxation Code criminalize the failure to pay other taxes, such as bank and corporation taxes, sales and use taxes, liquor taxes, fuel taxes, and cigarette taxes.[4]

PEOPLE v. WAYNE LYNN PEDERSEN
86 Cal.App.3d 987; 150 Cal.Rptr. 577
[Nov. 1978]

Defendant, Wayne Lynn Pedersen, appeals from a judgment of conviction for embezzlement (Pen. Code, §§ 487, 503) and for signing a false income tax return with intent to evade the payment of taxes (Rev. & Tax. Code, § 19406).

* * *

Defendant's third contention is that the court erred in refusing to give his requested instructions to the effect that a partner cannot steal from his partnership. He argues that the trial court was bound by the doctrine of *stare decisis* to follow *People v. Foss* (1936) 7 Cal.2d 669 [62 P.2d 372], where the Supreme Court stated ...: "The rule that a partner cannot steal from the partnership is, of course, well settled ..." and *People v. Oehler* (1970) 7 Cal.App.3d 685 [86 Cal.Rptr. 703], in which Division One of this District Court of Appeal reiterated the rule, noted that it also applies to embezzlement, and then applied it to the case before it.

The People point to *People v. Sobiek* (1973) 30 Cal.App.3d 458 [106 Cal.Rptr. 519], where the court held that a partner may indeed embezzle from partnership funds.

* * *

We have examined the California Supreme Court cases involving the rule and find that the statements of the rule contained therein are dicta, thus we are not required to follow such statements. *People v. Oehler* ... states the rule, notes that it has been disparaged and is subject to exceptions but has not been overruled, and then applies it. This is hardly an enthusiastic embracement of the rule. We find the reasoning of *People v. Sobiek* ... persuasive, and see no reason to repeat or add to what was said in that opinion, and thus hold that the trial court did not err in refusing defendant's requested instructions.

* * *

Finally, defendant contends there was insufficient evidence to find him guilty of violating Revenue and Taxation Code section 19406, i.e., signing a false income tax return with intent to evade the payment of taxes. He first argues that had the court given his requested instructions on the defense of being a partner, he would not have been convicted of embezzlement, and a conviction on this charge probably would not have occurred. The logic of defendant's argument escapes us; the income must be reported whether or not it is obtained through embezzlement. In any case, we have already determined that the requested instructions were properly refused.

Defendant asserts that the income not reported on his tax returns was reimbursement for expenses. He argues that if a taxpayer makes an accounting to an employer for expenses and is reimbursed, it is not necessary to report either the expenses or reimbursement on the taxpayer's tax return. However, defendant fails to point to any showing that reimbursements were for expenses or that he made an accounting to his employer. There was ample evidence from which to conclude that no accounting of expenses was made; examination of numerous financial statements failed to reveal such an accounting. According to the testimony of a state income tax auditor, defendant did not report $32,054 in income in 1975. The jury apparently did not believe that this sum was reimbursement for unaccounted expenses. There was substantial evidence to support the conviction.

The judgment is affirmed.

Obstruction of Justice

Obstruction of justice refers to any number of unlawful acts. As a general proposition, any act that interferes with the performance of a public official's duties obstructs justice. However, the crime is most commonly associated with law enforcement and judicial officials. The Penal Code contains a multitude of offenses generally classified as crimes of obstructing justice.

Interference with Judicial Proceedings   A number of provisions of the Penal Code are designed to assure the integrity of judicial proceedings. The offenses of bribery of judicial officers, jurors, and witnesses were mentioned in the section on bribery. Other offenses include: offering false written evidence in judicial proceedings (see Penal Code § 132); willful destruction of evidence (see Penal Code § 135); acceptance of payment by a witness to a crime for providing information about the crime (see Penal Code § 132.5); and interfering with a victim or witness to a crime in an attempt to prevent or dissuade the victim or witness from reporting the crime or attending a trial and testifying (see Penal Code § 136.1).

Interference with Law Enforcement   Penal Code § 148(a) makes it a crime to resist, delay, or obstruct a public officer, peace officer, or emergency medical technician in the discharge of any duty of his or her office or employment. The offense is a general-intent crime. The courts have read a knowledge element into the crime: the defendant must know, or reasonably should know, that the person being resisted, delayed, or obstructed is a public officer, peace officer, or emergency medical technician. The offense under § 148(a) includes **resisting arrest.** In California, one does not have the right to resist an arrest by a peace officer, even if the person believes that the arrest is in error.

Other subdivisions of Penal Code § 148 make it a crime to take or attempt to take a weapon away from a public officer or peace officer during commission of an offense described in subdivision (a). In the *Wilkins* case, the defendant, Theodore Wilkins, was convicted of, among other things, taking a police officer's baton while obstructing him in the performance of his duties and forcibly resisting a police officer in the performance of his duties. Wilkins appealed, arguing that the jury had not been properly instructed by the trial judge. Specifically, claimed Wilkins, the offenses occurred inside his home after police officers

---

PEOPLE v. THEODORE ALBERT WILKINS
14 Cal.App.4th 761; 17 Cal.Rptr.2d 743
[Mar. 1993]

Officer Bruce Donaldson of the Marysville Police Department arrived at 131 Johnson Avenue to investigate a report of a domestic dispute. The victim, Pamela Wilkins, met Donaldson outside the residence. She was "very upset" and "crying uncontrollably." Her face and nose were red. Police Sergeant Kenneth Kauk arrived shortly thereafter. The victim stated she had been in an "altercation" with her husband (defendant) and he "had hit her a few times in the face." She told the officers her nose and neck were sore and requested them "to go inside the residence to arrest [defendant]."

The officers instructed the victim to remain outside. They intended to enter the residence and arrest defendant for corporal injury to a spouse. The officers, who were in uniform, knocked and defendant opened the door approximately one-quarter to

one-half way. He appeared calm. Donaldson informed defendant they needed to come in and talk with him. Defendant refused to allow more than one officer to enter. Donaldson said both officers needed to come in. Defendant attempted to close the door, but Donaldson blocked it with his foot and hand, forced the door open, and reached for defendant's wrist. Defendant backed away and began flailing his arms and yelling at the officers to get out.

Defendant retreated, Donaldson followed and Kauk got behind defendant and grabbed him by the arms in a "semi-bear hug." Kauk tried to calm defendant but defendant continued to yell at the officers and "lunged forward," grabbing Donaldson's baton. Holding the baton like a baseball bat, defendant "charged at" Donaldson and threatened to kill him. Defendant and the two officers crashed into a wall of the room, bounced off and fell against another wall. The victim, who by this time had entered the residence, shouted at defendant to stop and put down the baton. Defendant eventually lost control of the baton and it fell to the floor where the victim retrieved it.

During the fray, defendant "went for" Donaldson's gun. Donaldson pushed defendant's hand away and drew the gun out of its holster. Defendant again grabbed at the gun. There was more wrestling around until Kauk put pressure on defendant's neck and he stopped struggling. The officers then placed handcuffs on him.

Defendant still refused to cooperate and had to be dragged from the residence. Defendant refused to get into the police car and leg restraints were applied. When he tried to kick the officers, defendant was "maced," forcibly strapped onto an ambulance board and placed in the vehicle. Defendant was transported to a hospital for examination because he complained that his back hurt. During the trip, defendant told an officer: "When this is all over, I will see you in my cross hairs." When asked if this was a threat, defendant indicated: "Damn right, I'm threatening you."

* * *

Defendant was charged with infliction of corporal injury on a spouse (§ 273.5), taking a peace officer's weapon (baton) while obstructing him in the performance of his duties (§ 148, subd. (b)), attempting to take a peace officer's firearm while obstructing him in the performance of his duties (§ 148, subd. (d)), and forcibly resisting a peace officer in the performance of his duties (§ 69). ... The matter was tried to a jury which returned a verdict of guilty on all but the charge of attempting to take a peace officer's firearm in violation of section 148, subdivision (d). Imposition of sentence was suspended for three years and defendant was placed on probation.

* * *

Violation of section 148, subdivision (b) and violation of section 69 each require as an element that the officer at the time of the offense be engaged in the lawful performance of his duties. This means, where the offense is committed upon an officer effecting an arrest, the arrest must have been lawful.

The jury was instructed on the engaged-in-duty element as follows:

* * *

"A lawful arrest may be made by a peace officer without a warrant whenever the officer has reasonable cause to believe that the person arrested has committed a felony, whether or not a felony has, in fact, been committed.

* * *

Defendant contends this instruction is incomplete as it fails to address the additional requirement of exigent circumstances. ...

We agree with defendant. In order for the officers to have effected a lawful nonconsensual entry into the house to make a warrantless arrest, they must not only have had reasonable cause to believe defendant had committed a felony but there must also have been exigent circumstances justifying the officers' immediate entry without obtaining a warrant.

* * *

Having concluded the court erred in failing to instruct on the existence or not of exigent circumstances, we must decide whether reversal is required. Instructional error affecting an element of the offense warrants reversal unless we are able to conclude beyond a reasonable doubt that the jury's verdict was not affected by the error.

Under that standard, we conclude beyond a reasonable doubt the verdict would not have been more favorable to defendant had the jury been instructed on exigent circumstances as part of the necessary criteria for determining the lawfulness of the arrest. The evidence on that issue before the jury was substantial and it was not in conflict.

The officers arrived at the scene shortly after midnight in response to a report of domestic violence in progress. They encountered the victim on her porch. She had been assaulted and injured by her husband who was still in the house. The victim had fled from her house and was waiting outside for the police to arrive. The officers had probable cause to arrest defendant for felony violation of section 273.5. Had the officers withdrawn to obtain a warrant instead of acting immediately to arrest defendant, the victim would have been unprotected and exposed to risk of further physical harm. In light of this substantial, uncontradicted evidence, we are satisfied beyond a reasonable doubt that the instructional omission did not prejudice defendant, i.e., that the verdict of the jury would have been no different even had the erroneously omitted instruction been given. ...

The judgment is affirmed.

entered without a warrant. Entry of a home by police without a warrant is lawful only in exigent circumstances. In the absence of exigent circumstances, entry of the home by the officers would be unlawful, and the officers would not be engaged in the performance of their lawful duties while inside. Wilkins argued that the trial judge was required to instruct the jury to make a finding as to whether exigent circumstances existed, but failed to do so, thereby committing prejudicial error. The appellate court agreed that the trial judge had erred, but held the error to be harmless under the circumstances of the case.

Other obstruction-of-justice offenses that may be categorized as interference with law enforcement include: willfully resisting a peace officer in the discharge of the peace officer's duties resulting in death or serious bodily injury to a peace officer (see Penal Code § 148.10); falsely identifying oneself to a peace officer upon lawful detention or arrest by the peace officer, if the purpose of the false identification is either to evade the process of the court (e.g., an arrest warrant) or to evade proper identification by the officer (see Penal Code § 148.9); and refusal to come to the aid or assistance of a peace officer when lawfully ordered by the officer to do so (see Penal Code § 150). With regard to the last offense, certain peace officers, such as sheriffs and police officers, have the common-law authority to require citizens to aid them in a law enforcement situation. This is known as the *posse comitatus* power.

False Reports   A number of types of false reports are made criminal by the Penal Code. A false report of emplacement of a bomb in any public or private place is a felony-misdemeanor under § 148.1. A false report of the existence of an emergency is a misdemeanor under § 148.3, unless the report results in great bodily injury or death to another person, in which event the offense is a felony. A false report of the commission of a criminal offense is a misdemeanor under § 148.5. A false allegation of police misconduct made to a law enforcement agency is a misdemeanor under § 148.6.

Contempt

Contempt consists of acts or omissions in violation of court orders or that undermine or disrupt the judicial process. Two types of contempt are recognized: criminal contempt and civil contempt. Criminal contempt is contempt declared to be a crime under Penal Code § 166. Criminal contempt is prosecuted in the same manner as any other crime. Civil contempt is contempt that is not treated as a crime. Civil contempt is governed by Code of Civil Procedure §§ 1209 through 1222.

Criminal Contempt   Penal Code § 166(a) provides that commission of any of eight enumerated acts constitutes a misdemeanor. Briefly described, the acts are: (1) disorderly, contemptuous, or insolent behavior in court; (2) similar conduct in the presence of a court referee or a jury; (3) breach of the peace, noise, or other disturbance that disrupts court proceedings; (4) willful disobedience of any process or order lawfully issued by a court; (5) willful resistance to the lawful order or process of a court; (6) refusal to be sworn as a witness or, if sworn, refusal to answer a material question; (7) publication of a false or grossly inaccurate report of the proceedings of a court; and (8) presenting evidence of aggravating or mitigating circumstances in a criminal case in a manner not authorized by the Penal Code. Other forms of criminal contempt include violation by a convicted stalker of a court order not to contact the victim (see Penal Code § 166(b)), and violation by one convicted of domestic violence of a court order that he or she stay away from a named family member or the family dwelling (see Penal Code § 166(c)).

As previously stated, criminal contempts are charged and prosecuted in the same manner as other crimes.

Civil Contempt   The principal distinction between civil contempt and criminal contempt is that civil contempt is not charged and prosecuted as a crime. However, a person who commits civil contempt may be incarcerated. Some of the acts constituting criminal contempt may also be treated as civil contempt. Other forms of criminal contempt are not included within the civil contempt statutes. The civil contempt statutes, however, include certain acts that are not covered by Penal Code § 166.

Under Code of Civil Procedure § 1209, and subsequent sections, the following acts constitute civil contempt: (1) disorderly, contemptuous, or insolent behavior in court; (2) breach of the peace, boisterous conduct, or violent disturbance that disrupts court proceedings; (3) misbehavior by certain officials (sheriffs, attorneys, etc.) with respect to court proceedings; (4) abuse of process or proceedings of a court; (5) disobedience of any lawful judgment, order, or process of a court; (6) rescuing any person or property in the court-ordered custody of an officer; (7) unlawfully detaining a witness from appearing in court; (8) other unlawful interference with the process or proceedings of a court; (9) disobedience of a subpoena, or refusing to be sworn or answer as a witness; (10) failure to appear as a juror when summoned; (11) disobedience by an inferior court or tribunal of the order of a superior court; (12) failure of a parent to comply with a court order to provide care or support to a child; and (13) reentry onto property after being ejected by order of a court.

Certain forms of civil contempt may be committed in the presence of a judge, either in court or in the judge's chambers. Code of Civil Procedure § 1211 provides that these forms of contempt may be punished summarily by the judge. Other forms of civil contempt will necessarily be committed outside of court. In such cases, a hearing is scheduled to determine whether the offender is guilty of contempt. If the court finds the person guilty, it may impose a fine of not more than $1,000, imprisonment of not more than five days, or both.

Another civil contempt sanction is imprisonment to compel performance of an act ordered by the court. Section 1219(a) provides that the person may be imprisoned until he or she performs the act. An example would be imprisonment of a witness who refuses to testify after being ordered by the court to do so. Section 1219(b) makes an exception for sexual assault victims, providing that such persons may not be imprisoned for refusing to testify concerning the sexual assault.

The legislature also has the power to cite for contempt. The legislature, usually through committees, conducts hearings and other proceedings when considering bills and amendments to statutes. The contempt power serves the same function for the legislature that it does for courts. It furthers the orderly performance of legislative duties. Refusal to testify before a legislative body (usually a committee), to produce documents or other items, and disruption of a proceeding are examples of legislative contempt. The contempt power of the legislature is provided for in Government Code §§ 9405–9412.

§ 8.2 Crimes Against the Environment

With the modernization of the United States has come a threat to the environment. The air and water that people depend upon for sustenance have become polluted. Many species of flora and fauna have been lost and many more are threatened.

Modernization threatens the environment in several ways. By "developing" land, habitats are lost. Also, the use of dangerous chemicals and toxins has become commonplace. In many industries, toxic byproducts of manufacturing are common. Toxic wastes and substances pose use, transportation, and disposal problems. The release of dangerous substances into the air or into water endangers the health and safety of the public. It is estimated that air pollution kills 14,000 people annually in the United Sates, and that 100,000 workers die annually from exposure to toxins.[5] The increased population aggravates the problem. Greater numbers of people place greater stress on natural systems. Resources are depleted faster and nature's cleansing process becomes strained and less effective.

Today, there is a large body of environmental law that, to some extent, addresses these problems. The objective of environmental law is to create and maintain conditions in which man and nature can exist in productive harmony. Both the federal and state governments play a role in regulation of the environment, although the federal government has the larger part currently.

Several federal and state administrative agencies are charged with overseeing the enforcement and administration of environmental laws. Both federal and state law provide for imposition of administrative, civil, and criminal sanctions on environmental law violators.

There are two classes of environmental laws. One class of laws is intended to further the public health and safety. A second class of laws is intended to protect the environment itself, for its aesthetic, recreational, and other value. Of course, many laws serve both objectives.

Until recently, environmental offenses were not usually treated as criminal; rather, they were viewed as civil or administrative infractions. Enforcement agencies relied almost exclusively on administrative and civil processes to enforce environmental laws. Fines were the most common penalty sought by the government against offenders.

The belief that environmental violations are serious and should be prosecuted as criminal offenses is a recent development. For example, one of the most notorious environmental cases was Love Canal, where it was discovered in 1978 that the improper disposal of toxins was causing death and illness to local residents. An entire community was forced to relocate to escape the danger—yet not one person was prosecuted in the Love Canal case.

The fear of another Love Canal, or an accident like the one involving Union Carbide in Bhopal, India, where 2,000 people were killed and 200,000 people were injured, and the dangers posed by other environmental wrongs led Congress and the California legislature to strengthen environmental laws. The measures included added criminal sanctions. Relying on civil remedies alone had proved ineffective. Individuals were not being held accountable and corporations found it more cost-effective to violate the law and pay any fines than to comply with the law.

Therefore, although most violations continue to be handled through civil and administrative proceedings, the number of environmental criminal cases is increasing. Of the 500 largest corporations in the United States, one-fourth have been convicted of an environmental crime or have been subject to civil penalties for violating environmental laws.[6]

Unlike at common law, today business entities, such as corporations, may be charged with crimes. Fines and dissolution of a corporation are examples of the penalties that may be imposed. Charging corporations for environmental violations is common. Of course, individuals may also be charged with violating environmental laws and corporate employees may be charged for actions taken on behalf of a corporation. It is not a defense for an employee to claim that he or she was following a supervisor's directive, nor may it be a defense for the supervisor to claim that he or she is innocent because he or she delegated performance of the act to an employee. In *People v. Matthews* (1992) 7 Cal.App.4th 1052, for example, the president of a large corporation claimed that he could not be held responsible for environmental violations committed by employees at one of the corporation's facilities who were four management levels removed from him. The court rejected the executive's contention.

Some environmental crimes are strict liability. Others, and of course those that can be punished with jail time, require some mens rea, usually a knowing violation.

Several federal and California environmental laws contain criminal sanctions. Because of the federal predominance in the area of environmental law, federal environmental laws are discussed here with corresponding references to California laws.

Clean Water Act

The Federal Water Pollution Control Act, commonly known as the Clean Water Act (CWA),[7] regulates the discharge of pollutants into the nation's navigable waters. The CWA establishes a scheme of permits and reporting. The contamination of water with a pollutant, without a permit or exceeding the limits of a permit, is criminal under the Clean Water Act.

Both negligent and knowing acts are criminalized and may be punished with fines and imprisonment. A knowing act is punished more severely than a negligent act. Offenders who have acted negligently may be sentenced to one year in prison, whereas knowing offenders may be sentenced to three years in prison.[8] Fines may also be imposed for both, in addition to any civil remedies.

Also, the CWA contains a "knowing endangerment" provision. If a person violates the CWA with knowledge that the violation "places another person in imminent danger of death or serious bodily injury," the offender may be sentenced to up to fifteen years in prison, and significant fines may be imposed.

Finally, false reporting under the Act is criminal and may be punished by up to two years in prison, in addition to a fine.

The CWA provides that states may administer their own permit programs for discharges of pollutants into navigable waters.[9] The CWA also provides that states are free to adopt standards and limitations regarding discharges of pollutants and requirements respecting control or abatement of pollution, provided such standards, limitations, and requirements are at least as stringent as those established by the federal government.[10] California regulates discharges of pollutants into navigable waters, as well as other forms of water pollution, through the California Water Code. Responsibility for formulating and adopting state policy for control of water quality resides in the California Water Resources Control Board. Regional water policy is developed by nine regional water quality control boards.

Section 13387 of the Water Code criminalizes, under state law, violations that are criminal under the CWA, as well as violations of other provisions of the Water Code. The penalty structure is almost identical to that contained in the CWA.

Clean Air Act

The goal of the Clean Air Act (CAA) is to preserve air quality. It does this by regulating emissions of dangerous substances into the air.

Similar to the CWA in its criminal aspects, the CAA criminalizes negligent and knowing violations of its mandates, punishing the latter more severely.[11] Further, it contains knowing endangerment and false reporting provisions.

In California, air quality is regulated under the provisions of Division 26 of the Health and Safety Code, beginning with § 39000. The State Air Resources Board is responsible for controlling emissions from motor vehicles and coordinating, encouraging, and reviewing the efforts of all levels of government as they affect air quality. County air pollution control districts are responsible for control of air pollution from all sources other than emissions from motor vehicles. Violations of air quality standards can result in imposition of criminal sanctions or civil penalties.[12] Somewhat similar to the penal provisions of the Water Code, the penal provisions of Division 26 of the Health and Safety Code punish willful and negligent violations of air quality standards, as well as falsification of records.

Comprehensive Environmental Response, Compensation and Liability Act

The Comprehensive Environmental Response, Compensation and Liability Act (CERCLA) is commonly known as *Superfund*. The purpose of CERCLA is to identify and clean up existing hazardous waste sites.

Any person who knowingly falsifies or destroys any required record or who fails to report a spill of hazardous materials may be punished with fines and imprisonment.[13]

CERCLA provides that states are to share in the cost of cleaning up hazardous waste sites within their borders. In response to CERCLA, California enacted the Hazardous Substances Account Act in 1981. The Act, found at § 25300 *et seq.* of the Health and Safety Code, establishes an account that the state may use to pay for hazardous waste cleanup, including paying the state's share of cleanup costs under CERCLA. The account is funded through a number of sources, including fees paid by persons or companies disposing of hazardous waste in the state, monies received from the federal government in implementation of CERCLA, civil penalties collected from violators, and amounts recovered by the attorney general from persons or companies liable for pollution cleanup costs. The Hazardous Substance Account is administered by the State Department of Toxic Substances Control. The Act does not provide for criminal penalties, but does provide for civil penalties of up to $25,000 per violation for failure to comply with an order to remove or remedy hazardous substances, failure to report reportable releases of hazardous substances into the environment, intentional failure to make required reports, or intentional falsification of reports.[14] If a violation is of a continuing nature, each day constitutes a separate violation.

Resource Conservation and Recovery Act

The Resource Conservation and Recovery Act (RCRA) is similar to CERCLA in that they regulate the same subject matter: hazardous materials. However, CERCLA is an after-the-fact regulation intended to clean up existing sites, whereas RCRA is intended to regulate the day-to-day use, storage, transportation, handling, and disposal of hazardous materials.

There are no negligent violations under RCRA; rather, the mens rea for conviction of its prohibitions is knowledge. For example, the knowing transportation of hazardous waste to an unlicensed facility; the knowing treatment, storage, or disposal of hazardous waste without a permit; and the knowing violation of a permit are criminal and may be punished with both imprisonment and fines. As with the CWA and the CAA, knowingly endangering another enhances the punishment for a violation of RCRA.[15]

The California counterpart of RCRA is the Hazardous Waste Control Act (HWCA), found in Chapter 6.5 of Division 20 of the Health and Safety Code, beginning with § 25100. The HWCA establishes a state hazardous waste program in lieu of the federal program established in RCRA. RCRA specifically authorizes states to establish such programs. Under the HWCA, the State Department of Toxic Substances Control classifies and prepares lists of hazardous wastes, and regulates the storage, transportation, and disposal of hazardous wastes. Knowing violation of the regulations of the State Department of Toxic Substances Control pertaining to disposal, transportation, treatment, or incineration of hazardous wastes is subject to penalties ranging from civil penalties to fines to misdemeanor and felony convictions. Also criminalized under the HWCA are the falsification, alteration, or destruction of records relating to generation, storage, treatment, transportation, disposal, or handling of hazardous wastes.[16]

Occupational Safety and Health Act

The Occupational Safety and Health Act (OSHA) regulates the work environment of the American worker. The objective of the law is to create safe working conditions. There is a plethora of regulations enforcing this mandate.

Any employer who causes the death of an employee as a result of noncompliance with OSHA may be prosecuted and sentenced to imprisonment and a fine. Of course, the employer may also be liable under other criminal laws, such as negligent manslaughter.

Additionally, OSHA requires employers to notify their employees of potential exposure to dangerous chemicals and to provide information and resources to protect the employees. Failure to notify employees of this risk is a criminal omission under OSHA. False reporting is also a crime under this statute.

OSHA permits states to assume responsibility for occupational safety and health matters, and California has done so through enactment of the California Occupational Safety and Health Act of 1973, commonly known as Cal/OSHA. The statute is found at Labor Code § 6300 *et seq.* The California Department of Industrial Relations is the state agency responsible for administering Cal/OSHA; the Division of Occupational Safety and Health within the Department of Industrial Relations is specifically charged with this function. Violations of Cal/OSHA may result in imposition of civil penalties. Criminal sanctions are imposed for willful violations causing death or permanent injury to an employee; negligent, knowing, or repeat violations of Cal/OSHA safety standards; false statements and representations in reports or records required by Cal/OSHA; and failure to determine the presence of asbestos in a structure prior to performing construction work.[17] In addition, an employer may be prosecuted for manslaughter under Penal Code § 192 if an employee dies as a result of Cal/OSHA violations by the employer.

Toxic Substances Control Act

The Toxic Substances Control Act (TSCA) is the most comprehensive federal law concerning dangerous substances. The Environmental Protection Agency (EPA) is delegated considerable authority under the TSCA to regulate the sale, manufacture, development, processing, distribution, and disposal of toxic substances. Under the TSCA, the EPA is empowered to ban, or otherwise control, the production and distribution of chemicals. Asbestos and radon are examples of chemicals that the EPA has heavily regulated under the TSCA.

Any person who knowingly or willfully violates the TSCA concerning the manufacture, testing, or distribution of a chemical may be punished with both a fine and imprisonment. Also, false reporting, failing to maintain records, and failing to submit records as required by law are criminal acts under the TSCA.[18]

Unlike many federal environmental statutes, TSCA does not provide for state implementation of its provisions. States are free to regulate chemical substances, mixtures, or articles containing chemical substances or mixtures, provided that they do not regulate those regulated by the Environmental Protection Agency. Some exceptions are provided to this restriction, including a provision permitting states to request an exemption permitting the state to regulate a substance regulated by the EPA if the state requirement would provide a higher degree of protection from the risks posed by the substance than the federal regulation, and the state regulation would not unduly burden interstate commerce.[19] California regulates toxic substances under the provisions of the Hazardous Waste Control Act, found in Chapter 6.5 of Division 20 of the Health and Safety Code, beginning with § 25100 (this statute was addressed previously in the discussion of

RCRA). Because of the restrictive nature of TSCA, limiting regulation by the states of toxic substances that are already regulated by the EPA, a number of cases have arisen in which California regulations were challenged as intruding into regulatory areas reserved to the EPA. *People v. Todd Shipyards Corp.* is such a case. In that case, the defendants attempted to argue that California's regulation of PCBs under the Hazardous Waste Control Act was **preempted** by EPA regulations on the same subject. The appellate court, the Appellate Department of the Los Angeles Superior Court, disagreed.

PEOPLE v. TODD SHIPYARDS CORPORATION
192 Cal.App.3d Supp. 20; 238 Cal.Rptr. 761
[Apr. 1987]

In this case, we must decide whether federal law prohibits California from regulating the storage of a hazardous substance, polychlorinated biphenyls (PCB's). We conclude that the applicable federal law does not preempt California laws on the subject, and that, as a result, the trial court erred in sustaining defendants' demurrers to the complaint.

Defendants, officers and employees of Todd Shipyards Corporation and the corporation (hereafter Todd Shipyards or defendants), are charged with multiple counts of violating the California Hazardous Waste Control Act (Health & Saf. Code, § 25100 et seq.) specifically, transporting a hazardous waste without a permit, and storing a hazardous waste without a permit.

The trial court sustained defendants' demurrers to the unlawful storage counts. ... [T]he People appeal from the order sustaining defendants' demurrers.

* * *

On September 11, 1983, [Daniel] Fresquez [a senior environmental health officer in the Hazardous Waste Control Program of the Los Angeles County Department of Health Services] was called to a residential street in Van Nuys where fellow health inspectors showed him an oily black stain in the street, approximately one foot by three feet, and a long trail of the same substance approximately two blocks long. The substance was analyzed and found to contain an extremely hazardous level of PCB contamination.

Fresquez went to the residence nearest the spill and spoke to a man who told him that five days earlier, a friend had picked him up in a truck which contained drums of an oily material which was leaking into the street. This truck was traced to a company, Park Metals, in Chatsworth.

Fresquez went to Park Metals that same day and spoke to the owner, William Park. Park stated that he had picked up some transformers at Todd Shipyards in San Pedro and was in the process of draining the transformers, dismantling them, and disposing of the drained transformer oil.

Fresquez saw six large transformers at the location. The identification plates which usually indicate whether the transformers contain PCB's had been removed. Park was unable to produce the manifests which are required for the transportation of hazardous wastes by Health and Safety Code section 25160. Park did produce a routine shipping manifest which indicated that the transformers had been picked up at Todd Shipyards on August 31 .... Samples of a black, oily substance gathered from a large puddle near one of the transformers and from the truck which had been earlier identified revealed extremely hazardous levels of PCB's.

* * *

On October 14, 1983, Fresquez contacted the California Department of Health Services and learned that ... Todd Shipyards [was not] licensed to transport hazardous wastes. Fresquez also learned that [the company was not] licensed to treat, store, or dispose of PCB's or other hazardous wastes.

* * *

Defendants are charged with storing PCB's, a hazardous substance, in 1982 and 1983, in violation of the California Hazardous Waste Control Act (HWCA). (Health & Saf. Code, § 25191, subd. (d).) The storage of PCB's is also regulated by federal law. (15 U.S.C. § 2601 et seq.) Under California law at that time, hazardous wastes could be stored for 60 days without a permit. (Health & Saf. Code, § 25201; Stats. 1980, ch. 878.) Under federal law at the time, such wastes could be stored until January 1,

1984, or for a year without a permit. (40 C.F.R., § 761.76(a).)

The trial court, in sustaining defendants' demurrers to 277 counts of violating Health and Safety Code section 25191, subdivision (b)(2), ruled that California's hazardous waste storage regulations, as applied to PCB's, are preempted by the federal Toxic Substances Control Act (TSCA) (15 U.S.C. § 2601 et seq.). The trial court erred.

It is well settled that Congress may, within constitutional limits, preempt state authority by so stating in express terms. In areas that are traditionally part of the police powers of the state, preemption will be found only if the clear and manifest purpose of Congress is to preempt.

* * *

Section 2616 [of TSCA] says that if the EPA exercises its rule-making power, state laws are preempted, unless the state laws regulate the disposal of certain substances or the state laws are adopted under the authority of any other federal law. However, ... the federal legislation does not clearly decide the issues involved in this case. ...

No case has squarely decided whether the storage of PCB's is exempted from preemption .... The existing authority, however, supports our conclusion that California laws regulating the storage of PCB's are exempt from preemption.

* * *

There is no merit to defendants' contention that the federal and California rules governing PCB storage are in "actual conflict." An actual conflict will exist when it is impossible to comply with both federal and state law, or where the state law stands as an obstacle to the accomplishment of the full purposes and objectives of Congress. Defendants could have complied with both California and federal law by obtaining a permit, and it is beyond dispute that the purposes of the TSCA and HWCA are the same: to protect the public health and environment from exposure to certain chemical substances. (15 U.S.C. § 2601; Health & Saf. Code, § 25101, subd.(a).)

* * *

The trial court erred in sustaining defendants' demurrers to the complaint. ... The orders relating to defendants' demurrers are reversed.

Federal Insecticide, Fungicide, and Rodenticide Act

Chemicals that are lethal to pests may also be lethal or at least harmful to humans. In addition to being inhaled, pesticides find their way into human drinking water and food.

The Federal Insecticide, Fungicide, and Rodenticide Act (FIFRA) delegates to the EPA the task of regulating the manufacture, sale, distribution, and use of these chemicals. Some chemicals are forbidden; there are limits on the use of others. There are labelling and reporting requirements.

Knowing violations of any of FIFRA's requirements are criminal and may be punished with fines and imprisonment.[20]

FIFRA permits states to regulate the sale and use of federally registered pesticides or devices, provided the state regulation does not permit any sale or use prohibited by FIFRA. California regulates those who are in the business of recommending, selling, and applying pesticides. The applicable statutory provisions are found in Division 6 of the Food and Agricultural Code, beginning with § 11401. Division 7 of the Food and Agricultural Code, beginning with § 12501, regulates the use of agricultural chemicals. Violations of the provisions of Divisions 6 or 7, or any regulation issued pursuant to Divisions 6 or 7, are punishable as misdemeanors or through the imposition of civil penalties.[21] An intentional or negligent violation of Division 7 that creates, or reasonably could create, a hazard to human health or the environment is a felony-misdemeanor.[22]

Emergency Planning and Community Right-to-Know Act

Bhopal, India; Chernobyl; and closer to home, Three Mile Island—all three are reminders that accidents happen, or that the actions of one person, such as a terrorist, can cause a tragedy of enormous proportion. In both the Chernobyl and Bhopal incidents, there was no planning or preparation for an accident.

The purpose of the Emergency Planning and Community Right-to-Know Act is to better prepare the community in which a facility is sited for disaster and to inform the community about emissions of hazardous substances by the facility. The Act requires facilities that use or produce chemicals to report both accidental and routine releases of substances into the air or water. Further, facilities are required to provide local officials (e.g., hospitals) with information about the chemicals used.

Knowing or willful failure to give notice of a release may be punished by both imprisonment and a fine.[23]

There is no California equivalent to the Emergency Planning and Community Right to Know Act.

Endangered Species Act

The Endangered Species Act (ESA)[24] and the Marine Mammal Protection Act represent a different form of environmental law from those discussed so far. The purpose of these laws is not to protect the public health; rather, the intent is to preserve the integrity of the environment itself.

The ESA establishes a program of conservation of threatened and endangered species of plants and animals and the habitats where they are found. The law is co-administered by the Departments of Interior, Commerce, Agriculture, and Justice.

The ESA prohibits the sale, taking, possession, importation, and exportation of endangered species and the products of those species. Violations of the law are punishable by both fines and imprisonment.

Marine Mammal Protection Act

Similar to the ESA, the Marine Mammal Protection Act (MMPA)[25] is intended to protect and conserve marine mammals. The taking of such creatures without a permit by a U.S. flag vessel while on the high seas is a crime. The taking, possession, and trade of animals protected under the law is prohibited within the United States unless a permit has been obtained. Fines and imprisonment may be imposed on violators.

California Conservation Laws

Like the federal government, California has a number of statutes which have as their principal object the protection of the state's natural resources. These laws, referred to as *conservation laws,* are administered by a number of administrative agencies. Many of the state's conservation statutes are found in the Public Resources Code. Other codes, such as the Government Code, the Water Code, and the Fish and Game Code, also contain significant conservation provisions.

Among the many topics addressed by the conservation provisions in the California codes are the designation and protection of threatened and endangered species of animals and plants; the establishment of conservancies to protect environmentally fragile areas; development and use of coastal areas; preservation of agricultural land; conservation and development of energy resources; and water conservation.[26] Conservation laws are frequently enforced prospectively, through requirements for approvals or permits before activities regulated by the laws may be undertaken. Violations of conservation laws incur varying sanctions, ranging from injunctions against continuance of violations to imposition of civil penalties to, under some laws, imposition of criminal penalties.

One law with a significant effect on conservation of natural resources is the California Environmental Quality Act, found at Public Resources Code § 21000 *et seq.* The California Environmental Quality Act requires that an environmental impact report be prepared for any proposed project involving a public agency or the use of public funds, if the project may have a significant impact on the environment. Among the stated purposes of the Act are to provide the people of the state with clean air and water; enjoyment of aesthetic, natural, scenic, and historic environmental qualities; and freedom from excessive noise. It is also aimed at preventing the elimination of fish or wildlife species due to human activities and preserving plant and animal communities.[27] The Act does not set out criminal sanctions for noncompliance with its provisions, but does provide that public agencies involved in a project void any noncomplying determinations, findings, or decisions made with respect to the project and that all activity on the project related to the noncomplying determination, finding, or decision be suspended until the noncompliance is corrected.[28]

Key Terms

bribery The crime of giving, offering to give, requesting, receiving, or agreeing to receive anything of value or advantage, with a corrupt intent to influence the recipient in the discharge of his or her official or public duty.

commercial bribery The crime involving bribery of an employee with the specific intent to injure or defraud the employee's employer, the employer of the person paying the bribe, or a competitor of any such employer.

contempt Acts or omissions specified by statute that violate court orders or that undermine or disrupt the judicial process. Some contempts are crimes, whereas others are punished through civil proceedings.

perjury The crime involving the willful making of a material statement under oath or penalty of perjury that the maker of the statement knows to be false, with the specific intent to make the false statement under oath or penalty of perjury.

preemption The doctrine that once Congress has enacted on a subject, a state may not enact a legislation on the same subject.

resisting arrest The crime of resisting arrest by a peace officer under circumstances in which the arrested person knows or should know that the arresting person is a peace officer. In California, a person does not have the right to resist arrest by a peace officer, even if the person believes that the arrest is in error.

solicitation of perjury The crime committed by one who, with intent that perjury be committed, solicits another to commit perjury. If the person solicited actually commits perjury, the solicitor becomes guilty of subornation of perjury, a more serious offense.

subornation of perjury The offense involving the willful procuring of another to commit perjury. The person procured must actually commit perjury for the procuring person to be guilty of subornation of perjury.

Review Questions

1. What is the difference between the offenses of subornation of perjury and solicitation of perjury?

2. List the categories of persons specified in the Penal Code who may be bribed.

3. The governor is considering a number of candidates for a high-level executive position in the state government. Max, a wealthy construction contractor, secretly offers to build the governor an expensive home at no cost if the governor will appoint his son to the executive position. The governor refuses the offer. Has Max committed the offense of bribery?

4. What criminal offenses associated with the California personal income tax are prescribed by Revenue and Taxation Code § 19701?

5. Myra witnesses a murder committed by a prominent media personality. She reports the offense to the police, who immediately arrest and charge the offender with the crime. A media sensation follows, and Myra is soon contacted by Penelope, a writer, who wants to write a magazine article about the murder. Penelope offers Myra $10,000 for information about the murder. At the time Penelope makes the offer, it has been three weeks since commission of the offense. Can Myra accept the money and provide the information?

6. Jack, wanting to add some excitement to his afternoon, picks up the telephone, dials 911, and falsely reports that he has just seen a person break into the house across the street. The police arrive within minutes, sirens wailing and lights flashing. Has Jack committed a criminal offense?

7. What is the principal distinction between criminal contempt and civil contempt?

8. The California Assembly is debating a bill that would raise property taxes. Phil, a citizen who is adamantly opposed to the bill, is in the gallery observing the debate. Suddenly Phil stands up, begins shouting obscenities, and hurls tomatoes at the legislators. True or false: Phil cannot be charged with contempt because the offense of contempt applies only to court proceedings. Briefly explain your answer.

9. Where will one find California statutes setting forth water pollution offenses?

10. What acts involving air pollution are made criminal by the California Health and Safety Code?

11. Briefly describe the functions performed by the California Department of Toxic Substances Control in implementing the Hazardous Waste Control Law (found in Chapter 6.5 of Division 20 of the Health and Safety Code).

12. What types of violations of Cal/OSHA are criminal offenses?

13. What California code regulates the sale and use of pesticides and agricultural chemicals?

14. What procedure is used under the California Environmental Quality Act to protect the environment?

Review Problems

1. Hector is on trial for murder. Helga witnessed the killing and is on the witness stand testifying. The prosecuting attorney asks her, "Did you see the defendant kill the victim?" Helga knows that Hector has an identical twin brother, and is not certain whether the killing was committed by Hector or by his brother. She has a romantic interest in the brother, however, and does not want him to go to prison. Helga answers the prosecutor's question with an unqualified "Yes." Has Helga committed perjury?

2. Marisa is the president of ABC Corporation. She is aware of a valuable opportunity for the corporation to expand its business. Larry, the president of XYZ Corporation, a competitor of ABC Corporation, secretly offers Marisa $50,000 for her personal use if she will cause ABC Corporation to refrain from pursuing the corporate opportunity so that XYZ Corporation may pursue it. Marisa agrees and accepts the money from Larry. Have either Marisa or Larry committed a criminal offense? If so, what offense?

3. Mark owns and operates a dry cleaning establishment that employs five persons. For some reason, he is unaware that he is required to withhold state income tax from the pay of his

employees. Has Mark committed a criminal offense? If Mark knows he is required to withhold state income tax and willfully fails to do so, has he committed a criminal offense?

4. Paul, a police officer, receives a report on his car radio that a man has attempted to rob a local bank and has fled the bank on foot. The report provides a physical description of the offender. Paul drives up and down the streets in the vicinity of the bank and observes Buford, who fits the description of the offender. In fact, Buford is not the offender. Paul stops the car, gets out, and informs Buford that he is under arrest for attempted bank robbery. Paul is wearing his police uniform. Buford protests that he did not commit any such crime. Paul states that Buford is nevertheless under arrest. Buford then tells Paul that he will not allow Paul to arrest him and assumes a fighting stance. Paul then draws his service revolver and orders Buford to "spread-eagle" up against a nearby wall. Instead, Buford attempts to grab Paul's revolver, but is unsuccessful. Paul then forces Buford against the wall, frisks him, forcibly places Buford in the squad car, and takes him to the police station. Later that day, the actual offender is apprehended and Buford is released. Three days later, Buford files a formal accusation with the police department that Paul used excessive force when arresting him. The report is false. Has Buford committed any crime or crimes?

5. Brian has an obsession with Sylvia Silhouette, a popular movie actress. Brian has been convicted of stalking Sylvia. In addition to imprisoning Brian for the offense, the court ordered him not to contact her for any reason. After being released from prison, Brian begins telephoning Sylvia. What type of contempt is Brian committing by disobeying the court's order? What is the maximum sentence he can receive for this offense?

6. What procedure is used to determine whether a person is guilty of civil contempt when the contemptuous act is committed outside the presence of a judge? What is the maximum penalty a court may impose if it finds a person guilty of civil contempt?

7. The California Water Code and the federal Clean Water Act categorize violations of their provisions in the same manner. The penalties prescribed by both the California and federal laws are almost identical. Briefly describe the categorization of violations and the penalty structures under the two laws.

8. Bart owns a manufacturing plant in which a number of hazardous conditions exist. All of these conditions violate Cal/OSHA. Bart is aware of the conditions and the hazards they present to his employees. He is also aware that the conditions are in violation of Cal/OSHA. Because of a desire to save money, Bart does not remedy the conditions. One day, an employee is killed as a direct result of one of the hazardous conditions. Can Bart be charged with a criminal offense or offenses? If so, with what offense or offenses can he be charged?

9. Assume that the federal Environmental Protection Agency regulates the use of asbestos in the construction of buildings under the authority of the Toxic Substances Control Act (TSCA). Assume further that California enacts regulations under the Hazardous Waste Control Law which also regulate the use of asbestos in the construction of buildings. California enacts the regulations without having obtained an exemption from the Environmental Protection Agency permitting the state to regulate this type of asbestos use. If a contractor is prosecuted in a California court for violation of the California regulations, what defense is she likely to raise?

Notes

[1] CALJIC Nos. 7.20 and 7.21.

[2] *See, e.g.,* CALJIC No. 7.00 and No. 7.02.

[3] *People v. Allen* (1993) 20 Cal.App.4th 846; *People v. Jones* (1983) 149 Cal.App.3d Supp. 41.

[4] For a discussion of California tax crimes, *see generally* 2 Witkin & Epstein, *California Criminal Law,* §§ 1232–1236 (2d ed. Bancroft-Whitney 1988).

[5] Michael Norton, *Federal Environmental Criminal Law Enforcement in the 1990's* 1 (ALI-ABA, C868, 1993).

[6] *Id.*

[7] 3 U.S.C. § 1319(a).

[8] 33 U.S.C. § 1319(c).

[9] 33 U.S.C. § 1342.

[10] 33 U.S.C. § 1370.

[11] 42 U.S.C. § 7413.

[12] Cal. Health & Safety Code §§ 39674, 42400–42409.

[13] 42 U.S.C. § 9603.

[14] Health & Safety Code §§ 25359.2, 25359.4, 25367.

[15] 42 U.S.C. § 6928.

[16] Health and Safety Code §§ 25189.2, 25189.5, 25189.7, 25190, 25191.

[17] Labor Code §§ 6425, 6423, 6426, 6505.5.

[18] 15 U.S.C. §§ 2614–2615.

[19] 15 U.S.C. § 2617.

[20] 7 U.S.C. § 136l.

[21] Cal. Food & Agric. Code § 11891 *et seq.,* and § 12996 *et seq.*

[22] Food & Agric. Code § 12996(b).

[23] 42 U.S.C. § 11045.

[24] 16 U.S.C. §§ 1531–1543.

[25] 16 U.S.C. §§ 1361–1384, 1401–1407.

[26] California conservation laws are discussed in 50 *Cal. Jur. 3d,* "Pollution and Conservation Laws," pt. III. *See also* 34 *Cal. Jur. 3d,* "Fish and Game," § 51.

[27] Pub. Res. Code § 21001.

[28] Pub. Res. Code § 21168.9.

CHAPTER 9

Parties and Inchoate Offenses

OUTLINE

§ 9.1   Parties to Crimes

Not all crimes are committed by only one person. Not all planned crimes are completed. This chapter examines the two issues of group criminal responsibility and uncompleted crimes. Those who participate in a crime are referred to as *parties*. Uncompleted crimes are referred to as *inchoate crimes*.

At common law, there were four parties to crimes: principals in the first degree; principals in the second degree; accessories before the fact; and accessories after the fact.

Consider the following example. A, B, and C plan a bank robbery. C works in the bank and obtains diagrams of the bank's security system. C is unwilling to actually go to the bank and participate in the robbery, but meets ahead of time with A and B to teach them about the bank's security system and how to break into the bank. When the day of the planned bank robbery arrives, A and B go to the bank after it has closed. B waits outside in the car with the engine running for a quick getaway. A breaks into the bank and successfully steals a quantity of money. A accidentally trips an alarm as he is leaving the bank, whereupon A and B flee to the house of D, a friend of A. D has had no previous involvement in the robbery or its planning. When A and B explain their predicament, D hides them in his basement for three days to assist them in avoiding apprehension by the police. At the end of the three days, the police discover the whereabouts of A and B and arrest them. The police also arrest D. Based on information given to the police by A, the police apprehend C.

Under the common law, a person who committed the actus reus of the crime was a *principal in the first degree*. In the foregoing example, A broke into the bank and stole the money. A, having committed the actus reus of bank robbery, would be a principal in the first degree.

A *principal in the second degree* was a person who aided, abetted, counseled, assisted, or encouraged the principal in the first degree during the commission of the crime. To be a principal in the second degree, one must have been present at the scene of the crime. "Constructive" presence was sufficient, i.e., the person could be physically absent from the crime scene, but aid from a distance. In the foregoing example, B, although not in the bank, was constructively present because he aided A in the commission of the offense by waiting outside in the getaway car with the engine running for the purpose of facilitating a fast getaway. B would be a principal in the second degree.

An *accessory before the fact* was a person who aided, counseled, encouraged, or assisted in the preparation of a crime, but was neither physically present at the crime scene at the time of commission of the offense nor aided from a distance. In the preceding example, C would be an accessory before the fact.

Finally, an *accessory after the fact* was a person who had no involvement in the offense as a principal or accessory before the fact, but who intentionally aided or assisted an offender to evade apprehension. In the foregoing example, D would be an accessory after the fact.

Under the common law, principals of the first and second degree and accessories before the fact were punished equally. Accessories after the fact were punished less severely than the other three classes of parties.

Principals

California has abrogated the distinctions between and among principals of the first and second degree and accessories before the fact.[1] All are now simply termed **principals** and all are liable for the same punishment for the crime committed. Penal Code § 31 defines *principals* in the following language (bracketed notations have been added to refer to the former common-law party classifications):

> All persons concerned in the commission of a crime, whether it be felony or misdemeanor, and whether they directly commit the act constituting the offense [principal in the first degree], or aid and abet in its commission [principal in the second degree], or, not being present, have advised and encouraged its commission [accessory before the fact] … are principals in any crime so committed.

The concept of "aiding and abetting" in the statutory definition has received some judicial interpretation. A person aids and abets the commission of a crime when he or she aids, promotes, encourages, or instigates the commission of the crime: (1) with knowledge of the unlawful purpose of the perpetrator, and (2) with the intent or purpose of committing, encouraging, or facilitating the commission of the crime.[2] Knowledge of the unlawful purpose of the perpetrator, alone, is not sufficient. To be an aider and abettor (i.e., a principal, formerly in the second degree), one must possess the intent or purpose of committing, encouraging, or facilitating the commission of the crime. Also, mere presence at the scene of a crime which does not assist the commission of the crime is not sufficient to constitute one an aider and abettor. Consider the following example. Joe and Sam go to a liquor store and, before they enter, Sam tells Joe, "I'm going to rob this place." Joe enters the store with Sam and Sam, true to his word, commits the robbery. Joe does nothing to assist Sam in the commission of the offense. He also does nothing to prevent Sam from committing the crime. Joe had knowledge that Sam was going to commit the offense and was present when Sam committed it. Joe is not a party to the crime as an aider and abettor, however, because he did not possess the intent or purpose of committing, encouraging, or facilitating the commission of the crime. In short, Joe did not possess criminal intent.

Accessories

Parties formerly termed "accessories after the fact" are now called simply **accessories**. Penal Code § 32 defines *accessory* as follows:

> Every person who, after a felony has been committed, harbors, conceals, or aids a principal in such felony, with the intent that said principal may avoid or escape from arrest, trial, conviction or punishment, having knowledge that said principal has committed such felony or has been charged with such felony or convicted thereof, is an accessory to such felony.

As should be apparent from the language of § 32, one may be an accessory only to a felony. There is no offense of being an accessory to a misdemeanor. Being an accessory is an offense separate and distinct from the underlying felony. In other words, it is an offense in and of itself: the offense of being an accessory to a felony. Penal Code § 33 prescribes the punishment for the offense of being accessory to a felony as a fine of up to $5,000, imprisonment in the state prison or in a county jail not exceeding one year, or by both such fine and imprisonment, unless a different punishment is prescribed by a specific statute.

Accomplices

The term **accomplice**, in California law, is not used to describe a party to a crime. The only significance of the term is evidentiary. Penal Code § 1111 requires that, if testimony of an accomplice is used by the prosecution in a criminal trial, the defendant may not be convicted based on such testimony unless the testimony is independently corroborated. An *accomplice* is defined in Penal Code § 1111 as "one who is liable to prosecution for the identical offense charged against the defendant on trial in the cause in which the testimony of the accomplice is given." An *accomplice,* thus defined, is a principal to the crime for which the defendant is being tried, and the person's status as an accomplice becomes material only if his or her testimony is going to be used in an effort to convict the defendant.

§ 9.2 Inchoate Crimes

Not all planned crimes are completed. Because of the danger posed by substantial planning, accompanied by an intent to carry out a plan, some uncompleted crimes may be punished.

By punishing inchoate acts, the deterrent purpose of the criminal justice system is furthered. If the rule were otherwise, law enforcement officials would have no incentive to intervene in a criminal enterprise before it is completed. By punishing attempt, conspiracy, and solicitation, an officer may prevent a planned criminal act from occurring without risking losing a criminal conviction.

Attempt

An **attempt** to commit a crime is defined in Penal Code § 21a, as follows: "An attempt to commit a crime consists of two elements: a specific intent to commit the crime, and a direct but ineffectual act done toward its commission." The specific-intent element of attempt is not conceptually difficult: the defendant acts with the intent to achieve a specific result. The second element—a direct but ineffectual act done toward commission of the crime—is more problematic. The difficulty lies in the fact that the law does not punish mere preparation for the commission of a crime. Thus, in an attempt case, the question becomes: Did the defendant's actions amount to more than mere preparation? That is, did they constitute a "direct but ineffectual act done toward commission of the crime"? There is no simple test for determining when a defendant's acts cross the line between preparation and attempt. Some examples may prove illustrative. First, suppose that George, intending to kill Sue, fires a rifle at Sue from across the street. Just as George pulls the trigger, a car passes between him and Sue and deflects the bullet, causing it to miss Sue. Next, move back in time to the point at which George took up a position across the street from which he could shoot Sue. Before he was able to shoot at Sue, a police officer arrived on the scene, and George was afraid to fire at Sue when she walked by. Finally, moving farther back in time, assume that the day before George was going to kill Sue, he went to a sporting goods store and purchased the rifle and a box of cartridges for the purpose of using them to murder Sue the next day. On his way home from the sporting goods store, George was involved in an automobile accident and was hospitalized. As a result of his hospitalization, George was unable to go to the scene of the intended crime the next day and commit the intended murder of Sue.

The question in each of the foregoing scenarios is: Did George's act amount only to preparation to commit the murder of Sue, or did it amount to an attempt? The first scenario—George's firing at Sue with deflection of the bullet by a car—is the easiest to analyze. Clearly, George's act constituted a "direct but ineffectual act" done toward commission of the intended crime. Because George possessed the intent to kill Sue, his firing of the rifle constituted attempted murder.

What about the second scenario? George takes up a position from which to shoot at Sue, but desists because of the unexpected arrival of a police officer. Assume, for purposes of this example, that but for the arrival of the police officer, George would have fired at Sue. Has George's taking up of the firing position crossed the line between mere preparation to commit murder and become an attempt to commit murder? The law, unfortunately, is not entirely clear on this point, but the answer is probably yes. As was stated by one California court:

the acts proximately leading up to the consummation of the intended crime need not include the last proximate act for its completion. It is sufficient if the overt acts reach far enough toward the accomplishment of the intended offense to amount to the *commencement* of its consumption.[3]

In the scenario, the last proximate act for completion of the murder of Sue would have been the firing of the rifle by George. If George's taking up of the firing position were considered to constitute commencement of the consummation of the killing of Sue, or an act beyond commencement of the consummation of the offense, then George has crossed the line from mere preparation and has committed attempted murder of Sue, despite the fact that he did not fire the rifle. In fact, a number of California judicial decisions have held that a defendant committed attempt despite the fact that he or she desisted from completion of the intended crime because of the unexpected arrival of a police officer or other person.

The third scenario, George's purchasing of the rifle and cartridges, is subject to the same analysis as the second. One factor that becomes significant when the defendant's act is remote from actual consummation of the intended offense is the nature of the defendant's intent at the time of the act. If the defendant has formed a fixed and irrevocable intent to commit the offense at the time of the remote act, some courts would view the act as an attempt despite its remoteness from the completed offense. Put another way, such courts would view George's purchasing of the rifle and cartridges as the commencement of the act of killing Sue. Other courts, however, would hold George's act to constitute mere preparation. The third scenario is the most conceptually difficult of the three, and is susceptible to more than one answer.

Certain provisions of the Penal Code address attempts to commit particular crimes. Section 181 is such a provision, providing, in pertinent part: "Every person who ... buys, or attempts to buy, any person ... is punishable by imprisonment in the state prison for two, three, or four years." In *People v. Delvalle*, defendant Luis Delvalle was convicted of attempting to buy a four-year-old girl from her mother. Delvalle appealed his conviction, asserting that his actions did not constitute attempt. The appellate court's decision is illustrative of the analysis used by California courts in attempt cases.

Two defenses often raised in the context of attempt are legal and factual impossibility. **Legal impossibility** refers to the situation in which the act intended by the defendant is actually lawful, despite the defendant's belief that it is unlawful. The law of attempt does not punish one for attempting to do a lawful thing, even if the person has an evil mind. For instance, John believes that driving on a Sunday is a crime. He attempts to start his car on a Sunday for the purpose of driving it, but the ignition fails. John has not committed the crime of attempted driving of a car on Sunday because the intended act is not a crime.

Factual impossibility, in contrast, involves the situation in which the act intended by the defendant is a crime, but the circumstances are such that it cannot be committed. Unlike legal impossibility, factual impossibility is not a defense to the crime of attempt. Suppose, in the George-Sue scenario, that Sue arranges department store windows. George fires at a mannequin, thinking it is Sue. George has committed attempted murder of Sue because the act that George intended to commit is a crime.

Another defense sometimes raised in attempt cases is **voluntary withdrawal**. Voluntary withdrawal occurs when the defendant decides not to complete the crime. Voluntary withdrawal is not a valid defense to the crime of attempt. If the defendant's acts have reached the point at which they constitute attempt, voluntary withdrawal thereafter does not erase the completed attempt. If the defendant voluntarily withdraws before his or her acts amount to attempt—i.e., during the mere preparation stage—no crime has been committed.

Unless otherwise prescribed by a particular provision of the Penal Code, such as § 181 discussed in the *Delvalle* case, the punishment for the crime of attempt is set forth in Penal Code § 664. Most attempts are punishable by one-half of the punishment authorized for the offense the defendant attempted to commit. Section 664 prescribes heavier penalties for attempts to commit crimes punishable by life imprisonment or death.

PEOPLE v. LUIS ALBERTO MOLINA DELVALLE
26 Cal.App.4th 869; 31 Cal.Rptr.2d 725
[July 1994]

KLEIN, P.J.—Defendant and appellant Luis Alberto Molina Delvalle appeals the judgment (order granting probation) entered following his conviction of two counts of attempting to buy a person. (Pen. Code, § 181.)

* * *

[T]he evidence established that Orozco lived in Lynwood. Her four-year-old daughter attended kindergarten a short distance from their home. Orozco walked the child to and from school each day. On July 14, 1992, at 11:30 A.M., Orozco saw Delvalle outside the school in his car. Orozco had never seen Delvalle before. He called to Orozco and "asked [her] to give him the girl." Orozco said " 'No,' " and continued walking. Orozco recalled his exact words were " 'Could you give me the girl?' " Delvalle then asked "[i]f [Orozco] would sell her to him." When Orozco again said no, Delvalle offered her money although he did not say how much. Orozco again said no and walked home "fast."

Delvalle followed Orozco and her child home in his car and repeated his demands two or three more times that day. Orozco testified, "All the time he would tell me to give him the girl." "The first time [he said] to give him the girl. To sell her to him. And how much I wanted [¶] I went towards my house. When I arrived to my house—he was parked in front of the house. I didn't get to my house. I went inside my neighbor's house, right by my house. I was afraid to go to my house. Because he was parked there."

Two days later, on July 16, 1992, Orozco again walked her daughter home from school and saw Delvalle driving the same car. Orozco tried to avoid Delvalle but he drove up to her and again asked Orozco to sell the child to him. He also told Orozco "to give him the girl." Delvalle asked Orozco for the girl twice that day. ...

On Monday, July 20, 1992, Delvalle followed Orozco and the child home from school in a blue pickup truck and said "the same words, if I would give him the girl, or if I would sell her to him." Orozco continued walking quickly. Delvalle drove ahead of them and moved over in the truck to the passenger door which was closest to the sidewalk. Orozco told her daughter to run. Delvalle asked Orozco for the child three or four times that day.

* * *

Orozco reported the matter, and on July 23, 1992, sheriff's Detective Elizabeth Smith walked home with Orozco and her child. Delvalle drove next to them and stopped. Orozco pointed Delvalle out to Smith. Delvalle looked at Smith with a startled expression and drove away quickly. Smith made a radio broadcast and Delvalle was arrested.

* * *

Delvalle contends his conduct did not "establish an 'attempt' under ... section 181, as his requests, if anything, amounted to nothing more than a mere 'solicitation' to purchase the minor child." He claims "the evidence revealed unsolicited, harassing conduct by appellant" but not an 'attempt' to buy another person ... ." He asserts he never got out of his car or displayed any money. He contends his conduct amounts to nothing more than preparation and does not constitute an attempt.

This claim lacks merit.

" 'It is settled that an attempt to commit a crime is compounded of two elements, viz., intent and a direct ineffectual act done toward its commission. It is equally well settled that there is a material difference between the preparation antecedent to an offense and the actual attempt to commit it. The preparation consists of devising or arranging the means or measures necessary for the commission of the offense, while the attempt is the direct movement toward its commission after the preparations are made. In other words, to constitute an attempt the acts of the defendant must go so far that they would result in the accomplishment of the crime unless frustrated by extraneous circumstances." (*People v. Memro* (1985) 38 Cal.3d 658, 698 [214 Cal.Rptr. 832, 700 P.2d 446].)

"[A]n attempt, as distinguished from acts preparatory to that offense, requires 'some appreciable fragment of the crime ... accomplished.' However, '[a]n overt act need not be the ultimate step toward the consummation of the design; it is sufficient if it is the first or some subsequent act directed towards that end after the preparations are made.' " (*People v. Memro, supra,* 38 Cal.3d at p. 698.)

* * *

The pertinent portion of section 181 declares it a felony to buy or attempt to buy any person. The evidence produced at trial, viewed in the light most favorable to the judgment, clearly was sufficient to allow a rational trier of fact to find Delvalle guilty beyond a reasonable doubt.

Delvalle repeatedly approached Orozco and asked her to give or sell the child to him. Orozco testified Delvalle was frightening and clearly was referring to her child. This conduct went beyond mere preparation. But for Orozco's resolute refusal of Delvalle's overtures, the crime would have been committed.

* * *

Each case must be decided on its own merits. "[N]one of the various 'tests' used by the courts can possibly distinguish all preparations from all attempts." (*People v. Memro, supra,* 38 Cal.3d at p. 699.) On the facts presented here, the trial court properly could conclude Delvalle had violated section 181.

* * *

The evidence supports Delvalle's conviction of two counts of attempting to buy a person ....

Conspiracy

The offense of **conspiracy** is covered in Penal Code §§ 182 through 184. Section 182 criminalizes conspiracies but does not actually define the term *conspiracy*. The definition is taken from case law, and is stated in CALJIC No. 6.10, as follows:

> A conspiracy is an agreement entered into between two or more persons with the specific intent to agree to commit a public offense and with the further specific intent to commit such offense, followed by an overt act committed in this state by one or more of the parties for the purpose of accomplishing the object of the agreement.

Agreement   The actus reus of conspiracy is an agreement between two or more persons to accomplish a criminal act, followed by an overt act in furtherance of the agreement. (The overt act requirement is discussed later.) The agreement need not be a formal written or oral agreement. Nor must it be shown that the parties met together to discuss the unlawful design. There must, however, be a mutual understanding between the parties regarding accomplishment of the unlawful objective.

Intent   The mens rea of conspiracy involves two types of specific intent: (1) a specific intent to agree to commit a criminal act, and (2) a specific intent to commit the criminal act. As to the first type of specific intent, because the actus reus of conspiracy is the agreement, there must be an intent on the part of the parties to enter into the agreement. The second type of specific intent is the intent to accomplish the criminal objective of the conspiracy. Both types of specific intent must be proved by the prosecution to obtain a conviction on a conspiracy charge.

Intent is to be distinguished from mere knowledge when determining whether a person is a conspirator. One who furnishes legal goods or services, knowing that the recipient will use them for illegal purposes, does not become a co-conspirator with the other person unless, in addition to the knowledge, the furnisher intends to further the unlawful purpose of the other person. For example, one who operates a telephone answering service, knowing that some of his or her clients are prostitutes, does not engage in a conspiracy with the prostitutes unless he or she intends to further the unlawful activities of the prostitutes.

Parties   Because the essence of conspiracy is an agreement, at least two persons are required for commission of the offense. This requirement has produced some legal principles unique to the crime of conspiracy. One such principle is that at least two defendants must be convicted on a conspiracy charge, or none of them can be convicted. If, for example, Phil and Jeff are tried for conspiracy, and Phil is acquitted, Jeff cannot be convicted. If Jeff is convicted, the conviction will be reversed on appeal. A similar principle holds that, if the convictions of all defendants but one are reversed on appeal, or all defendants but one are granted a new trial, the conviction of the remaining defendant is invalid. If there are more than two defendants, and at least two of them are convicted, and remain convicted after appeal, those convictions will stand. Another principle, known as **Wharton's Rule**, provides that, if an offense requires two persons for its commission, and only two defendants are involved, they cannot be charged with conspiracy to commit the offense, although they may be charged with commission of the offense itself. If more than two defendants are involved, they may be charged both with conspiracy and with the substantive offense. Bribery is a good example. Recall that one form of bribery involves the actual payment of a bribe to another. This offense requires two persons for its commission. Applying Wharton's Rule, if only two persons are involved in a bribery offense—the giver and the receiver of the bribe—they may be charged with bribery, but not with conspiracy to commit bribery. If, however, two persons agree to bribe a third person, and actually pay the bribe to the third person, they may be charged both with conspiracy to commit bribery and with the substantive offense of bribery, because there are more than two persons involved in the offense.

Distinction Between Conspiracy and Object of Conspiracy   Except when Wharton's Rule is applicable, when two or more persons agree to commit a crime, and then commit the crime, they may be charged with both conspiracy to commit the crime and the crime itself. This is true because conspiracy is a crime in and of itself. As an inchoate offense, it may be committed even if the unlawful purpose of the conspiracy is not achieved. If Stephanie kills Amanda, Stephanie may be charged with murder, assuming the elements of murder are present. If Stephanie agrees with Vicki that they will kill Amanda, and they then kill Amanda, they may be charged with both conspiracy to commit murder and murder. If Stephanie and Vicki agree that they will kill Amanda and take steps to carry out their plan, but are unsuccessful, they may be charged with conspiracy to commit murder (and possibly attempt).

Objects of Conspiracy   Under the common law, an agreement to accomplish an unlawful end or to accomplish a lawful end by unlawful means constituted a criminal conspiracy. These standards were considered vague. Penal Code §§ 182 and 183 were written with specificity to rectify the vagueness problem under the common-law definition. Section 182 describes six types of agreements that constitute criminal conspiracies, and § 183 provides that no conspiracies other than those enumerated in § 182 are punishable criminally. Section 182 prohibits agreements:

1. To commit any crime
2. Falsely and maliciously to indict another for any crime, or to procure another to be charged or arrested for any crime
3. Falsely to move or maintain any suit, action, or proceeding
4. To cheat and defraud any person of any property, by any means which are in themselves criminal, or to obtain money or property by false pretenses or by false promises with fraudulent intent not to perform such promises
5. To commit any act injurious to the public health or public morals, or to pervert or obstruct justice or the due administration of the laws
6. To commit any crime against the person of the President or Vice President of the United States, the governor of any state or territory, any United States justice or judge, or the secretary of any of the executive departments of the United States.

Overt Act   Penal Code § 184 provides that no agreement amounts to a conspiracy unless an **overt act** is committed by one of the conspirators for the purpose of accomplishing the object of the conspiracy. The act must be committed within the state of California. The overt act does not have to be unlawful in itself. If, for example, Larry and Sheila agree to plant a bomb in a local shopping mall, and Sheila, in furtherance of the agreement, purchases chemical fertilizer from which the bomb is to be made, Sheila has committed an overt act. The purchase of the fertilizer is not unlawful, but nevertheless constitutes the overt act that transforms the agreement into a criminal conspiracy.

Voluntary Withdrawal from Conspiracy   If a party withdraws from a conspiracy after the agreement is made, but before the overt act is committed, the party is not guilty of conspiracy. If the party withdraws from the conspiracy after the overt act is committed, the guilt or innocence of the party is unsettled under California law. Withdrawal after the overt act is considered a defense by some authorities, but not by others. In any event, for withdrawal to be effective, the withdrawing party must do more than manifest an intent to withdraw. He or she must communicate the fact of withdrawal to the other parties in time for them also to abandon the scheme. In the Larry and Sheila example, if Larry changes his mind and decides not to participate in the plot to detonate a bomb at the shopping mall, and communicates that fact to Sheila before Sheila purchases the fertilizer, Larry will not be guilty of conspiracy. If Larry changes his mind, but does not tell Sheila until after she has purchased the fertilizer, Larry may or may not be guilty of conspiracy, depending on the view in the judicial district with jurisdiction over the offense.

Punishment   Penal Code § 182, which defines the six types of criminal conspiracies recognized by California law, also prescribes differing levels of punishment for the various types of conspiracies. Conspiracy to commit any crime against an official listed in the sixth category is a felony punishable by imprisonment in the state prison for five, seven, or nine years. If the parties conspire to commit any other felony, they are punishable in the same manner as for commission of the felony. All other conspiracies defined in § 182 are felony-misdemeanors, punishable by imprisonment in the state prison, in the county jail for up to one year, by a fine of up to $10,000, or by both fine and imprisonment.

As discussed in Chapter 4, a felony-misdemeanor is an offense that may be charged and prosecuted as either a felony or a misdemeanor, within the discretion of the prosecutor. By making all conspiracies (other than those against specified government officials and conspiracies to commit felonies) felony-misdemeanors, § 182 makes it possible for a prosecutor to charge a conspiracy to commit a misdemeanor as a felony. In other words, even if the object of the conspiracy is a misdemeanor, a prosecutor may still charge the conspiracy itself as a felony. The courts have placed some limits on the discretion of prosecutors to "convert" misdemeanors into felonies by charging the participants with conspiracy, but for the most part prosecutors retain the discretion to charge defendants in this manner, provided the elements of conspiracy are present.

Another effect of the punishment provisions of § 182 is to make it possible to punish persons who conspire to commit a felony in the same manner as if they had actually committed the felony. Thus, if Barbara and Evelyn agree to rob a local bank, and Evelyn goes to a sporting goods store and buys a gun and ski masks for use in the robbery, Barbara and Evelyn can, at that point, be punished to the same degree as if they had carried out the bank robbery. This is true even if Barbara and Evelyn do not actually carry out the bank robbery. This aspect of conspiracy law, together with the discretion conferred upon prosecutors to convert misdemeanors into felonies by charging them as conspiracies, make conspiracy a powerful weapon in the arsenal of prosecutors.

Finally, the distinction between conspiracy and attempt should be noted. An obvious distinction is the fact that attempt may be committed by one person, whereas conspiracy requires at least two participants. Another distinction, which may not be quite so obvious, is that attempt requires the commission of acts going beyond mere preparation. In contrast, if two persons agree to commit a crime, and one of them commits an act in furtherance of the agreement that amounts only to preparation, the crime of conspiracy has been committed. Yet another distinction is that, if a crime is successfully committed, the defendant cannot be guilty of both attempt to commit the crime and actual commission of the crime. In contrast, if a crime is successfully committed after two persons agree to commit the crime, the two persons may be convicted of both the crime and the conspiracy. Finally, attempts are generally subject to less severe punishment than conspiracies. For example, attempted robbery is punishable by one-half the punishment prescribed for robbery, whereas conspiracy to commit robbery is punishable by the full punishment for robbery.

Solicitation

You have already encountered **solicitation** in the discussion of prostitution. But solicitation is much broader than attempting to engage someone in prostitution. Solicitation is the encouraging, requesting, or commanding of another to commit a crime.

The crime of solicitation is prescribed in Penal Code § 653f, and is limited to solicitation of the offenses enumerated in that section. These offenses are generally serious felonies, including murder, bribery, carjacking, robbery, burglary, grand theft, receiving stolen property, extortion, perjury, subornation of perjury, forgery, kidnapping, arson, assault with a deadly weapon, witness intimidation, sex offenses, and drug offenses. Solicitation is a specific-intent crime; the solicitation must occur with the specific intent that the crime solicited be committed. The solicitation itself is a crime, regardless of whether the person solicited agrees to commit the offense proposed by the solicitor. If the person solicited agrees to commit the proposed offense, and an overt act is committed by one of the parties in furtherance of the agreement, the parties commit conspiracy, in addition to the solicitation committed by the solicitor. If the person solicited commits the proposed crime, both that person and the solicitor become principals to the completed crime. The solicited person is a principal because he or she actually commits the crime. The solicitor is a principal under Penal Code § 31 because he or she advised and encouraged commission of the crime.

Punishment for solicitation is prescribed in § 653f, and depends on the crime solicited. Solicitation of certain enumerated crimes, such as murder, is a felony. Solicitation of other enumerated crimes is a felony-misdemeanor.

In *Miley*, the defendant, Roy Lee Miley, was convicted of soliciting one Michael Douglas (not the movie star) to rape and murder Miley's wife Carole, from whom Miley was estranged, and to murder Carole's two daughters if they were at home when Carole was murdered. The purpose of the rape was to cover up the true nature of the offense, i.e., to make it appear that a rapist had entered

---

PEOPLE v. ROY LEE MILEY
158 Cal.App.3d 25; 204 Cal.Rptr. 347
[July 1984]

Appellant was a deputy sheriff for the Ventura County Sheriff's Department from 1962 to 1980. While so employed, he met Michael Douglas, also a deputy sheriff. Douglas left the department in 1979 and moved out of the area. Appellant resigned in 1980 and opened a sporting goods store specializing in guns and fishing tackle.

In late 1980, Douglas returned to Ventura and met up with appellant in appellant's store. Appellant employed him as a part-time clerk during the 1980 Christmas season and on occasional weekends for the next few months. Douglas also worked as an investigator for appellant's private investigation agency.

During this period, both appellant and Douglas were experiencing marital difficulties. They developed a social relationship, complaining to each other about their respective wives. On several occasions, appellant expressed his desire that "something happen to [Carole]" and that he "get rid of her."

* * *

[A]ppellant offered Douglas $2,500 to kill Carole. He told Douglas that he could use a gun from the store, one which had been sold but which was being held for the 15-day registration waiting period. Douglas told appellant that he would have to think about it.

Fortunately for Carole, Douglas contacted an investigator for the district attorney's office. The sheriff's department was called in, and listened-in by telephone or "Fargo" unit on the remainder of Douglas' conversations with appellant.

On October 12, 1981, at the request of law enforcement, Douglas arranged a meeting with appellant. Douglas was instructed to obtain the details of appellant's proposal. He did.

Appellant reiterated that Douglas could use a gun from the store and explained that the weapon could be cleaned and the barrel "reworked" so that the weapon could not be traced. He showed Douglas two guns which he thought would be suitable.

... Douglas was instructed to make the killing appear to have occurred during a robbery or rape. Appellant was not sure whether Carole's daughters would be home on the evening in question; his statement to Douglas was: "They're no use. You're going to have to kill them too."

* * *

On October 15, 1981, appellant met with Douglas and gave him a bag containing $50, a .38 revolver, a box of ammunition, and a key to Carole's residence. Appellant drew a diagram of the house and the lighting system, explaining Carole's habits and where she would most likely be found. There was further discussion regarding Douglas' setting up the crime to look like a rape/murder.

Appellant described the cars driven by Carole's daughters; he could not "guarantee" that they would be gone. If either of the girls were home, appellant instructed Douglas: "better do her too. You don't want any witnesses. They both know you."

Appellant assured Douglas that he had no qualms about the plan. Douglas then left appellant's office and delivered the money, gun, ammunition and key to the officers waiting outside. Appellant was arrested shortly thereafter.

* * *

Appellant does not challenge the sufficiency of the evidence to sustain his conviction for soliciting the murder and rape of Carole. He attacks only the solicitation of the murders of her daughters, and argues (a) that the class of victims was too indefinite,

i.e., that the killing of the daughters was contemplated only because "there were to be no witnesses," and (b) that the solicitation was not "unconditional"; i.e., the girls were to be murdered *only if* they were at home when Douglas killed Carole. We disagree.

Solicitation consists of the asking of another to commit one of the crimes specified in Penal Code section 653f with the intent that the crime be committed. Intent may be inferred from the circumstances attendant to the request.

The crime is complete once the request is made, and no steps need be taken to consummate the target offense. That is so because one of the purposes of the statute is to *avoid citizen exposure to inducements to commit crime.*

Unlike other criminal offenses, in the crime of "solicitation" the harm *is* the asking—nothing more need be proven.

* * *

The real problem here, if any there be, is that the girls were to be killed *only if* they were home. Appellant characterizes this as a "contingent solicitation," and therefore no solicitation at all.

We note initially that neither the statute nor the cases which construe it require that a solicitation be "unconditional." It is probably fair to say that a great many solicitations for murder are "conditional"; the payment of a certain sum is the condition precedent to the killing. Yet, it could not be argued that the solicitation is not complete until the money is paid; the payment merely affects whether or not the object of the solicitation will be consummated.

The same is true in this case. The "contingency" affects whether the girls will be murdered; the solicitation is complete upon the asking. Appellant cannot save himself from a conviction for solicitation merely because, due to some circumstance entirely beyond his control, his intended victims may save themselves from death.

* * *

[T]he judgment is affirmed.

Carole's house and raped and murdered her. The purpose of murdering the daughters was to eliminate any witnesses to the crimes. Miley appealed his conviction of soliciting the murder of Carole's daughters, arguing that he had solicited Douglas to murder them only if they were at home. Because the request that Douglas murder the daughters was conditional, Miley argued that it did not constitute the crime of solicitation. The appellate court did not agree.

Key Terms

accessory A person who, after a felony has been committed, harbors, conceals, or aids a principal in such felony, with the intent that said principal may avoid or escape from arrest, trial, conviction, or punishment, having knowledge that said principal has committed such felony or has been charged with such felony or convicted thereof. Formerly termed *accessory after the fact.*

accomplice A person called to testify in the trial of a defendant who himself or herself is a principal to the crime with which the defendant is charged. A defendant may not be convicted on accomplice testimony unless the testimony is independently corroborated.

attempt A direct but ineffectual act done toward the commission of a crime by one having the specific intent to commit the crime.

conspiracy An agreement entered into between two or more persons with the specific intent to agree to commit a public offense and with the further specific intent to commit such offense, followed by an overt act committed in California by one or more of the parties for the purpose of accomplishing the object of the agreement.

factual impossibility As applied to the crime of attempt, means that the act intended by the defendant is a crime, but the circumstances are such that the crime cannot successfully be committed. Factual impossibility is not a defense to the crime of attempt. For example, if John points a replica of a gun at Sue, thinking it is a real gun, and tries to shoot Sue with it, John can be convicted of attempted murder despite the fact that shooting Sue with a replica of a gun is not possible.

legal impossibility A defense to the crime of attempt; means that the act attempted is not a crime, despite the belief of the actor that it is a crime.

overt act A necessary element of the crime of conspiracy; an act committed by one of the conspirators within the state of California in furtherance of the conspirators' agreement. An agreement to commit a crime, if not followed by an overt act in furtherance of the agreement, does not amount to a conspiracy.

principal A person involved in the commission of a crime. Such involvement may include: (1) directly committing the offense (formerly, a principal in the first degree); (2) aiding and abetting the person directly committing the offense while present at the scene of the crime (formerly, a principal in the second degree); or (3) advising or encouraging the commission of the crime, usually prior to actual commission of the crime (formerly, an accessory before the fact).

solicitation The crime of encouraging, requesting, or commanding of another person to commit a crime.

voluntary withdrawal As applied to the crime of attempt, means voluntary cessation of the criminal act by the defendant before the crime is completed. If the defendant's acts have reached the point at which they constitute an attempt, voluntary withdrawal thereafter is not a defense.

Wharton's Rule The legal principle applicable to the crime of conspiracy which provides that if an offense requires two persons for its commission, and only two defendants are involved, they cannot be charged with conspiracy to commit the offense, although they may be charged with commission of the offense itself.

Review Questions

1. Distinguish the common-law concepts of a principal in the first degree and a principal in the second degree. Which was punished more severely?

2. Under the common law, what was a person called who helped principals to commit a crime, but was not present during the commission?

3. Under present-day California law, how are principals of the first and second degree and accessories before the fact categorized? How are accessories after the fact categorized?

4. What is the significance of the term *accomplice* in California law?

5. What is an "inchoate" crime?

6. Has Jan committed attempted murder if she decides to kill her sister and mentally works out the details of when, how, and where?

7. What are the two types of specific intent required for the crime of conspiracy?

8. Briefly explain the requirement under California law that, for an agreement to constitute conspiracy, one of the conspirators must commit an overt act to effect the object of the conspiracy.

9. Is solicitation of any crime an offense in California?

10. What is the difference between solicitation and attempt?

Review Problems

1-3. Use the following facts to answer questions 1 through 3.

Abel and Baker were inmates sharing a cell in state prison. During their stay they planned a convenience store robbery for after their release. They decided which store to rob, when they would rob it, and what method they would use. Having frequented the store on many occasions, Abel knew that the store had a safe and that the employees did not have access to its contents. Neither Abel or Baker had any experience with breaking into safes, so they decided to seek help.

Accordingly, they sought out "Nitro," a fellow inmate who was a known explosives expert. They requested his assistance and promised to pay him one-third of the total recovery. He agreed. However, he would only be able to teach the two how to gain entry to the safe, because he was not scheduled for release until after the day they had planned for the robbery. He added that he owned a house in the area and that it would be available for them to use as a "hide-out until the heat was off."

The two were released as planned and drove to the town where the store was located. As instructed by Nitro, the two went to a store and purchased the materials necessary to construct an explosive, which was to be used to gain entry to the safe. That evening Abel and Baker went to the store with their homemade explosive. They left the car they were traveling in and went to the rear of the store to gain entry through a back door. However, as they entered the alley behind the store, they encountered a police officer. The officer, suspicious of them, examined their bag and discovered the bomb. Abel and Baker escaped from the officer and stayed in Nitro's house for three days before being discovered and arrested.

1. What crimes has Abel committed? Under common-law party classifications, what type of party or parties is Abel with respect to each crime? Under present-day party classifications, what type of party or parties is Abel with respect to each crime?

2. Answer the same questions as in #1 for Baker.

3. Answer the same questions as in #1 for Nitro.

4. John and Tyrone have a fight in a bar. Tyrone returns home, climbs into bed, and suffers a fatal heart attack. John, still angry from the earlier fight, climbs through a window into Tyrone's room and shoots Tyrone twice in the head. Has John committed a murder? Attempted murder? Explain your answer.

5. Mark wants to kill Deborah.
   a. Mark approaches Andrew and offers Andrew $5,000 if he will kill Deborah. What crime has Mark committed? If Andrew refuses Mark's offer, has Andrew committed a crime?
   b. Assume that Andrew tells Mark he accepts the offer and will kill Deborah. Andrew then goes to a sporting goods store and purchases a box of cartridges for his handgun so that he can use the handgun to kill Deborah. What crime or crimes have Mark and/or Andrew committed at this point in time?
   c. Andrew knows that Deborah goes jogging every morning along a certain path. Andrew lies in wait for Deborah and, as she runs by, points the gun at her and pulls the trigger. However, the gun fails to fire. What crime has Andrew committed? Is Mark guilty of this crime as well?

Notes

1 Penal Code § 971.

2 CALJIC No. 3.01.

3 *People v. Lanzit* (1925) 70 Cal.App. 498, 505.

CHAPTER 10

Factual and Statutory Defenses

OUTLINE

§ 10.1 "Defense" Defined

Criminal defendants usually claim that they are innocent of the charges against them. A defendant's reason for asserting that he is innocent is called a *defense*. Defenses can be factual: "I didn't do it!" They can also be legal: "I did it, but the case was filed after the statute of limitation had run." Many defenses have been developed under the common law; however, many others have been created by legislation. Some defenses are complete (perfect); that is, if successful, the defendant goes free. Other defenses are partial; the defendant avoids liability on one charge, but may be convicted of a lesser offense.

§ 10.2 Defense by Denial and Affirmative Defenses

In any trial, civil or criminal, the defendant has two lines of defense available. The first line of defense is defense by denial of the allegations made against him or her. In a criminal case, the government, and in a civil case, the plaintiff, have the burden of proving the allegations made against the defendant. By denying the allegations made against him or her, the defendant puts them in issue. This means that the defendant refuses to admit the allegations and cannot be held criminally or civilly liable unless the allegations are proven by the government or the plaintiff. In a criminal case, the government must prove each element of the charged offense beyond a reasonable doubt. (This standard of proof is discussed in more detail in Chapter 17.) Theoretically, a criminal defendant can do nothing at the trial and hope that the government will fail to prove its case, i.e., fail to establish each element of the charged offense beyond a reasonable doubt. Should the government fail to establish any element of the offense, the defendant must be acquitted.

The defendant's second line of defense is made up of what are known as **affirmative defenses**. Affirmative defenses are principles of law that completely or partially absolve the defendant of guilt in situations in which the defendant has committed the act with which he or she has been charged. Affirmative defenses are a defendant's second line of defense because they can be raised by a defendant even when the prosecution has otherwise proved its case. Put another way, the prosecution may have introduced sufficient evidence to convict the defendant of the charged offense, but an affirmative defense nonetheless results in complete or partial exoneration of the defendant. For example, in a battery case, the prosecution may introduce evidence establishing all the elements of the offense of battery. At the conclusion of the prosecution's evidence, it appears the defendant will be convicted. The defendant, however, presents evidence that he or she struck the victim in self-defense. Self-defense is a complete defense to a charge of battery and, if the defendant successfully raises the defense, he or she must be acquitted.

Affirmative defenses are of two types. Most affirmative defenses tend to negate an element of the charged offense. Self-defense is an example of this type of affirmative defense, because it negates the unlawfulness of the striking of the victim. Other affirmative defenses do not negate an element of the charged offense, but exonerate the defendant on public policy grounds. Entrapment, which is discussed later in this chapter, is an example of such a defense.

The prosecution in a criminal trial bears the **burden of proof** as to all elements of the charged offense and, as previously stated, must prove the existence of each element beyond a reasonable doubt. The beyond-a-reasonable-doubt standard is the highest standard of proof in the American judicial system. The burden of proof really has two components: **the burden of production**, also known as the burden of going forward with the evidence, and the **burden of persuasion**. The burden of production refers to the law's allocation of the obligation to introduce evidence tending to show the existence or nonexistence of a particular fact. The burden of persuasion refers to the designation of the party who has the burden of persuading the trier of fact of the existence or nonexistence of a fact once some evidence of the existence or nonexistence of the fact (burden of production) has been introduced.

The two burdens are distinct. It is one thing to introduce evidence tending to show the possible existence or nonexistence of a fact. It is quite another thing to persuade the trier of fact of the actual existence or nonexistence of the fact.

In a criminal trial, the prosecution always has both the burden of production and the burden of persuasion with respect to each element of the charged offense. A defendant wishing to raise an affirmative defense always has the burden of production, which means that the defendant must introduce some evidence tending to show the possible existence of the defense. If the affirmative defense is one that negates an element of the offense, such as self-defense, the burden of persuasion remains with the prosecution. All the defendant need do is introduce enough evidence to raise a reasonable doubt regarding the existence of that particular element of the offense.

If the affirmative defense is one that does not relate to an element of the offense, such as entrapment, the defendant has both the burden of production and the burden of persuasion. What this means is that the defendant must both introduce some evidence tending to show the existence of the defense and then follow through by persuading the trier of fact of the existence of the defense. The burden of proof is entirely on the defendant with an affirmative defense of this type. The standard of proof, however, is different from that borne by the prosecution. A defendant is required to prove this type of defense by a preponderance of the evidence. The preponderance of the evidence standard is the lowest of the three common standards of proof recognized in American jurisprudence.

Some authorities limit the term *affirmative defense* to defenses that exonerate the defendant on public policy grounds. Defenses that tend to negate an element of the charged offense are regarded as forms of defense by denial. These categorizations are not critical as long as the allocations of the burdens of production and persuasion are understood.

§ 10.3 Insanity

Few aspects of criminal law have received as much public attention as the insanity defense. The defense has also been the subject of considerable scholastic research and discussion. Some critics charge that the defense should not be available. Others criticize not the availability of such a defense, but the particular tests employed to determine sanity. Despite its critics, insanity is recognized by nearly all jurisdictions as a defense. At least three states—Montana, Utah, and Idaho—have abolished the insanity defense. In 1994, the U.S. Supreme Court denied certiorari in a case challenging such a law as violative of due process.

The theory underlying the defense of insanity is that no purpose of criminal law is served by subjecting insane persons to the criminal justice system. Because they have no control over their behavior, they cannot be deterred from similar future behavior. Similarly, no general deterrence will occur, as others suffering from a mental or physical disease of the mind cannot alter their behavior. The one purpose that may be served, incapacitation, is inappropriate if the defendant no longer suffers from a mental disease, or if the disease is now controlled. If the defendant continues to be dangerous, there is no need to use the criminal justice system to remove him or her from society, because this can be accomplished using civil commitment.

Something that must be remembered is that criminal law has its own definition of insanity. Other areas of law (e.g., civil commitment) use different tests, as do other professions (e.g., psychiatry). Each jurisdiction is free to use whatever test it wishes to determine insanity. Among the various jurisdictions in the United States, three tests are used to determine sanity in the criminal law context: M'Naghten; irresistible impulse; and the Model Penal Code. A fourth test, the Durham, is no longer used in any jurisdiction, but is mentioned because of its historical significance.

Although California currently uses the M'Naghten test for insanity, the Model Penal Code and irresistible impulse tests have been recognized in California in the past. They are discussed for purposes of comparison with the current California test, as well as for their historical significance. Finally, a defense related to the insanity defense, known as *diminished capacity,* is discussed. The diminished capacity defense was at one time widely accepted in California; it has since been abolished.

SIDEBAR

Twinkies, Witchcraft, PMS, and More

A number of interesting insanity-related defenses have been raised by defendants. Although some are in the nature of full insanity defenses, most are asserted as diminished-capacity defenses.

One of the most famous is the so-called "Twinkie defense," raised by a defendant in California who was charged with murdering a mayor and another official. He claimed that his large consumption of white sugar, primarily through snack foods, caused him to have a diminished capacity. The defense was successful in reducing the crime from murder to manslaughter. He was sentenced to a short prison term and committed suicide after his release. The California legislature responded to the decision by barring diminished-capacity defenses in future cases.

In addition to the Twinkie defense, all of the following have been pleaded by defendants in support of either an insanity or diminished-capacity defense: premenstrual syndrome, involuntary subliminal television intoxication, brainwashing syndrome, and posttraumatic stress disorder. One defendant even asserted a witchcraft defense, claiming that witchcraft made him do it.

Many states have followed California's lead and eliminated the diminished-capacity defense. Others require defendants to choose between asserting insanity or diminished capacity.

M'Naghten

In 1843 Daniel M'Naghten was tried for killing the British prime minister's secretary. M'Naghten was laboring under the paranoid delusion that the prime minister was planning to kill him, and he killed the minister's secretary, believing him to be the prime minister. The jury found M'Naghten not guilty by reason of insanity.[1] The decision created controversy, and the House of Lords asked the justice of the Queens Bench to state what the standards for acquittal on the grounds of insanity were.[2] Those standards were attached to the decision and set forth the following standard, known as the **M'Naghten test.**

1. At the time that the act was committed

2. the defendant was suffering from a defect of reason, from a disease of the mind, which caused

3. the defendant to not know
   a. the nature and quality of the act taken or
   b. that the act was wrong.

This test has become known as the M'Naghten, or the right-wrong test. The M'Naghten test is incorporated in the California Penal Code at § 25(b), in the following language:

> In any criminal proceeding, including any juvenile court proceeding, in which a plea of not guilty by reason of insanity is entered, this defense shall be found by the trier of fact only when the accused person proves by a preponderance of the evidence that he or she was incapable of knowing or understanding the nature and quality of his or her act and of distinguishing right from wrong at the time of the commission of the offense.

Unlike the common-law M'Naghten test, the language of § 25(b) does not explicitly state that the defendant must be suffering from a defect of reason or a disease of the mind. This requirement is, however, impliedly included by use of the words "incapable of." Another apparent difference between the § 25(b) test and the traditional common-law M'Naghten test is the use in § 25(b) of the word "and," rather than "or," between the two types of specified mental defects. The courts in California have viewed the use of the word "and" as a drafting error, and interpret it to mean "or."[3] Thus, as with M'Naghten, a defendant may be found not guilty by reason of insanity if he or she was incapable of knowing or understanding the nature and quality of his or her act *or* of distinguishing right from wrong at the time of commission of the offense.

Section 25(b) is of relatively recent origin, having been added to the Penal Code in 1982. From 1864 to 1978, the California courts employed the common-law M'Naghten test, i.e., the test developed by the courts rather than by statute. In its 1978 decision in *People v. Drew,* 22 Cal.3d 333, the California Supreme Court, declaring that the M'Naghten test was outdated, adopted the Model Penal Code test (discussed in a following section). In 1982, however, Proposition 8, an initiative measure, appeared on the ballot. Proposition 8 proposed abrogation of the Model Penal Code test and reinstatement of M'Naghten by addition of the language now found at § 25(b) of the Penal Code. Proposition 8 was approved by the electorate, and California has, as a result, returned to use of the M'Naghten test.

Irresistible Impulse

Under the M'Naghten test, a defendant who knows that his or her actions are wrong, but cannot control his or her behavior because of a disease of the mind, is not insane. This has led a few jurisdictions that follow M'Naghten to supplement the rule. These states continue to follow the basic rule, but add that a defendant is not guilty by reason of insanity if a disease of the mind causes the defendant to be unable to control his or her behavior. This is true even if the defendant understands the nature and quality of the act or knows that the behavior is wrong. This is known as **irresistible impulse**.

The California courts rejected the irresistible impulse defense as early as 1882, and maintained their rejection of it until adoption of the Model Penal Code test of insanity in 1978. The Model Penal Code test incorporates the irresistible impulse defense. When the Model Penal Code test became the test for insanity in 1978, irresistible impulse began to be recognized as a defense by the California Courts. In 1981, however, the legislature repudiated the defense of irresistible impulse in California. (See Penal Code § 28(b).)

Durham

In 1871 the New Hampshire Supreme Court rejected the M'Naghten test and held that a defendant was not guilty because of insanity if the crime was the "product of mental disease." No other jurisdictions followed New Hampshire's lead until 1954, when the District of Columbia Court of Appeals handed down *Durham v. United States,* 214 F.2d 862 (D.C. Cir. 1954). Generally, the **Durham test** requires an acquittal if the defendant would not have committed the crime if he or she had not been suffering from a mental disease or mental defect.

Durham was overturned in 1972 by the District of Columbia Court of Appeals in favor of a modified version of the Model Penal Code test.[4] Today, Durham is not used by any jurisdiction.

The Model Penal Code Test

As previously mentioned, the **Model Penal Code test** for insanity was adopted by the California Supreme Court in 1978 and experienced a brief existence until repudiated by the electorate by adoption of Proposition 8 in 1982. The Model Penal Code contains a definition of insanity similar to, but broader than, the M'Naghten and irresistible impulse tests. This test is also referred to as the *substantial capacity test.* The relevant section of the Code reads:[5]

> A person is not responsible for criminal conduct if at the time of such conduct as a result of mental disease or defect he lacks substantial capacity either to appreciate the criminality [wrongfulness] of his conduct or to conform his conduct to the requirements of law.

The Code is similar to M'Naghten in that it requires that mental disease or defect impair a defendant's ability to appreciate the wrongfulness of his or her act. The final line, "conform his conduct to the requirements of law," incorporates the irresistible impulse concept.

The Code's approach differs from the M'Naghten and irresistible impulse test in two important regards. First, the Code requires only substantial impairment, whereas M'Naghten requires total impairment of the ability to know the nature or wrongfulness of the act. Second, the Code uses the term "appreciate," rather than "know." The drafters of the Code clearly intended more than knowledge, and, as such, evidence concerning the defendant's personality and emotional state are relevant.

Diminished Capacity

Insanity, if established, is a complete defense to the crime charged. The defense will apply, however, only if the defendant is found to have been incapable of knowing or understanding the nature and quality of his or her act or of distinguishing right from wrong. If a defendant's ability to know or understand the nature and quality of the act or to distinguish right from wrong is partially, but not fully, impaired, the insanity defense does not apply, and the defendant is held fully responsible for the offense. Put another way, there is no defense of "partial insanity" in California.

Prior to 1981, a partial insanity defense was recognized in California, and was known as the defense of **diminished capacity**. The diminished capacity defense recognized that a defendant who was not legally insane might nevertheless be suffering from a mental disease or defect that affected his or her ability to possess the mental state required for the crime charged. Diminished capacity could be the result of intoxication, trauma, disease, or other factor affecting mental capacity. It was a defense to specific-intent crimes and other crimes requiring a mental state more than general intent. Diminished capacity was not a defense to general-intent crimes. If a defendant successfully raised the defense of diminished capacity in a trial for a specific-intent offense, he or she could be found guilty of a lesser included general-intent crime, or, if the specific-intent crime had no lesser included offense, could be acquitted.

The emphasis in the diminished capacity defense was on the defendant's *capacity* to form the mental state required for the charged offense. The defense did not address whether the defendant actually possessed the mental state required for the crime. The inquiry stopped at capacity: if the defendant lacked the capacity to form the required mental state, he or she presumably could not have possessed that mental state during commission of the offense.

In 1981, the legislature expressed its dissatisfaction with the diminished capacity defense and eliminated it as a defense in California. (See Penal Code §§ 28(a) and (b).) In 1982, the voters added their voice to that of the legislature by approving Proposition 8 which, among its provisions, expressly repudiated the diminished capacity defense. (See Penal Code § 25(a).) Diminished capacity continues to be admissible at the time of sentencing, after the question of the defendant's guilt has been determined.[6] Also note that, although evidence of mental disease, mental defect, or mental disorder is not admissible to negate the *capacity* to form a mental state, it is admissible on the issue whether the defendant *actually formed* a required specific intent, or premeditated, deliberated, or harbored malice aforethought, when a crime involving those mental states is charged.

Procedures of the Insanity Defense

Insanity is an affirmative defense. Unlike most other affirmative defenses, however, a defendant raising the insanity defense must do more than produce evidence creating a reasonable doubt as to his or her sanity. A defendant claiming that he or she is not guilty by reason of insanity bears the burden of persuasion as well as the burden of production. This means that the defendant must prove that he or she was insane at the time of commission of the offense. However, whereas the prosecution must prove the elements of the charged offense beyond a reasonable doubt, a defendant may establish insanity by a preponderance of the evidence.[7]

Establishing insanity as a defense in a criminal trial requires opinion testimony. Under Evidence Code § 870, opinion testimony regarding the sanity or insanity of a defendant may be given by a witness who is an intimate acquaintance of the defendant, by a witness who rationally concluded that the defendant was insane based on the witness's perception of the defendant, or by a witness who is qualified as an expert, such as a psychiatrist.

As discussed in Chapter 16, a defendant may enter a number of pleas in response to the formal charges against him or her. Pleas of guilty or not guilty are two examples. A defendant claiming the insanity defense must plead not guilty by reason of insanity. By making this plea, the defendant is claiming that he or she is not guilty of the offense charged because he or she was insane at the time he or she committed the offense. If the defendant merely pleads not guilty, the issue of the defendant's sanity is not raised, and the defendant is conclusively presumed to have been sane at the time of commission of the offense. A not guilty plea by the defendant requires the prosecution to prove every element of the offense beyond a reasonable doubt. If the defendant pleads not guilty by reason of insanity, he or she admits commission of the offense charged. The defendant is tried on the issue of sanity alone and, if he or she is found to be sane, judgment of conviction is entered without any trial on the issue of guilt.

Defendants are permitted to double-plead, that is, to plead both not guilty and not guilty by reason of insanity. In this situation, the defendant is first tried on the not guilty plea and, for that purpose, is conclusively presumed to have been sane at the time the offense was committed. If the defendant is found guilty of the offense, the question of his or her sanity at the time of commission of the offense is then tried.[8]

Disposition of the Criminally Insane

If a defendant is adjudged not guilty by reason of insanity, he or she becomes subject to the procedures specified in § 1026 *et seq.* of the Penal Code. Section 1026(a) provides that the defendant is to be confined to a state hospital for the care and treatment of the mentally disordered, other appropriate public or private treatment facility, or placed on an outpatient status. An exception to this requirement exists if it appears to the court that the defendant has fully recovered his or her sanity. In that case, the defendant is held in custody pending a final determination on that issue. If the defendant is found to have fully recovered his or her sanity, he or she is released.

In the usual case, in which the defendant has not fully recovered his or her sanity, the court orders the community program director to evaluate the defendant and to recommend to the court the type of treatment facility to which the defendant should be committed or, alternatively, to recommend that the defendant be placed on an outpatient status. The community program director is a person or agency designated by the State Department of Mental Health. After the court receives the recommendation of the community program director, it directs the disposition of the defendant.[9]

The defendant must remain in the court-ordered treatment program until his or her sanity is fully restored. The court's initial order committing a defendant to a treatment facility or outpatient status specifies the maximum term of commitment. If the defendant was charged with a felony, the maximum term of commitment is the longest term of imprisonment that could have been imposed on the defendant for the offense committed. If the defendant was charged with a misdemeanor, the maximum term of commitment is the longest term of county jail confinement that could have been imposed on the defendant.[10] The general rule is that the defendant may not be committed longer than the maximum term of commitment. If the defendant has not fully recovered his or her

Insanity and
Criminal
Procedure

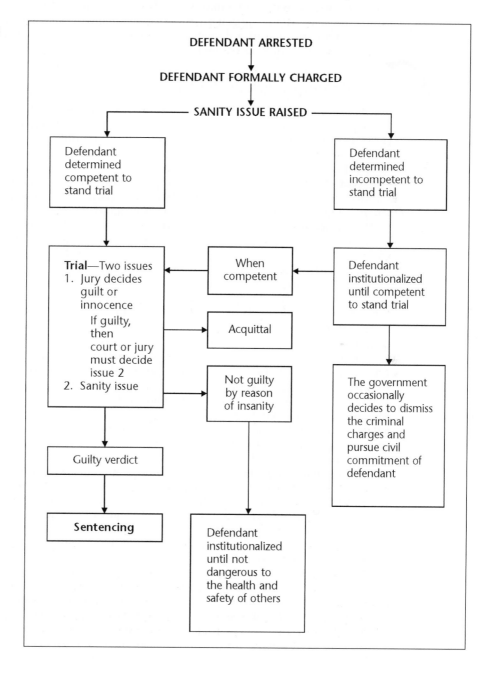

sanity at the expiration of the maximum term of commitment, the rule conflicts with the requirement that the defendant not be released until his or her sanity is fully restored. For cases of this nature, Penal Code § 1026.5(b) provides for extension of the defendant's commitment for successive two-year increments if the defendant was convicted of a felony. The Penal Code does not provide for extension in a case in which the defendant was convicted of a misdemeanor, although if the defendant remains a danger to himself, herself, or others, civil commitment proceedings may be available.

Mental Competence at the Time of Trial

The United States Supreme Court has held that a defendant who is mentally incompetent at the time of trial may not be tried.[11] The Court found that the Due Process Clauses of the Fifth and Fourteenth Amendments require that a defendant be able to assist in his or her defense and understand the proceedings against him or her.

The test for determining mental competence in this context is different from that for insanity at the time of the offense. Incompetence to stand trial exists when a defendant lacks the capacity to understand the proceedings or assist in his or her defense. This simply means that defendants must be rational, possess the ability to testify coherently, and be able to meaningfully discuss their cases with their lawyers.

In California, if a defendant's mental competence at the time of trial is questionable, the court must suspend the criminal proceedings and hold a hearing on the issue. (See Penal Code § 1368.) If the defendant is found mentally competent, the trial resumes. If he or she is found mentally incompetent, the court orders that he or she be committed to a psychiatric facility or placed in an outpatient program until his or her mental competence is restored. If the defendant is committed to a psychiatric facility or outpatient program, the court must receive a report on the defendant's progress within ninety days and each six months thereafter. The court periodically evaluates the defendant's mental competence and, if it appears that the defendant will not regain mental competence, may order that the charges be dismissed. In such a case the defendant remains subject to commitment under the state's civil commitment laws.[12] The foregoing rules apply equally to a defendant who is mentally competent during his or her trial but becomes mentally incompetent prior to sentencing.

The United States Supreme Court has held that a person who has become insane after being sentenced to death may not be executed until his or her sanity is regained.[13] The constitutional basis of the Court's decision was the Eighth Amendment's prohibition of cruel and unusual punishment. Justice Marshall has stated that "It is no less abhorrent today than it has been for centuries to exact in penance the life of one whose mental illness prevents him from comprehending the reasons for the penalty or its implications."[14]

California law comports with the principles enunciated by the United States Supreme Court. If a defendant who has been sentenced to death becomes insane before the sentence is carried out, the execution must be suspended and a hearing held on the defendant's sanity. If the defendant is found to be insane, he or she is committed to a medical facility of the State Department of Corrections until his or her sanity is restored. If the defendant appears to regain his or her sanity, another hearing is held before the court. If the court concludes that sanity has been restored, the defendant is returned to the state prison for execution of the sentence. If the court concludes that the defendant has not recovered his or her sanity, the defendant is returned to the medical facility. (See Penal Code § 3701 *et seq.*)

§ 10.4 Duress and Necessity

Duress

Penal Code § 26 provides, in part:

> All persons are capable of committing crimes except those belonging to the following classes:
> … Six—Persons (unless the crime be punishable with death) who committed the act or made the omission charged under threats or menaces sufficient to show that they had reasonable cause to and did believe their lives would be endangered if they refused.

The language of § 26(Six) describes what is known as the defense of **duress**. Consider, for example, the case of Terry Teller, a bank teller, who is ordered at gunpoint by a bank robber to place the money in her drawer in a bag and give it to the bank robber. The robber states that if Terry does not comply, he will kill her. If Terry complies with the bank robber's demand, she has not committed theft, although the elements of theft may be present, because she was acting under duress.

A person who engages in otherwise criminal conduct as the result of a threat may successfully raise the defense of duress if the threat was to his or her life. The defense requires that the actor's fear of danger to his or her life be reasonable. An honest but unreasonable fear that one's life is threatened is not sufficient to constitute the defense. In contrast, if the actor's fear is reasonable, it will support the defense of duress even if the person communicating the threat has no intention of actually carrying it out. For example, if the bank robber threatening Terry Teller did not really intend to shoot her, Terry has the defense of duress if a reasonable person would have feared for his or her life as a result of the robber's words and conduct. Although Penal Code § 26(Six) does not explicitly so state, judicial decisions have held that the defense of duress is available to a person who acts in response to a threat to the life of a third person. Also, there is some case authority that a threat of serious bodily injury will suffice, but the law is unsettled on this point.

To constitute duress, the threat to life must be immediate. Threats of future harm are insufficient to support the defense. Suppose that the bank robber in the Terry Teller example stated that, if Terry did not comply with his demand, he would send his brother after her to kill her. This threat would not constitute duress, and Terry would not be justified in complying with the robber's demand.

Duress is a defense to all crimes except homicide. One is not justified in taking the life of another even if one's own life is threatened. If one kills under duress, however, the coercion may negate malice aforethought, reducing the offense from murder to manslaughter.

Necessity

The defense of **necessity** is similar to the defense of duress, and recent cases in California have tended to blur the distinction between the two. Nonetheless, necessity, as a matter of law, remains a defense distinct from the defense of duress. The traditional distinction between duress and necessity has to do with the source of the threat to the life of the actor. If the actor commits what would otherwise be a criminal act in response to a threat from another person, he or she is acting under duress. If the actor commits such an act in response to a threat caused by natural forces, he or she is acting under necessity. The Terry Teller example in the discussion of duress illustrates a threat situation created by another person. Assume now that Terry is mountain climbing and is stranded on the mountain by a sudden snowstorm. After two days of wandering, she comes upon a cabin. To avoid freezing to death and starving, she breaks into the cabin, uses it for shelter, and consumes food she finds within. These acts would ordinarily be criminal but, because Terry committed them to save her life, she may successfully raise the defense of necessity.

The elements of the defense of necessity were derived from the case of *People v. Pena* (1983) 149 Cal.App.3d Supp. 14, and form the basis for CALJIC No. 4.43. The following discussion is based on the CALJIC instruction.

First, to serve as the basis for a necessity defense, the act charged as criminal must have been done to prevent a significant and imminent evil. In Terry's case, the evil to be prevented was death from exposure or starvation. Second, there must have been no reasonable legal alternative to commission of the act. Terry was stranded on a snow-covered mountain and had no recourse but to enter the cabin and consume the food. The third requirement for the necessity defense is that the harm caused by the actor's act not be disproportionate to the harm avoided. Again, using Terry as an example, the harm caused by her actions was the invasion of the cabin owner's property rights and the taking of the food. The harm avoided was loss of human life. Clearly, in Terry's case, the harm caused to the cabin owner was not disproportionate to the harm avoided. The fourth element of the necessity defense requires that the actor have entertained a good faith belief that his or her act was necessary to prevent the greater harm. In Terry's case, this element is easily met. The fifth element of the defense is related to the fourth and requires that the belief be objectively reasonable. *Objectively reasonable* means that the belief is one that would be entertained by a reasonable person in the same circumstances as the actor. The final element requires that the actor not have substantially contributed to creation of the emergency. This element could be problematic for Terry if the snowstorm was predicted, and she was aware of the forecast but recklessly disregarded it. In such circumstances, a jury might conclude that she substantially contributed to the creation of the predicament which she is trying to assert as a defense at trial.

The necessity defense is not a defense of wide applicability in California, and there are relatively few cases in which it has been an issue on appeal.

§ 10.5 Use-of-Force Defenses

In some situations, the law permits actors to use physical force against others. Self-defense, defense of others, defense of property, and use of force to make arrests fall into this area. Self-defense, defense of others, and defense of property, when successful, are complete defenses. Imperfect self-defense (including defense of another) does not lead to acquittal; however, it does reduce murder to manslaughter.

Self-Defense

A person is entitled by law to use force to protect himself or herself against injury or death at the hands of another. The degree of force that may be used depends on the severity of the threat.

Use of Deadly Force The use of deadly force in self-defense was briefly alluded to in Chapter 4 in the discussion of justifiable homicide. A killing is not unlawful if it occurs as the result of the lawful exercise of the right of self-defense. The circumstances under which one may use deadly force in self-defense are stated in the Penal Code. (See Penal Code § 197(3).)

The use of deadly force to repel an attack is justified only if the attack creates an imminent danger that a felony or great bodily injury is about to be committed upon the defender. This limitation reflects the general principle inherent in all use-of-force defenses that the degree of force used must be limited to that which is reasonable under the circumstances. The degree of force which is reasonable under a given set of circumstances is that degree of force which is necessary to repel the attack. If the defender uses a greater degree of force than is necessary, he or she becomes the assailant, and the original assailant becomes entitled to use the same degree of force to repel the defender's attack. In other words, the roles of aggressor and defender can change if the original victim responds with excessive force. Consider, for example, Eric and Bob, who become engaged in a verbal argument in a bar. The argument becomes heated and Eric attacks Bob with his fists. Generally, Bob would not be permitted to respond to the attack with deadly force because deadly force is not normally necessary to repel a simple assault. If Bob defended himself with his fists, his act would be justified as lawful self-defense. If, however, Bob pulled a handgun out of his coat pocket and fired at Eric, his use of force would not constitute lawful self-defense because it would be excessive. Bob would, at that point, become the assailant, and Eric would have the right to defend himself with the use of deadly force. Thus, Eric, threatened with infliction of death by Bob, could kill Bob in self-defense, despite the fact that Eric was the initial attacker. If Eric did kill or seriously wound Bob, however, his defense of self-defense would exonerate him only from the homicide or aggravated battery. It would not exonerate him from his initial assault upon Bob, because the initial assault was not justified.

The authorization conferred by § 197(3) to use deadly force to repel commission of a felony does not refer to all felonies. Rather, it refers to **forcible and atrocious crimes.**[15] A *forcible and atrocious* crime is defined by CALJIC No. 5.16 as:

> A forcible and atrocious crime, as the term is used in these instructions, is any felony, the character and manner of the commission of which threatens, or is reasonably believed by the defendant to threaten, life or great bodily injury so as to instill in [him] [her] a reasonable fear of death or great bodily injury.

The CALJIC instruction then cites as nonexclusive examples murder, mayhem, rape, and robbery.

Section 197(3) also reflects another principle common to use-of-force defenses—that the threat be imminent. One may not respond with deadly force to a threat of future harm. Use of force in self-defense is lawful only if the threat will result in immediate injury unless responded to with force.

The necessity to use force in self-defense, as well as the degree of force that is reasonably necessary, is governed by the principle known as **apparent necessity**. In the case of deadly force, apparent necessity means that the situation, as it appears to the defender, creates in the defender a reasonable fear of imminent danger that a felony or great bodily injury is about to be perpetrated upon him or her. Apparent necessity is to be contrasted with actual necessity. This means that the defender may use deadly force in self-defense when he or she is not actually threatened with imminent commission of a felony or great bodily injury if the circumstances are such that he or she honestly believes that such a threat exists and a reasonable person, in the same situation, would possess the same belief. Consider, for example, the Eric and Bob situation. If Bob pulled out a realistic-looking toy gun and told Eric he was going to kill him, Eric would be justified in using deadly force to repel the apparent attack if he honestly believed that Bob was about to inflict deadly force upon him and a reasonable person in the same situation would possess the same belief.

Many states require that a defender retreat, if possible, before using deadly force in self-defense. In California, there is no such requirement. A person is entitled to stand his ground in the face of an attack, even if doing so will necessitate the use of deadly force in self-defense.[16] An exception to this principle exists if the defender created the situation by initially attacking the assailant with deadly force. In that case, the defender must attempt to withdraw or retreat, and must inform the assailant that he or she is doing so, before using deadly force. For example, if an attacker attacks his victim with deadly force, and the victim defends with deadly force, the attacker does not thereby become entitled to continue the deadly attack and claim he is lawfully defending against the victim's use of deadly force. If, however, the initial attacker attempts to withdraw or retreat in response to the use of deadly force by the victim, and informs the victim that he is withdrawing or retreating, and the victim persists in his use of deadly force, the attacker then becomes entitled to defend himself with deadly force.

Contrast this situation with that of Eric and Bob, in which Eric attacked Bob with nondeadly force. In that case, if Bob responded with deadly force, Eric had the immediate right to defend with deadly force without the necessity of prior retreat or withdrawal. The requirement that a defender attempt to withdraw or retreat before using deadly force also applies in cases of mutual combat. If, for example, two persons are mutually engaged in a gunfight, and one shoots the other, he or she cannot successfully claim that the shooting was in lawful self-defense. If, however, one of the persons attempts to break off the gunfight, and so informs the other person, and the other person continues to fire at the person attempting to terminate the combat, the person attempting to break off the gunfight becomes entitled to use deadly force in self-defense.

The right to use deadly force in self-defense terminates if the defense is so successful that the attacker is rendered incapable of inflicting further injury on the defender. The right also terminates if the threat of being subjected to a felony or serious bodily injury terminates, such as by a discontinuation of the attack by the assailant. A victim who uses deadly force against an attacker after the attack has ceased is not regarded as acting under the influence of the fear created by the attack. Rather, he or she is considered to be acting in retaliation or revenge. Retaliation and revenge are never grounds for self-defense.

Use of Nondeadly Force One may use nondeadly force to repel any unlawful attack upon one's person. (See Penal Code §§ 692 and 693).[17]) Many of the principles discussed with respect to the use of deadly force in self-defense apply to the use of nondeadly force. As with the use of deadly force, the degree of non-deadly force used to repel an attack must be reasonable, i.e., not excessive. Also, as with the use of deadly force, the necessity to engage in self-defense and the degree of force necessary to repel the attack are determined by the principle of apparent necessity. Finally, as with the use of deadly force, the threat responded to must be imminent.

Defense of Others

It is also a justified use of force to defend another. The rules are similar to that of self-defense: there must be a threat of immediate danger to the other person; the perception of threat must be reasonable; the amount of force used must be reasonable; and deadly force may be used only to repel an attack that threatens commission of a forcible and atrocious crime or infliction of great bodily injury.

Penal Code § 197, subdivisions (1) and (3), authorize the use of deadly force in defense of others. Penal Code §§ 692 and 694, and Civil Code § 50, authorize the use of nondeadly force in defense of others. Some of these provisions limit those whom one may defend to relatives and members of his or her household. This limitation appears to be out of date. The current view is expressed in CALJIC No. 5.32, which cites as its basis all of the foregoing statutory provisions. According to CALJIC No. 5.32:

> It is lawful for a person who, as a reasonable person, has grounds for believing and does believe that bodily injury is about to be inflicted upon _____ to protect that individual from attack.
>
> In doing so, [he] [she] may use all force and means which such person believes to be reasonably necessary and which would appear to a reasonable person, in the same or similar circumstances, to be necessary to prevent the injury which appears to be imminent.

The CALJIC instruction reflects that one may use force in the defense of any person in a situation that would justify the use of force in the defense of oneself.

Defense of Property and Habitation

One is permitted by law to use force to defend property. The right to defend one's property extends to both real and personal property. The general right to defend property is found in Penal Code § 693 and Civil Code § 50. The rules applicable to self-defense apply to defense of property, that is, the force used must be reasonable, apparent necessity must exist, and the threat must be immediate. As a general rule, the life of the wrongdoer is of more importance than the property right which he or she is invading, and the owner or possessor of the property may not use deadly force to defend the property. If, for example, a wrongdoer enters a person's driveway and begins damaging the person's car, the car owner may not use deadly force to stop the wrongdoer. The owner may, of course, use reasonable nondeadly force.

Some specific applications of the right to defend property appear in the Penal Code and case law. These principles generally have to do with defense of real property. An owner or occupier of real property, for example, has the right to eject a trespasser. The trespasser should first be requested to leave. If he or she fails to comply within a reasonable time, the owner or occupier may use reasonable force to eject the trespasser. The amount of force that is reasonable depends on the amount and degree of resistance offered by the trespasser. If the trespasser were to resist in a way that threatened physical harm to the owner or occupant, the usual rules of self-defense would apply, even to the point of using deadly force if the trespasser resisted ejection with deadly force.[18] The right to use deadly force in such a situation would proceed from the threat to the person of the owner or occupant, not from the threat to the property rights of the owner or occupant. If the threat caused by the trespasser were limited to the property rights of the owner or occupant, only nondeadly force could be used to remove him or her.

The habitation has traditionally been accorded special protection under the law, and special legal principles have developed with respect to defense of habitation. Penal Code § 197(2), for example, addresses the right of the owner or occupier of a residence to use deadly force against an intruder. As with all use-of-force defenses, only reasonable force may be used. One may not, for example, intentionally kill an intruder who does not threaten violence to the person of one inside the residence or the commission of a felony (a forcible and atrocious crime). If, however, the presence of the intruder within the residence, or the attempt by the intruder to violently enter the residence, threatens the infliction of death or serious bodily injury to, or commission of a forcible and atrocious crime against, a person within the residence, the owner or occupier may use deadly force to defend against the intruder. Penal Code § 198.5, known as the "Home Protection Bill of Rights," creates a presumption that the owner or occupier of a residence using deadly force against an intruder who has unlawfully and forcibly entered the residence does so under a "reasonable fear of imminent peril of death or great bodily injury to self, family, or a member of the household." By so providing, § 198.5 presumes that the basis for use of deadly force in self-defense exists. However, the presumption is rebuttable, which means that it can be overcome by evidence that the person using the force did not actually entertain a fear of death or great bodily injury to himself or herself, to his or her family, or to a member of the household. (See Penal Code § 198.5.)

A final legal principle which has developed with respect to defense of real property has to do with the use of mechanical devices, such as electric fences and spring guns (guns rigged to discharge automatically when a door or window is opened). Mechanical devices are more often used to protect nonresidential real property, such as warehouses, than residential real property. The law regarding such devices is the same for both residential and nonresidential property: deadly mechanical devices are prohibited, whereas nondeadly mechanical devices generally are not prohibited. Thus, if a business owner surrounds his or her premises with an electrified fence using a voltage that is not designed to kill or seriously injure persons touching the fence, the owner is engaging in lawful defense of his or her property. If, however, the owner uses a voltage designed to kill or seriously injure, or emplaces spring guns that will automatically shoot any person entering a door or window, the owner has used excessive force and will be criminally liable for any resulting death or injury to another. As has been observed by the courts, mechanical devices are unable to discriminate between persons lawfully and unlawfully on the property. A spring gun, for example, could as easily wound or kill a firefighter responding to a fire on the premises as a criminal unlawfully breaking into the premises.

Imperfect Self-Defense

As has already been discussed, the lawfulness of using force in self-defense and the permissible degree of force which may be employed are governed by the principle of apparent necessity. With respect to the use of deadly force in self-defense, apparent necessity requires that the actor entertain an honest and reasonable belief that he or another is threatened with commission of a felony (a forcible and atrocious crime) or infliction of serious bodily injury. The belief must be both honest and reasonable. If a defender has an honest, but unreasonable, belief that he or another is threatened with commission of a felony or infliction of serious bodily injury, and responds with deadly force, the resulting injury to or death of the assailant is not justified. If the assailant is actually killed, the defender's honest but unreasonable belief in the necessity of defending with deadly force may negate malice aforethought and reduce the killing from murder to voluntary manslaughter. In this situation, the defender's self-defense is "imperfect" in the sense that it does not completely exonerate the defender from culpability. For example, Sue is walking on a dark street late at night when she is approached by a man who asks her what time it is. Fearing robbery or rape, Sue pulls a pistol out of her purse and kills the man. In fact, no conduct on the part of the man indicated that he intended to rob or rape Sue. Accordingly, Sue cannot escape criminal liability for the homicide. If, however, her belief that she was in danger was honest, although unreasonable, the element of malice is negated and the homicide is reduced from murder to voluntary manslaughter.

Prevention of Crime and Apprehension of Criminals

The Penal Code and decisional law authorize the use of force to prevent the commission of crimes and to apprehend persons who have committed crimes.

This authorization is distinct from the right of self-defense. If, however, one is using force to prevent the commission of a crime or to apprehend a criminal, he or she is privileged to use force in self-defense if the person committing the crime or the criminal being apprehended responds in a manner that gives rise to a threat of harm to the actor.

Prevention of Crime

The principles of California law directly addressing the use of force to prevent commission of a crime are stated in two of the justifiable homicide provisions of Penal Code § 197: § 197(1) and § 197(4). Under § 197(1), a homicide is justifiable when committed by any person "when resisting any attempt to murder any person, or to commit a felony, or to do some great bodily injury upon any person." Under § 197(4), a homicide is justifiable when "necessarily committed in ... lawfully suppressing any riot, or in lawfully keeping and preserving the peace." Both sections, dealing as they do with justifiable homicide, address the use of deadly force to prevent commission of the crimes described in their provisions.

The decisional law and commentary on the use of force to prevent commission of crimes focuses principally on § 197(1), although the principles expressed in § 197(4) have been embodied in CALJIC No. 5.25. The provisions of § 197(1) authorizing the use of deadly force to resist an attempt to murder or inflict great bodily injury on another do not present conceptual problems because common sense dictates that deadly force could be used in such situation. The provision authorizing the use of deadly force to prevent the commission of a felony is conceptually problematic because, under the modern Penal Code, there are many felonies which are nonviolent, and the use of deadly force to prevent their commission would offend common sense. For example, thefts of certain items exceeding $100 in value may be prosecuted as felony grand theft. In response to this problem, the courts have limited the types of felonies that may be prevented by the use of deadly force to the same types that give rise to a right to use deadly force in self-defense. These felonies are the forcible and atrocious crimes discussed in the section on self-defense.[19]

Deadly force may not be used to resist the commission of a misdemeanor; only nondeadly force may be used. (See Penal Code § 692.) It must be kept in mind, however, that resisting the commission of any crime may expose one to a threat of harm that gives rise to a right of self-defense. Also, resisting the commission of a crime may involve the defense of others. If resisting the commission of a crime gives rise to a right of self-defense or involves the defense of others, the actor is entitled to use the degree of force necessary to protect himself or those whom he has a right to defend, regardless of whether the crime resisted is a felony or a misdemeanor. For example, Ed discovers Dennis stealing a used television set worth $150 (petty theft). Ed may not use deadly force to prevent Dennis from completing the crime. Assume that Ed tries to prevent completion of the crime by attempting to pull the television from Dennis' hands, and Dennis responds by drawing a gun. Ed is now privileged to use deadly force against Dennis, not to prevent the theft of the television set but to defend himself from the deadly threat arising from Dennis' use of the gun.

Apprehension of Criminals

Arrests by Law Enforcement Officers   It is well known that peace officers may use force to effect the arrest of one suspected of a crime. The authority of peace officers to use force when arresting a person is addressed in the Penal Code. Under Penal Code § 835, an arresting officer may employ "such restraint as is reasonable for [the arrestee's] arrest and detention." Under § 835a, an arresting officer may "use reasonable force to effect the arrest, to prevent escape or to overcome resistance." Both § 835 and § 835a impose a reasonableness standard on the degree of force that may be employed by a peace officer when effecting an arrest. Under the statutory provisions, a peace officer may use only that degree of force reasonably necessary to accomplish the purposes authorized by such provisions: to effect the arrest, to detain the arrestee, to prevent escape, and to overcome resistance. The amount of force that is reasonable in any given case is determined largely by the conduct of the arrestee. The greater the resistance offered, the greater the amount of force a peace officer may use. This principle is not without its limits, however, particularly when a peace officer uses deadly force. If a peace officer uses more force in effecting an arrest than is reasonable under the circumstances, he or she may be subjected to criminal and civil liability.

Penal Code §§ 835 and 835a address use of force generally. Penal Code § 196(3) specifically addresses use of deadly force by peace officers in arrest situations. (See Penal Code § 196(3).) Judicial decisions have interpreted this section as authorizing the use of deadly force in two situations: (1) when a felony has actually been committed, and (2) when a peace officer reasonably believes that a suspect has committed a felony.[20] As previously mentioned, there are many types of felonies in California, ranging from murder to theft of relatively small dollar amounts. The use of deadly force by a peace officer to apprehend a suspect for a felony such as the theft of avocados exceeding $100 in value offends common sense, and several California appellate courts have limited the use of deadly force under § 196(3) to apprehension of offenders who have committed felonies that threaten death or great bodily harm. No definitive statement of the principle has yet been made by the California Supreme Court.

The United States Supreme Court has imposed limits on the use of force, particularly deadly force, by law enforcement personnel when apprehending criminal suspects. In 1974, a Memphis, Tennessee, police officer shot and killed a fifteen-year-old boy who was fleeing a burglary. The boy had stolen $40. The family of the deceased boy sued the police department in federal court for violating his constitutional rights. The case, *Tennessee v. Garner* 471 U.S. 1 (1985), was ultimately reviewed by the United States Supreme Court. The Court held that the use of deadly force by a police officer is a "seizure" under the Fourth Amendment. Accordingly, the test used to determine whether the use of deadly force is proper is the Fourth Amendment's test: reasonableness. The Court then held that the use of deadly force is reasonable only when the person fleeing is a dangerous felon. The Court did not state what standard must be applied in cases of nondeadly force.

In 1989 the Court handed down *Graham v. Connor,* in which the standard was set for all preconviction arrests. In that opinion, the Court held that all seizures are to be evaluated under the Fourth Amendment reasonableness standard.

In *Graham*, the United States Supreme Court imposed the Fourth Amendment reasonableness standard on all uses of force by law enforcement personnel when effecting any restraint of a private citizen. *Tennessee v. Garner* limited the use of deadly force to situations in which the suspect is a dangerous felon. It is presently unclear whether the *Graham* decision nullified this limitation. In other words, a question remains as to whether deadly force is reasonable only when the suspect is a dangerous felon, or whether deadly force may be reasonable in other circumstances. However, in view of the California appellate court decisions previously mentioned, together with the United States Supreme Court's rulings, the sound approach for California law enforcement personnel would be to limit the use of deadly force to situations in which the arrestee is suspected of an offense that threatens death or great bodily harm, or there is a substantial risk that the suspect will cause death or serious bodily harm if his or her apprehension is delayed.[21]

GRAHAM v. CONNOR
490 U.S. 386 (1989)

This case requires us to decide what constitutional standard governs a free citizen's claim that law-enforcement officials used excessive force in the course of making an arrest, investigatory stop, or other "seizure" of his person. We hold that such claims are properly analyzed under the Fourth Amendment's "objective reasonableness" standard. ...

On November 12, 1984, Graham, a diabetic, felt the onset of an insulin reaction. He asked a friend, William Berry, to drive him to a nearby convenience store so he could purchase some orange juice to counteract the reaction. Berry agreed, but when Graham entered the store, he saw a number of people ahead of him in the checkout line. Concerned about the delay, he hurried out of the store and asked Berry to drive him to a friend's house instead.

Respondent Connor, an officer of the Charlotte, North Carolina, Police Department, saw Graham hastily enter and leave the store. The officer became suspicious that something was amiss and followed Berry's car. About one-half mile from the store, he made an investigatory stop. Although Berry told Connor that Graham was simply suffering from a "sugar reaction," the officer ordered Berry and Graham to wait while he found out what, if anything, had happened at the convenience store. When Officer Connor returned to his patrol car to call for backup assistance, Graham got out of the car, ran around it twice, and finally sat down on the curb, where he passed out briefly.

In the ensuing confusion, a number of other Charlotte police officers arrived on the scene in response to Officer Connor's request for backup. One of the officers rolled Graham over on the sidewalk and cuffed his hands tightly behind his back, ignoring Berry's pleas to get him some sugar. Another officer said: "I've seen a lot of people with sugar diabetes that never acted like this. Ain't nothing wrong with the M.F. but drunk. Lock the S.B. up." Several officers then lifted Graham up from behind, carried him over to Berry's car, and placed him face down on the hood. Regaining consciousness, Graham asked the officers to check in his wallet for a diabetic decal that he carried. In response, one of the officers told him to "shut up" and shoved his face down against the hood of the car. Four officers grabbed Graham and threw him head-first into the police car. A friend of Graham's brought some orange juice to the car, but the officers refused to let him have it. Finally, Officer Connor received a report that Graham had done nothing wrong at the convenience store, and the officers drove him home and released him.

At some point during the encounter with the police, Graham sustained a broken foot, cuts on his wrists, a bruised forehead, and an injured shoulder; he also claims to have developed a loud ringing in his right ear that continues to this day. ... [The Court then discussed previous cases which held that a due process standard should be applied in all cases of excessive force. To be successful using the due process standard, a plaintiff had to prove the actions of the police were "sadistic and malicious."]

We reject this notion that all excessive force claims brought under § 1983 [a federal statute permitting cases against government officials to be brought in federal court] are governed by a single generic standard. As we have said many times, § 1983 "is not itself a source of substantive rights," but merely provides a method for vindication of federal rights elsewhere conferred. ... In addressing an excessive force claim brought under § 1983, analysis begins by identifying the specific constitutional right allegedly infringed by the challenged application of force. ... In most instances, that will be either the Fourth Amendment's prohibition against unreasonable seizures of the person, or the Eighth Amendment's ban on cruel and unusual punishments, which are the two primary sources of constitutional protection against physically abusive governmental conduct. ...

Today we make explicit what is implicit in *Garner's* analysis, and hold that *all* claims that law-enforcement officers have used excessive force—deadly or not—in the course of an arrest, investigatory stop, or other "seizure" of a free citizen should be analyzed under the Fourth Amendment and its "reasonableness" standard. ...

The "reasonableness" of a particular use of force must be judged from the perspective of a reasonable officer on the scene, rather than with the 20/20 vision of hindsight. ... The calculus of reasonableness must embody allowance for the fact that police officers are often forced to make split-second judgments—in circumstances that are tense, uncertain, and rapidly evolving—about the amount of force that is necessary in a particular situation.

As in other Fourth Amendment contexts, however, the "reasonableness" inquiry in an excessive force case is an objective one: the question is whether the officer's actions are "objectively reasonable" in light of the facts and circumstances confronting them, without regard to their underlying intent or motivation.

Use of force in effecting the arrest of one suspected of a misdemeanor is, as a general rule, limited to nondeadly force. This rule is, however, not absolute. The language of Penal Code § 835a makes it clear that a peace officer is not required to retreat or desist from his or her efforts to arrest a suspect by reason of the resistance offered by the suspect. (See Penal Code § 835a.) The provision envisions the use of reasonable force to effect the arrest and, if the resistance of the suspect becomes so extreme that deadly force is required, the peace officer may use deadly force.

It should be kept in mind that, in addition to the foregoing principles governing the use of force to effect an arrest, a peace officer has the same right of self-defense as any other person if the suspect puts the peace officer's physical well-being in jeopardy.

Arrests by Citizens   California recognizes the right of citizens' arrest. According to Penal Code § 834, "[a]n arrest may be made by a peace officer or by a private person." Under Penal Code § 837, a private person may arrest another: (1) when any offense, including a misdemeanor, has been committed in his or her presence, (2) when the person arrested has committed a felony, although not in the arresting citizen's presence, or (3) when a felony has in fact been committed, and the citizen has reasonable cause for believing that the person being arrested committed it. A private citizen may use reasonable force to effect a citizens' arrest, subject to the limitation that deadly force may not be used by a private citizen to arrest one who has committed only a misdemeanor.[22] Use of deadly force by a private citizen is addressed in Penal Code § 197(4), certain provisions of which were previously discussed in the context of prevention of

crimes. The portion of § 197(4) pertinent here provides that a homicide is justifiable when committed by *any* person "[w]hen necessarily committed in attempting, by lawful ways and means, to apprehend any person for any felony
committed." The use of deadly force by a citizen to effect an arrest is limited by
the principle that deadly force may not be used unless a felony has been committed that threatens death or great bodily harm. There appears to be no legal
principle similar to that appearing in § 835a with respect to peace officers,
which authorizes the use of escalating force by a citizen in response to escalating
resistance by the offender. Several judicial decisions have upheld manslaughter
convictions of citizens who used deadly force in effecting arrests when the use of
such force was not necessitated by a threat of death or great bodily injury arising
from the offense committed by the arrestee. Also, it should be noted that, unlike
a peace officer who may use deadly force to arrest one whom he or she reasonably suspects has committed a felony warranting the use of deadly force, even if
a felony has not actually been committed, a private citizen may not arrest a
felon, or use deadly force in effecting the arrest, unless a felony has actually been
committed. Thus, if a private citizen uses deadly force to arrest a person whom
he or she reasonably suspects has committed a felony when, in fact, a felony has
not been committed, the private citizen is criminally and civilly liable for the results of his or her actions.

The use-of-force rules applicable to private citizens are potentially different if
the citizen is aiding a peace officer in effecting an arrest. Penal Code § 839 authorizes any person making an arrest to orally summon others to assist him or her.
As mentioned briefly in Chapter 8, if the person summoning aid is among the
categories of peace officers described in Penal Code § 150, the citizen summoned
is required to aid the peace officer. Failure to do so is a criminal offense. Arguably, in such a situation, the citizen should be privileged to use the same degree
of force the peace officer is privileged to use, although there appears to be no explicit statement of this principle in California law.

 Use of Force to Resist an Unlawful Arrest   In California, one subjected to an
unlawful arrest by a peace officer is not authorized to use force to resist the arrest
if the person knows, or should know, that the arresting person is a peace officer.
(See Penal Code § 834a.) Knowing resistance to arrest by a peace officer constitutes the offense of obstruction of justice under Penal Code § 148(a). Currently
no statutory provision prohibits resistance to an unlawful citizens' arrest.

§ 10.6   Infancy

At common law, it was a complete defense to a charge that the accused was
a child under the age of seven at the time the crime was committed. It was conclusively presumed that children under seven were incapable of forming the requisite mens rea to commit a crime. A rebuttable presumption of incapacity
existed for those between seven and fourteen years of age. The presumption
could be overcome for those between seven and fourteen if the prosecution
could prove that the child understood that the criminal act was wrong.

The Penal Code eliminates the conclusive presumption applicable to children under the age of seven and creates a rebuttable presumption that children under the age of fourteen are incapable of committing crimes. (See Penal Code § 26(One).) In a particular case, the presumption may be overcome by "clear proof" that the child offender, including an offender under the age of seven, knew the wrongfulness of his or her act. The clear proof requirement was formerly held by the courts to require proof beyond a reasonable doubt, i.e., the highest standard of proof. In a 1994 decision, however, the California Supreme Court held that *clear proof* means proof by clear and convincing evidence,[23] a lower standard than proof beyond a reasonable doubt, but a higher standard than proof by a preponderance of the evidence.

In actual practice, the defense of **infancy** is rarely raised in criminal trials because most minor offenders are dealt with by the juvenile courts and are not subjected to criminal prosecution. The purpose of the juvenile justice system differs from that of the criminal justice system. In contrast to the criminal justice system, which has punishment as one of its major purposes, the purpose of the juvenile justice system is not to punish, but to reform the delinquent child.

Minors aged fourteen and over do not enjoy the rebuttable presumption of incapacity to commit a crime applicable to children under the age of fourteen, although minors aged fourteen and over, like younger children, are generally dealt with by the juvenile courts. However, the fact that most minor offenders are dealt with by the juvenile courts does not mean that all are. There are numerous cases in which minors have been prosecuted as criminals.[24]

§ 10.7 Intoxication

In its treatment of **intoxication** as a defense, the law distinguishes between voluntary intoxication and involuntary intoxication. *Voluntary intoxication* is defined as "the voluntary ingestion, injection, or taking by any other means of any intoxicating liquor, drug, or other substance." (See Penal Code § 22.) CALJIC No. 4.23 provides that "[i]ntoxication is involuntary when it is produced in a person without [his] [her] willing and knowing use of intoxicating liquor, drugs or other substance and without [his] [her] willing assumption of the risk of possible intoxication."

Voluntary Intoxication Penal Code § 22 states the general rule that "[n]o act committed by a person while in a state of voluntary intoxication is less criminal by reason of his or her having been in that condition." What this language means is that voluntary intoxication is not a complete defense—that is, it will not completely exonerate the defendant. Under Penal Code § 22, however, voluntary intoxication may have the effect of negating the mental state required when a specific-intent crime or murder is charged. Negation of the requisite mental state does not exonerate the defendant, but may result in his or her conviction of a lesser crime not requiring the specified mental state, such as a general-intent crime. This result, however, is not assured. If the jury finds beyond a reasonable doubt that, despite his or her voluntary intoxication, the defendant formed the requisite specific intent, or premeditated, deliberated, or harbored express malice aforethought, the defendant may be found guilty of the offense charged. Voluntary intoxication is never a defense to a general-intent crime.

Involuntary Intoxication   Involuntary intoxication, as previously stated, is intoxication produced in a person without his or her willing and knowing use of intoxicating liquor, drugs, or other substances and without his or her willing assumption of the risk of possible intoxication. Like voluntary intoxication, involuntary intoxication can negate the mental state required for a specific-intent crime or murder. In addition, however, if involuntary intoxication produces a state of unconsciousness in the defendant, it can be a complete defense to the charged offense. Voluntary intoxication is not a complete defense even if the defendant was so intoxicated that he or she was in a state of unconsciousness when the crime was committed.

Involuntary intoxication has been successfully raised as a complete defense in relatively few cases. These cases have generally involved situations in which the defendant was tricked into ingesting a hallucinogenic drug such as, for example, by someone secretly putting it in a glass of beer the defendant was drinking. Recall the final words of the first paragraph of CALJIC No. 4.23, which provide that the defendant must not have willingly assumed the risk of possible intoxication. If a defendant is tricked into ingesting an illegal drug capable of producing a state of unconsciousness when, for example, he or she is engaged in using other illegal drugs, he or she may be deemed to have assumed the risk of intoxication by a hallucinogenic drug, and will not be completely exonerated by his or her unconscious state. For example, in *People v. Velez* (1985) 175 Cal.App.3d 785, the defendant testified that he had smoked a marijuana cigarette which, unknown to him, contained PCP. The defendant's involuntary intoxication defense was rejected on the ground that it is common knowledge that marijuana may be laced with PCP.

§ 10.8 Mistake

Just as the law recognizes two types of intoxication, it also recognizes two types of **mistake**: mistake of law and mistake of fact. The two types of mistake are treated differently when they are asserted by a defendant as a defense to a criminal act.

Mistake of Law   The term *mistake of law* really involves two concepts: ignorance of the law and mistake of law. It is a well-known maxim that ignorance of the law is no excuse for a violation of the law. Everyone is presumed to know the law, and it is not a defense to a crime that one did not know that his or her act was prohibited by law. Were the courts to hold otherwise, the result would be chaos in the criminal justice system and in its objective of maintaining an ordered society. Defendants could escape criminal liability by claiming that they had not read the statute they were accused of violating or did not otherwise know their conduct was illegal.

In contrast to ignorance of the law, an honest mistake of law can sometimes be a defense. Situations in which mistake of law is a defense usually are those in which the defendant acts under a mistaken belief that he or she has the legal right to commit the act in question. The offense must be one requiring a mental state more than general intent, and the mistake of law must negate the required mental state. For example, larceny requires an intent to steal, i.e., to permanently deprive another of his or her property. Assume that Bob owes Max money, but is refusing to repay it. Max, erroneously but honestly believing that he has a right to take Bob's property in satisfaction of the debt, takes Bob's car and sells it, retaining the proceeds in payment of the debt. Because Max entertained an honest, though erroneous, belief that he had a right to take Bob's property, he did not possess the intent to steal and thus has not committed larceny. The effect of Max's belief was to negate the mens rea element of the offense.

Despite the fact that mistake of law can be a defense to an offense requiring a particular mental state, reliance on the erroneous advice of an attorney has long been held not to constitute a defense. Accordingly, if one acts under an honest mistake of law emanating from one's own mind, the mistake may constitute a defense, but if the mistake of law was the result of legal advice given by an attorney, the mistake will not constitute a defense.

In contrast to erroneous advice given by an attorney, erroneous advice given by a government official regarding a matter within the scope of his or her responsibilities can be a defense to one acting in reliance on such advice. So, too, can reliance on a statute or administrative regulation that is later held to be invalid, or a judicial decision that is later overruled. The rationale is that one is entitled to, and in fact should, adhere to the rulings of government officials and official government institutions, and should not be penalized for doing so if the advice, statute, regulation, or court decision later turns out to be wrong.

Mistake of Fact   Mistake of fact is a more common defense than mistake of law. A *mistake of fact* is a mistake in the mind of the defendant regarding a fact or circumstance involved in the commission of the offense with which he or she is charged. (See Penal Code § 26(Three).) In other words, the defendant's perception of the factual situation is erroneous. If the facts, as believed by the defendant, would negate criminal liability, the mistake of fact is a defense. For example, if an attorney leaving the courthouse picks up another attorney's briefcase, believing it to be his or her own, the attorney has not committed larceny. The facts believed by the attorney negate criminal intent, in this case the intent to steal, and the attorney is not criminally liable for taking the briefcase.

To constitute a defense, a mistake of fact must negate criminal intent. As discussed in Chapter 3, there is a class of crimes that do not require criminal intent—strict liability offenses—and the general rule is that mistake of fact is not a defense to this category of crimes. If, however, the statute prescribing a strict liability offense requires that the defendant act willfully or with knowledge, mistake of fact may constitute a defense if it negates the defendant's willfulness or knowledge.

Also, certain statutes require criminal negligence rather than criminal intent for conviction. Involuntary manslaughter is such an offense. Mistake of fact is not a defense to such a crime unless it negates the element of negligence. In a number of cases, for example, persons have negligently killed other persons by pointing firearms at their victims and pulling the trigger under the mistaken belief that the firearms either were unloaded or would not fire. In some of these cases, the defendants have attempted to raise a mistake-of-fact defense, i.e., a mistaken belief regarding whether the weapon would fire. The courts have rejected the defense in such cases holding that pointing a weapon at another person and pulling the trigger under the mistaken belief that the weapon is unloaded or will not fire constitutes criminal negligence, which is the mens rea of involuntary manslaughter.

An honest and reasonable, but mistaken, belief regarding the consent of the victim in a rape case has been held to constitute a defense. So, too, has an honest and reasonable belief regarding the age of the victim in an unlawful sexual intercourse (statutory rape) case. In contrast, an honest and reasonable belief that a minor victim of a sex offense is over the age of fourteen, thereby potentially taking the act out of Penal Code § 288 (lewd and lascivious act with a child under age fourteen), has been held not to be a defense because of the strong public policy favoring protection of young children. Finally, as was discussed in Chapter 7, in a drug possession case, if the defendant knows he or she is in possession of a substance, but entertains a mistaken belief that it is something other than a controlled substance, he or she has a valid mistake-of-fact defense. To be guilty of possession of a controlled substance, a defendant must both be aware of the fact of possession and must know that the item possessed is a controlled substance.

§ 10.9 Entrapment

To what extent should police officers be permitted to induce someone to commit a crime? This question underlies the defense of entrapment. *Entrapment* occurs when law enforcement officers induce another to commit a crime with the intent of arresting and prosecuting that person for the commission of that crime.

Entrapment is a defense of recent development, although all states and the federal government recognize some form of the defense today. There is no constitutional basis for the entrapment defense, so each jurisdiction is free to structure the defense in any manner. Of course, a state may also do away with the defense, although none have done so. This is a sound policy decision, as most people would agree that there must be some limit on police conduct. The California Supreme Court explained its recognition of the entrapment defense as follows:

> [O]ut of regard for its own dignity, and in the exercise of its power and the performance of its duty to formulate and apply proper standards for judicial enforcement of the criminal law, the court refuses to enable officers of the law to consummate illegal or unjust schemes designed to foster rather than prevent and detect crime ... . Entrapment is a defense not because the defendant is innocent but because ... "it is a less evil that some criminal should escape than that the Government should play an ignoble part."[25]

As indicated by this statement, the rationale underlying the entrapment defense is not so much protection of the defendant as it is a refusal to permit the government to trap and convict people using inappropriate means.

Two tests are used in the United States to determine whether a defendant has been entrapped: the subjective and objective tests. Until 1979, California used the subjective test, also called the *origin of intent test.* This test is currently used in the federal system and most other states. The subjective test, as its name implies, examines the subjective mental state of the defendant at the time he or she is encouraged to commit the offense by law enforcement personnel. If the defendant is predisposed to commit the crime, and is only awaiting the opportunity to do so, the providing of that opportunity by law enforcement personnel does not constitute entrapment. If, however, the defendant is not predisposed to commit the offense, and does so only because of inducement by law enforcement personnel, he or she has been entrapped.

Under the subjective test, as well as under the objective test used today in California, it was and is permissible for law enforcement personnel to use decoys and feigned accomplices, or to furnish opportunities to commit crime, as a means of detecting and apprehending criminals. If such methods result in the capture of those predisposed to commit crimes, there was no entrapment. What was not permitted was the use by law enforcement of tactics that resulted in the commission of crimes by persons not predisposed to commit them. For example, it was perfectly acceptable for an undercover police officer to purchase drugs from a drug dealer for the purpose of arresting the dealer for the illegal sale. It was not permissible, however, for an undercover police officer to encourage a person not predisposed to sell drugs to acquire and sell drugs to the officer, and to badger the person until he or she finally succumbed to the pressure imposed by the police officer's badgering.

Under the subjective approach, evidence of the defendant's criminal record may be relevant to show predisposition. For example, recent drug convictions may evidence a predisposition to enter into future drug purchases or sales.

The second method of determining whether a person has been entrapped is the *objective test,* adopted by the California Supreme Court in its 1979 decision in *People v. Barraza* (1979) 23 Cal.3d 675. A similar test has been adopted in the Model Penal Code and in a minority of the other states. The objective test does not inquire into the actual mental state of the defendant at the time of the encouragement by law enforcement personnel to commit the crime. Rather, the question to be answered under the objective test is: Was the conduct of the law enforcement agent likely to induce a normally law-abiding person to commit the offense? If the answer to this question is in the affirmative, the defendant has been entrapped, regardless of his or her actual predisposition or lack of predisposition to commit the offense.

Because the defendant's actual state of mind is not relevant under the objective test, evidence of the defendant's character, predisposition to commit the crime, and his or her subjective intent are similarly irrelevant.[26] As a result, under the objective test, it is possible for a defendant who was predisposed to commit the offense to raise the defense of entrapment if the police conduct was such as would have led a normally law-abiding citizen to commit the offense. Consider, for example, a prostitute who normally charges $50 for her services. If an undercover officer approaches her and offers her $50 to have sex with him, and she accepts, she has not been entrapped because a normally law-abiding person would not consent to an act of prostitution for $50. If, however, the undercover officer offers the prostitute $10,000, and the prostitute accepts, she can raise the defense of entrapment if a normally law-abiding person would have been induced to engage in an act of prostitution for that price. The defense would be available to the prostitute in that situation despite the fact that she was predisposed to commit acts of prostitution.

Finally, as discussed earlier in this chapter, the defense of entrapment is based on public policy and does not tend to negate an element of the charged offense. As a result, a defendant raising the defense of entrapment bears both the burden of production and the burden of persuasion. The standard of proof is proof by a preponderance of the evidence. In other words, the defendant has the burden of proving by a preponderance of the evidence that the conduct of the law enforcement agents was such as would likely induce a normally law-abiding person to commit the offense.[27]

§ 10.10   Alibi

An **alibi** is a claim by a defendant that he or she was not present at the scene of the crime at the time it was committed. Whenever a defendant asserts an alibi, he or she is simply contesting the government's factual claims. CALJIC No. 4.50 addresses the alibi defense as follows:

> The defendant in this case has introduced evidence for the purpose of showing that [he] [she] was not present at the time and place of the commission of the alleged crime for which [he] [she] is here on trial. If, after consideration of all the evidence, you have a reasonable doubt that the defendant was present at the time the crime was committed, you must find [him] [her] not guilty.

§ 10.11   Consent

Consent of the victim of a crime to the act committed by the perpetrator is not a defense unless lack of consent is an element of the charged offense. For example, consent is not a defense to assault and battery. If Joe and Ed voluntarily engage in a fight, and Joe strikes Ed, Joe cannot defend against a battery charge on the ground that Ed consented to being struck by voluntarily participating in the fight. This rule does not, of course, apply to contact sports. Physical blows received during such activities are normally lawful.

Crimes such as rape, theft, and robbery have as one of their elements lack of consent of the victim. Proof that the "victim" consented in such cases constitutes a defense. Consent, however, involves more than passive assent. According to CALJIC No. 1.23:

> To consent to an act or transaction, a person (1) must act freely and voluntarily and not under the influence of threats, force or duress; (2) must have knowledge of the true nature of the act or transaction involved; and (3) must possess sufficient mental capacity to make an intelligent choice whether or not to do something proposed by another person.

> [Mere passivity does not amount to consent.] Consent requires a free will and positive cooperation in act or attitude.

Thus, apparent consent to intercourse or the taking of property induced by threats, force, or duress is not a defense. Similarly, apparent consent induced by fraud, without knowledge of the facts, is not a defense. Finally, apparent consent of a person without legal capacity to give consent, such as a child or insane person, is ineffective.[28]

§ 10.12 Statutes of Limitation

Many crimes must be prosecuted within a specified time after being committed. A **statute of limitation** sets the time limit. If prosecution is initiated after the applicable statute has expired, the defendant is entitled to a dismissal.

Statutes of limitation vary in length, generally based on the seriousness of the crimes to which they apply. The following statutory scheme is established by §§ 799 through 802 of the Penal Code.

There is no period of limitations for prosecution of an offense punishable by death or by imprisonment in the state prison for life or life without the possibility of parole, or for the embezzlement of public money. (See Penal Code § 799.) Except as provided in § 799, prosecution for an offense punishable by imprisonment in the state prison for eight years or more must be commenced within six years after commission of the offense. (See Penal Code § 800.) Except as provided in §§ 799 and 800, prosecution for an offense punishable by imprisonment in the state prison must be commenced within three years after commission of the offense. (See Penal Code § 801.)

Notwithstanding the foregoing provisions, the limitations period for certain offenses is four years after discovery of the offense or four years after completion of the offense, whichever is later. (See Penal Code § 801.) These offenses are felonies involving fraud, breach of a fiduciary obligation, or misconduct in office by a public officer, employee, or appointee. (See Penal Code § 803(c).) Offenses of this nature are frequently not discovered until after they are committed, and the law recognizes this fact by permitting the limitation period to begin running at the time the offense is discovered.

Prosecution for a misdemeanor generally must be commenced within one year after commission of the offense. (See Penal Code § 802.) Section 802 provides a two-year limitations period for the following misdemeanors: (1) a misdemeanor violation of § 647.6 (molesting or annoying a child under age eighteen) if the child is under fourteen years of age; and (2) a misdemeanor violation of § 729 of the Business and Professions Code (sexual exploitation of client or patient by psychotherapist or alcohol and drug abuse counselor).

A limitations period may be tolled in certain situations. **Tolling** refers to exclusion of time from the computation of the limitations period. For example, under § 803(d), if the defendant is outside the state of California when or after the offense is committed, the period of limitations applicable to the offense may be tolled for the period of time the defendant is outside the state, up to a maximum of three years. If a person commits an offense having a six-year limitations period on June 1, 1990, prosecution for the offense normally must commence no later than June 1, 1996. If, however, the person, after committing the offense, flees the state for two years and then returns, the two years during which he or she was absent are not counted. In that event, prosecution must commence no later than June 1, 1998.

Sections 803(f) and (g) toll the statute of limitations in child sexual abuse cases. Under § 803(f), a criminal complaint may be filed within one year after the date of a report to a responsible adult or agency (a person or agency required to report the offense) by a child under eighteen years of age of an act of sexual abuse if: (1) the period of limitations for the offense has expired, and (2) the same defendant has committed another act of sexual abuse on the child within the applicable limitations period. Under § 803(g), a criminal complaint may be filed within one year after the date of a report to a law enforcement agency by a person of any age alleging that he or she, while under the age of eighteen, was the victim of sexual abuse. Section 803(g) applies only if three conditions are met. First, the limitations period applicable to the offense must have expired. Second, the crime must have involved substantial sexual conduct other than masturbation. (See Penal Code § 1203.0(6).) Third, there must be independent evidence that clearly and convincingly corroborates the victim's allegation.

Key Terms

affirmative defense A principle of law that completely or partially absolves the defendant of guilt when the defendant has committed the act with which he or she has been charged.

alibi A claim by the defendant that he or she was not present at the scene of the crime at the time the crime was committed.

apparent necessity A legal principle applicable to the law of self-defense which provides that a person is entitled to use deadly force in self-defense to repel an attack when the circumstances are such that he or she honestly and reasonably believes that he or she is being attacked with deadly force or that the attacker is attempting to perpetrate a "forcible and atrocious crime" upon him or her, even if such belief is mistaken.

burden of persuasion The duty to persuade the trier of fact of the existence or nonexistence of a fact.

burden of production The duty to introduce evidence tending to show the existence or nonexistence of a particular fact. The burden of production does not require that the party having the burden actually persuade the trier of fact of the existence or nonexistence of the fact.

burden of proof The duty to prove the existence or nonexistence of a fact or facts material to the outcome of a case.

consent Free and voluntary assent, based upon knowledge of the true nature of the act or transaction involved, by one possessing sufficient mental capacity to make an intelligent choice. Consent by the victim is a defense to a crime only if lack of consent is an element of the crime.

diminished capacity A form of partial insanity defense under which a defendant claims that, although not sufficiently mentally impaired to be entitled to a defense of insanity, he or she may have been impaired to the point that he or she lacked the capacity to form the mental state necessary for commission of the crime. The diminished capacity defense is not recognized in California on the issue of guilt of the defendant.

duress A defense to a crime other than homicide, involving commission of an otherwise criminal act or omission under a threat to the defendant's life if he or she does not comply. The threat must be one that would cause a reasonable person to fear for his or her life, and the person threatened must have actually entertained such fear. There is some authority that a threat of serious bodily injury also constitutes duress.

Durham test A test for insanity of a defendant, which provides that the defendant will not be guilty of the crime charged, by reason of insanity, if his or her act was the product of mental disease. The Durham test is not recognized in California.

forcible and atrocious crime A concept applicable to the use of deadly force in self-defense. A forcible and atrocious crime is a felony, the character and manner of commission of which threatens, or is reasonably believed by the person against whom it is directed to threaten, life or great bodily injury, so as to instill in the person a reasonable fear of death or great bodily injury. One is legally authorized to use deadly force to defend oneself against commission of a forcible and atrocious crime.

infancy   A defense to crime based on age. Under California law, a person under the age of fourteen is presumed incapable of forming the mental state required to commit a crime. The presumption may be rebutted by a showing of clear proof that, at the time of committing the act, the child knew its wrongfulness.

intoxication   As a defense to crime, intoxication is categorized as voluntary or involuntary. *Voluntary intoxication* involves the voluntary ingestion, injection, or taking by any other means of any intoxicating liquor, drug, or other substance. Intoxication is involuntary when it is produced in a person without his or her willing and knowing use of intoxicating liquor, drugs, or other substance, and without his or her willing assumption of the risk of possible intoxication. Voluntary and involuntary intoxication have differing legal effects as defenses to crimes.

irresistible impulse   A defense to a criminal charge, which asserts that the defendant is not guilty of the crime because, although he knew the act was wrong, he was unable to control his behavior because of a disease of the mind. The irresistible impulse defense is not recognized in California.

mistake   As a defense to crime, the law distinguishes between mistake of law and mistake of fact. Ignorance of the law is never a defense. A mistaken belief that the law authorizes the act for which the defendant has been charged may constitute a defense if the offense is more than a general-intent crime and the mistake negates the mental state required for the offense. Mistake of fact may be a defense if the factual circumstances, as believed by the defendant, would mean that the act did not constitute a crime.

M'Naghten test   The test for insanity used in the California criminal justice system to determine whether a defendant is not guilty by reason of insanity. The defense may be established only when the defendant proves by a preponderance of the evidence that he or she was incapable of knowing or understanding the nature and quality of his or her act or of distinguishing right from wrong at the time of commission of the offense.

Model Penal Code test   A test for insanity under the Model Penal Code, which provides that a person is not responsible for criminal conduct if, at the time of such conduct, as a result of mental disease or defect, he or she lacked substantial capacity either to appreciate the criminality of his or her conduct or to conform his or her conduct to the requirements of law. The Model Penal Code test is not recognized in California.

necessity   A defense of limited applicability in California to acts that would otherwise be criminal but which are necessary to avoid a threat to human life imposed by natural forces.

statutes of limitation   Statutorily prescribed time limits within which prosecution for a crime must be commenced.

tolling   Exclusion of time from computation of a period prescribed by a statute of limitation.

Review Questions

1. What are the two lines of defense available to a defendant in a criminal case? Briefly explain.

2. What are the two components of the burden of proof? Who has these burdens when the defendant raises an affirmative defense?

3. Briefly describe the history of the insanity defense in California, from 1864 to the present.

4. What is the irresistible impulse defense? Is this defense recognized in California?

5. What is the diminished capacity defense? Is this defense recognized in California?

6. What is the traditional distinction between the defenses of duress and necessity?

7. Briefly explain the principle of apparent necessity which applies to the defense of self-defense.

8. May one use deadly force to prevent the theft or destruction of his or her automobile? Briefly explain.

9. May one use deadly force to protect his or her home? Briefly explain.

10. What is the constitutional limitation on the use of force by peace officers when effecting arrests or other restraints of private citizens?

11. Is a child under the age of seven capable of committing a crime under California law? Briefly explain.

12. Briefly explain the differences between the defenses of voluntary intoxication and involuntary intoxication.

13. When can mistake of law constitute a defense?

14. Briefly distinguish between the subjective and objective tests for entrapment.

15. When is the consent of the victim of a crime a defense to the crime?

16. What is a statute of limitations? What is meant by "tolling" the statute of limitations?

Review Problems

1. Ira stabbed his good friend, inflicting a fatal wound. At trial, a psychiatrist testified that Ira could not control his behavior, as he has a brain tumor that causes him to act violently. The doctor also testified that the condition did not impair Ira's ability to know what he was doing or that it was wrong. Assume that the jury believes the psychiatrist's explanation. Would Ira be convicted in a jurisdiction which uses the M'Naghten test? The irresistible impulse test? The Model Penal Code? Would Ira be convicted in California?

2. Jane was attacked by an unknown man. She was able to free herself and ran to a nearby house, with the man chasing close behind. She screamed and knocked at the door of the house. The occupant of the house opened the door and she requested refuge. The occupant refused, but Jane forced her way into the house. To gain entry, Jane had to strike the occupant. Once inside, she used the telephone to contact the police, who responded within minutes. At the insistence of the occupant of the house, Jane has been charged with trespass and battery. Does she have a defense?

3. Gary and Gene were both drinking at a bar. Gary became angered after Gene asked Gary's wife to dance. Gary walked up to Gene and struck him in the face. Gene fell to the floor, and as he was returning to his feet Gary hit him again. In response, Gene took a knife out of his pocket and attacked Gary with it. Gary then shot Gene with a gun he had hidden in his coat. The injury proved fatal. What crime has Gary committed?

4. One night, at 3 A.M., George was awakened by the sound of breaking glass, followed by the sound of his front door opening. Alarmed, George took a pistol from his closet, stealthily went to the area of the house where he heard the noise, and observed a shadowy figure moving about as if looking for something. Without saying a word, George shot and killed the person. The decedent turned out to be George's next-door neighbor who, in a drunken stupor, had mistakenly entered George's house by breaking a window next to the front door, and then reaching in and opening the door from the inside. The neighbor was apparently wandering about trying to understand where he was when George shot him. Has George committed criminal homicide in this situation?

5. Rebecca is a police officer in the city of Cownard, California. She receives a report on her radio that a farm worker has stolen $5,000 worth of avocados and is fleeing with the avocados in his truck. The radio report describes the truck and, as Rebecca is carefully listening, a truck matching the description of the farm worker's vehicle speeds by Rebecca. The truck is a pickup, and Rebecca observes a large pile of what appear to be avocados in the rear portion of the truck. Rebecca immediately pursues the truck with siren activated and lights flashing. The truck comes to a sudden stop and the driver jumps out and begins running on foot. Rebecca stops her vehicle, exits, draws her service revolver, and orders the fleeing suspect to "stop or I'll shoot." The suspect continues running, whereupon

Rebecca fires her weapon, killing the suspect. Was Rebecca's use of deadly force against the suspect lawful? Explain your answer.

6. Please refer to the fact situation in problem 5. Assume that after Rebecca shouts, "Stop or I'll shoot," she fires at the suspect and misses, and the suspect continues fleeing. Theodore, a private citizen, who happens to be carrying a firearm on his person, observes the situation, pulls out his firearm, and shouts, "Citizen's arrest; stop or I'll shoot." The suspect ignores Theodore's warning and continues fleeing, whereupon Theodore shoots the suspect, killing him. Rebecca did not request Theodore's assistance. An investigation of the incident reveals that, in fact, there was no theft of avocados and the report of the crime was in error. It is never determined why the suspect fled rather than surrender to Rebecca. Was Theodore's shooting of the suspect justifiable? Why or why not?

7. Mike is at a party at a friend's home. Illegal drugs are being freely used by the guests, including Mike. Mike is aware that LSD, a hallucinogenic drug, is available at the party; however, he is limiting his use to cocaine. Someone at the party decides it would be fun to spike the punch with LSD and does so. Mike drinks some of the punch, not knowing that it contains LSD. All of a sudden, he observes a giant insect-like creature grasping a beautiful princess. Mike grabs a kitchen knife and attacks the creature, killing it. What Mike actually observed was two party guests dancing. Unfortunately, Mike really did kill the guest who appeared to him to be an insect-like creature. If Mike is charged with murder, what defense or defenses is he likely to raise? Will he be successful?

8. Rachel is walking in the business district of her town when she sees an envelope lying on the sidewalk. She picks up the envelope and looks inside. The envelope contains Sam's paycheck. Sam has already endorsed it on the back. Rachel takes the check to Harley's Check Cashing Palace and cashes the check. She is later arrested and prosecuted for theft. Discuss her likely success if she raises the following defenses:
   a. "I didn't know it was against the law to cash a check I found on the sidewalk."
   b. "I remembered from my Business Law course in college that, under the Uniform Commercial Code, a check that has been endorsed in blank [Sam endorsed in blank] can be cashed by any person in possession of the check. So, I thought I could legally cash the check." [Note: although Rachel is correct about the Uniform Commercial Code, she is mistaken in her belief that it gives her the right to take someone else's money.]

9. A city ordinance requires that all restaurants maintain fire extinguishers capable of extinguishing grease fires in their kitchens. Violation of the ordinance is a misdemeanor. Reynaldo is the owner of a restaurant. He has fire extinguishers in the kitchen which he believes are capable of extinguishing grease fires. Unfortunately, he is incorrect. During an inspection of the restaurant's kitchen, a city inspector discovers the violation and cites Reynaldo. What defense is Reynaldo likely to raise when he is prosecuted for the violation? Is he likely to be successful?

10. Peter works for a large food manufacturer. For years, he has skillfully stolen food products from the company and resold them to black-market distributors in foreign countries. The company management begins to suspect wrongdoing by Peter and consults with the local police. The police decide to conduct a "sting" operation through which they hope to implicate Peter in the theft of the company's products. Two police officers visit Peter in his office and, after being assured that they cannot be overheard, inform Peter that they are representatives of a foreign black-market organization which is seeking a supplier of food products on a long-term basis. They inform Peter that their organization will purchase all the food products he can steal from his employer. They also inform Peter that, in addition to paying his price for the food products he sells to their organization, their organization will pay Peter $100,000 per year as compensation for participating in "the program." After thinking the offer over for a few days, Peter agrees. When he makes the first delivery to the police officers, they arrest him and charge him with grand theft. At his trial, Peter raises the defense of entrapment. Discuss the subjective and objective tests for entrapment, and Peter's likelihood of success under each.

Notes

1 *M'Naghten's Case,* 8 Eng. Rep. 718 (H.L. 1843).

2 LaFave & Scott, *Criminal Law* § 4.2A(a) (West 1986).

3 1 Witkin & Epstein, *California Criminal Law* § 205 (2d ed., Bancroft-Whitney 1988).

4 *United States v. Brawner,* 471 F.2d 969 (D.C. Cir. 1972).

5 Model Penal Code § 4.01(1).

6 Cal. Penal Code § 25(c).

7 Penal Code § 25(b). *See also* Evidence Code § 522.

8 Penal Code § 1026(a).

9 Penal Code § 1026(b).

10 Penal Code § 1026.5.

11 *Dusky v. United States,* 362 U.S. 402 (1960).

12 Penal Code § 1370.01.

13 *Ford v. Wainwright,* 477 U.S. 399 (1986).

14 *Id.* at 417.

15 CALJIC No. 5.13.

16 *See* CALJIC No. 5.50.

17 *See also* Civil Code § 50.

18 *See* CALJIC No. 5.40.

19 *See* CALJIC No. 5.10.

20 1 Witkin & Epstein, *supra* note 3, at § 252.

21 *See generally* 1 Witkin & Epstein, *supra* note 3, at § 253.

22 1 Witkin & Epstein, *supra* note 3, at § 256.

23 *In re Manuel L.* (1994) 7 Cal.4th 229.

24 *See, e.g.,* 1 Witkin & Epstein, *supra* note 3, at § 186.

25 *People v. Benford* (1959) 53 Cal.2d 1, 9.

26 *See, e.g.,* CALJIC No. 4.61.

27 CALJIC No. 4.60.

28 1 Witkin & Epstein, *supra* note 3, at § 259.

CHAPTER 11

Constitutional Limits on the Power of Government to Define and Prosecute Offenses

OUTLINE

Introduction

Chapter 10 examined the two lines of defense available to a defendant at trial: defense by denial and affirmative defenses. These means of defense presuppose the legal validity of the defendant's trial and the penal statutes upon which the trial is based. A defendant raising such defenses in essence asserts that he or she either did not commit the charged offense or, if he or she did commit the offense, that he or she has a defense that negates criminal culpability.

In addition to the foregoing means of defense, a criminal defendant may raise constitutional principles if warranted by the circumstances of the case. For example, if the defendant has been previously put in jeopardy for the offense for which he or she is being tried, he or she may raise the defense of double jeopardy. If the defendant wishes to refrain from testifying, he or she may invoke the right against self-incrimination. In some situations, a criminal defendant may go so far as to attack the validity of the criminal statute under which he or she is

255

being prosecuted. A challenge of this nature claims that the statute is unconstitutional for one or more reasons, such as:

- It amounts to a denial of due process or equal protection of the law
- It is void because it is vague or overbroad
- It constitutes an ex post facto law or bill of attainder
- It violates certain fundamental rights, such as freedom of religion, freedom of speech, the right of privacy, or certain other fundamental rights.

This chapter examines these constitutional principles and their effect on the power of government to define and prosecute criminal offenses.

In prosecutions in California state courts, adherence to the principles of two constitutions is involved: the United States Constitution and the California Constitution. As discussed in more detail in Chapter 13, the principles of the United States Constitution applicable to criminal prosecutions are found primarily in the first ten amendments, commonly known as the *Bill of Rights*. Although initially considered applicable only to trials in the federal courts, most of the rights guaranteed by the Bill of Rights have been applied to state court proceedings through decisions of the United States Supreme Court. The legal basis for these decisions has been primarily the Fourteenth Amendment to the United States Constitution, which provides that no state "shall deprive any person of life, liberty, or property, without due process of law, nor deny to any person within its jurisdiction the equal protection of the laws." As a result of the application of federal constitutional rights to state court prosecutions, criminal prosecutions in California state courts are subject to the rights accorded criminal defendants by both the United States and California Constitutions.

The California Constitution contains provisions affording many of the same rights to criminal defendants as does the United States Constitution. If criminal defendants in California state courts have the rights guaranteed by the United States Constitution, what is the role of the California Constitution? In *People v. Brisendine* (1975) 13 Cal.3d 528, the California Supreme Court squarely addressed this issue. According to the court, even California constitutional provisions that mirror those in the United States Constitution do not necessarily have the same meaning or effect as their federal counterparts. All that is required in the relationship of the two constitutions is that the California constitutional provisions accord at least the same degree of protection as the federal constitutional provisions. Beyond that, the California courts are free to interpret California constitutional provisions in a manner that accords greater protection than their federal counterparts. In 1974, § 24 was added to article I of the California Constitution. That section states: "Rights guaranteed by this Constitution are not dependent on those guaranteed by the United States Constitution." Thus, in any California criminal case in which the defense has raised a constitutional issue, two bodies of constitutional law must be consulted: that which has evolved under the federal Constitution and that which has evolved under the California Constitution.

The constitutional rights discussed in this chapter are restricted to those that limit the power of government to define and prosecute criminal offenses. Many other rights are guaranteed to those suspected or accused of crimes by the United States and California constitutions, such as the right to a speedy trial, the right to confront adverse witnesses, and the right to counsel. These and other rights applicable during the various stages of a criminal prosecution are discussed in Part II of this text.

§ 11.1 Double Jeopardy

The Fifth Amendment to the United States Constitution provides that "no person shall be subject for the same offense to be twice put in jeopardy of life or limb." Article I, § 15, of the California Constitution states that "Persons may not twice be put in jeopardy for the same offense." What these two constitutional provisions mean is that a person may not be put "in jeopardy"—i.e., at risk of a criminal conviction—for the same offense more than one time. The operative legal term in both the United States and California constitutional provisions is **jeopardy**. If a double jeopardy claim is raised by a defendant, the court will inquire as to whether jeopardy has "attached" in both the former and present proceedings. If the answer is in the affirmative, the defendant has been twice put in jeopardy for the same offense, and the second proceeding must be dismissed.

Generally, jeopardy *attaches* when the trial of the defendant commences. Completion of the trial is unnecessary. If the trial is by jury, jeopardy attaches when jury selection is completed and the members of the jury have been sworn. If the trial is a court trial (i.e., a trial by the judge without a jury), jeopardy attaches when the trial is "entered upon." A court trial is *entered upon* when the first witness is sworn. Once a jury trial has commenced by the selection and swearing of the jury, or once a court trial has commenced by the swearing of the first witness, the defendant has been put in jeopardy (i.e., at risk of conviction of the charged offense) and cannot be put in jeopardy for the same offense again. If for some reason the trial of the case is not completed, the defendant cannot be retried for the same offense.

Because jeopardy attaches when the trial of the defendant commences, pretrial proceedings do not place a suspect or accused in jeopardy. A person may be subjected to the full range of pretrial criminal procedures (which are discussed in Part II) only to have the government decide not to commence a trial in the case. In such a situation, the suspect or accused may be tried at a later date because jeopardy has not attached.

Double jeopardy, also called *former jeopardy*, may appear to be a simple concept, but, in actuality, it is relatively complex in its application. The remainder of this section deals with specific applications of the double jeopardy principle to particular attributes of a criminal trial.

Mistrial   The first attribute of a criminal trial that may raise double jeopardy issues is the phenomenon known as **mistrial**. A *mistrial* is a termination of a trial by the judge before the trial's conclusion for some legally recognized reason. The usual basis for a mistrial is the occurrence of a procedural defect in the conduct of the trial which cannot be corrected and which creates the risk that the defendant will not receive a fair trial or will not be accorded all of his or her procedural rights. Inflammatory arguments by the prosecutor that appeal to the prejudices of jury members and absence of a juror are two examples of circumstances that will justify declaration of a mistrial. The inability of the jury to reach a verdict, termed a *hung jury,* is another common ground for a mistrial.

When a judge declares a mistrial, a question arises as to whether the defendant may be tried again for the offense that was the subject of the first trial. The general rule is that once a trial has commenced, the defendant is in jeopardy, and may not be retried after a mistrial unless: (1) the defendant consented to declaration of the mistrial, or (2) mistrial was declared for reasons of "legal necessity." A defendant is deemed to consent to declaration of a mistrial if the defendant is the party who requests the court to declare the mistrial. In some situations, a defendant may be deemed to impliedly consent to a motion for mistrial made by the prosecution or a mistrial declared by the court on its own motion. If the defendant is deemed to have consented to declaration of the mistrial, the claim of double jeopardy is waived and the defendant may be retried for the same offense.

Legal necessity for declaration of a mistrial can exist in a number of situations. Legal necessity is the standard used in the California courts and means that there is some recognized, proper cause for declaration of a mistrial. Federal courts use a standard known as *manifest necessity,* which is less strict than California's legal necessity standard. Legal necessity may arise from such causes as: illness, other incapacity, or absence of a juror when no alternate juror is available (see Code of Civil Procedure § 233; Penal Code § 1147); inability of jurors to agree on a verdict (a hung jury) (see Penal Code § 1140); absence of the defendant from the trial proceedings; discovery by defense counsel of a conflict of interest during trial; and disqualification of the judge during the trial.[1] If a mistrial is declared because of legal necessity, there is no jeopardy and the defendant may be retried. It is unnecessary for the defendant to consent to declaration of a mistrial based on legal necessity.

Acquittal   Penal Code § 1023 provides that if a defendant is acquitted of a charged offense, the acquittal is a bar to another prosecution for the same offense, as well as for any included offense. An *included offense* is a lesser offense consisting of some, but not all, of the elements of the greater offense with which a defendant is charged. For example, a charge of assault with intent to commit rape necessarily includes the lesser offense of simple assault. Simple assault contains some, but not all, of the elements of assault with intent to commit rape. It is possible that the trier of fact will acquit the defendant on the more serious charge of assault with intent to commit rape, but find the defendant guilty of simple assault. This result is possible even if the defendant has not been separately charged with simple assault. If simple assault has not been separately charged, however, it is also possible that the trier of fact will simply acquit the defendant of the assault with intent to commit rape charge and render no verdict on the uncharged lesser offense of simple assault. In that situation, the acquittal on the greater charge operates as a bar to future prosecution for that charge or for the uncharged lesser included offense.

Other situations are also possible. For example, the jury may acquit the defendant of the assault with intent to commit rape charge, and attempt to reach a verdict on the lesser included offense of simple assault, but find that it cannot agree on a verdict for the lesser offense. The jury, in effect, becomes a hung jury with respect to the lesser included offense. In such a case, the court may declare a mistrial with respect to the lesser included offense, and the defendant may be retried for that offense.

Note that the reverse of this situation cannot occur; that is, if the jury finds the defendant not guilty of a lesser included offense, it *must* find the defendant not guilty of the greater offense. The reason for this rule is that the lesser included offense contains some elements of the greater offense. By acquitting the defendant of the lesser offense, the jury is finding that one or more of these elements has not been established. If even one element of the greater offense is not established, the jury must acquit the defendant of the greater offense. Put in terms of double jeopardy, if the jury acquits the defendant of a lesser included offense, the acquittal operates as an acquittal of the greater offense, and the defendant cannot be retried for the greater offense.

In *People v. Orr,* the defendant was charged with murder in the beating death of the man with whom she lived. Voluntary manslaughter and involuntary manslaughter are lesser included offenses of murder. The defendant was not separately charged with the lesser included offenses, but the jury addressed them nonetheless. The jury acquitted the defendant of murder and involuntary manslaughter, but could not reach a verdict on the offense of voluntary manslaughter. After the trial court declared a mistrial as to the voluntary manslaughter offense, the defendant was retried for voluntary manslaughter and convicted. The defendant appealed, claiming that involuntary manslaughter is a lesser

---

PEOPLE v. CONNIE MARIA ORR
22 Cal.App.4th 780; 27 Cal.Rptr.2d 553
[Feb. 1994]

Appellant contends that the principle of double jeopardy barred the second trial, asserting that involuntary manslaughter is a lesser included offense of voluntary manslaughter and her acquittal of the former offense served as an implied acquittal of the latter. We affirm the judgment. …

The essence of appellant's contention that her conviction must be reversed is as follows. Involuntary manslaughter is a lesser included offense of voluntary manslaughter because involuntary manslaughter has two elements in common with voluntary manslaughter—a human being was killed and the killing was "unlawful." Because the jury acquitted her of involuntary manslaughter in the first trial, it necessarily determined that the respondent failed to prove at least one of those elements, presumably that the killing was "unlawful." Thus, her acquittal of involuntary manslaughter should have served to prevent the subsequent trial. We conclude that the argument fails because the "unlawful" element of involuntary manslaughter differs from that of voluntary manslaughter.

"[W]here an offense cannot be committed without necessarily committing another offense, the latter is a necessarily included offense." The jury was instructed that both voluntary and involuntary manslaughter were lesser included offenses of murder (CALJIC No. 17.10 (1989 re-rev.)). In addition it was instructed, pursuant to CALJIC Nos. 8.40 and 8.45, regarding the elements of each of those offenses.

* * *

[T]o convict a person of voluntary manslaughter, the jury must find that the killing was intended and was *unlawful* in that it was *neither justifiable,* that is, did not constitute lawful defense of self, others, or property, prevention of a felony, or preservation of the peace; *nor excusable,* that is, the killing did not result from a lawful act done by lawful means with ordinary caution and a lawful intent, and did not result from accident and misfortune under very specific circumstances, including that no dangerous weapon was used. In order to convict a person of involuntary manslaughter, the jury must find that the killing was *unlawful* in that it occurred in the commission of an ordinary lawful act which inherently involved a high degree of risk of death or great bodily harm and was accomplished in a criminally negligent manner. The definition of *unlawful* as an element of involuntary manslaughter differs significantly from that of voluntary manslaughter and requires the trier of fact to make substantially different findings. Voluntary manslaughter can be committed without committing involuntary manslaughter, and thus the latter is not a lesser included offense of voluntary manslaughter.

While both voluntary and involuntary manslaughter are lesser included offenses of murder, it does not follow that involuntary manslaughter is a lesser included offense of voluntary manslaughter. They are merely siblings who have a common parent.

Both federal and state Constitutions provide that a person cannot be subjected to more than one prosecution for the same offense. (U.S. Const., 5th and 14th Amends.; Cal. Const., art. I, § 15.) In addition, [Penal Code §] 1023 provides: "When the defendant is convicted or acquitted or has been once placed in jeopardy upon an accusatory pleading, the conviction, acquittal, or jeopardy is a bar to another prosecution for the offense charged in such accusatory pleading, or for an attempt to commit the same, *or for an offense necessarily included therein,* of which he might have been convicted under that accusatory pleading." (Italics added.) Appellant contends that her conviction must be reversed "premised in double jeopardy considerations because her acquittal of the lesser included crime of involuntary manslaughter operated as an 'implied acquittal' of the greater charge of voluntary manslaughter." The contention is without merit since, as discussed above, involuntary manslaughter is not a lesser included offense of voluntary manslaughter.

The judgment is affirmed.

included offense of voluntary manslaughter and that her acquittal of involuntary manslaughter operated as an acquittal of the voluntary manslaughter offense. Therefore, argued the defendant, she could not, under principles of double jeopardy, be retried for the voluntary manslaughter offense because she had been acquitted of it. The appellate court disagreed for the reasons stated in the case excerpt.

Dismissal If a case is dismissed after commencement of the trial for a reason involving the merits of the charge against the defendant, such as insufficiency of the evidence, the defendant may not be tried again. If, however, dismissal is on a technical ground, such as a defect in an accusatory pleading (to be discussed in a later chapter) or some other procedural defect, the commencement of the dismissed proceeding does not, as a general rule, bar a second prosecution for the same offense.

Conviction Conviction of a defendant may occur after a trial or after entry of a plea of guilty by the defendant. In either case, conviction of the defendant is a bar to any further trial of the defendant for the same offense or for any included offense.

Particular Issues with Appeals and Reversals If a defendant is charged with an offense, is convicted of that offense, and then appeals, and the appellate court reverses the conviction, the defendant may be retried for the same offense. There is one exception to this rule: when the appellate court reverses the conviction because the prosecution produced insufficient evidence at trial to support a conviction. In such a case, the double jeopardy provisions of the United States and California Constitutions bar retrial of the defendant. In the words of the United States Supreme Court, the Double Jeopardy Clause "forbids a second trial for the purpose of affording the prosecution another opportunity to supply evidence which it failed to muster in the first proceeding."[2]

Not infrequently, a defendant is charged with an offense but is convicted of a lesser offense at trial. If the defendant appeals the conviction and succeeds in obtaining a reversal, can he or she can be retried for the originally charged offense, or only for the lesser offense for which he or she was actually convicted? The rule in both the federal and California courts is that the defendant may be retried only for the lesser offense of which he or she was actually convicted. Conviction of the lesser offense is deemed tantamount to an acquittal of the greater offense originally charged—and, as has been previously discussed, an acquittal is an absolute bar to retrial for an offense. For example, if Melinda is charged with first-degree murder, but is convicted at trial of voluntary manslaughter, and the voluntary manslaughter conviction is reversed on appeal, Melinda is subject to retrial on a charge of voluntary manslaughter, but not on a charge of first-degree murder. Her conviction of voluntary manslaughter is deemed to be an acquittal on the more serious first-degree murder charge.

A related question is whether a defendant whose conviction is reversed on appeal, and who is subsequently retried and reconvicted, can receive a greater punishment than he or she received at the first trial. The federal and California rules differ on this point. Under the federal rule, the defendant may receive a greater sentence if convicted on retrial, provided it is not imposed as a penalty for seeking appellate review of the initial conviction. The California rule, applicable in the California courts, is contrary to the federal rule: a greater sentence may not be imposed on retrial. The California rule provides greater protection to a defendant than does the federal rule and is one of many examples in California criminal procedure of California legal principles that do so.

Proceedings in Other Jurisdictions   Under both federal and state constitutional principles, a defendant is not subjected to double jeopardy if he or she is tried for the same offense by two different sovereigns. For example, if a defendant commits a kidnapping in California and takes his victim to Nevada, he has committed the offense of kidnapping under both California and Nevada law. Because he has transported his victim across the California-Nevada state line, he has also committed kidnapping under federal law. The defendant may be tried for the offense of kidnapping by the states of California and Nevada, as well as by the federal government, without violating the double jeopardy provisions of the federal and state constitutions involved.

Although there is no constitutional bar to multiple trials for the same offense by differing sovereigns, a number of states, including California, have enacted statutes affording defendants a statutory (as opposed to constitutional) double jeopardy defense if they were previously subjected to trial for an offense in another jurisdiction. The California statute is Penal Code § 656. Section 656 requires more than that the defendant have been put in jeopardy in the other jurisdiction. The defendant must have actually been acquitted or convicted of the charged offense. If this requirement is met, however, the defendant cannot be prosecuted for the same offense in California.

Single Act Constituting Multiple Offenses   A single act or transaction by a defendant may constitute more than one criminal offense. For example, a defendant who blows up an airliner, killing all persons on board, has committed as many homicides as there were persons on the airplane. The killing of each victim constitutes a separate crime. Similarly, a single act or course of conduct by a defendant against a single victim may violate several criminal statutes. The violation of each statute is a separate offense. The double jeopardy provisions of the United States and California Constitutions do not prohibit separate trials of the defendant for each offense, with one exception: in the case of violations of multiple statutes, if the offenses are lesser included offenses of the most serious offense committed, separate trials are not permitted. The constitutional double jeopardy provisions also do not prohibit separate punishments for each offense. However, as it has done with respect to trials by several sovereigns, the legislature has enacted statutory provisions limiting the seeming harshness of the constitutional rule. Penal Code § 654, read together with Penal Code § 954, generally requires that all offenses arising out of an act or course of conduct be prosecuted in a single proceeding. Under § 654 and the judicial decisions interpreting it, if a single act or "indivisible course of conduct" by a defendant violates more than one statute, the defendant may be charged with and convicted of each separate statutory violation, but only one punishment may be imposed. The punishment that may be imposed in such a situation is the punishment prescribed for any one of the violations for which the defendant is convicted. Generally, the court will sentence the defendant to the punishment for the most serious offense of which the defendant was convicted.

As stated, these principles apply when the defendant's act or indivisible course of conduct may be charged as a violation of two or more statutes. The foregoing principles do not apply when the defendant has committed distinct acts constituting separate offenses. In such cases, the defendant may be sentenced for each offense of which he or she is convicted.

§ 11.2 Self-Incrimination and Immunity

The Fifth Amendment to the United States Constitution states that no person "shall be compelled in any criminal case to be a witness against himself." This protection applies to state court proceedings through the Fourteenth Amendment to the United States Constitution. In addition, article I, § 15, of the California Constitution states that "[p]ersons may not ... be compelled in a criminal cause to be a witness against themselves." As interpreted by the courts, the constitutional provisions regarding **self-incrimination** yield two distinct privileges: (1) the privilege of a defendant in a criminal case to refuse to testify at all, and (2) the privilege of a witness in any type of proceeding to refuse to answer a question that will tend to incriminate him or her, i.e., to subject him or her to criminal prosecution. These two privileges are recognized in California Evidence Code §§ 930 and 931.

Privilege of Criminal Defendant Not to Testify A defendant in a criminal case has the constitutional right to refuse to be called as a witness by the prosecution. If a defendant is not represented by counsel, and is called as a witness by the prosecution, the court must advise him or her of the right to refuse to testify. The privilege protects against *testimonial compulsion.* This means that a criminal defendant cannot be compelled to give evidence of a testimonial nature; that is, he or she may not be compelled to give evidence that would be tantamount to testifying against himself or herself. Evidence of a testimonial nature has been described by the United States Supreme Court as evidence that reveals a defendant's own knowledge of facts relating him or her to the charged offense, or evidence that discloses his or her thoughts and beliefs to the government.[3] A defendant may be required to give evidence of a nontestimonial nature. Such evidence is usually given during the investigative phase of a criminal proceeding, before trial commences, although it may be given at trial as well. A defendant, for example, may be compelled to put on clothes similar to those worn by the perpetrator of the charged offense, to speak for voice identification by a witness, to submit to fingerprinting, to submit to the taking of hair samples, to give handwriting exemplars, or to participate in police lineups and other investigative procedures that may produce incriminating evidence, but that do not involve the defendant's disclosure of his or her own knowledge of facts relating him or her to the charged offense, or evidence that discloses his or her thoughts and beliefs to the government. The scope of the privilege against self-incrimination during the investigative stage of a criminal proceeding is discussed in greater detail in Chapter 15. A recent, and well-known, example of compelled nontestimonial evidence was the "bloody gloves" incident during the murder trial of a well-known sports personality. The defendant was required by the prosecution to put on a pair of bloody gloves that had allegedly been found outside his home. The scene was televised, and many readers will remember the defendant standing before the jury struggling to don the gloves—which did not fit! This demonstration turned out to be very damaging to the prosecution's case. Had the gloves fit, the demonstration would undoubtedly been quite damaging to the defense's case, and the incriminating evidence produced thereby would not have violated the defendant's right against self-incrimination.

A defendant may waive the privilege against self-incrimination at trial by voluntarily testifying in his or her own behalf. The waiver is not a complete waiver, but is limited to answering questions by the prosecutor that are within the permissible scope of cross-examination or that are permissible for purposes of impeaching the defendant's testimony. When a defendant testifies in his or her own behalf, he or she may be cross-examined by the prosecutor regarding the matters to which he or she testified, that is, he or she may be asked questions designed to refute or explain his or her testimony. *Impeachment* of a witness involves demonstrating his or her lack of credibility, and a defendant who voluntarily testifies may be asked questions on cross-examination that are designed to show that he or she should not be believed. Once the defendant has "opened the door," so to speak, to this type of questioning, he or she may not refuse to answer the prosecutor's questions on the ground of self-incrimination. The possibility of such damaging cross-examination requires a defendant and his or her attorney to carefully consider whether the defendant should take the stand and testify in his or her own defense.

A corollary to the privilege against self-incrimination is that, if a defendant decides not to testify in his or her own behalf, that fact may not be unfavorably commented upon by the prosecutor or the court. Thus, prosecutors, in their arguments to the jury, or judges, in their instructions to the jury, may not urge or advise the jury to consider that the defendant had the opportunity at trial to explain the evidence against him or her and did not do so. In fact, if a defendant does not testify, he or she is entitled to a jury instruction that no inference may be drawn from that fact (CALJIC No. 260).

Privilege of Witness in any Proceeding Not to Give Incriminating Testimony

In contrast to the broad privilege of a criminal defendant to refuse to testify at all, other witnesses in criminal proceedings, and all witnesses (including parties) in civil proceedings, may be required to testify. All witnesses, however, retain the constitutional right to refuse to answer specific questions if the answers would tend to incriminate them. The courts recognize two types of incriminating questions: those which, if answered, will directly incriminate the witness, and those which, if answered, will form a link in the chain of evidence of guilt and thus indirectly incriminate the witness.

For example, assume a defendant is on trial for bank robbery and the defense calls as a witness a close associate of the defendant. On cross-examination, the prosecutor asks the witness: "Have you ever participated in a bank robbery?" If the witness has participated in a bank robbery in the past, or in the robbery for which the defendant is on trial, the answer to the question (if truthful) will directly incriminate the witness. Assume further that it has been established that the defendant planned the bank robbery with a number of other persons, and that one of the meetings occurred at the defendant's home on the evening of July 7. If the prosecution asks the witness whether he was at the defendant's home on the evening of July 7, and the truthful answer is "yes," the answer will indirectly incriminate the witness because it shows a possible association with the bank robbery; it shows that the witness may have participated in the planning of the crime, although it does not fully establish that the witness participated in the crime. The answer to the question, if given, will provide the prosecution with a link in an evidentiary chain that could lead to prosecution of the witness for the bank robbery.

An answer to a question will not be deemed incriminatory if the witness cannot be prosecuted for the offense to which the answer relates. A witness who has already been convicted of an offense, for example, may not refuse to testify about his or her participation in the offense once his or her time to appeal the conviction expires. The witness may be ordered to testify because the principle of double jeopardy protects him or her from another prosecution for that offense. Similarly, if the applicable statute of limitations would prevent prosecution for an offense, a witness may not refuse to testify about it on the ground of self-incrimination. Finally, a witness may be compelled to testify about an offense if he or she has been granted immunity from prosecution.

Immunity

Notwithstanding the right against self-incrimination contained in the federal and California constitutions, a witness who is granted immunity from prosecution may be compelled to testify as to matters that could be incriminatory. There are two types of immunity: transactional and derivative use. The latter is frequently referred to as *use immunity.*

Transactional immunity shields a witness from prosecution for the offense about which he or she is compelled to testify. For example, if a witness testifies concerning a robbery, the government may not prosecute the witness for that robbery, even though the government may have evidence of guilt independent of the witness's testimony.

Use immunity is more limited than transactional immunity. A grant of use immunity prohibits the government from using the witness's testimony or any evidence derived from that testimony to prosecute the witness. However, all evidence that is independently obtained may be used against the witness.

The general rule regarding immunity is that the grant of immunity must protect the witness from prosecution to the same degree as invocation of the right against self-incrimination. It is said that the scope of the immunity must be coextensive with the protection afforded by the right against self-incrimination. Transactional immunity clearly meets this requirement and, in fact, exceeds it because the witness is not only protected from adverse criminal consequences he or she could avoid by invoking the right against self-incrimination, but is also protected from the use of incriminating evidence independently obtained by the government. Use immunity has been challenged as not meeting the coextensiveness requirement, but such challenges have been rejected by the courts. By prohibiting the government from using the witness's testimony against him or her, as well as any evidence derived from that testimony, the witness receives the same protection from prosecution he or she would receive, if he or she refused to testify, through assertion of the right against self-incrimination. Use immunity therefore meets the coextensiveness requirement.

In California, the Penal Code accords differing treatment to grants of immunity in felony and misdemeanor proceedings. Penal Code § 1324 applies to felony proceedings and provides that if a witness refuses to testify on the ground that he or she may be incriminated by the testimony, the prosecutor may request that the court order the witness to answer. If the court issues the order, the witness must testify, but is granted use immunity. (See Penal Code § 1324.) If the witness, after having been ordered by the court to testify, continues to refuse to testify, he or she may be held in contempt of court.

Penal Code § 1324.1 applies to misdemeanor proceedings. Under § 1324.1, the witness is not compelled by court order to testify. Instead, he or she can voluntarily decide to testify; if so, the witness enters into a written agreement with the district attorney that he or she will do so. If the witness then testifies, he or she is granted transactional immunity. (See Penal Code § 1324.1.) If the witness refuses to testify after entering into the agreement with the district attorney, the witness is not subject to contempt of court because he or she has not been ordered by the court to testify. The witness, however, forfeits any grant of immunity under the agreement and can be prosecuted for the offense to which his or her testimony was to relate.

Not infrequently, a defendant calls a witness to testify on his or her behalf, but the witness, after taking the witness stand, invokes the right against self-incrimination and refuses to testify. In such a situation, the defendant may claim that the prosecutor has an obligation to seek immunity for the witness under Penal Code §§ 1324 or 1324.1 so that the witness's testimony may be made available to the defense. Some defendants have also argued that if the prosecution refuses to seek immunity for the witness, the court has the inherent power to grant use immunity to the witness. In *In re Stanley Williams,* the defendant was convicted of robbery and murder of a convenience store employee, and of murder of three members of a family who owned and operated a motel. The convictions were upheld on appeal. The defendant then sought review of his convictions by petitioning the California Supreme Court for a writ of habeas corpus. (Habeas corpus proceedings are discussed in Chapter 19.) In his petition for writ of habeas corpus, the defendant challenged the constitutionality of the proceedings in the trial court. One of the defendant's constitutional challenges involved the fact that several witnesses called by the defendant asserted the right against self-incrimination and refused to testify. The defendant claimed that he was denied a fair trial because neither the prosecutor nor the court

---

In re STANLEY WILLIAMS
7 Cal.4th 572; 29 Cal.Rptr.2d 64; 870 P.2d 1072
[Apr. 1994]

Petitioner insists that in light of his witnesses' invocation of their Fifth Amendment rights, either the prosecution, or the court, had an obligation to grant his witnesses immunity sufficient to allow them to testify at the hearing.

Petitioner's claim of a right to compulsory prosecutorial immunity for his witnesses is easily rejected. Petitioner has no such right. As [prior] cases disclose, although the prosecution has a statutory right, incident to its charging authority, to grant immunity and thereby compel testimony (Pen. Code, § 1324), California cases have uniformly rejected claims that a criminal defendant has the same power to compel testimony by forcing the prosecution to grant immunity.

Petitioner insists, nevertheless, that the court ... had inherent power to grant his witnesses whatever immunity might be necessary to compel their testimony. He relies on *People v. Hunter* (1989) 49 Cal.3d 957, 972 et seq. [264 Cal.Rptr. 367, 782 P.2d 608], in which we *declined to decide* whether "in appropriate circumstances an essential witness for a criminal defendant should be granted judicial use immunity," but concluded that, even if available, such immunity was not required in that case.

As *Hunter* makes clear, the vast majority of cases, in this state and in other jurisdictions, reject the notion that a trial court has "inherent power" to confer immunity on a witness called by the defense. We noted and discussed the "one case which has clearly recognized such a right, *Government of Virgin Islands v. Smith* (3d Cir. 1980) 615 F.2d 964," and

concluded that even under *Smith,* the defendant's offer of proof "fell well short of the standards set forth" in that case. (*People v. Hunter,* 49 Cal.3d at p. 974.) We reach the same conclusion, by the same reasoning, in this case.

As we explained in *Hunter, supra,* although the *Smith* court recognized the possibility of judicially conferred immunity in special cases, it "also recognized that 'the opportunities for judicial use of this immunity power must be clearly limited; ... the proffered testimony must be clearly exculpatory; the testimony must be essential; and there must be no strong governmental interests which countervail against a grant of immunity ... [¶] [T]he defendant must make a convincing showing sufficient to satisfy the court that the testimony which will be forthcoming is both clearly exculpatory and essential to the defendant's case. Immunity will be denied if the proffered testimony is found to be ambiguous, not clearly exculpatory, cumulative or it is found to relate only to the credibility of the government's witnesses.' " (People v. Hunter, 49 Cal.3d at p. 974.)

In *Hunter,* we concluded the proffered testimony failed to meet *Smith's* first two requirements, because it was not " 'clearly exculpatory and essential' " to his defense. (49 Cal.3d at p. 974.) We reach the same conclusion here: Petitioner does not explain how his witnesses' testimony might meet that stringent requirement; in fact, as suggested above, it is unclear whether his witnesses' testimony would have been favorable to petitioner.

* * *

... The petition for a writ of habeas corpus is denied.

granted immunity to his witnesses and, as a result, they could not be compelled to testify in his behalf. The excerpt contains the California Supreme Court's discussion of this argument.

Note that the California Supreme Court in *Williams* holds the law is well-settled in California that a prosecutor is not required to seek immunity for defense witnesses who refuse to testify on the ground of self-incrimination. The court also indicates that the law remains unsettled in California as to whether a trial court has the inherent power to grant use immunity in order to compel the testimony of witnesses called by the defendant.

§ 11.3 Due Process and Equal Protection

The constitutional protection against double jeopardy focuses on the permissibility of a second prosecution of a defendant for the same offense. The privilege against self-incrimination protects a defendant or witness from being compelled to be a witness against himself or herself. The constitutional rights discussed in the remainder of this chapter are directed to the constitutional validity of statutes defining crimes and the validity of procedures used by the government to prosecute those accused of criminal offenses.

Due Process

The Fifth Amendment to the United States Constitution provides that no person shall be "deprived of life, liberty, or property, without due process of law." This constitutional principle applies to the federal government. The Fourteenth Amendment contains a similar provision that applies to the states. The California Constitution, at article I, §§ 7 and 15, contains due process provisions in language almost identical to the language used in the United States Constitution. Deprivation of life, liberty, or property is inherent in criminal proceedings. For example, a defendant in a capital murder case may be deprived of life by imposition of the death penalty. A defendant in almost any criminal case may be deprived of liberty by a sentence to imprisonment or confinement in the county jail. A criminal defendant may also be deprived of property through imposition of a fine, a sentence to pay restitution, or forfeiture of property involved in the commission of the crime. The United States and California Constitutions provide that these governmental actions may not be taken against criminal defendants without due process of law.

Due process has been subdivided by the courts into two types: substantive due process and procedural due process. **Substantive due process** applies to the content of statutes, local ordinances, and the regulations of administrative agencies. To meet the requirements of substantive due process, a statute, ordinance, or agency regulation must constitute a reasonable exercise of the power conferred on the enacting governmental body by the constitution or enabling statute from which the governmental body derives its power to legislate. If the legislative act is unreasonable or arbitrary, i.e., not sufficiently justified by public necessity or too drastic in its methods, it is a violation of substantive due process. The courts, when reviewing a challenge to unreasonable and arbitrary legislation, will usually declare it to be "arbitrary and capricious." If, for example, the California legislature added a provision to the Vehicle Code stating that the California state color is declared to be blue and that, in the future, it will be a misdemeanor for any person to own an automobile that is any color other than blue, the new provision could easily be challenged on the ground that it is not a reasonable exercise of a power granted to the legislature by the California Constitution. Such a statute would be arbitrary and capricious, and would be unconstitutional as a violation of substantive due process. Procedurally, the challenge to the statute would in all likelihood occur in the context of a criminal prosecution of a person accused of violating the statute, and the statute's unconstitutionality would be declared by the courts.

Substantive due process, as its name implies, sets a constitutional standard for the *substance* or content of legislative enactments and administrative agency regulations. **Procedural due process** applies to the procedures used by the government when depriving a persons of life, liberty, or property. These procedures must be fair and reasonable and must, at a minimum, afford the affected person advance notice of the intended adverse action and a reasonable opportunity to be heard on the matter before a governmental decision is made.

The principle of legality, discussed in Chapter 2, is an example of procedural due process. Recall that the principle of legality requires that criminal laws, and the prescribed punishments for violations of those laws, be written and enacted before an individual may be prosecuted for violation of them. The principle of legality is an application of the notice requirement of procedural due process. It would be unfair to announce that an act is illegal, or to increase its punishment, after the act has been committed.

The Due Process Clause of the Fourteenth Amendment to the United States Constitution has been interpreted by the United States Supreme Court as applying to the states most of the individual rights guaranteed by the first ten amendments to the United States Constitution. What this means is that with a very few exceptions, states must accord their citizens the same constitutional protections as are guaranteed by the Bill of Rights in the United States Constitution. This principle is known as *incorporation:* federal constitutional rights are incorporated into the due process requirement of the Fourteenth Amendment and applied to the states. These rights are discussed in more detail in Part II of this text.

Equal Protection

The Fourteenth Amendment to the United States Constitution provides that no state shall "deny to any person within its jurisdiction the equal protection of the laws." Although there is no similar provision in the United States Constitution applicable to the federal government, the United States Supreme Court has found an **equal protection** requirement in the Due Process Clause of the Fifth Amendment. Article I, § 7, of the California Constitution provides that a person "may not be ... denied equal protection of the laws." Equal protection requires that the federal and state governments accord equal treatment to persons similarly situated. To do otherwise constitutes unconstitutional discrimination.

Not all discrimination by a government is unlawful. In fact, governments engage in a substantial amount of discriminatory activity. For example, persons with differing income levels are subjected to differing income tax brackets. Blind persons are not permitted to drive cars, whereas other persons are permitted to drive. Children are not permitted to vote, but adults are. Repeat criminal offenders may receive sentence enhancements, whereas first-time offenders may not. The list goes on and on. What is immediately apparent from these examples is that the discrimination is among persons who are not similarly situated, and it is reasonable.

Governmental discrimination necessarily involves classifications. A *classification* is a designation of a group of persons sharing similar characteristics, such as aliens, members of minority groups, women, the poor, the elderly, and any other group designation one might imagine. Legislation or other governmental action aimed at persons because they are members of a particular class is constitutionally suspect. If the classification does not touch upon fundamental constitutional values (such as free exercise of religion) or use a criterion for classification which itself violates a constitutional value (such as race or religious preference), it will be upheld by the courts if it bears a rational relationship to the end sought by the legislation or governmental action. The differing treatment of the groups mentioned in the preceding paragraph involves classifications of this sort. If a classification touches upon fundamental constitutional values or uses a criterion for classification which itself violates a constitutional value, the legislation or governmental action will be subjected to strict scrutiny by the courts and will be upheld only if the classification is necessary to promote a compelling governmental interest. Classifications based on race, gender, or religion are examples of classifications of this sort. Thus, if legislation prohibits or compels conduct by a particular racial group, while not prohibiting or compelling it with respect to other racial groups, the statute will be struck down as unconstitutional unless it is necessary to promote a compelling governmental interest.

Perceptions regarding permissible discrimination can change with evolving societal attitudes. For example, in the first half of this century, interracial marriage was a crime in California. Few would dispute that such a law today would be unconstitutional. By way of further example, as this text is being written, two state-sponsored military academies on the east coast of the United States are dealing with a United States Supreme Court decision that their all-male admissions policies violate the Equal Protection Clause of the United States Constitution.

A criminal defendant who believes that the law he or she is accused of violating unlawfully discriminates against him or her may challenge the constitutionality of the law as a violation of the equal protection guarantees of the federal and state constitutions. It is unlikely that such a challenge will be successful in the trial court, because trial courts are generally reluctant to rule on the constitutionality or unconstitutionality of a law. The constitutional challenge will be given a fuller hearing at the appellate level and may ultimately carry the case to the United States Supreme Court.

§ 11.4 Vagueness and Overbreadth

A criminal defendant may challenge the statute under which he or she is charged if the statute is unconstitutionally vague or overbroad. The Due Process Clauses of the Fifth and Fourteenth Amendments to the United States Constitution are the foundation of the void-for-vagueness and overbreadth doctrines.

A statute is void for **vagueness** whenever "men of common intelligence must necessarily guess at its meaning and differ as to its application."[4] As to the meaning of a statute, confusion among lower courts resulting in varying interpretations is evidence of vagueness.[5] The Supreme Court has held that uncertain statutes do not provide notice of what conduct is forbidden and are violative of due process. The Court has also found statutes that permit arbitrary or discriminatory enforcement void. That is, if the police or courts are given unlimited authority to decide who will be prosecuted, the statute is invalid.

It is under the void-for-vagueness doctrine that many vagrancy laws have been attacked. If it were not for the doctrine, legislatures could draft statutes so that nearly everyone would risk being engaged in criminal activity at one time or another, and police and prosecutors would have unfettered discretion to decide who would be arrested and prosecuted.

A closely related doctrine is **overbreadth**. A statute is overbroad if it includes within its scope not only unprotected activity, but also activity protected by the Constitution. For example, in one case a city ordinance made it illegal for "one or more persons to assemble" on a sidewalk and conduct themselves in an annoying manner. The United States Supreme Court found that the law was unconstitutional not because it made unprotected activity illegal (fighting words or riotous activity), but because it also included activity that is protected by the First Amendment's free assembly and association provisions.[6] It is possible for a statute to be clear and precise (not vague), but overbroad.

§ 11.5 Ex Post Facto and Bills of Attainder

Article I, § 9, of the United States Constitution prohibits the state and federal governments from enacting both ex post facto laws and bills of attainder. Article I, § 9, of the California Constitution contains similar provisions.

An **ex post facto law** is one that (1) makes an act illegal after the act was committed, (2) increases the punishment or severity of a crime after it occurred, or (3) changes the procedural rules so as to increase the chances of conviction after the crime occurs. In short, a government may not make criminal law retroactive if doing so is detrimental to the defendant. However, changes that benefit a defendant may be applied retroactively. So, if a legislature increases the prosecution's burden of proof after a defendant has committed a crime, but before trial, the legislature may make the change applicable to the defendant.

A **bill of attainder** is a legislative act punishing a person without a judicial trial. This provision reinforces the concept of separation of powers. It is the duty of the legislative branch to make the laws, and it is the duty of the judicial branch to determine who has violated those laws.

In a few instances, however, Congress and the California legislature may act in judicial roles. These legislative bodies may punish those who disrupt their functions for contempt. In addition, Congress and the California legislature are authorized by the United States Constitution and the California Constitution, respectively, to conduct impeachment hearings of high federal and state officials and to discipline their own members.

§ 11.6 First Amendment and Religion

The First Amendment to the United States Constitution provides that "Congress shall make no law respecting an establishment of religion, or prohibiting the free exercise thereof." Article I, § 4, of the California Constitution contains similar provisions. The language of the federal and state constitutions addresses two subjects. First, it provides that the government may not establish, sponsor, or give preference to a religion. This provision, known as the **Establishment Clause**, is the basis for the well-known principle of separation of church and state. Second, the constitutional language states that the government may not prohibit the free exercise of religion by individual citizens. This provision is known as the **Free Exercise Clause**. Criminal cases, involving as they do acts committed by individual citizens, are more likely to be affected by the Free Exercise Clause than the Establishment Clause.

The courts have long recognized a distinction between religious beliefs and religious practices. Generally, the individual's freedom to believe is absolute—the government may not regulate the religious beliefs of its citizens. However, when those religious beliefs are put into practice, some regulation may be permissible if the religious practice may be harmful to society or individual members of society. In the area of constitutional law, freedom of religion has been determined by the courts to be a fundamental right. The federal government or a state government may interfere with the exercise of a fundamental right only if the interference is justified by a compelling governmental interest.

At the state level, compelling governmental interests generally involve the state's exercise of its power and responsibility to enact and enforce laws for the public health, morals, safety, and welfare. When determining whether a compelling interest exists which will justify governmental interference with a specific religious practice, the courts engage in a balancing analysis. The importance of the religious practice to its adherents is balanced against the importance of the governmental interest in regulating or prohibiting the practice. Put another way, the importance of the religious practice to its adherents is balanced against the degree to which the practice constitutes a threat to public health, safety, morals, or welfare. In *Wollershiem v. Church of Scientology* (1989) 212 Cal.App.3d 872, the California Court of Appeal explained that for the government to constitutionally impose a burden on a religious practice, a four-part test must be satisfied. First, the government must be seeking to further an important or compelling state interest. Second, the burden on the exercise of religion must be essential to further the state interest. Third, the type and level of burden imposed must be the minimum required to achieve the state interest. Finally, the measure imposing the burden must apply to everyone, not merely to those who have a religious belief; that is, it may not be directed only against the religious practice.

There have been a number of cases in which criminal defendants claimed that the acts for which they were being prosecuted were religious practices. Some of these claims have been successful; others have not. In *Walker v. Superior Court* (1988) 47 Cal.3d 112, a mother claimed she could not be prosecuted for involuntary manslaughter for withholding medical treatment from her child and treating the child by prayer alone. The California Supreme Court rejected her claim. The court reached a different result in *People v. Woody* (1964) 61 Cal.2d 716. In that case, the court held that the defendants, members of an Indian tribe, could not be prosecuted under the state's drug laws for using peyote in their religious rituals.

§ 11.7   First Amendment and Speech

The First Amendment to the United States Constitution states, in part: "Congress shall make no law ... abridging the freedom of speech." As with most other rights guaranteed by the federal Bill of Rights, the First Amendment right of freedom of speech applies to the states through the Fourteenth Amendment to the United States Constitution. The California Constitution also contains a guarantee of freedom of speech. Article I, § 2, states: "Every person may freely speak, write and publish his or her sentiments on all subjects, being responsible for the abuse of this right. A law may not restrain or abridge liberty of speech or press."

The term *freedom of speech* raises a primary question: What is *speech?* In the context of the constitutional guarantee of freedom of speech, *speech* means expression by any means. Some means of expression included under the constitutional guarantee are verbal expression, written expression, pictorial expression, and expression by conduct. Because of this broad coverage of the constitutional freedom, it is frequently referred to as *freedom of expression*. This term reflects the principal focus of the constitutional protection, which is to protect the right of the people to express ideas free from interference by the government.

As with the right to practice one's religion, the right to freely express ideas is not absolute. For example, speech that creates a clear and present danger of serious public harm is not protected. States such as California may, and do, prohibit conduct such as incitement to riot (see Penal Code § 404.6) and fighting words (see Penal Code § 415). These offenses were discussed in Chapter 7. When evaluating any statute that prohibits expression, the courts apply three principles. First, in balancing the governmental interest sought to be promoted by the statute against the right of freedom of expression, the right of freedom of expression is given preference. Second, to justify a restriction on the right of freedom of expression, there must be a clear and present danger of serious public harm. Third, any restriction on the right of freedom of expression must be clear and confined to an area of legitimate public interest, that is, the statute must not be uncertain or overbroad.[7]

In some instances, a state may regulate expression, not because of its content, but by the time, place, and manner of expression. In these cases, it is not what is said that is regulated, but the circumstances in which the expression may be made. For example, the state may make it unlawful to stand in the middle of the street to make a speech. The governmental interest in maintaining a safe, consistent flow of traffic outweighs the interest of the speaker in freedom of expression. The result would be different, however, if the state attempted to prohibit all speeches made in a public place.

As stated earlier, one type of expression protected by both the federal and California constitutions is expressive conduct. *Expressive conduct* is conduct that is intended by the actor to convey an idea. Examples include activities such as wearing a black armband as a symbol of protest against a war, marching in protest against racial prejudice, or even the use of a well-known hand gesture to insult another person.

Expressive conduct has two components: the idea expressed and the conduct used to express it. The idea is always constitutionally protected, but the conduct used to express the idea may not be protected. Numerous cases have arisen in which persons have been prosecuted for expressing ideas in a manner that violates a criminal statute. Many of these cases have been appealed on the ground that the conduct was constitutionally protected because it involved the expression of an idea. Some appeals have been successful and others have not, depending largely on a balancing of the importance of the governmental interest promoted by the statute against the defendant's right of freedom of expression. *Texas v. Johnson,* 491 U.S. 397 (1989), is a case in point. In that case, the defendant, Johnson, burned an American flag outside of the 1984 Republican Convention in Dallas, Texas, as a means of political protest. Johnson was convicted of desecration of the flag, a crime under Texas law. The United States Supreme Court overturned Johnson's conviction, holding that his burning of the flag constituted political expression protected by the First Amendment. In another case, *R.A.V. v. City of St. Paul,* 505 U.S. 377 (1992), the United States Supreme Court reversed the conviction of a defendant who had been prosecuted for burning a cross in the yard of a black family. The statute under which the defendant had been charged made it a crime to burn a cross, or take certain other actions, for the purpose of expressing racial or other prejudice. The Supreme Court held the statute violative of the First Amendment because it defined the offense in terms of expression of ideas.

As can be seen from the *Johnson* and *R.A.V.* cases, freedom of expression includes the freedom to express offensive, obnoxious, and outrageous ideas. The protection by the courts of freedom to express such ideas often leads to results that many persons consider unacceptable. Even the United States Supreme Court, in the *Johnson* and *R.A.V.* decisions, expressed its disapproval of the conduct of the defendants. Such, however, is the operation of the First Amendment. It protects the freedom of expression of all persons, not just persons whose ideas are in the mainstream.

The lesson to be learned from *Johnson, R.A.V.,* and other judicial decisions is that any crime that is defined in terms of the expression of ideas is subject to challenge on First Amendment grounds. Acts prohibited by constitutionally valid statutes, which are motivated by ideas such as racial prejudice, are a different matter. Many states, including California, have statutes providing for sentence enhancement in hate crimes cases, and the United States Supreme Court has upheld the constitutional validity of statutes of this nature. Recall, for example, the discussion in Chapter 5 of Penal Code §§ 422.7 and 422.75 which provide sentence enhancements for hate crimes.

§ 11.8 Right of Privacy

The United States Supreme Court has recognized the existence of certain constitutional rights that are not specifically included in the Bill of Rights. Chief among these is the **right of privacy**. In the context of criminal law, the significance of the right of privacy has been its use to challenge the validity of penal statutes that inappropriately intrude into the personal affairs of private citizens. The first United States Supreme Court decision to definitively enunciate this principle was the 1965 decision in *Griswold v. Connecticut*.[8] In *Griswold*, the defendants, officers of the Planned Parenthood League, had given advice on contraceptive devices to married persons, in violation of a Connecticut statute that made it a criminal offense to use a contraceptive device or to assist another person in using such a device. The Court held that the statutory prohibition on the use of contraceptive devices invaded the constitutional right to privacy of married couples and was therefore invalid. In reaching its decision, the Court was initially faced with the task of determining whether there is a constitutional right of privacy at all. Justice Douglas, writing for the Court, stated that there is such a constitutional right, and that it is to be found in the "penumbras" of other constitutional rights.

The right to privacy is essentially the right of the individual to be free from unwarranted governmental intrusion into his or her private life. The right has been invoked as the basis for invalidation of a number of state penal statutes. Among these are statutes prohibiting interracial marriage[9] and statutes prohibiting the sale and distribution of contraceptives to unmarried persons.[10] Perhaps the most prominent application of the right to privacy has been with respect to abortion.[11] The United States Supreme Court has not found a right to privacy in all situations. For example, in *Bowers v. Hardwick*, (discussed in Chapter 7), the Court upheld a Georgia statute that criminalized sodomy between consenting adults.

Unlike the United States Constitution, the California Constitution expressly recognizes the existence of a right of privacy. Article I, § 1, of the Constitution, which states the "inalienable rights" of all "people," includes, without elaboration, the "right of privacy." Unlike the right of privacy under the United States Constitution, which has been invoked to create zones of activity that the government may not regulate, the right of privacy under the California Constitution is aimed principally at the improper collection and dissemination of personal information by government agencies. With a few exceptions, the California right of privacy has not been used to challenge prohibitions on individual conduct imposed by penal statutes; in the few cases in which it has been invoked, the penal statutes have been upheld. Thus, for example, the right of privacy was unsuccessfully invoked in an attempt to overturn a conviction for sale of the unapproved drug laetrile,[12] in an attempt to overturn a conviction for oral copulation in a public place,[13] and in an attempt to invalidate the Health and Safety Code provisions prohibiting the private possession and use of marijuana.[14]

Key Terms

bill of attainder An act by a legislature that imposes punishment on a person without the use of court proceedings.

double jeopardy A rule originating in the Fifth Amendment to the United States Constitution and Article I, § 15, of the California Constitution that prohibits a second punishment or a second trial for the same offense. It is sometimes referred to as *former jeopardy or prior jeopardy.*

equal protection The constitutional requirement that the government accord equal treatment to persons similarly situated.

Establishment Clause The provision of the First Amendment to the United States Constitution that prohibits the government from establishing, sponsoring, or giving preference to any religion.

ex post facto law A law that makes illegal past acts that were legal at the time they were committed.

Free Exercise Clause The provision of the First Amendment to the United States Constitution that prohibits the government from interfering with the free exercise of religion by individual citizens.

jeopardy In a criminal case, the danger of conviction and punishment to which a defendant is exposed when he is brought to trial.

mistrial Termination of a trial by the judge before the trial's conclusion for some legally recognized reason.

overbreadth doctrine A principle of constitutional law which provides that a statute is unconstitutional if, in addition to regulating conduct the government may constitutionally regulate, it attempts to regulate activity that the government may not constitutionally regulate.

procedural due process The constitutional requirement that any procedure used by the government to deprive a person of life, liberty, or property must be fair and reasonable and must, at a minimum, afford the affected person advance notice of the intended adverse action

and a reasonable opportunity to be heard on the matter before a governmental decision is made.

right of privacy The constitutional right of the individual to be free from unwarranted governmental intrusion into his or her private life. The right to privacy is not specifically enumerated in the United States Constitution, but emanates from the penumbras of other specifically enumerated constitutional rights.

self-incrimination Testimony by a defendant or other witness constituting evidence that he or she committed a crime. Under the United States and California Constitutions, a person may not be compelled to give such testimony, with one exception: a witness may be compelled to give self-incriminating testimony if he or she has been granted immunity from prosecution.

substantive due process The constitutional requirement that laws enacted by the government which may have the effect of depriving a person of life, liberty, or property must constitute a reasonable exercise of governmental power. If a person is deprived of life, liberty, or property on the basis of a law that is unreasonable or arbitrary, the deprivation constitutes a violation of substantive due process.

transactional immunity Immunity that shields a witness from prosecution for the offense about which he or she is compelled to testify, even if the prosecution has independent evidence against the witness.

use immunity A form of immunity, more limited than transactional immunity, that prohibits the government from using a witness's testimony or any evidence derived from that testimony to prosecute the witness. However, all evidence that is independently obtained may be used against the witness.

vagueness doctrine A principle of constitutional law which provides that a statute is constitutionally invalid if it is so ambiguous that it fails to put citizens on notice of the act that it mandates or prohibits.

Review Questions

1. When is a person put in jeopardy (when does jeopardy attach) in a jury trial? In a court trial (a trial without a jury)?

2. What is a mistrial? After a mistrial, can the defendant be tried again for the same offense?

3. In view of the double jeopardy provisions in the United States and California Constitutions, how could the police officers who arrested and beat Rodney King in Los Angeles lawfully be tried in federal court after they were tried and acquitted in a California state court?

4. What are the two distinct privileges included in the constitutional right against self-incrimination?

5. What is the difference between transactional immunity and use immunity?

6. Explain the distinction between substantive and procedural due process.

7. What is the principle of incorporation?

8. Under the Equal Protection Clause of the Fourteenth Amendment to the United States Constitution, may the state of California ever enact legislation that is discriminatory (i.e., that favors or disfavors a particular group of persons)?

9. Differentiate overbreadth from vagueness. Give an example of each.

10. Differentiate a bill of attainder from an ex post facto law.

11. May religious beliefs be regulated by the state? May religious practices be regulated by the state?

12. May racially derogatory statements be made criminal? May racial motives be used to enhance the punishment for crimes such as assault and battery?

13. Is a right to privacy specifically expressed in the United States Constitution? In the California Constitution?

Review Problems

1. The California Constitution contains provisions affording many of the same rights to criminal defendants as does the United States Constitution. If criminal defendants in California state courts have the rights (or most of them) guaranteed by the United States Constitution, what is the role of the California Constitution?

2. Mark is charged with assault with intent to commit rape and simple assault. Mark is a member of a minority group. During final argument, the prosecutor tells the jury that statistics show that a disproportionately high number of the rapes in the state of California are committed by persons in Mark's minority group. Then the prosecutor points at Mark and says: "Look at the defendant. Now, there's a rapist if I ever saw one." Based on these comments, Mark's attorney moves for a mistrial. Should the court declare a mistrial? If the judge declares a mistrial, can Mark be tried again for the same offenses?

3. In the fact situation in question 2, assume that the prosecutor did not make the inflammatory comments. The jury, after careful deliberation, reaches a verdict of not guilty of assault with intent to commit rape, but guilty of simple assault. Mark appeals the conviction for simple assault and the conviction is reversed by the court of appeal. Can the government retry Mark for assault with intent to commit rape? For simple assault?

4. Continuing with the scenario from question 2, assume that Mark, rather than committing attempted rape, actually raped the victim. The victim was taken to a hospital immediately after the offense and was examined by doctors who found hair fragments from another person on her body, blood from another person on her body, and semen in and around her vagina. At the police station, Mark was searched by police who observed what appeared to be fragments of skin under his fingernails. The victim was scratched by the

rapist during commission of the offense. Also, during commission of the offense, the rapist uttered certain words. The police investigators want to compel Mark to do the following: allow hair, blood, and semen samples to be taken for comparison to the hair, blood, and semen found on the victim; allow scrapings under Mark's fingernails to be taken, to compare the skin there with the victim's skin; and to utter the same words used by the rapist for comparison by the victim of Mark's voice with the rapist's voice. Mark objects to all of the foregoing, claiming his privilege against self-incrimination. To which, if any, of the police demands can Mark successfully interpose his privilege against self-incrimination?

5. The California legislature enacts a law stating: "Any person who goes upon a state beach improperly attired shall be guilty of a misdemeanor." What constitutional challenges could be raised against this statute?

6. On the same day it enacts the statute in question 5, the legislature enacts the following statute: "It shall be unlawful for any person age 70 or older to operate a motor vehicle." What constitutional challenges could be raised against this statute? Do you think they would be successful?

7. The legislature is truly having a busy day. On the same day it enacts the statutes in questions 5 and 6, it conducts a debate on a bill that would outlaw the handling of poisonous snakes during religious rituals. The legislature is concerned that persons in certain religious denominations are exposing themselves to serious injury or death by the handling of poisonous snakes during religious ceremonies. As proposed, the bill reads: "Any person who handles a poisonous snake during a religious ritual shall be guilty of a misdemeanor." A number of legislators state their

opinion that, if the bill were enacted in its present form, the resulting statute would be an unconstitutional violation of the free exercise of religion provisions of the United States and California Constitutions. Do you agree or disagree with them?

8. On this most busy day of the year, the legislature, after dealing with the statutes in questions 5, 6, and 7, next considers the problem of graffiti. The legislature is particularly concerned about graffiti containing racial slurs. It is considering two versions of a proposed statute.

   Version 1 reads: "Any person who sprays or writes graffiti on any building, bridge, highway overpass, or billboard containing language disparaging to any racial or ethnic group shall be guilty of a misdemeanor."

   Version 2 reads: "Any person who sprays or writes graffiti on any building, bridge, highway overpass, or billboard shall be guilty of a misdemeanor. If the graffiti contains language disparaging to any racial or ethnic group, the person, upon conviction, shall receive a sentence of ninety (90) days imprisonment in the county jail in addition to the sentence that would normally be imposed for such offense."

   Evaluate the constitutionality or unconstitutionality of the two proposed statutes.

9. The legislature's day is almost over. As its final task, it considers one more proposed piece of legislation, which reads: "Any person who consumes an alcoholic beverage within his or her home and, as a result of such consumption, attains a blood-alcohol level of .08% or higher, shall be guilty of a misdemeanor." Do you think the proposed statute, if enacted, will be constitutional?

Notes

1 *See* 1 Witkin & Epstein, *California Criminal Law* § 298 (2d ed., Bancroft-Whitney 1988).

2 *Burks v. United States,* 437 U.S. 1 (1978).

3 *Doe v. United States,* 487 U.S. 201 (1988) (see 108 S. Ct. at 2349).

4 *Connally v. General Construction Co.,* 269 U.S. 385 (1926).

5 *United States v. Cardiff,* 344 U.S. 174 (1952).

6 *Coates v. Cincinnati,* 402 U.S. 611 (1971).

7 7 Witkin, *Summary of California Law*, § 289 (9th ed., Bancroft-Whitney 1988).

8 381 U.S. 479 (1965).

9 *Loving v. Virginia*, 388 U.S. 1 (1967). Interracial marriage was prohibited in California under Civil Code § 60 until the statute was repealed in 1959.

10 *Eisenstadt v. Baird*, 405 U.S. 438 (1972).

11 *Roe v. Wade*, 410 U.S. 113 (1973).

12 *People v. Privitera* (1979) 23 Cal.3d 697.

13 *People v. Baldwin* (1974) 37 Cal.App.3d 385.

14 *National Organization for Reform of Marijuana Laws v. Gain* (1979) 100 Cal.App.3d 586.

PART II

CRIMINAL PROCEDURE

CHAPTER 12

Introduction and Participants

OUTLINE

§ 12.1   Criminal Procedure Defined

The second part of this text addresses criminal procedure. Criminal procedure, as a field of law, prescribes the methods used to bring an alleged criminal to justice. To state it another way, criminal procedure puts substantive criminal law into action.

Each state and the federal government has its own procedural rules. The emphasis in this text is, of course, on California criminal procedure. As was discussed in Chapter 11, many federal constitutional principles apply to the states through the Fourteenth Amendment to the United States Constitution. As a result, a number of principles of criminal procedure applied in the California justice system are derived from the United States Constitution, as well as from corresponding provisions in the California Constitution. Other procedural principles governing the criminal justice system are derived from statutes enacted by the legislature and rules of court adopted at the state and local levels. As was discussed in Chapter 2, the state-level rules are entitled the *California Rules of Court*. The California Rules of Court are uniformly applicable in courts throughout the state. At the local level, individual courts may adopt rules that refine or add detail to the procedural matters covered by the California Rules of Court or impose local requirements not addressed in the California Rules of Court.

What follows in this part of the text is a discussion of the constitutional aspects of criminal procedure; the law of searches, seizures, and arrests; the law governing interrogation and other law enforcement practices; the pretrial process; trial; sentencing; and postconviction remedies.

§ 12.2 A Common-Law, Adversarial, and Accusatorial System

The colonists on the eastern seaboard brought with them the common law of England. Before 1850, the legal system of California was based upon Mexican and Spanish law. In 1850, the legislature, by statute, declared that henceforth the common law of England would be the rule of decision of the courts of the state of California, "so far as it is not repugnant to or inconsistent with the Constitution of the United States, or the Constitution or laws of this State." Recall that a common-law legal system recognizes judicial decisions as a source of law, whereas a civil law system does not. As was mentioned in Chapter 3, common-law crimes (those defined by judicial decisions) have been abolished in California and replaced with statutorily defined crimes. Many rules of criminal procedure, however, particularly those dealing with the rights of persons suspected or accused of crime, derive from the decisions of the appellate courts. The common law continues to be a direct source of legal principles in the field of criminal procedure.

In addition to being common-law in nature, the legal system is **adversarial**. Adversarial adjudications resemble sporting events. There are two opposing parties and a neutral umpire. In criminal adjudications, these roles are played by the defendant, prosecutor, and judge. The judge in criminal adjudications is a passive participant, usually becoming involved only as needed by the parties or as required by law. Of course, the approach of judges varies and some are more proactive than others. A pure adversarial system is not employed in the United States and judges are expected to supervise the proceedings to assure fairness. The adversary system is built upon the fundamental theory that the truth is more likely to be discovered when there are two competing parties, each conducting its own investigation, asserting differing theories of law, and presenting its own case to the court. From this adversarial stance, it is expected that all theories and facts will be discovered and developed.

Also, the role of the judge as impartial, neutral, and detached is believed to increase the fairness of the proceedings, unlike in an inquisitorial system, where the judges sometimes develop an opinion or theory and then work toward proving that theory to be true. In the adversarial system, the parties are largely responsible for development of the case, that is, discovery of the evidence and, accordingly, the issues of law as well.

The adversarial system has its critics. Opponents contend that the truth is not found because the system encourages the opposing parties to present a distorted, misleading, and sometimes untruthful account of the facts. The factfinder, who is not part of the investigative process, is often left to choose between polarized versions of the same event. The adversarial system is also challenged as being unfair because it rests upon the theory that there will be two equally competent competing parties. However, because of differences in the ability of counsel and the respective powers of the parties, this premise is questionable.

In addition to being adversarial, the criminal justice system is **accusatorial**. This means that the government, as the accuser, bears the burden of proving a defendant's guilt. If the government fails in its burden, then a defendant is entitled to a directed verdict or a judgment of acquittal. The accusatorial nature of the system extends beyond placing the burden of proof on the government at trial. The entire process is designed to minimize the risk of convicting an innocent person. The belief that it is better to free several guilty persons than to convict one innocent person is a major theme of the criminal justice system. Accordingly, the system is designed so that the accused enjoys several advantages, the most critical one being the presumption of innocence. The freedom from self-incrimination, the right to a jury trial, and the right to counsel are among the many other protections afforded criminal defendants in the American legal system.

The fact that a defendant enjoys certain advantages does not mean that the defendant has the advantage on the whole. The government, unlike an individual defendant, is in the business of prosecuting criminal cases and has, for this purpose, investigative and prosecutorial agencies staffed with experienced and capable personnel. Defendants faced with prosecution by the government have a formidable opponent and, were it not for the protections afforded to them by law, would have little likelihood of successfully defending themselves against criminal charges.

§ 12.3 The Due Process Model

Criminal justice systems are commonly characterized as adhering to either a *crime control model* or a *due process model*. The repression, detection, and efficient prosecution of crime are central to the crime control model. Failure to detect and successfully prosecute criminals is perceived as a failure of government. This failure leads to a loss of individual liberties because citizens live in constant fear of, and are actually subject to, criminal conduct. A secondary consequence is a loss of confidence in government by the public, thereby further hindering its ability to detect and prevent crime. Prosecution in such systems tends to be bureaucratic, that is, a form of "assembly-line" justice. Some civil law and socialist nations employ the crime control model.

The due process model focuses on the integrity of individual rights, not the rights of the community to be free from crime. Because of the importance afforded individual rights, legal guilt is at issue, as opposed to factual guilt in the crime control model. *Factual guilt* refers to whether a defendant has in fact committed a crime. *Legal guilt* is concerned not only with factual guilt, but also with whether the defendant's rights were observed and respected by the government in the processes of investigation and prosecution. It is possible, under the due process model, for there to be sufficient evidence to prove a defendant factually guilty, but because of a civil rights violation the defendant must be declared legally not guilty. The due process model has little tolerance for conviction of the innocent; the crime control model equally abhors crimes going unsolved and defendants unpunished. The investigation and adjudication of defendants is less efficient and more costly under the due process model than under the crime control model.

This is a simplification of the two models.[1] No system falls squarely into one of the two models, although most systems can be generally characterized as adhering to the principles of one more than the other. The United States follows the due process model. Individual rights and fair procedures are the hallmark of the U.S. system of criminal justice. All individuals are innocent until proven guilty. The process itself presumes innocence, and deprivations of liberties are sharply limited and regulated before guilt is found.

Also, as the severity of the government's intrusions or deprivations increases, so must the evidence of guilt. For example, less evidence is required to establish probable cause to support a search of an automobile than to bind a defendant over to trial. This is because binding a defendant over to trial entails greater losses of liberty (possible pretrial detention and the cost and humiliation of being publicly tried) than does the search. You will learn many procedures that support the conclusion that the United States adheres to the due process model. Attempt to identify these characteristics as you read the following chapters. Chapters 13 through 19 examine the basic procedures and constitutional aspects of bringing criminals to justice. First, however, you must become familiar with the participants in this process.

§ 12.4 The Participants

Besides the accused and witnesses, there are five primary participants in criminal adjudications: law enforcement officers, prosecutors, judges, defense attorneys, and victims.

Law Enforcement Officers

The front line of law enforcement in the United States is what the public commonly refers to as the *police*. Law enforcement officers exist at the national, state, and local levels.

Federal law enforcement agencies include the Federal Bureau of Investigation, the Drug Enforcement Administration, Customs, the Coast Guard, U.S. Marshals, the Secret Service, and the Bureau of Alcohol, Tobacco, and Firearms, to name only a few.

California has more than 600 law enforcement agencies, at the state, county, and local levels. Among these agencies are: the California Highway Patrol, county sheriffs, local police departments, specialized police forces such as the University of California and California State University police departments, the Department of Fish and Game, Bay Area Rapid Transit (BART) police, park rangers, and numerous other organizations. Law enforcement officers in California are designated **peace officers**. Specific categories of peace officers are enumerated in Penal Code § 830 and following sections. (See Penal Code §§ 830–832.9.)

Discretion

Law enforcement personnel are expected to keep the peace, investigate possible wrongdoing, enforce the laws, and further crime prevention. Although it is generally held that the police must enforce the laws, it is also recognized that officers may exercise a certain amount of discretion when performing their daily duties. This is particularly true in the case of warrantless arrests, as discussed in more detail in Chapter 14. However, the conduct of police officers must comply with constitutional, statutory, and departmental policy standards.

Ethics

As is true of prosecutors and defense attorneys, the police officer's paramount ethical code is the Constitution. Police officers have a legal and ethical obligation to keep themselves within constitutional limits when performing their duties.

The International Association of Chiefs of Police (IACP) has formulated a set of ethical principles intended to guide the law enforcement officer in the performance of his or her duties. The IACP has actually issued two documents, the "Law Enforcement Code of Ethics" and the "Police Code of Conduct." The Law Enforcement Code of Ethics is taught in all the police academies in California. The text reads:

> As a law enforcement officer, my fundamental duty is to serve mankind; to safeguard lives and property; to protect the innocent against deception, the weak against oppression or intimidation, and the peaceful against violence or disorder; and to respect the Constitutional rights of all men to liberty, equality, and justice.
>
> I will keep my private life unsullied as an example to all; maintain courageous calm in the face of danger, scorn, or ridicule; develop self-restraint; and be constantly mindful of the welfare of others. Honest in thought and deed in both my personal and official life, I will be exemplary in obeying the laws of the land and the regulations of my department. Whatever I see or hear of a confidential nature or that is confided to me in my official capacity will be kept ever secret unless revelation is necessary in the performance of my duty.
>
> I will never act officiously or permit personal feelings, prejudices, animosities or friendships to influence my decisions. With no compromise for crime and with relentless prosecution of criminals, I will enforce the law courteously and appropriately without fear or favor, malice or ill will, never employing unnecessary force or violence and never accepting gratuities.
>
> I recognize the badge of my office as a symbol of public faith, and I accept it as a public trust to be held so long as I am true to the ethics of the police service. I will constantly strive to achieve these objectives and ideals, dedicating myself before God to my chosen profession ... law enforcement.

The IACP Police Code of Conduct is not taught in California's police academies. However, the California Peace Officers' Association has promulgated a "Code of Professional Conduct and Responsibility for Peace Officers" which is required in the curriculum of the police academies. The Code of Professional Conduct and Responsibility is more lengthy than the Code of Ethics, and is intended to provide a degree of specificity for the general concepts expressed in the Code of Ethics. Among its many provisions, the Code of Professional Conduct and Responsibility calls upon peace officers to always uphold the law; to be aware of the extent and limitations of their law enforcement authority; to respect and uphold the dignity, human rights, and constitutional rights of all persons; to use only the degree of force reasonably necessary in discharging their duties; to be truthful in all official matters; to observe the legal principles applicable to interrogations, arrests, searches, and seizures; to avoid official actions motivated by personal beliefs or prejudices; to maintain a knowledge of current developments in the law; to cooperate with other agencies engaged in law enforcement; to avoid receiving gifts or gratuities that could influence their official actions; and to respect the confidentiality of official information.

Prosecutors

Prosecutors are also central to the administration of justice. *Prosecutors* are government attorneys responsible for prosecuting violators. This role includes preparing and filing documents; engaging in pretrial activity, such as discovery; and appearing in court. Prosecutors also act as legal counsel to law enforcement officers, rendering advice on the law of searches, seizures, arrests, surveillance techniques, and similar matters. Prosecutors appear at grand jury hearings, where they present evidence and assist the grand jury in other ways. Finally, in some jurisdictions, prosecutors act in a supervisory capacity as the head of a law enforcement agency, such as the Attorney General of the United States, who is the head of the Department of Justice.

In California, the highest law enforcement official is the Attorney General, who heads the State Department of Justice. The Attorney General is an elected official.

Within each county is one district attorney who, like the Attorney General, is an elected official. "The district attorney is the public prosecutor, except as otherwise provided by law."[2] The district attorney, with the assistance of his or her staff of deputy district attorneys, institutes proceedings before magistrates for the arrest of persons charged with or suspected of public offenses; attends grand jury sessions and advises the grand jurors on cases presented for their consideration; draws all indictments and informations; and conducts prosecutions for public offenses.[3] The institution of a criminal proceeding must be authorized and approved by the district attorney.[4]

The district attorney is a county official. Government Code § 72193 authorizes a city, by charter, to create the office of "city prosecutor," or to provide that a deputy city attorney will act in that capacity for the prosecution of all misdemeanors committed within the city.

Prosecutorial Discretion

The term prosecutorial **discretion** reflects the discretionary authority possessed by a prosecutor to decide whether to initiate a criminal prosecution; to decide what crime to charge; and, in some states, to discontinue a prosecution that has already been commenced. As regards the last of these concepts, in some jurisdictions a prosecutor may decide on his or her own authority to discontinue a criminal case after prosecution has begun. In such jurisdictions, a prosecutor frequently has authority to make this decision prior to the filing of a formal charge against the defendant by indictment or information. The decision to discontinue prosecution is implemented by the entry of a *nolle prosequi* in the court records.

In California, a prosecutor generally lacks the authority to discontinue a criminal prosecution once it has been commenced. The decision whether to initiate a prosecution is another matter, and California prosecutors exercise considerable discretion at this stage of a criminal proceeding. Prosecutorial discretion is recognized in Government Code § 26500, which provides in part:

> The public prosecutor shall attend the courts, and *within his or her discretion* shall initiate and conduct on behalf of the people all prosecutions for public offenses [italics added].

According to the California Supreme Court: "The public prosecutor has sole responsibility and discretion in deciding whom to charge, what charges to file, what punishment to seek, and how to conduct a prosecution after it is begun."[5] As is illustrated in the case of *People v. Smith*, this power of the prosecutor may not be infringed, even by the courts.

The rationale behind prosecutorial discretion is twofold. First, the prosecutor's ethical obligation requires that he or she seek justice, not convictions. Prosecutors are not to pursue a prosecution simply because there is a probability of prevailing. Rather, the totality of the facts must be examined and it must be determined that a prosecution will further justice. The justice obligation continues through the entire adjudicative process. This obligation is reflected in the California Rules of Professional Conduct, which govern the legal profession. Rule 5-110 provides:

> A member [of the state bar] in government service shall not institute or cause to be instituted criminal charges when the member knows or should know that the charges are not supported by probable cause. If, after the institution of criminal charges, the member in government service having responsibility for prosecuting the charges becomes aware that those charges are not supported by probable cause, the member shall promptly so advise the court in which the criminal matter is pending.

Economics is the second reason why prosecutors cannot pursue every case. The resources of the prosecutor and law enforcement agencies are limited. Not every case can be prosecuted, because there are insufficient numbers of investigators, police officers, prosecutors, and other resources. Prosecutors must prioritize cases for prosecution. The decision of whether to prosecute is influenced by many factors. The facts of the case; the accused's criminal, social, and economic history; the likelihood of success; the cost of prosecution, including the probable time investment; public opinion; the seriousness of the crime; the desires of the victims; police expectations and desires; political concerns; and the question of whether the prosecution will further the administration of justice are all considered.

The California District Attorney's Association has adopted the Uniform Crime Charging Standards, which are intended to guide prosecutors in the exercise of their discretion in determining whether to initiate the prosecution of a given case. The standards provide:

> The prosecutor should charge only if the following four basic requirements are satisfied:
>
> a. Based on a complete investigation and a thorough consideration of all pertinent data readily available, the prosecutor is satisfied that the evidence shows the accused is guilty of the crime to be charged.

b. There is legally sufficient, admissible evidence of a corpus delicti.

c. There is legally sufficient, admissible evidence of the accused's identity as the perpetrator of the crime charged.

d. The prosecutor has considered the probability of conviction by an objective fact-finder hearing the admissible evidence. The admissible evidence should be of such convincing force that it would warrant conviction of the crime charged by a reasonable and objective fact-finder after hearing all the evidence available to the prosecutor at the time of charging and after hearing the most plausible, reasonably foreseeable defense that could be raised under the evidence presented to the prosecutor.[6]

PEOPLE v. MICHAEL RAY SMITH
53 Cal.App.3d 655; 126 Cal.Rptr. 195 (1975)

The People appeal from an order admitting Michael Ray Smith to probation. Respondent had been charged by information with assault by means of force likely to produce great bodily injury (Pen. Code, § 245). Respondent at first pleaded not guilty. During pretrial proceedings, the court granted respondent's motion to withdraw his former plea of not guilty and, over the objection of the prosecutor, permitted him to plead guilty to violation of Penal Code section 242 (battery). The prosecutor objected on the basis that it was improper for the court in effect to negotiate its own plea bargain with the defendant; it was also pointed out that the offense to which a plea of guilty was being accepted had not been charged by the prosecutor and was not a lesser offense included within the charged assault. Nevertheless, the court accepted the plea and admitted Smith to probation.

* * *

"Plea bargaining" is a process by which the People, represented by the prosecutor, and a defendant negotiate an agreement for the disposition of criminal charges against the defendant. The approval of the trial judge is an essential element to the effectiveness of the plea bargain eventually worked out between the prosecutor and the defendant. "However, the court has no authority to substitute itself as the representative of the People in the negotiation process and under the guise of 'plea bargaining,' to 'agree' to a disposition of the case over prosecutorial objection."

* * *

The powers of state government are separated among the legislative, executive, and judicial branches, and the powers of one branch may not be exercised by another branch. (Cal. Const., art. III, § 3.) ...

[T]he district attorney, part of the executive branch, is the public prosecutor charged with conducting all prosecutions on behalf of the People. This function includes instituting proceedings against persons suspected of criminal offenses, and drawing up informations and indictments. The discretionary decision to bring criminal charges rests *exclusively* in the grand jury and the district or other prosecuting attorney. The choice of the appropriate offense to be charged is also within the discretionary power of the prosecuting attorney. "The charging decision is the heart of the prosecution function. The broad discretion given to a prosecutor in deciding whether to bring charges and in choosing the particular charges to be made requires that the greatest effort be made to see that this power is used fairly and uniformly." The trial court, by allowing respondent to withdraw his plea of not guilty to Penal Code section 245 and enter a plea of guilty to Penal Code section 242 instead, encroached upon the prosecutor's function of charging offenses. ... [T]he court took it upon itself to charge the respondent with an otherwise uncharged and nonincluded, although related, lesser offense than that which had been charged by the People. That action was unlawful; just as the executive may not exercise judicial power, so the judiciary is prohibited from entering upon executive functions. (Cal. Const., art. III, § 3.) The court acted beyond its authority in accepting a plea of guilty to a lesser nonincluded but related offense over the prosecutor's objection.

* * *

The probation order is reversed with directions to vacate the plea of guilty to violating Penal Code section 242 and reinstate the plea of not guilty to violating Penal Code section 245.

The decision of whether to charge a person with a crime must be fairly and impartially made. Decisions to prosecute that are motivated by improper criteria may violate equal protection. As discussed in Chapter 11, the United States and California Constitutions prohibit the state from taking actions that deny persons equal protection of the law. However, a claim that it is unfair to prosecute a person because other known violators are not prosecuted will not be successful unless it can be shown that the accused was singled out for an improper reason.

Ethics

All attorneys are bound by ethical rules. Many states have adopted the ethical rules promulgated by the American Bar Association. These rules are found in the American Bar Association's Model Code of Professional Responsibility and its Model Rules of Professional Conduct. California has long had its own body of ethical principles applicable to the legal profession, and thus has not adopted the American Bar Association Rules. California ethical principles are found primarily in the California Rules of Professional Conduct, which are promulgated by the Board of Governors of the California State Bar. Not surprisingly, many of the California ethical rules are similar to those adopted by the American Bar Association. Also, the American Bar Association rules are relevant and useful in interpreting and applying the California Rules of Professional Conduct.

Ethical violations may result in discipline by the bar, an offended court, or both. Common sanctions include private and public reprimands, suspension, and disbarment. Under court rules and rules of procedure, other sanctions, such as monetary penalties, may be assessed. Also, all courts possess the authority to punish for contempt.

Prosecutors have special ethical responsibilities. Unlike other attorneys, who need only focus on "representing their clients zealously within the bounds of the law"—which essentially means using all legal means at their disposal to win their cases—prosecutors must be more objective. A prosecutor must be less focused than other attorneys on achieving a win, or a conviction, than on seeing that justice is done in each case. The initial decision to charge or not charge a suspect, and the factors considered in making that decision, are examples of this special ethical obligation of the prosecutor. A prosecutor is not to charge every suspect, regardless of the strength or weakness of the case against the suspect, and let the "chips fall where they may" at trial. To do so would be an abuse of the prosecutor's discretion and a violation of the prosecutor's ethical obligations. The unique ethical duties of the prosecutor were summarized by the California Court of Appeal in *People v. Kelley*:

> As the representative of the government, a public prosecutor is not only obligated to fight earnestly and vigorously to convict the guilty, but also to uphold the orderly administration of justice as a servant and representative of the law. Hence, a prosecutor's duty is more comprehensive than a simple obligation to press for conviction. As the court said in *Berger v. United States*: "[The Prosecutor] is the representative not of an ordinary party to a controversy, but of a sovereignty whose obligation to govern impartially is as compelling as its obligation to govern at all; and whose interest, therefore, in a criminal prosecution is not that it shall win a case, but that justice shall be done. As such, he is in a peculiar and very definite sense the servant of the law, the twofold aim of which is that guilt shall not escape or innocence

suffer. He may prosecute with earnestness and vigor—indeed, he should do so. But, while he may strike hard blows, he is not at liberty to strike foul ones. It is as much his duty to refrain from improper methods calculated to produce a wrongful conviction as it is to use every legitimate means to bring about a just one."

... Thus a prosecutor is required to meet standards of candor and impartiality not demanded of defense counsel. For example, a prosecutor must disclose unfavorable aspects of his case; defense counsel can remain silent. A prosecutor must disclose unfavorable evidence relating to the accusation and must make available impeaching evidence relating to witnesses. Defense counsel need not do either. A conviction in a criminal cause may be reversed if the prosecutor suppresses material evidence, makes improper comments during cross-examination, makes improper references to extrinsic matters, or fails to disclose important information to the defense. Lapses by defense counsel in these and other respects can never bring about reversal of an acquittal. To this extent the Attorney General's complaint about a double standard is correct, for "[t]he duty of the district attorney is not merely that of an advocate."[7]

On the other side, prosecutors have an obligation to pursue a prosecution when the facts of the case demand it. At trial, unless a prosecutor becomes convinced that the accused is innocent, the prosecutor is to zealously pursue a conviction.

Judges

Judges are not executive branch officials, as are prosecutors and law enforcement officers. Judges are part of the judiciary, a separate and independent branch of government. Generally, the judiciary is responsible for the resolution of disputes and the administration of justice. In regard to criminal law, judges are responsible for issuing warrants, supervising pretrial activity, presiding over hearings and trial, deciding guilt or innocence in some cases, and passing sentence on those convicted.

Having a fair and impartial party make these determinations is an important feature of the U.S. criminal justice system, and is mandated by the Constitution in many instances, as you will learn in the following chapters. A judge has the obligation to remain unbiased, fair, and impartial in all cases before the bar.

Ethics

Like attorneys, judges are subject to a code of ethics. The California Judges Association has adopted the California Code of Judicial Conduct, which is derived from the American Bar Association's Model Code of Judicial Conduct. The California Code of Judicial Conduct requires that judges conduct themselves ethically in both their judicial and personal capacities. Specific applications of this principle called for by the California Code of Judicial Conduct include, but are not limited to, the following:

1. Judges should uphold the integrity and independence of the judiciary.
2. Judges should avoid impropriety and the appearance of impropriety in all their activities.

3. Judges should perform the duties of their office impartially and diligently.

4. Judges should regulate their extrajudicial activities to minimize the risk of conflict with their judicial duties.

Defense Attorneys

Because of the complexity of the legal system and the advantage of having an advocate, competent legal counsel has become an important feature of the American system of criminal justice. The Sixth Amendment to the Constitution provides that all persons have a right to be represented by counsel in criminal cases. Today, under the United States Constitution, indigent defendants have a right to court-appointed counsel in all cases that may result in incarceration.

Ethics

Defense attorneys have high, and sometimes morally challenging, ethical responsibilities. Unlike the prosecutor, whose duty is to see that justice is achieved, the defense attorney must zealously represent the accused, within the bounds of the law, regardless of innocence or guilt.

This obligation is the cause of some public disrespect for the legal profession. Attorneys are perceived as hired guns, not as advocates of civil liberties. Defense lawyers are frequently asked how they can defend people they know are guilty. There are two responses to this inquiry. First, defense attorneys often do not know whether their clients are in fact guilty, as this question is rarely asked. Second, defense attorneys are not defending the actions that the defendant is accused of committing; rather, defense attorneys are defending the rights of the accused, specifically, the right to have the government prove its case beyond a reasonable doubt using lawfully obtained evidence. By defending the rights of one person against governmental oppression, the rights of all the people are defended.

This approach, which is a vital part of the United States criminal justice system, is often misunderstood by the public. The defense attorney who fulfills this constitutional and ethical mission is sometimes the target of public animosity and ridicule.

As previously stated, a defense attorney is obligated to represent his or her client zealously *within the bounds of the law*. Thus, the scope of permissible conduct by a defense counsel is not without its limits. Defense attorneys, like all attorneys, are required to maintain the decorum of the court and may be cited for contempt of court if they fail to do so. Also, like other attorneys, defense attorneys are governed by the California Rules of Professional Conduct. Rule 5-200, entitled "Trial Conduct," provides:

In presenting a matter to a tribunal, a member:

(A) Shall employ, for the purposes of maintaining the causes confided to the member, such means only as are consistent with truth;

(B) Shall not seek to mislead the judge, judicial officer, or jury by an artifice or false statement of fact or law;

(C) Shall not intentionally misquote to a tribunal the language of a book, statute, or decision;

(D) Shall not, knowing its invalidity, cite as authority a decision that has been overruled or a statute that has been repealed or declared unconstitutional; and

(E) Shall not assert personal knowledge of the facts at issue, except when testifying as a witness.

An ethical dilemma is presented when a defense attorney knows or suspects that the defendant intends to give perjured testimony. On the one hand, the attorney is an officer of the court and is prohibited by law and by Rule of Professional Conduct 5-200 from deceiving the court. On the other hand, the defense attorney has an obligation to his or her client. The following course of action has been recommended to deal with such a situation. First, the attorney should advise the client that a criminal defendant does not have the right to commit perjury, that perjury is a criminal offense, that fabricated testimony is strategically risky, and that the attorney cannot assist in presenting perjury or arguing perjured testimony to the court or jury. If the client still insists on lying while testifying, the attorney might ask the court in camera (in the judge's chambers) to be permitted to withdraw from the case because of an irreconcilable conflict in representing the defendant. The prosecutor should not be present during the in camera session. If the court refuses to permit the attorney to withdraw, the attorney should state, on the record and outside the jury's presence, that the defendant is taking the stand against the attorney's advice and that the "free narrative" approach will be used during direct examination, i.e., the defendant will simply tell his or her story, rather than respond to questions from his or her attorney.[8]

The rule regarding perjured testimony by defense witnesses is more stringent than that pertaining to perjured testimony by the defendant. A defense attorney may not knowingly permit a defense witness to give perjured testimony. However, if a defense witness unexpectedly perjures himself or herself while testifying, there appears to be no obligation on the part of the defense attorney to disclose the fact of the perjury to the court or jury. In contrast, prosecuting attorneys have a duty to disclose witness perjury.[9] Of course, the defense attorney may not attempt to exploit the perjured testimony through further development of the witness's false testimony or by using the perjured testimony when presenting argument to the jury.

Defense attorneys are sometimes asked to represent co-defendants. This can create a conflict of interest for a defense attorney if the defendants have conflicting or antagonistic defenses. Because of the inherent dangers of representing co-defendants, many defense attorneys refuse joint representation. It is a violation of a defendant's Sixth Amendment right to the assistance of effective counsel to have a lawyer with divided loyalties.

If a defense attorney undertakes to represent co-defendants with potential or actual conflicting interests, the attorney must obtain the informed written consent of each defendant and must inform the court of the existence of the potential or actual conflict. The court must then question the defendants to determine whether they understand that they have the right to conflict-free representation and, if so, whether they have freely and voluntarily waived the potential or actual conflicts of interest.[10]

Rule of Professional Conduct 5-120, which became effective on October 1, 1995, provides that an attorney may be disciplined for making statements regarding a case to the news media when the attorney knows or reasonably should know that the statement will have a "substantial likelihood of materially prejudicing an adjudicative proceeding in the matter." This rule raises freedom-of-speech issues under the First Amendment to the United States Constitution and article I, § 2, of the California Constitution. At the time of this writing, the constitutionality of Rule 5-120 had not been tested in the courts.

One of the ethical obligations of any attorney, including defense counsel, is to provide effective representation to his or her client. In a criminal case, ineffective assistance of counsel may be a ground for reversal of a conviction and/or the grant of a new trial. In *People v. Day*, the defendant, Valoree Jean Day, was convicted of involuntary manslaughter for killing Steve Brown, the man with whom she was living. Over the term of their relationship, Brown had repeatedly subjected Day to physical abuse consisting of violent assaults on her person and threats to kill her. Day claimed that she killed Brown in self-defense. The prosecution contended that Day's conduct (engaging in violent conduct toward Brown during the relationship, failing to escape the relationship, and fleeing after the killing) was inconsistent with self-defense. Day's defense attorney, Martell, was unfamiliar with battered woman syndrome (BWS) and thus failed to present any evidence regarding this condition at trial. After her conviction, Day retained new counsel and moved for a new trial on the ground that she was denied effective assistance of counsel, because of Martell's failure to introduce evidence of BWS that would have demonstrated that her conduct was not inconsistent with her claim of self-defense.

PEOPLE v. VALOREE JEAN DAY
2 Cal.App.4th 405; 2 Cal.Rptr.2d 916
(Jan. 1992)

After her conviction, appellant sought alternate counsel, who moved for a new trial on the ground appellant did not receive constitutionally adequate representation because her trial counsel had been unaware of and made no effort to explore the implications of her status as a battered woman. Defense counsel asserted evidence of battered woman syndrome (BWS) would serve to ... permit the jury to evaluate appellant's testimony free of common misconceptions regarding battered women.

Several affidavits were filed in support of appellant's motion. First, trial counsel Martell admitted in court and in letters on file with the court that he was unaware of the existence of BWS before and during trial and never considered investigation, research, or presentation of expert witness testimony regarding BWS on appellant's behalf. ...

The declaration of legal expert witness M. Gerald Schwartzbach submitted in support of appellant's motion for new trial established that in 1981 Schwartzbach successfully used the expert witness testimony of psychologist Lenore E. Walker to obtain an acquittal on self-defense grounds of a client in a homicide case.

Psychologist Dr. Lee H. Bowker, dean of behavioral and social sciences at Humboldt State University and an authority on BWS, submitted an affidavit in support of appellant's motion for new trial. Based on his lengthy interview with appellant and review of materials provided by Attorney Mikelich, Dr. Bowker concluded appellant suffered from BWS.

Dr. Bowker stated "[o]ne does not have to be 'docile, submissive, humble, ingratiating' et cetera to be a victim of the Battered Woman Syndrome." According to Dr. Bowker, "[t]wo of the personal strategies commonly employed by battered women are flight and active self-defense, more commonly known as counter-violence." Dr. Bowker "found counter-violence to be the least effective of all personal strategies used by the one thousand battered wives in [his] most recent wife abuse study. It was also the personal strategy most likely to stimulate the batterer to increase the level of his violence." Dr. Bowker stated that while counterviolence was one of "the least effective methods of attempting to stop the abuse, it is a method commonly used by women suffering from the syndrome."

Pat Cervelli, a counselor with extensive experience in the field of domestic violence, counseled appellant after her conviction. Based on her experience and her interviews with appellant, she concluded appellant suffered from BWS. Ms. Cervelli explained that it is common for battered women not to recall severe beatings perpetrated by the batterer. She explained "[t]his amnesia is very common in battered women, because they block out and minimize the danger that they feel from the battering partner in order for them to justify continuing to live with that person. By forgetting and minimizing the danger, they can cope with and remain in a very dangerous relationship." She also explained that "[t]he battered woman typically views her batterer as far more powerful and stronger than he actually is. This reinforces the battered woman's sense of helplessness [and] sense of futility ... ." A "perception of a lack of protection by law enforcement (or by anyone else) is part of the Battered Woman Syndrome." "Attempts to stop the violence usually fail, because the battered woman has a belief that it is useless, a previous experience with law enforcement officials that was unsupportive, fear of retaliation by the batterer, and lastly, fear of loss of the relationship."

Ms. Cervelli explained "[s]ome of the reasons a woman stays in a battering relationship are: she loves the batterer; she hopes/believes the violence will end; she grew up in a household where violence was the norm; she is a substance abuser who does not feel adequate on her own; she thinks the violence is her fault; and she is economically dependent on the batterer."

* * *

The trial court denied appellant's new trial motion. The court ruled appellant had established counsel was ineffective in failing to investigate and to present evidence of the BWS. However, the court found appellant had not been prejudiced by counsel's failings.

* * *

Appellant asserts, as she did below, that BWS evidence was admissible to rehabilitate her in light of the prosecution's impeachment by urging that her conduct, both before and after the incident, was inconsistent with having acted in self-defense. In effect, she argues that if BWS evidence had been admitted it would have demonstrated her conduct was consistent with self-defense. As a consequence of BWS not being presented to the trier of fact the prosecutor was able to draw inferences from her conduct that disparaged her credibility as to her version of the incident. Her argument concludes that if the jury had understood her conduct in light of BWS evidence, then the jury may well have concluded her version of the events was sufficiently credible to warrant an acquittal on the facts as she related them.

* * *

BWS evidence would have deflected the prosecutor's challenge to appellant's credibility. Such evidence would have assisted the jury in objectively analyzing appellant's claim of self-defense by dispelling many of the commonly held misconceptions about battered women. As the record reflects, the prosecutor exploited several of these misconceptions in urging the jury to reject appellant's self-defense claim.

First, the prosecutor presented evidence to support the notion that appellant and Brown were engaged in mutual combat. The prosecutor argued: "Valoree's in mutual combat here. It's Valoree and Steve in the ring again, just like happened so many other times. She's in it and this other is a lie."

Expert testimony on BWS would have disabused the jury of the notion that because a woman strikes back at her batterer, she is engaging in "mutual combat." As Dr. Bowker stated, it is not uncommon for a battered woman to resort to counterviolence.

* * *

The prosecutor also argued appellant could have left Brown if she really was being beaten by him. ...

"Expert testimony on the battered woman syndrome would help dispel the ordinary lay person's perception that a woman in a battering relationship is free to leave at any time." ...

The prosecutor further argued appellant's conduct after the incident was inconsistent with a self-defense claim. The prosecutor argued appellant's flight after stabbing Brown evidenced a consciousness of guilt. The prosecutor also argued appellant's expression of fear and her request to turn off the lights in response to the sound of sirens after she reached Olson's home was an expression of a consciousness of guilt.

As appellant argued in her new trial motion, BWS evidence could have explained that:

"Some women after the death of their mates suffer intense fear based upon their perceptions that the abuser was much stronger than they were and able to retaliate against them, even after the abuser was dead. Some women are unable to realize that they are safe even after the abuser is dead and take further protective measures against the retaliation that they expect to follow an aggressive attack."

* * *

In order to prevail on her claim of ineffective assistance of counsel, appellant must demonstrate she was prejudiced by counsel's failings. Prejudice is demonstrated when there is a "reasonable probability that, but for counsel's unprofessional errors, the result of the proceeding would have been different. A reasonable probability is a probability sufficient to undermine confidence in the outcome. …"

In the present case, evidence of BWS was relevant not only on the issue of whether appellant honestly believed she needed to use deadly force in self-defense, but also to explain a behavior pattern that might otherwise appear unreasonable to the average person. Evidence of BWS not only explains how a battered woman might think, react, or behave, it places the behavior in an understandable light.

One of the most commonly made arguments by prosecutors in urging rejection of a defense is that the person's behavior is inconsistent with that defense. … Jurors are told to evaluate and react to evidence by what a reasonable person would do or not do. Frequently, conduct appears unreasonable to those who have not been exposed to the same circumstances. … It is only natural that people might speculate as to how they would react and yet be totally wrong about how most people in fact react. If the average person's thinking is that a person who acted in self-defense would not have run away, then the argument of the prosecutor that running away is inconsistent with self-defense is very appealing. This is precisely the type of argument made by the

prosecutor in the instant case. Evidence that flight was a common reaction for a battered woman would have allowed the jury to question and evaluate the logic of the prosecutor's argument in light of evidence that supported her defense.

Evidence that explains rape trauma syndrome, child sexual abuse accommodation syndrome and BWS informs the finders of fact that how they think the average reasonable person would behave and/or how they think they personally would behave are not necessarily the same way that people who have been raped, molested or battered in fact behave. It bears repeating that we have difficulty accepting what we do not understand. Depriving the finder of fact of such understanding may well lead to a conclusion based on misconceptions held in good faith. That such conceptions are held in good faith in no way lessens the magnitude of the error and the injustice that may result.

We conclude the failure to present BWS evidence was prejudicial: the evidence was not only relevant, but critical in permitting the jury to evaluate appellant's testimony free of the misperceptions regarding battered women. … The prosecutor repeatedly relied on misconceptions about battered women in urging the jury to reject appellant's claim of self-defense. Because counsel was unaware of the BWS he was unable effectively to counter the prosecutor's contention that appellant's conduct was inconsistent with self-defense. … Had evidence of the BWS been introduced, [the defense attorney] effectively could have countered the battered woman myths on which the prosecutor built his case.

BWS evidence would have bolstered appellant's credibility and lent credence to her self-defense claim. Moreover, the lengthiness of deliberations, the jurors' request to review certain testimony, and the jurors' request for clarification of the self-defense instructions establish that the case was close. Under these circumstances, counsel's failure to investigate and present BWS evidence must be deemed prejudicial. …

The judgment is reversed.

Legal Assistants

Legal assistants are employed by both prosecutors and defense attorneys, with the latter being more common.[11] In the defense context, legal assistants may be asked to perform several tasks, including conducting initial interviews, conducting legal research, preparing drafts of motions and other documents, maintaining and organizing files, acting as a contact with incarcerated clients, assisting in preparing the defendant and other witnesses for trial, and preparing the defendant for the presentence investigation interview. Some paralegals are called upon to conduct investigations.

As employees of attorneys, legal assistants must also follow ethical guidelines and responsibilities. Although no state has yet established mandatory licensing of legal assistants, and therefore there is no enforceable set of ethics rules beyond what is required by law, the National Association of Legal Assistants (NALA) has promulgated a Code of Ethics.

First, legal assistants may not engage in the practice of law.[12] This includes rendering legal advice, establishing an attorney-client relationship, setting fees, and appearing in court on behalf of a client. Although some administrative agencies permit legal assistants to represent clients at hearings, this is never so in criminal law. The unauthorized practice of law is both criminal and unethical. Further, legal assistants are to act prudently in determining the extent to which a client may be assisted without the presence of a lawyer.[13] Finally, it is imperative that the attorney directly supervise the legal assistant's work in criminal law.[14]

Second, all employees of an attorney are bound by the confidentiality rule.[15] All communications made by a client to a legal assistant fall within the scope of the attorney-client privilege and may not be disclosed by the legal assistant.

Third, legal assistants must be careful not to suborn perjury when preparing the client and witnesses for trial. Instructing a witness in effective techniques, including dress and personal appearance, and methods of responding to inquiries (e.g., answer directly, honestly, and as succinctly as possible; look at the jury during your response) is proper. Suggesting, urging, encouraging, or directing a witness to lie or mislead a court is suborning perjury.

Fourth, the NALA Code of Ethics calls upon legal assistants to comply with the bar associations' codes of professional responsibility and rules of professional conduct.[16]

Victims

Recall that the victim of crimes is the citizenry. That is why criminal prosecutions are brought in the name of the "People." However, most crimes have another victim, the victim-in-fact. This is the person assaulted, battered, raped, or robbed. Victims affect criminal adjudications in a number of ways.

First, law enforcement officers may decline to make an arrest or conduct an investigation if the victim is disinterested in having the matter pursued. Second, the prosecutor may, in the exercise of prosecutorial discretion, decide not to charge the offender if that is the victim's desire. Third, if the matter proceeds to trial, the victim may be required to testify at both pretrial hearings and trial. A victim may choose to attend even if his or her testimony is not required. Fourth, the victim may participate in the sentencing portion of the trial. As you will learn, statements concerning how a victim and a victim's family have been affected may be considered by judge and jury when passing sentence.

Victims' rights have received considerable attention since the mid-1980s. Victims' rights organizations have strenuously—and successfully—lobbied to introduce both state constitutional amendments and legislation concerning victims' rights. In June 1982, Proposition 8, an initiative measure, was adopted by the electorate. Proposition 8 added § 28, entitled the "Victims' Bill of Rights," to article I of the California Constitution. Section 28 states the recognition by the people of the state that the

> rights of victims pervade the criminal justice system, encompassing not only the right to restitution from the wrongdoers for financial losses suffered as a result of criminal acts, but also the more basic expectation that persons who commit felonious acts causing injury to innocent victims will be appropriately detained in custody, tried by the courts, and sufficiently punished so that the public safety is protected and encouraged as a goal of highest importance.

Among its specific provisions, § 28 of article I states that: (1) all persons who suffer losses as a result of criminal activity are entitled to restitution from the person convicted of the crime, unless compelling and extraordinary reasons exist to the contrary; (2) all students and staff of schools have the right to attend campuses that are safe, secure, and peaceful; (3) relevant evidence is not to be excluded from criminal proceedings (this provision does not overrule any established rule of evidence); (4) persons accused of capital crimes may not be released on bail; (5) persons accused of serious felonies may not be released on their own recognizance; and (6) prior felony convictions of defendants may be used without limitation for purposes of impeachment or enhancement of a sentence.

Penal Code § 679.02 contains a number of provisions conferring rights on victims of crimes. Among the rights enumerated in § 679.02 are: (1) the right of victims to be notified of their rights and other information specified in various provisions of the Penal Code and other statutes; (2) the right, upon request, to be informed by the prosecuting attorney of the final disposition of a case; (3) the right to be notified of sentencing proceedings and of the right to appear and reasonably express their views and have the court consider their statements in determining the appropriate sentence; (4) the right to be notified of a parole eligibility hearing and of the right to appear and reasonably express their views and have those views considered in determining whether to grant parole to the offender; (5) the right, upon request, to be notified of an inmate's placement in a reentry or work furlough program, or to be notified of the inmate's escape; and (6) the right to be notified if the offender is to be placed on parole. The foregoing list is not all-inclusive; see the text of § 679.02 for a full enumeration of the rights granted to crime victims by that section. (See Penal Code § 679.02.)

Rape shield legislation is another form of victims' rights law. Rape shield laws, which were discussed in Chapter 5, generally exclude from trial evidence of a rape victim's sexual history (except evidence of sexual history with the accused) and reputation in the community. These laws were enacted to protect the rape victim from embarrassing, harassing, and intimidating inquiries.

Victims also have civil remedies against perpetrators. These remedies involve civil litigation based on traditional civil law theories, such as intentional tort actions for assault, battery, invasion of privacy, and conversion.

Finally, *victim assistance organizations* are available in California. These organizations provide information, counseling, and other assistance to victims.

Also, California has established a *victim compensation program*. In many instances restitution proves inadequate, such as when the perpetrator is indigent. In these instances, a victim can request compensation from the state victim compensation fund, known as the Restitution Fund. This program reimburses victims for medical expenses, loss of income, and property losses.

Key Terms

accusatorial A type of legal system in which the government brings charges against a defendant and bears the burden of proving them.

adversarial A method of conducting trials in which the opposing parties advocate their respective positions before a neutral trier of fact.

discretion The use of one's own judgment when making a decision, based on consideration of the circumstances pertinent to the decision.

district attorney The government official in each county having primary responsibility to prosecute persons accused of crimes.

nolle prosequi A legal document filed by a prosecutor with a court by means of which the prosecutor discontinues criminal proceedings against a defendant.

peace officer In California, a person having authority to enforce the law; a law enforcement officer.

Review Questions

1. Was the common law of England always the law in California?

2. Does the American criminal justice system adhere to a crime control model or a due process model? Briefly explain your answer.

3. Is a peace officer ethically obligated to be aware of changes in the law?

4. List some of the functions performed by a district attorney and his or her staff of deputy district attorneys.

5. Briefly explain the rationale behind permitting prosecutors to exercise discretion when

determining whether to bring criminal charges against a suspect.

6. Briefly explain the difference between a prosecutor's ethical responsibilities and the ethical responsibilities of other attorneys.

7. Is there any ethical restriction on a prosecutor or a defense attorney speaking to the media about an ongoing criminal case?

8. What are some of the activities legal assistants must refrain from performing to avoid engaging in the unauthorized practice of law?

9. Describe five of the rights conferred on victims of crime by the Penal Code.

Review Problems

1. Create a set of facts under which co-defendants could not be represented by the same attorney. Explain why separate counsel is necessary under your scenario.

2. Do you believe that a defense attorney should be required to zealously represent a client who has admitted guilt to the lawyer? What if the result is the release of a violent criminal (i.e., acquittal or dismissal of charges)? Can you suggest an alternative method?

3. Do you believe that police officers should arrest every violator they encounter, discover, or are made aware of? Support your answer. What factors should an officer consider when making the decision whether to arrest or otherwise pursue a prosecution?

4. In some nations, prosecutors are required to file a criminal charge if sufficient evidence exists. Should this form of compulsory prosecution replace the U.S. model of prosecutorial discretion? Explain your answer.

5. In some nations, individual victims are permitted to file a criminal charge against the person(s) who committed the alleged act(s). In these nations, the victim may prosecute the case or a public prosecutor may prosecute on the victim's behalf. Should such a method be employed in the United States? Explain your answer.

6. Melinda, a prosecutor in the district attorney's office, brings a criminal prosecution against Wilbur for grand theft auto. Shortly after the trial commences, an investigator for the district attorney's office discovers that the crime was actually committed by Filbert, Wilbur's identical twin brother. The investigator informs Melinda of this fact. Melinda firmly believes that even if Wilbur did not commit the crime charged in this case, he has stolen other cars and belongs behind bars. She is of the opinion that she can convict Wilbur of the present offense if she does not disclose the investigator's discovery to the court. Assuming that Melinda is correct in her belief that Wilbur has committed other auto thefts and is a menace who should be removed from society, may she ethically refrain from disclosing the investigator's discovery to the court?

7. Bob, a manufacturer of shaving cream, is the defendant in a lawsuit arising from an automobile accident. Bob knows that the case will be heard by Judge Harry Beard. Bob has his advertising agency contact Judge Beard and offer to have the judge do a television commercial for Bob's shaving cream. The advertising agency offers to pay the judge $20,000 for making the commercial. May Judge Beard make the commercial and accept payment for doing so?

8. Boswell, an attorney, is defending Mack, who is being tried for bank robbery. Boswell knows that Mack committed the offense, but Mack insists that he wants to take the stand and testify that he was fifteen miles from the scene of the crime with his girlfriend, Nicole, at the time the robbery was committed. Mack wants to call Nicole as a defense witness to corroborate his story. What should Boswell do in response to Mack's intention to perjure himself and present the perjured testimony of Nicole?

9. Marilyn was the victim of an armed robbery perpetrated by Steve, and was seriously injured by Steve during the robbery. As a result of her injuries, Marilyn incurred $5,000 in medical expenses and lost two months' income. Steve is tried for and convicted of the armed robbery. Marilyn also lost $100 that was taken from her by Steve during the robbery. Does Marilyn have a right to be present and make a statement at Steve's sentencing hearing? May she ask the court to order Steve to make restitution to her for her monetary losses? What if Steve is indigent?

Notes

1 For more information concerning the due process and crime control models, *see* N. Gary Holten & Lawson Lamar, *The Criminal Courts* ch. 1 (McGraw-Hill 1991).

2 Government Code § 26500.

3 *See* 4 Witkin & Epstein, *California Criminal Law* § 1789 (2d ed., Bancroft-Whitney 1989).

4 *Id.*

5 *Dix v. Superior Court* (1991) 53 Cal.3d 442, 451–52.

6 Uniform Crime Charging Standards (California District Attorney's Association), reprinted with permission of the California District Attorneys Association.

7 *People v. Kelley* (1977) 75 Cal.App.3d 672, 680, 688–90 (citations omitted).

8 California Continuing Education of the Bar (CEB), *California Criminal Law Procedure and Practice* § 18.31 (3d ed., CEB 1996).

9 *Id.* at § 18.32.

10 *Id.* at §§ 18.9–8.10.

11 Approximately 13 percent of all paralegals in the United States work in criminal law. *See* Angela Schneeman, *Paralegals in American Law* (Lawyers Cooperative/Delmar Publishers 1994).

12 NALA Code of Ethics, Cannons 1, 3, 4, and 6.

13 *Id.*, Canon 5.

14 *Id.*, Canon 2.

15 *Id.*, Canon 7.

16 *Id.*, Canon 19.

CHAPTER 13

The Constitutional Aspects of Criminal Procedure

Introduction

Criminal justice is a subject that belongs largely to the states. Nearly 95 percent of all criminal prosecutions occur in state courts. Not only do the states conduct most of the prosecutions, but each state is free, with few limitations, to design its criminal justice system in any manner it chooses. This was especially true in the early years of the United States. For the most part, the national government did not involve itself in state criminal law for 150 years.

This began to change in the 1950s, and today the federal government plays a major role in defining the rights of criminal defendants in state prosecutions, as well as federal. The source of federal involvement is the United States Constitution, and two developments account for its increased role in state criminal law. First, the reach of the Constitution has been extended to the states through what is known as *incorporation*. Second, the rights found in the Bill of Rights have been significantly expanded.

§ 13.1 Incorporation

Prior to the adoption of the Fourteenth Amendment, the Bill of Rights guarantees were interpreted by the United States Supreme Court as restricting only the power of the federal government. That meant that fundamental rights, such as the right to counsel and the right to be free from unreasonable searches and seizures, were only guaranteed to a defendant when prosecuted in federal court. If a state did not have a constitutional or statutory provision granting the right, the defendant was not entitled to its protection when prosecuted in state court.

In 1868 the Fourteenth Amendment to the United States Constitution was adopted. One objective of the Fourteenth Amendment is to protect certain civil liberties from state action. Section One of that amendment reads:

> All persons born or naturalized in the United States, and subject to the jurisdiction thereof, are citizens of the United States and of the State wherein they reside. No State shall make or enforce any law which shall abridge the privileges or immunities of citizens of the United States; nor shall any State deprive any person of life, liberty, or property, without due process of law; nor deny to any person within its jurisdiction the equal protection of the laws.

The language of the Fourteenth Amendment is similar to that found in the Fifth Amendment, insofar as they both contain a Due Process Clause. It is through the Due Process and Equal Protection Clauses that the powers of the states are limited. However, what is meant by *due process* has been the subject of great debate among jurists.

Note that the language of the Fourteenth Amendment does not include any of the specific guarantees found in the Bill of Rights, except that it requires the states to afford due process whenever depriving a person of life, liberty, or property. Thus, one of the most important issues raised in the context of the Fourteenth Amendment is whether the due process guaranteed by that Amendment includes the rights found in the Bill of Rights, such as the rights to counsel, to freedom of the press, to freedom of speech, to be free from self-incrimination, to be free of unreasonable searches and seizures, and to be free from cruel and unusual punishments.

One position, which was held by the Supreme Court until the 1960s, is known as *fundamental fairness*. Those rights that are "fundamental" and "essential to an ordered liberty" are incorporated into the due process required by the Fourteenth Amendment and become applicable to the states. The fundamental fairness doctrine held that no relationship existed between the Bill of Rights and those deemed fundamental, although the rights recognized under the fundamental fairness doctrine may parallel rights recognized by the Bill of Rights.

The Supreme Court rejected the fundamental fairness doctrine in the 1960s and replaced it with the *selective incorporation doctrine*. Similar to the fundamental fairness doctrine, a right is incorporated under this doctrine if it is both fundamental and essential to the concept of ordered liberty. Like the fundamental fairness approach, independent rights are also recognized under selective incorporation analysis.

However, the two approaches differ in two major respects. First, under the fundamental fairness approach, cases were analyzed case-by-case. That is, it was possible to have essentially the same facts with different outcomes under the fundamental fairness doctrine. Critics charged that the approach was too subjective. Under the selective incorporation method, rules are established to act as precedent for all similar cases in the future. In addition, the entire body of precedent interpreting a federal amendment becomes applicable to the states as a result of an amendment's incorporation.

Second, selective incorporation gives special attention to the rights contained in the Bill of Rights. A right secured by the Bill of Rights is more likely to be protected by the Fourteenth Amendment's Due Process Clause than others. Selective incorporation continues to be the approach of the Supreme Court today.

Nearly the entire Bill of Rights has been incorporated under the selective incorporation doctrine. The right to grand jury indictment has not been incorporated,[1] nor has the right to a jury trial in civil cases. Once incorporated, a right applies against the states to the extent and in the same manner as it does against the United States. Also, several independent due process rights have been declared. You will learn many of these in the following chapters.

§ 13.2   Expansion of Rights

Another major development in the area of constitutional criminal procedure has been the expansion of many rights. The language of the Constitution is concise. It refers to "unreasonable searches and seizures," "due process," "equal protection," "speedy and public trial," and so on. No further definition or explanation of the meaning of these provisions is provided. The process of determining the meaning of such phrases is the responsibility of the courts, primarily the United States Supreme Court, and is known as *constitutional interpretation*. It is possible to make each right ineffective by reading it narrowly. The opposite is also true.

During the 1960s, many rights found in the Bill of Rights were expanded by court decisions. *Expansion* refers to extending a right beyond its most narrow reading. The effect of expansive interpretation is to increase defendants' rights. An example of an expansive interpretation is the *Miranda v. Arizona* decision, 384 U.S. 436 (1966). Although the language of the Fifth Amendment does not explicitly state that a defendant must be advised of the right to remain silent, to have the assistance of counsel, and so forth, the United States Supreme Court now requires that such admonishments be given because of an expanded interpretation of the Fifth Amendment.

Another example of expanded individual rights is the right to privacy. No explicit constitutional language provides for a right to privacy. However, as was briefly discussed in Chapter 11, the United States Supreme Court has found a right to privacy to be implicit in the Federal Constitution.

The scope of other individual rights under the United States Constitution has been expanded by decisions of the United States Supreme Court. Many of these rights apply to defendants in the criminal justice system and are discussed in this and succeeding chapters. In recent years, there appears to be a trend away from expansive interpretation. This is in large part because the composition of the United States Supreme Court is more conservative than it was during the 1960s. Some believe that the trend toward increasing individual rights was hindering law enforcement and welcome the current, less expansive, view of the Court. Others believe that individual rights should be further expanded and would welcome a Supreme Court that would do so.

§ 13.3 Exclusionary Rule

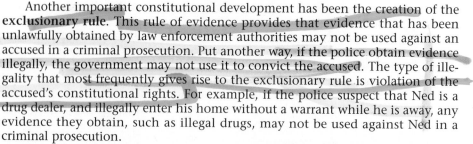

Another important constitutional development has been the creation of the **exclusionary rule.** This rule of evidence provides that evidence that has been unlawfully obtained by law enforcement authorities may not be used against an accused in a criminal prosecution. Put another way, if the police obtain evidence illegally, the government may not use it to convict the accused. The type of illegality that most frequently gives rise to the exclusionary rule is violation of the accused's constitutional rights. For example, if the police suspect that Ned is a drug dealer, and illegally enter his home without a warrant while he is away, any evidence they obtain, such as illegal drugs, may not be used against Ned in a criminal prosecution.

The rule was first announced by the United States Supreme Court in 1914.[2] However, at that time the rule had not been incorporated into the Due Process Clause of the Fourteenth Amendment, and therefore the exclusionary rule did not apply to state court proceedings. This changed in 1961 when the Supreme Court declared that evidence obtained in violation of the United States Constitution could not be used in state or federal criminal proceedings. The case was *Mapp v. Ohio.*

The exclusionary rule has been the subject of intense debate. There is no explicit textual language establishing the rule in the United States Constitution. For that reason, many contend that the Supreme Court exceeded its authority by creating it; that it is the responsibility of the legislative branch to make such laws.

On the other side is the argument that without the exclusionary rule, the Bill of Rights is ineffective. Why have constitutional standards if there is no method to enforce them? For example, why require that the officers in the *Mapp* case have a search warrant, yet permit them to conduct a warrantless search and use the evidence obtained against the defendant? These questions go to the purpose of the exclusionary rule: it discourages law enforcement personnel from engaging in conduct that violates the constitutional rights of private citizens.

The exclusionary rule works to prevent the admission of any evidence that was obtained by law enforcement officers in violation of the constitutional rights of the accused.

The exclusionary rule applies only to evidence obtained by law enforcement authorities in an unlawful manner. If a private citizen working on her own obtains evidence illegally and then turns it over to the police, it may be used against the accused at trial.[3] However, persons hired or authorized to assist the police are considered agents of the government, and therefore the exclusionary rule applies to their actions.

California, as did most other states, at one time held that illegally obtained evidence was admissible at the trial of an accused. The rationale behind this holding was that illegally obtained evidence, if otherwise admissible under the rules of evidence, should not be excluded, because the illegal conduct of law enforcement personnel does not affect the fairness and impartiality of subsequent court proceedings.[4] An otherwise guilty criminal defendant should not be allowed to escape conviction because of the fortuitous circumstance that the evidence against him or her was obtained in violation of his or her constitutional rights.

The view of the California courts changed with the California Supreme Court decision in *People v. Cahan*[5] in 1955, six years before the United State Supreme Court's decision in *Mapp v. Ohio.* In *Cahan,* the California Supreme Court reconsidered the arguments and policies for and against the exclusionary rule and declared that henceforth, evidence obtained in violation of the constitutional rights of an accused may not be used against the accused in a criminal proceeding. As will be discussed, there are certain exceptions to this rule.

Although any evidence obtained in violation of the constitutional rights of an accused is excludable from criminal proceedings brought against the accused,

MAPP v. OHIO
367 U.S. 643 (1961)

Appellant stands convicted of knowingly having had in her possession and under her control certain lewd and lascivious books, pictures, and photographs in violation [of Ohio law]. …

On May 23, 1957, three Cleveland police officers arrived at appellant's residence in that city pursuant to information that "a person [was] hiding out in the home, who was wanted for questioning in connection with a recent bombing." …

Upon their arrival at that house, the officers knocked on the door and demanded entrance but appellant, after telephoning her attorney, refused to admit them without a search warrant. They advised their headquarters of the situation and undertook a surveillance of the house.

The officers again sought entrance some three hours later when four or more additional officers arrived on the scene. When Miss Mapp did not come to the door immediately, at least one of the several doors to the house was forcibly opened and the policemen gained admittance. Meanwhile Miss Mapp's attorney arrived, but the officers, having secured their own entry, and continuing in their defiance of the law, would permit him neither to see Miss Mapp nor to enter the house. It appears that Miss Mapp was halfway down the stairs from the upper floor to the front door when the officers, in this highhanded manner, broke into the hall. She demanded to see the search warrant. A paper, claimed to be a warrant, was held up by one of the officers. She grabbed the "warrant" and placed it in her bosom. A struggle ensued in which the officers recovered the piece of paper and as a result of which they handcuffed appellant because she had been "belligerent" in resisting their official rescue of the "warrant" from her person. Running roughshod

over appellant, a policeman "grabbed" her, "twisted [her] hand," and she "yelled [and] pleaded with him" because "it was hurting." Appellant, in handcuffs, was then forcibly taken upstairs to her bedroom where the officers searched a dresser, a chest of drawers, a closet and some suitcases. They also looked into a photo album and through personal papers belonging to the appellant. The search spread … . The obscene materials for possession of which she was ultimately convicted were discovered in the course of that widespread search.

At the trial no search warrant was produced by the prosecution, nor was the failure to produce one explained or accounted for. At best, "There is, in the record, considerable doubt as to whether there ever was any warrant for the search."…

We hold that all evidence obtained by searches and seizures in violation of the Constitution is, by that same authority, inadmissible in a state court.

Since the Fourth Amendment's right of privacy has been declared enforceable against the States through the Due Process Clause of the Fourteenth, it is enforceable against them by the same sanction of exclusion as it used against the Federal Government. …

Moreover, our holding that the exclusionary rule is an essential part of both the Fourth and Fourteenth Amendments is not only the logical dictate of prior cases, but it also makes very good sense. There is no war between the Constitution and common sense. Presently, a federal prosecutor may make no use of evidence illegally seized, but a State's attorney across the street may, although he supposedly is operating under the enforceable prohibitions of the same Amendment. Thus the State, by admitting evidence unlawfully seized, serves to encourage disobedience to the Federal Constitution which it is bound to uphold.

the term *exclusionary rule* is most frequently applied to the exclusion of evidence obtained through an illegal search or seizure. In the remainder of this chapter, discussion of the exclusionary rule is in the context of illegal searches and seizures. (The legal principles governing searches and seizures are discussed in detail in Chapter 14.)

Raising the Exclusionary Rule   In California, a defendant wishing to prevent the use of illegally seized evidence against him or her will usually make a motion to return property or suppress evidence under Penal Code § 1538.5. This motion is frequently referred to as a "1538.5 motion." (See Penal Code § 1538.5.) The motion is to be made as early in the criminal proceedings as feasible. If the motion is granted, the property or evidence is, with certain limited exceptions, not admissible against the defendant at trial or other hearing.

Standing to Raise the Exclusionary Rule   Before a defendant can assert the exclusionary rule to exclude illegally obtained evidence from his or her trial, he or she must have standing to do so. There are two aspects to standing. First, for a person to have standing to challenge illegally obtained evidence, he or she must be a person who would be harmed by introduction of the evidence. In a criminal trial, the defendant's interests will be adversely affected by the introduction of illegally obtained evidence, so he or she meets the first requirement for standing to challenge the evidence. Under this first aspect of standing, a third person, such as a relative of the defendant, would not have standing to make a 1538.5 motion to suppress the introduction of illegal evidence at the defendant's trial, because the third person's interests would not be put at risk by introduction of the evidence. Thus, only the defendant may make the motion.

The Fourth Amendment to the United States Constitution provides that all persons have the right to be free from unreasonable searches and seizures. The second aspect of standing has to do with whose Fourth Amendment rights have been violated by the illegal search and seizure that produced the evidence the defendant wishes to suppress. Both the federal and California courts formerly held that a defendant had standing to move to suppress illegally obtained evidence even if the evidence had been seized in violation of the Fourth Amendment rights of another person. For example, assume the police conducted an illegal search of the home of Frank's mother, thereby violating her constitutional right to be free from unreasonable searches and seizures, and seized evidence of criminal activity by Frank. If Frank were prosecuted for the criminal activity, he could, under the former rule, move to suppress the evidence on the ground that it was seized in violation of his mother's constitutional rights. The rationale behind permitting a defendant to assert the constitutional rights of another was that the exclusionary rule is intended primarily to deter misconduct by law enforcement personnel; if such misconduct occurred, it was irrelevant whether the defendant's or a third party's constitutional rights were violated. In either event, the evidence was the result of unlawful activity by law enforcement personnel and the defendant had standing to move to suppress the evidence.

The United States Supreme Court began moving away from its expansive concept of standing in 1969. In its 1980 decision in *United States v. Salvucci*,[6] the Court stated:

We are convinced that the automatic standing rule ... has outlived its usefulness in this Court's Fourth Amendment jurisprudence. The doctrine now serves only to afford a windfall to defendants whose Fourth Amendment rights have not been violated. We are unwilling to tolerate the exclusion of probative evidence under such circumstances since we adhere to the view ... that the values of the Fourth Amendment are preserved by a rule which limits the availability of the exclusionary rule to defendants who have been subjected to a violation of their Fourth Amendment rights.[7]

The California courts, under the doctrine that state courts may grant greater rights to defendants than required by the federal constitution, did not immediately follow the lead of the United States Supreme Court, and continued to hold that a defendant in a criminal proceeding had standing to suppress evidence seized in violation of any person's Fourth Amendment rights. In June 1982, the electorate adopted Proposition 8, which added § 28 to article I of the California Constitution. Section 28 provides in part that "relevant evidence is not to be excluded from criminal proceedings." This language is known as the **"Truth-in-Evidence"** provision of article I, § 28. This amendment of the California Constitution forced the California courts to adopt the United States Supreme Court's narrowed position on standing to assert the exclusionary rule. Under the "Truth-in-Evidence" principle, the only limits on the use of relevant evidence are those imposed on California by a higher authority, i.e., those imposed by the United States Constitution. Because the United States Supreme Court, which is the ultimate expositor of federal constitutional principles, now holds that evidence is excludable only if the *defendant's* Fourth Amendment rights were violated, the California courts have had to abandon their more expansive reading of the exclusionary rule. The rule in California is now the same as the federal rule: a defendant has standing to move to suppress illegally seized evidence only if the search or seizure that produced the evidence violated the defendant's Fourth Amendment rights (and corresponding rights under the California Constitution).

The law of search and seizure is discussed in greater detail in Chapter 14. For the present, it is sufficient to state that a search or seizure will violate a defendant's Fourth Amendment rights only if the defendant has a reasonable expectation of privacy in the place searched or the place from which the evidence was seized and the search or seizure was without lawful authority. Under the current federal and California exclusionary rules, Frank would not have standing to move to suppress evidence illegally seized from his mother's house, assuming he did not live there, and the evidence could be used against him at trial.

The current view that a defendant has standing to assert the exclusionary rule only if his or her constitutional rights were violated requires that the defendant, at the motion to suppress, present evidence connecting him or her with the place from which the evidence was seized and, possibly, with the illegally obtained evidence itself. Establishing a connection with the place or the illegally obtained evidence could be incriminating and damaging to the defendant's ability to defend against the criminal charge. This situation was also possible under the former expansive exclusionary rule if the defendant were claiming a violation of his or her own constitutional rights. In *Simmons v. United States*, 390 U.S. 377 (1968), the United States Supreme Court held that a defendant may testify at a suppression hearing without waiving the right not to testify at trial and that any testimony given at a suppression hearing by a defendant may not be used against him or her at trial. This decision eliminated the quandary faced by many defendants: should they testify at a suppression hearing, thereby possibly connecting them with the crime, or should they refrain from challenging the evidence in order to avoid the risk of incriminating themselves at the suppression hearing? The United States Supreme Court held that defendants should be free from such dilemmas.

Exceptions to and Limitations on the Exclusionary Rule

The exclusionary rule is subject to a number of exceptions and limitations.

Reasonable Reliance on Defective Warrant A search warrant may be issued by a magistrate only after facts are presented by law enforcement personnel to the magistrate which persuade the magistrate that probable cause exists to believe that the person or thing to be seized is located in the place to be searched. The factual presentation is usually made by means of a written affidavit of a law enforcement officer. If a magistrate issues a warrant based on an inadequate affidavit, the defendant may challenge the validity of the warrant by pretrial motion and, if necessary, at later stages of a criminal proceeding. If a police officer executes the warrant (i.e., conducts a search pursuant to the warrant) in good faith reliance on the warrant, must any evidence seized during the search be excluded at the trial of the defendant? The United States Supreme Court, in *United States v. Leon*,[8] held that evidence obtained in objectively reasonable reliance on a defective search warrant is admissible. The Court noted that the purpose of the exclusionary rule is to deter police misconduct, not the errors of judges and magistrates. If an officer's reliance on a defective warrant is "objectively reasonable," there is no police misconduct to deter. The Court indicated that an officer's reliance would not be considered objectively reasonable in four situations: (1) when the affidavit supporting the warrant contains information the officer knows or should know is false; (2) when the magistrate has abandoned his or her role as a neutral and detached officer; (3) when the affidavit is so lacking in indicia of probable cause as to make belief in its existence entirely unreasonable; and (4) when the warrant is so facially deficient that the officer cannot reasonably presume it to be valid.[9] The rule of admissibility adopted by the United States Supreme Court in *Leon* has been adopted by the California courts.[10]

Grand Jury Proceedings Penal Code § 939.6(b) provides that: "The grand jury shall receive none but evidence that would be admissible over objection at the trial of a criminal action." This language appears to apply the exclusionary rule to grand jury proceedings. In *United States v. Calandra,* however, the United States Supreme Court held that the exclusionary rule does not apply to grand jury proceedings.[11] According to the Court, a grand jury is not trying the guilt or innocence of the person being investigated and there is no valid purpose to impede the orderly progress of a grand jury by rules of evidence such as the exclusionary rule. As has been previously mentioned in this chapter, states such as California may grant greater protections to criminal suspects and defendants than are granted under the United States Constitution. The United States

Supreme Court's holding in *Calandra* does not, therefore, invalidate the requirement of Penal Code § 939.6(b) that a grand jury consider only evidence which would be admissible at trial. Recall, however, that the "Truth-in-Evidence" provision, added to article I, § 28, of the California Constitution by Proposition 8, provides in part that "relevant evidence is not to be excluded from criminal proceedings." Evidence subject to the exclusionary rule may be, and usually is, relevant, that is, probative of the guilt or innocence of the accused. Constitutional provisions always prevail over conflicting statutes. Although the issue is not completely resolved in California, the concurrence of the United States Supreme Court's holding in *Calandra* and the addition of § 28 to article I of the California Constitution appear to have rendered the exclusionary rule inapplicable to grand jury proceedings, despite the conflicting language in Penal Code § 939.6(b).[12]

Parole Revocation Hearings   The California Supreme Court has held that illegally obtained evidence may be considered when determining whether to revoke the parole of a convicted criminal. The court noted that police misconduct is unlikely to be deterred by application of the exclusionary rule to parole revocation proceedings.[13]

Probation Revocation Proceedings   Based on reasoning similar to that applicable to parole revocation proceedings, the California courts have held that illegally obtained evidence may be considered by a judge at a proceeding to revoke the probation of a convicted criminal, if the evidence has not been suppressed pursuant to a Penal Code § 1538.5 motion, and if the evidence has not been obtained in a manner so egregious as to shock the conscience.[14]

Sentencing Proceedings   Trial of the guilt or innocence of an accused and sentencing after conviction of an accused are distinct phases of a criminal proceeding. The general rule in the United States is that illegally obtained evidence may be considered during the sentencing phase of a trial. In California, this rule is limited by Penal Code § 1538.5, which provides that, upon motion by an accused, illegally obtained evidence may not be used against him or her at trial "or other hearing." The sentencing phase of a trial is considered a hearing within the meaning of § 1538.5. Accordingly, in California, if illegally obtained evidence has been suppressed pursuant to a § 1538.5 motion, and the prosecution has not sought review of the court's ruling, the evidence may not be considered at sentencing. Otherwise, illegally obtained evidence may be considered during the sentencing phase of a trial.

Impeachment of Defendant   Illegally obtained evidence may be used by the prosecution to *impeach* (attack the credibility of) a defendant who chooses to testify. This is true even if the evidence has been suppressed pursuant to a 1538.5 motion.

Evidence Obtained by a Private Citizen   As mentioned earlier, the purpose of the exclusionary rule is to deter unlawful police conduct in the obtaining of evidence against persons suspected or accused of crimes. This rationale does not extend to evidence obtained unlawfully by private persons. For example, if

Kimberly, without Amber's consent or knowledge, goes through the contents of Amber's purse, discovers a bag of cocaine, and turns it over to the police, the cocaine may be used against Amber at her trial for possession of a controlled substance. The result would be different if Kimberly were acting at the direction of a police officer when she surreptitiously examined the contents of Amber's purse; in that situation, she would be considered an agent of the police.

§ 13.4   Fruit of the Poisonous Tree

The exclusionary rule applies to evidence obtained during an illegal search or seizure. It also applies to additional evidence discovered through evidence obtained during an illegal search or seizure. If law enforcement personnel conduct an illegal search and seizure, and the evidence seized leads them to other evidence, the other evidence is also inadmissible under the exclusionary rule. This rule of law is given the colorful name *fruit of the poisonous tree*. For example, assume that police officers unlawfully enter Bob's home and conduct an illegal search for stolen money. In a desk drawer, they find a hand-drawn map. The police officers seize the map, proceed to the location indicated on it, and there find the stolen money. The stolen money is evidence of Bob's guilt but, because it was discovered as the result of evidence (the map) obtained during an unlawful search and seizure, it may not be used against Bob at trial.

As just discussed, there are exceptions to the exclusionary rule. Similarly, there are exceptions to the fruit of the poisonous tree doctrine.

Independent Source Exception   If the discovery of evidence is the result of an unlawful search or seizure of other evidence, the evidence is normally inadmissible at trial. However, if law enforcement personnel had a second, lawful source of information that led them to the evidence, the evidence is admissible. Consider the preceding example in which a map illegally seized from Bob's house resulted in seizure of money stolen by Bob. Assume instead that Bob had an accomplice in the theft of the money who confessed to the crime and told the police where the money was. As long as the confession was not the result of unlawful coercion, it constitutes an independent and lawful source of information from which the police could find and seize the money. This is an example of the independent source rule.

The rationale behind the independent source rule is that the exclusionary rule is intended to put the police in the same position they would have been in had the unlawful search or seizure not occurred. The exclusionary rule is not intended to put the police in a worse position than they would have been in absent the illegal search and seizure. In Bob's case, had the illegal search and seizure not occurred, the police would have found and seized the stolen money based on the accomplice's confession. Because the police had a lawful, independent source of information leading them to the money, the money may be admitted into evidence at Bob's trial in spite of the illegal search of Bob's home.

Attenuation of "Taint"   In the words of the United States Supreme Court, if the causal connection between the illegal search and seizure and the evidence subsequently discovered has become "so attenuated as to dissipate the taint" caused by the illegal search and seizure, the subsequently discovered evidence is admissible against the defendant. What this means is that evidence is not rendered inadmissible by a prior illegal search and seizure if the connection between the illegally seized evidence and the subsequently obtained evidence is only marginal. In one California case, for example, a police officer illegally seized certain tools from the defendant's home. The seizure was determined to be unlawful and the police were required to return the tools to the defendant. Before returning the tools, the police stamped them with small identifying marks and photographed them. Two years later, the same tools were found abandoned at the scene of a burglary. Based on recognition of the tools, the police obtained a search warrant and searched the defendant's home. As a result of the search, the police discovered and seized evidence that was later used against the defendant in a prosecution for the burglary. The defendant challenged the seizure of the evidence from his home on the ground that, but for the illegal search and seizure of the tools two years previous, followed by the marking and photographing of the tools, the police could not have used the tools to connect him to the burglary. The appellate court held that although the defendant's contention was true, his commission of the burglary and his abandonment of the tools at the scene were intervening independent acts that attenuated any taint between the prior illegality and the evidence from the defendant's home after the burglary.[15]

Inevitable Discovery Exception   If, as a result of an illegal search and seizure of evidence, police are led to other evidence which, in the normal course of investigation, they would have discovered despite the initial illegal search and seizure, the evidence is admissible against the defendant. In other words, if the prosecution can show that the evidence would ultimately and inevitably have been discovered by the police even without the unlawful search and seizure, the evidence may be used against the accused. Consider the previous example of Bob and the stolen money. Assume, however, that rather than a map, the police illegally seize a handwritten note indicating a safety deposit box number at a particular bank. The police obtain a search warrant, examine the contents of the safety deposit box, and find the stolen money. If the prosecution can establish at trial that routine investigative techniques would have led police to discovery of the safety deposit box without the aid of the illegally seized note, the money may be admitted into evidence at the defendant's trial. As mentioned with respect to the independent source rule, the exclusionary rule is not supposed to put the government in a worse position than it would have been in had the illegal search and seizure not occurred. To deprive the government of the use of illegally obtained evidence it would ultimately have discovered through lawful investigative techniques would violate this principle.

§ 13.5 State Constitutions and the "New Federalism"

As you already know, California has its own constitution. The California Constitution contains many provisions conferring individual rights on persons within the state. Some of these rights were discussed in Chapter 11. Individual rights are addressed in article I of the California Constitution. Section 1 of that article states:

> All people are by nature free and independent and have inalienable rights. Among these are enjoying and defending life and liberty, acquiring, possessing, and protecting property, and pursuing and obtaining safety, happiness, and privacy.

Succeeding sections of article I specify particular individual rights. Provisions applicable to criminal law and procedure include:

- freedom of speech and press (art. I, § 2)
- freedom of assembly and petition (art. I, § 3)
- freedom of religion (art. I, § 4)
- due process of law, equal protection, and privileges and immunities (art. I, § 7)
- prohibition of bills of attainder and ex post facto laws (art. I, § 9)
- bail and release on own recognizance (art. I, § 12)
- search and seizure (art. I, § 13)
- prosecution of felonies and arraignment (art. I, § 14)
- safeguards in criminal prosecutions (art. I, § 15)
- trial by jury (art. I, § 16)
- cruel or unusual punishment or excessive fines (art. I, § 17)
- grand juries (art. I, § 23)
- provisions concerning the death penalty (art. I, § 27).

As has been previously mentioned in this text, states may grant greater rights to defendants than are required by the United States Constitution. They may not, however, restrict rights granted by the federal Constitution. In California, this authority of the courts and the legislature to accord rights to defendants based on California constitutional principles is known as the **independent grounds doctrine.** The California Constitution provides a basis for individual rights independent of the United States Constitution. In this second part of the text, you will learn of a number of rights that are granted to criminal defendants by California law which are not required by the federal Constitution. Two examples are the requirement for a unanimous jury verdict and the right to appointed counsel in all criminal cases. The federal Constitution does not require a unanimous jury verdict (although it is required by federal statute) and does not require the appointment of counsel to represent indigent defendants in certain cases.

Until recently, state constitutions have not played an important role in defining civil liberties. This is because both state and federal courts have looked almost exclusively to the federal Constitution as a source of individual rights. It is also because there has been a tendency on the part of state courts to interpret state constitutional rights as identical to those secured by the federal Constitution.

Increasingly, this is no longer so. During recent decades, commentators, judges, and attorneys have exhibited a renewed interest in state constitutional law. The resurgence in state constitutional law is known as the *New Federalism.*

As was discussed in Chapter 11, the California Constitution is a document of independent force, and the California Supreme Court is the ultimate interpreter of the meaning of that document. *People v. Brisendine* (1975) 13 Cal.3d 528, a California Supreme Court decision, squarely addressed this issue. According to the Court, even California constitutional provisions that mirror those in the United States Constitution do not necessarily have the same meaning or effect as their federal counterparts. All that is required in the relationship of the two constitutions is that the California constitutional provisions accord at least the same degree of protection as the federal constitutional provisions. Beyond that, the California courts are free to interpret California constitutional provisions in a manner that accords greater protection than their federal counterparts. In 1974, § 24 was added to article I of the California Constitution. That section states: "Rights guaranteed by this Constitution are not dependent on those guaranteed by the United States Constitution." Thus, in any California criminal case in which the constitutional rights of the defendant are in issue, two bodies of constitutional law must be consulted: federal constitutional law, based on the United States Constitution and developed primarily by the United States Supreme Court; and California constitutional law, based on the California Constitution and developed primarily by the California Supreme Court. If the particular constitutional right in issue is covered by both the federal and California Constitutions, the federal Constitution establishes the minimum standard of protection to be afforded the defendant. California constitutional principles may exceed the federal standard, thereby conferring on the defendant greater protections than are afforded by federal constitutional law, but (as previously stated) may not so restrict the rights of the defendant that they fail to meet the minimum standard set by the federal Constitution.

In the *Brisendine* case, for example, the defendant was arrested in a remote wooded area and subjected to a search of his knapsack. The purpose of the search was to determine whether the knapsack contained any weapons that could endanger the arresting officers. The officers did not find any weapons in the knapsack, but did discover some sealed envelopes and opaque glass containers. The officers opened the envelopes and containers and discovered illegal drugs, for which Brisendine was ultimately prosecuted. The opening of the envelopes and containers without a search warrant was lawful under federal constitutional standards, but was unlawful under California constitutional standards. Stating that the California Constitution imposes a "higher standard" than the federal Constitution, the California Supreme Court reversed Brisendine's conviction on the grounds that the opening of the envelopes and containers constituted an illegal search and seizure under California constitutional law and that the evidence of their contents should have been excluded under the exclusionary rule.

One exception to the independent grounds doctrine is the "Truth-in-Evidence" provision of Proposition 8, mentioned several times in this chapter. Proposition 8 added the "Truth-in-Evidence" provision to article I of the California Constitution in 1982. Its effect is to prevent California from expanding the exclusionary rule beyond the scope of the exclusionary rule under the United States Constitution. Thus, since 1982, defendants in California state courts have had no greater right to exclude illegally obtained evidence than they would in federal court. Were the *Brisendine* case being decided today, the California courts would be required to measure the legality of the search and seizure by federal constitutional standards—under which (as previously stated) the search and seizure would have been deemed lawful. Thus, through the initiative process, California, although not required to do so, has curtailed its own power to grant defendants the right to exclude evidence that is admissible under the federal Constitution.

Under the exclusionary rule, evidence is to be excluded if it was obtained as the result of a search or seizure that violated the defendant's right under the federal and California Constitutions to be free from unreasonable searches and seizures. The focus in an exclusionary rule inquiry is whether the search or seizure was reasonable. Prior to Proposition 8, California law required exclusion of evidence unless the search and seizure were both "subjectively" and "objectively" reasonable. *Subjective reasonableness* required that the law enforcement officer conducting the search and seizure do so for a proper motive. *Objective reasonableness* required that the search and seizure be justified by the circumstances. In contrast to the California rule, federal constitutional principles require only that the search and seizure be objectively reasonable; the motive of the officer is irrelevant as long as the search and seizure were justified by the circumstances. The excerpt from *People v. Hull* illustrates the deference to the federal constitutional standard shown by the California courts in post-Proposition 8 exclusionary rule cases. The case also illustrates the analytical process used by the courts when the defendant raises the exclusionary rule.

In *Hull,* the police placed a "bait vehicle" on a city street. The vehicle contained two speakers in which had been placed electronic tracking devices. Each speaker had also been coated with a fluorescent green powder which was visible only through ultraviolet light and which would stick to the hands of those who touched the speakers. The vehicle was equipped with an alarm that would activate if the vehicle were broken into. In this case, the vehicle was broken into

---

PEOPLE v. JOHN DAVID HULL
34 Cal.App.4th 1448; 41 Cal.Rptr.2d 99
(May 1995)

The defendant claims the evidence obtained in the search of the home should have been suppressed as an unreasonable search or seizure in violation of the Fourth Amendment. We first recite the exclusionary rule and then summarize the appropriate method of dealing with such claims. ...

"When evidence is obtained in violation of the Fourth Amendment, the judicially developed exclusionary rule usually precludes its use in a criminal proceeding against the victim of the illegal search and seizure. ... The [United States Supreme] Court has stressed that the 'prime purpose' of the exclusionary rule 'is to deter future unlawful police conduct and thereby effectuate the guarantee of the Fourth Amendment against unreasonable searches

and seizures.' ... As with any remedial device, application of the exclusionary rule properly has been restricted to those situations in which its remedial purpose is effectively advanced."

When a defendant asserts relevant evidence should be suppressed under the exclusionary rule, the trial court, after resolving factual conflicts, undertakes a legal test which has two parts. In the first part of the test, the court assesses whether the actions of the officer in obtaining the evidence were objectively reasonable. The officer's state of mind is irrelevant to this inquiry.

* * *

If this first part of the test shows a violation of the Fourth Amendment, that is, an objectively unreasonable search or seizure, prosecutorial use at trial of the evidence obtained from the search or seizure is "usually preclude[d]." However, the second part of the test, to determine whether exclusion of the evidence would advance the remedial purpose of the exclusionary rule, is undertaken only if the search or seizure fails the first part of the test.

In this case, as we explain in detail later, the search and seizure were objectively reasonable. Therefore, we do not consider the second part of the test, and the officer's state of mind during the time period in question is irrelevant. ...

The law concerning arrests within the home is clear: the Fourth Amendment of the United States Constitution and article I, section 13 of the California Constitution prohibit warrantless arrests within the home absent exigent circumstances. As pertinent here, " '[e]xigent circumstances' justifying a warrantless, in-home arrest for felony refer to an emergency situation requiring swift action ... to forestall the imminent ... destruction of evidence. ... 'There is no ready litmus test for determining whether such circumstances exist, and in each case the claim of an extraordinary situation must be measured by the facts known to the officers.' " ...

The defendant claims we must determine the officer's entry was both objectively and subjectively reasonable before we can uphold it. Testing the entry for subjective reasonableness, however, is an obsolete California approach superseded by the passage of Proposition 8. When a defendant moves to suppress evidence citing a violation of the Fourth Amendment, the federal standard for exclusion must be applied. There is no independent California standard. The federal standard finds a violation of the Fourth Amendment and requires exclusion of the evidence only if the search and seizure were objectively unreasonable.

In an exigent circumstances case applying pre-Proposition 8 law, the Court of Appeal regarded as relevant the following question: "[W]as this officer ... motivated primarily by a desire to save lives and property?" An officer's motivation, however, is no longer a part of determining whether there is an unreasonable search or seizure in violation of the Fourth Amendment, although it may become relevant, under the second part of the exclusionary rule test, to whether evidence obtained by an *unreasonable* search or seizure should be excluded. ...

In *People v. Ortiz*, a police officer saw the defendant and a woman in a hotel room, which is treated the same as a home for Fourth Amendment purposes, counting tinfoil bindles. The police officer was in the hallway and observed the room's occupants through an open door. He immediately entered the room, seized the contraband, and arrested the defendant and the woman. The trial court denied the defendant's motion to suppress the contraband, and the defendant appealed after conviction. We held exigent circumstances justified the warrantless entry into the hotel room. "[V]iewed objectively, the facts known to the officer[ ] and the inferences drawn therefrom were sufficient to lead a reasonable officer to conclude that there was an imminent danger the contraband would be destroyed if he did not act immediately to arrest defendant and seize the evidence."

The circumstances are similar here. An occupant of the residence appeared to see Officer Herring outside and moved toward the front of the house. While the speakers, the main evidence indicating the defendant's guilt, were not as readily disposable as drugs might be, the occupants of the house, knowing police action was imminent, could have disassembled or destroyed the speakers during the time it would have taken to obtain a warrant to search the residence. They also could have hidden the speakers.

Most importantly, fluorescent powder invisible to the unaided eye coated the speakers. This powder tagged each person who touched the speakers. Officer Herring saw one of the speakers on the coffee table. He also saw the defendant enter the living room and sit down on the couch near the coffee table. If the defendant were to reach out and touch the speaker, he could claim he had nothing to do with the vehicle burglary, even though green powder fluoresced on his hands. He could claim he touched the speaker only after Officer Herring arrived. Furthermore, the defendant and others could have used the time it took the officers to obtain a warrant to wash the powder off their hands and clothing. By immediately entering the residence and arresting the defendant, Officer Herring preserved the state of the ephemeral evidence.

Without immediate action, the state of the evidence could have been lost and, perhaps, the speakers themselves. This imminent danger of losing vital evidence made immediate entry into the residence reasonable.

* * *

The judgment is affirmed.

and the speakers were stolen. Officer Herring responded to the vehicle alarm and tracked the speakers to a residence. Officer Herring radioed for backup, but one of the occupants of the residence noticed the backup police car arriving. The occupant, Aaron, exited the front door of the residence and spoke to Officer Herring. Officer Herring told Aaron to remain outside with another officer. Aaron had left the front door standing open, and Officer Herring observed one of the speakers on a table. The defendant, Hull, was sitting on a couch next to the speaker. Officer Herring entered the residence without a search warrant and arrested the defendant. He then searched the house and found the other speaker in a bedroom. Officer Herring seized both speakers. At his trial for vehicle burglary and receiving stolen property, Hull moved to exclude the speakers as evidence under Penal Code § 1538.5, claiming that the search and seizure without a warrant violated his right to be free from unreasonable searches and seizures under the federal and California Constitutions.

The "Truth-in-Evidence" provision affects only the exclusion of evidence. There are many other constitutional rights granted by both the state and federal constitutions, and California continues to possess the authority to grant defendants greater protection than is afforded by the federal Constitution with respect to these rights. One such right is the right to a speedy trial, guaranteed by the Sixth Amendment to the United States Constitution and by article I, § 15, of the California Constitution. As the excerpt from *People v. Hannon* illustrates, the right to a speedy trial under the federal Constitution has a different meaning than the right to a speedy trial under the California Constitution; the California Constitution grants greater protection to a criminal defendant than does the federal Constitution.

PEOPLE v. LEE ROY HANNON
19 Cal.3d 588; 138 Cal.Rptr. 885, 564 P.2d 1203 (1977)

Lee Roy Hannon appeals from a judgment following convictions by jury of attempted robbery (Pen. Code, §§ 211, 664) and assault with a deadly weapon (Pen. Code, § 245, subd. (a)). He contends initially that he was denied his constitutional right to a speedy trial ... .

* * *

Defendant bases his contention that he was denied his constitutional right to a speedy trial on our decision in *Jones v. Superior Court* (1970) 3 Cal.3d 734 [91 Cal.Rptr. 578, 478 P.2d 10], and on the fact that while the criminal complaint against him was filed on February 1, 1974, and an arrest warrant was secured on that same date, the warrant was not served on him until September 3, 1974. He argues that he was prejudiced in the preparation of his defense by virtue of this seven-month delay and that

the People have failed to provide an adequate justification for the delay.

* * *

In order to assess defendant's speedy trial claim we must evaluate the effect which subsequent decisions of the United States Supreme Court have had on our earlier interpretation of the Sixth Amendment's speedy trial provision in *Jones v. Superior Court.* In *Jones* we focused our analysis of the speedy trial issue on the key word "accused" in the relevant portions of both the United States Constitution and the California Constitution, noting that those provisions "provide only that an 'accused' shall enjoy the right to a speedy trial." (*Id.,* at p. 739.) We observed that California courts had long followed the rule that "a person does not become an 'accused' until he has been publicly charged with a crime." Thus, "[o]ne does not become an 'accused' until the filing of a complaint or other charge."

It was suggested in *Jones* however that the constitutional speedy trial provisions should not apply to prearrest delays because the exclusive protection in that context was supplied by the applicable statute of limitations. In addition, we were told that application of the right to a speedy trial in the case of prearrest delay would unduly hamper effective police investigation. We firmly and unequivocally rejected both suggestions, holding that the speedy trial provisions of the United States Constitution and the California Constitution came into play no later than the time at which the complaint against Jones was filed. ...

Shortly after we rendered our decision in *Jones* the United States Supreme Court addressed a similar speedy trial question in *United States v. Marion* (1971) 404 U.S. 307 [30 L. Ed. 2d 468, 92 S. Ct. 455]. The high court focused its attention, as had we, on the use of the word "accused" in the Sixth Amendment. In contrast to the conclusion we reached in *Jones*, however, the language used by the Supreme Court in delineating the scope of protection afforded by the federal charter was more limited than that which we adopted in *Jones*: "[I]t is either a formal indictment or information *or else the actual restraints imposed by arrest and holding to answer a criminal charge* that engage the particular protections of the speedy trial provision of the Sixth Amendment." ... [W]e conclude that the Supreme Court intended by its use of the foregoing phrase to hold that the filing of a complaint is by itself insufficient to trigger the protection of the right to a speedy trial under the federal Constitution. To that extent a conflict exists between our interpretation of the Sixth Amendment in Jones and the high court's reading of that provision in *Marion*, for as previously indicated, we held in *Jones* that the defendant became an "accused" for Sixth Amendment purposes at the time that the complaint was filed. It is that discrepancy which we next address.

It is an elemental principle of our system of federalism that ultimate responsibility for interpretation of the federal Constitution rests with the United States Supreme Court. Thus that court's pronouncement in *Marion* delineating the scope of protection afforded by the Sixth Amendment's guarantee of the right to a speedy trial is binding on this court as well as all other state and federal courts in our nation. At the same time, the Supreme Court's decision in *Marion* did not, and indeed could not, determine the constitutional requirements of the right to a speedy trial guaranteed by the analogous

portion of the California Constitution. As we noted in *People v. Longwill* (1975) 14 Cal.3d 943, 951, footnote 4 [123 Cal.Rptr. 297, 538 P.2d 753]: "[I]n the area of fundamental civil liberties—which includes not only freedom from unlawful search and seizure but all protections of the California Declaration of Rights—we sit as a court of last resort, subject only to the qualification that our interpretations may not restrict the guarantees accorded the national citizenry under the federal charter. In such constitutional adjudication, our first referent is California law and the full panoply of rights Californians have come to expect as their due. Accordingly, decisions of the United States Supreme Court defining fundamental civil rights are persuasive authority to be afforded respectful consideration, but are to be followed by California courts only when they provide no less individual protection than is guaranteed by California law." We have consistently adhered to the foregoing rule of interpretation and in our nation's system of federalism it is as fundamental a principle of constitutional law as that which rests ultimate authority for interpretation of the federal Constitution in the United States Supreme Court.

Our analysis in *Jones* revealed that the established rule in California governing the application of the constitutional right to a speedy trial was that such protection extended to the prearrest stage in cases in which a complaint has been filed against an individual not yet apprehended by law enforcement authorities. ... No new justifications have been presented to us which warrant rejection of the rule reaffirmed in *Jones* and the People concede as much, expressly stating in their brief, "The right to a speedy trial encompasses pre-arrest delays in criminal prosecutions." ... Upon due consideration the United State Supreme Court has apparently concluded that the Sixth Amendment guarantee of the right to a speedy trial does not extend to the prearrest stage when the sole accusation against an individual consists of the filing of a criminal complaint. Nevertheless, our independent examination of the speedy trial question, *in light of California law* and "the full panoply of rights Californians have come to expect as their due," has led us to conclude that the right to a speedy trial guaranteed by article I, section 15 of the California Constitution applies once a criminal complaint is filed. We continue to adhere to that higher standard of protection against the abuses of pretrial delay.

Key Terms

exclusionary rule A principle of law which provides that evidence that has been illegally obtained by law enforcement authorities may not be used against a defendant at trial or other hearing in a criminal case.

independent grounds doctrine The legal principle providing that the California Constitution constitutes a basis for individual rights independent of the United States Constitution. Under the independent grounds doctrine, the California courts and legislature may accord

rights to individuals which exceed the rights granted by the United States Constitution.

"Truth in Evidence" The name given to a provision of Article I, § 28, of the California Constitution which provides that "relevant evidence is not to be excluded from criminal proceedings." The effect of this provision is to limit the application of the exclusionary rule in the California courts to evidence that is excludable under federal constitutional principles.

Review Questions

1. What is meant by the term *selective incorporation?*

2. Briefly explain what is meant by the phrase *expansion of rights.*

3. What is a 1538.5 motion?

4. Briefly explain the two aspects of standing to raise the exclusionary rule.

5. What is the "fruit of the poisonous tree" doctrine?

6. Name five individual rights guaranteed by the California Constitution.

7. What is the independent grounds doctrine in California constitutional law?

8. What impact did the "Truth-in-Evidence" provision of Proposition 8 have on the California exclusionary rule?

Review Problems

1. Assume, hypothetically, that the California Constitution contained no grant of individual rights to the people of the state. One of the individual rights granted by the federal Constitution is free exercise of religion. Under these circumstances, is the following statement true or false? "If the California Constitution does not grant the right of free exercise of religion, a California statute making it a crime to use any language but English in a religious service cannot be challenged on constitutional grounds by a person being prosecuted for violating the statute." Explain your answer.

2. Fifty years ago, it was a crime in California for a person of one race to marry a person of another race. The statute prescribing this offense has long since been repealed. Assume,

hypothetically, that the statute is still in effect and that a Caucasian man and an Oriental woman are being prosecuted under the statute for marrying each other. Do you think the defendants could raise a constitutional challenge against the statute? If so, what constitutional right would they claim the statute violates? How could they persuade a court that the statute violates a constitutional right, considering that neither the federal Constitution nor the California Constitution addresses the subject of mixed-race marriages?

3. The police suspect that Albert is a drug dealer but do not know where Albert is obtaining his supply of drugs. One day the desk sergeant at the police station receives an anonymous telephone call. The caller says that Albert is receiving his drugs from Bert, who

manufactures the drugs in a makeshift laboratory in the garage of his home. The desk sergeant swears out an affidavit reciting that he received the anonymous telephone call and stating what the caller told him. He presents the affidavit to a magistrate and requests that the magistrate issue a search warrant authorizing the police to search Bert's garage. The affidavit is defective because it fails to provide information from which the magistrate can determine that the informant and the informant's information are reliable. Nevertheless, the magistrate issues the warrant. The affidavit is attached to the warrant and is read by the police who are executing the search warrant. The police search Bert's garage and discover the laboratory and a quantity of illegal drugs. The district attorney initiates criminal prosecutions of Albert and Bert. Albert and Bert both make Penal Code § 1538.5 motions to suppress the evidence found during the police search of Bert's garage. Do you think the motions will be successful? Explain your answers.

4. The police suspect that Patti is the perpetrator of a recent bombing of a government building. They surveil her home and see her leaving in her automobile. After she leaves, they enter the house without a search warrant to search for bomb-making materials. During the search, one of the officers finds a key to unit 3-A in a commercial self-storage facility. The officers take the key to the storage facility and open unit 3-A, again without a search warrant. Inside they find chemicals commonly used in the making of bombs. Patti is charged with the bombing. At her preliminary hearing, she makes a Penal Code § 1538.5 motion to prevent the prosecution from using the key or the chemicals as evidence at her trial. Assume for the purposes of this question that the search of Patti's house violated her constitutional right to be

free from unreasonable searches and seizures. The violation consisted in the failure of the police to obtain a search warrant before conducting the search. What do you think the result of Patti's motion will be? Explain your answer.

5. Please refer to the fact situation in question 4. At the hearing on Patti's 1538.5 motion, the prosecution presents evidence that, as part of their investigation of the bombing, the police were checking the customer listings of all self-storage facilities in the city and would ultimately have discovered that Patti had rented the storage unit. The prosecutor also presents evidence that the police had enough legally obtained evidence connecting Patti to the bombing to have obtained a search warrant for unit 3-A once they discovered that she was renting it. What effect do you think the prosecutor's evidence will have on the outcome of the hearing on Patti's motion?

6. Linda works part-time in a convenience store at minimum wage. She has been charged with selling an alcoholic beverage to a person under the age of twenty-one. The offense is a misdemeanor punishable by a fine and community service, but not by imprisonment. Because of her income level, Linda meets the California courts' indigency standard for entitlement to court-appointed counsel. Under California constitutional law, an indigent defendant is entitled to court-appointed counsel in all misdemeanor and felony cases. Under the federal Constitution, an indigent defendant is entitled to court-appointed counsel in all felony cases, but only in those misdemeanor cases in which a sentence of imprisonment is imposed. As stated, a sentence of imprisonment is not possible in Linda's case. If Linda is to be tried in the California Superior Court, is she entitled to court-appointed counsel?

Notes

1 *Hurtado v. California*, 110 U.S. 516 (1884).

2 The rule, as it applied in federal courts, was announced in *Weeks v. United States*, 232 U.S. 383 (1914). However, it appears that the rule was applied in at least one case prior to that

date. *See* LaFave & Israel, *Criminal Procedure* 78 (West 1985).

3 *Burdeau v. McDowell*, 256 U.S. 465 (1921).

4 4 Witkin & Epstein, *California Criminal Law* § 2232 (2d ed., Bancroft-Whitney 1988).

5 (1955) 44 Cal.2d 434.

6 48 U.S. 83 (1980).

7 48 U.S. at 95.

8 68 U.S. 897 (1984).

9 *See* 4 Witkin & Epstein, *supra* note 4, at § 2239.

10 *See People v. Camarella* (1991) 54 Cal.3d 592.

11 414 U.S. 338 (1974).

12 *See* 4 Witkin & Epstein, *supra* note 4, at § 2244.

13 *In re Martinez* (1970) 1 Cal.3d 641.

14 *People v. Hayko* (1970) 7 Cal.App.3d 604.

15 *People v. Coe* (1991) 228 Cal.App.3d 526.

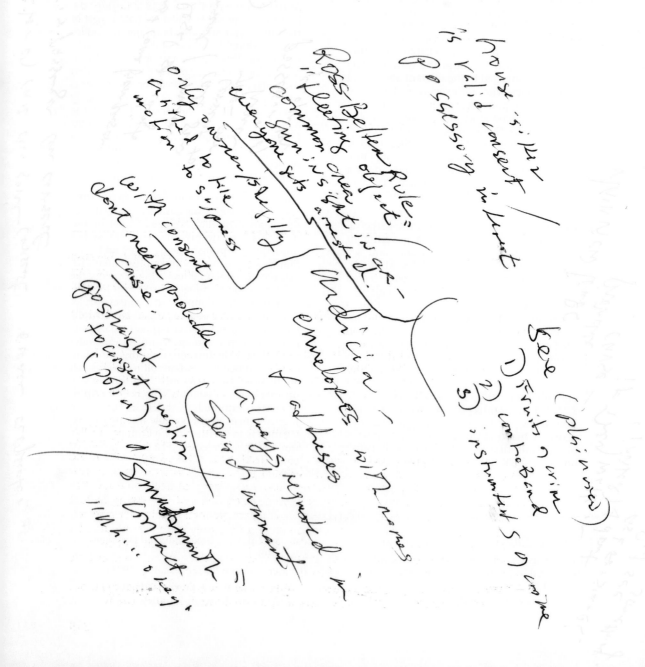

CHAPTER 14

Searches, Seizures, and Arrests

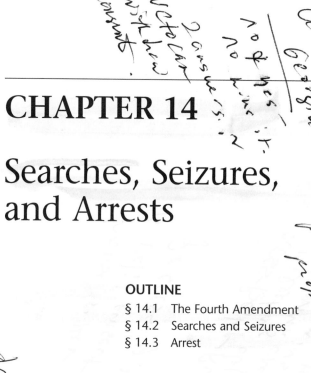

§ 14.1   The Fourth Amendment

Searches, seizures, and arrests are vital aspects of law enforcement. Because they involve significant invasions of individual liberties, limits on their use can be found in the constitutions, statutes, and other laws of the states and federal government.

The most important limitation is the Fourth Amendment of the United States Constitution, which reads:

The right of the people to be secure in their persons, papers and effects, against unreasonable searches and seizures, shall not be violated, and no warrants shall issue but upon probable cause, supported by oath or affirmation, and particularly describing the place to be searched and the persons or things to be seized.

Article I, § 13, of the California Constitution contains a substantially similar provision. Both the federal and California constitutions protect against unreasonable searches and seizures. Reasonableness is the standard against which the lawfulness of a search or seizure is measured. What is reasonable in one situation may not be reasonable in another, and a vast body of decisional law has resulted from application of the reasonableness requirement to varying factual situations. Under the law of search and seizure, the general rule is that a search by law enforcement officials is not reasonable unless they have first obtained a search warrant. The courts have developed numerous exceptions to this rule, which are discussed later in this chapter. These exceptions permit warrantless searches under specified circumstances.

Another aspect of reasonableness is the general requirement that searches and seizures are lawful only if based upon probable cause. As with the warrant requirement, the courts have developed exceptions to the probable cause requirement in certain situations. Because of the judicially created exceptions to the warrant and probable cause requirements, the law of search and seizure has become one of the most intricate areas of criminal procedure.

Recall from Chapter 13 that the constitutional principles underlying the law of search and seizure apply only to government action. If a private citizen conducts a search or seizure that would be unlawful if conducted by government officials, the evidence thus obtained is admissible against the accused. This principle does not apply, however, if the private citizen is acting under the direction of a government official, because in that situation the private citizen would be an agent of the government.

The exclusionary rule is the primary remedy of a criminal defendant whose constitutional rights have been violated by an illegal search or seizure. Other remedies may include a right to sue the offending law enforcement official under a civil rights statute or under common-law tort theory. In 1971, the United States Supreme Court recognized the concept of a "constitutional" tort, that is, a right to sue a government official for violation of one's constitutional rights independent of state common-law tort theories.[1]

The discussion in this chapter on the law of search and seizure focuses initially on searches of places and persons and the seizure of items from the place or person searched. The legal principles governing arrests, which are seizures of persons, are somewhat different from those governing searches and seizures generally, so the subject of arrest is treated separately at the end of the chapter.

When does government action constitute a search? Until 1967, the constitutional protection against unreasonable searches and seizures was interpreted to apply to physical "areas." A search was a governmental intrusion into a constitutionally protected area. This standard was changed in *Katz v. United States*.

In *Katz*, the United States Supreme Court established a standard known as the "reasonable expectation of privacy." The Court recognized that an individual may have a reasonable expectation of privacy in his or her activities, such as speaking on a public telephone, as well as in physical areas. A later United States Supreme Court decision has stated that a **search** occurs "when an expectation of privacy that society is prepared to consider reasonable is infringed." In the same opinion, the Court defined a **seizure** as "a meaningful interference with an individual's possessory interest" in property.[2]

If law enforcement officials infringe a person's reasonable expectation of privacy, they have engaged in a search within the scope of the federal and California constitutions. In *People v. Dumas* (1973) 9 Cal.3d 871, the California Supreme Court provided examples of places in which a person might have a reasonable expectation of privacy. Such places include homes, offices, hotel rooms, automobiles, and luggage, among others. The enumeration was not intended to be exhaustive, and a person may have a reasonable expectation of privacy in any number of places or activities. For example, it was held by one court that a person had a reasonable expectation of privacy in his backyard, which was enclosed by two fences, one six feet high and one ten feet high. Another court decision held that a defendant had a reasonable expectation of privacy in a paper bag in his car. There have even been decisions holding that a person has a reasonable expectation of privacy in a garbage or trash receptacle.[3]

KATZ v. UNITED STATES
389 U.S. 347 (1967)

The petitioner was convicted in the District Court for the Southern District of California under an eight-count indictment charging him with transmitting wagering information by telephone from Los Angeles to Miami and Boston, in violation of a federal statute. At trial the Government was permitted, over the petitioner's objection, to introduce evidence of the petitioner's end of telephone conversations, overheard by FBI agents who had attached an electronic listening and recording device to the outside of the public telephone booth from which he had placed his calls. In affirming his conviction, the Court of Appeals rejected the contention that the recordings had been obtained in violation of the Fourth Amendment, because "[t]here was no physical entrance into the area occupied by [the petitioner]." We granted certiorari in order to consider the constitutional questions thus presented.

The petitioner has phrased those questions as follows:

A. Whether a public telephone booth is a constitutionally protected area so that evidence obtained by attaching an electronic listening recording device to the top of such booth is obtained in violation of the right to privacy of the user of the booth.
B. Whether physical penetration of a constitutionally protected area is necessary before a search and seizure can be said to be violative of the Fourth Amendment to the United States Constitution.

We decline to adopt this formulation of the issues. In the first place, the correct solution of Fourth Amendment problems is not necessarily promoted by incantation of the phrase "constitutionally protected area." Secondly, the Fourth Amendment cannot be translated into a general constitutional "right to privacy." That Amendment protects individual privacy against certain kinds of governmental intrusion, but its protections go further, and often have nothing to do with privacy at all. Other provisions of the Constitution protect personal privacy from other forms of governmental invasion. But the protection of a person's *general* right to privacy—his right to be left alone by other people—is, like the protection of

property and of his very life, left largely to the law of the individual States.

Because of the misleading way the issues have been formulated, the parties have attached great significance to the characterization of the telephone booth from which the petitioner placed his calls. The petitioner has strenuously argued that the booth was a "constitutionally protected area." The Government has maintained with equal vigor that it was not. But this effort to decide whether or not a given "area," viewed in the abstract, is "constitutionally protected" deflects attention from the problem presented by this case. For the Fourth Amendment protects people, not places. What a person knowingly exposes to the public, even in his own home or office, is not a subject of Fourth Amendment protection. ... But what he seeks to preserve as private, even in an area accessible to the public, may be constitutionally protected. ...

The Government stresses the fact that the telephone booth from which the petitioner made his calls was constructed partly of glass, so that he was as visible after he entered it as he would have been if he had remained outside. But what he sought to exclude when he entered the booth was not the intruding eye—it was the uninvited ear. He did not shed his right to do so simply because he made his calls from a place where he might be seen. No less than an individual in a business office, in a friend's apartment, or in a taxicab, a person in a telephone booth may rely upon the protection of the Fourth Amendment. One who occupies it, shuts the door behind him, and pays the toll that permits him to place a call is surely entitled to assume that the words he utters into the mouthpiece will not be broadcast to the world. To read the Constitution more narrowly is to ignore the vital role that the public telephone has come to play in private communication.

The Government contends, however, that the activities of its agents in this case should not be tested by Fourth Amendment requirements, for the surveillance technique they employed involved no physical penetration of the telephone booth from which the petitioner placed his calls. It is true that the absence of such penetration was at one time thought to foreclose further Fourth Amendment inquiry ... for that Amendment was thought to limit only searches and seizures of tangible property ... we have since departed from the narrow view on which that decision rested. Indeed, we have expressly held that the Fourth Amendment governs not only the seizure of tangible items, but extends as well to the recording of oral statements, overheard without any "technical trespass under ... local property law." *Silverman v. United States*, 365 U.S. 505, 511. Once this much is acknowledged, and once it is recognized that the Fourth Amendment protects people—and not simply "areas"—against unreasonable searches and seizures, it becomes clear that the reach of that Amendment cannot turn upon the presence or absence of a physical intrusion into any given enclosure.

We conclude that the underpinnings of [prior decisions] have been so eroded by our subsequent decisions that the "trespass" doctrine there enunciated can no longer be regarded as controlling. ...

[The Court then held that the warrantless search was conducted in violation of the Fourth Amendment.]

If there is no invasion of a reasonable expectation of privacy, there is no search within the scope of the Fourth Amendment to the United States Constitution and article I, § 13, of the California Constitution. For example, a police officer's observations made from a public place, such as a sidewalk, are not searches. Observing the exterior of an automobile, including a license plate, is not a search, nor is a dog sniff of an item or person. The rationale behind the principle that a dog sniff is not a search is that the dog is sniffing the air around the item or person, and a person does not have a reasonable expectation of privacy in the air surrounding his person or items. It has also been held that a prisoner has no reasonable expectation of privacy in his or her prison cell.[4]

An area of considerable judicial activity has been the use of aerial surveillance by police to detect criminal activity, often the growing of marijuana crops. The courts have taken varying positions on this subject over the years. The principal question is: does a person growing marijuana have a reasonable expectation of privacy against observation of the marijuana crop from the air? The current view of the federal and California courts is that a person may have a reasonable expectation of privacy if he or she carries on an activity in such a manner that it would not be visible from an aircraft flying at a normal altitude. If, however, the activity is visible from an aircraft flying at a normal altitude, the person does not have a reasonable expectation of privacy. Accordingly, aerial surveillance from a normal altitude does not involve a search and is not subject to the constitutional restrictions applicable to searches. In practice, aerial surveillance is used to establish probable cause for issuance of a warrant to conduct a ground-level search of property on which the marijuana is growing and seize the marijuana.[5]

Another subject frequently discussed in the context of the reasonable expectation of privacy is the use of mechanical or electronic aids to observe criminal activity or evidence. Binoculars and telescopes are examples of such aids. Is it lawful, for example, for a police officer to secretly observe persons engaged in criminal activity from a distance using a telescope? According to judicial decisions, if the criminal activity is conducted in such a manner that it would be observable by the unaided eye or ear, the perpetrators have no reasonable expectation of privacy, and the police may use mechanical or electronic aids to enhance their ability to observe the activity. If, however, the perpetrators conduct the activity in such a manner that it would be imperceptible without mechanical or electronic aids, they have a reasonable expectation of privacy, and the police may not observe it unless they obtain a search warrant or an exception to the warrant requirement applies.

If John and Sue are discussing their criminal plans inside Sue's apartment, and the conversation cannot be heard outside the apartment with an unaided ear, law enforcement officials using sound-amplifying equipment to listen in on the conversation are conducting a search and must have a warrant. If, however, Sue has left a window open and a person would be able to hear the conversation from outside the window, John and Sue do not have a reasonable expectation of privacy, and police using sound-amplifying equipment to listen in from across the street are not conducting a search within the meaning of the federal and California constitutional protections. The police are merely using the equipment to enhance their ability to perceive what John and Sue are exposing to observation from outside the apartment.

Probable Cause

Probable Cause Defined

The Fourth Amendment requires the existence of **probable cause** before law enforcement authorities may conduct a search, i.e., before they may infringe a person's reasonable expectation of privacy. When a warrant is obtained prior to a search, the probable cause determination is made by a judge. When a judge is performing the function of issuing a search warrant, he or she is generally referred to as a *magistrate*. In situations in which a police officer acts without a warrant, the officer makes that determination. In both cases, as you will see, probable cause is required.

 Probable cause is a phrase describing the minimum amount of evidence necessary before a search, seizure, or arrest is proper. Whether the issue concerns a search and seizure or an arrest, the same quantity of evidence is necessary to establish probable cause.

There is no one universal definition of probable cause. In fact, the definition of probable cause differs depending on the context. In all situations, it is more than mere suspicion and less than the standard required to prove a defendant guilty at trial (beyond a reasonable doubt). As the United States Supreme Court has expressed, probable cause is present when the trustworthy facts within the officer's knowledge are sufficient in themselves to justify a "person of reasonable caution" in the belief that seizable property will be found or that the person to be arrested committed the crime in question.[6]

Sources Used to Establish Probable Cause

When making the probable cause determination, a magistrate considers information provided by law enforcement authorities. As will be discussed in the section on search warrants, this information is provided to the magistrate in the form of a written affidavit or by oral testimony under penalty of perjury. When a police officer makes his or her own probable cause determination in a situation in which a search warrant is not required, the officer must consider the information of which he or she has been made aware through sources available to him or her. The information relied upon by the magistrate or police officer need not be evidence that would be admissible at trial, but it must be reliable. Innuendo or conjecture that is not supported by facts may not be considered.

Information frequently relied upon by magistrates and law enforcement officers when making probable cause determinations includes the personal observations of the police officer preparing the affidavit, testifying before the magistrate, or making his or her own probable cause determination; statements of other law enforcement officers; and information obtained from other persons, such as witnesses, victims, and informants. Hearsay evidence is frequently relied upon by magistrates and police officers when making probable cause determinations. *Hearsay evidence* is a statement made by a person to the magistrate or a police officer about something another person has said. For example, suppose that officer A writes an affidavit in support of a search warrant application and states in the affidavit that a witness told him that the suspect was seen selling drugs from his home. The officer's repetition of the witness's statement is hearsay. Officer A does not have first-hand personal knowledge of the suspect's activities, but knows of them only because a third person, the witness, told him so. Hearsay evidence is generally inadmissible at trial. It may, however, be used to support a probable cause determination for a search if it has sufficient indicia of reliability.

Information obtained from informants has been a matter of particular concern for the courts. Informants are frequently persons who associate with criminals and the courts have historically been cautious in accepting them as sources of information for probable cause determinations. However, because they do associate with criminals, informants have access to valuable information regarding criminal activity, making the use of informant-provided information highly desirable from a law enforcement perspective. In *Aguilar v. Texas,* 378 U.S. 108 (1964), the United States Supreme Court established a two-prong test for the use of informant information when making a probable cause determination for the issuance of a search warrant. First, the affidavit submitted to the magistrate had to contain information establishing the basis of the informant's knowledge about the alleged criminal activity. For example, did the informant personally observe the criminal activity, or hear about it from another person? This prong of the *Aguilar* test was designed to assure that the informant's own perceptions were reliable and that his or her allegations were well founded. Second, the affidavit had to provide the magistrate with a basis for believing that the informant was being truthful in what he or she told the police. This could be done, for example, by showing that the informant had previously given truthful information. Thus, the *Aguilar* test enabled a magistrate to determine whether the informant's information was reliable and whether the informant himself or herself was believable. If the magistrate was satisfied that both of these requirements had been met, and that the information provided by the informant established probable cause, the magistrate possessed a sound basis for issuance of a search warrant.

In *Illinois v. Gates,* decided in 1983, the United States Supreme Court abandoned the two-prong *Aguilar* test as the sole method of assessing the credibility and reliability of informant-provided information. The Court adopted what is known as the **totality of the circumstances test,** which is the standard used today in the federal and California courts. In the words of the Court:

> The task of the issuing magistrate is simply to make a practical, common-sense decision whether, given all the circumstances set forth in the affidavit before him, including the "veracity" and the "basis of knowledge" of persons supplying hearsay information, there is a fair probability that contraband or evidence of a crime will be found in a particular place.[7]

Note that the standard enunciated by the Court in *Gates* includes the "veracity" and "basis of knowledge" elements of the *Aguilar* test. Under the *Gates* standard, however, these elements are not determinative, but are only factors to be considered in the mix of factors termed the *totality of the circumstances.*

Probable cause may be established by an animal, as well as a human. Dogs can be trained to discover bombs, drugs, and people. At the borders, dogs are used to sniff vehicles for the presence of illegal aliens. At airports, dogs are used to detect explosives and contraband. Many police departments depend on dogs to detect drugs and track fugitives. The United States Supreme Court has stated that the act of having a dog sniff a person or thing is not a search.[8] The California Supreme Court reached a similar result in *People v. Mayberry* (1982) 31 Cal.3d 335, a case involving the use of a sniffer dog to detect illegal drugs in airport luggage. In *Mayberry,* the court reasoned that "the passenger's reasonable expectation of privacy does not extend to the airspace surrounding the luggage." Accordingly, governmental intrusion into the airspace through the use of the dog does not constitute a search. In a "canine olfactory investigation," as the California Supreme Court calls it, the role of the dog is to establish probable cause sufficient to support the issuance of a search warrant, or to support a search without a warrant if an exception to the warrant requirement applies.

§ 14.2 Searches and Seizures

The Warrant Requirement

According to Penal Code § 1523, a **search warrant** is "an order in writing, in the name of the people, signed by a magistrate, directed to a peace officer, commanding him or her to search for a person or persons, a thing or things, or personal property, and, in the case of a thing or things or personal property, bring the same before the magistrate." *Personal property,* in this context, means anything that is not real estate or a thing permanently attached to real estate. The United States Supreme Court has expressed that there is a strong preference for the use of warrants over warrantless searches and seizures.[9] The warrant preference serves an important purpose: it protects citizens from overzealous law enforcement practices.

> The presence of a search warrant serves a high function. Absent some grave emergency, the Fourth Amendment has interposed a magistrate between the citizen and police. This was done not to shield criminals nor to make the home a safe haven for illegal activities. It was done so that an objective

mind might weigh the need to invade the privacy in order to enforce the law. The right of privacy was deemed too precious to entrust to the discretion of those whose job is the detection of crime and the arrest of criminals.[10]

A search conducted pursuant to a valid search warrant is per se reasonable. Warrantless searches are permitted only in special circumstances, and it is the responsibility of the government to prove that the facts of the case fit into one of the exceptions to the warrant requirement.

To give this preference some "teeth," the United States Supreme Court, in *Aguilar v. Texas,* 378 U.S. 108, 111 (1964), announced that "when a search is based upon a magistrate's, rather than a police officer's determination of probable cause," reviewing courts are to accept lesser competent evidence than if the officer made the determination personally, so long as there was a "substantial basis" for the magistrate's decision. To say it another way, less evidence is required to sustain a search if a warrant was obtained prior to the search.

"Reviewing courts" are referred to because the determination that probable cause exists by a magistrate when issuing a warrant is not final. A defendant may later attack any evidence seized pursuant to a warrant through a motion to suppress. In California courts, the motion to suppress is made pursuant to Penal Code § 1538.5, discussed in Chapter 13. As stated, determinations by a magistrate are less likely to be overturned than those made by police officers.

Requirements for Obtaining a Warrant

Federal and California constitutional principles establish the requirements that must be met before a search warrant can be issued. Article I, § 13, of the California Constitution, which is almost identical to corresponding language in the federal Fourth Amendment, provides that "a warrant may not issue except on probable cause, supported by oath or affirmation, particularly describing the place to be searched and the persons and things to be seized." These requirements are implemented through procedures established in Penal Code § 1524 and following sections.

Under the federal and California constitutional principles, a warrant must be issued by a "neutral and detached magistrate." This means that the official who determines whether to issue the warrant must not be involved in law enforcement. The requirement is met in California by having municipal and superior court judges issue warrants. Law enforcement authorities desiring a search warrant initiate the process by submitting an application for a search warrant to the magistrate.

Penal Code § 1525 reflects the basic constitutional standards for issuance of a warrant:

> A search warrant cannot be issued but upon probable cause, supported by affidavit, naming or describing the person to be searched or searched for, and particularly describing the property, thing or things, and the place to be searched.

The statute incorporates a number of requirements. First, the evidence presented to the magistrate must establish probable cause to believe that the items or persons sought are in the area to be searched. Second, there must be probable cause to believe that the items or persons sought are connected with criminal activity. Third, the evidence must be presented to the magistrate by affidavit. Fourth, the affidavit must name or describe the person to be searched for, if the search is to be for a person; and must "particularly describe" any property to be searched for and, in the case of both persons and property, the place to be searched.

With regard to the fourth requirement, the amount of specificity required varies from case to case. An affidavit that describes the property sought as "unauthorized contraband" is clearly insufficient. In contrast, an affidavit that describes the property as, for example, a"nine-inch knife with an ivory handle" is sufficient. According to Witkin and Epstein, the description need not be exact; it is sufficient if it imposes a "meaningful restriction" on the objects to be seized.[11] With regard to the location to be searched, a street address is normally sufficient. If there is no street address, the affidavit should describe the location, owner, color, and architectural style of the property. Of course, any additional information that aids in describing property should be included. If the building to be searched is an apartment building or similar multiunit structure, the specific subunit to be searched must be stated in the affidavit.

Penal Code § 1524(a) specifies the types of items for which a search warrant may issue. The affidavit submitted to the magistrate must show that the property to be searched for and seized is of one of the specified types. The following categories of items are stated in § 1524(a):

1. Stolen or embezzled property
2. Property that was used as a means of committing a felony
3. Property in the possession of a person who intends to use it as a means of committing an offense, or in the possession of another person for the purpose of concealment or prevention of discovery
4. Evidence showing that a felony has been committed or that a particular person committed a felony
5. Evidence of sexual exploitation of a child

Section 1524.1 provides that a warrant may issue, upon the request of a crime victim, compelling the accused to submit to a blood test for the HIV virus if the crime was such that the accused, if infected, could have transmitted the HIV virus to the victim. The "property" to be seized in such a case is a sample of the accused's blood. In the remainder of this section, reference will be limited to § 1524(a).

The affidavit or affidavits submitted to a magistrate with a warrant application must set forth facts establishing the grounds of the application, or probable cause for believing that they exist. (*See* Penal Code § 1527.) What this means is that the facts stated in the affidavit or affidavits must persuade the magistrate that seizable items—i.e., items enumerated in Penal Code § 1524(a)—are located in the place or on the person to be searched. If the affidavit or affidavits meet this requirement, the magistrate is to issue the search warrant. (*See* Penal Code § 1528.)

The contents of a search warrant are prescribed in Penal Code § 1529. According to that section, a search warrant must contain the following: (1) a description of the person or place to be searched and the person or things to be seized, with reasonable particularity; (2) the names of every person, except confidential informers, providing an affidavit in support of the warrant application; (3) a statement of the grounds for issuing the warrant (i.e., that the items to be seized fall within one of the categories specified in § 1524(a)); (4) a command to the peace officer to whom the warrant is directed to conduct the search and seizure; and (5) the signature of the magistrate.

Scope of Warrants

As previously discussed, a warrant may be issued to search for and seize items described in Penal Code § 1524(a). A warrant may authorize a search of a place and seizure of property belonging to an innocent third party, as well as to places and property belonging to suspected criminals. (*See* Penal Code § 1524(b).)

The particularity requirement acts to limit the breadth of a warrant. A peace officer executing a warrant may search only the place specified and may search for only the things specified in the warrant. For example, an officer executing a warrant directing her to search a suspect's home for stolen televisions would not be authorized to search places that are too small to contain televisions, such as drawers in the suspect's desk. If an officer exceeds the scope of a warrant and discovers evidence of a crime, the exclusionary rule will make the evidence inadmissible at trial. If, in the stolen television example, the officer searched the suspect's desk drawers and found illegal drugs, the drugs would not be admissible against the suspect at trial.

In some circumstances the particularity requirement is heightened. For example, because of the importance of protecting the press from government intrusion, warrants to search newsrooms or similar areas must be drafted with "particular exactitude."[12]

As a general proposition, a warrant to search premises does not authorize the police to search the occupants of the premises.[13] Of course, a search may be conducted if an independent basis exists justifying that action. Generally, the occupants of an area to be searched may be detained until the search is complete. However, occupants cannot be detained for an "unduly prolonged" period of time.[14] Once the evidence sought is found or the threat of loss or destruction of evidence by an occupant has passed, he or she should be released.

Executing the Warrant

The warrant may direct a particular officer or an entire unit of peace officers to conduct the search. Only the officers identified in the warrant may conduct the search, although the officers may be assisted by other persons if the named officers direct the others and remain present during the search.[15]

As a general rule, a search warrant must be executed (carried out) during the day or in the evening. Penal Code § 1533 provides that, absent a specific direction in the warrant, it must be executed between the hours of 7 A.M. and 10 P.M. Upon a showing of good cause, a magistrate may insert a direction in a warrant allowing it to be served at any time of the day or night. When determining the existence of good cause, the magistrate is to consider the safety of the peace officers serving the warrant and the safety of the public as a valid basis for nighttime endorsements. Other grounds for authorizing nighttime searches might include evidence that a daytime search would not be successful, such as when illegal activities are occurring on the premises to be searched only during the night, or when the items to be searched for are likely to be destroyed or disposed of during the night.

Under Penal Code § 1534, a search warrant must be executed and returned to the issuing magistrate within ten days after the date of issuance. In some jurisdictions, the law provides that if probable cause dissipates before the statutory period for executing the warrant has expired, a search violates the Fourth Amendment. The rule in California is different. Penal Code § 1534(a) provides that "[a] warrant executed within the 10-day period shall be deemed to have been timely executed and no further showing of timeliness need be made." If a warrant is not executed within the ten-day period, it automatically becomes void.

The general rule is that officers executing a search warrant must give the occupant of the premises notice of their authority and purpose and provide the occupant an opportunity to admit them. If, however, after giving notice of their authority and purpose, they are refused admittance, the officers may use force to enter the premises.[16] Notice of authority and purpose are also excused in exigent circumstances of which the officers executing the warrant are aware, such as the likely destruction of evidence by the occupant or the risk of injury to the officers by an armed and dangerous suspect.[17]

Penal Code § 1535 requires peace officers who execute a search warrant and seize property to give a receipt for the property to the person from whom it was taken or in whose possession it was found. If no person is present, the receipt must be left in the place where the property was found. The receipt must specify the property in detail. Under § 1536, all property or things seized pursuant to a warrant must be retained by the officers in their custody, subject to order of the court. Section 1537 requires that the officers return the warrant to the issuing magistrate accompanied by an inventory of the property and things seized. As discussed in Chapter 13, a defendant may move for return of the property or to suppress its use as evidence under § 1538.5. If the magistrate finds that the property taken is not the same as that described in the warrant, or that there is no probable cause to believe the existence of the grounds on which the warrant was issued, the magistrate must cause the property to be restored to the person from whom it was taken.[18] The property need not be restored if its possession would be illegal, such as in the case of illegal drugs.

Exceptions to the Search Warrant Requirement

A search must be made pursuant to a warrant unless an exception to the warrant requirement applies. This section discusses the numerous exceptions to the warrant requirement that have been developed by the courts.

Consent Searches

A person may consent to a search of his or her person or property. Effective consent to a search renders a warrant unnecessary. To be effective, a person's consent to a search must be voluntary. There is, however, no requirement that law enforcement officers advise the person that he or she may refuse to consent.

The fact that they are requesting the person's consent to submit to a search carries with it the implication that the person may refuse to consent to the search. A person who allows a search may choose to give only limited consent. The scope of a **consent search** must be kept within the limits imposed by the consent. In one case, for example, the defendant consented to a search of the inside of his automobile, but did not consent to a search of the trunk. A police officer searched both the inside of the automobile and the trunk and found illegal drugs in the trunk. The defendant was convicted of possession of the illegal drugs. On appeal, the appellate court reversed the conviction. The court held that the search of the trunk was illegal because it exceeded the scope of the consent given by the defendant, and that the evidence seized from the trunk should have been excluded at trial.[19] In the same case, the defendant asked the police officer to stop when the officer began searching the trunk. The appellate court held that a person who has consented to a search may withdraw the consent; if consent is withdrawn, the search must stop. Although there is some contrary authority on the right of a person to withdraw consent to a search, once given, the majority of California courts appear to recognize the right.[20]

As stated, consent to a search must be voluntary to be effective. Consent influenced by illegal conduct on the part of law enforcement officers is considered involuntary and ineffective. Thus, consent to a search obtained by police immediately after an illegal entry, arrest, search, or interrogation is ineffective to support a warrantless search.

Consent obtained by coercion is likewise involuntary and ineffective. It is not coercion for a person to be told that if he or she does not consent to a search, the police will obtain a search warrant. It is, however, coercion for the police to state that when they search pursuant to the warrant, they will ransack the person's home. The courts have found some situations inherently coercive, despite the lack of threats by police. In *People v. McKelvy* (1972) 23 Cal.App.3d 1027, the defendant was detained, but not arrested, at 3:00 A.M. as he was walking through residential front yards. While surrounded by four officers armed with shotguns and carbines, one of the officers asked the defendant to hand over an object that the defendant had put in his pocket. The defendant gave the object, which was a bottle containing an illegal drug, to the officer. On appeal of his conviction, the appellate court noted that no matter how politely the police officer might have phrased his request for the object, the situation was coercive and the defendant's consent was not voluntary.

Consent obtained by fraud is similarly ineffective to support a warrantless search. For example, assume the police interrogate a suspect but obtain no admission of criminal activity. They keep the suspect in custody and go to the suspect's house. When the suspect's wife answers the door, the police falsely tell her that the suspect confessed to certain crimes and request permission to search the house. If the wife consents to the search because of the police deception, the consent is invalid and any evidence discovered during the search will be inadmissible against the suspect at trial.

Another common issue in consent search situations involves the question of who may consent to the search. This issue arises in cases in which someone other than the suspect has the physical ability to allow the police access to the premises to be searched. For example, if Jed and Ned are college roommates, and the police want to search the room for evidence of criminal activity by Jed, can

Ned consent to a search of the room? If Martha owns an apartment building or a hotel, can she consent to a search of a tenant's apartment or a hotel guest's room?

The Jed and Ned example is called a "co-inhabitant" situation. In *United States v. Matlock,* 415 U.S. 164 (1974), the United States Supreme Court held that the nonsuspect co-inhabitant may consent to a search of the premises if the parties share access, use, and control of the area searched. If the co-inhabitants have exclusive use of certain parts of the premises (such as their own bedrooms) or certain items in the premises (such as their own desks), only the co-inhabitant having exclusive use of the part of the premises or the item to be searched may consent to the search. If Jed and Ned are sharing an apartment, Ned could consent to a search of areas commonly used by both himself and Jed, such as the living room and kitchen. However, only Jed could consent to a search of Jed's separate bedroom, assuming the bedroom was an area of exclusive use by Jed.

A spouse has the authority to consent to a search of the home when the police are seeking evidence of criminal activity by the other spouse.

What about Martha, who owns an apartment building or a hotel? Can she consent to a search of a tenant's apartment or a hotel guest's room? The answer in both cases is no. In both situations, the tenant or hotel guest has hired or purchased the use of the apartment or hotel room from Martha and has a right to possess the premises during the period of the tenancy or hiring. In cases such as these, ownership of the property does not carry with it the authority to consent to a search. Rather, the person with the possessory interest has the right to consent.

Plain View

Another exception to the warrant requirement is the **plain view doctrine.** Under this rule, a warrantless seizure of evidence by an officer who is lawfully in a position to see the evidence is valid.

A large body of cases discusses the plain view doctrine. From those cases it can be gleaned that for a seizure to be lawful under the doctrine, the following must be shown: (1) The officer must lawfully be in an area (2) from which the object to be seized is in plain view (3) and the officer does in fact see the item, (4) there is probable cause to believe the object is connected to a crime, and (5) the officer has a right to access the object itself.

First, the officer must be in a place where he or she has a right to be. An officer, as is true of anyone, has a right to be in public places. Thus, evidence seen in a public park, on the street, or in a business open to the public may be seized without a warrant.

Evidence located on private property is different. As a general rule, the police have no right to enter private property to seize evidence that is in plain view from a public area. In such cases the officer is expected to obtain a warrant; the officer's observation provides the requisite probable cause. However, if an exception applies, such as preventing destruction of the evidence, the officer may immediately seize the evidence.

If an officer is on private property for a lawful reason, then the officer may seize evidence in plain view without first obtaining a warrant. There are many reasons why an officer might be in a position to see evidence. Many of these were discussed in *Coolidge*. An officer who has to enter a home to execute an arrest warrant is not expected to overlook illegal objects in plain sight. The same is true if the officer is executing a search warrant, is in hot pursuit, is responding to an emergency, or is conducting a stop and frisk.

Second, the evidence seized must be in plain view. As the term implies, *plain view* generally means observation using the sense of sight. The officer, from a vantage point where he or she has a legal right to be, must see the evidence. This requirement is strictly enforced by the courts. For example, in *Arizona v. Hicks*, 480 U.S. 321 (1987), the police entered an apartment in response to a gunshot. Once inside, they observed expensive stereo equipment which they suspected to be stolen. They moved the stereo equipment to check the serial number and thereby confirmed that the stereo was stolen. The United States Supreme Court held that the serial number was not in plain view because the police officers had to move the stereo to observe it.

A few California cases have applied the plain view analysis to the sense of hearing, holding that if police are in a place they have a right to be, and hear conversations or other sounds indicating that a narcotics transaction is in progress, the statements made by the defendants are admissible.[21]

The plain view analysis has not been applied to the sense of smell in California. The issue has arisen in cases involving marijuana and hashish, which have distinctive odors. The decisions in these cases have essentially held that if police officers are in a place they have a right to be, and smell marijuana or hashish, but do not visually observe it, they cannot seize the drugs. In *People v. Marshall*

COOLIDGE v. NEW HAMPSHIRE
403 U.S. 443 (1971)

It is well established that under certain circumstances the police may seize evidence in plain view without a warrant. But it is important to keep in mind that, in the vast majority of cases, *any* evidence seized by the police will be in plain view, at least at the moment of seizure. The problem with the "plain view" doctrine has been to identify the circumstances in which plain view has legal significance rather than being simply the normal concomitant of any search, legal or illegal.

An example of the applicability of the "plain view" doctrine is the situation in which the police have a warrant to search a given area for specified objects, and in the course of the search come across some other article of incriminating character. ... Where the initial intrusion that brings the police within plain view of such an article is supported, not by a warrant, but by one of the recognized exceptions to the warrant requirement, the seizure is also

legitimate. Thus, the police may inadvertently come across evidence while in "hot pursuit" of a fleeing suspect. ... And an object that comes into view during a search incident to arrest that is appropriately limited in scope under existing law may be seized without a warrant. ... Finally, the "plain view" doctrine has been applied where a police officer is not searching for evidence against the accused, but nonetheless inadvertently comes across incriminating evidence. ...

What the "plain view" cases have in common is that the police officer in each of them had a prior justification for an intrusion in the course of which he came inadvertently across a piece of evidence incriminating the accused. ... Of course, the extension of the original justification is legitimate only where it is immediately apparent to the police that they have evidence before them; the "plain view" doctrine may not be used to extend a general exploratory search from one object to another until something incriminating at last emerges.

(1968) 69 Cal.2d 51, officers lawfully in the defendant's apartment smelled marijuana and observed that the source of the odor was a cardboard box. The officers went to the box, looked inside, and found marijuana. The California Supreme Court held that the officers should have obtained a search warrant before looking into the box because the marijuana was not in plain view. The court held that the sense of smell may provide probable cause for issuance of a warrant, but it does not provide grounds for an exception to the warrant requirement under the plain view doctrine. In the words of the court, there is no "plain smell" doctrine in California.

Third, the officer must see the item. In *Coolidge*, the Court stated that:

> [T]he discovery of evidence in plain view must be inadvertent. The rationale of the exception to the warrant requirement, as just stated, is that a plain-view seizure will not turn an initially valid (and therefore limited) search into a "general" one, while the inconvenience of procuring a warrant to cover an inadvertent discovery is great. But where the discovery is anticipated, where the police know in advance that location of the evidence and intend to seize it, the situation is altogether different. The requirement of a warrant imposes no inconvenience whatever.[22]

In most cases, the discovery will be inadvertent. However, in *Horton v. California*, 496 U.S. 128 (1990), the Supreme Court rejected inadvertence as a requirement of plain view, although it recognized that, in most instances, a discovery will be inadvertent. In *Horton*, an officer sought a search warrant for both the proceeds of a robbery and the weapons used during the robbery. The warrant was issued, but only for the proceeds. During the search, the officer discovered the weapon, as expected, in plain view. The Court held that even though expected, the gun was properly seized.

Fourth, the officer must have probable cause to believe that the object is subject to seizure, or, as the Court stated in *Horton*, the incriminating character of the object must be immediately apparent. *Contraband* (an item that is illegal itself, such as drugs) can be seized, as can property used to commit crimes, that has been used in a crime, or that has been stolen.

Fifth, the officer must be located such that he or she has a legal right to access the object. If not, the officer must obtain a warrant. For example, a police officer has a warrant to search a suspect's garage. While in the garage, he observes evidence of a crime inside the suspect's home through an open door or window, but in this situation he may not enter the home to seize the evidence. He must obtain a warrant unless an exception to the warrant requirement, other than the plain view doctrine, applies. In such a case, observation of the object in plain view establishes probable cause to issue a warrant, but does not confer authority on the officer to enter the house. If, however, the officer is searching the garage for a gun, and sees illegal drugs in the garage in plain view, the officer may seize the drugs because he has access to them; that is, they are in the garage, which is where the officer has a legal right to be pursuant to the warrant.

Stop and Frisk

On October 31, 1963, a Cleveland, Ohio, police detective observed three men standing on a street corner. Suspicious of the men, the detective positioned himself to watch their behavior. After some time the officer concluded that the men were "casing a job, a stick-up."

The officer approached the men, identified himself, and asked them to identify themselves. After the men "mumbled something," the officer grabbed one of the men and conducted a frisk, or a pat-down, of the man's clothing. The officer felt a pistol in the man's coat pocket. He removed the gun from his coat and then "patted down" the other two men. Another gun was discovered during those frisks.

The officer testified that he conducted the frisks because he believed the men were carrying weapons. The first man frisked was defendant Terry. At trial he was convicted of carrying a concealed weapon and was subsequently sentenced to one to three years in prison. His appeal made it to the United States Supreme Court.

In *Terry v. Ohio,* 392 U.S. 1 (1968), the Supreme Court was confronted with these issues: Did the officer's behavior amount to a search or seizure under the Fourth Amendment? If so, was the search or seizure by the officer reasonable?

The Court decided that defendant Terry had been seized under the Fourth Amendment. "It must be recognized that whenever a police officer accosts an individual and restrains his freedom to walk away, he has 'seized' that person." As to the frisk, the Court stated that "it is nothing less than sheer torture of the English language to suggest that a careful exploration of the outer surfaces of a person's clothing all over his or her body in an attempt to find weapons is not a search." With these statements, the Court made it clear that the police practice of stopping and frisking people is governed by the Fourth Amendment.

A **stop and frisk** involves two occurrences that bring the constitutional protections against unreasonable searches and seizures into play. The first occurrence is the stop—the detention of an individual by a law enforcement officer. The stop is an interference with the individual's freedom of movement. It is not, however, an arrest, which is a taking of a person into custody. A stop, unlike an arrest, is only temporary. As the Court explained in *Terry,* a stop constitutes a "seizure" of the person. As will be explained in the discussion of arrest, a police officer conducting a warrantless arrest must have probable cause to believe that a crime has been committed and that the person being arrested committed the crime. In *Terry,* the United States Supreme Court held that a police officer conducting a stop need not have the probable cause required to support an arrest. The officer must, however, have a "reasonable suspicion" that the person to be stopped has committed, is committing, or is about to commit a crime. The officer's suspicion must be supported by "specific and articulable facts which, taken together with rational inferences from those facts, reasonably warrant that intrusion."[23] An officer's intuition alone is not enough suspicion to support a *Terry* seizure. The California courts have held similarly.[24]

In *United States v. Mendenhall,* 446 U.S. 544 (1980), it was stated that a seizure occurs whenever a reasonable person believes that he or she is not free to leave. There need not be an attempt to leave. A person may feel restrained by physical contact from a police officer, by tone of voice, by threatening language, or by the threatening presence of many officers. However, not all contacts between an officer and a citizen amount to a seizure. A police officer may speak to an individual for many reasons that do not involve any suspicion that the person has been, is, or is about to become engaged in criminal activity. For example, an officer might wish to speak to a person because the person is a witness to a crime, or because the person appears to need assistance. However, if a police officer's questioning becomes accusatory or its duration lengthy, Fourth Amendment principles become applicable.

The first element of a stop and frisk that brings constitutional principles into play is the stop. The second element is the frisk. As discussed, the stop is a seizure of the person akin to, but falling short of, an arrest. The frisk is a form of search, and involves a pat-down of the outer clothing of the detained individual. The purpose of a frisk is protection of the detaining officer and others from the person being detained. When conducting a frisk, the officer may search only for the presence of weapons on the detained person. He or she may not search for contraband or other evidence of criminal activity.

A stop does not always justify a frisk. The purpose behind permitting investigatory stops is crime detection and prevention. The purpose of a frisk, as stated, is protection of the officer and others from potential harm by the person detained. Searches normally must be supported by probable cause to believe that an item subject to seizure is in the place to be searched. A frisk is less intrusive than a full search and does not require probable cause. To conduct a frisk, though, an officer must have a reasonable belief that the detained person is armed and dangerous. The officer must be able to point to articulable facts to support her belief, and may draw upon her experience in forming the belief that the person is armed and dangerous. Mere intuition—that is, suspicion not supported by facts—is not sufficient. If, for example, an officer stops an individual and notices an unusual bulge under the person's coat that might be a handgun, the officer may frisk the individual, (i.e., conduct a pat-down of the person's outer clothing).

Initially, a frisk is limited to a pat-down of the outer clothing of the detained individual. An officer conducting a frisk may not initially reach into the individual's pockets or interior clothing. If, during the pat-down, the officer feels an item that might be a weapon, he or she may reach into the clothing of the person to seize the item. Any item seized, whether a weapon, contraband, or other item associated with a crime, may be used as evidence. If, during the pat-down, the officer feels evidence of another crime, such as contraband, he or she may reach into the person's clothing to seize the evidence, under the plain feel doctrine discussed in the next section.

If a lawful stop of a vehicle is made, the driver may be ordered out of the vehicle. In *People v. Maxwell* (1988) 206 Cal.App.3d 1004, the court held that a passenger may be ordered out of the vehicle as well. If the officer has a reasonable belief, supported by specific and articulable facts, that the driver or passenger is armed and dangerous, he or she may conduct a pat-down of such person or persons. Under such circumstances, the officer may also search those areas of the passenger compartment in which a weapon may be hidden.[25]

Plain Feel

You have learned both the plain view doctrine and the *Terry* exception to the warrant and probable cause requirements of the Fourth Amendment. The **plain feel doctrine** is the product of their combination. That is, what happens when an officer who is conducting a Terry pat-down discovers, through the sense of touch, not a weapon, but contraband? May this information be used to establish probable cause allowing a more intrusive search? This question was answered in the *Dickerson* case.

If an officer discovers contraband through the sense of touch during a *Terry* frisk, probable cause exists to search further. If contraband is recovered, it is admissible at trial. The rules set out in *Terry* apply. First, stops must be supported by reasonable suspicion. Second, pat-downs may be conducted only when an officer possesses a reasonable suspicion based on specific and articulable facts that the suspect may be armed and dangerous. Third, the pat-down must be limited. Exploration of the clothing beyond what is necessary to determine dangerousness is not permitted, unless probable cause to believe that there is contraband is created through the officer's sense of touch.

Note the United States Supreme Court's requirement in *Dickerson* that the identity of the object felt must be "immediately apparent" to the officer conducting the pat-down. The seizure of the crack cocaine in *Dickerson* was held unconstitutional because its identity was not immediately apparent to the officer. The officer was able to identify the object only after "squeezing, sliding and otherwise manipulating the contents of the defendant's pocket." These actions on

---

MINNESOTA v. DICKERSON
113 S. Ct. 2130 (1993)

On the evening of November 9, 1989, two Minneapolis police officers were patrolling an area on the city's north side in a marked squad car. At about 8:15 P.M., one of the officers observed respondent leaving a 12-unit apartment building on Morgan Avenue North. The officer, having previously responded to complaints of drug sales in the building's hallways and having executed several search warrants on the premises, considered the building to be a notorious "crack house." According to testimony credited by the trial court, respondent began walking toward the police but, upon spotting the squad car and making eye contact with one of the officers, abruptly halted and began walking in the opposite direction. His suspicion aroused, this officer watched as respondent turned and entered an alley on the other side of the apartment building. Based upon respondent's seemingly evasive actions and the fact that he had just left a building known for cocaine traffic, the officers decided to stop respondent and investigate further.

The officers pulled their squad car into the alley and ordered respondent to stop and submit to a patdown search. The search revealed no weapons, but the officer conducting the search did take an interest in a small lump in respondent's nylon jacket. The officer later testified: "As I pat-searched

the front of his body, I felt a lump, a small lump, in the front pocket. I examined it with my fingers and it slid and it felt to be a lump of crack cocaine in cellophane." The officer then reached into respondent's pocket and retrieved a small plastic bag containing one fifth of one gram of crack cocaine. Respondent was arrested and charged in Hennepin County District Court with possession of a controlled substance.

Before trial, respondent moved to suppress the cocaine. The trial court first concluded that the officers were justified under *Terry v. Ohio* ... in stopping respondent ... . The court further found that the officers were justified in frisking respondent to ensure that he was not carrying a weapon. Finally, analogizing to the "plain-view" doctrine ... the trial court ruled that the officers' seizure of the cocaine did not violate the Fourth Amendment ... . [The Minnesota Court of Appeals and Supreme Court reversed, rejecting the trial court's "plain feel" theory. In addition, the Supreme Court held that the search itself went beyond the frisk authorized by *Terry*.]

Most state and federal courts have recognized a so-called "plain feel" or "plain touch" corollary to the plain-view doctrine. ... Some state courts, however, like the Minnesota court in this case, have rejected such a corollary. ...

We have already held that police officers, at least under certain circumstances, may seize contraband detected during the lawful execution of a *Terry* search. In *Michigan v. Long,* for example, police approached a man who had driven his car into a ditch and who appeared to be under the influence of some intoxicant. As the man moved to reenter the car from the roadside, police spotted a knife on the floorboard. The officers stopped the man, subjected him to a patdown search, and then inspected the interior of the vehicle for other weapons. During the search of the passenger compartment, the police discovered an open pouch containing marijuana and seized it. This Court upheld the validity of the search and seizure under *Terry.* The Court held first that, in the context of a roadside encounter, where police have reasonable suspicion based on specific and articulable facts to believe that a driver may be armed and dangerous, they may conduct a protective search for weapons not only of the driver's person but also of the passenger compartment of the automobile. ... "If, while conducting a legitimate *Terry* search of the interior of the automobile, the officer should, as here, discover contraband other than weapons, he clearly cannot be required to ignore the contraband, and the Fourth Amendment does not require its suppression in such circumstances." ...

We think this doctrine has an obvious application by analogy to cases in which an officer discovers contraband through sense of touch during an otherwise lawful search. The rationale of the plain view doctrine is that if contraband is left in open view and is observed by a police officer from a lawful vantage point, there has been no invasion of a legitimate expectation of privacy and thus no "search" within the meaning of the Fourth Amendment—or at least no search independent of the initial intrusion that gave the officers their vantage point. ... The warrantless seizure of contraband that presents itself in this manner is deemed justified by the realization that resort to a neutral magistrate under such circumstances would often be impracticable and would do little to promote the objectives of the Fourth Amendment. ... The same can be said of tactile discoveries of contraband. If a police officer lawfully pats down a suspect's outer clothing and feels an object whose contour or mass makes its identity immediately apparent, there has been no invasion of the suspect's privacy beyond that already authorized by the officer's search for weapons; if the object is contraband, its warrantless seizure would be justified by the same practical considerations that inhere in the plain view context. ...

The Minnesota Supreme Court rejected an analogy to the plain-view doctrine on two grounds: first, its belief that "the sense of touch is inherently less immediate and less reliable than the sense of sight," and second, that "the sense of touch is far more intrusive into the personal privacy that is at the core of the Fourth Amendment." We have a somewhat different view. First, *Terry* itself demonstrates that the sense of touch is capable of revealing the nature of an object with sufficient reliability to support a seizure. The very premise of *Terry,* after all, is that officers will be able to detect the presence of weapons through the sense of touch ... . The court's second concern—that touch is more intrusive into privacy than is sight—is inapposite in light of the fact that the intrusion the court fears has already been authorized by the lawful search for weapons. ...

It remains to apply these principles to the facts of this case. ... Thus, the dispositive question before this Court is whether the officer who conducted the search was acting within the lawful bounds marked by *Terry* at the time he gained probable cause to believe the lump in respondent's jacket was contraband. ...

Under the State Supreme Court's interpretation of the record before it, it is clear that the court was correct in holding that the police officer in this case overstepped the bounds of the "strictly circumscribed" search for weapons allowed under *Terry.* [In *Terry*], as here, "an officer who is executing a valid search for one item seizes a different item," [and] this Court rightly "has been sensitive to the danger ... that officers will enlarge a specific authorization, furnished by a warrant or an exigency, into the equivalent of a general warrant to rummage and seize at will." ...

Although the officer was lawfully in a position to feel the lump in respondent's jacket, because *Terry* entitled him to place his hands upon respondent's jacket, the court below determined that the incriminating character of the object was not immediately apparent to him. Rather, the officer determined that the item was contraband only after conducting a further search, one not authorized by *Terry* or by another exception to the warrant requirement. Because this further search of respondent's pocket was constitutionally invalid, the seizure of the cocaine that followed is likewise unconstitutional.

For these reasons, the judgment of the Minnesota Supreme Court is affirmed.

the part of the officer exceeded the limits of the pat-down search authorized under *Terry*. In one California case, an officer conducting a stop and frisk felt an unusual lump in the defendant's clothing and, without further manipulation of the lump, formed a reasonable suspicion that the item was contraband. Seizure of the item was upheld by the California Court of Appeal.

Search Incident to Arrest

Two search issues arise during and immediately following an arrest. First, may officers search the arrestee's person without first obtaining a warrant? Second, may officers search the arrestee's home, apartment, or other structure where the defendant is arrested?

The issue of search of the defendant's person was addressed in *United States v. Robinson,* 414 U.S. 260 (1973). In *Robinson* the United States Supreme Court held that, after a lawful arrest, the defendant's person may be fully searched without first obtaining a warrant. The rationale behind the holding was that an arrested suspect might be in possession of a weapon that could be used to harm the arresting officers or effect an escape, as well as evidence that the suspect could destroy. The Court held that to require officers to obtain a warrant would needlessly endanger their lives and would increase the risk of escape and destruction of evidence. A **search incident to arrest** is more intrusive than the pat-down search permitted in a stop-and-frisk situation, and includes a full search of the defendant's clothing. If a closed container, such as a tobacco pouch or a pill box, is found on the person of the arrestee, the arresting officer may open it and examine the contents.[26] There is no probable cause requirement for a search incident to arrest.

The second issue concerns search of the area where the defendant is arrested. The premier case in this area is *Chimel v. California*. *Chimel* significantly changed the law; before *Chimel* was decided, officers had the authority to search a much greater area as incident to arrest. The "within the defendant's immediate control" test continues to be the governing law. As with any other lawful search and seizure, any evidence obtained may be used to prosecute the defendant.

Finally, "when a policeman has made a lawful custodial arrest of the occupant of an automobile, he may, as a contemporaneous incident of that arrest, search the passenger compartment of that automobile," including the contents of any containers found in that area.[27]

Preservation of Evidence

In some instances evidence may be destroyed before a warrant can be obtained. In such cases an officer may make a warrantless search and seizure.

Although the typical case involves the destruction of evidence, the preservation-of-evidence theory also has been applied to evanescent evidence (evidence that may vanish on its own). For example, in one case a defendant, who was arrested for drunk driving, was subjected to a warrantless blood alcohol test. The Court concluded that the warrantless test was reasonable under the Fourth Amendment.

The officer in the present case, however, might reasonably have believed that he was confronted with an emergency, in which the delay necessary to

CHIMEL v. CALIFORNIA
395 U.S. 752 (1969)

This case raises basic questions concerning the permissible scope under the Fourth Amendment of a search incident to a lawful arrest.

The relevant facts are essentially undisputed. Late in the afternoon of September 13, 1965, three police officers arrived at the Santa Ana, California, home of the petitioner with a warrant authorizing his arrest for the burglary of a coin shop. The officers knocked on the door, identified themselves to the petitioner's wife, and asked if they might come inside. She ushered them into the house, where they waited 10 to 15 minutes until the petitioner returned home from work. When the petitioner entered the house, one of the officers handed him the arrest warrant and asked for permission to "look around." The petitioner objected, but was advised that "on the basis of the lawful arrest," the officers would nonetheless conduct the search. No search warrant had been issued.

Accompanied by the petitioner's wife, the officers then looked through the entire three-bedroom house, including the attic, the garage, and a small workshop. In some rooms the search was relatively cursory. In the master bedroom and sewing room, however, the officers directed the petitioner's wife to open drawers and "to physically remove contents of the drawers from side to side so that [they] might view items that would have come from [the] burglary." After completing the search, they seized numerous items—primarily coins, but also several medals, tokens, and a few other objects. The entire search took between 45 minutes and an hour. ...

When an arrest is made, it is reasonable for the arresting officer to search the person arrested in order to remove any weapons that the latter might seek to use in order to resist arrest or effect his escape. Otherwise, the officer's safety might well be endangered, and the arrest itself frustrated. In addition, it is entirely reasonable for the arresting officer to search for and seize any evidence on the arrestee's person in order to prevent its concealment or destruction. And the area into which an arrestee might reach in order to grab a weapon or evidentiary items must, of course, be governed by a like rule. A gun on a table or in a drawer in front of one who is arrested can be as dangerous to the arresting officer as one concealed in the clothing of the person arrested. There is ample justification, therefore, for a search of the arrestee's person and the area "within his immediate control"—construing that phrase to mean the area from within which he might gain possession of a weapon or destructible evidence.

There is no comparable justification, however, for routinely searching any room other than that in which an arrest occurs—or, for that matter, for searching through all the desk drawers or other closed or concealed areas in the room itself. Such searches, in the absence of well-recognized exceptions, may be made only under the authority of a search warrant. ...

Application of sound Fourth Amendment principles to the facts of this case produces a clear result. ... The scope of the search was ... "unreasonable" under the Fourth and Fourteenth Amendments, and the petitioner's conviction cannot stand.

Reversed.

obtain a warrant, under the circumstances, threatened "the destruction of evidence."... We are told that the percentage of alcohol in the blood begins to diminish shortly after drinking stops, as the body functions to eliminate it from the system. Particularly in a case such as this, where time had to be taken to bring the accused to the hospital and to investigate the scene of the accident, there was no time to seek out a magistrate and secure a warrant. Given these special facts, we conclude that the attempt to secure evidence of blood-alcohol content in this case was an appropriate incident to petitioner's arrest.[28]

Any evidence that may be destroyed, intentionally or not, before a warrant can be obtained, can be the foundation of a warrantless search and seizure under the preservation-of-evidence exception to the Fourth Amendment's warrant requirement. For example, in *Cupp v. Murphy,* 412 U.S. 291 (1973), police questioning the husband of a homicide victim took scrapings from under his fingernails without a warrant and over the husband's objections. The scrapings revealed incriminating evidence. The United States Supreme Court upheld the police conduct on the grounds that probable cause existed for the seizure and that the evidence could easily have been destroyed by the husband during the time it would have taken to obtain a search warrant.

In a California case, *People v. Bullock* (1990) 226 Cal.App.3d 380, the defendant was being booked on narcotics charges. During the booking process, the defendant's pager "beeped" twenty times. Each time, a police officer pushed a button on the pager and recorded the telephone number that appeared. When an officer returned the calls, many of the callers requested that the defendant deliver rock cocaine. The California Court of Appeal held that this warrantless seizure of evidence was justified because, during the time it would have taken to obtain a search warrant, the evidence would have been lost. In *People v. Ortiz* (1995) 32 Cal.App.4th 286, a police officer observed the defendant in possession of what appeared to be contraband through the open door of a hotel room. The officer entered without a warrant and seized the items, which turned out to be contraband. The court of appeal held that the warrantless entry and seizure were justified because the evidence could easily have been destroyed by the defendant during the time it would have taken to obtain a warrant.

Emergency Searches and Hot Pursuit

Law enforcement personnel may conduct warrantless searches in emergency situations and other exigent circumstances. The purpose of the search in such situations is to respond to the emergency or exigent circumstance. A warrantless search is permitted because the situation does not allow the time required to obtain a warrant.

One type of permissible warrantless search in an emergency situation involves the identification of an injured person. In *People v. Gonzales* (1960) 182 Cal.App.2d 276, for example, a police officer found the defendant unconscious with a knife wound. The defendant was taken to the hospital and the officer searched the defendant's clothing for identification. During the search, the officer discovered marijuana. The defendant appealed after being convicted of possession of marijuana, claiming that the search violated his right to be free from unreasonable searches and seizures. The court of appeal upheld the conviction, reasoning that a police officer has a duty to identify the victim of a crime and that a search of an unconscious victim's clothing for such purpose is lawful. If during the lawful search, evidence of a crime is found, it is admissible.

Another exigent-circumstances exception to the warrant requirement is the **hot pursuit** of a fleeing felon or other dangerous criminal. If the person runs into a house or other structure, the police are not required to stop at the door. They may enter without a warrant to search for and arrest the person. If evidence of criminal activity comes into the officers' plain view while they are lawfully inside the structure, the evidence may be seized. Of course, a hot-pursuit entry does not authorize a general exploratory search of the premises without a warrant. To justify a warrantless entry under the hot pursuit exception, the pursuit of the suspect must be substantially continuous, and the officers must not have the opportunity to obtain a warrant.[29]

Finally, an exception to the warrant requirement exists in situations in which an immediate police response is necessary to prevent loss of life or property. A police officer may enter a house or other building without a warrant when someone inside is screaming for help. He or she may enter a burning structure to search for victims. An officer may also enter to prevent a crime in progress, such as an assault or rape, or to search for a kidnap victim upon reliable information that the victim is inside. Other emergency situations justifying warrantless entry into buildings are too numerous to mention. In all of these cases, evidence in plain view may be seized by the officers.

Open Fields

The open fields doctrine is not, technically, an exception to the search warrant requirement. That is because, to be an exception to the Fourth Amendment warrant requirement, the Fourth Amendment must apply to the conduct of the officers. The Supreme Court has held that the **open fields** around one's home are not protected by the Fourth Amendment, so officers are free to intrude upon such areas without first obtaining a warrant. In addition, officers will not be liable for trespass if they make such an intrusion while performing a lawful duty.[30]

The reason that open fields are not protected is because of the language of the Fourth Amendment itself: "The right of the people to be secure in their persons, houses, papers, and effects ... ." The Supreme Court has found that this extends the Fourth Amendment's protection only to a person's home and the curtilage of that home.

Curtilage is the area directly around one's home. It is treated as part of the home, as the Court has recognized that a person's privacy interest does not end at the front door of the home. The proximity of the area in question to the home, the fact that it is enclosed by fencing, that it is commonly used by the residents, and that the residents have taken measures to assure privacy in the area all increase the probability that the area will be determined to be curtilage. The issue is whether the residents have a reasonable expectation of privacy in the area.

There have been numerous decisions in the California courts involving the reasonable expectation of privacy in areas adjacent to the home. The courts have held, for example, that a person has a reasonable expectation of privacy in an enclosed backyard patio and in a fenced backyard, assuming the fence is made of material that prevents observation into the yard. Police observation of these areas without a warrant, such as by peeping through a knothole in a fence, is unlawful unless an exception to the warrant requirement applies. With respect to the fenced backyard, however, recall that while one may have a reasonable expectation of privacy against observation from the ground, one may *not* have a reasonable expectation of privacy against observation from an aircraft flying at a normal altitude. Court decisions have also held that there is no reasonable expectation of privacy in a yard surrounded by a chain-link fence or in a condominium complex garage that is open to the public.[31]

The issue of reasonable expectation of privacy in areas adjacent to the home has been debated in cases involving trash containers. In *People v. Edwards* (1969) 71 Cal.2d 1096, police entered the defendant's backyard without a warrant and proceeded to examine the contents of trash containers two or three feet from the back porch door. They found a bag of marijuana in one of the containers. The California Supreme Court held the search and seizure without a warrant unlawful because a person has a reasonable expectation of privacy in a trash container in his or her yard. The existence or nonexistence of a reasonable expectation of privacy in trash that has been left at the curb for pickup, or that has already been picked up, has been the subject of two California cases that went to the United States Supreme Court. In the second of these cases, *California v. Greenwood,* 486 U.S. 35 (1988), the California Supreme Court held that the warrantless search and seizure of garbage bags left at the curb violated the Fourth Amendment. The United States Supreme Court reversed the California Supreme Court, holding that a person does not have a reasonable expectation of privacy in trash bags placed at the curb outside his or her home. The Court pointed out that it is common knowledge that trash bags placed at a curb are susceptible to intrusion by animals, children, and others. Also, the bags are placed at the curb to be collected by the refuse company, which itself might sift through the trash. Expecting that the contents of trash bags placed at the curb for disposal will remain private is not "reasonable," according to the United States Supreme Court.

Border Searches

Unlike ordinary searches, searches at the borders of the United States do not require probable cause. In fact, no suspicion is required whatsoever. This rule applies to searches of both luggage and persons.[32] However, these searches must comply with the reasonableness requirement of the Fourth Amendment.[33]

For a strip search to be conducted, a customs official must have a "real suspicion" that illegality is afoot. As for more invasive searches, such as cavity searches, more suspicion is required. A customs official must be aware of a "clear indication" of illegality before such searches are conducted. Further, these searches must be conducted in a private and medically safe environment. A *clear indication* is less than probable cause, but more than either the *Terry* reasonable suspicion or the border strip-search "real suspicion" standards.

The **border search** exception to the Fourth Amendment actually extends beyond the border. For example, first arrival ports in the United States of international flights are treated as borders for purposes of the Fourth Amendment. Roadblock-style checkpoints miles from a border intended to discover illegal aliens have been approved,[34] but the authority to search is more limited than at the border. Officers may not search the occupants of the vehicles stopped at these checkpoints without probable cause.[35] Random stops of vehicles away from the border must be supported by reasonable suspicion, because they are treated as *Terry* detentions.

Motor Vehicles and Roadblocks

Privacy in automobiles is protected by the Fourth Amendment. However, the Supreme Court has not extended full Fourth Amendment protection to the occupants of automobiles. The Court's rationale for decreased protection is two-fold. First, because of the mobile nature of automobiles, evidence can disappear quickly. Second, automobiles are used on the public roads where they and their occupants are visible to the public; thus, an occupant of an automobile has a lesser expectation of privacy than does the occupant of a home.

A police officer may stop a motorist if he or she has probable cause to believe that the motorist is committing an offense. The offense may range from a traffic violation to a serious felony. Under the stop-and-frisk authority, if the officer has a reasonable suspicion, supported by articulable facts, that the motorist is armed and dangerous, the officer may require the motorist (or a passenger) to get out of the vehicle, and may conduct a pat-down of the person's outer clothing. Under such circumstances, the officer may also search those portions of the interior of the vehicle in which a weapon could be located. This authority is granted to the officer for his or her protection, and does not authorize the officer to open closed containers in the vehicle or look into the vehicle's trunk. The scope of a search of a vehicle under the stop-and-frisk authority is limited.

If the officer stopping the motorist arrests the motorist, the officer may conduct a search incident to arrest. As discussed earlier in this chapter, a *search incident to arrest* is a full search of the person, as well as a search of any area into which the person might reach to seize a weapon or destroy evidence. If the arrestee is an occupant of a motor vehicle, the arresting officer may search the passenger compartment of the automobile, including a closed glove compartment and closed containers. The reason a search incident to arrest may be more intrusive than a stop-and-frisk search is because a search incident to arrest is a search for evidence as well as a search for weapons, whereas a stop-and-frisk search is only a search for weapons. A search incident to arrest does not, however, authorize the arresting officer to search areas of the vehicle not readily accessible to the arrestee, such as a closed trunk.

There are situations in which an officer may have probable cause to believe that an item subject to seizure (i.e., an item in one of the categories in Penal Code § 1524(a)) is located in a motor vehicle. This situation is conceptually distinct from the search incident to arrest and stop-and-frisk situations in which the focus of police activity is a person in the vehicle. In 1982, the United States Supreme Court set forth the principles governing warrantless searches of motor vehicles.[36] According to the holding of the Court, if an officer has probable cause to believe that a seizable item is located in a motor vehicle, the officer may conduct a warrantless search of all parts of the vehicle in which the item could be located. The officer may also open any container in the vehicle that could contain the evidence.

For example, if an officer has probable cause to believe that a shotgun used in a crime will be found in a car, he or she may search the parts of the car in which a shotgun could be placed. A search of other parts of the car, such as the glove compartment, would not be authorized, and any evidence of a crime found in the glove compartment would be inadmissible as the product of an illegal search. If the **motor vehicle search** were for a stolen piece of jewelry, a search of the glove compartment would be proper. The same holds true for containers in the vehicle. If the container is large enough to hold the item being sought, it may be opened and searched. Otherwise, the container may not be searched.

May the occupants of a vehicle be searched incident to a proper search of the vehicle? The answer is no[37]—but if an officer has probable cause to believe that one of the occupants has hidden the item sought on his or her person, a search of that occupant is permissible.

Fourth Amendment issues also arise in the context of roadblocks, which are used by law enforcement officers in two situations. First, they assist in the apprehension of particular suspects being sought by police. Second, serving the regulatory function of protecting the public from unsafe drivers, officers may stop vehicles to determine if the car satisfies the state's safety requirements, whether the driver is properly licensed, and whether the vehicle is properly registered. In regard to the first purpose, reasonable suspicion is required before a stop can be made. As to the latter, temporary regulatory detentions are permitted so long as they are both objectively random and reasonable. That is, the police must use an objective system in deciding what automobiles will be stopped. Every car, or every tenth car, or some similar method is permissible.

The United States Supreme Court has also upheld roadblocks intended to discover drunk drivers. *Michigan State Police v. Sitz,* 496 U.S. 444 (1990), upheld a highway sobriety checkpoint program where 126 vehicles passed through the checkpoint, the average delay for each vehicle was 25 seconds, and 2 intoxicated drivers were arrested. The Court found that the stops were seizures under the Fourth Amendment, but that they were reasonable. In support of this conclusion, the Court stressed that the stops were of limited duration; that drunk drivers are a serious problem in the nation, and accordingly Michigan had a compelling interest in performing the sobriety checks; that all stops were governed by objective guidelines; that the guidelines required all vehicles to be stopped, thereby preventing arbitrary decisions by individual officers; that all officers were fully uniformed, thereby lessening motorists' concerns; and finally, that data support the conclusion that sobriety checkpoints are effective in apprehending drunk drivers. The California Supreme Court reached a similar conclusion in *Ingersoll v. Palmer* (1987) 43 Cal.3d 1321.

Although systematic roadblocks are proper, discretionary spot checks are not. In the *Prouse* case, the Supreme Court held that arbitrary stops of automobiles by law enforcement officers violate the Fourth Amendment.

Inventory Searches

Police officers may impound vehicles whenever the driver or owner is arrested. *Impoundment* means towing the vehicle to a garage or parking lot for storage.

Although the decision to impound a vehicle is generally left to the discretion of the police officer, an officer may not refuse a less intrusive manner of caring for the vehicle. For example, if a husband and wife are riding together, and the husband is arrested for drunk driving, the wife is to be permitted to drive the vehicle home, provided she is capable.

Once a vehicle has been impounded, an **inventory search** may be conducted. The purpose of an inventory search is to protect the owner of the vehicle from vandalism, protect the safety of the officers and others, and to protect the police department from claims of theft.

DELAWARE v. PROUSE
440 U.S. 648 (1979)

At 7:20 P.M. on November 30, 1976, a New Castle County ... patrolman in a police cruiser stopped the automobile occupied by respondent. The patrolman smelled marihuana smoke as he was walking toward the stopped vehicle, and he seized marihuana in plain view on the car floor. Respondent was subsequently indicted for illegal possession of a controlled substance. At a hearing on respondent's motion to suppress the marihuana seized as a result of the stop, the patrolman testified that prior to stopping the vehicle he had observed neither traffic or equipment violations nor any suspicious activity, and that he made the stop only in order to check the driver's license and registration. The patrolman was not acting pursuant to any standards, guidelines, or procedures pertaining to document spot checks, promulgated by either his department or the State Attorney General. Characterizing the stop as "routine," the patrolman explained, "I saw the car in the area and wasn't answering any complaints, so I decided to pull them off." The trial court granted the motion to suppress, finding the stop and detention to have been wholly capricious and therefore violative of the Fourth Amendment. ...

The Delaware Supreme Court affirmed. ...

But the State of Delaware urges ... these stops are reasonable under the Fourth Amendment because the State's interest in the practice as a means of promoting public safety upon its roads more than outweighs the intrusion entailed. Although the record discloses no statistics concerning the extent of the problem of highway safety, in Delaware or in the Nation as a whole, we are aware of danger to life and property posed by vehicular traffic and the difficulties that even a cautious and experienced driver may encounter. We agree that the States have a vital interest in ensuring that only those qualified to do so are permitted to operate motor vehicles, that these vehicles are fit for safe operation, and hence that licensing, registration, and vehicle inspection requirements are being observed. ...

The question remains, however, whether in the service of these important ends the discretionary spot check is a sufficiently productive mechanism to justify the intrusion upon Fourth Amendment interests which stops entail. On the record before us, that question must be answered in the negative.

Given the alternative mechanisms available, both those in use and those that might be adopted, we are unconvinced that the incremental contribution to highway safety of the random spot check justifies the practice under the Fourth Amendment.

The foremost method of enforcing traffic and vehicle safety regulations, it must be recalled, is acting upon observed violations. Vehicle stops for traffic violations occur countless times each day; and on these occasions, licenses and registration papers are subject to inspection and drivers without them will be ascertained. Furthermore, drivers without licenses are presumably the less safe drivers whose propensities may well exhibit themselves. ...

Much the same can be said about the safety aspects of automobiles as distinguished from drivers. Many violations of minimum vehicle-safety requirements are observable, and something can be done about them by the observing officer, directly and immediately. Furthermore, in Delaware, as elsewhere, vehicles must carry and display current license plates, which themselves evidence that the vehicle is properly registered; and, under Delaware law, to qualify for annual registration a vehicle must pass the annual safety inspection and be properly insured. ...

The marginal contribution to roadway safety possibly resulting from a system of spot checks cannot justify subjecting every occupant of every vehicle on the roads to a seizure—limited in magnitude compared to other intrusions but nonetheless constitutionally cognizable—at the unbridled discretion of law enforcement officials. To insist neither upon an appropriate factual basis for suspicion directed at a particular automobile nor upon some other substantial and objective standard or rule to govern the exercise of discretion "would invite intrusions upon constitutionally guaranteed rights based on nothing more substantial than inarticulable hunches ... . This kind of standardless and unconstrained discretion is the evil the Court has discerned when in previous cases it has insisted that the discretion of the official in the field be circumscribed, at least to some extent. ...

Accordingly, we hold that except in those situations in which there is at least articulable and reasonable suspicion that a motorist is unlicensed or that an automobile is not registered, or that either the vehicle or an occupant is otherwise subject to seizure for violation of law, stopping an automobile and detaining the driver in order to check his driver's license and the registration of the automobile are unreasonable under the Fourth Amendment. This holding does not preclude the State of Delaware or other States from developing methods for spot checks that involve less intrusions or that do not involve unconstrained exercise of discretion.

Questioning of all oncoming traffic at roadblock-type stops is one possible alternative. We hold only that persons in automobiles on public roadways may not for that reason alone have their travel and privacy interfered with at the unbridled discretion of police officers. The judgment below is affirmed.

The United States Supreme Court has held that, because inventory searches are not conducted for the purpose of discovering evidence, there is no requirement of probable cause.[38] Prior to Proposition 8's addition of the Truth-in-Evidence provision to the California Constitution, California law prohibited inventory searches unless they were supported by probable cause. Since the adoption of Proposition 8, inventory searches without probable cause are lawful in California because they are lawful under the United States Constitution. An exception to the rule, under both federal and California law, is so-called *pretextual impoundment*. A pretextual impoundment is an impoundment of a vehicle that is not justified and is made for the purpose of affording law enforcement authorities the opportunity to conduct an inventory search of the vehicle. A search in this situation is unlawful, and any evidence of a crime discovered during the search must be suppressed.[39]

Inventory searches are limited in scope. Although it is reasonable to search unlocked glove compartments and trunks, it is unreasonable under the Fourth Amendment if they are locked. A search of a vehicle's seats, floor area, and dashboard are routine. The Supreme Court has also stated that closed items found in impounded vehicles are subject to inventory searches.[40]

To avoid arbitrary inventory searches, police departments are expected, if not required, to establish an inventory search policy and procedure. All items discovered during an inventory search are to be recorded.

Prisoners

The Fourth Amendment is not fully applicable in prisons, for three reasons. First, security concerns outweigh privacy concerns. Second, loss of privacy is considered by our society to be an attribute of confinement and punishment. Third, inmates generally do not have reasonable expectations of privacy.

Hence, the Fourth Amendment is not implicated in the search of an inmate's cell, as there is no reasonable expectation of privacy in that area. The Supreme Court stated:

A prison "shares none of the attributes of privacy of a home, an automobile, an office, or a hotel room." ... We strike the balance in favor of institutional security, which we have noted is "central to all other correctional goals." ... A right of privacy in traditional Fourth Amendment terms is fundamentally incompatible with the close and continual surveillance of inmates and their cells required to ensure institutional security and internal order. We are satisfied that society would insist that the prisoner's expectation of privacy always yield to what must be considered the paramount interest in institutional security. We believe that it is accepted by our society that "[l]oss of freedom of choice and privacy are inherent incidents of confinement."[41]

Although the Fourth Amendment does not apply to searches of inmates' cells, it does apply to searches of their persons. However, the probable cause and warrant requirements are dispensed with in the prison context. Rather, they are tested by the Fourth Amendment's reasonableness provision. Prisoners may be searched without any particular suspicion if the search is part of a routine system. Analogous to roadblocks, if the custodians search every prisoner, or every other prisoner, or use some other system, no suspicion is required. Prisoners may also be searched without suspicion if they have recently come into contact with visitors. In *Bell v. Wolfish,* 441 U.S. 520 (1979), the Supreme Court held that strip searches of prisoners, conducted after they have contact with visitors or upon their return to the institution from outside, are permissible even without individualized suspicion. Otherwise, individual searches of inmates are allowed only when an officer has a reasonable suspicion that the inmate possesses contraband.

Although searches of inmates' cells are not included within the grasp of the Fourth Amendment, repeated searches intended to harass an inmate may be violative of the Eighth Amendment's prohibition of cruel and unusual punishment, as may searches of an inmate's person.

§ 14.3 Arrest

One of the most extreme interferences with a person's liberty is to be arrested. An **arrest** is a seizure of the person and, as such, is governed by the Fourth Amendment to the United States Constitution and article I, § 13, of the California Constitution.

Defining Arrest

As you have already learned, seizures by the police take two primary forms. First, at the lower end of the spectrum is the *Terry v. Ohio* seizure. Such seizures occur whenever a person reasonably believes that he or she is not free to leave. In addition, the seizure must be as brief as possible and be of limited intrusion to the person detained.

Any seizure that goes beyond the *Terry* standard is an arrest. A *Terry* investigatory detention may be transformed into an arrest if the person is detained for an unreasonable length of time or the police use intrusive investigatory tactics. Whether an officer intends to arrest is not dispositive, nor is an announcement to the citizen that he or she is or is not under arrest. The totality of the facts will determine whether the intrusion amounts to an arrest under the federal and California constitutions.

Penal Code § 834 defines an *arrest* as "taking a person into custody, in a case and in the manner authorized by law." Section 835 provides that "[a]n arrest is made by an actual restraint of the person, or by submission to the custody of an officer."

Police can only arrest for misdemeanor if they witness it.

Who May Arrest

An arrest may be made by a peace officer, by certain other public officers or employees, or by a private person. (*See* Penal Code §§ 834, 836.5, 837.) A peace officer may arrest a person with or without a warrant, depending on the circumstances of the case. An arrest by a private citizen will always be without a warrant, because a private citizen has no authority to obtain an arrest warrant.

As with search warrants, the general rule is that, unless an exception applies, an arrest by a law enforcement officer must be made pursuant to an arrest warrant. Arrests pursuant to warrants are covered after the following discussion of warrantless arrests.

A peace officer may arrest a person without a warrant under the following circumstances. (*See* Penal Code § 836(a).) First, a peace officer may arrest a person without a warrant when the person to be arrested has committed a felony. It is not necessary that the officer have observed the commission of the felony or that the felony have been committed in the officer's presence. Second, a peace officer may make a warrantless arrest when he or she has reasonable cause to believe that the person to be arrested has committed a felony, whether or not a felony has in fact been committed. Reasonable cause exists if a person of ordinary caution or prudence would be led to believe and consciously entertain a strong suspicion of guilt of the suspect.[42] Third, a peace officer may arrest a person without a warrant when the person commits any offense, including a misdemeanor, in the arresting officer's presence. Note that this third basis is the only one that permits warrantless arrests for misdemeanors. An offense is committed in the arresting officer's presence if it is committed within the officer's immediate physical presence or within the perception of the officer's senses, such as the senses of hearing and smell.

A private person may arrest another person under three circumstances. (*See* Penal Code § 837.) First, a private person may arrest another person when the person has committed or attempted to commit a public offense in the presence of the arresting person. A public offense may include a felony or a misdemeanor. Second, a private person may arrest a person who has committed a felony within or outside the presence of the arresting person. Third, a private person may arrest another person when a felony has in fact been committed and the arresting person has reasonable cause for believing that the person arrested committed it. These grounds for *citizen's arrest* are similar to those for a warrantless arrest by a peace officer, with one important distinction. A peace officer may arrest a person whom he or she reasonably believes has committed a felony, whether or not a felony has in fact been committed. In contrast, a private citizen may arrest a person whom he or she reasonably believes has committed a felony only if a felony has actually been committed. Thus, a peace officer can be mistaken regarding whether a felony has actually been committed, whereas a private citizen cannot.

Arrest Pursuant to Warrant

Arrests by peace officers frequently occur under the circumstances enumerated in Penal Code § 836(a) and are therefore accomplished without an arrest warrant. In circumstances other than those listed in § 836(a), a peace officer must obtain an **arrest warrant** before he or she may arrest a person. In addition, if the arrest is to occur within the suspect's home, an arrest warrant is required even if the grounds for a warrantless arrest are present.[43] If an arrest is to occur within the home of a person other than the suspect, a search warrant is required.[44] Warrants are not required to enter the home of the suspect or a third person if entry is consented to by a person authorized to consent or if exigent circumstances exist, such as entry in hot pursuit of a fleeing suspect or to prevent the destruction of evidence.

As with a search warrant, an arrest warrant is issued by a magistrate; in California, this is a municipal or superior court judge.[45] The written submission used to request an arrest warrant is called a *complaint*. A complaint is a document, made under oath and submitted to a magistrate, that accuses a person of a criminal offense. More will be said about the function of the complaint in Chapter 16. If the magistrate, after reviewing the complaint, is satisfied that the offense alleged in the complaint has been committed and that there is reasonable ground to believe that the person named in the complaint committed it, the magistrate must issue a warrant for the arrest of the person.[46] A *warrant* is a command issued by a court to a government official directing the official to take a specified action. An arrest warrant is a command that the official arrest a particular person. An arrest warrant is directed to any peace officer of the state.

Penal Code § 813 provides that, subject to certain limitations (*see* Penal Code § 813), a prosecutor may request a magistrate to issue a **summons** rather than an arrest warrant. A summons is a command directed to the defendant ordering him or her to appear before the magistrate, rather than a command to a peace officer to arrest the defendant. Summonses are used more frequently in misdemeanor cases than in felony cases. If a defendant has been properly served with a summons and fails to appear on the specified date, the court is to issue a bench warrant for the defendant's arrest. A **bench warrant** is a warrant of arrest issued by a judge on the judge's own initiative, that is, without the filing of a complaint by the prosecutor.

Arrest Procedures

A person making an arrest is required to inform the person to be arrested of the intention to arrest him or her, the cause of the arrest, and the authority to make it. These formal requirements need not be complied with if the person to be arrested is actually engaged in the commission of or an attempt to commit an offense, or if the person to be arrested is pursued immediately after commission of a crime or an escape. The person making the arrest must, on request of the person being arrested, specify the offense for which the person is being arrested. (*See* Penal Code § 841.)

An arrest pursuant to an arrest warrant is lawful even if the arresting officer does not have the warrant in his or her possession at the time of the arrest. If the arrested person requests, the warrant must be shown to him or her as soon as practicable. (*See* Penal Code § 842.)

An arrest for a felony may be made at any time of the day or night. An arrest for a misdemeanor or an infraction cannot be made between the hours of 10 P.M. and 6 A.M. except under certain circumstances, such as when the offense is committed in the arresting officer's presence or when an arrest warrant specifies that the arrest may be made at any time. (*See* Penal Code § 840.)

The law requires that a person submit peaceably to a lawful arrest. If the arrest is made by a peace officer, the arrestee must submit even if he or she believes that the arrest is unlawful or mistaken. There is no right to resist an unlawful arrest by a peace officer in California. Penal Code § 834a provides: "If a person has knowledge, or by the exercise of reasonable care should have knowledge, that he is being arrested by a peace officer, it is the duty of such person to refrain from using force or any weapon to resist such arrest." If a person resists an arrest by a peace officer, he or she is guilty of resisting or obstructing an officer in the discharge of his or her duties, an offense under Penal Code § 148. Currently, no statute criminalizes resistance to an unlawful citizen's arrest.

Rules governing the use of force by persons effecting an arrest are discussed in Chapter 10. You should review those rules now.

A peace officer or private citizen who is arresting a person inside private premises is generally required first to demand admittance and explain the purpose for which admittance is desired. If admittance is not granted, the arresting person may use force to gain entry. Penal Code § 844 provides:

> To make an arrest, a private person, if the offense is a felony, and in all cases a peace officer, may break open the door or window of the house in which the person to be arrested is, or in which they have reasonable grounds for believing the person to be, after having demanded admittance and explained the purpose for which admittance is desired.

The courts have created exceptions to the demand-and-explanation requirement explained. The courts have held that the announcement requirement need not be met in situations in which: (1) the arresting person's peril will be increased by the announcement, (2) the warning will allow the suspect to escape, destroy incriminating evidence, or otherwise frustrate the arrest, and (3) the knocking on the door and announcement elicit no response.[47]

Search Incident to Arrest and the Protective Sweep

As you learned earlier in this chapter, an officer may search an arrestee fully incident to arrest. In addition, the area within the arrestee's immediate control may also be searched. The scope of a search incident to arrest, however, is limited to areas where a weapon might be obtained or evidence destroyed by the person arrested. Clearly, a search of any room other than the one where a defendant is being held is not supported by the doctrine of search incident to arrest.

The search-incident-to-arrest doctrine does not consider the possibility that other potentially dangerous persons may be present, but out of sight, when an arrest is made. Must police take the risk that no other dangerous persons are on the premises when making a lawful arrest? This question was answered by the Supreme Court in *Maryland v. Buie.*

It is important to note that the **protective sweep** may not be automatically conducted by the police, unlike a search incident to arrest. An officer must have a reasonable belief, supported by specific and articulable facts, that a dangerous person may be hiding in the home, before a protective sweep may be conducted. There need not be a belief of dangerousness to conduct a search incident to arrest.

Also a protective sweep must be limited to searching those areas where a person might be hiding. How far this will be permitted to go by the courts remains to be seen.

MARYLAND v. BUIE
494 U.S. 325 (1990)

A "protective sweep" is a quick and limited search of a premises, incident to an arrest and conducted to protect the safey of police officers or others. It is narrowly confined to a cursory visual inspection of those places in which a person might be hiding. In this case we must decide what level of justification is required by the Fourth and Fourteenth Amendments before police officers, while effecting the arrest of a suspect in his home pursuant to an arrest warrant, may conduct a warrantless protective sweep of all or part of the premises. ...

On February 3, 1986, two men committed an armed robbery of a Godfather's Pizza restaurant in Prince George's County, Maryland. One of the robbers was wearing a red running suit. The same day, Prince George's County police obtained arrest warrants for respondent Jerome Edward Buie and his suspected accomplice in the robbery, Lloyd Allen. Buie's house was placed under police surveillance.

On February 5, the police executed the arrest warrant for Buie. They first had a police department secretary telephone Buie's house to verify that he was home. The secretary spoke to a female first, then to Buie himself. Six or seven officers proceeded to Buie's house. Once inside, the officers fanned out through the first and second floors. Corporal James Rozar announced that he would "freeze" the basement so that no one could come up and surprise the officers. With his service revolver drawn, Rozar twice shouted into the basement, ordering anyone down there to come out. When a voice asked who was calling, Rozar announced three times: "this is the police, show me your hands." Eventually, a pair of hands appeared around the bottom of the stairwell and Buie emerged from the basement. He was arrested, searched, and handcuffed by Rozar. Thereafter, Detective Joseph Frolich entered the basement "in case there was someone else" down there. ... He noticed a red running suit lying in plain view on a stack of clothing and seized it.

The trial court denied Buie's motion to suppress the running suit, stating in part: "The man comes

out from a basement, the police don't know how many other people are down there."...

It goes without saying that the Fourth Amendment bars only unreasonable searches and seizures. ... Our cases show that in determining reasonableness, we have balanced the intrusion on the individual's Fourth Amendment interests against its promotion of legitimate governmental interests. ... Under this test, a search of the house or office is generally not reasonable without a warrant issued on probable cause. There are other contexts, however, where the public interest is such that neither a warrant nor probable cause is required. ...

The *Terry* case is most instructive for present purposes. There we held that an on-the-street "frisk" for weapons must be tested by the Fourth Amendment's general proscription against unreasonable searches because such a frisk involves "an entire rubric of police conduct—necessarily swift action predicated upon the on-the-spot observations of the officer on the beat—which historically has not been, and as a practical matter could not be, subjected to the warrant procedure." ...

The ingredients to apply the balance struck in *Terry* and *Long* are present in this case. Possessing an arrest warrant and probable cause to believe Buie was in his home, the officers were entitled to enter and to search anywhere in the house in which Buie might be found. Once he was found, however, the search for him was over, and there was no longer that particular justification for entering any rooms that had not yet been searched.

That Buie had an expectation of privacy in those remaining areas of his house, however, does not mean such rooms were immune from entry. In *Terry* and *Long* we were concerned with the immediate interest of the police officers in taking steps to assure themselves that the persons with whom they were dealing were not armed with or able to gain immediate control of a weapon that could unexpectedly and fatally be used against them. In the instant case, there is an analogous interest of the officers in taking steps to assure themselves that the house in which the suspect is being or has just been arrested is not harboring other persons who are dangerous and who could unexpectedly launch an attack. The risk of danger in the context of an arrest in the home is as great as, if not greater than, it is in the on-the-street or roadside investigatory encounter. ...

We should emphasize that such a protective sweep, aimed at protecting the arresting officers, if justified by the circumstances, is nevertheless not a full search of the premises, but may extend only to a cursory inspection of those spaces where a person may be found. The sweep lasts no longer than is necessary to dispel the reasonable suspicion of danger and in any event no longer than it takes to complete the arrest and depart from the premises.

... The Fourth Amendment permits a properly limited protective sweep in conjunction with an in-home arrest when the searching officer possesses a reasonable belief based on specific and articulable facts that the area to be swept harbors an individual posing a danger to those on the arrest scene.

Illegal Arrests

Does the exclusionary rule apply to people as it does to things? That is, should a defendant be excluded from trial because he or she has been arrested unlawfully? Generally, the United States Supreme Court has said no.[48] However, evidence obtained as a result of an unlawful arrest is excludable. For example, if there is a causal connection between an illegal arrest and a subsequent confession, the confession must be excluded.[49] Similarly, if evidence is obtained through a search incident to an illegal arrest, it must also be suppressed. In short, any evidence obtained as a result of an illegal arrest must be excluded unless an independent basis for its discovery can be shown by the government.

Key Terms

arrest Taking a person into custody, in a situation and in the manner authorized by law.

arrest warrant A written command issued by a magistrate to a peace officer to take the person identified therein into custody.

bench warrant A warrant of arrest issued by a judge on the judge's own initiative, that is, without the filing of a complaint by the prosecutor.

border search A search of incoming persons and vehicles at the borders and other entry points to the United States. Border searches do not require a warrant and may be made without probable cause.

consent search A search authorized by the consent of a person having lawful authority to permit law enforcement officers to search the premises. A consent search is an exception to the usual requirement that a search must be pursuant to a warrant.

curtilage The area directly around one's home in which one has a reasonable expectation of privacy.

hot pursuit The substantially continuous pursuit of a fleeing felon or other dangerous criminal. During hot pursuit, the pursuing officers may enter a house or other structure without a warrant to search for and arrest the fleeing person if they have a reasonable belief that he or she is inside.

inventory search A routine inventorying of the contents of an impounded vehicle by law enforcement personnel. An inventory search does not require a warrant or probable cause.

motor vehicle search A search of a motor vehicle that may be made without a warrant if the searching officer has probable cause to believe that an item subject to seizure is located in the vehicle.

open fields Areas around the home that are outside the curtilage. One does not have a reasonable expectation of privacy in these areas, and they are not protected by the United States or California Constitutions from government searches.

plain feel doctrine The legal principle holding that an officer conducting a pat-down for weapons during a stop and frisk may seize contraband that he or she feels inside the detained person's clothing if the nature of the object as contraband is immediately apparent, that is, is apparent without further intrusion into the clothing of the detained person or manipulation of the object through the clothing of the detained person.

plain view doctrine A principle of the law of search and seizure that permits a law enforcement officer to seize evidence without a search warrant if the evidence is in plain view from a place where the officer has a legal right to be.

probable cause In the law of search, seizure, and arrest, a basis for believing that seizable property will be found in a particular location or that a particular person committed a crime, which is founded upon facts that are sufficiently reliable that a person of ordinary caution would be justified in believing them.

protective sweep A limited search of the interior of a building for the purpose of discovering the presence of dangerous persons who might constitute a threat to law enforcement officers who are conducting the arrest of a person within the building.

search Governmental infringement of a person's reasonable expectation of privacy.

search incident to arrest A search of a person being arrested, and of the area within the person's immediate control, for weapons and destructible evidence. A search incident to arrest does not require probable cause.

search warrant An order in writing, in the name of the people, signed by a magistrate, directed to a peace officer, commanding him or her to search for personal property and bring it before the magistrate.

seizure A meaningful interference with an individual's possessory interest in property.

stop and frisk The police practice of temporarily detaining a person suspected of criminal activity (*stop*) accompanied by a pat-down of the person's outer clothing to detect the presence of weapons (*frisk*). To be lawful, the stop must be supported by a reasonable suspicion that the person has committed, is committing, or is about to commit a crime. The frisk is lawful only if the detaining officer has a reasonable belief that the person is armed and dangerous.

summons A command directed to an individual ordering him or her to appear before the magistrate. A summons may be used in lieu of an arrest warrant, subject to limitations specified in the Penal Code.

totality of the circumstances test The test currently used by courts when determining whether information received from an informant by law enforcement officers is sufficient to support a determination that probable cause exists to issue a search warrant or arrest warrant.

Review Questions

1. Define the term *search* under constitutional legal principles developed in *Katz v. United States* and later cases.

2. In the context of search and seizure law, what is meant by the term *probable cause*?

3. Describe the two-prong test for the use of informant information as a basis for establishing probable cause created by the United States Supreme Court in *Aguilar v. Texas*. How has the Aguilar two-prong test been affected by the "totality of the circumstances" test established in *Illinois v. Gates*?

4. How is *search warrant* defined in the California Penal Code?

5. What are the types of items for which a search warrant may issue under the California Penal Code?

6. What are the required contents of a search warrant under the California Penal Code?

7. Does the California Penal Code impose any limits on the hours during which law enforcement officers may execute a search warrant? If so, describe the limits.

8. Judy and Sue are co-tenants in an apartment. The police have probable cause to believe that evidence of criminal activity by Sue is present in the apartment. The police approach Judy while Sue is out and ask Judy if they can

search the apartment. Briefly describe the legal principles governing the scope of consent Judy may give.

9. Briefly describe the plain view doctrine.

10. What is a stop? What is a frisk? Briefly describe the legal principles applicable to each.

11. What is the permissible scope of a search incident to arrest?

12. Describe the types of situations in which an officer may conduct a warrantless search under the exigent circumstances exception to the warrant requirement.

13. Describe three types of warrantless searches that may be conducted with respect to an automobile and its occupants.

14. What is the definition of *arrest* under the California Penal Code?

15. Under what circumstances may a peace officer conduct a warrantless arrest?

16. What document is used by police to request the issuance of an arrest warrant? Who issues arrest warrants?

17. What is a summons?

18. May a peace officer ever use deadly force to effect an arrest?

19. When making an arrest of a person located within private premises, is the arresting officer required to demand admittance and explain the purpose for which admittance is desired? If so, are there any exceptions to this rule?

20. What is a protective sweep?

Review Problems

1. Two police officers receive a tip that Farmer John is growing marijuana on his farm. The officers take a police helicopter and fly over Farmer John's farm at an altitude of 500 feet, looking for signs of a marijuana crop. (Assume that 500 feet is an altitude at which helicopters normally fly.) Soon one of the officers spots a field of growing marijuana. Upon their return to headquarters, the officers obtain a search warrant and, pursuant to the warrant, enter the farm and seize the marijuana. The district attorney charges Farmer John with growing marijuana. Farmer John moves to suppress the marijuana as evidence, claiming that the overflight of his farm constituted an unlawful warrantless search. What will be the result of Farmer John's motion? Discuss your reasoning.

2. Officer Smith, a police officer in the County of Golden, searches the home of Elmer Gentry pursuant to the following warrant issued by Judge Milton Pilton of the Golden County Municipal Court:

   County of Golden

   The people of the State of California to any sheriff, constable, marshal, or police officer in the County of Golden:

   Proof, by affidavit, having been this day made before me by Officer Frank Jones that seizable items are located in the home of Elmer Gentry, you are therefore commanded, in the daytime, to make search in the home of Elmer Gentry for any item which may lawfully be seized, and if you find the same or any part thereof, to bring it forthwith before this court.

   Given under my hand, and dated this fifth day of March, A.D. 1998.

   (Signed) Milton Pilton, Judge of the Municipal Court.

   Officer Smith knows that Elmer Gentry owns two homes in Golden County. He believes that Elmer Gentry is conducting illegal bookmaking activities from the home on Oak Street. Officer Smith uses the warrant to search Gentry's home on Oak Street and finds and seizes evidence of illegal bookmaking activities, as expected. Gentry is prosecuted but moves to suppress the bookmaking evidence on the ground that the search warrant was invalid. The prosecution argues that the warrant was valid and that, even if it were invalid, officer Smith was acting in good faith reliance on it. What will be the result of Gentry's motion to suppress? Discuss your reasoning.

3. Assume that police officers have a valid search warrant for the defendant's apartment. The warrant specifies that the officers may search

for stolen stereos. May the officers do the following?

    a. Search the defendant's desk drawers in his study?

    b. Search the defendant's closets in his bedroom?

    c. Search the defendant's body?

    d. Seize a transparent bag of cocaine found lying on the defendant's dining room table?

4. Police officers receive reliable information that Max is selling drugs from a motel room. While Max is away from the room, the officers ask permission from the motel owner to search the room. The owner consents and opens the room for the officers. The search reveals a quantity of cocaine, which the officers seize. Max is charged with possession of the cocaine and moves to suppress the cocaine as evidence, claiming the search and seizure were illegal. What will be the likely result of Max's motion?

5. While on patrol, officer Mahoney observes Arlo standing in an alley next to an apartment building. While officer Mahoney is watching from her patrol car, three different persons approach Arlo and hand him something. In return, Arlo hands something back to each of the persons. Both Arlo and the other persons seem anxious during these transactions and look around as if to assure that no one sees what they are doing. After the third transaction, officer Mahoney leaves the patrol car and approaches Arlo. She orders Arlo to turn around and "spread-eagle" against the wall of the apartment building. Officer Mahoney then frisks Arlo. During the frisk, officer Mahoney feels a bulge in one of Arlo's pockets which she recognizes as the feel of marijuana. She reaches into Arlo's pocket and retrieves the item, which in fact is marijuana. Arlo is charged with selling marijuana. He moves to suppress the marijuana as evidence claiming that the search of his clothing was illegal. What is the likely result of Arlo's motion?

6. Refer to the fact situation in question 5, except this time assume that before ordering Arlo to spread-eagle, officer Mahoney notices an unusual bulge under Arlo's jacket, which appears to be a concealed handgun. During the frisk, officer Mahoney feels the bulge and recognizes it as marijuana. She removes the

item from Arlo's clothing and finds that it is in fact marijuana. If Arlo moves to suppress the marijuana, what do you think the result of the motion will be?

7. Refer to the fact situation in question 6. When officer Mahoney seized the marijuana, she informed Arlo that he was under arrest for possession and sale of marijuana. Officer Mahoney then noticed a tote bag lying on the ground next to Arlo's feet. Officer Mahoney picked up the tote bag and opened it. Inside she found several one-ounce packets of marijuana. If Arlo moves to suppress this evidence, what will be the likely result?

8. After taking Arlo to the police station, officer Mahoney received a call on the car radio directing her to respond to a domestic disturbance. She arrived at the residence and knocked on the door, but received no answer. A neighbor came up to officer Mahoney and stated that the husband had hurriedly left the house a few minutes earlier. Officer Mahoney noticed what appeared to be drops of blood on the front porch. Concerned that the wife was still inside and might be seriously injured, officer Mahoney entered the house. She found the wife lying on the kitchen floor with serious stab wounds. Paramedics were summoned. While the paramedics were preparing to transport the wife to a hospital, officer Mahoney observed a clear plastic bag containing a white powdery substance on the kitchen table. Also on the table were items that officer Mahoney immediately recognized as paraphernalia used for cocaine ingestion. Officer Mahoney seized the bag containing the powder and the paraphernalia. Subsequent tests on the contents of the bag established that the substance was cocaine. The husband and wife were both charged with possession of cocaine. They moved to suppress the cocaine and paraphernalia as evidence on the ground that officer Mahoney had entered the residence without a search warrant. What do you think the result of this motion will be?

9. Dawnblossom is a middle-aged woman who has never quite gotten over her life as a flower child during the 1960s. In an area of the backyard of her home, she cultivates a small marijuana crop. Her backyard is completely surrounded by a wood fence which prevents observation of the yard by other persons

at ground level. Officer Smith has received reliable information that Dawnblossom is growing marijuana in her backyard. He approaches Dawnblossom's next-door neighbor and asks permission to enter the neighbor's backyard so that he can look into Dawnblossom's backyard. The neighbor consents, whereupon officer Smith enters the neighbor's backyard, places a ladder against the fence, climbs the ladder, and gazes into Dawnblossom's yard. Officer Smith immediately spots the marijuana crop. He then obtains a search warrant, enters Dawnblossom's backyard, and seizes the marijuana. The district attorney charges Dawnblossom with cultivation of marijuana. Dawnblossom moves to suppress the marijuana as evidence on the ground that officer Smith searched her backyard without a warrant. The prosecution argues that the backyard of Dawnblossom's home was not an area protected by the Fourth Amendment to the United States Constitution or article I, § 13, of the California Constitution. What do you think the result of the motion to suppress will be?

10. Officer Williams is on patrol in his squad car. He listens to a report broadcast by the police dispatcher, which advises that a bank robbery has just occurred near his location. The report states that the robbery was perpetrated by three males, that they stole a large quantity of cash from the bank, and that they fled the scene in a blue Chevrolet sedan. While Williams is listening to the report, a blue Chevrolet sedan occupied by three males passes his location at a high rate of speed. The sedan is proceeding from the direction of the bank. Officer Williams pursues and stops the sedan. He orders the occupants to exit the vehicle and place their hands on the top of the car. He then calls for backup. When a backup police officer arrives, officer Williams conducts a full search of all parts of the vehicle that could contain stolen money, including the trunk. The occupants have not consented to the search. Officer Williams finds a large quantity of cash in the trunk. He seizes the cash and places the occupants of the vehicle under arrest. It is later confirmed that the cash was money stolen from the bank. The vehicle occupants are charged with bank robbery. They move to suppress the cash as evidence, claiming that officer Williams

did not have probable cause to search the vehicle and that, even if he did have probable cause, the search should have been limited to the passenger compartment. What do you think the result will be?

11. John Q. Citizen, a private citizen, is walking down the sidewalk when he hears what he believes to be a gunshot followed by a scream. He then observes an adult male running from the area where the sound occurred. Believing that this person has shot someone, John orders him to stop, shouting "this is a citizen's arrest." The person does not stop. John, being very athletic, overtakes the person and tackles him. The person continues to resist, so John beats him until he submits to the arrest. A police officer arrives and John turns the person over to the custody of the officer. Investigation reveals that the sound John heard was a firecracker, which exploded in a teenager's hand. The scream John heard was a scream of pain from the teenager. The person John arrested was running because he was being threatened by a street gang. John is charged with assault and battery upon the person he arrested. Is it likely that John will be convicted?

12. What is wrong with the following situation? Officer Keystone has a warrant to arrest Charlie Chaplet. The warrant reads as follows:

> County of Boondoggle
>
> The people of the State of California to any peace officer of said State:
>
> Complaint on oath having this day been laid before me that the crime of petit theft, a misdemeanor, has been committed and accusing Charlie Chaplet thereof, you are therefore commanded forthwith to arrest the above-named defendant and bring him before me at Department 5 of this court, or in case of my absence or inability to act, before the nearest or most accessible magistrate in this county.
>
> Dated at the City of Boon, County of Boondoggle, this 12th day of July, 1998.
>
> (Signed)
>
> Signature and title

Officer Keystone proceeds to Chaplet's home at midnight and knocks on the front door. The door is opened by Chaplet's wife, who informs officer Keystone that Chaplet is at a friend's house. Officer Keystone goes to the friend's house and knocks on the door but receives no response. He observes that the lights are on inside the house. He knocks again and shouts, "Open up, this is the police." Again, he receives no response. Officer Keystone then breaks open the front door and enters. He searches through the house and discovers Chaplet hiding in a bedroom, whereupon officer Keystone arrests him. The friend, who owns the house, is also present in the bedroom. Officer Keystone observes a plastic bag containing marijuana on the dresser. He seizes the marijuana and arrests the friend for possession of marijuana.

13. After the episode described in question 12, officer Keystone attends a refresher course on arrest procedures. Later, he is directed to arrest Milton Burly in his home pursuant to an arrest warrant. The offense for which Burly is to be arrested is armed robbery. Keystone and two other officers arrive at Burly's home. They observe a car parked in front of the house which they recognize as belonging to Theodore Thug, a known criminal. The officers have no basis to arrest Thug at that time, but they know Thug to be a violent person. The officers knock on the front door, announce their purpose, and are granted admittance by Burly's wife. Burly is seated in the living room, and one of the officers immediately arrests him. Keystone proceeds through the house looking for Thug. Keystone limits his search to places where a person could hide. He finds Thug hiding in the bathroom. After briefly detaining Thug, Keystone suggests that he leave the house. Thug readily complies. While in the bathroom, Keystone sees illegal drugs lying on the counter. He seizes the drugs. Burly is prosecuted for both the armed robbery and possession of the drugs. His wife is also prosecuted for possession of the drugs. Both move to suppress the drugs as evidence, on the ground that officer Keystone had no right to search the house because he did not have a search warrant. They argue that if Keystone had not improperly searched the house, the drugs would never have been in his plain view. What do you think the result of the motion to suppress will be?

Notes

1 *Bivens v. Six Unknown Named Agents,* 403 U.S. 388 (1971).

2 *United States v. Jacobsen,* 466 U.S. 109, 113 (1984).

3 4 Witkin & Epstein, *California Criminal Law* § 2330 (2d ed. Bancroft-Whitney 1988), and cases cited.

4 *Hudson v. Palmer,* 468 U.S. 517 (1984).

5 *See, e.g., Florida v. Riley,* 109 S. Ct. 693 (1989); *People v. McKim* (1989) 214 Cal.App.3d 766.

6 *Carroll v. United States,* 267 U.S. 132 (1934).

7 462 U.S. 213, 233 (1983).

8 *United States v. Place,* 462 U.S. 696 (1983). A dog sniff of a person or thing, assuming no more intrusion, is not a search under the Fourth Amendment because no reasonable expectation of privacy has been violated.

9 *Beck v. Ohio,* 379 U.S. 89 (1964).

10 *McDonald v. United States,* 335 U.S. 451, 455–56 (1948).

11 4 Witkin & Epstein, *supra* note 3, at § 2447.

12 *Zurcher v. Stanford Daily,* 436 U.S. 547 (1978).

13 *Ybarra v. Illinois,* 444 U.S. 85 (1979).

14 *Michigan v. Summers,* 452 U.S. 692 (1981).

15 Penal Code § 1530.

16 Penal Code § 1531.

17 4 Witkin & Epstein, *supra* note 3, at §§ 2454, 2455.

18 Penal Code § 1540.

19 *People v. Martinez* (1968) 259 Cal.App.2d Supp. 943.

20 *See* 4 Witkin & Epstein, *supra* note 3, at § 2294; 20 Cal. Jur. 3d, *Criminal Law,* § 2559.

21 4 Witkin & Epstein, *supra* note 3, at § 2380.

22 403 U.S. at 470–71.

23 *Terry,* 392 U.S. at 21.

24 *See In re Tony C.* (1978) 21 Cal.3d 888, 893.

25 *Michigan v. Long,* 463 U.S. 1032 (1983).

26 *People v. Gutierrez* (1984) 163 Cal.App.3d 332.

27 *New York v. Belton,* 453 U.S. 454 (1981).

28 *Schmerber v. California,* 384 U.S. 757, 770–71 (1966).

29 4 Witkin & Epstein, *supra* note 3, at § 2374, citing *People v. Escudero* (1979) 23 Cal.3d 800.

30 *Oliver v. United States,* 466 U.S. 170 (1984).

31 *See* 4 Witkin & Epstein, *supra* note 3, at § 2342.

32 *United States v. Ramsey,* 431 U.S. 606 (1977).

33 *See* Torcia, *Wharton's Criminal Evidence* § 733 (13th ed., Lawyers Co-operative, 1986 Supp.).

34 *United States v. Martinez-Fuerte,* 428 U.S. 543 (1976).

35 *United States v. Ortiz,* 422 U.S. 891 (1975).

36 *United States v. Ross,* 456 U.S. 798 (1982).

37 *United States v. DiRe,* 332 U.S. 581 (1948).

38 *South Dakota v. Opperman,* 428 U.S. 364 (1976).

39 *See, e.g., People v. Aguilar* (1991) 228 Cal.App.3d 1049.

40 *Colorado v. Bertine,* 479 U.S. 367 (1986).

41 *Hudson v. Palmer, supra* note 4.

42 *People v. Fischer* (1957) 49 Cal.2d 442, 446.

43 *People v. Ramey* (1976) 16 Cal.3d 263.

44 *Stealgald v. United States,* 451 U.S. 204 (1981).

45 Penal Code § 808 provides that justices of the California Supreme Court and the courts of appeal, and judges of the superior and municipal courts, are magistrates. In actual practice, the magistrate function is performed by municipal and superior court judges.

46 Penal Code §§ 813(a), 1427(a).

47 *See* 4 Witkin & Epstein, *supra* note 3, at § 1935.

48 *Frisbie v. Collins,* 342 U.S. 519 (1952).

49 *Taylor v. Alabama,* 457 U.S. 687 (1982).

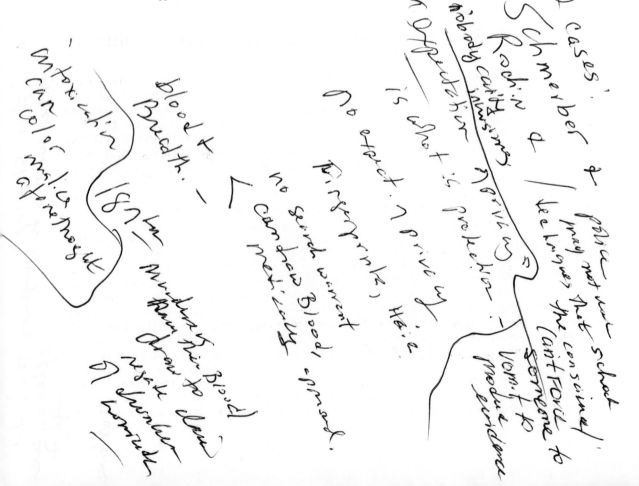

CHAPTER 15

Interrogation and Other Law Enforcement Practices

OUTLINE

§ 15.1 Interrogations, Confessions, and Admissions

This chapter deals with the legal requirements pertaining to certain investigative techniques used by law enforcement agencies, such as police interrogations, confessions, electronic surveillance, lineups, showups, and other identification procedures. Many of the matters dealt with in this chapter affect the individual constitutional rights of the persons against whom they are directed. These rights may arise under the Fourth, Fifth, or Sixth Amendments to the United States Constitution and corresponding provisions of the California Constitution.

The first topic discussed in this chapter is the subject of interrogations, confessions, and admissions. As is well known, a common police investigative procedure involves the questioning of persons suspected of crimes. This type of questioning is frequently referred to as interrogation. The term **interrogation** implies more than routine questioning of a witness or uninvolved third party. It is a questioning directed toward a specific person for the purpose of eliciting incriminating information. If, during a police interrogation, a person admits that he or she has committed a crime, the admission is known as a **confession**. If a person makes a statement that connects him or her with the crime being investigated—that is, it tends to show that he or she may have committed the crime—but does not actually admit commission of the crime, he or she has made an **admission**. For example, if a suspect admits that he deliberately killed a murder victim, he or she has confessed to murder. If, however, the suspect admits only to being at the scene of the crime at the time the offense was committed, he or she has not confessed to the crime, but has made an admission, because the statement tends to show that he or she may have committed the crime. The suspect has admitted one of the facts that will be necessary to convict him or her of the offense.

As a matter of evidence law, admissions or confessions are admissible, even though hearsay, as statements against interest. However, the use of interrogations, confessions, and admissions to prove guilt is controversial. The United States Supreme Court has recognized that admissions are highly suspect when relied upon alone to obtain a conviction. The Court stated, in *Escobedo v. Illinois*, 378 U.S. 478 (1964), that a "system of criminal law enforcement which comes to depend on the 'confession' will, in the long run, be less reliable and more subject to abuses than a system which depends on extrinsic evidence independently" obtained through other means of investigation.

At common law, confessions and admissions could be used freely, as long as they were made voluntarily. The early basis for excluding involuntary confessions was the Due Process Clauses of the Fifth and Fourteenth Amendments.[1]

Today, interrogations, confessions, and admissions are governed by these constitutional provisions, as well as two broader rights: the Fifth Amendment right to be free from self-incrimination and the Sixth Amendment right to counsel, together with corresponding provisions of the California Constitution.

Miranda

In *Escobedo v. Illinois,* the United States Supreme Court held that a suspect undergoing interrogation in police custody has a right to counsel, i.e., to have an attorney present during the questioning. *Escobedo* was decided as a Sixth Amendment "right to counsel" case. Two years later, the United States Supreme Court elaborated on the rights of a suspect during a custodial interrogation in the case of *Miranda v. Arizona*. The *Miranda* decision established the current law regarding an suspect's right to remain silent and to have the assistance of counsel during an interrogation. Unlike *Escobedo*, *Miranda* was a Fifth Amendment case; that is, it involved the right to remain silent and to have counsel present, which were considered essential to protect the suspect's right against self-incrimination.

Anyone who has watched a police program on television is familiar with the *Miranda* warnings. Before a person in custody may be interrogated, the required warnings must be given. Specific language need not be used, as long as the suspect is fully and effectively apprised of each right. Specifically, the suspect must be advised of the following:

1. That he or she has a right to remain silent.
2. That any statement the suspect makes may be used against him or her as evidence.
3. That the suspect has the right to consult with an attorney and to have an attorney present during questioning.
4. That if the suspect is indigent, an attorney will be appointed to represent him or her.

The warnings must be given to all persons in custody who are to be interrogated. The law does not presume that any person, including an attorney, knows these rights. The warnings should be given in a timely manner and stated at such a speed that the suspect can fully understand them.

MIRANDA v. ARIZONA
384 U.S. 436 (1966)

The cases before us raise questions that go to the roots of our concepts of American criminal jurisprudence: the restraints society must observe consistent with the Federal Constitution in prosecuting individuals for crime. More specifically, we deal with the admissibility of statements obtained from an individual who is subjected to custodial police interrogation and the necessity for procedures which assure that the individual is accorded his privilege under the Fifth Amendment to the Constitution not to be compelled to incriminate himself. ...

Our holding will be spelled out with some specificity in the pages which follow but briefly stated it is this: the prosecution may not use statements, whether exculpatory or inculpatory, stemming from custodial interrogation of the defendant unless it demonstrates the use of procedural safeguards effective to secure the privilege against self-incrimination. By custodial interrogation, we mean questioning initiated by law-enforcement officers after a person has been taken into custody or otherwise deprived of his freedom of action in any significant way. As for the procedural safeguards to be employed, unless other fully effective means are devised to inform accused persons of their right of silence and to assure a continuous opportunity to exercise it, the following measures are required. Prior to any questioning, the person must be warned that he has a right to remain silent, that any statement he does make may be used as evidence against him, and that he has a right to the presence of an attorney, either retained or appointed. The defendant may waive effectuation of these rights, provided the waiver is made voluntarily, knowingly, and intelligently. If, however, he indicates in any manner and at any stage of the process that he wishes to consult with an attorney before speaking there can be no questioning. Likewise, if the individual is alone and indicates in any manner that he does not wish to be interrogated, the police may not question him. The mere fact that he may have answered some questions or volunteered some statements on his own does not deprive him of the right to refrain from answering any further inquiries until he has consulted with an attorney and thereafter consents to be questioned.

The constitutional issue we decide in each of these cases is the admissibility of statements obtained from a defendant questioned while in custody or otherwise deprived of his freedom of action in any significant way. In each, the defendant was questioned by police officers, detectives, or a prosecuting attorney in a room in which he was cut off from the outside world. In none of these cases was the defendant given a full and effective warning of his rights at the outset of the interrogation process. In all of the cases, the questioning elicited oral admissions, and in three of them, signed statements as well which were admitted at their trials. They all thus share salient features—incommunicado interrogation of individuals in a police-dominated atmosphere, resulting in self-incriminating statements without full warnings of constitutional rights.

An understanding of the nature and setting of this in-custody interrogation is essential to our decisions today. The difficulty in depicting what transpires at such interrogations stems from the fact that in this country they have largely taken place incommunicado. From extensive factual studies undertaken in the early 1930s ... it is clear that police violence and the "third degree" flourished at that time. In a series of cases decided by the Court long after those studies, the police resulted to physical brutality—beating, hanging, whipping—and to sustained and protracted questioning incommunicado in order to extort confessions. ...

Again we stress that the modern practice of in-custody interrogation is psychologically rather than physically oriented. As we have stated before "... this court has recognized that coercion can be mental as well as physical, and that the blood of the accused is not the only hallmark of an unconstitutional inquisition." ...

The circumstances surrounding in-custody interrogation can operate very quickly to overbear the will of one merely made aware of his privilege [against self-incrimination] by his interrogators. Therefore, the right to have counsel present at the interrogation is indispensable to the protection of the Fifth Amendment privilege under the system we delineate today. Our aim is to assure that the individual's right to choose between silence and speech remains unfettered throughout the interrogation process. A once-stated warning, delivered by those who will conduct the interrogation, cannot itself suffice to that end among those who most require knowledge of their rights. A mere warning given by the interrogators is not alone sufficient to accomplish that end. Prosecutors themselves claim that the admonishment of the right to remain silent without more "will benefit only the recidivist and the professional." Even preliminary advice given to the accused by his own attorney can be swiftly overcome by the secret interrogation process. ... Thus, the need for counsel to protect the Fifth Amendment privilege comprehends not merely a right to consult with counsel prior to questioning, but also to have counsel present during any questioning if the defendant so desires.

The presence of counsel at the interrogation may serve several significant subsidiary functions as well.

If the accused decides to talk to his interrogators, the assistance of counsel can mitigate the dangers of trustworthiness. With a lawyer present the likelihood that the police will practice coercion is reduced, and if coercion is nevertheless exercised the lawyer can testify to it in court. The presence of a lawyer can also help to guarantee that the accused gives a fully accurate statement to the police and that the statement is rightly reported to the prosecution.

Custodial Interrogation

Not all questioning by law enforcement officers must be preceded by the *Miranda* warnings. A defendant must be "in custody" and "interrogated" by police before *Miranda* becomes applicable. This is known as the "custodial interrogation" requirement.

The Court used the phrase "taken into custody or otherwise deprived of his freedom of action in any significant way" to define the custody element of *Miranda*. Although a statement by a police officer to a suspect that he is not under arrest is not dispositive, it may be considered. Of course, a person is in custody if an officer announces that an arrest is being made or that the person is not free to leave. The Court made it clear that the in-custody element may be satisfied anywhere—it is not required that the defendant be at the police station to be in custody. For example, in *Orozco v. Texas,* 394 U.S. 324 (1969), the United States Supreme Court held that a murder suspect was in custody in his room at his boarding house, when police questioned him there, because he was not free to leave during the questioning.

All of the surrounding facts must be considered in making the custody determination. The location of the interrogation, though not determinative, is significant. There is a greater chance of finding that a person is in custody if the questioning takes place in a police station or prosecutor's office rather than the suspect's home or in public. The presence of other persons during the interrogation decreases the odds of the suspect being in custody. The Court was troubled by the fact that the suspects in *Miranda* were "cut off from the outside world." The length and intensity of the questioning are also relevant. A brief encounter between a citizen and a police officer is generally not a custodial situation.

In addition to being in custody, a defendant must be subjected to an interrogation before *Miranda* applies. Clearly, interrogation includes questioning by law enforcement officers, but this is not all. In *Rhode Island v. Innis,* 446 U.S. 291 (1980), the Supreme Court held that any "functional equivalent" to express questioning is also interrogation. That is, all actions or words by police officers that can reasonably be expected to elicit an incriminating response are interrogation.

The nature of the information elicited is not relevant; the *Miranda* court stated that the decision applies to both inculpatory and exculpatory statements.

Thus, not only incriminating statements, but also statements made by the defendant in an attempt to exonerate himself or herself, are inadmissible as evidence by the prosecution unless preceded by the *Miranda* warnings.

Exceptions to *Miranda*

Not every communication between a police officer and a suspect amounts to an interrogation under *Miranda*. First, volunteered statements are not the product of interrogation. The *Miranda* decision explicitly states that officers are under no duty to interrupt a volunteered confession in order to read a suspect his or her *Miranda* rights.

Second, routine questions that are purely informational normally do not lead to incriminating responses and need not be preceded by a reading of the *Miranda* warnings. Questions about one's name, age, address, and employment are not treated as interrogation.

Third, questions made by officers in the interest of public safety need not be preceded by a *Miranda* warning. In one case, a woman told two police officers that she had just been raped by a man carrying a gun and that the rapist had gone into a nearby grocery. The officers went to the store and arrested the man. However, he did not have the gun on his person. One of the police officers asked the arrestee where the gun was, and the arrestee responded by indicating the location where the gun was hidden in the store. The Supreme Court decided that, despite the facts that the question was interrogation and the defendant had not been mirandized, the evidence could be used at trial. The Court recognized that in such situations, when there is a danger to the officers or the public, officers must be permitted to extinguish the public threat. Thus, the relatively rigid *Miranda* rules are relaxed when there is a public safety exigency that is the impetus of a brief and limited interrogation designed to meet that exigency.[2]

Fourth, and related to the public safety exception, is spontaneous questioning by police. If a question is asked spontaneously, such as in response to an emergency or a confusing situation, there is no interrogation. For example, assume that police officers arrive at the scene of a homicide and find several people present. An officer asks a person in the group, "What happened here?" The person responds, "I killed him." The statement would be admissible because the person was not in custody and was not being interrogated.

Fifth, and also related to the public safety exception, is what is known as the *rescue doctrine*. This doctrine is frequently invoked in kidnapping cases in which the police arrest a suspect and ask him or her where the victim is located. The question is not preceded by *Miranda* warnings. In such situations, the life and safety of the victim is deemed more important than the suspect's right to counsel or right to remain silent.

Sixth, the *Miranda* warnings do not have to be given by undercover officers because there is no custody, no "police-dominated atmosphere."[3] However, once criminal charges have been filed, undercover officers may not be used to extract information from a defendant.[4]

Seventh, the Supreme Court has determined that *Miranda* warnings do not have to be recited during routine traffic stops, even though an interrogation occurs. The Court concluded that although traffic stops are seizures for Fourth Amendment purposes, they are not custodial for Fifth Amendment purposes.

The "noncoercive aspect of ordinary traffic stops prompts us to hold that persons temporarily detained pursuant to such stops are not 'in custody' for the purposes of *Miranda*."[5]

Eighth, *Miranda* warnings are not required during a temporary detention such as that authorized under the United States Supreme Court's holding in *Terry v. Ohio*, discussed in Chapter 14.

Invocation of *Miranda* Rights

Miranda clearly states that if a suspect invokes the right to remain silent, he or she may not be interrogated. Similarly, if the suspect states that he or she wants counsel present, he or she may not be interrogated until the attorney is present. A suspect may initially waive his or her *Miranda* rights and then invoke them during questioning. At that point, interrogation must cease.

Once a suspect has invoked his or her right to remain silent under *Miranda*, he or she may not be reinterrogated about the same offense. In *Michigan v. Mosely*, 423 U.S. 96 (1975), the defendant was arrested and questioned about a number of robberies. In response to a reading of his *Miranda* rights, the defendant invoked the right to remain silent, whereupon the interrogation ceased. The defendant did not request the assistance of counsel. Later the same day, another police officer readvised the defendant of his *Miranda* rights and questioned the defendant about a murder unrelated to the robberies. The defendant made an incriminating statement which was later used against him in a trial for the murder, at which he was convicted. The United States Supreme Court held that the second interrogation about an offense unrelated to the first interrogation, accompanied by a readvisement of the defendant's *Miranda* rights, was permissible.

In *Miranda*, the United States Supreme Court clearly stated that once a suspect has invoked the right to counsel, the police are prohibited from interrogating him or her until he or she has had an opportunity to confer with an attorney, and that the suspect may have the attorney present during any subsequent questioning. In a later decision, *Edwards v. Arizona*, 451 U.S. 477 (1981), the Court stated that a suspect who has invoked his or her right to counsel may not be questioned further until counsel has "been made available" to him or her. This language in *Edwards* muddied the waters, so to speak, because it raised an issue as to whether the right to counsel could be satisfied by permitting the suspect to confer with counsel and then reinterrogating the suspect without counsel present. This issue was settled by the United States Supreme Court in *Minnick v. Mississippi*, 498 U.S. 146 (1990). *Minnick* makes it clear that once a suspect has asserted the right to counsel, all police-initiated interrogations must occur with counsel present.

The foregoing principles were restated by a California appellate court in *People v. DeLeon* (1994) 22 Cal.App.4th 1265. The court in *DeLeon* distinguished between the two rights guaranteed under *Miranda:* the right to remain silent and the right to counsel. According to the court, invocation of the right to remain silent applies only to the offense for which the suspect is being interrogated and does not preclude later interrogation regarding an unrelated offense. Of course, the suspect must be readvised of his or her *Miranda* rights and knowingly and voluntarily waive them. The right to counsel is a different matter. If a suspect invokes the right to have counsel present, he or she may not be reinterrogated for any offense unless counsel is present.

Waiver

A defendant may waive the rights to have the assistance of counsel or to remain silent. The waiver must be made voluntarily and knowingly. In *Miranda*, the Supreme Court said that the "heavy burden" of proving that a defendant made a knowing and voluntary waiver rests with the prosecution; courts are to presume no waiver.

In determining whether there has been a waiver, the totality of the circumstances is considered. The actions of the police, as well as the defendant's age, intelligence, and experience, are all relevant to this inquiry.

An express waiver, preferably written, is best for the prosecution. However, a defendant's waiver does not have to be express to be valid. In *North Carolina v. Butler,* 441 U.S. 369 (1962), the Court held that "in at least some cases waiver can be clearly inferred from the actions and words of the person interrogated." For example, in *People v. Sully* (1991) 53 Cal.3d 1195, the defendant was advised of his *Miranda* rights and asked if he understood them. He answered, "Yes, I do." The defendant did not expressly state that he waived his *Miranda* rights, but proceeded to answer the questions put to him by the interrogating police officers. The California Supreme Court held that the defendant had indicated waiver of his rights by his statement that he understood his rights followed by his answering of the questions. Contrast this situation with the situation in which a suspect remains completely nonresponsive after being advised of his or her rights—the suspect neither indicates that he or she understands them nor waives them. In such a case, waiver will not be presumed.

Violating *Miranda*

Any statement obtained in violation of *Miranda* is inadmissible at trial to prove guilt. This rule applies even if the defendant's confession was otherwise voluntary. In other words, if the police interrogate a defendant without first giving him or her the *Miranda* warnings, and the defendant voluntarily confesses to the crime, the confession is inadmissible for the simple reason that the *Miranda* warnings were not given.

Although statements that are illegally obtained may not be admitted to prove a defendant's guilt, the United States Supreme Court has held that statements violating *Miranda* may be admitted, under certain circumstances, to impeach a defendant (to challenge the truthfulness of the defendant's testimony).[6]

Sixth Amendment

Miranda rights arise as soon as a person is in custody and subject to interrogation. This can occur long before, or directly prior to, the filing of a formal charge. After an adversary judicial proceeding has been formally initiated against a person, the right to be represented by counsel arises under the Sixth Amendment rather than under the Fifth Amendment *(Miranda)*.

In *Michigan v. Jackson,* 475 U.S. 625 (1986), the United States Supreme Court held that the Sixth Amendment provides the same protections as *Miranda, Edwards,* and similar cases. The Court reasoned that interrogation of a defendant after criminal charges have been filed constitutes a "critical stage" of a criminal proceeding at which counsel is necessary to protect the defendant's rights. More will be said about the Sixth Amendment right to counsel in Chapter 17.

Voluntariness Requirement

As was true at common law, all confessions must be made voluntarily. This is required by the Due Process Clauses of the Fifth and Fourteenth Amendments. The totality of the circumstances must be examined when making the voluntariness determination.

Police officers do not have to physically coerce a confession for it to be involuntary. Mental or emotional coercion by law enforcement also violates a defendant's due process rights. Confessions induced by false promises of leniency are similarly involuntary.

Involuntary confessions are to be excluded at trial. For years, the admission of a coerced confession resulted in an automatic reversal of conviction. This was changed in *Arizona v. Fulminante,* 499 U.S. 279 (1991), in which the United States Supreme Court decided that a conviction is not to be automatically reversed because a coerced confession was admitted at trial. Rather, the Court held that if the prosecution can show beyond a reasonable doubt that the trial court error was harmless, the conviction is to be affirmed. That is, if there was sufficient other evidence to sustain the conviction, then it stands.

The requirement that a confession be voluntary is separate and distinct from the requirements under *Miranda.* An example would be a defendant who is given the *Miranda* warnings, but waives the right to counsel and states that he or she will discuss the offense with the investigating officers. The officers then induce the defendant to confess by making false promises that, if he confesses, they can persuade the prosecutor to "go easy" on him. The resulting confession is involuntary, although it does not violate *Miranda.*

§ 15.2 Electronic Surveillance

Many forms of electronic surveillance are used by law enforcement agencies. Wiretaps and highly sensitive microphones are examples. When the Supreme Court first addressed the issue of wiretapping, it concluded that there was no Fourth Amendment protection because there was no trespass into a constitutionally protected area. This changed when the Court issued the *Katz* decision, which advanced the idea that the Fourth Amendment protects people, not places. Now, if a person has a justifiable expectation of privacy, the Fourth Amendment applies.

Despite the constitutional aspect of using such devices, this area of law is highly regulated by statute at both the federal and state levels.

Title III of the Omnibus Crime Control Act

Title III of the Omnibus Crime Control and Safe Streets Act of 1968[7] is a federal statute that regulates the use of electronic surveillance by both federal and state law enforcement authorities. It is also known as the Federal Wiretap Act.

The act regulates wiretapping, bugging, or other electronic surveillance of a conversation by law enforcement officials when the parties to that conversation possess a reasonable expectation of privacy. Violation of the act may result in civil and criminal penalties. Evidence obtained in violation of the act is excluded at trial.

The statute permits states to enact their own electronic surveillance laws; however, those laws cannot provide less protection of individual rights than the federal statute. A state may, however, provide greater protection of individual rights through its surveillance law than does the federal statute.

California Penal Code

In 1995, the legislature added Chapter 1.4 to Title 15 of Part 1 of the California Penal Code. The subject of Chapter 1.4, which includes Penal Code §§ 629.50 through 629.98, is "Interception of Wire, Electronic Digital Pager, or Electronic Cellular Telephone Communications." The authority and procedures established in Chapter 1.4 are similar to those found in Title III of the Omnibus Crime Control and Safe Streets Act, although there are some differences.

Chapter 1.4 authorizes interception of wire, digital pager, or cellular telephone communications by law enforcement authorities investigating the following crimes: certain crimes involving large quantities of specified drugs, murder, solicitation to commit murder, crimes involving the bombing of public or private property, aggravated kidnapping, and conspiracy to commit any of the foregoing offenses.

Law enforcement authorities wishing to engage in electronic surveillance under the authority of Chapter 1.4 must obtain a court order authorizing the surveillance. The court's order may not authorize interception of communications "for a period longer than is necessary to achieve the objective of the authorization, nor in any event longer than 30 days." Extensions subject to the same duration limitations may be granted by the court. (*See* Penal Code § 629.58.) The order must direct that interception activities occur as soon as practicable, that they be conducted in such a way as to minimize interception of communications not otherwise subject to interception under Chapter 1.4, and that they terminate upon attainment of the authorized objective, or, in any event, at the expiration of the authorization as designated in the order.

Progress reports must be made to the judge no less often than every seventy-two hours by the officials conducting the interception. If the judge finds that satisfactory progress has not been made toward interception of the communications or that no need exists for continued interception, he or she must order that the interception immediately terminate.

Interceptions of communications must be recorded, if possible, on tape or other comparable device. Immediately upon expiration of the period of authorized interception specified in the court's order, the recordings are to be made available to the judge issuing the order and sealed under his or her directions.

No later than ninety days after termination of the period of an interception order, the issuing judge must cause an inventory to be served on the persons named in the court order and any other known person whose communications were intercepted. The inventory is to include notice of the following: (1) the fact of entry of the interception order; (2) the date of entry of the order and the period of authorized interception; and (3) the fact that, during the period, communications were or were not intercepted. The serving of the inventory may be postponed by the judge upon a showing of good cause for the postponement. Upon receiving the inventory, a person named in the interception order or whose communications were intercepted may make a motion to inspect the intercepted communications, the application, and the court's interception order. The judge may grant the motion in whole or in part, as the judge determines to be in the interest of justice.

Intercepted communications, or evidence derived from intercepted communications, may not be used in any trial, hearing, or other proceeding, except a grand jury proceeding, unless each party is provided a transcript of the intercepted communications and a copy of the application and interception order at least ten days before the trial, hearing, or other proceeding. A person may move to suppress the contents of intercepted communications or evidence derived therefrom, but only on the ground that the contents or evidence were obtained in violation of the Fourth Amendment to the United States Constitution or in violation of Chapter 1.4.

Penal Code § 629.89 expressly prohibits covert entry by law enforcement officers into a residential dwelling, hotel room, or motel room for installation or removal of an interception device.

An order authorizing the interception of communications may require that a public communications company providing service to the person whose communications are to be intercepted, or a landlord, custodian, or other person, cooperate with and render technical assistance to law enforcement authorities conducting the interception.

Violation of the provisions of Chapter 1.4 is a felony-misdemeanor punishable by a fine not exceeding $2,500, or imprisonment in the county jail not exceeding one year, or by imprisonment in the state prison, or by both such fine and imprisonment in the county jail or state prison. Any person whose communication is intercepted, disclosed, or used in violation of Chapter 1.4 has a civil cause of action against the violator in which he or she may recover actual damages, punitive damages, costs, and attorneys' fees. Good faith reliance on a court order is a complete defense to any civil or criminal action brought under Chapter 1.4.

§ 15.3 Pretrial Identification Procedures

Law enforcement officers use a variety of techniques to identify a person as a criminal, such as eyewitness identifications, fingerprinting, blood tests, and, recently, deoxyribonucleic acid (DNA) tests. The use of any of these procedures raises certain constitutional issues, such as the right to be free from self-incrimination and the right to counsel.

There is also another concern: reliability. Eyewitness identification, though powerful, has a few inherent problems. First, each person will testify to his or her perception of an event, and people often perceive the same event differently. Second, not every person will use the same language to describe what was witnessed. Third, a witness may simply have a faulty memory and unintentionally testify to an untruth. Fourth, for a variety of reasons, a witness may intentionally lie.

Scientific testing may also prove to be invalid or unreliable. How accurate is the test when performed properly? Was the test performed properly in this case? Is the evidence tested actually the defendant's? These types of questions are asked of expert witnesses who testify to the results of scientific testing. This discussion begins with eyewitness identification procedures.

Lineups and One-Man Showups

A **lineup** is an investigative technique in which a suspect is included in a group of people that is viewed by the victim or other witness. The victim or witness is asked by law enforcement authorities whether the perpetrator of the crime is among the individuals in the group and, if so, to identify the perpetrator. A one-man **showup** is similar to a lineup except that only the suspect is exhibited to the victim or witness.

In practice, police first conduct a lineup and then, if the suspect is identified, the witness is asked at trial to testify that he or she identified the perpetrator of the crime at the lineup. Therefore, if the initial identification is faulty, the subsequent in-court identification is also faulty. Even if the witness is asked to identify anew the perpetrator of the crime, such an identification is tainted by the witness's earlier identification. In the landmark case of *United States v. Wade,* the Supreme Court addressed the problems inherent in pretrial identification procedures.

The Right to Counsel

In *Wade,* the United States Supreme Court held that because a defendant may be irreparably damaged by an improperly conducted lineup, he or she has a right to have an attorney present at the lineup. As will be discussed in Chapter 17, a defendant has a right to counsel at each critical stage of the prosecution. The Court in *Wade* held that a pretrial lineup is a critical stage, thereby entitling the defendant to the assistance of counsel. However, because the lineup in *Wade* occurred after Wade had been formally charged by means of an indictment, it was unclear whether the Court meant to hold that *all* lineups (even those occurring before the defendant is formally charged, so-called **pre-accusatory lineups**) constitute critical stages of a criminal proceeding at which the defendant is entitled to counsel. *Kirby v. Illinois,* 406 U.S. 682 (1972), resolved this issue. In *Kirby,* the United States Supreme Court held that a defendant participating in a pretrial lineup has a right to counsel only after initiation of "adversary judicial proceedings—whether by way of formal charge, preliminary hearing, indictment, information, or arraignment." Thus, under *Kirby,* a suspect participating in a lineup after he or she has been arrested, but before he or she has been formally charged, does not have a right to counsel. This is so despite the fact that identification of the suspect by a victim or other witness may constitute the basis for an in-court identification at a later trial of the suspect for the offense.

UNITED STATES v. WADE
338 U.S. 218 (1967)

The question here is whether courtroom identifications of an accused at trial are to be excluded from evidence because the accused was exhibited to the witness before trial at a post-indictment lineup conducted for identification purposes without notice to and in the absence of the accused's appointed counsel.

The federally insured bank in Eustace, Texas, was robbed on September 21, 1964. A man with a small strip of tape on each side of his face entered the bank, pointed a pistol at the female cashier and the vice president, the only persons in the bank at the time, and forced them to fill a pillowcase with the bank's money. The man then drove away with an accomplice who had been waiting in a stolen car outside the bank. On March 23, 1965, an indictment was returned against respondent, Wade, and two others for conspiring to rob the bank, and against Wade and accomplice for the robbery itself. Wade was arrested on April 2, and counsel was appointed to represent him on April 26. Fifteen days later an FBI agent, without notice to Wade's lawyer, arranged to have the two bank employees observe a lineup made up of Wade and five or six other prisoners and conducted in a courtroom of the local county courthouse. Each person in the line wore strips of tape such as allegedly worn by the robber and upon direction each said something like "put the money in the bag," the words allegedly uttered by the robber. Both bank employees identified Wade in the lineup as the bank robber.

At trial, the two employees, when asked on direct examination if the robber was in the courtroom, pointed to Wade. The prior lineup identification was then elicited from both employees on cross examination. ... But the confrontation compelled by the State between the accused and the victim or witnesses to a crime to elicit identification evidence is peculiarly riddled with innumerable dangers and variable factors which might seriously, even crucially, derogate from a fair trial. The vagaries of eyewitness identification are well-known; the annals of criminal law are rife with instances of mistaken identification. ... The identification of strangers is proverbially untrustworthy. ... A major factor contributing to the high incidence of miscarriage of justice from mistaken identification has been the degree of suggestion inherent in the manner in which the prosecution presents the suspect to witness for pretrial identification. A commentator has observed that "[t]he influence of improper suggestion upon identifying witnesses probably accounts for more miscarriages of justice than any other single factor—perhaps it is responsible for more such errors than all other factors combined." ... Suggestion can be created intentionally or unintentionally in many subtle ways. And the dangers for the suspect are particularly grave when the witness' opportunity for observation was insubstantial, and thus his susceptibility to suggestion the greatest.

> Moreover, "[i]t is a matter of common experience that, once a witness has picked out the accused at the line-up, he is not likely to go back on his word later on, so that in practice the issue of identity may (in the absence of other relevant evidence) for all practical purposes be determined there and then, before the trial." ...

What facts have been disclosed in specific cases about the conduct of pretrial confrontations for identification illustrate both the potential for substantial prejudice to the accused at that stage and the need for its revelation at trial. A commentator provides some striking examples:

> In a Canadian case ... the defendant had been picked out of a line-up of six men, of which he was the only Oriental. In other cases, a black-haired suspect was placed among a group of light-haired persons, tall suspects have been made to stand with short non-suspects, and, in a case where the perpetrator of the crime was known to be a youth, a suspect under twenty was placed in a line-up with five other persons, all of whom were forty or over.

Similarly, state reports, in the course of describing prior identifications admitted as evidence of guilt, reveal numerous instances of suggestive procedures, for example, that all in the lineup but the suspect were known to the identifying witness, that the other participants in a lineup were grossly dissimilar in appearance to the suspect, that only the suspect was required to wear distinctive clothing which the culprit allegedly wore. ...

Since it appears that there is grave potential for prejudice, intentional or not, in the pretrial lineup, which may not be capable of reconstruction at trial, and since presence of counsel can often avert prejudice and assure a meaningful confrontation at trial, there can be little doubt that for Wade the post-indictment lineup was a critical stage of the prosecution at which [he] was [entitled to counsel]. ...

[The Court then concluded that in-court identifications must be excluded if they follow a lineup at which a defendant is not permitted counsel, unless the in-court identification has an independent origin.]

The Fairness Right

In addition to having a right to counsel at postindictment lineups, an accused is entitled to a fair lineup, one that is not unnecessarily suggestive of guilt. In *Stoval v. Denno*, 388 U.S. 293 (1967), the United States Supreme Court held that the Due Process Clauses of the Fifth and Fourteenth Amendments prohibit identifications that are so unnecessarily suggestive that there is a real chance of misidentification. When making the determination of whether an identification violates due process, a court is to examine the "totality of the circumstances" surrounding the identification. Examples of impermissibly suggestive lineups were mentioned in the *Wade* opinion. For example, if a witness states that a white male committed a crime, it would be improper to exhibit four black men and one white man in a lineup. Of course, in a lineup consisting of several persons, not all differences among the participants can be eliminated. Differences that do not impermissibly draw the attention of the witness or victim to the suspect are allowable. For example, it is not required that all participants in a lineup wear the same type of clothing. Also, it is not necessary that all participants be of the same height and weight, as long as the variance among them is not extreme. In most cases, lineups are found by the courts to have been fairly conducted.[8]

One-man showups, obviously, are more suggestive of guilt than lineups. Thus, they should be used with caution. Generally, a one-man showup should occur within a short period of time after the crime (minutes or hours). If there is time to organize a lineup, this is the preferable method of identification.

Self-Incrimination

It is not violative of the Fifth Amendment's privilege against self-incrimination for a defendant to be compelled to appear in a lineup. As stated in Chapter 11, the privilege against self-incrimination protects against testimonial compulsion. This means that a criminal defendant cannot be compelled to give evidence of a testimonial nature; that is, he or she may not be compelled to give evidence that would be tantamount to testifying against himself or herself. A defendant may, however, be required to give evidence of a nontestimonial nature.

Such evidence may include physical acts such as appearing in a lineup, walking, gesturing, or speaking certain words for identification purposes.[9] If a defendant has changed in appearance, he or she may be made to shave, to don a wig or hairpiece, or wear a certain article of clothing.

Exclusion of Improper Identification

The consequences of not providing counsel during an identification procedure after the adversary judicial proceeding has begun were discussed in *Wade*. First, testimony about an illegal identification must be excluded at trial. Second, in-court identifications must be excluded if tainted by the pretrial identification. However, if the government can show, by clear and convincing evidence, that an in-court identification has a source independent of the illegal pretrial identification, then it is to be allowed. The *Wade* Court said the following factors are to be considered when making the taint or no-taint determination:

1. The prior opportunity to observe the criminal act
2. The difference between a witness's pre-lineup description and actual description of an accused
3. Whether the witness identified another person as the criminal before the lineup
4. Whether the witness identified the accused by photograph prior to the lineup
5. Whether the witness was unable to identify the accused on a previous occasion
6. The lapse of time between the crime and the identification.

In most cases, a court will find an independent source for an in-court identification and will allow a witness to identify the defendant during trial, while prohibiting mention of the pretrial identification.

The same rules apply to identifications that are impermissibly suggestive and unreliable. They must be excluded, as must the fruits thereof, unless an independent basis for an in-court identification can be shown.

Photographs

Police may show a witness photographs to obtain an identification. The due process test discussed earlier applies to the use of photos; that is, the event must not be impermissibly suggestive and unreliable. The showing of one picture is likely to be determined improper, absent an emergency. If the photographic identification procedure is impermissibly suggestive, the photographic identification may not be used as a basis for identification of the defendant at trial.

As with lineups, the people in the pictures should be somewhat alike in appearance, although absolute similarity is not required. Victims and witnesses may be asked to look through police **mug-shot files** to determine whether a picture of the offender is contained there. However, a mug-shot of the suspect should not be mixed with ordinary photos of nonsuspects because the procedure would thereby unduly focus attention on the suspect and be impermissibly suggestive. Police may also conduct a **simulated lineup** in which they photograph a lineup of individuals and then show the photograph to the victim or witness and ask if the offender is among the individuals photographed. This practice, although upheld by the courts, is not favored.[10] Any photographic identification procedure should be conducted in such a manner that the suspect's picture does not stand out.

The United States Supreme Court has determined that there is no right to counsel at a photo identification session, either before initiation of adversarial judicial proceedings or thereafter.

Scientific Identification Procedures

Law enforcement officials may use scientific methods of identification to prove that a defendant committed a crime. Fingerprinting, blood tests, genetic tests (deoxyribonucleic acid, or DNA, testing), voice tests, and handwriting samples are examples of such techniques.

Such tests are not critical stages of the criminal proceedings; therefore, there is no right to counsel. There is also no right to refuse to cooperate with such testing on Fifth Amendment grounds, because the defendant is not being required to give testimony. However, if a test involves an invasion of privacy (i.e., a search or seizure), then the Fourth Amendment requires probable cause before the procedure may be forced on an unwilling defendant.

Validity and Reliability

Scientific evidence must be reliable before it may be introduced at trial. In a landmark case, *Frye v. United States*, 293 F. 1013 (D.C. Cir. 1923), it was held that scientific techniques must be generally accepted as valid and reliable by the scientific community to be admissible. The principle enunciated in the *Frye* decision applies to the admissibility of new types of scientific evidence. Once a particular type of scientific evidence becomes firmly established as admissible by the courts, it is not generally subject to challenge under *Frye*.

In *People v. Kelly* (1976) 17 Cal.3d 24, the California Supreme Court discussed the admissibility of scientific evidence. The Court noted that in any case involving scientific evidence, whether of a new or established type, the reliability of the method used must be established, usually by expert testimony, and the witness furnishing the testimony must be properly qualified to give an opinion on the subject. Also, the proponent of the evidence must demonstrate that correct scientific procedures were used in the particular case. The Court then held that when scientific evidence involving new scientific techniques is proffered by a party, the *Frye* standard must be met as well. In other words, the evidence will be admissible only if the technique is generally accepted in the applicable scientific community. This rule of California law is known as the **Kelly-Frye rule** or, alternatively, the "Frye-Kelly rule."

Techniques that are experimental and not highly reliable are not admissible. A few common scientific techniques are discussed here. Note that the results of a specific test may be denied admission, even if the scientific basis of the testing is valid, if the test is administered incorrectly. Further, scientific testing also raises Fourth, Fifth, Sixth, and Fourteenth Amendment issues, some of which are discussed later.

Fingerprinting

A fingerprint consists of several identifiable characteristics, such as loops, arches, whorls, islands, and bifurcations. The arrangement, frequency, and design of these features are among the many characteristics used to distinguish fingerprints. Although it is common to state that every person has a unique set of prints, there is a possibility of duplication. However, the odds of that occurring has been estimated to be as low as one in 64 billion.[11]

Fingerprint identification is a highly accurate science and is universally accepted by federal and state courts.[12] Federal and state law enforcement agencies, as well as international agencies, possess libraries of fingerprints. Through the use of computers, fingerprints lifted from crime scenes, weapons, and other objects can be matched to a particular individual's fingerprints in a matter of minutes. Lifted prints may be matched to a print already on file or to a print taken from a suspect.

The taking of fingerprints does not implicate the Fifth Amendment because the accused is not compelled to give testimony or provide evidence of a testimonial or communicative nature. Further, it is not a search to take a suspect's fingerprints. This being so, neither probable cause nor a warrant is required to take the suspect's prints. Courts have analogized fingerprints to physical characteristics such as hair and eye color. Because it is not an invasion of a reasonable expectation of privacy (search) for an officer to visually observe a defendant, courts have reasoned that it is not an invasion of privacy to observe and record a suspect's fingerprints.

In California, palmprints and footprints are also considered reliable means of identification.[13]

Blood Testing

Blood testing is commonly employed and universally accepted by courts in the United States. Although the science of blood testing is generally beyond scrutiny, individual blood tests are not. Laboratories make mistakes, and both the defense and the prosecution may challenge a particular test.

Securing a suspect's blood is different from rolling a fingerprint. The process of withdrawing blood involves a bodily invasion and the possibility of pain and infection. Therefore, a person's expectation of privacy is higher when the government seeks blood rather than fingerprints. Whether the government possesses the authority to compel a suspect to undergo a blood test was the subject of *Schmerber v. California.*

Schmerber stands for the principle that the withdrawal of blood, as well as other bodily-intrusive procedures, constitutes a search under the Fourth Amendment. Probable cause is required, as is a warrant, unless exigent circumstances, such as those in *Schmerber*, justify bypassing the warrant requirement. In addition, such procedures must be conducted in a safe, discrete, medical environment.

In *People v. Superior Court (Hawkins)* (1972) 6 Cal.3d 757, the defendant, Hawkins, was in the hospital for treatment following an automobile accident. He was given a blood-alcohol test for intoxication and was found to be intoxicated. Hawkins had not been arrested prior to administration of the blood-alcohol test. He later successfully moved to suppress the results of the test. Reviewing the trial court's decision to suppress the evidence, the California Supreme Court held that the United States Supreme Court's decision in *Schmerber* justified the compulsory seizure of the defendant's blood, on the ground that it constituted a search incident to arrest. The California Supreme Court held that because Hawkins had not been arrested before being subjected to the test, the blood-alcohol test was illegal and the results could not be used as evidence against Hawkins. This principle of California law became known as the *Hawkins rule.* The Hawkins rule has been questioned in court of appeal decisions, although it has not yet been reexamined by the California Supreme Court. Two courts of appeal have held that *Schmerber* required only probable cause to arrest, rather than actual arrest, to justify a warrantless administration of a blood-alcohol test for intoxication.[14] Until the issue is revisited by the California Supreme Court, it will remain an unsettled area of California law.

SCHMERBER v. CALIFORNIA
384 U.S. 757 (1966)

Petitioner was convicted in Los Angeles Municipal Court of the criminal offense of driving an automobile while under the influence of intoxicating liquor. He had been arrested at a hospital while receiving treatment for injuries suffered in an accident involving the automobile that he was apparently driving. At the direction of a police officer, a blood sample was then withdrawn from petitioner's body by a physician at the hospital. The chemical analysis of this sample revealed a percent by weight of alcohol in his blood at the time of the offense which indicated intoxication, and the report of this analysis was admitted in evidence at trial. ...

II. The Privilege Against Self-Incrimination Claim

... We ... must now decide whether the withdrawal of the blood and admission in evidence of the analysis involved in this case violated petitioner's privilege. We hold that the privilege protects an accused only from being compelled to testify against himself, or otherwise provide the State with evidence of a testimonial or communicative nature, and that the withdrawal of blood and use of the analysis in question in this case did not involve compulsion to these ends. ...

IV. The Search and Seizure Claim

The overriding function of the Fourth Amendment is to protect personal privacy and dignity against unwarranted intrusion by the State. ...

The values protected by the Fourth Amendment thus substantially overlap those the Fifth Amendment helps to protect. ...

Because we are dealing with intrusions into the human body rather than with state interferences with property relationships or private papers—"house, papers, and effects"—we write on a clean slate. ...

In this case, as will often be true when charges of driving under the influence of alcohol are pressed, these questions arise in the context of an arrest made by an officer without a warrant. Here, there was plainly probable cause for the officer to arrest petitioner and charge him with driving an automobile while under the influence of intoxicating liquor. The police officer who arrived at the scene shortly after the accident smelled liquor on petitioner's breath, and testified that petitioner's eyes were "bloodshot, watery, sort of a glassy appearance." The officer saw petitioner again at the hospital, within two hours of the accident. There he noticed similar symptoms of drunkenness. He thereupon informed petitioner "that he was under arrest and that he was entitled to the services of an attorney, and that he could remain silent, and that anything he told me would be used against him in evidence." ...

Although the facts which established probable cause to arrest in this case also suggested the required relevance and likely success of a test of petitioner's blood for alcohol, the question remains whether the arresting officer was permitted to draw these inferences himself, or was required instead to procure a warrant before proceeding with the test. Search warrants are ordinarily required for searches of dwellings, and, absent an emergency, no less could be required where intrusions of the human body are concerned. ... The importance of informed, detached and deliberate determinations of the issue whether or not to invade another's body in search of evidence of guilt is indisputable and great.

The officer in the present case, however, might reasonably have believed that he was confronted with an emergency, in which the delay necessary to obtain a warrant, under the circumstances, threatened "the destruction of evidence" ... . We are told that the percentage of alcohol in the blood begins to diminish shortly after drinking stops, as the body functions to eliminate it from the system. Particularly in a case such as this, where time had to be taken to bring the accused to a hospital and to investigate the scene of the accident, there was no time to seek out a magistrate and secure a warrant. ...

Finally, the records show that the test was performed in a reasonable manner. Petitioner's blood was taken by physician in a hospital environment according to accepted medical practices. We are thus not presented with the serious questions which would arise if a search involving use of a medical technique, even of the most rudimentary sort, were made by other than medical personnel or in other than a medical environment—for example, if it were administered by police in the privacy of the stationhouse. To tolerate searches under these conditions might be to invite an unjustified element of personal risk of infection and pain.

DNA Testing

Deoxyribonucleic acid (DNA) is a complex compound with two strands that spiral around one another, forming a double helix. Within the helix are molecules, called *nucleotide bases*, that connect the strands. There are four bases, identified by the letters A, T, G, and C. The A base of one strand attaches to the T base of its counterpart strand. In the same manner, the G base of one strand connects to the C base of the opposing strand. There are more than three billion base pairs in human DNA. However, only three million of these differ from person to person. The precise vertical ordering of these pairs determines a person's genetic code.

Through biological specimens, such as hair, blood, tissue, and semen, evidence from crime scenes can be compared with specimens from suspects. This testing is known as *DNA printing* or *genetic fingerprinting*. DNA printing compares the codes and determines if they are from the same individual. DNA testing is sophisticated and, if properly performed, nearly conclusively establishes identity.

DNA has proven to be an effective weapon for both prosecutors and defendants. In recent years, several convicted felons have used DNA testing to prove their innocence and secure their release. This has occurred, for example, in rape cases where blood and semen were used as prosecution evidence, but DNA testing was unavailable. After conviction, and from prison, these men used DNA testing to establish their innocence and set aside their verdicts.

DNA testing is not perfect. The testing method is sophisticated and errors can be made. For instance, methodology was hotly contested in the O.J. Simpson murder trial of 1995. Further, interpretations of test results differ. It is, therefore, imperative that a reliable laboratory do the testing. Further, in some cases, the defense and prosecution may have independent DNA testing conducted. In spite of the possibility of error (false positive and false negative findings), courts in many jurisdictions have held that DNA evidence is sufficiently reliable for admission into evidence.

The admissibility of DNA evidence in the California courts has, at the time of this writing, not yet been conclusively established. There are conflicting decisions among the courts of appeal, and the California Supreme Court has not yet rendered a definitive decision on the issue. The California Supreme Court has granted review of a number of court of appeal decisions involving the admissibility of DNA evidence,[15] and it is hoped that it will set the parameters for use of such evidence in the future.

Voice Tests

Compelling a suspect to speak for the purposes of audio identification is not violative of the Fifth Amendment's prohibition against compelled self-incrimination. This is because the purpose in compelling the statements is identification, not to secure testimony. Again, the voice is considered a physical characteristic that is readily observable to the ordinary person; accordingly, it is not a search under the Fourth Amendment to compel a suspect to speak.

Voice is also at issue whenever a party intends to introduce audio records that purport to be a particular individual's, such as the defendant. For example, assume John is charged with murdering Henry. The police have in their possession a tape from Henry's telephone answering machine. The tape contains a threat to Henry's life that the government claims was made by John. To prove that John made the threat, the prosecutor plans to introduce voice spectrographic identification evidence, also referred to as a **voiceprint.**

This test involves a comparison of the recording and a voice sample provided by the defendant. It compares the complex sound waves of the two for similarity. The accuracy of voice spectrographics is questionable, and thus this type of evidence is not universally accepted by courts. In some jurisdictions, admissibility is prohibited, whereas in others the decision is left to the trial judge. California is one of the states that have not accepted the admissibility of voiceprints as evidence in criminal trials.

Polygraph Tests

Polygraph testing, also known as lie detection testing, measures a subject's physical responses, such as heartbeat, blood pressure, and perspiration, during questioning. This is not a new concept. The Chinese monitored the heartbeat of suspects as long as 4,000 years ago. If a suspect's heartbeat increased during a response, he was presumed to have lied.[16]

Until recently, courts have held that the results of polygraph evidence are too unreliable to be admitted at trial, unless the parties have stipulated to admission. Today, however, a few jurisdictions permit the introduction of polygraph evidence if it is determined reliable. That is, polygraph evidence is not automatically excluded, but may be if found to be unreliable in a specific case.

California is one of the majority of jurisdictions in which polygraph evidence is inadmissible at trial except under the limited circumstance when both the prosecution and the defense stipulate to its admissibility. Absent a stipulation, polygraph evidence may not be offered by either the prosecution or the defense. Thus, a defendant who has "passed" a polygraph examination may not introduce evidence of that fact at trial. If a defendant is offered, and refuses, a polygraph test, that fact may not be introduced or commented on by the prosecution at trial.[17]

In addition to the issue of reliability, a Fifth Amendment self-incrimination issue surfaces when a prosecutor seeks an order requiring a defendant to undergo a polygraph examination. The Supreme Court has stated in dictum,[18] and the lower courts have similarly ruled directly, that lie detector tests involve communications and, accordingly, that the Fifth Amendment applies. Defendants may refuse to respond to questions when the answers may be incriminating, and *Miranda*-type warnings should be given before the test begins, assuming that custody exists.

Chain of Custody

To assure that physical evidence discovered during an investigation remains unchanged and is not confused with evidence from other investigations, police must maintain the **chain of custody**. The officer who discovered the evidence must mark it, and all subsequent contacts with the evidence, such as by forensics officers, must be recorded. This creates a record known as the chain of custody. Chain-of-custody records must be kept from the time the evidence is seized until the evidence is introduced at trial. Breaks in the chain of custody may result in exclusion of the evidence at trial.

In California, the effect of a break in the chain of custody on the admissibility of evidence is evaluated using the "reasonable certainty" standard enunciated by the California Supreme Court in *People v. Riser* (1956) 47 Cal.2d 566.

THE PEOPLE v. RICHARD G. RISER
47 Cal.2d 566 (Dec. 1956)

As a further error, defendant complains of the admission in evidence of a bottle and a glass bearing fingerprints testified to be the fingerprints of Richard Riser. Deputy Sheriff Lochry identified the bottle and glass as articles that he had taken from the Hilltop Café. When he arrived at the Café, early in the morning of July 12th, he found several bottles, glasses, and salt cellars on the bar. He dusted them for fingerprints, put them in a box, and locked the box in the sheriff's identification truck. About 4 or 5 A.M. he returned to the sheriff's office and put the articles in an open book case in an office that he shared with another police officer. This office was unlocked; it was flanked on one side by an office shared by two or three persons, and on the other side by a hall leading to a general office. According to Lochry, the evidence remained in the book case approximately four hours, until about 8:30 A.M., when it was removed and thereafter kept under lock and key or in the custody of specific persons.

Defendant contends that in view of these facts the prosecution failed to establish continuous possession, which is a necessary foundation for the admission of demonstrative evidence; that since someone could have altered the prints or imposed wholly new ones during the four hours the glass and bottle were left unguarded in the book case, the prosecution has not sufficiently identified the prints as those that existed when the articles were removed from the bar. Defendant would require the prosecution to negative all possibility of tampering.

Undoubtedly the party relying on an expert analysis of demonstrative evidence must show that it is in fact the evidence found at the scene of the crime, and that between receipt and analysis there has been no substitution or tampering, but it has never been suggested by the cases, what the practicalities of proof could not tolerate, that this burden is an absolute one requiring the party to negative all possibility of tampering.

The burden on the party offering the evidence is to show to the satisfaction of the trial court that, taking all the circumstances into account including the ease or difficulty with which the particular evidence could have been altered, it is reasonably certain that there was no alteration.

The requirement of reasonable certainty is not met when some vital link in the chain of possession is not accounted for, because then it is as likely as not that the evidence analyzed was not the evidence originally received. Left to such speculation the court must exclude the evidence. Conversely, when it is the barest speculation that there was tampering, it is proper to admit the evidence and let what doubt remains go to its weight. In the present case defendant did not point to any indication of actual tampering, did not show how fingerprints could have been forged, and did not establish that anyone who might have been interested in tampering with the prints knew that the bottles and glasses were in Deputy Sheriff Lochry's book case. There was no error in the court's ruling.

Key Terms

admission A statement made by a person, other than at his or her trial, which does not by itself acknowledge guilt of a crime, but which tends to prove guilt when considered with other evidence.

chain of custody A method of maintaining accountability for evidence whereby a record is made of all persons having possession of the evidence from the time of seizure by law enforcement personnel to use of the evidence at trial. Maintenance of the chain of custody assures that the evidence presented at trial is the same evidence originally seized by law enforcement personnel.

confession A statement made by a person, other than at his or her trial, in which he or she acknowledges guilt of a crime.

interrogation Questioning of a person suspected of committing a crime by law enforcement officials, for the purpose of eliciting incriminating information.

Kelly-Frye rule A rule of procedure in California pertaining to the admissibility of novel types of scientific evidence. Under the Kelly-Frye rule, new types of scientific evidence are admissible only if the techniques used are generally accepted in the applicable scientific community. This determination is usually made through the testimony of expert witnesses, who must be properly qualified to give an opinion on the subject. Also, the proponent of the evidence must demonstrate that correct scientific procedures were used in the particular case.

lineup An investigative technique in which a suspect is included in a group of people that is viewed by the victim or witness. The victim or witness is asked whether the perpetrator of the crime is in the group and, if so, to identify the perpetrator.

mug-shot files Files maintained by law enforcement agencies of photographs of persons who have been arrested and booked.

showup An investigative technique in which the victim or witness is asked to observe the suspect alone and then to indicate whether the suspect is the person who committed the crime under investigation.

simulated lineup A photograph of a lineup of individuals, which is shown to a victim or witness to determine whether the offender is among the persons photographed.

voiceprint An analysis of the complex sound waves of a person's voice for the purpose of comparing the voice with a voice on a recording, such as an answering-machine tape.

Presently, voiceprint evidence is inadmissible in a criminal trial because its reliability has not yet been sufficiently demonstrated.

Review Questions

1. List the rights included in the *Miranda* warnings. When must these rights be read to a suspect?

2. What happens if an officer fails to read a suspect his or her rights prior to obtaining a confession?

3. Briefly explain the exception to the *Miranda* warning requirement known as the "rescue doctrine."

4. If a suspect is read his or her *Miranda* rights and waives them, but then, after a period of interrogation, states that he or she does not wish to answer any more questions, must the police interrogation cease?

5. What legal principle was established by the United States Supreme Court in *Minnick v. Mississippi?*

6. What must law enforcement authorities do if they wish to engage in electronic surveillance under the authority of Chapter 1.4 of Title 15 of Part 1 of the California Penal Code (interception of wire, electronic digital pager, or electronic cellular telephone communications)?

7. What procedural step is required by Chapter 1.4 of Title 15 of Part 1 of the Penal Code before intercepted communications, or evidence derived therefrom, may be used in a trial, hearing, or other proceeding, other than a grand jury proceeding? What procedural right is granted to persons who may be affected by the use of such communications or derivative evidence in a trial, hearing, or proceeding?

8. Is a criminal suspect appearing in a lineup always entitled to have counsel present during the lineup? Briefly explain your answer.

9. What is a one-man showup?

10. What is the difference between a suspect's right to counsel at a lineup and at a photographic identification procedure?

11. Under California's Kelly-Frye rule, what standards must evidence involving new scientific techniques meet to be admissible in court?

12. Are the results of polygraph tests admissible as evidence in criminal trials in California?

Review Problems

1. While on patrol, officer Norman heard a scream from the backyard of a house. The officer proceeded to the back of the house where he observed two people, a badly beaten victim and a young man (Tom) standing over her. Shocked by the sight of the victim, the officer exclaimed, "What happened here?" Tom responded, "I killed her and threw the baseball bat over the fence." Officer Norman restrained the young man, called for an ambulance, and retrieved the bat. While waiting for the ambulance to arrive, officer Norman asked the young man what his motive was for injuring the woman. Tom explained his motive to the officer. The officer never mirandized Tom. A motion to suppress the statement, "I killed her and threw the baseball bat over the fence," as well as the statement explaining his motive, has been filed. Additionally, Tom claims that the bat should be excluded because it is a fruit of an illegal interrogation. What should be the outcome? Explain your answer.

2. Joe telephones a local train station and states that a bomb has been planted there and will explode unless he is paid $1 million by 5:00 P.M. that day. In subsequent telephone conversations, Joe and station officials agree that an official will meet Joe at an agreed

location at 4:00 P.M. to make the payment. At 4:00 P.M., Joe goes to the agreed location and is promptly arrested by the police. A police officer looks Joe in the eye and says, "Now, I want you to tell me where the bomb is. Then I want you to take me to the bomb and defuse it." Joe, his will to resist crushed by the arrest, tells the officer where the bomb is located, takes the officer to that location, and defuses the bomb while several police officers and station officials watch. Joe is charged with several offenses involving destructive devices. He files a motion under Penal Code § 1538.5 to suppress his statement telling the officer where the bomb was located, on the ground that he was not read his *Miranda* rights before the officer demanded that he reveal the location of the bomb. Joe also moves to suppress any evidence relating to his taking the officer to the location of the bomb and his defusing of the bomb, on the ground that these acts were the product of his statement informing the officer where the bomb was located. What do you think the result of Joe's motion will be? Explain your answer.

3. Richard is arrested as a suspect in a series of burglaries. He is taken to the police station where he is to be questioned about the burglaries by Detective Smith. Detective Smith reads Richard his *Miranda* rights, whereupon Richard tells Detective Smith that he is willing to talk and does not want a lawyer. During the questioning, Richard becomes uncomfortable and informs Detective Smith that he does not want to answer any further questions.

Later the same day, Detective Jones decides to question Richard about a recent homicide. The homicide is unrelated to the burglaries for which Richard was arrested. Detective Jones reads Richard his rights, and Richard again waives them. During the questioning by Detective Jones, Richard makes some incriminating statements. Richard is then charged with murder. He files a motion to suppress the statements he made to Detective Jones, on the ground that, when he was questioned by Detective Smith, he asserted the right to remain silent and therefore could not be questioned about any offense thereafter. What do you predict the result of Richard's motion will be? Explain your answer.

4. Officer Green obtains a court order authorizing interception of wire communications originating from the home telephone of Maxwell. Maxwell is suspected of operating a methamphetamine factory in the garage of his house. In order to install the wiretap, officer Green surreptitiously enters Maxwell's house while Maxwell is away and puts a miniature transmitter in the receiver of Maxwell's telephone. Officer Green then begins his electronic surveillance of Maxwell. In his seventy-two-hour status report to the court, officer Green tells the judge about his entry into Maxwell's home to place the miniature transmitter. What do you expect the judge's reaction will be?

5. Officer Day is participating in a search in a remote mountainous region for Barney Barnowitz, who has failed to return home from a camping trip. Officer Day observes a gaping hole in the guardrail along the side of a mountain road. Peering down, he observes Barney's car at the bottom of a ravine. Officer Day immediately radios for assistance and then climbs to the bottom of the ravine, where he observes Barney, still alive and conscious, pinned inside his car. An open bottle of whiskey is on the floor of the car and Barney smells of alcohol. Officer Day suspects that Barney has been driving under the influence of alcohol. Knowing that it may be hours before Barney can be transported to a hospital, officer Day decides to take a blood sample himself. He takes out his pocket knife, opens it, and, in spite of Barney's vehement objections, cuts Barney's finger, letting the blood drip into a small vial. Barney screams in pain when officer Day cuts his finger. The cut later becomes infected. The blood analysis, done later at a laboratory, reveals that Barney's blood-alcohol content at the time officer Day removed the blood was 0.2 percent, far in excess of the legal rate for intoxication. Barney is later charged with drunk driving. He moves to suppress the results of the blood-alcohol test. What do you think the result of Barney's motion will be? Explain your answer.

6. Zeb has been arrested for kidnapping. Fortunately, the victim was found and rescued by police when the kidnapper was away from the premises where the victim was being kept. The kidnapper had communicated his ransom demands by means of an audiotape. Zeb,

with his attorney present, states that he would like to take a polygraph test. The police administer a polygraph test to him during which he denies committing the kidnapping. The test is tape-recorded with Zeb's consent. Analysis of the polygraph test results by an expert indicates that Zeb was lying. The police then take the tape containing the ransom demands and the tape recording of Zeb's polygraph answers and conduct a voiceprint analysis. The voiceprint analysis indicates that the voice on the ransom tape is Zeb's. At Zeb's trial for the kidnapping, the prosecutor seeks to introduce both the results of Zeb's polygraph test and the results of the voiceprint analysis. Zeb's attorney objects to the admission of either into evidence. How should the judge rule regarding the admissibility of this evidence?

Notes

1 *Brown v. Mississippi,* 295 U.S. 278 (1936).

2 *New York v. Quarles,* 467 U.S. 649 (1984).

3 *Illinois v. Perkins,* 496 U.S. 292 (1990).

4 *Massiah v. United States,* 377 U.S. 201 (1964).

5 *Pennsylvania v. Bruder,* 488 U.S. 9 (1988).

6 *Oregon v. Haas,* 420 U.S. 714 (1975).

7 18 U.S.C. § 2510 *et seq.*

8 2 Witkin, *California Evidence,* § 1337 (3d ed., Bancroft-Whitney 1986).

9 *Schmerber v. California,* 384 U.S. 757 (1966).

10 2 Witkin, *California Evidence, supra* note 8, at § 1344.

11 Braun, "Quantitative Analysis and the Law: Probability Theory as a Tool of Evidence in Criminal Trials," 1982 *Utah L. Rev.* 41, 57 n.82.

12 *See, e.g., People v. Corral* (1964) 224 Cal.App.2d 300.

13 *See People v. Atwood* (1963) 223 Cal.App.2d 316 (palmprints); *People v. Corral, supra* note 12 (footprints).

14 *People v. Trotman* (1989) 214 Cal.App.3d 430; *People v. Deltoro* (1989) 214 Cal.App.3d 1417.

15 *See, e.g., People v. Burks* (1995) 37 Cal.App.4th 652; *People v. Venegas* (1995) 35 Cal.App.4th 1258; *People v. Marlow* (1995) 34 Cal.App.4th 460.

16 Morland, *An Outline of Scientific Criminology* 59–60 (2d ed. 1971).

17 Cal. Evid. Code § 351.1.

18 *Schmerber v. California,* 384 U.S. 757, 764 (1966).

CHAPTER 16

The Pretrial Process

OUTLINE

Introduction

In this and the following three chapters, we will examine the progress of a criminal case in the California judicial system. This chapter discusses the criminal case from before arrest to before trial. Chapter 17 examines the trial of the case. Chapter 18 discusses sentencing, and Chapter 19 covers postconviction remedies, such as appeal.

§ 16.1 Discovery and Investigation of Criminal Activity

Law enforcement authorities may learn of criminal activity in a number of ways. For example, a crime may be committed in the presence of an officer, or may be reported to an officer or the police department by a private citizen. Crimes committed in the presence of an officer and many crimes reported to the police by private citizens result in the immediate arrest of a suspect or suspects. In other cases, the perpetrator is unknown to the police, so investigation begins.

Sometimes police suspect criminal activity by a person, but determine that further investigation is warranted before any action is taken against the person. In all cases, police attempt to gather sufficient evidence to establish the identity of the perpetrator of the offense, together with sufficient evidence to convict the perpetrator if and when the case goes to trial.

§ 16.2 Arrest

Whether a crime is one requiring an immediate police response or one warranting a preliminary police investigation, the ultimate result, generally, is that a suspect is arrested. As was discussed in Chapter 14, an arrest may be made without an arrest warrant in some situations. Other situations require the issuance of an arrest warrant by a magistrate (usually a municipal or superior court judge). As an alternative to an arrest warrant, a prosecutor may request a magistrate to issue a summons to a suspect, commanding the suspect to appear before the magistrate in certain types of cases. (*See* Penal Code § 813.)

Penal Code §§ 853.5 through 853.85 prescribe special procedures applicable to infraction and misdemeanor cases. Although there are exceptions, the general rule in infraction cases is that the arresting officer may require only that the person present his or her driver's license or other satisfactory evidence of identity and sign a written **promise to appear** before a magistrate.

A person arrested for a misdemeanor must be released unless one of the circumstances enumerated in Penal Code § 853.6 exists (*see* Penal Code § 853.6), in which case the arresting officer may either release the person or take the person into custody. A person released after arrest for a misdemeanor must be given a **notice to appear** by the arresting officer. The notice to appear, frequently referred to as a *citation*, must contain the name and address of the person, the offense charged, and the time and place at which the person must appear in court. The arresting officer may book the arrested person before release or may indicate on the citation that the person must appear at the arresting agency for **booking** or fingerprinting before the court appearance date. *Booking* is defined in Penal Code § 7(21) as "the recordation of an arrest in official police records, and the taking by police of fingerprints and photographs of the person arrested, or any of these acts following an arrest." When the individual appears in court, he or she must provide satisfactory evidence to the court that he or she has been booked or fingerprinted, as required by the notice to appear.

If the suspect is not released, he or she is held in custody until being brought before a magistrate. The suspect is booked, searched (sometimes deloused and showered), and held in jail.

A person being held in custody has certain rights. Penal Code § 825(b) provides that, at the request of the prisoner, he or she may be visited by an attorney or a relative. Under Penal Code § 851.5, a prisoner, immediately upon being booked and, except where physically impossible, no later than three hours after arrest, has the right to make three completed telephone calls. The calls may be made to the following categories of persons: an attorney, a bail bondsman, and a relative or other person.

§ 16.3 The Complaint

Although law enforcement is the responsibility of the executive branch of the government, the judicial branch becomes involved very early in the processing of a criminal case. This involvement is brought about by the filing of a **complaint with a magistrate**. Justices of the California Supreme Court, justices of the courts of appeal, and judges of the superior and municipal courts are magistrates. In actual practice, complaints are usually filed with judges of the municipal courts.

No particular form is prescribed by law for the complaint. The complaint must, however, be made in writing and under oath. Also, it must contain sufficient factual information from which the reviewing magistrate can determine whether an offense has been committed and whether there is reasonable ground to believe that the defendant committed the offense.

In both felony and misdemeanor cases, the complaint is the document used by law enforcement authorities to apply for an arrest warrant. Naturally, this function of the complaint is needed only if the defendant has not already been lawfully arrested without a warrant.

Before an accused may be brought to trial, he or she must be formally charged with an offense. A formal charge is made by filing an **accusatory pleading** with the court in which the defendant may be tried. Recall from Chapter 1 that misdemeanors are tried in the municipal courts, whereas felonies are tried in the superior courts. Remember also that the complaint is usually filed in the municipal court. In misdemeanor cases, the complaint constitutes the accusatory pleading, and the defendant is formally charged at the time a properly drawn complaint is filed in the municipal court. No further accusatory pleading is required to bring a defendant to trial on a misdemeanor charge in the municipal court. In felony cases, the complaint serves as the application for an arrest warrant, but does not constitute the accusatory pleading. A defendant may be tried for a felony only if he or she has been formally charged by indictment or information filed in the superior court. These procedures are discussed later in this chapter.

In misdemeanor cases in which the defendant has been arrested without a warrant and issued a notice to appear, and in infraction cases in which the defendant has signed a written promise to appear, the notice or promise to appear serves as the complaint once it has been filed with the municipal court. However, because the notice is not sworn by the arresting officer and does not contain any factual allegations, the defendant is limited, under Penal Code § 853.9, to pleading either guilty or nolo contendere (no contest) to the charged offense. If the defendant pleads other than guilty or nolo contendere; or if the defendant violates his or her promise to appear; or if the defendant does not deposit lawful bail, the prosecuting attorney must file a formal complaint charging the defendant with the offense.

Finally, in warrantless arrest situations in which the arrestee has been taken into custody, a complaint will not have been filed in the municipal court before the arrest. Penal Code § 849(a) provides that in such a situation, a complaint is to be filed against the person when he or she is brought before a magistrate at his or her initial appearance, discussed in § 16.4.

§ 16.4 Initial Appearance

A defendant in custody following arrest must be promptly brought before a magistrate. The purposes of this **initial appearance** requirement are protection of the defendant's rights, specifically to prevent unwarranted police interrogation; to make it possible for the defendant to be promptly advised of his or her right to counsel; to enable the defendant to obtain bail; and to have the issue of probable cause for his or her arrest determined by a judicial officer.[1] The requirement is imposed by Penal Code § 825, which also establishes a dual timeliness standard. First, it requires that the defendant be taken before a magistrate "without unnecessary delay." Second, it states that, in any event, the defendant *must* be taken before a magistrate within forty-eight hours after his or her arrest, excluding Sundays and holidays. Judicial decisions have made it clear that bringing a defendant before a magistrate within the forty-eight-hour period does not necessarily comply with the "without unnecessary delay" requirement. It is possible for unnecessary delay to exist even within the forty-eight hours after a defendant's arrest.

The time requirements imposed by § 825 do not apply in misdemeanor cases in which the defendant has been released upon signing a notice to appear, because the defendant is not being held in custody.

Municipal Court Arraignment   **Arraignment** means a formal reading of the charges to the defendant. The magistrate then asks the defendant how he or she pleads to the charges. An arraignment of the defendant occurs during the initial appearance. If the defendant is charged with a misdemeanor, the arraignment during the initial appearance is the only arraignment he or she will have. If the defendant in a misdemeanor case pleads guilty or nolo contendere before the magistrate, the court must pronounce judgment not less than six hours nor more than five days after the plea. (*See* Penal Code §§ 1445, 1449.)

If the defendant is charged with a felony and pleads guilty or nolo contendere before the magistrate, the magistrate may accept the plea, but only if the defendant is represented by counsel.[2] In such a case, the magistrate will then certify the case to the superior court and set a time for pronouncement of judgment in the superior court. If a felony defendant is not represented by counsel, or enters a plea other than guilty or nolo contendere, the case will continue to proceed as a normal felony prosecution.

Probable Cause Determination in Misdemeanor Case   If a defendant who is charged with a misdemeanor pleads not guilty during the municipal court arraignment, the magistrate must then determine whether probable cause exists to believe that a public offense has been committed and that the defendant is guilty of the offense. In making this determination, the magistrate may rely on the arrest warrant, the complaint, any documents appended thereto, and documents of similar reliability. If the magistrate determines that probable cause exists to believe that an offense has been committed and that the defendant committed it, he or she then sets the case for trial. If the magistrate determines that probable cause does not exist, he or she must dismiss the complaint and discharge the defendant.[3]

Scheduling Preliminary Examination in Felony Case If a defendant who is charged with a felony pleads other than guilty or nolo contendere, the magistrate schedules a hearing known as a **preliminary examination.** The magistrate must set the preliminary examination no less than two days nor more than ten court days after the defendant is arraigned or pleads in the municipal court, whichever is later.[4] The times for arraignment and plea can be different because a defendant must, on request, be given a reasonable time after arraignment to enter a plea.

Informing Defendant of Right to Counsel In all felony and misdemeanor cases, the magistrate must inform the defendant that he or she has a right to be represented by counsel at all stages of the criminal prosecution.[5] The magistrate is required to ask the defendant if he or she desires to be represented by counsel and, if so, whether he or she is financially able to employ counsel. If the defendant indicates that he or she wishes to be represented by counsel, and is financially able to employ counsel, he or she must be given a reasonable time to send for his or her attorney. If the defendant wishes to be represented by counsel, but is not financially able to retain counsel, the magistrate must appoint counsel to represent him or her.

Determining Whether to Release Defendant from Custody Another matter addressed at the initial appearance is whether a defendant in custody should be released pending further proceedings in the case. This subject is addressed in § 16.5.

§ 16.5 Pretrial Release and Detention

In many instances, defendants are released from custody during the pendency of criminal proceedings. Release is accomplished by admission to bail or the defendant's own recognizance.

Release by Admission to Bail Penal Code § 1268 states: "Admission to bail is the order of a competent Court or magistrate that the defendant be discharged from actual custody upon bail." A defendant **admitted to bail** will be discharged from custody upon the taking of **bail**, which is the provision of an undertaking by a surety or a deposit by the defendant that will be forfeited if the defendant fails to appear in court when required. Bail is considered and granted separately for each stage of a criminal proceeding.

The taking of bail by means of an undertaking involves the use of sureties. Sureties may be private persons or bail bond companies (bail bondsmen). The defendant enters into a contract with the surety pursuant to which the surety files a **bail bond** with the court. The bond is a promise to pay the amount of bail to the court if the defendant fails to appear at the proceeding to which the bail applies. Commercial sureties require that the defendant pay a fee for the bond. The fee is usually set as a percentage of the amount of the bail.

As an alternative to the provision of an undertaking by a surety on behalf of a defendant, the defendant or any other person may deposit a sum of money equal to the amount of the bail with the court.

A criminal defendant has a right to be released on bail prior to conviction except in the following situations enumerated in article I, § 12, of the California Constitution: (1) capital crimes; (2) felony offenses involving acts of violence on another person when there is a substantial likelihood that the defendant's release would result in great bodily harm to others; and (3) felony offenses when the defendant has threatened another with great bodily harm and there is a substantial likelihood that he or she would carry out the threat if released.

Under Penal Code § 1272, bail after conviction pending imposition of judgment is a matter of right if the defendant has been convicted of a misdemeanor. After imposition of judgment, pending appeal, bail is a matter of right if the defendant has been sentenced to imprisonment for a misdemeanor or has only been sentenced to a fine for either a felony or a misdemeanor. In other cases, bail is a matter within the discretion of the court.

When a magistrate issues an arrest warrant for a defendant, the amount of bail is specified by the magistrate in the warrant. If a defendant is arrested without a warrant, the magistrate sets the defendant's bail at his or her initial appearance. Once the defendant posts the bail with the court, by undertaking or deposit, he or she is released from custody.

 Release on Defendant's Own Recognizance An *own recognizance release* from custody, also referred to as an O.R. release, is a release without bail upon the defendant's promise to appear in court at the next scheduled appearance. In felony cases, other than those for which bail may not be granted, an O.R. release is a matter of discretion with the court. In misdemeanor cases, a defendant is entitled to an O.R. release unless the court makes a finding that an O.R. release will compromise public safety or will not reasonably assure the appearance of the defendant as required. If the court makes such a finding, it may release the defendant only upon setting bail. (*See* Penal Code § 1270.)

 The Eighth Amendment to the United States Constitution states that "excessive bail shall not be required." The applicability of the Eighth Amendment to the states through the Fourteenth Amendment Due Process Clause has not been definitively determined by the United States Supreme Court. California has its own constitutional requirement in article I, § 12, of the California Constitution, which prohibits imposition of "excessive" bail. Imposition of an amount of bail in excess of the amount necessary to assure the presence of the defendant in court is excessive. The courts are directed to consider certain criteria when fixing the amount of bail: the protection of the public, the seriousness of the offense charged, the previous criminal record of the defendant, and the probability of his or her appearing at trial or hearing of the case. (*See* Penal Code § 1275.)

Under Penal Code § 1305, a court must declare bail forfeited if the defendant fails to appear at the court proceeding for which release on bail was granted. In all cases of nonappearance by a defendant released on bail or on his or her own recognizance, the court may order the defendant to be arrested and recommitted to the custody of the law enforcement agency to which he or she was committed prior to release from custody.[6]

§ 16.6 Preliminary Examination

In a felony case, the complaint does not serve as the formal charge, which is also known as the **accusatory pleading.** If the defendant pleads not guilty or not guilty by reason of insanity at the initial appearance, the district attorney must then initiate procedures to formally charge the defendant. The formal charge may be by indictment or information, both of which are discussed later in this chapter. Under California law, if the prosecution elects to charge the defendant by information rather than by indictment, a **preliminary examination** must first be conducted. Generally, the preliminary examination must be held not less than two days (excluding Sundays and holidays) and not more than ten court days after the defendant is arraigned or enters a plea at the initial appearance, whichever is later.

The preliminary examination is a hearing held before a magistrate in the municipal court. It is generally open to the public, except under certain circumstances specified in the Penal Code. Among those circumstances are: protection of the right of the defendant to receive a fair trial, protection of the interests of minor victims of sexual offenses, and protection of the safety of witnesses.

The primary purpose of the preliminary examination is to permit a neutral third party, the magistrate, to examine the evidence and determine whether probable cause exists to believe that a crime has been committed and that the defendant committed it. Recall that, in a misdemeanor case, this determination is made by the magistrate at the initial appearance. The preliminary examination is an adversarial hearing at which the evidence is considered by the magistrate in greater depth than at the initial appearance. Evidence, including the testimony of witnesses, is presented by the prosecution. The defendant is entitled to be present at the preliminary examination and to be represented by counsel. The defendant may present his or her own witnesses and other evidence. In addition, the defendant, or his or her attorney, may cross-examine prosecution witnesses.[7]

Penal Code § 861 requires that the preliminary examination be completed in one session unless the magistrate postpones it for good cause. The prosecution must present evidence of every element of the charged offense. However, it is not necessary that the prosecution present the quantum of evidence required to prove the defendant guilty beyond a reasonable doubt at trial. Rather, the prosecution must establish that there is probable cause to believe that a crime has been committed and that the defendant committed it. *Probable cause* may be defined as "a state of facts as would lead a man of ordinary caution or prudence to believe, and conscientiously entertain a strong suspicion of the guilt of the accused."[8] If the prosecution fails to meet its burden, the magistrate must order the complaint dismissed and the defendant discharged. (*See* Penal Code § 871.) If the prosecution does establish probable cause to believe that a crime has been committed and that the defendant committed it, the magistrate is to order that the defendant be held to answer. (*See* Penal Code § 872.) The term **held to answer** means that the magistrate orders the defendant to respond to a formal accusatory pleading, which will be an information filed by the prosecutor.

If the magistrate determines that sufficient evidence has been presented at the preliminary examination to hold the defendant to answer, the magistrate must address the matter of custody of the defendant. The defendant may have been released on bail at the initial appearance, but that bail ceases to be applicable once the preliminary examination is conducted. The question of release or custody must be addressed anew. However, the standards for releasing a defendant on bail or his or her own recognizance are the same after a preliminary examination as they are at an initial appearance.

Delivery of a defendant into the custody of a law enforcement agency is known as **commitment** of the defendant. If the defendant is held to answer, the magistrate is required by Penal Code § 877 to commit the defendant into the custody of the sheriff. If the defendant has been admitted to bail, custody will, of course, cease once the defendant posts the bail.

If the complaint charges the defendant with more than one offense, the magistrate may find that the prosecution has presented sufficient evidence of some offenses but not of others. In such instances, the magistrate may dismiss the charges insufficiently established and hold the defendant to answer on the others.

§ 16.7 The Formal Charge

As stated earlier, the complaint serves as the formal charge, also known as the accusatory pleading, in a misdemeanor case. In a felony case, the complaint does not formally charge the defendant. It serves as the basis for issuance of an arrest warrant and for conduct of the initial appearance in the municipal court, including arraignment of the defendant before the magistrate. Before a defendant may be tried for a felony in the California courts, though, he or she must be formally charged by indictment or information. An **indictment** is a charge issued by a grand jury and filed with the superior court. An **information** is a charge issued by the district attorney and filed with the superior court. The indictment or information causes a felony defendant's case to move from the municipal court into the superior court. (Recall that only the superior court has jurisdiction to try felony cases.)

Indictment and Grand Jury

In early American history, **grand juries** were used to guard against unfair and arbitrary government prosecutions. The framers of the United States Constitution believed grand jury review so important that they stated in the Fifth Amendment: "[N]o person shall be held to answer for a capital, or otherwise infamous, crime, unless on a presentment or indictment of a Grand Jury." Based on this language of the Fifth Amendment, a defendant may not be prosecuted for a "capital" or "infamous" crime in the federal courts unless he or she has first been indicted by a grand jury. A *capital crime* is a crime punishable by death; an *infamous crime* is one punishable by one year or longer in prison.[9]

The United States Supreme Court has held that grand jury review is not a fundamental right. Therefore, the Fifth Amendment requirement for indictment is not applicable to the states. California, for example, does not mirror the federal requirement that persons be charged with capital or infamous crimes by means of grand jury indictment. However, grand juries are available in California for this purpose. California Constitution article I, § 23, provides that "[o]ne or more grand juries shall be drawn and summoned at least once a year in each county." Penal Code § 888 states that: "A grand jury is a body of the required number of persons returned from the citizens of the county before a court of competent jurisdiction, and sworn to inquire of public offenses committed or triable within the county." Presently, Los Angeles County has a grand jury consisting of twenty-three persons; other counties have grand juries consisting of nineteen persons.

The grand jury has the power of independent investigation, which means that it may investigate offenses that come to its attention by any means. However, cases prosecuted by grand jury indictment are almost always brought before the grand jury by the district attorney. Cases in which prosecutors elect grand jury indictment rather than charging by information tend to be murder and sex crimes. The main factors affecting the decision to utilize the grand jury in individual cases include: (1) high public interest in a case; (2) the fact that a preliminary examination takes more time than a grand jury hearing; (3) the need to call children or timid witnesses who would be subject to cross-examination at a preliminary examination; (4) the existence of a weak or doubtful case which the district attorney wishes to test; (5) the fact that a case involves malfeasance in office; and (6) the fact that witnesses are in prison.[10]

The framers of the United States Constitution, in including the requirement for grand jury indictment in cases involving capital and infamous crimes, intended primarily to protect innocent persons from unwarranted prosecutions. Because grand jury proceedings are closed, individuals investigated but not charged are not subjected to the public humiliation and damage to reputation that often results from a more public investigation. In California, the grand jury serves these purposes.

A grand jury proceeding is a hearing at which the testimony of witnesses and other forms of evidence, such as writings and other physical evidence, are presented by a prosecuting attorney from the district attorney's office. Witnesses may be subpoenaed to appear and must testify under oath. Witnesses do not have the right to have counsel with them in the hearing room. Unlike in some states and the federal system, a California grand jury may receive and consider only evidence that would be admissible at trial.[11] Thus, evidence not authorized by the Evidence Code and illegally obtained evidence subject to the exclusionary rule may not be presented to or considered by the grand jury.

A witness before a grand jury possesses the right against self-incrimination. Under Penal Code § 939.3, if a witness refuses to answer a question or produce other evidence on the ground that he or she may thereby be incriminated, proceedings may be had under Penal Code § 1324. Section 1324, as discussed in Chapter 11, involves granting immunity to a witness if he or she is required to present testimony or other evidence that could tend to incriminate him or her.

The defendant who is the subject of the grand jury proceeding may be called as a witness by the prosecuting attorney. As with other witnesses before a grand jury, the defendant does not have the right to be represented by counsel at the grand jury hearing. Aside from the fact that he or she might be called by the prosecutor as a witness before the grand jury, the defendant is not entitled to appear before the grand jury or even to be informed that the grand jury is considering his case. The rationale behind this principle is that the grand jury is performing an investigatory, not a judicial, function. The grand jury proceeding is not a trial of the defendant and the rights of the defendant applicable to trial do not apply to grand jury hearings. The prosecuting attorney conducting the grand jury hearing is not required to present evidence favorable to the defendant (exculpatory evidence) on his or her own initiative. However, the grand jury has the power to require the prosecutor to present exculpatory evidence if it has reason to believe that such evidence exists.

As previously mentioned, grand jury proceedings are made secret by statute. Penal Code § 939 generally limits presence at grand jury proceedings to the members of the grand jury and witnesses who are called to testify. Certain other categories of persons whose presence is necessitated by the nature of the proceedings may also be present during the taking of testimony. No person, other than members of the grand jury, may be present during the deliberations of the grand jury after presentation of the evidence. Penal Code § 924.2 provides, in part, that "[e]ach grand juror shall keep secret whatever he himself or any other grand juror has said, or in what manner he or any other grand juror has voted on a matter before them."

After presentation of the evidence by the prosecuting attorney, and after hearing any other evidence compelled by the grand jury, the grand jurors deliberate and then vote on the question of indictment. Penal Code § 889 defines an *indictment* as "an accusation in writing, presented by the grand jury to a competent court, charging a person with a public offense." If the grand jury votes to indict a person, it is said to *find an indictment.* A grand jury must indict if it finds that there is probable cause to believe that a crime has been committed and that the person to be indicted committed it.

When an indictment is found, it is presented by the foreman of the grand jury, in the grand jury's presence, to the superior court, and is filed with the clerk of court. This procedure is known as *presentment of the indictment.*

An indictment may contain accusations of more than one offense against the defendant. Each accusation of an offense is stated in a separate count of the indictment.

Whenever a grand jury is investigating a criminal offense, the grand jury must appoint a stenographic reporter to report all testimony taken. The stenographic record must be transcribed by the reporter in cases in which an indictment is found, and a copy given to the defendant for use in the preparation of his or her defense.[12]

Grand jury proceedings are usually convened by the district attorney, are conducted by prosecuting attorneys, and are not required to hear evidence for the defendant. Furthermore, the defendant has no right to appear or present evidence on his or her behalf. Because of these facts, the grand jury system has been criticized as being too heavily weighted in favor of the prosecution. Despite such criticism, however, the grand jury system continues to be an important part of the criminal justice system in California, as well as in the federal system and the criminal justice systems of other states.

Information

The district attorney may elect to charge a defendant in a felony case by information rather than by indictment. In fact, most felony cases in the California courts are prosecuted pursuant to informations rather than indictments.

We have already considered the preliminary examination. A preliminary examination is a prerequisite to charging a defendant by information. The preliminary examination theoretically serves a purpose similar to that of a grand jury, in that it permits a review of the case by a person (the magistrate) outside of the law enforcement system and a determination by that person of whether probable cause exists to believe that a crime has been committed and that the defendant committed it. In practice, as opposed to theory, the preliminary examination affords the defendant a more neutral review of the case than does a grand jury proceeding because, as noted, a grand jury proceeding is controlled by the prosecutor and the defendant has no right to present evidence on her own behalf.

 If the magistrate at the preliminary examination finds that there is probable cause to believe that a crime has been committed and that the defendant committed it, he or she holds the defendant to answer and commits the defendant to the custody of the sheriff until the defendant posts bail, or until trial if the offense is one for which bail is not authorized. No later than fifteen days after commitment of the defendant, the district attorney must file an information in the superior court charging the defendant with either the offense or offenses named in the order of commitment or any offense or offenses shown by the evidence taken before the magistrate to have been committed. (*See* Penal Code § 739.) The fifteen-day period for the filing of the information is strictly enforced. Penal Code § 1382(a) provides that a criminal case must be dismissed when a person has been held to answer for a public offense but an information has not been filed within fifteen days thereafter, "unless good cause to the contrary is shown."

Challenging Accusatory Pleadings

 A defendant may challenge defects in an indictment or information by means of a motion to set aside (*see* Penal Code § 995) or a demurrer (*see* Penal Code § 1002 *et seq.*).

Motion to Set Aside

A **motion to set aside** an indictment may be brought on the grounds that the grand jury was illegally constituted or conducted, or that the defendant was indicted without probable cause. A motion to set aside an information may allege that, before the filing of the information, the defendant was not legally committed by a magistrate (i.e., that there was a defect in the preliminary examination), or that the defendant was committed without probable cause.

A defendant must bring a motion to set aside an indictment or information under Penal Code § 995 prior to trial. If the defendant brings a timely motion under § 995, and the motion is granted, the court must order the defendant discharged from custody, if he or she is in custody, or the defendant's bail exonerated, if he or she has posted bail, unless the court orders that the case be resubmitted to a grand jury or that a new information be filed.[13] A defendant is not put in jeopardy by the filing of an indictment or an information, and an order setting aside an indictment or information is not a bar to future prosecution of the defendant for the same offense.[14]

Demurrer

Another means of challenging an indictment or information is the **demurrer**. (*See* Penal Code § 1004.) In contrast to a motion to set aside, which challenges the proceedings that produced an indictment or information, a demurrer challenges the form of the indictment or information itself. A demurrer is said to be limited to challenging errors that "appear on the face" of the indictment or information; the defect must be apparent from reading the indictment or information without the need for reference to the proceedings that produced the accusatory pleading. For example, an indictment or information would be subject to demurrer if it charged the defendant with acts that do not constitute a crime, or if the facts stated in the indictment or information revealed the existence of a defense such as expiration of the statute of limitations.

A demurrer generally must be made before the defendant enters a plea. If the court sustains (grants) the demurrer, and if the defect in the accusatory pleading can be remedied, the court must permit the prosecution to amend the indictment or information within a period not exceeding ten days. If the defect cannot be remedied by amendment, the court may direct the filing of a new information or resubmission of the case to a grand jury.[15] If the demurrer is sustained and the defect in the accusatory pleading cannot be remedied, the criminal action must be dismissed. The same holds true if the prosecution has been given time to amend the accusatory pleading and has failed to do so.[16]

§ 16.8 Arraignment

Once an accusatory pleading has been filed with the court, Penal Code § 976 requires that the defendant be arraigned before that court.

Arraignment and Plea **Arraignment** in the superior court consists of reading the accusatory pleading to the defendant, providing the defendant with a true copy of the pleading, and asking the defendant how he or she pleads in response to the charge or charges in the accusatory pleading.[17]

In California, a defendant may enter the following **pleas** to a criminal charge: (1) guilty, (2) not guilty, (3) former judgment of conviction or acquittal, (4) once in jeopardy, (5) not guilty by reason of insanity, and (6) nolo contendere.[18]

A plea of guilty is authorized by Penal Code § 1016(1). A defendant who pleads guilty is deemed to admit every element of the charged offense, and no other proof of the offense is required. A guilty plea is also a waiver of any defects in the accusatory pleading which could have been raised by demurrer. A guilty plea is equivalent to a verdict of guilty and results in conviction of the defendant. No trial is required.

Because of these consequences of a guilty plea, a court may not accept such a plea unless there is an affirmative showing by the defendant that the guilty plea is knowing and voluntary. This requirement was made a matter of federal constitutional law by the United States Supreme Court in *Boykin v. Alabama*, 395 U.S. 238 (1969). In *Boykin*, the United States Supreme Court held that the record must show that a defendant entering a guilty plea has knowingly and voluntarily waived his or her constitutional rights against self-incrimination, to trial by jury, and to confront adverse witnesses. In the same year, the California Supreme Court decided *In re Tahl* (1969) 1 Cal.3d 122. In that case, the California Supreme Court, applying the requirement set forth in *Boykin*, held that the record must show that the court explained to the defendant that, in pleading guilty, he or she is waiving the three constitutional rights; and that the defendant, after receiving the explanation, waived the rights.

Later court decisions in California have developed a rule that before a court may accept a plea of guilty, it must advise the defendant of the three constitutional rights and obtain express waivers of those rights. As part of this process, the court must explain to the defendant the nature of the charges against him or her and the potential direct consequences of a plea of guilty to the charged offense, such as the range of possible sentences.[19]

In contrast to a plea of guilty, a plea of not guilty, authorized by Penal Code § 1016(2), puts in issue every material allegation of the accusatory pleading which relates to guilt or innocence of the charged offense.[20] A not guilty plea places the burden on the prosecution to prove every element of the charged offense at trial beyond a reasonable doubt.

A plea of **nolo contendere**, authorized by Penal Code § 1016(3), means that the defendant does not contest the accusatory pleading. In effect, a plea of nolo contendere informs the court that the defendant, though not admitting guilt, does not intend to defend against the charge or charges in the accusatory pleading. A plea of nolo contendere is treated by the courts in the same manner as a plea of guilty, so it cannot be accepted unless the requirements applicable to acceptance of a guilty plea are met. If accepted, the plea results in conviction of the defendant. One limited advantage of a plea of nolo contendere over a plea of guilty has to do with misdemeanor cases. In such cases, a plea of guilty may be used as an admission against the defendant in a later civil suit arising out of the acts or omissions constituting the offense, whereas a plea of nolo contendere may not be so used. This limitation on use of a nolo contendere plea does not apply in felony cases.[21]

Pleas of former judgment of conviction or acquittal of the offense charged and once in jeopardy, authorized by Penal Code §§ 1016(4) and 1016(5) respectively, assert the bar of double jeopardy to prosecution for the charged offense. (The principles pertaining to the constitutional right against double jeopardy are discussed in Chapter 11.)

A plea of not guilty by reason of insanity, authorized by Penal Code § 1016(6), alleges that the defendant is not guilty of the crime charged because he was insane at the time he is alleged to have committed the offense. This plea was discussed in Chapter 10. As was stated in that chapter, if the defendant merely pleads not guilty, the issue of the defendant's sanity is not raised, and the defendant is conclusively presumed to have been sane at the time of commission of the offense. A not guilty plea by the defendant requires the prosecution to prove every element of the offense beyond a reasonable doubt. If the defendant pleads not guilty by reason of insanity, he admits commission of the offense charged. The defendant is tried on the issue of sanity alone and, if he is found to have been sane, judgment of conviction is entered without any trial on the issue of guilt.

Defendants are permitted to "double plead," i.e., to plead both not guilty and not guilty by reason of insanity. In this situation, the defendant is first tried on the not guilty plea. If the defendant is found guilty of the offense, the question of her sanity at the time of commission of the offense is then tried. If the defendant is found to have been sane, her conviction stands. If the defendant is found to have been insane, she will be found not guilty by reason of insanity.

Plea Bargaining Not surprisingly, most defendants are not interested in acquiescing in criminal proceedings against them by simply pleading guilty to the offense or offenses charged in the accusatory pleading. Many defendants do, however, plead guilty as the result of a process known as **plea bargaining**. In fact, although statistics vary, it is widely accepted that approximately 90 percent of all felony cases in the United States are disposed of by pleas of guilty. The number is probably higher for misdemeanors. Plea bargaining is a procedure through which the defendant and the prosecutor enter into an agreement that the prosecutor will dismiss a more serious charge if the defendant will plead guilty to a lesser charge, or that the defendant will receive a sentence no more severe than specified in the agreement if the defendant will plead guilty to the charged offense.

Although the general public appears to disfavor plea bargaining, there is no question but that plea bargaining is essential to the efficient functioning of the criminal justice system. Warren Burger, past Chief Justice of the United States Supreme Court, estimated that judicial resources in the United States would have to be doubled if only 20 percent of the criminal cases went to trial.[22] This conclusion was in large part a matter of simple mathematics and has been criticized, but plea bargaining is nonetheless an important part of the criminal justice system. It is so important that the United States Supreme Court has stated that it "is not only an essential part of the process but a highly desirable part."[23]

In California, plea bargaining is both authorized and restricted by the Penal Code. Section 1192.5 provides that a plea bargain involving a felony, other than certain specifically enumerated felonies (*see* Penal Code § 1192.5), may specify the punishment the defendant will receive in return for a plea of guilty. The plea agreement must be approved by the court to be effective. By initiative measure adopted by the electorate in June 1982, § 1192.7 was added to the Penal Code. Section 1192.7(a) provides:

> Plea bargaining in any case in which the indictment or information charges any serious felony, any felony in which it is alleged that a firearm was personally used by the defendant, or any offense of driving while under the influence of alcohol, drugs, narcotics, or any other intoxicating substance, or any combination thereof, is prohibited, unless there is insufficient evidence to prove the people's case, or testimony of a material witness cannot be obtained, or a reduction or dismissal would not result in a substantial change in sentence.

The term "serious felony" used in § 1192.7(a) includes twenty-eight categories of offenses. At first glance, it would appear that § 1192.7 effectively eliminated most plea bargaining in felony cases in California. In practice, however, the prosecutor and defendant frequently stipulate that one of the three exceptions exists. If the stipulation is accepted by the court, a plea bargain in a case governed by § 1192.7 remains possible.

§ 16.9 Pretrial Activity

Discovery

Discovery is the pretrial acquisition by one party to a criminal proceeding of evidence and information in the possession of the other party. Discovery is not as broad in criminal cases as in civil. Before 1990, the law governing discovery in criminal proceedings in California was primarily a product of the courts. In 1990, the electorate adopted Proposition 115, which added §§ 1054 through 1054.7 to the Penal Code. Discovery is now governed by these statutory provisions.

Section 1054.1 addresses discovery by defendants of evidence and information in the possession of prosecuting attorneys, in the following language:

> The prosecuting attorney shall disclose to the defendant or his or her attorney all of the following materials and information, if it is in the possession of the prosecuting attorney or if the prosecuting attorney knows it to be in the possession of the investigating agencies:
>
> (a) The names and addresses of persons the prosecutor intends to call as witnesses at trial.
>
> (b) Statements of all defendants.
>
> (c) All relevant real evidence seized or obtained as a part of the investigation of the offenses charged.
>
> (d) The existence of a felony conviction of any material witness whose credibility is likely to be critical to the outcome of the trial.
>
> (e) Any exculpatory evidence.
>
> (f) Relevant written or recorded statements of witnesses or reports of the statements of witnesses whom the prosecutor intends to call at the trial, including any reports or statements of experts made in conjunction with the case, including the results of physical or mental examinations, scientific tests, experiments, or comparisons which the prosecutor intends to offer in evidence at the trial.

Section 1054.1(e) reflects the requirement established by the United States Supreme Court in *Brady v. Maryland,* 373 U.S. 83 (1963), that prosecutors disclose exculpatory evidence in their possession to defendants. This principle is known as the **Brady doctrine.**

Disclosure directly to a defendant of the names and addresses of persons a prosecutor intends to call as witnesses at trial pursuant to § 1054.1(a) may pose a risk to such persons of harassment, intimidation, or physical harm by the defendant or persons acting on the defendant's behalf. Because of this risk,

§ 1054.2 attempts to preclude disclosure directly to the defendant. Under § 1054.2, if the defendant is represented by counsel, disclosure is made only to the attorney; the attorney is prohibited from disclosing the information to the defendant unless specifically permitted to do so by the court. If the defendant is not represented by counsel, disclosure is made to a licensed private investigator appointed by the court. The defendant may contact victims or prosecution witnesses only through the private investigator.

Section 1054.3 addresses discovery by the prosecution of information and evidence in the possession of the defense. The categories of information and evidence a defendant is required to disclose to the prosecuting attorney correspond to four of the six categories that the prosecuting attorney is required to disclose to the defense (categories (a), (b), (c), and (f) of § 1054.1). The defendant is not obligated to disclose to the prosecution the existence of a felony conviction of a material defense witness or exculpatory evidence in the possession of the defendant.

Section 1054.6 exempts from disclosure during pretrial discovery "materials or information which are work product as defined in subdivision (c) of § 2018 of the Code of Civil Procedure, or which are privileged pursuant to an express statutory provision, or are privileged as provided by the Constitution of the United States." Under Code of Civil Procedure § 2018, an attorney's work product includes "any writing that reflects an attorney's impressions, conclusions, opinions, or legal research or theories." Thus, for example, the notes made by a defense attorney or prosecutor outlining her strategy for the upcoming trial would not be discoverable by the other side. Materials or information that are "privileged pursuant to an express statutory provision" appear to be those falling within one of the privilege provisions of the Evidence Code. One such provision, for example, provides that confidential communications between an attorney and his client are privileged. If a defendant wrote a confidential letter or made a confidential written statement to his attorney, the letter or statement would not be discoverable by the prosecution because its contents fall within the attorney-client privilege. Materials and information privileged "as provided by the Constitution of the United States" appear to be those covered by federal constitutional privileges, such as the privilege against self-incrimination.

As in civil cases, the discovery provisions of the Penal Code envision a system of voluntary cooperation in which the parties exchange information and evidence without the need for court participation. The court is to become involved only if one or both parties fail to comply with the statutory discovery requirements. Discovery is initiated by a party's making an informal request for the desired materials and information. The other party has fifteen days to comply with the discovery request by providing the requested materials and information. If the party receiving the discovery request fails to comply within the fifteen-day period, the requesting party may then seek a court order compelling the party to comply. (See Penal Code § 1054.5.)

Section 1054.7 requires that pretrial discovery disclosures be made at least thirty days before trial, "unless good cause is shown why a disclosure should be denied, restricted, or deferred." If the requested material or information becomes known to or comes into the possession of a party after the thirtieth day before trial, disclosure must be made immediately, again "unless good cause is shown why a disclosure should be denied, restricted, or deferred." According to

§ 1054.7, " '[g]ood cause' is limited to threats or possible danger to the safety of a victim or witness, possible loss or destruction of evidence, or possible compromise of other investigations by law enforcement."

Motion Practice

In both civil and criminal practice, a *motion* is a request made to a court that the court do something. In most cases a party who files a motion is seeking an order from the court. Generally, when a person desires something from a court, a formal motion must be filed and copies sent to opposing counsel. On occasion, oral motions are made. This is most common during trials and hearings. Some of the most common motions are discussed here.

Motion to Set Aside and Demurrer

If a defendant believes that the indictment or information is fatally flawed, the appropriate remedy is a **motion to set aside** under Penal Code § 995—if the defendant claims that the proceedings that produced the indictment or information were defective. If the defendant challenges the indictment or information based on a defect apparent on the face of the document, the proper remedy is a demurrer under Penal Code § 1002 *et seq.* (The motion to set aside and the demurrer were discussed in § 16.7.)

Motion to Suppress

You have learned that illegally obtained evidence may not be used against a defendant at trial. This principle is known as the *exclusionary rule*. If the prosecutor attempts to introduce illegally obtained evidence at trial, the defendant may object. If the objection is sustained by the judge, the evidence will be excluded. A common defense procedure is to challenge the admissibility of evidence before trial. An advantage of this procedure is that it adds an element of certainty to the trial; the defendant knows before trial whether the challenged evidence will be admitted into evidence by the judge. A pretrial challenge to the admissibility of illegally seized evidence is accomplished by means of a **motion to** return property or **suppress** evidence under Penal Code § 1538.5. This motion was discussed in detail in Chapter 13.

Motion for Change of Venue

In California, any superior court has the power to hear and determine cases involving felonies. Municipal courts have the power to hear and determine cases involving misdemeanors. This power is an aspect of the subject-matter jurisdiction of the court. In any given criminal case, however, the following question may arise: among the many courts having jurisdiction to hear and determine the case, which is the correct court for this particular case? This question involves the concept of venue, that is, the proper court in which to bring a criminal proceeding. Although there are exceptions, the general rule is that for a felony case, the proper court is the superior court of the county in which the crime was committed. In the case of a misdemeanor, the proper court is the municipal court for the judicial district in which the crime was committed.[24]

In certain limited situations, a change of venue may be appropriate. For example, a criminal proceeding may have been brought initially in the court of the county or judicial district in which the crime was committed, but for some reason the proceeding should be transferred to another court. Such a situation is addressed in Penal Code §§ 1033 and 1034, which provide that, upon motion of the defendant, the court is to order a change of venue "when it appears that there is a reasonable likelihood that a fair and impartial trial cannot be had in the county." Determination by the court that there is "a reasonable likelihood that a fair and impartial trial cannot be had in the county" involves the assessment of a number of factors: (1) the nature and gravity of the offense, (2) the nature and extent of the publicity given to the offense and the proceedings against the defendant, (3) the size of the community, (4) the status of the defendant in the community, and (5) the popularity and prominence of the victim.[25] Another factor that may warrant a change of venue is the politicization of the case. In *Maine v. Superior Court* (1968) 68 Cal.2d 375, all of these factors were considered by the court in determining that a change of venue was warranted. The court stated:

> We hold that where, as here, the defendants are friendless in the community, the victims prominent, the occurrence of the crime probably fortuitous as to locale, community-wide interest and generosity are expressed on behalf of the victim, newspaper publicity includes accounts of a purported confession, and two opposing counsel are also election opponents, a change of venue is clearly necessary to assure a fair trial to the defendants.[26]

A **motion for change of venue** must be filed with the court at least ten days before the date set for trial.

Motion to Sever

A **motion to sever** is a motion made by a defendant requesting the court to order that the defendant be tried separately from other defendants or that one or more multiple charges against him be tried separately from other offenses for which he has been charged. Penal Code § 1098 addresses the situation in which two or more defendants have been jointly charged with the same offense. Under § 1098, joint defendants must be tried jointly (in the same trial) unless the court, in its discretion, orders that the defendants be granted separate trials. Thus, for example, if Bonnie and Clyde are jointly charged with the murder of Sam, the general rule under § 1098 is that they should be tried together at the same trial.

If a defendant moves for a separate trial and can establish that she will be prejudiced by a joint trial, the court may exercise its discretion to *sever* the cases, i.e., to order that the defendant be tried separately from the other defendant or defendants. For example, assume that, in the Bonnie and Clyde murder case, Clyde confessed to the murder and, in his confession, stated that Bonnie also participated in the murder. Bonnie did not confess. If the prosecution intends to introduce Clyde's confession at the defendants' joint trial for the purpose of convicting Clyde, Bonnie will be prejudiced because Clyde's confession implicates her. If Bonnie were tried separately, Clyde's confession would not be admissible at her trial. In such a situation, if Bonnie moves to sever, the court should grant the motion and order that Bonnie be tried separately from Clyde.[27]

Another situation in which a motion to sever may be granted is the misjoinder of offenses. Misjoinder of offenses may involve one defendant or multiple defendants. Penal Code § 954 provides that "[a]n accusatory pleading may charge two or more different offenses connected together in their commission, or different statements of the same offense or two or more different offenses of the same class of crimes or offenses." If an indictment or information charges a defendant with two or more offenses that are not "connected together in their commission," are not "different statements of the same offense," and are not "different offenses of the same class of crimes or offenses," the defendant may make a motion to sever. The granting of such a motion is not automatic. Generally, to prevail on such a motion, the defendant must show that he or she will be substantially prejudiced by failure to grant a separate trial as to the unrelated offenses. Substantial prejudice could exist, for example, if evidence presented as to one offense would inflame the jury against the defendant, thereby rendering the jury unable to reach a fair and impartial verdict on another unrelated offense.

A third situation in which a motion to sever is appropriate is when the accusatory pleading charges multiple defendants with unrelated offenses. For example, an information charging Albert with grand theft of jewelry, Betty with arson, and Charles with extortion would be improper and would be subject to motions to sever by each of the defendants. The general rule is that it is error to try different defendants together for different crimes unless at least one count of the accusatory pleading charges all the defendants with a single crime.[28] Remember that even if this requirement is met, a defendant may be successful on a motion to sever if she can establish that she will be prejudiced by a joint trial.

Motion in Limine

The prosecuting or defense attorney may anticipate that the other side will attempt to offer evidence at trial that is inadmissible. Evidence may be inadmissible because it has been illegally obtained; because it is privileged under the Evidence Code; because it is not competent (for example, hearsay evidence); because it is inflammatory and unduly prejudicial; or because of some other reason. The attorney opposing the admission of such evidence may wait until the other side attempts to offer it at trial and then object to it. The problem with this approach is that the jury may become aware of the evidence and may be affected by it even if the objection to admission of the evidence is sustained by the trial judge. The **motion in limine** is designed to avoid this problem. *In limine* means "at the threshold" or "at the beginning." A motion in limine is typically made immediately before the trial commences. In the motion, counsel requests the court to rule in advance that opposing counsel and witnesses be instructed not to mention objectionable matters specified by the moving counsel in the motion.

A motion in limine is broader in scope than a motion to suppress. The motion to suppress is limited to exclusion of evidence that has been illegally obtained by the government. The motion in limine may seek the exclusion of evidence that is inadmissible for any reason. Also, the motion in limine may be made by the prosecution as well as by the defense.

The motion in limine serves a tactical purpose as well. The attorney making the motion will learn, prior to trial, whether the court will admit or exclude the challenged evidence. This knowledge will assist the attorney in preparing for and conducting the trial.

Other Motions

A great many types of motions may be filed by the defense or prosecution during the course of a criminal proceeding. Some motions, such as motions to set aside, demurrers, and motions to suppress, are filed and heard at the pretrial stage. Also filed and heard at the pretrial stage are motions such as motions to continue (postpone) the trial date and motions for protective orders (to avoid complying with discovery requests when valid reasons exist for refusing to comply). Other motions may be filed during trial. Examples of such motions include motions for acquittal, made by defendants when the prosecution has arguably failed to prove its case, and motions for mistrial. Finally, motions may be filed and heard after conclusion of the trial and before entry of judgment against the defendant. A motion for a new trial is an example of such a motion. Selected trial and posttrial motions are discussed in Chapter 17. The foregoing list names only a small number of the possible motions which may be made, particularly during the pretrial and trial stages of a criminal proceeding.

§ 16.10 Extradition and Detainers

If wanted persons are located outside the jurisdiction where they are, or will be, charged, **extradition** is one method of securing their presence in the charging jurisdiction. *Extradition* is the surrender of a person from one jurisdiction to another where the person has been charged or convicted of a crime.

Extradition may be between nations or between states within the United States. International extradition is accomplished pursuant to treaties or other international agreements between the United States and other countries. Interstate extradition is governed by the internal law of the United States and the fifty states. The discussion in this section is limited to interstate extradition.

Article IV, § 2, clause 2, of the United States Constitution provides: "A person charged in any state with treason, felony, or other crime, who shall flee from justice, and be found in another state, shall on demand of the executive authority of the state from which he fled, be delivered up to be removed to the state having jurisdiction of the crime." This provision has been implemented by a federal statute (18 U.S.C. § 3182). Further implementing provisions have been enacted in the Uniform Interstate Criminal Extradition Act, a uniform act that has been adopted in almost all states, including California. California's enactment of the uniform act is found at Penal Code §§ 1547 through 1556.2.

Pursuant to the Uniform Interstate Criminal Extradition Act, the request for extradition is made between governors. If a governor determines that the person sought should be delivered, an arrest warrant is issued by that governor.

Once seized, the arrestee is brought before a magistrate and informed of the demand made for his or her surrender, of the crime with which he or she has been charged in the requesting state, and of his or her right to counsel. The arrestee has the right at that point to petition for habeas corpus. (Habeas corpus is discussed in more detail in Chapter 19.) In the context of extradition, habeas corpus enables the arrestee to seek court review of the legality of his or her seizure by the executive authority of the sending state for the purpose of extraditing him or her to the requesting state.

During extradition proceedings, release on bail is permitted, unless the crime charged is one punishable by death or life imprisonment in the state where the crime was committed. If the person sought is under charge in the sending state, the governor may order his or her surrender immediately or may wait until the prosecution and punishment is completed in the sending state.

Generally, the guilt or innocence of the accused may not be considered by the governor or courts during the proceedings; that issue is left to the requesting jurisdiction. It is the obligation of the governor and courts of the sending state to be sure that the correct person is seized and that proper procedures are followed.

Defendants may waive extradition, that is, they may voluntarily agree to be returned to the requesting state. This waiver must be made in court, and defendants must be informed of their rights, including habeas corpus, for waivers to be valid.

A **detainer** is a request (or order) for the continued custody of a prisoner. For example, suppose California charges are pending against a Utah prisoner. California would issue a detainer requesting that Utah hold the prisoner after his or her sentence is completed so that California may take custody.

Procedures for requesting and implementing detainers are established by the Interstate Agreement on Detainers (IAD), an agreement among all the states that has been enacted into the legislation of each state. California's enactment of the IAD is found at Penal Code §§ 1389 through 1389.8. Pursuant to the IAD, a state may request the temporary custody of a prisoner of another state in order to try the person. Once the trial is completed, the prisoner is returned, regardless of the outcome. If convicted, a detainer is issued for the prisoner and he or she is again returned after the sentence is completed in the sending state.

The IAD also provides that prisoners are to be notified of any detainers against them. Further, if a state issues a detainer for a prisoner, that prisoner may request to be temporarily transferred to that state for final disposition of that case. A request for final disposition by a prisoner is deemed a waiver of extradition to and from the sending state. Also, it is deemed a waiver of extradition to the receiving state to serve any resulting sentence after the sentence in the sending state is completed.

The United States Supreme Court has held that the exclusionary rule does not exclude persons who have been illegally seized from trial. In *Frisbie v. Collins*, 342 U.S. 519 (1952), the fact that Michigan police officers kidnapped a defendant from Illinois and returned him to Michigan, disregarding extradition laws, did not affect the court's jurisdiction to try the defendant. The same result was reached in a case in which international extradition laws were not followed.[29] Today, if the government's conduct in seizing a defendant is outrageous or shocking, there is a possibility that a court will bar prosecution.[30]

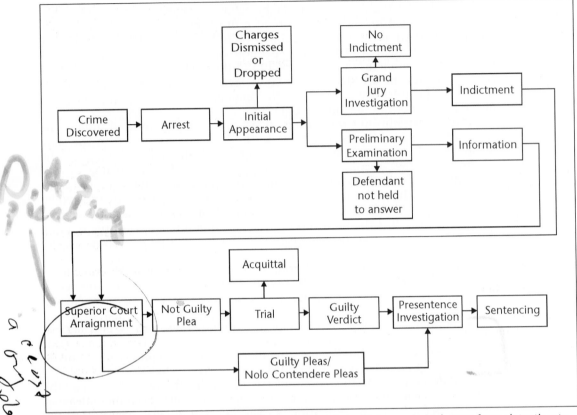

The Basic Criminal Process This charts the basic progress of felony criminal cases from detection to sentencing. Misdemeanor cases normally progress through the system faster, as many stages are omitted.

Key Terms

accusatory pleading The formal charge that must be filed with the proper court before a defendant may be brought to trial. In misdemeanor cases, the accusatory pleading is the complaint filed in the municipal court. In felony cases, the accusatory pleading is the indictment or information filed in the superior court.

admission to bail The order of a competent court or magistrate that a defendant be discharged from custody upon bail.

arraignment A procedure that consists of reading the accusatory pleading to the defendant, providing the defendant a true copy, and asking

him or her how he or she pleads in response to the charge or charges in the accusatory pleading.

bail A deposit of money, property, or a bond with a court to assure the presence of the defendant at court proceedings.

bail bond A promise made by a surety, pursuant to a contract with the defendant, to pay the amount of the defendant's bail to the court if the defendant fails to appear at the proceeding to which the bail applies.

booking The recordation of an arrest in official police records, and the taking by police of fingerprints and photographs of the person arrested, or any of these acts following an arrest.

Brady doctrine The rule developed by the United States Supreme Court that prosecutors must disclose exculpatory evidence to defendants.

commitment An order of a court directing that a defendant be delivered into the custody of a law enforcement agency.

complaint The initial document filed with the court in a criminal proceeding that accuses the defendant of a crime. The complaint is the document used to request an arrest warrant. It also serves as the accusatory pleading in a misdemeanor case.

demurrer A challenge by a defendant to an indictment or information based on a defect apparent on the face of the pleading.

detainer A request made by one state to another state that the latter state retain custody of a prisoner so that the prisoner may be tried for an offense in the requesting state.

discovery The pretrial acquisition by one party to a criminal proceeding of evidence and information in the possession of the other party.

extradition The surrender of a person from one jurisdiction to another where the person has been charged with or convicted of a crime.

grand jury A body of the required number of persons drawn from the citizens of a county, before a court of competent jurisdiction, and sworn to inquire of public offenses committed or triable within the county.

held to answer A term describing the contents of an order issued by a magistrate after a preliminary examination, requiring the defendant to respond to a formal accusatory pleading.

indictment An accusation in writing, presented by the grand jury to a competent court, charging a person with a public offense.

information An accusation in writing, presented by the district attorney to a competent court, charging a person with a public offense.

initial appearance The appearance of an in-custody defendant before a magistrate without unnecessary delay, and in no case longer than forty-eight hours after arrest. The purpose of the initial appearance is protection of the defendant's rights, specifically: to prevent unwarranted police interrogation, to make it possible for the defendant to be promptly advised of his or her right to counsel, to enable the defendant to obtain bail, and to have the issue of probable cause for his or her arrest determined by a judicial officer.

magistrate A judicial officer having power to issue a warrant for the arrest of a person charged with a public offense. This power is held by justices of the California Supreme Court, justices of the courts of appeal, and judges of the superior and municipal courts.

motion for change of venue A motion made to change the location of a trial on the grounds that the defendant cannot receive a fair and impartial trial in the originally scheduled location or that all the jury panels in the originally scheduled location have been exhausted.

motion in limine A motion requesting the court to rule, prior to trial, that opposing counsel and witnesses are to be instructed not to make reference during the trial to inadmissible evidence specified in the motion.

motion to set aside A motion made by a defendant prior to trial requesting the court to set aside an indictment or information charging the defendant with a crime. The motion challenges the proceedings that produced the indictment or information rather than the form of the indictment or information itself.

motion to sever A motion made by a defendant requesting the court to order that he or she be tried separately from other defendants, or that one or more multiple charges against him or her be tried separately from other offenses with which he or she has been charged.

motion to suppress Technically known as a *motion to return property or suppress evidence,* a motion, made pursuant to Penal Code § 1538.5, that requests the court to exclude from admissibility at trial evidence that was illegally obtained by the government.

nolo contendere A plea to a criminal charge which informs the court that the defendant, though not admitting guilt, does not intend to defend against the charge or charges in the accusatory pleading.

notice to appear Frequently referred to as a *citation;* a written notice given to a person arrested for a misdemeanor that states the name and address of the person, the offense charged, and the time and place at which the person must appear in court.

plea A defendant's formal answer to charges in an accusatory pleading.

plea bargain An agreement between the defendant and the prosecutor, which is subject to approval by the court, that the prosecutor will dismiss a more serious charge if the defendant will plead guilty to a lesser charge, or that the defendant will receive a sentence no more severe than specified in the agreement if the defendant will plead guilty to the charged offense.

preliminary examination A hearing conducted before a magistrate in the municipal court in a felony case at which evidence is presented by the prosecution for the purpose of establishing probable cause to believe that an offense has been committed and that the defendant committed it. The defendant is entitled to be present and to present evidence on his or her behalf. A preliminary examination is required if the prosecution intends to formally charge the defendant by information.

promise to appear A written promise to appear before a magistrate signed by a person arrested for an infraction.

Review Questions

1. What is a notice to appear? What information must it contain?

2. This chapter discussed certain rights possessed by a person being held in custody. What are these rights?

3. What are the differing functions of the complaint in felony and misdemeanor cases?

4. What are the purposes of the requirement that a defendant in custody be brought before a magistrate following arrest? What are the time requirements for bringing the defendant before a magistrate at this stage in the proceedings?

5. What functions are performed by the magistrate during the initial appearance of the defendant?

6. Briefly discuss the ways in which a defendant may post bail.

7. What is an "own recognizance" release?

8. If things do not go well for the defendant at the preliminary examination, he will probably be "held to answer" and "committed." What do these terms mean?

9. What is a defendant's role in a grand jury proceeding investigating allegations that she engaged in criminal conduct?

10. What is the difference between an indictment and an information?

11. An indictment or information may be challenged by a motion to set aside under Penal Code § 995 or a demurrer under Penal Code § 1002 *et seq.* The two types of challenges address different aspects of the accusatory pleadings. What aspect of the accusatory pleadings is challenged by a motion to set aside? By a demurrer?

12. What are the six possible pleas a defendant may enter to a criminal charge in California?

13. Briefly describe the effect of Penal Code § 1192.7, added by initiative measure in June 1982, on the practice of plea bargaining in California.

14. What are the six categories of evidence and information the prosecution must disclose to the defense, upon request, under the discovery provisions of Penal Code § 1054.1?

15. What is extradition? What is a detainer? What laws specify the procedures for extradition and detainers, and where are they found in the California Penal Code?

Review Problems

1. Officer Jones observes Frank Smith commit a misdemeanor and immediately arrests Smith. Must officer Jones take Smith into custody? If not, what is the proper procedure for officer Jones to follow in this situation?

2. Officer Lopez is on patrol when an agitated person runs up to him and reports that she has just been robbed at gunpoint. She says the assailant fled into a nearby alley. Officer Lopez and the victim enter the alley and the victim identifies Max, the man they find there, as the robber. Officer Lopez immediately arrests Max and takes him into custody. When must a criminal complaint be filed against Max? When must Max be brought before a magistrate? What will occur when Max is brought before a magistrate?

3. Maggie the magistrate is having a busy morning. She is conducting the municipal court arraignments, also known as the initial appearances, for a courtroom full of defendants. At the moment, Maggie is deciding whether to release three defendants from custody pending their next court appearance and, if so, whether to release them on bail or on their own recognizance. What should be her decision with respect to each of the following? Explain your reasoning.
   a. Abel Baker—charged with shoplifting a watch with a value of $30.
   b. Charlie Delta—charged with attempted murder of his estranged wife. The prosecutor presents evidence to Maggie that when Charlie was arrested, he shouted at his wife: "They can't hold me forever. When I get out, I'll be back."
   c. Elvis Foxtrot—charged with embezzlement from his employer of approximately $80,000 over a period of three years.

4. If you were a defendant in a felony case, would you prefer to be charged by indictment or information? Explain your answer.

5. The Golden County Grand Jury has an indictment against Merton Melroid charging him with intentionally killing Fido, a dog owned by Matilda Petunia. At the grand jury hearing, only one witness testified, Matilda Petunia, who is Merton's next-door neighbor. Matilda testified that, late one night, about a week before Fido was killed, she heard Merton speaking to his wife through an open window and saying: "We are not going to get a dog. I can't stand dogs." Approximately one week later, Matilda returned from the store and found Fido shot to death. Other than Merton's alleged words to his wife, there is no evidence connecting Merton with Fido's death. If Merton wants to challenge the indictment, what

is the correct procedure for him to use, and upon what ground should he base his challenge? If Merton's challenge is successful, what must the court do?

6. After a preliminary examination at which Ace Hart has been held to answer and committed, the Golden County District Attorney has filed the following information with the Clerk of the Golden County Superior Court:

> The People of the State of California against Ace Hart.

> In the Superior Court of the State of California in and for the County of Golden.

> The District Attorney of the County of Golden hereby accuses Ace Hart of a felony, to wit: obscenity, in that, on or about the 18th day of July, 1997, in the County of Blackjack, State of Nevada, he did maliciously and intentionally teach Polly, a parrot and the property of Ace Hart, to utter the words "go to hell," a profanity.

At the preliminary examination, four witnesses testified that they accompanied Ace and his pet parrot, Polly, on a trip to Nevada in July 1997. They also testified that they were in Ace's hotel room in Blackjack County, Nevada, on July 18, 1997, and watched him teach Polly to say the foul (pun intended) words. If Ace wants to challenge the information, what is the correct procedure for him to use, and upon what ground should he base his challenge? If Ace's challenge is successful, what must the court do?

7. At his superior court arraignment on a charge of rape, Jack pleads guilty. What must court do before it can accept Jack's guilty plea?

8. Timothy Timid is charged with the first-degree murder of his wife, Nagatha. Timothy tells his defense attorney, in confidence, that he is a victim of spousal abuse, having been constantly subjected to nagging by his deceased wife. He further states that on the night of the killing, Nagatha's friend, Malicia, was visiting, and that they were discussing his lack of character, laughing at him, and directing derogatory comments toward him. According to Timothy, a rising crescendo of fury welled up within him and, before he fully realized what he was doing, he attacked Nagatha with a rolling pin and bludgeoned

her to death. Malicia, the only witness to the crime, ran from the house screaming, "Murder, murder!" The next day, Malicia's husband found her in a catatonic state, from which she has not recovered. She is completely uncommunicative and, according to her doctor, may remain that way indefinitely. Timothy's attorney negotiates with the prosecuting attorney, offering to plead guilty to voluntary manslaughter if the prosecuting attorney will dismiss the first-degree murder charge and will agree to a maximum sentence of three years. The prosecuting attorney agrees. At Timothy's superior court arraignment, the plea bargain is presented to the court. May the court approve it? Explain your answer.

9. Medford Bedford has been charged with first-degree burglary in an information filed with the superior court by the prosecutor. Medford's attorney sends a written request to the prosecutor for the following:

   a. The names and addresses of all witnesses the prosecutor intends to call at trial.

   b. Any statement made by Medford to law enforcement authorities relating to the first-degree burglary charge.

   c. All objects seized during a search of Medford's apartment by police when they searched pursuant to a warrant.

   d. Any information or evidence that might exculpate Medford.

    e. Any internal memorandum in the prosecutor's office reflecting the legal issues the prosecutor perceives to be involved in the case.

 f. All notes made by the prosecutor reflecting the manner in which he intends to present the case at trial.

   g. Any report issued by a fingerprint expert, analyzing fingerprints found at the scene of the crime, which the prosecutor intends to offer as evidence at trial.

Must the prosecutor disclose each of the requested categories of information and evidence? If not, which categories must the prosecutor disclose, and which may the prosecutor refuse to disclose? What is the time requirement for disclosure by the prosecutor of information and evidence in response to the request? What remedy does Medford have if the prosecutor fails to comply with the time requirement?

10. Penelope Envelope is about to be tried for the murder of her boyfriend, Hunk Hulk. The prosecutor plans to call as a witness a police officer, who is expected to testify that he was told by Starr Chambers, a friend of Hunk's who was present when he died, that Hunk said to Starr that "Penelope did it." Unfortunately, Starr died shortly thereafter from a drug overdose. Penelope's attorney believes that the officer's testimony will constitute inadmissible hearsay and wants to act to exclude any reference at trial to Starr's alleged statement, by the officer, any other witness, or the prosecutor. What is the best course of action for Penelope's attorney to take in an effort to protect his client from this damaging evidence?

Notes

1 4 Witkin & Epstein, *California Criminal Law* § 1939 (2d ed., Bancroft-Whitney 1989).

2 Penal Code § 859a(a).

3 Penal Code § 991.

4 Penal Code § 859b.

5 Penal Code § 858.

6 Penal Code § 1310 *et seq.*

7 Penal Code §§ 865, 866.

8 4 Witkin & Epstein, *supra* note 1, at § 1989, quoting *People v. Nagle* (1944) 25 Cal.2d 216, 222.

9 *Ex parte Wilson,* 114 U.S. 417 (1884). *See also* Fed. R. Crim. P. 7.

10 4 Witkin & Epstein, *supra* note 1, at § 1804, *citing* 8 Stan. L. Rev. 644.

11 Penal Code § 939.6(b).

12 Penal Code §§ 938, 938.1.

13 Penal Code § 997.

14 Penal Code § 999.

15 Penal Code § 1007.

16 Penal Code § 1008.

17 Penal Code § 988.

18 Penal Code § 1016.

19 *See generally* 4 Witkin & Epstein, *supra* note 1, at §§ 2149–2162.

20 Penal Code § 1019.

21 Penal Code § 1016(3).

22 Burger, "The State of the Judiciary," 56 *A.B.A. J.* 929 (1970); Note, "Is Plea Bargaining Inevitable?," 97 *Harv. L. Rev.* 1037 (1984).

23 *Santobello v. New York,* 404 U.S. 257, 261 (1971).

24 Penal Code §§ 777 and 691(c).

25 4 Witkin & Epstein, *supra* note 1, at § 1893.

26 *Maine,* 68 Cal.2d at 388.

27 *See Bruton v. United States,* 391 U.S. 123 (1968); *People v. Aranda* (1965) 63 Cal.2d 518.

28 *People v. Ortiz* (1978) 22 Cal.3d 38.

29 *Ker v. Illinois,* 119 U.S. 436 (1886).

30 *See United States v. Toscanino,* 500 F.2d 267 (2d Cir. 1974).

CHAPTER 17

Trial

OUTLINE

Introduction
§ 17.1   Trial Rights of Defendants
§ 17.2   Trial Procedure

Introduction

After the pretrial procedures discussed in Chapter 16 have been completed, the defendant is brought to trial. *Trial* is the proceeding at which evidence for and against the defendant is presented to a "trier of fact," which then determines the defendant's guilt or innocence. In a jury trial, the jury is the trier of fact. In a trial by judge alone, sometimes referred to as a **court trial** or a **bench trial**, the trier of fact is the judge. Pronouncement of judgment and sentencing are technically not part of the trial and thus are discussed in the next chapter. This chapter discusses trial of a defendant from two perspectives. First, the constitutional rights of a defendant at trial are considered. Next, a discussion of trial procedures follows.

§ 17.1   Trial Rights of Defendants

The Right to a Jury Trial

The Sixth Amendment to the United States Constitution guarantees the right to trial by jury in criminal cases. In 1968, the United States Supreme Court held that trial by jury is required by due process of law and is therefore applicable to the states under the Due Process Clause of the Fourteenth Amendment.[1] Later United States Supreme Court decisions have further refined federal constitutional principles applicable to the right of trial by jury, holding that the right exists in all criminal cases except those involving "petty" offenses. A *petty offense* in this context is an offense for which the maximum authorized imprisonment is six months or less.[2]

In keeping with the general constitutional principle that states may grant greater protections to defendants than the federal Constitution, the California Constitution, at article I, § 16, grants defendants a right of trial by jury in all felony and misdemeanor cases, without regard to the amount of imprisonment that may be imposed. In fact, criminal defendants in the California courts are entitled to trial by jury in cases in which the offense is one for which no imprisonment is authorized (for example, an offense punishable only by a fine). There is, however, no right to a jury trial in infraction cases. Recall that an infraction is a minor offense of lesser severity than a misdemeanor.

In most states, juries consist of twelve persons. This number is not required by the United States Constitution. The California Constitution, however, at article I, § 16, requires a twelve-person jury in all felony cases. That section also requires a twelve-person jury in misdemeanor cases, but provides further that the prosecution and defense may agree to a jury of fewer than twelve persons in open court.

In a jury trial, the jury serves as the trier of fact. In this capacity, the jury hears the evidence and determines whether the defendant is guilty or not guilty of the offense charged. When determining whether to find the defendant guilty, the jury must vote. Most jurisdictions require a unanimous vote of the jurors to convict the defendant. As with the twelve-person jury requirement, a unanimous vote of the jury is not mandated by the United States Constitution.[3] Unanimity of the jury is, however, mandated by the California Constitution. Thus, in the trial of a defendant in a California state court, the defendant may be convicted only if all jurors vote for conviction.

The Sixth Amendment to the United States Constitution requires that the defendant be tried by an "impartial jury of the State and district wherein the crime shall have been committed." Generally, this requirement is met by drawing jurors from the county or judicial district in which the crime was committed. The concept of jury impartiality requires that the jury be drawn from a fair cross-section of the community. Systematic exclusion of potential jurors based on racial, social, or economic factors, or gender, is prohibited.

There are two exceptions to the general requirement of trial by jury in criminal cases: (1) cases in which the defendant waives a jury, and (2) cases in which the defendant pleads guilty. (*See* Penal Code § 689.) Guilty pleas were discussed in Chapter 16. In a case in which the defendant waives trial by jury, he or she is tried by the judge alone; the judge serves as the finder of fact and determines whether sufficient evidence has been presented to convict the defendant. Waiver of trial by jury is effective only if it is expressly stated by the defendant in open court, and only if it is consented to by both the defendant's attorney and the prosecutor.[4]

The Right to a Public Trial

The right to a public trial has two aspects. First, a defendant is entitled to a public trial by the United States Constitution; by article I, § 15 of the California Constitution; and by Penal Code § 686(1). Second, the people—i.e., the public—have a right to attend and be made aware of proceedings in the state's criminal courts.

Defendant's Right to a Public Trial   As the United States Supreme Court stated in *Estes v. Texas*, 381 U.S. 532 (1965), "[h]istory has proven that secret tribunals were effective instruments of oppression." The right of defendants to have their trials held in public is intended to assure that the government does not take action against individuals in secret and thereby turn the criminal justice system into an instrument of oppression. Violation of a defendant's right to a public trial is reversible error per se; that is, the defendant is entitled to reversal of any conviction regardless of whether he can prove that he was actually prejudiced by the exclusion of the public. The right to a public trial extends to pretrial proceedings, such as a hearing on a motion to suppress evidence.

A defendant may waive the right to a public trial. Unlike a waiver of trial by jury, which must be expressly made in open court, waiver of the right to a public trial may be effectively made by acquiescing in an order of the court excluding the public.

Right of the Public to Open Proceedings   There is a public interest in the criminal justice system, and the public has a right to attend and to know what transpires during criminal proceedings. This right includes the right of the media to report the details of trials and other proceedings to the public. Generally, a defendant may not require the court to close criminal proceedings to the public or the media.

Restrictions on the Right to a Public Trial   Under certain circumstances, a court may close a criminal proceeding, or part of a criminal proceeding, to the public without violating the defendant's right to a public trial or the public's right to attend. Also, a court may, under limited circumstances, restrict media reporting of a criminal proceeding. The trial judge has the duty to maintain order and security in the courtroom. If spectators cause a disturbance that threatens the integrity of the proceedings, the judge may order the courtroom cleared, or at least order the unruly spectators removed. Also, there is authority that, in the interest of protecting the right of a defendant to a fair trial, a court may exclude the public during the testimony of a witness if necessary to protect the witness from embarrassment that might inhibit the witness from fully and freely testifying.[5] Penal Code § 686.2 permits a court to exclude a spectator who is intimidating a witness. Penal Code § 859.1 permits the court to exclude the public from portions of proceedings involving sexual offenses against minors under the age of sixteen in order to protect the reputation of the minor.

Cases that capture the attention of the media, especially in the early stages, present special problems. Extensive pretrial publicity may affect public attitudes to such an extent that impaneling of an impartial jury becomes almost impossible. In addition, inflammatory or inaccurate publicity during trial can expose jurors to unproven allegations about the defendant or the case and may thus affect their ability to decide the case based solely on the evidence presented in court. In such situations, two constitutional rights may come into conflict: the defendant's right to a fair trial, guaranteed as a matter of due process of law, and the

First Amendment guarantee of freedom of the press. The courts have had difficulty reconciling these two rights.

One principle that has emerged from judicial decisions dealing with the problem of publicity is that the right of the defendant to a fair trial must predominate over the right of the media to report the proceeding. It is established that the judge can, and is required to, control the activities of the media and trial participants who provide information to the media if necessary to assure the defendant a fair trial. One means of exercising this control is the issuance by the court of protective orders, commonly known as gag orders. A **gag order** is an order by the court restricting participants in the criminal proceeding from discussing specified aspects of the case with news media representatives. Violation of a gag order may be punished as a contempt of court.

After the jury is impaneled, another means of protecting the jury from exposure to out-of-court commentary about the trial is a **sequestration order**. *Sequestration* means keeping the jury in custody between court sessions. An unusual and extreme example of sequestration occurred in the famous O.J. Simpson trial of 1995, conducted in the Los Angeles County Superior Court. In that case, the jury was sequestered for several months.

With the age of electronic communication has come the desire of the media to broadcast trial proceedings that have caught the public interest. Like most other states, California initially prohibited photography, recording, and broadcasting in the courtroom. Since 1980, however, film or electronic media coverage of court proceedings has been permitted under California Rule of Court 980, but only on written order of the court. The court may refuse, limit, or terminate film or electronic media coverage if necessary to protect the rights of the parties and the dignity of the court, or to assure the orderly conduct of court proceedings.

The Right to Confrontation and Cross-Examination

Under the Sixth Amendment to the United States Constitution, a defendant has the right "to be confronted with the witnesses against him." A similar right is guaranteed by article I, § 15, of the California Constitution, and by Penal Code § 686(3). The right of confrontation essentially means the right of a defendant to cross-examine prosecution witnesses. **Cross-examination** is questioning of an opposing party's witnesses, and it occurs after the witness has testified on direct examination for the side that called him or her as a witness. Direct examination is designed to elicit testimony about the facts in issue in the case. Cross-examination is designed to test the truthfulness and accuracy of the witness's testimony on direct examination. The right of confrontation thus affords the defendant the opportunity to challenge the testimony of those who testify against him or her.

The right of confrontation requires the presence of prosecution witnesses in court. There are two exceptions to this rule. First, hearsay evidence may be admitted to the extent that it is admissible under the Evidence Code. Second, a written deposition of a witness's testimony made at a prior proceeding may be read into evidence, in lieu of the live testimony of the witness, if the witness is unavailable. A witness is *unavailable* if he or she is dead, unable to attend the trial, absent, or cannot be found with reasonable diligence.[6] In such circumstances, use of the witness's prior statement does not violate the defendant's right of confrontation.

The requirement that the witness testify in open court in the presence of the defendant has proven particularly problematic in child sexual abuse cases. In such cases, particularly those involving young children, the victim is frequently intimidated by the presence of the defendant in court. The defendant's presence may so affect the child witness that he or she cannot coherently testify. If the court finds that this is so, it may permit the child to testify in a separate room via either one-way or two-way closed-circuit television. (*See* Penal Code § 1347.) If the court determines that conditions exist warranting the use of closed-circuit television, the preference is for a two-way setup (i.e., an arrangement whereby persons in the courtroom may observe the witness on television and the witness may observe persons in the courtroom on television, particularly the defendant). If the court finds that observing the defendant on television would be so traumatic for the minor that he or she would still be unable to testify competently, the court may allow the minor to testify through one-way closed circuit television. One-way closed-circuit television arrangements were upheld by the United States Supreme Court in *Maryland v. Craig*, 497 U.S. 836 (1990).

The Right to Be Present at Trial

Related to the right of confrontation is the defendant's right to be present at trial. This right is implicitly guaranteed by the Confrontation Clause of the Sixth Amendment to the United States Constitution, and is explicitly guaranteed by article I, § 15, of the California Constitution. The Penal Code recognizes this right of the defendant and, in addition, contains provisions requiring the presence of the defendant at trial in certain circumstances and dispensing with the necessity of the personal presence of the defendant in others. The principal Penal Code provisions on this subject are §§ 1043 and 977.

Section 1043 states the general requirement that a defendant in a felony case be personally present at trial. Once a trial has commenced in the defendant's presence, however, it may proceed in her absence if she is removed from the courtroom for disruptive behavior or if the defendant voluntarily absents herself. If the defendant absents herself in a misdemeanor case, the court may do one or more of the following: (1) continue the matter, (2) order bail forfeited or revoke release on the defendant's own recognizance, (3) issue a bench warrant, or (4) proceed with the trial if the court finds that the defendant has absented herself voluntarily with full knowledge that the trial is to be held or is being held.

The focus of § 1043 is on the right of the court to proceed in the absence of the defendant. Section 977 deals with the right of the defendant to elect to be absent from criminal proceedings. Under § 977, the defendant in a misdemeanor case may absent himself from all court proceedings and appear by counsel only. There is an exception to this rule in domestic violence cases if the court requires the personal presence of the defendant for the purpose of serving a restraining order. Section 977 provides that a defendant in a felony case is required to be present at the arraignment, at the time of plea, during the preliminary examination, during those portions of the trial when evidence is taken before the trier of fact, and at the time of imposition of sentence. The defendant is permitted to waive appearance at all other proceedings. The waiver must be in writing, executed in open court, and approved by the court. If a felony defendant does not execute a written waiver, he is required to be present at all proceedings in his case.

The Right to a Speedy Trial

The government may not delay the trial of a defendant indefinitely. A defendant has a right to a speedy trial, as guaranteed by the Sixth Amendment to the United States Constitution and article I, § 15, of the California Constitution. The Penal Code also contains speedy trial provisions.

The federal constitutional right sets the standard that the California constitutional and statutory provisions must at least meet. Neither the United States Constitution nor the United States Supreme Court has defined the speedy trial right in terms of a specific time period. Instead, the United States Supreme Court has established standards for determining whether a defendant's speedy trial right has been violated in a particular case. In *Barker v. Wingo*, 407 U.S. 514 (1972), the Court stated that the following four factors must be evaluated: (1) the length of the delay, (2) the reason for the delay, (3) whether the defendant invoked his or her right to a speedy trial, and (4) how seriously the defendant was prejudiced by the delay. If, upon evaluation of these factors, a court finds that a defendant's right to a speedy trial has been violated, the case must be dismissed with prejudice (i.e., it cannot be brought against the defendant again).

The factors specified by the United States Supreme Court in *Barker v. Wingo* are applied by the California courts when evaluating whether a delay by the prosecution constitutes a violation of the California constitutional right to a speedy trial. There is, however, a difference between the federal and California systems regarding when the right to a speedy trial arises. The United States Supreme Court has held that the right to a speedy trial guaranteed by the United States Constitution arises when an individual becomes an "accused," that is, when an accusatory pleading is filed or the individual is actually arrested.[7] The California Supreme Court has held that the California constitutional right to a speedy trial arises at the time the complaint is filed.[8] In a felony case, the filing of the complaint precedes the filing of an accusatory pleading (indictment or information) and may precede the arrest of the defendant. Accordingly, in many felony cases in California, the right to a speedy trial arises at an earlier stage of the proceedings than it would under federal constitutional principles.

A lengthy delay by the government in filing a complaint (California) or in filing an accusatory pleading or arresting a defendant (federal) does not violate the constitutional right to a speedy trial provided that, once the speedy trial right arises, the defendant is tried promptly. Such a delay may, however, violate a defendant's right to due process of law under the United States and California Constitutions if the delay prejudices the right of the defendant to a fair trial. This is particularly true if the prosecution purposefully engages in delay to gain a tactical advantage over the defendant.[9] If a court finds the existence of such circumstances, dismissal is warranted.

In addition to the federal and California constitutional guarantees of the right to a speedy trial, the Penal Code contains provisions establishing certain statutory speedy trial rights. These provisions are found in § 1382(a). Section 1382(a) requires dismissal of a criminal case in the following situations, unless the prosecution can establish good cause for failure to comply with the time requirements:

1. When the prosecution fails to file an information against a defendant within fifteen days after the defendant has been held to answer at a preliminary examination

2. In a felony case, when a defendant who is in custody is not brought to trial within sixty days after the finding of an indictment or the filing of an information

3. In a misdemeanor case, when a defendant who is in custody is not brought to trial within thirty days after he or she is arraigned or enters a plea, whichever occurs later

4. In a misdemeanor case, when a defendant who is not in custody is not brought to trial within forty-five days after he or she is arraigned or enters a plea, whichever occurs later.

Section 1382(a) does not mention prejudice to the defendant. Despite this fact, the courts have required prejudice to the defendant as a basis for dismissal of a case under those statutory provisions. The courts, however, presume that the defendant has been prejudiced when the statutory time limits are violated.

Government failure to meet the time requirements in § 1382(a) is excused if the government can show good cause for the delay, if the defendant enters a general waiver of the time requirement, or if a trial date is set beyond the required time period at the defendant's request or with his or her consent. In a felony case, failure to meet the statutory time requirements is also excused if the defendant has been ordered to appear in superior court for trial or a hearing prior to trial, and he or she fails to appear.

An additional statutory provision, applicable in felony cases, is found at § 1049.5 of the Penal Code, added by Proposition 115 in June 1990. Section 1049.5 provides, in pertinent part:

> In felony cases, the court shall set a date for trial which is within 60 days of the defendant's arraignment in the superior court unless, upon a showing of good cause as prescribed in Section 1050, the court lengthens the time.

Section 1049.5 is not entirely in harmony with § 1382(a). For example, § 1049.5 does not state that dismissal is required if the sixty-day time period is violated by the prosecution without good cause. Also, the sixty-day period is measured from the time of arraignment, whereas the sixty-day period under § 1382(a) is measured from the date of finding of an indictment or filing of an information. Arraignment occurs after the finding of an indictment or filing of an information; thus the two statutes establish differing time periods. These conflicts between §§ 1049.5 and 1382(a) have not been definitively resolved by the California courts at the time of this writing.

The Presumption of Innocence/Burden of Proof

One of the most basic rights underlying the right to a fair trial is the presumption of innocence. All those accused must be proven guilty by the government. Criminal defendants have no duty to defend themselves and may remain silent throughout the trial. In fact, the government is prohibited from calling defendants to testify, and defendants cannot be made to decide whether they will testify at the start of the trial.[10] The fact that a defendant chooses not to testify may not be mentioned by the prosecutor to the jury. Defendants may testify in their own behalf. If so, they are subject to full cross-examination by the prosecutor. The Fifth Amendment right to be free from self-incrimination is discussed more fully in Chapter 11.

To further the presumption of innocence, judges must be careful not to behave in a manner that implies to a jury that a defendant is guilty.

The United States Supreme Court has stated that the presence of a defendant at a jury trial in prison clothing is prejudicial to the presumption of innocence.[11] Additionally, a criminal defendant has a right not to appear before the jury in handcuffs or shackles.

This right to be free of restraint is not absolute. Judges have the authority to take whatever measures are necessary to assure safety in the courtroom and to advance the administration of justice. Accordingly, a defendant who is disorderly may be expelled from the trial. However, before exclusion is ordered the court should consider other alternatives. Defendants who are threatening may be restrained, and those who verbally interfere with the proceeding may be gagged.[12]

The standard imposed upon the government in criminal cases is to prove guilt **beyond a reasonable doubt**. The proof beyond a reasonable doubt standard is the highest standard of proof in the judicial system. There are two other standards of proof—the preponderance of the evidence standard and the clear and convincing evidence standard—which have been discussed previously in this text. Reasonable doubt is defined in Penal Code § 1096 as follows:

> "It is not a mere possible doubt; because everything relating to human affairs … is open to some possible or imaginary doubt. It is that state of the case, which, after the entire comparison and consideration of all the evidence, leaves the minds of jurors in that condition that they … *cannot* say they feel an abiding conviction … of the truth of the charge."

The reasonable doubt standard applies to each element of the offenses charged against the defendant; that is, the prosecution must prove each element beyond a reasonable doubt. Failure to prove any element of an offense beyond a reasonable doubt requires that the defendant be acquitted of that offense.

The Right to Counsel

The Sixth Amendment to the United States Constitution provides that "in all criminal prosecutions, the accused shall enjoy the right … to have the Assistance of Counsel for his defense." The right to counsel is one of the most fundamental rights guaranteed to criminal defendants and is fully applicable to the states.

The right to the assistance of counsel is found not only in the Sixth Amendment, but also in the Fifth and Fourteenth Amendments. These alternative sources are discussed later in the particular contexts within which they apply.

Indigency

It has always been clear that criminal defendants are entitled to retain the attorney of their choice. It was not until 1923 that the United States Supreme Court recognized a constitutional right to appointed counsel for indigent defendants, in *Powell v. Alabama*, 287 U.S. 45 (1923).

In the *Powell* case (commonly known as the Scottsboro case), nine young black males were charged with the rape of two white girls. Within one week of arrest, the defendants were tried. Eight of the "Scottsboro boys" were convicted and sentenced to death. The defendants appealed, claiming that they should have been provided counsel. The Supreme Court agreed.

However, the right to appointed counsel in *Powell* was founded not upon the Sixth Amendment, but upon the Fourteenth. The Court reasoned that the absence of counsel deprived the defendants of a fair trial and, accordingly, violated the defendants' due process rights. This decision was narrow: it applied only to capital cases in which the defendant was incapable of preparing an adequate defense and did not have the resources to hire an attorney.

The due process right to counsel was subsequently extended to all situations in which a defendant would not have a fair trial in the absence of defense counsel. Whether counsel was required depended on each particular case's "totality of facts." If denial of counsel was "shocking to the universal sense of justice," then the defendant's right to a fair trial, as guaranteed by the Fourteenth Amendment, was violated.[13] The Court refused to extend the right to counsel to all state criminal proceedings. Cases that involved complex legal issues or a defendant of low intelligence were the types of situations that required the appointment of counsel under the due process standard.

In 1938 the Court decided *Johnson v. Zerbst*, 304 U.S. 458 (1938), which held that the Sixth Amendment guarantees a right to counsel. The Sixth Amendment right to counsel was found to be broader than the right to counsel announced in *Powell*, as it applied to all criminal prosecutions. However, *Zerbst* did not apply to state proceedings. In 1963, the United States Supreme Court decided *Gideon v. Wainwright*. In that decision, the Court held that the Sixth Amendment right to counsel applies to all state felony proceedings and that counsel must be appointed for indigent defendants in such cases.

Powell established an indigent defendant's right to appointed counsel in state capital cases under the limited circumstances previously discussed. *Gideon* created a broader right and extended it to all state felony cases. In its 1972 decision in *Argersinger v. Hamlin*, 407 U.S. 25, the United States Supreme Court extended the right to appointed counsel yet further, holding that a right to counsel exists in all state criminal proceedings, including misdemeanor cases, in which the defendant is actually sentenced to imprisonment. The practical effect of *Argersinger* is that counsel must be appointed, if requested by an indigent defendant, in any case in which imprisonment is a possible sentence upon conviction.

GIDEON v. WAINWRIGHT
372 U.S. 335 (1963)

Petitioner was charged in Florida state court with having broken and entered a poolroom with intent to commit a misdemeanor. This offense is a felony under Florida law. Appearing in court without funds and without a lawyer, petitioner asked the court to appoint counsel for him, whereupon the following colloquy took place:

> THE COURT: Mr. Gideon, I am sorry, but I cannot appoint Counsel to represent you in this case. Under the laws of the State of Florida, the only time the Court can appoint Counsel to represent a defendant is when that person is charged with a capital offense. I am sorry, but I will have to deny your request to appoint Counsel to defend you in this case.

> THE DEFENDANT: The United States Supreme Court says I am entitled to be represented by Counsel.

Put to trial before a jury, Gideon conducted his defense about as well as could be expected from a layman. He made an opening statement to the jury, cross-examined the State's witnesses, presented witnesses in his own defense, declined to testify himself, and made a short argument "emphasizing his innocence to the charge contained in the Information filed in this case." The jury returned a verdict of guilty, and petitioner was sentenced to five years in the state prison. Since 1942, when *Betts v. Brady*, 316 U.S. 455, was decided by a divided Court, the problem of a defendant's federal constitutional right to counsel in a state court has been a continuing source of controversy and litigation in both state and federal courts. ... Since Gideon was proceeding in forma pauperis, we appointed counsel to represent him and requested both sides to discuss in their briefs and oral arguments the following: "Should this Court's holding in Betts v. Brady ... be reconsidered? ...

Governments, both state and federal, quite properly spend vast sums of money to establish machinery to try defendants accused of crime. Lawyers to prosecute are everywhere deemed essential to protect the public's interest in an orderly society. Similarly, there are few defendants charged with crime, few indeed, who fail to hire the best lawyers they can get to prepare and present their defenses. That government hires lawyers to prosecute and defendants who have the money to hire lawyers to defend are the strongest indications of the widespread belief that lawyers in criminal courts are necessities, not luxuries. The right of one charged with crime to counsel may not be deemed fundamental and essential to fair trials in some countries, but it is in ours. From the very beginning, our state and national constitutions and laws have laid great emphasis on procedural and substantive safeguards designed to assure fair trials before impartial tribunals in which every defendant stands equal before the law. This noble idea cannot be realized if the poor man charged with crime has to face his accusers without a lawyer to represent him. ... The Court in *Betts v. Brady* departed from sound wisdom upon which the Court's holding in *Powell v. Alabama* rested. Florida, supported by two other States, has asked that *Betts v. Brady* be left intact. Twenty-two states, as friends of the Court, argue that *Betts* was "an anachronism when handed down" and that it should now be overruled. We agree. ... Reversed.

The right-to-counsel principles developed by the United States Supreme Court are based on the United States Constitution and set the minimum standard that must be met by the states. As with many constitutional rights accorded defendants in criminal proceedings, the California Constitution grants greater protection than does the United States Constitution. In the California courts, an indigent defendant in any felony or misdemeanor case has a right to appointed counsel, regardless of whether imprisonment is or can be imposed. Article I, § 15, of the California Constitution provides that "[t]he defendant in a criminal cause has the right ... to have the assistance of counsel for the defendant's defense." Numerous provisions of the Penal Code refer to the right to counsel in all felony and misdemeanor cases, without reference to the type of punishment authorized for the offense charged.

Infraction cases, however, are treated differently. Penal Code § 19.6 provides that a person charged with an infraction is not entitled to appointed counsel unless she is arrested and not released on her written promise to appear, her own recognizance, or a deposit of bail.

Denial of the right to counsel is reversible error per se; that is, the defendant's conviction must be reversed even if he cannot establish that he was prejudiced by the court's failure to provide attorney representation.

When an indigent defendant requests appointment of counsel, he or she is entitled to appointment of a competent attorney. A defendant is not, however, entitled to choose the attorney the court will appoint. Counties are authorized to, and have, established **public defenders**. Many counties have created public defender offices that employ a number of attorneys. Under Penal Code § 987.2, if a court appoints counsel to represent an indigent defendant, and the county has a public defender, the court must appoint the public defender unless the public defender is unavailable.

The most common ground for unavailability is conflict of interest. For example, if two defendants are to be tried together for the same offense, and the public defender is appointed to represent one of the defendants, the public defender may be unavailable because of conflict of interest to represent the other defendant. A conflict of interest could arise if the two defendants have differing defenses or each is claiming that the other was the perpetrator of the offense.

If the public defender is unavailable, § 987.2 requires that the court appoint a private attorney who has contracted with the county and the court to provide defense services, if there is such an attorney in the county. Frequently, counties maintain panels of contracted private attorneys for this purpose. Finally, if no county-contracted private attorney is available, the court must appoint an attorney from among the private attorneys in the county. An attorney has an ethical duty to accept the appointment.

Effective Assistance of Counsel

A defendant is entitled not only to have an attorney, but also to the effective assistance of counsel. This entitlement applies to both appointed counsel and counsel retained by a defendant at his or her own expense. Ineffective assistance of counsel is a ground for appeal and reversal of a defendant's conviction.

In determining whether a defendant has received effective assistance of counsel, the California courts have consistently applied the federal standard, which is "reasonably effective assistance of counsel." This standard was established by the United States Supreme Court in *Strickland v. Washington*, 466 U.S. 668 (1984). In that decision, the Court stated that the criterion for deciding a claim of ineffective assistance of counsel is "whether counsel's conduct so undermined the proper functioning of the adversarial process that the trial cannot be relied upon as having produced a just result." To establish a claim of ineffective assistance of counsel, the defendant must make two showings. First, he must show that his attorney "failed to act in the manner to be expected of reasonably competent attorneys acting as diligent advocates." Second, the defendant must show that "it is reasonably probable that a more favorable determination would have resulted in the absence of counsel's failings."[14]

Ineffective assistance of counsel claims are rarely successful. Attorneys are expected to make legal and tactical decisions when defending their clients, and appellate courts are reluctant to second-guess defense counsels' decisions outside the context of the trial proceedings during which they were made. Also, even when a defendant persuades an appellate court that her attorney "failed to act in the manner to be expected of reasonably competent attorneys acting as diligent advocates," the court frequently finds that the defendant would have fared no better at trial with more competent representation; in other words, the court finds that it is not "reasonably probable that a more favorable determination would have resulted in the absence of counsel's failings."

Notwithstanding the difficulty of prevailing on a claim of ineffective assistance of counsel, defendants making such claims are sometimes successful. For example, the courts have found ineffective assistance of counsel in cases in which defense attorneys have failed to present a meritorious defense; have failed to object to the introduction of inadmissible and prejudicial evidence; have been ignorant of applicable law; and have failed to call a witness whose testimony would tend to exculpate the defendant.[15] In these cases, the defendant successfully established on appeal both the incompetence of the attorney *and* a reasonable probability of a more favorable result had the defendant been competently represented.

The Scope of the Right

In *United States v. Gouveia,* 467 U.S. 180 (1984), the United States Supreme Court held that the right to counsel under the Sixth Amendment to the United States Constitution arises at or after the time that adversary judicial proceedings have been initiated against the defendant, "whether by way of formal charge, preliminary hearing, indictment, information, or arraignment." Once such proceedings have been initiated, an indigent defendant has a right to appointed counsel at all "critical stages" of the proceedings. **Critical stages** are events that may affect substantial rights of the defendant. The right to counsel under the California Constitution, as applied through provisions of the Penal Code, applies at every stage of the proceedings against the defendant. In practical effect, the federal and California constitutional rights mean the same thing: an indigent defendant is generally entitled to appointed counsel beginning at the time of his or her initial appearance, because this is the point at which adversary judicial proceedings are commenced against him or her. The right continues through the pretrial stages, the trial, and sentencing. Once the right attaches, the defendant is entitled to appointed counsel whenever her contact with law enforcement officials or her participation in a court proceeding may affect her substantial rights.

This principle was applied by the United States Supreme Court in *Massiah v. United States,* 377 U.S. 201 (1964). In that case, the defendant was charged with conspiracy to import narcotics. After Massiah was indicted, a police officer used an undercover informant to engage the defendant in a conversation during which he incriminated himself. The informant was wearing a hidden radio transmitter and a police officer, sitting in an automobile not far away, monitored the conversation. The United States Supreme Court held that because the defendant had been formally charged (by indictment), he was entitled to be represented by counsel during any interrogation by the police, and the ruse employed by the police officer constituted a surreptitious interrogation. The Court reversed Massiah's conviction because of the violation of his right to counsel.

It is important to understand that the right to counsel addressed in the present discussion is the right to counsel guaranteed by the Sixth Amendment to the United States Constitution and the corresponding provision in article I, § 15, of the California Constitution. This right arises once adversarial judicial proceedings have been initiated against a defendant. Prior to the initiation of adversary judicial proceedings, a defendant generally has no right to counsel. An exception to this rule is the right to counsel at a custodial police interrogation. Recall from Chapter 15 that the United States Supreme Court established this right in its decision in *Miranda v. Arizona*. The right to counsel at this stage of the criminal process is, however, based on the Fifth Amendment to the United States Constitution, and the corresponding provision of the California Constitution, and is characterized as an essential safeguard to protect the defendant's right against self-incrimination. A right to counsel is also found in the Due Process and Equal Protection Clauses of the federal and California constitutions. These constitutional provisions have been held to confer a right to counsel on a defendant's first level of appeal, at probation revocation hearings, and (to a limited degree) at parole revocation hearings.

The Right to Self-Representation

A defendant may, for one reason or another, desire not to be represented by counsel during criminal proceedings. In *Faretta v. California*, 422 U.S. 806 (1975), the United States Supreme Court held that a criminal defendant has a constitutional right under the Sixth Amendment to choose *not* to be represented by counsel. The Court recognized that the assistance of trained legal counsel is essential to preparing and presenting a defense. However, on balance, the Court found that a defendant's right of choice is of greater importance. Therefore, a defendant may choose to act as his or her own counsel (pro se) even though the decision may increase the probability of conviction.

A court may permit a defendant to represent himself or herself only if it determines that the defendant's decision is knowingly and intelligently made. The court must make inquiry of the defendant for this purpose, and the inquiry must be made a part of the record of the case. If the court, upon inquiry, determines that the defendant's request to represent himself or herself is not knowingly or intelligently made, or that the defendant is so undereducated or inarticulate that his or her trial would be reduced to a sham, it may deny the defendant's request. Also, if a defendant representing himself or herself engages in misconduct or disrupts the court proceedings, the court may terminate the self-representation.

If a defendant chooses to represent himself and later changes his mind and requests appointment of counsel, the decision of whether to appoint counsel is a matter within the discretion of the trial judge.

Capital cases (cases in which the death penalty is authorized) are treated differently from other cases insofar as self-representation is concerned. If the offense with which the defendant is charged is a capital offense, the law requires that the defendant be represented by counsel, regardless of the desire of the defendant to be represented.

§ 17.2 Trial Procedure

Order for Trial

Penal Code § 1093 specifies the normal order for trial in a criminal case. That section provides that, unless otherwise directed by the court, a trial proceeds in the following order:

1. The jury is impaneled and sworn, unless the defendant has waived trial by jury.
2. If the defendant is charged with a felony, the clerk must read the accusatory pleading and inform the jury of the defendant's plea to the charge. In felony cases in which the defendant has elected to be tried by the judge alone, and in all other cases, this procedure may be dispensed with.
3. Each side may then make an opening statement, if desired. The prosecution makes its statement first. The defense may then make an opening statement, or may reserve making its opening statement until after the prosecution has presented its evidence.
4. The prosecution then presents its evidence in support of the charged offense or offenses. The defense may then present its case.
5. Both sides may then offer evidence in rebuttal of the evidence presented by the other side.
6. After all the evidence has been presented by both sides, each side may argue the case, if it chooses to do so. The prosecution argues first, followed by the defense. The prosecution is then given an opportunity to make a closing argument.
7. The judge then instructs the jury on the rules of law applicable to the case.

After the judge instructs the jury, the jury retires to deliberate and reach a verdict.

Formation of the Jury

Unless the defendant has waived trial by jury, the first step in a criminal trial is formation of the jury. Trial juries in both civil and criminal cases are formed in accordance with procedures established in the Code of Civil Procedure.[16] When jurors are summoned to court, they are grouped into *panels.* When a jury is needed in a courtroom, a panel of jurors is assigned to that courtroom, and the trial jury will be selected from that panel.

Code of Civil Procedure § 220 provides that a trial jury consists of twelve persons; in misdemeanor cases, the parties may agree to a lesser number. The discussion here presumes a twelve-person jury.

Twelve persons are randomly selected from the panel and seated in the courtroom. Examination of the prospective jurors is then conducted by means of a process known as **voir dire**. Voir dire involves questioning the prospective jurors to determine their competency and qualifications. The main concern is to select a fair and impartial jury. In criminal cases, voir dire is conducted by the judge. The judge may, upon a showing of good cause, allow attorneys for the parties to ask supplemental questions.

Voir dire is aimed at determining whether any juror is disqualified from serving or is biased in a manner that could deprive the defendant of a fair trial. Jurors may be biased in a number of ways. For example, a juror may have formed a preconceived opinion regarding the guilt of the defendant; may be prejudiced against persons of the defendant's race, religion, or ethnicity; or may have an abhorrence of the crime charged that renders him or her unable to act with objectivity and impartiality. There are many other potential forms of bias. In a capital case, for example, if a juror is so opposed to the death penalty that he or she would not vote for the death penalty under any circumstances, the juror is considered to be biased.[17]

At the conclusion of the voir dire, the parties may challenge jurors for the purpose of having them discharged from the jury. There are two types of challenges: challenges for cause and peremptory challenges. Challenges for cause are made first, followed by peremptory challenges. A **challenge for cause** is a challenge to a juror on the ground that his or her answers to the voir dire questioning reveal that he or she is disqualified from serving on the jury or is biased. A challenge for cause must be ruled upon by the judge. There is no numerical limit on the number of challenges for cause.

A **peremptory challenge** requires no showing of cause. Peremptory challenges are used by the parties to exclude jurors who are qualified but are not desired by the challenging party for some reason. For example, a potential juror may be peremptorily challenged by the defense because he or she is perceived to be too prosecution-oriented. Despite the fact that peremptory challenges require no grounds, jurors may not be peremptorily challenged based on group bias, such as a desire to eliminate all members of a racial minority from the jury. There are numerical limits on peremptory challenges.

If any of the original twelve randomly selected jurors are discharged through challenges for cause or peremptory challenges, they are replaced with other panel members who, in turn, are subjected to voir dire questioning. The process is repeated until a jury of twelve persons has been impaneled. The jury is then sworn.

If a trial is likely to be protracted, or if the parties stipulate, the court may appoint one or more alternate jurors from the jury panel. Alternate jurors are subject to the same voir dire and challenge procedures as the other jurors. Alternate jurors attend all sessions of the trial attended by the regular jurors. If a regular juror dies, becomes ill, or for other good cause is discharged prior to the rendering of the jury's verdict, the judge selects one of the alternate jurors to take the former juror's place on the jury.

Preliminary Instructions and Reading of Accusatory Pleading

The next stage in the trial proceeding is for the judge to give preliminary instructions to the jury. The subject matter of the preliminary instructions generally includes guidance regarding the jury's functions, duties, and conduct. The instructions are to include, among other matters, admonitions that the jurors not converse among themselves, or with anyone else, on any subject connected with the trial; that they not read or listen to any accounts or discussions of the case reported in the media; and that they not visit or view any premises or place involved in the case. The judge may also instruct on other matters intended to assure that the jury's decision will be based solely on the evidence presented in court. (*See* Penal Code § 1122.)

Penal Code § 1093(a) requires that, in a felony case, the clerk read the accusatory pleading to the jury and state the plea entered by the defendant. In all other cases, this procedure may be omitted. Even in a felony case, the defendant may, and frequently does, waive the reading.

Opening Statements

After the judge has given the preliminary instructions and the accusatory pleading and plea have been read to the jury (if they are read), the parties are given the opportunity to make an opening statement. Opening statements are optional, and either party may elect not to make an opening statement. Also, the defense may choose to postpone its opening statement until after the prosecution presents its case. The purpose of the opening statement is limited to advising the jury of the evidence to be presented in support of a party's case. At this point in the proceedings, counsel should not engage in argument designed to discredit the other party's case.

The Prosecution's Case in Chief

After any opening statements by the parties, the prosecution presents its case. The prosecution must present evidence establishing each element of the charged offense beyond a reasonable doubt. Evidence presented by the prosecution may take many forms, such as the testimony of witnesses, real evidence such as tangible objects, demonstrative evidence such as charts and pictorial depictions of the scene of the crime, documentary evidence, scientific evidence, and the opinions of experts. Evidence is commonly categorized in broad terms as direct or circumstantial. **Direct evidence** is evidence that directly establishes the fact to be proved. For example, a witness's testimony that he or she saw the defendant commit the offense would constitute direct evidence. **Circumstantial evidence** is evidence that does not directly establish the fact to be proved, but is consistent with or supports the fact to be proved. Contrary to popular belief, a defendant may be convicted in a case in which the only evidence is circumstantial evidence.

As you already know, only admissible evidence may be introduced by the parties at trial. The admissibility of evidence is governed by the Evidence Code and by constitutional principles developed by the courts, such as the exclusionary rule. As discussed in Chapter 16, a party may attempt to exclude evidence at the outset of the trial by means of a motion in limine. If inadmissible evidence has not been excluded in advance by a motion in limine, and a party attempts to introduce it, the other party may object to the evidence. The judge rules on the **objection** and either sustains or overrules it. In determining whether to sustain or overrule an objection, the judge may hear argument on the matter from the parties' attorneys. In some instances, the attorneys will want to argue the objection outside the hearing of the jury. In such instances, a **sidebar** may be held, or the judge may order that the jury be removed until the matter is resolved. If the judge sustains a party's objection, the evidence is excluded and the jury is instructed to disregard it. If the judge overrules the objection, the evidence is admitted. If the judge admits prosecution evidence over defense objection, the defendant may later assert the admission of the evidence as error on appeal. If the judge admits inadmissible evidence without defense objection, the defendant is precluded from relying on the admission of the evidence as a basis for appeal.

The constitutional right of confrontation guarantees the defendant the right to cross-examine prosecution witnesses. Cross-examination of each prosecution witness is conducted by the defendant's attorney after the witness testifies on direct examination. As stated earlier, the purpose of cross-examination is to highlight any weaknesses in the witness's testimony, such as the witness's faulty perception, bias, or lack of credibility.

When the prosecutor finishes presenting the government's case, he or she advises the court that the People "rest."

Motion for Judgment of Acquittal

If the prosecution fails to prove its case against the defendant, the court is empowered to order that the defendant be acquitted of the charged offense. Penal Code § 1118 applies to cases tried by the court without a jury and provides that after the evidence of the prosecution has been closed, the court, on its own motion or on the motion of the defendant, must order entry of a judgment of acquittal of one or more of the offenses charged if, upon weighing the evidence presented by the prosecution, the court finds the defendant not guilty of the offense or offenses. Penal Code § 1118.1 applies to jury trials and provides that the court must order entry of a judgment of acquittal at the close of the evidence on either side, and before the case is submitted to the jury for decision, if the evidence presented is insufficient to sustain a conviction of the charged offense or offenses on appeal. Evidence is insufficient to sustain a conviction of an offense if the prosecution has failed to present substantial evidence of any element of that offense.

If the judge grants a **motion for judgment of acquittal**, the defendant is acquitted; in a jury trial, the jury is discharged without having deliberated or rendered a verdict. Penal Code § 1118.2 provides that a judgment of acquittal entered pursuant to §§ 1118 or 1118.1 cannot be appealed by the government and is a bar to any other prosecution for the same offense.

If the judge denies a motion for judgment of acquittal, the trial proceeds and the defense may put on its case.

The Defense Case

If the defendant's motion for judgment of acquittal is denied, or if no such motion has been made, the defense may then put on its case. The defense is not required to put on a case, but usually does so. The defense may present witness testimony and all of the other types of evidence that the prosecution may present. The object of the defense case is to introduce evidence contradicting or discrediting prosecution evidence, in an attempt to raise a reasonable doubt in the minds of the jurors regarding the existence of one or more elements of the offense. Another defense objective may be to present evidence establishing one or more defenses. As with the prosecution's witnesses, defense witnesses are subject to cross-examination by the other side. The defendant, as you know, is not required to testify. If, however, the defendant chooses to testify, he or she is also subject to cross-examination by the prosecutor.

Rebuttal

After the defense has concluded, the prosecution may call rebuttal witnesses in an effort to disprove the evidence of the defense. No new issues may be raised during rebuttal. The defense is then permitted to rebut the prosecution's rebuttal evidence.

Argument

After the evidentiary phase of the trial is concluded, the parties may argue the case to the trier of fact. Penal Code § 1093(e) provides that the prosecution argues first, then the defense, followed by a closing argument by the prosecution. The parties are not required to present argument, but usually do so. In its argument, each party may argue that the evidence adduced supports its case and may generally attempt to persuade the trier of fact to find in its favor. There is not much law on what is improper in defense counsel's argument, because the issue is rarely raised on appeal. It has been held that defense counsel must not attempt in its argument to instruct the jury on the applicable law or to offer a personal opinion on the innocence of the defendant.[18]

There is, however, a considerable amount of law regarding what is improper in the prosecution's argument, because this issue is frequently raised on appeal by convicted defendants.[19] The prosecutor must not make inflammatory remarks about the defendant or defense counsel, nor attempt to influence the jury to decide the case based on prejudice or emotion. It is also improper for a prosecutor to comment on a defendant's decision not to testify. Improper argument by the prosecutor constitutes prosecutorial misconduct. If objected to by the defense, it is a ground for appeal of the defendant's conviction. If the appellate court finds that the improper argument was prejudicial (i.e., caused the outcome of the trial to be different than it would have been absent the argument), the appellate court may reverse the defendant's conviction. Alternatively, if the prosecutor's argument is so prejudicial that an admonition to the jury by the judge to disregard it is likely to be ineffective, the judge may declare a mistrial.

Final Instructions

After completion of the parties' arguments, the judge charges the jury by instructing them on the law applicable to the case. There are three fundamental requirements for instructions: (1) they must deal with the law rather than with the facts brought out by the evidence; (2) they must deal with legal principles relevant to the issues in the case; and (3) they must state the law correctly.[20] Errors of law in the instructions, if significant and prejudicial to the defendant, are grounds for reversal of the defendant's conviction on appeal.

Jury instructions may address all legal aspects of a criminal case. Subjects typically addressed by the court in its instructions to the jury include the elements of the charged offense, the elements of any lesser included offense, the meaning of particular terms, the elements of applicable defenses, procedural requirements pertaining to deliberation and verdicts, standards of proof, and principles of evidence.

Jury Deliberations and Verdict

After instructions are completed, the case is submitted by the judge to the jury. The jury then retires to deliberate. Courts typically have a jury room for this purpose. Jury deliberations are conducted in strict secrecy. In the California courts, the jury is permitted to take the evidence admitted at trial into the jury room.[21] The jury is not, however, permitted to take a transcript of the trial or the deposition of any witness into the jury room. The jury may also take into the jury room the written instructions given by the judge and their personal notes of the trial proceedings.

The object of jury deliberation is to reach a verdict of conviction or acquittal. Both require a unanimous vote of the jury members. Unanimous agreement is often difficult to attain and juries sometimes report to the judge that they are unable to reach a verdict. Penal Code § 1140 provides that the judge may discharge the jury if, after "the expiration of such time as the court may deem proper, it satisfactorily appears that there is no reasonable probability that the jury can agree." Before making a decision to discharge the jury, the judge may permissibly inquire about their numerical division, without specifying how many jurors are for conviction and how many are against. The judge may also urge the jury to continue to attempt to reach agreement, or order them to continue deliberation, provided the language used does not contain any element of coercion to reach a particular verdict.[22] The so-called "Allen charge" has been disapproved in California and may not be given by the judge. An Allen charge, approved by the United States Supreme Court in *Allen v. United States*, 164 U.S. 492 (1896), is an instruction by the judge encouraging jurors in the minority to consider the fact that the majority of the jurors are voting the other way and urging them to reexamine their positions in light of that fact.

If the point is reached at which "it satisfactorily appears that there is no reasonable probability that the jury can agree" on conviction or acquittal, the jury is said to be a **hung jury**. In this situation, the judge will declare a mistrial and discharge the jury. Penal Code § 1141 provides that the defendant may be retried for the charged offense. Recall from Chapter 11 that the constitutional prohibition against double jeopardy does not prevent retrial of a defendant when a mistrial has been declared because of a hung jury.

If the jury agrees on a verdict, they are conducted into the courtroom. The judge or clerk then asks the jury whether they have reached a verdict, and the foreman answers in the affirmative. The judge then asks what the verdict is, and the foreman states it. There are a number of types of verdict, but the most common is the general verdict. A general verdict simply states that the jury finds the defendant either guilty or not guilty as to each offense charged. At the request of either party, the jury may then be polled. **Polling the jury** means asking each juror individually whether the verdict is his or her verdict. If any juror answers in the negative, the jury must be sent out for further deliberation.[23] If all jurors confirm that the verdict is their verdict, or if the jurors are not polled, the court clerk enters the verdict in the minutes of the court.[24] The jury is then discharged.

Findings in Trial by Court

In cases in which the defendant has waived a jury (i.e., a court trial), the judge assumes the role of trier of fact. In a court trial, upon conclusion of the presentation of evidence and any argument by counsel, the judge announces his or her findings. The findings are to be rendered substantially in the form prescribed for a general verdict of a jury.[25] Thus, the judge will generally announce that he or she finds the defendant guilty or not guilty of the charged offense or offenses.

Acquittal

If the defendant has been found not guilty as to all charges, either by the jury or, in a court trial, by the judge, the court must enter a judgment of acquittal. If the defendant is in custody, he or she must be discharged.[26]

Conviction

If the defendant has been found guilty of any charge by the jury or the judge, or has pleaded guilty or nolo contendere, the judge must set a time for pronouncement of judgment and sentencing. In the superior court, the time set for pronouncement of judgment must be within twenty judicial days after the verdict. In the municipal court, judgment must be pronounced not less than six hours nor more than five days after the verdict. The defendant is permitted to waive the six-hour delay, thus enabling the municipal court to pronounce judgment immediately if the defendant so desires.[27]

New Trial

Penal Code §§ 1179 through 1182 permit a convicted defendant, under certain circumstances, to move the court for a new trial. The motion must be made and determined before pronouncement of judgment. A new trial "is a reexamination of the issue in the same Court, before another jury, after a verdict has been given."[28] If the court grants the defendant's **motion for a new trial**, it is as if the first trial never occurred. At the new trial, all evidence must be produced again, and the former verdict or finding cannot be used or referred to, either in evidence or in argument. Section 1181 states the exclusive grounds for the grant of a new trial. (*See* Penal Code § 1181.)

Key Terms

bench trial A trial by the judge alone, without a jury; also referred to as a *court trial.*

beyond a reasonable doubt The highest standard of proof in the judicial system. *Reasonable doubt* is defined in Penal Code § 1096 as follows: "It is not a mere possible doubt; because everything relating to human affairs ... is open to some possible or imaginary doubt. It is that state of the case, which, after the entire comparison and consideration of all the evidence, leaves the minds of jurors in that condition that they ... cannot say they feel an abiding conviction ... of the truth of the charge."

challenge for cause A challenge to a prospective juror on the ground that his or her answers to the voir dire questioning reveal that he or she is disqualified from serving on the jury or is biased.

circumstantial evidence Evidence that does not directly establish the fact to be proved, but that is consistent with or supports the fact to be proved.

court trial A trial by the judge alone, without a jury; also referred to as a *bench trial.*

cross-examination The questioning of a witness for one party by the attorney for the other party for the purpose of bringing out any weakness in the witness's testimony, such as faulty perception, bias, or lack of credibility.

direct evidence Evidence (such as eyewitness testimony) that directly establishes the fact to be proved.

gag order An order by the court restricting participants in the criminal proceeding from discussing specified aspects of the case with news media representatives.

hung jury A jury that is unable, after sufficient deliberation, to vote unanimously either for conviction or for acquittal.

motion for judgment of acquittal A motion made by the defendant in a criminal trial requesting the court to enter a judgment of acquittal before the normal termination of the trial, because of failure of the prosecution to prove its case.

motion for new trial A motion made by a defendant requesting a new trial because of judicial error or misconduct of the prosecutor or jury that is sufficiently serious to have prejudiced the defendant's right to a fair trial.

objection An assertion made by a party in a trial that the conduct of the other party is improper, that evidence offered by the other party is inadmissible, or that some other occurrence in the trial is not in accordance with law.

peremptory challenge A challenge to a prospective juror which requires no grounds.

polling the jury Questioning of each individual juror after the verdict is announced to assure that the verdict is his or her verdict.

public defender An attorney employed by a county to represent indigent defendants prosecuted in the courts situated in that county.

sequestration order An order by the trial judge that the jury be kept in custody between court sessions.

sidebar A discussion during a trial among the attorneys and judge, conducted outside the hearing of the jury.

voir dire The questioning of prospective jurors for the purpose of determining whether any are disqualified from serving or are biased in a manner that would deprive the defendant of a fair trial.

Review Questions

1. In what types of cases is a criminal defendant in the California courts entitled to a jury? In what type of case is a defendant not entitled to a jury?

2. What is a gag order? What is sequestration? What is the purpose of a gag order or sequestration?

3. Are photographing, recording, and broadcasting of criminal trials permitted in California? Does the judge have the authority to control the conduct of media representatives in the courtroom?

4. Under what circumstances may a child sexual-abuse victim testify against the defendant via closed-circuit television without violating the defendant's constitutional right to confront the witnesses against him or her?

5. Briefly describe the provisions of Penal Code § 977 that permit a defendant to elect to be absent during court proceedings in his or her case.

6. Penal Code § 1382(a) establishes certain statutory speedy trial rights. Briefly describe these rights.

7. What are the three standards of proof used in the California judicial system? Define the "beyond a reasonable doubt standard" of proof.

8. What is the difference between an indigent defendant's entitlement to appointed counsel under federal constitutional law and his or her right to appointed counsel under California constitutional law?

9. What are the two showings a defendant must make to establish a claim of ineffective assistance of counsel?

10. Briefly explain each of the following terms as they apply to the jury formation process: voir dire, challenge for cause, peremptory challenge.

11. What sort of subjects is the judge likely to cover in the preliminary instructions to the jury?

12. Briefly explain the terms *direct evidence* and *circumstantial evidence*.

13. What procedural step may a defendant's attorney take at the close of the prosecution's case if he or she believes that the prosecution has not established each element of the charged offense?

14. Give some examples of types of arguments that would be improper for a prosecuting attorney to make to the jury.

15. What subjects are typically covered in jury instructions?

16. What is a hung jury? What does the trial judge do if he or she determines that the jury is a hung jury?

17. List some of the grounds upon which a court may grant a defendant a new trial pursuant to Penal Code §§ 1179 through 1182.

Review Problems

1. Jane has been charged by complaint filed in the municipal court with selling an alcoholic beverage to a person under the age of twenty-one years. The offense is a misdemeanor punishable only by a fine and/or community service. Jane demands trial by jury. The prosecutor states that Jane does not have a right to a jury because the offense is a petty offense. Is the prosecutor correct? Explain your answer.

2. Waldo Knuttcase is an accused serial murderer. His case has attracted widespread media attention. Waldo's trial is about to begin. Citing the First Amendment right of freedom of the press, a prominent television network informs the judge that it intends to provide live coverage of the trial. The network's representative states that the network intends to place six television cameras in the courtroom and to bring in special lighting to support the cameras. The representative also advises the judge that the courtroom will have to be rearranged so that the cameras will have an optimum view of the proceedings. Finally, the

representative advises the judge that microphones will be placed on the judge's bench and in the judge's chambers to record all conversations between the judge and counsel conducted outside the hearing of the jury. May the judge refuse to permit the network to carry out its plans?

3. Hampton Figg is on trial for armed robbery. The prosecutor intends to call Robert Newton as a witness. Newton is expected to testify that his friend, Sara Teller, who works at the bank at which Figg maintains his accounts, told him that two days after the alleged robbery, Figg deposited a large sum of cash in the bank. Would Newton's testimony violate any constitutional right of Figg?

4. Myra Mercury has been charged with the theft of a telescope with a value of $250, a misdemeanor. She does not intend to testify at the trial and would prefer not to attend, leaving the matter in the hands of her attorney. Does the law permit Myra to decide that she will not attend the trial?

5. The district attorney files a criminal complaint in the municipal court against Sam, alleging that Sam committed the offense of battery on Joe, (a misdemeanor). Sam is not aware that the complaint has been filed. Four years pass without further action by the government. The district attorney then directs his staff to clear up all old cases, whereupon Sam is arrested and brought before a magistrate for his initial appearance. Sam's attorney asserts that to prosecute Sam now would violate his constitutional right to a speedy trial. The attorney states that there were witnesses to the incident who could have established that Sam was acting in self-defense, but none of them can now be located. How should the magistrate evaluate the attorney's claim? What decision do you think the magistrate should reach?

6. The district attorney has filed an information against Shirley Shmedlap, charging her with embezzlement of funds (theft) in the amount of $250,000. Shirley is being held in custody in the county jail awaiting her trial. One day, a new prisoner is brought in and Shirley is informed that the prisoner will be sharing her cell. Unknown to Shirley, the other "prisoner" is a police informant who has agreed to try to elicit incriminating statements from Shirley. The informant engages Shirley in conversation and eventually asks Shirley "what she is in for." Shirley tells the informant that she has been charged with embezzlement. The informant asks, "Well, did you do it?" Shirley answers, "Yeah, I did it, but they'll never prove it." Shirley tells her attorney about the conversation. At the commencement of her trial, Shirley's attorney makes a motion in limine requesting the court to prohibit any testimony about Shirley's conversation with the informant. Does the attorney have a valid legal basis to make the motion? Do you think the motion will be successful?

7. Malcolm is charged with several counts of assault with a deadly weapon and battery resulting in great bodily injury. All offenses have been charged as felonies (noncapital). Malcolm appears in court for trial without an attorney. When asked by the judge why he is not represented by counsel, Malcolm states that he wants to represent himself. The judge informs Malcolm that the law requires that he be represented by counsel and appoints an attorney to represent him. Is the judge correct? Explain your answer.

8. Voir dire is being conducted in a superior court case in which the defendant, a black male, is charged with the rape and murder of a white female. The prosecution is seeking the death penalty. Of the twelve jurors being questioned, four are black, two are oriental, one is hispanic, and five are white. The voir dire questioning produces the following results. Juror number 1, who is a white male, evidences racial bias toward blacks. Juror number 6, who is an oriental female, indicates an abhorrence of the crime of rape that may render her unable to act with objectivity and impartiality. Jurors number 2 through 5, who are the black jurors, all appear to be able to act objectively and impartially despite the race of the defendant and the race of the victim. Juror number 7 states that he has strong conscientious objections to the death penalty and that he does not believe he could vote for the death penalty even if the evidence indicated that grounds for imposition of the death penalty exist. When the voir dire is concluded, the defense counsel challenges jurors 1 and 6 for cause. The prosecutor challenges juror number 7 for cause. What is the correct legal basis for these challenges? What must the judge do when the challenges are

made? After the challenges for cause, the prosecutor peremptorily challenges the four black jurors. Is this challenge legal?

9. A defendant is being tried for murder. The prosecutor is attempting to prove that the defendant drove the victim to a remote area, killed the victim, and left the body there. The prosecutor offers the following evidence: (1) expert testimony that tire tracks at the scene of the crime match the tires on the defendant's automobile; (2) expert testimony that strands of hair found on the victim's clothing match the defendant's hair; (3) expert testimony that blood found on the defendant's coat matches that of the victim; and (4) testimony of a local resident that he saw a car matching the description of the defendant's car near the scene of the crime at the estimated time of the murder. Would this evidence be classified as direct or circumstantial? If you were on the jury, would you vote to convict the defendant based on this evidence?

10. Arlo is on trial for the offense of assault with intent to commit rape. During the final jury instructions, the judge gives the following instruction to the jury. "Given the late hour of the night and the fact that the complainant was alone and vulnerable, if you find that the defendant assaulted her, you may presume that he did so with the intent to commit rape. He could have had no other purpose." Is this jury instruction legally correct? If not, why not? If you feel the instruction is erroneous, what is the defendant's remedy if the jury finds him guilty of the offense?

Notes

[1] *Duncan v. Louisiana,* 391 U.S. 145 (1968).

[2] *Baldwin v. New York,* 399 U.S. 66 (1970).

[3] *Johnson v. Louisiana,* 406 U.S. 356 (1972); *Apodaca v. Oregon,* 406 U.S. 404 (1972).

[4] *See* 5 Witkin & Epstein, *California Criminal Law* §§ 2646–2647 (2d ed. Bancroft-Whitney 1989).

[5] *Id.* at § 2620.

[6] *Id.* at § 2671.

[7] *United States v. Marion,* 404 U.S. 307 (1971).

[8] *People v. Hannon* (1977) 19 Cal.3d 588, at 607, 608.

[9] *United States v. Marion, supra* note 7.

[10] *Brooks v. Tennessee,* 406 U.S. 605 (1972).

[11] *Estelle v. Williams,* 425 U.S. 501 (1976).

[12] *Stewart v. Corbin,* 850 F.2d 492 (9th Cir. 1988).

[13] *Betts v. Brady,* 316 U.S. 455 (1942).

[14] *People v. Lewis* (1990) 50 Cal.3d 262, 288.

[15] *See generally* 5 Witkin & Epstein, *supra* note 4, at §§ 2780–2788.

[16] Penal Code § 1046; Code of Civ. Proc. § 192.

[17] *See, e.g., People v. Kaurish* (1990) 52 Cal.3d 648.

[18] *People v. Baldwin* (1954) 42 Cal.2d 858; *People v. Tyler* (1991) 233 Cal.App.3d 1456.

[19] *See People v. Talle* (1952) 111 Cal.App.2d 650, 676.

[20] 5 Witkin & Epstein, *supra* note 4, at § 2921.

[21] Penal Code § 1137.

[22] 6 Witkin & Epstein, *supra* note 4, at § 3019.

[23] Penal Code § 1163.

[24] Penal Code § 1164.

[25] Penal Code § 1167.

[26] Penal Code § 1165.

[27] *See* Penal Code §§ 1191 (superior court) and 1449 (municipal court).

[28] Penal Code § 1179.

CHAPTER 18

Judgment and Sentencing

OUTLINE

Introduction

In this chapter we examine the legal principles that govern pronouncement of judgment on and sentencing of a defendant who has been convicted at trial or who has pled guilty.

§ 18.1 Judgment

If a defendant is acquitted at trial, the criminal proceeding against him or her is at an end. If, however, a defendant is convicted at trial, judgment must be pronounced and sentence imposed. Pronouncement of judgment and imposition of sentence are accomplished at a proceeding that is separate from, and that occurs after, the trial. Pronouncement of judgment and imposition of sentence are technically distinct concepts. *Pronouncement of judgment* refers to an adjudication of guilt by the court: the court adjudges that the defendant is guilty of the crime of which he or she has been convicted at trial. *Imposition of sentence* refers to the order of the court imposing on the defendant the penalty or penalties authorized by law for the crime(s) of which he or she has been adjudged guilty by the court. However, the Penal Code, Rules of Court, judges, attorneys, and commentators tend to use the terms interchangeably.

As mentioned in Chapter 17, the court must pronounce judgment and impose sentence in a felony case within twenty judicial days after the verdict, finding, or plea of guilty. (*See* Penal Code § 1191.) In a misdemeanor case, judgment must be pronounced and sentence imposed not less than six hours, nor more than five days, after the plea, finding, or verdict of guilty. The defendant may waive the six-hour postponement and request that judgment and sentence be imposed immediately. (*See* Penal Code § 1449.)

The court proceeding at which judgment is pronounced and sentence imposed begins with a procedure known as the **arraignment for judgment**. Penal Code § 1200 provides:

> When the defendant appears for judgment he must be informed by the Court, or by the Clerk, under its direction, of the nature of the charge against him and of his plea, and the verdict, if any thereon, and must be asked whether he has any legal cause to show why judgment should not be pronounced against him.

As is apparent from the statutory language, the defendant, although convicted at trial, is offered the opportunity to show why judgment should not be pronounced against him or her. This right of the defendant is known as the **right of allocution**. Penal Code § 1201 states two grounds why judgment should not be pronounced. The first ground is that the defendant is insane. As was briefly mentioned in Chapter 10, judgment may not be pronounced against a defendant who is insane. The second ground is that the defendant has grounds for arrest of judgment or a new trial. Procedurally, the defendant asserts these grounds by means of a motion. The motion for new trial was discussed in Chapter 17. A **motion in arrest of judgment** is a motion claiming that the accusatory pleading upon which the defendant was prosecuted is defective. (*See* Penal Code § 1185.) The grounds upon which the motion may be made are the same as the grounds for a demurrer (discussed in Chapter 16), and a motion in arrest of judgment may be made at the arraignment for judgment only if the defendant demurred to the accusatory pleading prior to trial. If at the arraignment for judgment the defendant moves for a new trial or arrest of judgment, the court may, in its discretion, order the judgment to be deferred, and proceed to hear and decide the motion. If the motion is granted, the relief sought therein (new trial or arrest of judgment) will be ordered and judgment will not be pronounced. If the motion is denied, the court will then pronounce judgment.

Judgment is pronounced orally by the judge and includes imposition of sentence. California law does not prescribe a particular form for the judgment. The judgment must, however, contain at least a statement of the offense of which the defendant has been convicted and the sentence of the court.[1]

§ 18.2 Sentencing

As stated in § 18.1, sentence is imposed by the court at the same time that judgment is pronounced. Pronouncement of judgment and imposition of sentence are functions of the judge, not the jury. In fact, at this point in the proceedings, there is no jury. (Recall that the jury is discharged after it renders its verdict.) There is an exception to this principle in death penalty cases. In such cases, the jury will remain impaneled to decide whether to impose a sentence of death.

The legislature prescribes the types and amounts of punishment authorized for crimes. Types of punishment authorized by the Penal Code and other codes containing penal provisions include imprisonment, fines, restitution, community service, and other forms of punishment. The authority of the legislature to prescribe punishment for crimes is broad, but not unlimited. The Eighth Amendment to the United States Constitution, applicable to the states through the Fourteenth Amendment, prohibits "cruel and unusual punishment." Article I, § 17, of the California Constitution contains a similar provision. Cruel and unusual punishment may include physical punishment of a barbarous nature, such as the maiming of the defendant or burning at the stake. Cruel and unusual punishment may also include other types of punishment that are not barbarous, such as a term of imprisonment that is excessive or disproportionate to the severity of the offense, corporal punishment of prisoners, deprivation of citizenship, and deliberate withholding of medical care from incarcerated persons.[2] The constitutionality of the death penalty has been challenged numerous times on the ground that it constitutes cruel and unusual punishment. These challenges experienced a period of success, as will be discussed more fully later.

Sentencing Procedure

Misdemeanor Cases

Sentencing in misdemeanor cases is a relatively simple process. After the arraignment for judgment has been accomplished, the judge conducts a sentencing hearing at which evidence may be presented in **aggravation** or **mitigation**. Evidence in aggravation concerns the circumstances of the offense or the criminal history of the defendant and supports imposition of a sentence at or near the maximum authorized by law. Evidence in mitigation supports imposition of a minimal sentence.

If the defendant is eligible for probation, the judge in a misdemeanor case may, but is not required to, refer the case to a probation officer for the preparation of a report. In most misdemeanor cases, the judge does not do so, and the sentencing hearing consists principally of statements to the court made by the prosecutor and defense attorney. The judge then determines the sentence to be imposed.

As at other stages of the proceedings against the defendant, he or she has the right to be represented by counsel at the arraignment for judgment and sentencing hearing, under the Sixth Amendment to the United States Constitution and article I, § 15, of the California Constitution.

Felony Cases

Presentence Investigation Report   In contrast to misdemeanor sentencing procedure, in which referral of the case to a probation officer is a matter within the judge's discretion, the court is required to refer the case to a probation officer prior to the sentencing hearing in any felony case in which the defendant is eligible for probation. (*See* Penal Code § 1203.) The function of the probation officer is to investigate and report on facts relevant to the sentencing of the defendant. If the defendant is not eligible for probation, the court is required to refer the case to the probation officer for preparation of a report which will assist the court in determining the amount of restitution the defendant should be ordered to pay, if any. If the defendant is not eligible for probation, the court may still, in its discretion, direct the probation officer to prepare a full report, as in the case of a defendant who is eligible for probation. The report, known as a **presentence investigation report**, advises the court of the circumstances surrounding the offense and the prior record and history of the defendant. The content of the probation officer's presentence investigation report is discussed in detail in California Rule of Court 411.5. Certain items are mandated by Penal Code § 1203 as well. Among the many items the report is required to contain are: the facts and circumstances of the crime; the defendant's prior criminal record; the defendant's social history, such as family, education, and employment information; statements of interested parties, such as the defendant himself, the victim, and family members; and an evaluation of factors relating to the appropriate sentence to impose on the defendant. At the sentencing hearing, the defendant does not have the right to cross-examine the probation officer who prepared the probation report. He does have the right, however, to present witnesses to counteract or correct the probation report.

Sentencing Hearing The disposition of the defendant is determined by the court at the sentencing hearing, which immediately follows the arraignment for judgment. California Rule of Court 433 requires that the court do the following at the hearing. First, the court must hear and determine any claim by the defendant that she is insane, and any motion for a new trial or motion in arrest of judgment pursuant to Penal Code § 1201. If the court denies the defendant's § 1201 claims (if any), it must then proceed with the sentencing hearing and accomplish the following:

1. Determine whether the defendant, if eligible for probation, should be granted or denied probation.
2. If the defendant is to be granted probation, determine the sentence of the defendant in the event probation is revoked.
3. If a sentence of imprisonment is to be imposed, or determined in the event of future revocation of probation:
   a. Hear evidence in aggravation and mitigation and, based upon such evidence, determine whether to impose the upper, middle, or lower term prescribed for the offense.
   b. Determine whether to strike any additional term of imprisonment provided for a sentence enhancement.
   c. Determine whether the sentences will be consecutive or concurrent if the defendant has been convicted of multiple crimes.
   d. Pronounce the court's judgment and sentence.

The sentencing hearing is designed to bring to the attention of the sentencing judge all matters pertinent to the appropriate sentence to be imposed on the defendant. Matters in aggravation and mitigation are generally required to be submitted to the court in the form of statements at least four court days before the sentencing hearing. Such statements may be submitted by the prosecution, the defense, and the victim or the victim's family if the victim is deceased. As previously stated, matters in aggravation and mitigation generally have to do with facts relating to the crime and facts relating to the defendant. For example, great violence used by the defendant in the commission of the crime would be a matter in aggravation (fact relating to the crime), as would a long history of prior convictions (fact relating to the defendant). Evidence that the defendant was provoked or induced to commit the crime would be a matter in mitigation (fact relating to the crime), as would the defendant's lack of a prior criminal record (fact relating to the defendant). California Rules of Court 421 and 423 contain detailed enumerations of matter that may be raised in aggravation and mitigation.

Penal Code § 1170(b) provides that the court, when determining whether to impose the upper, middle, or lower term of imprisonment for an offense at the sentencing hearing, may consider the record in the case, the probation officer's report, other reports, statements in aggravation or mitigation, and any further evidence introduced at the sentencing hearing. Section 1204 provides that evidence in aggravation and mitigation is to be presented at the sentencing hearing by the testimony of witnesses examined in open court. The sentencing hearing is, accordingly, a full adversarial hearing. The sentencing hearing is thus a critical stage of the proceedings against the defendant, and the defendant has a constitutional right to be represented by counsel at the hearing.[3]

A fairly recent development in California criminal law is the victim impact statement. Under Penal Code § 1191.1, the victim of the crime (or his or her parents or guardian if the victim is a minor, or his or her next of kin if the victim has died) has the right to attend the sentencing hearing and to express views concerning the crime, the defendant, and the need for restitution.

After considering the information presented to it at the sentencing hearing in the form of the probation officer's report, the record in the case, other reports, statements in aggravation or mitigation, and the testimony of witnesses (including the victim and his or her parents, guardian, or next of kin), the court must make its sentencing decisions. These decisions involve the matters specified in California Rule of Court 433. They include:

1. Whether the defendant, if eligible, is to be granted or denied probation
2. If a sentence of imprisonment is to be imposed, or suspended during a period of probation, whether the defendant is to be sentenced to the upper, middle, or lower term of imprisonment authorized for the offense
3. Whether any sentence enhancement is to be stricken
4. If the defendant has been convicted of multiple offenses, whether the terms of imprisonment for the offenses, if any, are to be served consecutively or concurrently

Once the court has made the required determinations, it pronounces judgment and sentence on the defendant. As previously mentioned, California law does not specify a particular format for the judgment (including the sentence). Penal Code § 1170(c) does require, however, that the court state its reasons for its sentence choice on the record at the time of sentencing. California Rule of Court 405(f) defines *sentence choice* as the "selection of any disposition of the case which does not amount to a dismissal, acquittal, or grant of a new trial."

Forms of Punishment

Although actual imposition of sentence is the function of the judge, the type of punishment that may be imposed for an offense is prescribed by the legislature. This section examines some of the numerous types of sentences authorized in the Penal Code and other codes containing criminal provisions.

Capital Punishment

Clearly the most controversial punishment is the death penalty. In early American history, capital punishment was commonly used. During the nineteenth century, use of the death penalty greatly declined. Today, more than half the states allow the death penalty, and its use has regained popular support. Although the number of inmates actually executed every year is small, the number is increasing.

The contention that the death penalty is inherently cruel and unusual and therefore violative of the Eighth Amendment has been rejected. However, the United States Supreme Court has struggled, as have state courts and legislatures, to establish standards for its use.

In *Furman v. Georgia,* 408 U.S. 238 (1972), the Court held that the death penalty cannot be imposed under a sentencing procedure that creates a substantial risk of being implemented in an arbitrary manner. It found that Georgia's law permitted arbitrary decisions and so declared it void. *Furman* required that the sentencer's discretion be limited by objective standards to eliminate unfairness—specifically, to eliminate racial and other bias from death sentence decisions.

States responded to *Furman* in a variety of ways. Some chose to eliminate discretion entirely by mandating capital punishment for certain crimes. The United States Supreme Court invalidated mandatory capital punishment laws in *Locket v. Ohio,* 438 U.S. 586 (1978). In *Locket* the Court held that individualized sentencing was constitutionally required. The Court stated that any law prohibiting a sentencer from considering "as a mitigating factor, any aspect of a defendant's character or record and any circumstances of the offense that the defendant proffers as a basis for a sentence less than death" creates an unconstitutional risk that the "death penalty will be imposed in spite of factors which may call for a less severe penalty."[4]

Georgia's new death penalty legislation was upheld in *Gregg v. Georgia,* 428 U.S. 153 (1976). The new law provided that the jury must find, in a sentencing hearing separate from the trial, an aggravating circumstance before the death penalty could be imposed. The statute enumerated possible aggravating circumstances. By requiring a jury to find an aggravating circumstance, arbitrariness is believed to be lessened.

In California, the death penalty is authorized only for the offense of first-degree murder. To be subject to the death penalty, the defendant must be charged with both first-degree murder and one or more **special circumstances** enumerated in Penal Code § 190.2. That enumeration is too lengthy to reproduce in full here, but consists of circumstances surrounding the killing that make it particularly heinous. (*See* Penal Code § 190.2.) Killing for financial gain, killing of a peace officer, and killing while engaged in the commission of certain felonies (such as robbery, kidnapping, rape, and burglary) are examples of special circumstances.

California has adopted a procedure in capital cases much like the procedure approved by the United States Supreme Court in *Gregg v. Georgia*. A capital case is divided into two phases: the guilt phase and the penalty phase. The guilt phase, as its name implies, is the trial of the defendant on the charge of first-degree murder and the special circumstance or circumstances. If the jury finds the defendant guilty of first-degree murder and finds, beyond a reasonable doubt, that one or more of the charged special circumstances exists, the defendant may be subject to a sentence of death.

Whether the defendant will be sentenced to death is decided by the jury during the penalty phase of the case. A capital case is the only type of criminal proceeding in which the jury decides the sentence. At the penalty phase, evidence is presented in aggravation and mitigation. (*See* Penal Code § 190.3.) If, after hearing the evidence, the jury determines that the aggravating circumstances outweigh the mitigating circumstances, the jury must impose a sentence of death on the defendant. If the jury determines that the mitigating circumstances outweigh the aggravating circumstances, it must impose a sentence of life without the possibility of parole.[5]

The decision of the jury to impose either a sentence of death or a sentence of life imprisonment without the possibility of parole is referred to as a *verdict*. If the jury returns a verdict imposing the sentence of death, the court must, under Penal Code § 190.4(e), independently review the evidence presented at the penalty phase and determine whether the jury's findings and verdict that the aggravating circumstances outweigh the mitigating circumstances are contrary to law or to the evidence presented. If the judge determines that the findings and verdict are contrary to law or not supported by the evidence, he or she must set aside the verdict and impose a sentence of life imprisonment without the possibility of parole, stating his or her reasons for the decision on the record. This decision by the judge may be appealed by the prosecution to the appropriate court of appeal. If the judge finds that the findings and verdict of the jury are in accordance with law and the evidence, the jury's verdict will be sustained and the judge will pronounce judgment, including the sentence of death, on the defendant.

When a judgment of death is rendered, Penal Code § 1217 requires that the court issue a commitment directing the sheriff to deliver the defendant to the state prison designated by the State Board of Prison Directors for the execution of the death penalty. The defendant is held there pending the decision upon the defendant's automatic appeal (discussed in the following paragraph). Under § 1218, the court must also transmit a complete record of the case to the governor, who may require the opinion of the Justices of the California Supreme Court or the Attorney General regarding the judgment of death in the particular case.

Under Penal Code § 1239(b), a judgment of death is automatically appealed to the California Supreme Court without any action on the part of the defendant or his or her counsel. Penal Code § 1193 provides that, in the event the California Supreme Court affirms the judgment of death, the superior court that pronounced the judgment must thereupon enter an order setting a date for execution of the judgment (carrying out of the death sentence) and a warrant directing that the sentence be executed. The date must be no less than sixty and no more than ninety days from the date of the order. Within five days thereafter, certified copies of the order and warrant must be sent by registered mail to the warden of the state prison having custody of the defendant and to the governor.

Once this point is reached, the defendant will be executed on the date set by the superior court unless he or she can obtain a stay of execution. Virtually all defendants do so, usually by claiming that their rights under the United States Constitution have been violated. Such claims enable defendants to appeal to the United States Supreme Court or to seek federal habeas corpus relief. Another method used by defendants to delay their executions is to apply to the governor for executive clemency (discussed in Chapter 19).

Penal Code § 3603 provides that "[t]he judgment of death shall be executed within the walls of the California State Prison at San Quentin." Section 3604 provides that the punishment of death shall be inflicted by the administration of a lethal gas or by an intravenous injection of a substance or substances in a quantity sufficient to cause death. The defendant is permitted to elect which method of execution will be used. The election must be made in writing and submitted to the warden at San Quentin. If the defendant fails to make the election, the death sentence is to be carried out by lethal gas.

The Eighth Amendment to the United States Constitution and article I, § 17, of the California Constitution both prohibit the imposition of "cruel and unusual" punishments on persons convicted of crimes. The definition of cruelty is an evolving concept. California's two methods, lethal gas and lethal injection, are currently approved methods of execution. So also are electrocution, hanging, and shooting. Other methods, such as starvation, would not pass constitutional muster.

Penal Code § 190.5 provides that the death penalty may not be imposed upon any person who was under the age of eighteen at the time of commission of the crime. Also, recall from Chapter 10 that a defendant who becomes insane prior to execution of a death sentence may not be put to death until he or she regains his or her sanity.

Corporal/Physical Punishment

The use of corporal or physical punishment raises issues under the Eighth Amendment to the United States Constitution and article I, § 17, of the California Constitution which, as previously mentioned, prohibit the imposition of cruel or unusual punishments. The constitutionality under the United States Constitution of some forms of corporal punishment of prisoners, such as whipping, has not been resolved by the courts. However, California, by statute, prohibits all forms of corporal punishment. (*See* Penal Code §§ 673, 2652, 147.) Also prohibited is the withholding of needed medical treatment and other forms of mistreatment of prisoners. In contrast, solitary confinement (i.e., the confinement of a prisoner in isolation from other prisoners) has been held by the California courts to be lawful when imposed as a disciplinary measure upon a prisoner.[6] Also, the prohibition against corporal punishment does not prevent custodial authorities from using force to quell riots or to prevent a prisoner from injuring an officer or another inmate.[7]

Imprisonment

Restraint is an effective method of dealing with dangerous persons. Imprisonment serves this purpose, and in some cases the offender is also rehabilitated. Regrettably, because rehabilitation is rare and (contrary to popular belief) prison conditions are often poor, many offenders leave prison angry, no more educated or employable, and occasionally more dangerous.

Nevertheless, imprisonment continues to be the most common method of punishing violent offenders. Offenders may be committed to the state prison, camps, or county jails. Those sentenced to short terms (one year or less) are usually housed in a county jail. Individuals sentenced to longer terms are committed to a state prison facility.

Imprisonment for Misdemeanors   Many penal statutes defining misdemeanors specify the maximum amount of imprisonment that may be imposed upon a person convicted of the offense. For example, Penal Code § 241(a), prescribing the punishment for simple assault, states: "An assault is punishable by a fine not exceeding one thousand dollars ($1,000), or by imprisonment in the county jail not exceeding six months, or by both the fine and imprisonment." Other penal statutes declare that a specified act is a misdemeanor but do not prescribe the punishment for the offense. In such a case, reference must be made to Penal Code § 19, a catch-all provision, which states:

> Except in cases where a different punishment is prescribed by any law of this state, every offense declared to be a misdemeanor is punishable by imprisonment in the county jail not exceeding six months, or by a fine not exceeding one thousand dollars ($1,000), or by both.

The maximum term of imprisonment specified in any statute for a misdemeanor is one year. A defendant may serve more than one year, however, if he or she is convicted of multiple misdemeanors and sentenced to serve consecutive terms of imprisonment.

Imprisonment for Noncapital Felony Offenses   As discussed previously, imprisonment for a capital offense is for a term of life without the possibility of parole. Terms of imprisonment authorized for noncapital felony offenses vary widely and are generally proportional to the severity of the crime. Prior to 1977, California used the **indeterminate sentence** to sentence convicted felons to state prison. Under the Indeterminate Sentence Law, found at Penal Code § 1168, the judge would sentence the defendant to imprisonment in the state prison but would not specify the term of imprisonment. The actual amount of time to be served by the defendant was determined by the Adult Authority, an administrative body, depending largely on the conduct of the defendant while in prison. The goal of the Indeterminate Sentence Law was to rehabilitate the offender.

In 1977, the legislature repealed the Indeterminate Sentence Law and replaced it with the **Determinate Sentence** Law, found in Penal Code § 1170. In a marked departure from the philosophy underlying the Indeterminate Sentence Law, the legislature, in the first sentence of § 1170(a)(1), states: "The Legislature finds and declares that the purpose of imprisonment for crime is punishment."

One of the problems the Determinate Sentence Law was intended to remedy was the disparity in terms served under the prior law by persons who had committed similar offenses. Because the actual term of imprisonment was determined by the Adult Authority and based largely on the offender's conduct in prison, two persons convicted of identical offenses could, and frequently did, serve different terms of imprisonment.

Under the Determinate Sentence Law, the statutory provisions prescribing punishments for most felonies now specify three possible terms of imprisonment, referred to as the lower term, the middle term, and the upper term. For example, Penal Code § 264(a) states the punishment for rape as follows: "Rape ... is punishable by imprisonment in the state prison for three, six, or eight years." Under the Determinate Sentence Law, if the punishment prescribed for an offense is three alternative time periods, the sentencing judge must sentence the offender to one of the specified time periods, "unless the convicted person is given any other disposition provided by law, including a fine, jail, probation, or the suspension of imposition or execution of a sentence." The requirement that the judge sentence the offender to one of the statutorily prescribed terms of imprisonment assures a certain degree of uniformity in the terms to be served by persons committing similar offenses.

Penal Code § 1170(b) provides that "[w]hen a judgment of imprisonment is to be imposed and the statute specifies three possible terms, the court shall order imposition of the middle term, unless there are circumstances in aggravation or mitigation of the crime." Recall that the court conducts a sentencing hearing at which evidence of circumstances in aggravation or mitigation may be presented. If the court finds the existence of aggravating circumstances, it may impose the upper term of imprisonment authorized for the offense. If it finds the existence of mitigating circumstances, the court may impose the lower term. Under § 1170(c), the court must state its reasons for its sentence choice on the record at the time of sentencing.

Not all statutory provisions prescribing punishment for felonies state three alternative terms of imprisonment. Some, for example, specify only one term. Penal Code § 1170(g) provides that a sentence to state prison for a determinate term for which only one term is specified is a sentence to state prison under the Determinate Sentence Law.

A defendant sentenced to a determinate term must serve the full term specified. There is no possibility of early release. Parole is available to the defendant only after he or she completes the full determinate term.[8]

Despite enactment of the Determinate Sentence Law, some felony statutes continue to provide for indeterminate sentences of imprisonment. For example, Penal Code § 190 provides that a defendant convicted of first-degree murder without special circumstances shall be imprisoned for a term of twenty-five years to life. The same section states that a defendant convicted of second-degree murder shall be sentenced to imprisonment for a term of fifteen years to life. Under § 205, a defendant convicted of aggravated mayhem is to be sentenced to imprisonment for life with the possibility of parole. The terms prescribed by these statutes are indeterminate in that, once the defendant has served the minimum specified number of years of imprisonment, if any, his or her continued incarceration is a matter within the discretion of the Board of Prison Terms. The Board of Prison Terms is the successor agency to the Adult Authority and is the administrative body that makes parole decisions in the California criminal justice system. A significant number of other felonies are punishable with indeterminate terms. These felonies are generally the most serious crimes, and are usually punishable "for life with the possibility of parole" or by imprisonment for a specified number of years "to life."

In addition to the continued existence of a number of indeterminate-sentence felonies, there are also many felonies for which no punishment is prescribed or for which punishment in the state prison is prescribed without any specification of a minimum term. Penal Code § 18 declares that, in such cases, the offense is punishable by imprisonment in the state prison for sixteen months, two years, or three years. The effect of § 18 is to bring these offenses within the Determinate Sentence Law.

Sentence Enhancements

In addition to requiring a sentencing judge to select one of the three alternative terms of imprisonment prescribed for an offense, Penal Code § 1170(a)(3) states that:

> The court, unless it determines that there are circumstances in mitigation of the punishment prescribed, shall also impose any other term which it is required by law to impose as an additional term.

The statutory language refers to what are known as **sentence enhancements.** A *sentence enhancement* is an additional term of imprisonment required or authorized by law under certain specified circumstances, which generally involve an aggravating factor in commission of the offense or the defendant's prior criminal history. Sentence enhancements are added to the punishment prescribed for the offense committed by the defendant, commonly referred to as the *base sentence.* Enhancement statutes generally provide that the enhancement is in addition and consecutive to the base sentence. This means that the defendant must serve the enhancement as a period of imprisonment added to the base sentence. The defendant cannot serve the base sentence and the enhancement concurrently.

Aggravating Factor in Commission of Offense   A number of penal statutes provide for sentence enhancements based on the defendant's conduct during commission of the offense or the manner in which the defendant committed the offense. Some examples of enhancements of this nature include:

- three years for infliction of great bodily injury during commission of the offense (*see* Penal Code § 12022.7)
- three, four, or ten years for use of a firearm in commission of the offense (*see* Penal Code § 12022.5)
- one to four years for the taking, damaging, or destroying of property during commission of a felony, depending on the value of the property (*see* Penal Code § 12022.6)
- three years for commission of a sex offense by one who knows he or she is infected with AIDS (*see* Penal Code § 12022.85)

- five years for a defendant who, during commission of a felony, knowing that the victim is pregnant, intentionally inflicts injury that results in termination of the pregnancy (*see* Penal Code § 12022.9).

Prior Criminal History of Defendant   Examples of enhancements based on the defendant's prior criminal history include:

- for a defendant convicted of a serious felony as defined in Penal Code § 1192.7, five years for each prior conviction of a serious felony (*see* Penal Code §§ 1192.7 and 667)
- for a defendant convicted of a violent felony as defined in Penal Code § 667.5, three years for each prison term he or she has served in the past upon conviction of a violent felony (*see* Penal Code § 667.5)
- for a defendant convicted of lewd acts upon a child under the age of fourteen, five years if he or she has a prior conviction for specified sex offenses (*see* Penal Code § 667.51)
- for a defendant convicted of a forcible or violent sex crime, five years for each prior conviction of a forcible or violent sex crime, plus a fine of up to $20,000 (*see* Penal Code § 667.6)
- for a defendant convicted of a specified felony sex offense who kidnapped the victim for the purpose of committing the offense, nine years or, if the victim was under the age of fourteen, fifteen years (*see* Penal Code § 667.8)

Some, but not all, of the statutes prescribing sentence enhancements for the prior criminal history of the defendant contain what is known as a **washout provision**. Such a provision states that the sentence enhancement does not apply if a specified period of years has passed since the prior conviction or prison term that is the basis for the enhancement.

Striking of Enhancements   Penal Code § 1170.1(h) permits the court to strike (not impose) sentence enhancements authorized under specified statutory provisions if the court determines that there are circumstances in mitigation of the additional punishment and states on the record its reasons for striking the additional punishment. Not all enhancement provisions are listed in § 1170.1(h). For example, of the enhancements discussed in this text, those prescribed in §§ 12022.5, 12022.85, 667, 667.51, and 667.6 are not included, and therefore may not be stricken by the court.

Special Sentencing Provisions for Habitual Offenders

Technically, the sentence enhancements discussed earlier, if based on prior convictions or prison sentences, are aimed at habitual offenders. The Penal Code contains additional sentencing provisions specifically applicable to habitual offenders. These provisions take the sentencing of such defendants out of the Determinate Sentence Law and impose indeterminate sentences, usually in the form of a specified number of years to life. Examples of the special sentencing provisions for habitual offenders follow, although these examples are not all-inclusive.

Lewd Acts with Minor after Previous Sex Offenses A person who commits a lewd act upon a child under the age of fourteen, and who has previously been convicted two or more times of a specified sex offense, is to be sentenced to imprisonment for fifteen years to life. (*See* Penal Code § 667.51.)

Habitual Violent Offender A person convicted of a felony involving the infliction of great bodily injury, or the use of force likely to produce great bodily injury, and who has served two or more prior prison terms for specified violent felonies, is to be sentenced to the greater of life with the possibility of parole no sooner than twenty years, or the sentence he or she would have received under the Determinate Sentence Law, including enhancements. If the person has served three or more prior prison terms for specified violent felonies, he or she is to be sentenced to life imprisonment without the possibility of parole. (*See* Penal Code § 667.7.)

Habitual Sexual Offender A person convicted of a specified type of sex offense, and who has been previously convicted of one of those types of offenses, is punishable by imprisonment in the state prison for twenty-five years to life. (*See* Penal Code § 667.71.)

Habitual Child Molester A person who has served at least one prison term for commission of a specified type of sex offense against a child under fourteen years of age, and who kidnapped the child in order to commit the offense, upon a second conviction of the same type of offense against at least two separate victims, accompanied by kidnapping, is to be sentenced to a term of twenty-five years or, at the request of the prosecutor, to a determinate sentence plus enhancements, or as a habitual violent offender under § 667.7 or a habitual sexual offender under § 667.71, if applicable. (*See* Penal Code § 667.72.)

Drug Offenses Involving Minors A defendant who is convicted of certain specified drug offenses involving minors, and who has served two or more prior prison terms for similar drug offenses, is to be sentenced either to a term of life imprisonment without the possibility of parole for seventeen years or to a determinate term for the offense plus enhancements, whichever is greater. (*See* Penal Code § 667.75.)

"Three Strikes and You're Out" Law Perhaps the most well-known of the habitual offender provisions of the Penal Code is the so-called "Three Strikes and You're Out" (or "Three Strikes") law. There are actually two forms of this law. In March 1994, the legislature enacted a "Three Strikes" law that appears at Penal Code § 667, subdivisions (b) through (i). In November 1994, the electorate approved an initiative measure, Proposition 184, which added a "Three Strikes" provision to the Penal Code as § 1170.12. Both "Three Strikes" provisions continue to exist in the Penal Code. Fortunately, they are almost identical. The provisions of § 1170.12 are the basis of our discussion here.

The sentencing scheme established by the "Three Strikes" law is straightforward. The law applies if a defendant is convicted of any felony and has one or more prior convictions for serious felonies (as defined in Penal Code § 1192.7) or violent felonies (as defined in Penal Code § 667.5). If a defendant is convicted of a felony, and has previously been convicted of one serious or violent felony, the determinate term or minimum indeterminate term for the present felony conviction is twice the term provided by law for the offense. Thus, if an offense carries a potential sentence of one, two, or three years, those periods will be doubled if the defendant has a prior conviction for a serious or violent felony. Similarly, if an offense carries an indeterminate term of ten years to life, the minimum indeterminate term would be doubled, resulting in a sentence of twenty years to life.

The "Three Strikes" concept becomes applicable when a defendant convicted of a felony has two or more convictions for serious or violent felonies. If, for example, a defendant convicted of a felony had two prior convictions for serious or violent felonies, the previous two convictions would be considered the first two "strikes." The present felony would be the third "strike," and the defendant would be "out" in the sense that the maximum penalty authorized by § 1170.12 would apply. That maximum penalty is an indeterminate sentence of life imprisonment, with the minimum term calculated as the greater of: (1) three times the term provided by law as punishment for each felony of which the defendant is convicted in the present proceeding; (2) twenty-five years; or (3) the determinate term for the felony or felonies of which the defendant is presently convicted, plus enhancements.

The practical effect of the "Three Strikes" law is that a defendant, on conviction of the third "strike," faces a prison term of at least twenty-five years. Particularly problematic from the defendant's point of view is the fact that the third "strike" may be *any* felony—it need not be a serious or violent felony. As has been mentioned several times in this text, the Penal Code and other California codes prescribe numerous offenses that may be charged as felonies. Any of them may constitute the third "strike" under the "Three Strikes" law.

Concurrent and Consecutive Sentencing

Frequently, defendants are tried for and convicted of more than one offense. For example, a defendant may be convicted of kidnapping and robbery. Another defendant may be convicted of multiple counts of child molestation. Each count would be considered a separate offense. The court must sentence the defendant for each offense on which he or she is convicted. When multiple sentences to imprisonment are imposed, the court must determine whether the sentences are to be served concurrently or consecutively. **Concurrent sentences** are served simultaneously. For example, if a defendant is sentenced to three five-year terms of imprisonment to be served concurrently, he or she serves five years in prison. **Consecutive sentences** are served one after the other. If the defendant is sentenced to three five-year terms and ordered to serve them consecutively, he or she serves fifteen years in prison.

Penal Code § 669 requires the court to determine whether multiple sentences are to be concurrent or consecutive. If the court does not do so, the sentences will be concurrent. In making its determination as to whether multiple sentences are to be concurrent or consecutive, the court is to consider whether the offenses were independent of each other or were part of a single period of aberrant behavior. Also to be considered are circumstances in aggravation and mitigation, except that the following may not be considered: (1) a fact used to impose the upper sentence term, (2) a fact used to otherwise enhance the defendant's prison sentence, and (3) a fact that is an element of the crime.

Suspended Sentence, Conditional Sentence, and Probation

As discussed earlier in this chapter, the judge, when setting the date for imposition of judgment in a felony case, must refer the case to the probation officer for preparation of a presentence probation report if the defendant is eligible for probation. This procedure is required by Penal Code § 1191. If the defendant is convicted of a misdemeanor, the judge may refer the case to the probation officer, but is not required to do so.

In a felony case, the key to the referral requirement is whether the defendant is eligible for probation. Generally, a defendant is eligible for probation unless otherwise provided in the Penal Code or, in the case of certain drug offenses, in the Health and Safety Code. The two codes contain a number of provisions stating that certain defendants are not eligible for probation. (The provisions are too numerous to be described in detail here.) In the Penal Code, they are found primarily at § 1203.06 and following sections, and tend to involve defendants convicted of use of firearms in the commission of violent offenses; the use of force, violence, or fear in the perpetration of sex offenses; intentional infliction of great bodily injury; manufacture or sale of certain illegal drugs; use of minors in the sale or manufacture of certain illegal drugs; and multiple prior felony convictions. (*See* Penal Code § 1203.06 *et seq.*) In addition to listing offenses for which probation is not allowed, the Penal Code, at § 1203(e), lists thirteen categories of offenses for which defendants are presumptively ineligible for probation. Such defendants are not to be granted probation. "except in unusual cases where the interests of justice would best be served" by a grant of probation. (*See* Penal Code § 1203.)

As discussed in the section on sentencing procedure, the court, after considering the information presented to it at the sentencing hearing, makes its sentencing decisions, including whether an eligible defendant is to be granted or denied probation. The decision on whether to grant or deny probation is a matter within the discretion of the judge, and such decisions are rarely reversed on appeal absent a clear showing of abuse of discretion.[9]

Probation involves suspension of the defendant's sentence; in misdemeanor or infraction cases, it may involve imposition of a conditional sentence. Sentence may be suspended in one of two ways: (1) imposition of sentence may be suspended, or (2) execution of sentence may be suspended.[10] If a court suspends imposition of sentence, it refrains from pronouncing judgment against the defendant. If a court suspends execution of sentence, it enters judgment and imposes sentence on the defendant, but then suspends execution of the sentence or some part of it. Penal Code § 1203(a) defines *probation* as "the suspension of the imposition or execution of a sentence and the order of conditional and revocable release in the community under the supervision of a probation officer." The same section defines *conditional sentence* as "the suspension of the imposition or execution of a sentence and the order of revocable release in the community subject to conditions established by the court without the supervision of a probation officer." The principal difference between probation and a conditional sentence is that probation involves supervision by a probation officer, whereas a conditional sentence does not. As noted, conditional sentences are used only in misdemeanor and infraction cases. When a conditional sentence is imposed, the defendant remains under the supervision of the court rather than a probation officer.

Probation in a felony case must generally be limited to a period of time that does not exceed the maximum possible term of the defendant's sentence. If, however, the maximum possible term of the sentence is five years or less, the court may order that probation continue for up to five years. In misdemeanor cases, probation generally may be ordered for up to three years. However, if the maximum sentence provided by law exceeds three years, probation may be ordered for a period up to the duration of the maximum sentence. This situation could arise if a defendant were convicted of multiple misdemeanors and sentenced to consecutive terms.

When granting probation (or a conditional sentence), the court may impose conditions on the defendant which, if violated, can result in revocation of probation. The judge has wide discretion in setting the conditions of probation. Conditions of probation typically imposed may include the requirement that the defendant:

- serve some period of time in the county jail
- pay a fine
- make monetary restitution to the victim
- pay probation or incarceration costs
- work at a public road camp or farm
- remain gainfully employed
- if convicted of child abuse or neglect, participate in counseling or education programs
- abstain from the use of intoxicants, if he or she was convicted of a sex offense committed while he or she was intoxicated
- perform community service
- participate in education or treatment, if convicted of possession of a controlled substance
- submit at any time to a warrantless search

The last condition, if imposed, generally refers to searches by the probation officer for the purpose of determining whether the defendant is complying with the terms of probation. It does not constitute carte blanche authority for law enforcement personnel to search the defendant for other purposes. Even searches by the probation officer must meet the reasonableness requirements of the United States and California constitutions.[11]

 If a defendant violates a condition of probation (or conditional sentence) or engages in criminal activity while on probation, his or her probation may be revoked. Revocation of probation is a two-step process. (*See* Penal Code § 1203.2.) The first step involves arrest of the defendant, followed by revocation of his or her probation by the court if the court finds that the defendant has violated any of the conditions of his or her probation, "has become abandoned to improper associates or a vicious life," or has committed new offenses. This procedure is known as *summary revocation of probation* because it occurs without a hearing.

The second step in the revocation of a defendant's probation is a hearing to determine whether the grounds asserted for revoking the defendant's probation are true. The hearing procedure is initiated by the court on its own motion, or by the filing of a petition by the probation officer or the district attorney. Notice of the filing of the petition or of the court's motion must be given to the defendant or the defendant's attorney of record. The court then refers the case to the probation officer for preparation of a report. After receiving the probation officer's report, the court conducts the hearing. The defendant has a right to be present at the hearing and to be represented by counsel. At the hearing, the court considers the petition filed by the probation officer or district attorney, if the revocation procedure was initiated in that manner; the report of the probation officer; and any other evidence presented by the parties. The defendant has a right to confront adverse witnesses, which means that he or she may cross-examine any witnesses against him or her.

If the judge determines at the hearing that probation should be revoked, and the probation was of the type that suspended the imposition of sentence, the court holds a hearing similar to a sentencing hearing and then pronounces judgment against the defendant. If the probation suspended the execution of sentence, the court revokes the suspension and orders that the sentence be served. In either case, the defendant is delivered into custody to serve his or her sentence. If as a result of the hearing the court finds that the defendant's probation should not be revoked, the court's initial order revoking probation (the first step) is set aside.[12]

Parole

Parole is a conditional release of a defendant from imprisonment. While on parole, the defendant technically remains in custody and may be reimprisoned if he or she violates the conditions of his or her parole. Parole is governed by the provisions of the Penal Code beginning with § 3000.

In many states, parole is an early release from imprisonment, that is, a release before the defendant has served the full term of imprisonment. Such is not the case in California for a defendant sentenced under the Determinate Sentence Law. A defendant who receives a determinate sentence must serve the full term of the sentence. After serving his or her full term, the defendant may then be released on parole. Parole may, however, constitute an early release for a defendant serving an indeterminate sentence. Under Penal Code § 3049, a defendant who receives an indeterminate sentence specifying a minimum term of imprisonment must serve at least one-third the specified minimum term, and then may be eligible for release on parole. However, many statutes providing for indeterminate sentences contain restrictions on the grant of parole, and these restrictions supersede the general rule stated in § 3049. Many of the habitual offender statutes contain such restrictions.

Recall also that the sentence for first-degree murder with special circumstances, if the death penalty is not imposed, is life without the possibility of parole. A defendant sentenced to life imprisonment with the possibility of parole, which does not specify a minimum term of imprisonment, is eligible for parole after serving seven years.[13] A defendant serving a determinate term of imprisonment is entitled to be released on parole at the end of the term. A defendant serving an indeterminate term is *not* entitled to be released on parole when he or she becomes eligible for parole. The decision to release or not release an eligible defendant serving an indeterminate term is a matter determined on a case-by-case basis by the Department of Corrections.

All defendants released from imprisonment are released on parole unless the parole authority for good cause waives parole. The duration of a defendant's parole is determined by the Department of Corrections within statutory limits. A defendant released on parole after serving a determinate sentence may be paroled for a period of up to three years. A defendant released after serving an indeterminate sentence may be paroled for up to three years (except a defendant convicted of first- or second-degree murder or a defendant serving a life sentence). For a defendant serving a life sentence, other than a defendant convicted of first- or second-degree murder, parole may be imposed for up to five years. Penal Code § 3000.1 provides that the period of parole for a defendant convicted of first-degree murder (without special circumstances) or second-degree murder is the remainder of the defendant's life. However, that section provides further that the defendant is to be discharged from parole after seven years in the case of first-degree murder and after five years in the case of second-degree murder, unless good cause exists to retain the defendant on parole.

A defendant on parole is subject to conditions imposed by the Department of Corrections. These conditions are similar to those that may be imposed on a person granted probation, and a violation of the conditions may result in reimprisonment of the defendant. The procedure used to reimprison a defendant who has violated his or her parole is known as *revocation of parole*. Revocation of parole is accomplished by means of a hearing conducted by the Board of Prison Terms or the Department of Corrections. The defendant is entitled to be present and to testify and present witnesses in his or her behalf. The defendant has only a limited right to counsel at a parole revocation hearing. Specifically, the defendant has a right to counsel only if the issues are sufficiently complex that the defendant cannot adequately present his or her side of the case without the aid of an attorney.[14] If the hearing results in a determination to revoke the defendant's parole, he or she may be reimprisoned. Penal Code § 3057 provides that the period of reimprisonment may not exceed twelve months. If, however, the defendant was on parole after serving a sentence for first- or second-degree murder, he or she need not be released at the end of twelve months if "the circumstances and gravity of the parole violation are such that consideration of the public safety requires a more lengthy period of incarceration." Such a defendant's suitability for parole must, however, be reviewed annually.[15] Upon release from reimprisonment following a parole violation, the defendant's period of parole may be extended.

Fines

From the discussion of specific crimes in Part I of this text, you know that a **fine** is a commonly authorized form of punishment for a criminal offense. Statutes prescribing punishment for minor offenses sometimes authorize only a fine, without imprisonment. Many statutes prescribing punishment for offenses authorize a fine, imprisonment, or both.

Statutes authorizing fines generally provide that the fine may be in an amount not to exceed a stated sum. The sentencing judge may set the fine within that range. Some statutes prescribing punishment for offenses do not specifically authorize imposition of a fine. They may, for example, simply state that, upon conviction, the defendant may be imprisoned in the county jail or state prison. Under Penal Code § 672, the court may impose a fine in such a case in an amount up to $1,000 if the offense is a misdemeanor, and up to $10,000 if the offense is a felony.

A fine imposed in a felony case is payable immediately. Under Penal Code § 1205, a fine in a misdemeanor case may be made payable within a limited time or in installments. In either a felony or a misdemeanor case, the court may order that the defendant be imprisoned until the fine is paid. If the court orders such imprisonment, it must specify the amount of credit toward the fine to be given for each day served. The term of imprisonment for nonpayment of a fine may not exceed one day for each $30 of the fine.

If a fine is payable immediately, and the defendant fails to pay, the court may order her imprisoned until the fine is paid. If time has been given by the court for payment of the fine, or it is payable in installments, and the defendant fails to pay on the day the fine is due or fails to pay an installment when due, the court is to immediately order the arrest of the defendant and order her to show cause why she should not be imprisoned until the fine or installment is paid.

There are constitutional limits on the courts' power to imprison a defendant for nonpayment of a fine. Both the California and United States Supreme Courts have held that it is a violation of equal protection of the law to imprison a defendant for nonpayment of a fine if nonpayment is the result of the defendant's indigency.[16] If nonpayment is for any other reason, such as a willful refusal to pay by a defendant who has the means to pay, imprisonment for nonpayment is constitutional.

Restitution

A fine is punishment and is payable to the court. **Restitution** is compensation payable to the victim of a crime. Proposition 8, adopted in June 1982, added § 28(b) to article I of the California Constitution; it provides, in part, that "[r]estitution shall be ordered from convicted persons in every case, regardless of the sentence or disposition imposed, in which the crime victim suffers a loss, unless compelling and extraordinary reasons exist to the contrary."

Penal Code § 1202.4(a)(3) requires that, when sentencing a defendant, the court order the defendant to pay both of the following: (1) a restitution fine, and (2) restitution to the victim, if there is a victim.

A **restitution fine** is paid into the **Restitution Fund**, which is maintained by the state to compensate victims of crimes for unreimbursed economic losses caused by the crimes. Penal Code § 1202.4(b) provides that the restitution fine is to be set at the discretion of the court and is to be commensurate with the seriousness of the offense. In the case of a felony conviction, the restitution fine must be at least $200 and not more than $10,000. If the defendant has been convicted of a misdemeanor, the restitution fine must be at least $100 and not more than $1,000. A restitution fine is to be imposed on the defendant in addition to any other fine imposed as part of his or her sentence.

Penal Code § 1202.4, subdivisions (f) through (j), provide for payment by the defendant of restitution directly to the victim (or victims) of his offense if the victim has suffered economic loss as the result of the defendant's commission of the offense. This restitution is in addition to the restitution fine payable to the Restitution Fund. The court is to order full restitution unless it finds clear and compelling reasons for not doing so and states them on the record. Restitution is, to the extent possible, to be sufficient to fully reimburse the victim (or victims) for every determined economic loss incurred as the result of the defendant's criminal conduct, including the following specifically enumerated losses: (1) the value of stolen or damaged property; (2) medical expenses; (3) wages or profits lost due to injury incurred by the victim; and (4) wages or profits lost by the victim as a result of time spent as a witness or in assisting the police or prosecution. In addition, if the conviction is for a felony violation of § 288 (lewd acts with a minor under the age of fourteen), restitution may also cover noneconomic losses, such as psychological harm. The defendant is entitled to a hearing before the judge to dispute the amount of restitution determined by the judge.

If a defendant is granted probation, Penal Code § 1202.4(m) requires that payment of both a restitution fine and restitution to the victim, if applicable, be a condition of probation.

Forfeiture

Certain California penal statutes authorize seizure and disposition by the government of real or personal property used in the commission of the offenses to which the statutes apply. For example, Penal Code § 312 provides that when a defendant is convicted of possession, sale, or distribution of obscene matter, the court may order the destruction of the obscene materials. Similarly, Penal Code § 480 provides that upon conviction of a defendant for counterfeiting, all "dies, plates, apparatus, paper, metal, or machine[s]" intended for use in counterfeiting must be destroyed. Other provisions of the Penal Code and provisions of other California codes provide for **forfeiture** in specified situations.

The most extensive forfeiture statutes are the Health and Safety Code provisions applicable to drug offenses. Health and Safety Code § 11470 lists the types of property subject to forfeiture, including: (1) illegally manufactured or distributed controlled substances; (2) raw materials and equipment used in the illegal manufacture of controlled substances; (3) property used as a container for illegal controlled substances; (4) books, records, and research products and materials used in violation of drug laws; (5) the interest of a registered owner of a boat, airplane, or vehicle used to facilitate the possession for sale of specified quantities of illegal drugs; (6) money and other things of value furnished in exchange for controlled substances or otherwise used in drug transactions; and (7) real property used in the illegal manufacture, sale, or distribution of controlled substances. Section 11470 allows an exception to forfeiture of some of the foregoing categories of property if the property is owned by more than one person and one of the co-owners is not involved in the drug offenses that would otherwise serve as a basis for forfeiture.

Under Health and Safety Code § 11488.4, if property is categorized as forfeitable under § 11470, but is not automatically forfeitable or subject to destruction, the property may be forfeited only if so ordered by the superior court. Notice of the proceeding must be given to interested persons and entities. An interested person might be a co-owner of the property; an interested entity might be a lending institution holding a mortgage on the property. If any person or entity files a claim of interest with the court, a hearing must be held at which the court will determine whether the property is to be forfeited or released to the person filing the claim of interest.

In 1993, the United States Supreme Court decided *Austin v. United States,* 113 S. Ct. 2801. In that case, the Court held that the Excessive Fines Clause of the Eighth Amendment applies to forfeitures of property used in drug offenses, despite the fact that forfeiture proceedings are civil rather than criminal in nature. Under the *Austin* decision, a forfeiture of property is unconstitutional if the value of the property forfeited is grossly disproportionate to the severity of the drug offense.

Registration

Certain classes of convicted criminals are subject to **registration** requirements imposed by law. The classes include certain sex offenders (*see* Penal Code § 290); persons convicted of arson or attempted arson (*see* Penal Code § 457.1); and persons convicted of certain drug offenses (*see* Health and Safety Code § 11590). A person in one of the foregoing categories is required to register with the law enforcement authorities having jurisdiction over the area in which he or she resides. If the person changes his or her address, he or she must register within a specified number of days with the law enforcement authorities having jurisdiction over his or her new place of residence. The registration requirements apply to sex offenders for life. Persons convicted of arson must register for life unless they obtain a Certificate of Rehabilitation (discussed in Chapter 19). Drug offenders required to register must do so for a period of five years after discharge from prison or termination of probation or parole.

Modern Sentencing Alternatives

In recent years, many new alternatives to incarceration have been developed. Several are discussed in this section.

Work Furlough   Penal Code § 1208 authorizes an arrangement under which selected county jail prisoners may leave jail to work or attend an educational program. This arrangement is known as **work furlough**. When not working or attending the educational program, prisoners return to jail. The work furlough program has many advantages. The prisoner continues to earn a living; this is particularly important if she has dependents. Also, the program is good for the self-esteem of the prisoner, because she feels that she is a useful part of the community. Finally, the cost to the public is lower because the offender may be required to use her earnings to pay for the costs of her incarceration and participation in the program.

Treatment   Treatment of persons convicted of certain alcohol and drug offenses is now a standard element of sentencing for those crimes. For example, Vehicle Code § 23161 provides that if a defendant is convicted of a first offense of drunk driving, and is granted probation, one of the conditions of probation must be that the person enroll in and successfully complete a licensed alcohol education and counseling program, if such a program exists in the person's county of residence or employment. If a person is convicted of a second or subsequent drunk driving offense, and is granted probation, he may be required by the court to participate in an alcohol treatment program.[17] Under Health and Safety Code § 11550, a person convicted of use or being under the influence of a controlled substance specified in that section may be permitted by the court to complete a licensed drug rehabilitation program in lieu of part or all of a sentence to imprisonment. Section 11550 applies only to those who use drugs. It does not apply to persons who manufacture or sell drugs.

Community Service   Another modern sentencing alternative, **community service**, may be imposed for a wide range of offenses, from infractions to more serious crimes. The type of work a person may be ordered to perform as community service is virtually unlimited, and may range from menial tasks, such as picking up trash from local roads, to rendering of professional services to the poor if the offender is a licensed professional.

Home Detention   Yet another modern sentencing alternative is **home detention**, a program under which eligible persons may voluntarily agree to be confined at home rather than in the county jail. This program, established by Penal Code § 1203.016, is limited to minimum-security inmates and low-risk offenders committed to a county jail or other county correctional facility or granted probation, or inmates participating in a work furlough program. An inmate may participate in the home detention program only if he or she agrees in writing to comply with certain rules and regulations, among which are the following:

1. That he or she will remain within the interior premises of his or her residence during the hours designated by the correctional administrator
2. That he or she will admit any person designated by the correctional administrator into his or her residence at any time for the purpose of verifying his or her compliance with the conditions of the home detention
3. That he or she agrees to the use of electronic monitoring or supervising devices designed to verify compliance with the conditions of the home detention
4. That he or she agrees that he or she may be retaken into custody to serve the balance of the sentence if the electronic monitoring or supervising devices are ineffective or he or she violates the conditions of the home detention.

The electronic monitoring or supervising device referred to in items 3 and 4 is frequently an electronic shackle worn on the inmate's leg, which transmits a radio signal. The radio signal can be monitored to determine the detainee's location.

Key Terms

aggravation Evidence regarding the circumstances of an offense or the criminal history of the defendant which supports imposition of a sentence at or near the maximum authorized by law.

arraignment for judgment The initial procedure at the court proceeding at which judgment is pronounced and sentence imposed on a convicted defendant. Arraignment for judgment involves informing the defendant of the nature of the charge against him or her; his or her plea; and the verdict, if any; followed by a question to the defendant whether he or she has any legal cause to show why judgment should not be pronounced.

community service A modern sentencing alternative under which a convicted defendant may be ordered to perform work beneficial to the community.

concurrent sentences Multiple sentences that are served simultaneously.

conditional sentence Suspension of the imposition or execution of a sentence and an order of revocable release in the community, subject to conditions established by the court, without the supervision of a probation officer.

consecutive sentences Multiple sentences that are served one after the other.

determinate sentence A sentence to a specified term of imprisonment under the Determinate Sentencing Law. The full term specified must be served by the defendant.

fine A monetary penalty imposed on a defendant as punishment for a crime, which is payable to the court.

forfeiture The seizure, destruction, or other disposition of real or personal property used in the commission of certain offenses, particularly drug offenses.

home detention A modern sentencing alternative under which eligible persons may voluntarily agree to be confined at home rather than in the county jail. The program is limited to minimum-security inmates and low-risk offenders committed to a county jail or other county correctional facility or granted probation, or inmates participating in a work-furlough program.

indeterminate sentence A sentence to imprisonment that does not specify the exact amount of time to be served by the defendant. An indeterminate sentence always specifies the maximum period of confinement authorized, and sometimes specifies the minimum amount of time that must be served. An example of an indeterminate sentence would be a sentence of from twenty-five years to life in a noncapital first-degree murder case.

mitigation Evidence regarding the circumstances of an offense or the criminal history of the defendant which supports imposition of a minimal sentence.

motion in arrest of judgment A posttrial motion in which the defendant claims that the accusatory pleading upon which he or she was prosecuted is defective.

parole The conditional release of a defendant from imprisonment.

presentence investigation report A report prepared by a probation officer for use by the court in determining the sentence to impose on a defendant. The report considers the circumstances surrounding the crime and the prior history and record of the defendant.

probation Suspension of the imposition or execution of a sentence and an order of conditional and revocable release of the defendant in the community under the supervision of a probation officer.

registration The requirement that persons convicted of certain sex, drug, and arson crimes register with the police in their municipality or the sheriff of the county in which they reside.

restitution Compensation a defendant is ordered to pay directly to the victim of his or her crime to compensate the victim for monetary loss sustained as a result of the crime.

restitution fine A monetary penalty imposed on a defendant as punishment for a crime, which is payable to the state Restitution Fund.

Restitution Fund A fund maintained by the state to compensate victims of crimes for unreimbursed economic losses caused by the crimes.

right of allocution The right of a defendant, before pronouncement of judgment, to show cause why judgment should not be pronounced against him or her.

sentence enhancement An additional term of imprisonment required or authorized by law under certain specified circumstances. Those circumstances generally involve an aggravating factor in the commission of the offense or the prior criminal history of the defendant.

special circumstances Circumstances enumerated in Penal Code § 190.2 which, if found by the jury to exist in a first-degree murder case, warrant imposition of the death penalty.

washout provision A provision stating that a sentence enhancement does not apply if a specified period of years has passed since the prior conviction or prison term which is the basis for the enhancement.

work furlough An arrangement under which county jail prisoners reside in jail, but may leave to work or attend an educational program.

Review Questions

1. When must judgment be pronounced against a defendant in a felony case? In a misdemeanor case?

2. What is meant by the term *arraignment for judgment*? What is the defendant's right of allocution?

3. What acts must the judge accomplish at a sentencing hearing under California Rule of Court 433?

4. What matters may the judge consider when determining whether to impose the upper, middle, or lower term of imprisonment for an offense at the sentencing hearing?

5. What findings must the jury make at trial and at the penalty phase in a capital case in order to impose the death penalty?

6. What is determinate sentencing? Under the Determinate Sentence Law, how does the judge select the appropriate term of imprisonment in a given case?

7. Give an example of an indeterminate sentence. Why is the sentence indeterminate?

8. Upon what two general categories of grounds are sentence enhancements prescribed by statute?

9. What is a habitual violent offender within the meaning of Penal Code § 667.7? What sentence enhancements are provided by that section?

10. What is the "Three Strikes and You're Out" law?

11. What factors are to be considered by a judge who is determining whether to impose consecutive terms of imprisonment on a defendant convicted of multiple offenses?

12. List some of the general categories of defendants who are ineligible for probation.

13. What is the general rule regarding when a prisoner serving an indeterminate sentence is eligible for parole if the indeterminate sentence specifies a minimum term of years of imprisonment? Why is the general rule frequently not applicable?

14. If a criminal statute states that an offense is punishable by imprisonment in the county jail or state prison, but says nothing about a fine, may the court impose a fine on a defendant who is convicted under that statute?

15. What is the difference between a restitution fine and restitution to the victim of an offense?

16. What types of property connected with drug offenses are subject to forfeiture under Health and Safety Code § 11470?

17. Describe three categories of offenders who are required to register with law enforcement authorities.

18. What is work furlough?

19. What is home detention?

Review Problems

1. The legislature enacts a statute that provides: "In any case in which a person is sentenced to death after a conviction of murder in the first degree, the convicted person shall be put to death in the same manner he or she used to kill his or her victim." Do you think this statute is constitutional? Why or why not?

2. Mortimer, a bookkeeper for a small company, has been convicted of felony embezzlement (grand theft) of his employer's funds. Mortimer has one previous misdemeanor conviction for petty theft. Assume that Mortimer is eligible for probation. He also is a single parent responsible for the support of three children. One of the children has a serious medical condition, and Mortimer claims that he committed the theft and embezzlement to obtain funds to pay for his child's medical care. What sort of documents should the court expect to receive prior to the sentencing hearing in Mortimer's case?

3. Continuing with Mortimer's situation in problem 2, the probation officer's report informs the court that, other than his prior conviction for petty theft and his present conviction, Mortimer has been a law-abiding citizen. He attends church regularly, coaches a children's soccer team, and is an active member of the PTA at his children's school. At the sentencing hearing, the prosecutor offers no additional evidence in aggravation. The president of Mortimer's company testifies that the financial damage done to his company by Mortimer's embezzlement will probably cause the company to have to file bankruptcy. Mortimer presents the testimony of three witnesses who testify to his good moral character. Penal Code § 489 provides: "Grand theft is punishable as follows: ... (b) ... by imprisonment ... in the state prison." Assume that the judge intends to sentence Mortimer to prison. What term of imprisonment do you think he or she will impose, and why?

4. A defendant has been arrested for allegedly kidnapping, raping, and then killing a twelve-year-old girl. There is evidence that the girl was tortured before she was killed. The prosecutor is trying to decide whether to seek the death penalty. Her main concern is the likelihood of success if she tries the case as a capital case. What do you think the prosecutor's

likelihood of success will be if she decides to seek the death penalty? Explain your answer.

5. Continuing the fact situation in question 4, assume that the defendant is convicted and sentenced to death. Where will the death sentence be carried out? In what manner will the death sentence be carried out?

6. The warden at one of the California state prison facilities asks his legal counsel to determine the legality of using whipping as a means of disciplining prisoners. What answer should the legal counsel give the warden?

7. Barbara is charged with theft of $150 worth of avocados. The prosecutor charges the offense as a felony. The information filed by the prosecutor alleges that Barbara has a prior conviction for burglary of an inhabited dwelling house (a serious felony under Penal Code § 1192.7), and a prior conviction for carjacking (a violent felony under Penal Code § 667.5). If Barbara is convicted of the theft of the avocados, and the prosecutor proves the prior convictions at trial, what is the minimum sentence Barbara can receive for the theft of the avocados?

8. Martin is arrested and charged with receiving stolen property of a value of $100,000 over a two-year period. He has been conducting this activity at a cabin he owns in the mountains. During investigation of the offense, the police discover evidence that Martin is also manufacturing illegal drugs in the garage of his home in the local municipality. He is charged with that offense as well. There is no relationship between the two offenses other than that they were both committed by Martin. Martin is convicted of both offenses at trial. A separate sentence of imprisonment is imposed by the court for each offense. Do you think the judge will order the sentences to be served concurrently or consecutively? If the court does not specify whether the sentences are to be concurrent or consecutive, which will they be?

9. Robert is convicted of a felony sex offense that he committed while intoxicated. It is his first offense. At the sentencing hearing, the victim testifies that she has incurred costs for medical care and psychiatric counseling as a result of the offense. If the judge decides to

grant probation, what are some of the conditions of probation that he will likely impose on Robert?

10. Jeff has been convicted of second-degree murder and sentenced to imprisonment for a term of from fifteen years to life. It is his first felony conviction. When will Jeff be eligible for parole? If he is released on parole, how long will he be on parole? May Jeff's parole be terminated earlier than the full period of his parole? If so, what is the earliest time at which his parole may be terminated?

11. Dorothy has been convicted of a misdemeanor and sentenced to pay a fine of $1,000, in monthly installments of $100, for 10 months. Dorothy is the single mother of three small children. She is poorly educated and is unable to obtain employment that pays enough to cover her child care expenses. Her only income is her welfare check, and she and the children live at or near the poverty level. Dorothy manages to make the first two monthly payments on the fine, but she fails to make the third payment. The court thereupon has Dorothy arrested and orders her to show cause why she should not be imprisoned until the installment is paid. At the show cause hearing, Dorothy explains to the judge that she is indigent and cannot obtain the money to make the monthly payment without depriving her children of the necessities of life. The judge, unmoved, orders Dorothy imprisoned until she makes the third monthly payment. Is the judge's action lawful? Briefly explain your answer.

12. Oscar is convicted of robbery and battery resulting in serious bodily injury to his victim, Felix. During the robbery, Oscar took Felix's Rolex watch and the contents of his wallet, which had a combined value of $3,200. As a result of his injuries, Felix incurred medical expenses of $15,000 and was out of work for one month, resulting in lost wages of $5,000. For which of these monetary losses should the court order Oscar to pay restitution to Felix? If the court orders Oscar to pay restitution directly to Felix, may the court also impose a restitution fine on Oscar?

Notes

1 22 Cal. Jur. *Criminal Law,* § 3322 (3d ed., Bancroft-Whitney 1985).

2 *See generally* 3 Witkin & Epstein, *California Criminal Law* §§ 1329–1344 (2d ed., Bancroft-Whitney 1989).

3 California Const., art. I, § 15; *Mempa v. Ray,* 389 U.S. 128 (1967); *In re Cortez* (1971) 6 Cal.3d 78.

4 *Locket,* 438 U.S. at 604–05.

5 Penal Code § 190.3.

6 *See People v. Eggleston* (1967) 255 Cal.App.2d 337.

7 *See O'Brien v. Olson* (1941) 42 Cal.App.2d 449.

8 Penal Code § 3000(b)(1).

9 *See* 3 Witkin & Epstein, *supra* note 2, at §§ 1653, 1658.

10 *See* Penal Code § 1203(a).

11 *See Griffin v. Wisconsin,* 483 U.S. 868 (1987); *United States v. Consuelo-Gonzalez,* 521 F.2d 259 (9th Cir. 1975).

12 *See* Penal Code § 1203.2; 3 Witkin & Epstein, *supra* note 2, at § 1695 *et seq.*

13 Penal Code § 3046.

14 *In re Love* (1974) 11 Cal.3d 179.

15 Penal Code § 3000.1(d).

16 *Williams v. Illinois,* 399 U.S. 235 (1970); *In re Antazo* (1970) 3 Cal.3d 100.

17 Vehicle Code §§ 23166, 23171.

CHAPTER 19

Postconviction Remedies

OUTLINE

Introduction

This chapter concludes the text with a discussion of the postconviction remedies available to a criminal defendant: appeal, habeas corpus, and executive clemency.

§ 19.1   Appeal

The Constitutions of the United States and the state of California do not expressly grant a right to appeal. The right is, however, conferred by statute: Penal Code § 1235 grants the right to appeal from criminal proceedings in the superior court. Such appeals are taken to the courts of appeal, which are the intermediate appellate courts in California. Penal Code § 1466 grants the right to appeal from criminal proceedings in the municipal court. Appeals from the municipal court are generally taken to the appellate department of the superior court. Recall that a judgment of death is automatically appealed to the California Supreme Court without any action on the part of the defendant or defense counsel. In California, the appealing party is called the **appellant** and the party responding to the appeal is called the **respondent**.

Appeals from the superior courts to the courts of appeal and from the municipal courts to the appellate departments of the superior courts are *appeals of right*. This means that the appealing party has a right to appeal, and the appellate court must hear the appeal unless it determines that the appeal should be dismissed because it is frivolous, or for some other reason authorized by law. A party dissatisfied with the results at this first level of appeal may attempt to appeal further. An appeal from a decision of the court of appeal is directed to the California Supreme Court. An appeal from the appellate department of the superior court is directed to the court of appeal. This second level of appeal is discretionary; that is, it is not an appeal of right.

When a case is appealed from the court of appeal to the California Supreme Court, the Supreme Court determines whether it will hear the appeal. In determining whether to entertain an appeal, the California Supreme Court weighs many factors, including the importance of the issues raised by the appellant, the need to settle a rule of law that has received conflicting treatment in the lower courts, and the existence of constitutional questions in the issues raised by the appellant.

Hearing an appeal of a decision of the appellate department of the superior court is also discretionary, but in this instance, the discretion lies with the superior court. Cases heard by the appellate department of the superior courts may be "certified" by the superior court to the court of appeal. The decision to certify a case to the court of appeal is discretionary, and the superior court may deny a defendant's request for certification.

California appellate courts may review all appellate issues raised by an appellant, including alleged violations of federal constitutional principles. If an appeal raises only issues of state law, it is dealt with exclusively by the state appellate courts. If an appeal raises issues of federal law, particularly federal constitutional law, the appellant may appeal to the United States Supreme Court once the appellate process in the California courts has been completed. As with second-level appeals in the California courts, review by the United States Supreme Court is discretionary.

Matters That May Be Appealed

The function of appellate courts is to review alleged errors of law committed at the trial-court level.[1] Appellate courts generally do not review the factual determinations made by the triers of fact in the trial courts. If the issue is raised by the appellant, however, the appellate court will examine the record of trial to determine whether the jury's verdict or the finding of the trial judge is supported by the evidence. If the appellate court finds that, based on the evidence presented at trial, the finder of fact could reasonably have reached the verdict or finding that was reached, the appellate court will not disturb the verdict or finding, even if it would have reached a different verdict or finding based on the same evidence.

Appeal by Defendant   Penal Code §§ 1237 (superior court) and 1466 (municipal court) provide that a defendant may appeal from a final judgment of conviction and from any order made after judgment that affects his or her substantial rights. On appeal from a final judgment, the court may also review any order denying a motion for a new trial. The requirement that an appeal be from a final judgment means that errors occurring before and during trial generally may not be appealed by the defendant at the time of their occurrence. Rather, the defendant must await the outcome of the trial and, if he or she is convicted, raise all issues in one appeal. For example, if a defendant's pretrial motion to suppress evidence is denied by the trial court, the defendant cannot appeal the denial until after final judgment in the case.[2] In addition to final judgments, orders after judgment affecting a defendant's substantial rights may be appealed. An example would be an order revoking a defendant's probation.

Appeal by Prosecution   The prosecution's right to appeal in a criminal case is considerably more limited than that of the defendant. For example, a defendant may appeal a final judgment of conviction, but the prosecution may not appeal an acquittal. The grounds upon which the government may appeal in a superior court case are specified in Penal Code § 1238. (*See* Penal Code § 1238.) The grounds for a government appeal in a municipal court case are specified in Penal Code § 1466. (*See* Penal Code § 1466.) Generally, these sections authorize the government to appeal pretrial disposition of a case, such as the granting of a motion to set aside the accusatory pleading or a demurrer, and posttrial orders, such as the grant of a new trial to the defendant or the imposition of a sentence not authorized by law. Anything occurring during the trial is generally not appealable by the government.

Filing the Appeal

Because the right to appeal is purely statutory, it may be lost if appeal is not timely filed. The filing of an appeal is a simple procedure accomplished by filing a notice of appeal with the clerk of the trial court. The notice of appeal must be filed within sixty days after rendition of the judgment or order being appealed in a superior court case, and within thirty days after rendition of the judgment or order in a municipal court case. No notice of appeal is required in a death penalty case, because of the automatic appeal to the California Supreme Court. A notice of appeal is sufficient if it states that the appealing party appeals from the trial court's judgment or order. The legal grounds for the appeal need not be specified. Upon receipt of a notice of appeal, the clerk of the trial court must transmit a copy to the appellate court and notify each party other than the appellant of the filing of the notice of appeal.

The **record on appeal** must then be prepared for use by the appellate court and the parties. The contents of the record on appeal are specified in the California Rules of Court.[3] In a typical case, the record on appeal consists of a **clerk's transcript** and a **reporter's transcript**. The clerk's transcript is prepared by the clerk of the trial court and consists of documents in the court's case file, such as the accusatory pleading, minutes of the trial court relating to the action, the verdict, the judgment or order appealed from, jury instructions, the transcript of the preliminary examination or grand jury hearing, and other documents required by the California Rules of Court.

The reporter's transcript is prepared by the court reporter or reporters who stenographically recorded the court proceedings in the case. It is a verbatim transcript of the oral proceedings at trial and other oral proceedings in the case, as specified in the California Rules of Court.

In addition to the clerk's transcript and the reporter's transcript, California Rule of Court 33 provides that the record on appeal is to contain any exhibit admitted in evidence or rejected at trial, if requested by the appellate court.

After the record on appeal has been assembled, the clerk of the trial court provides a copy to the appellant and the Attorney General and transmits the original record to the appellate court.

The appellant then prepares and files an opening **brief** with the appellate court and serves a copy on the respondent. A *brief* is an argumentative document in which the appellant states the grounds for appeal and the legal arguments supporting grant of the relief sought. The respondent may then file a respondent's brief in opposition to the appellant's opening brief. A copy of the respondent's brief must be served on the appellant. After being served with the respondent's brief, the appellant may file and serve a reply brief addressing the points raised by the respondent in the respondent's brief. Briefs are covered by California Rule of Court 37.

After the record on appeal and briefs have been filed with the appellate court, a hearing is scheduled at which the parties may orally present their positions to the court. This procedure is known as *oral argument.* No evidence is presented. The proceeding is limited to the presentation of argument by the parties, and often involves an active dialogue between the appellate justices or judges and the attorneys presenting the arguments.

Scope of Review

As previously discussed, an appellate court will not substitute its judgment for that of the trial court on the factual issues in the case. The appellate's court's function is to determine whether errors of law occurred at the trial court level. Errors of law frequently involve incorrect rulings by the trial judge.

From the defendant's perspective, opportunities for judicial error are numerous at the pretrial, trial, and posttrial stages of the proceedings. The defendant, for example, may claim that the judge erred by denying a motion to suppress evidence or a demurrer; by admitting inadmissible evidence over defense objection; by erroneously stating the law when instructing the jury; or by erroneously denying the defendant's motion for a new trial. The prosecution may claim error only within the scope of the matters that it may appeal under Penal Code §§ 1238 and 1466. The prosecution may claim, for example, that the court set aside an accusatory pleading or granted the defendant a new trial without adequate legal grounds to do so; that it imposed a sentence not authorized by law; or that it committed legal error with respect to one of the other matters listed in §§ 1238 or 1466.

Decision

After considering the arguments of the parties in their briefs and oral arguments, the appellate court renders its decision. If the court determines that the errors of law alleged by the appellant did not occur, it will affirm the trial court judgment or order being reviewed.

If the appellate court determines that an error of law occurred in the trial court, it must then determine whether the error was prejudicial or harmless. A **prejudicial error** is sufficiently serious that it is likely to have changed the outcome of the case. A **harmless error** is a trivial error that is not likely to have changed the outcome of the case. Article VI, § 13, of the California Constitution provides:

> No judgment shall be set aside, or new trial granted, in any cause, on the ground of misdirection of the jury, or of the improper admission or rejection of evidence, or for any error as to any matter of pleading, or for any error as to any matter of procedure, unless, after an examination of the entire cause, including the evidence, the court shall be of the opinion that the error complained of has resulted in a miscarriage of justice.

For error to be deemed prejudicial by an appellate court, it must be of the magnitude described in the constitutional provision. Prior to 1956, appellate courts in California applied a "possible prejudice" test when evaluating errors made in the trial court. In other words, an appellate court would find error prejudicial if it concluded that the error might "possibly" have resulted in a "miscarriage of justice." The test for prejudicial error was expressed in terms of a double negative: error was deemed prejudicial if it could not be said that a different result would not have been reached in the trial court in the absence of the error. In *People v. Watson*, the California Supreme Court disapproved the possible prejudice test and replaced it with a "probable prejudice" test, as the excerpt from that case illustrates. (Note that at the time of the *Watson* decision, the constitutional provision presently found at article VI, § 13, was designated article VI, § 4½.)

Since the California Supreme Court's decision in *People v. Watson*, the general test for prejudicial error has been the probable prejudice test, i.e., that prejudicial error will not be found by an appellate court unless it concludes that "it is reasonably probable that a result more favorable to the appealing party would have been reached in the absence of the error." An exception to this standard exists when the appellant is alleging constitutional error. The courts have held that when the alleged error is of constitutional dimensions, the appellate court must find prejudice unless it determines that the error was harmless beyond a reasonable doubt. The courts have gone even farther when a constitutional error has deprived the defendant of a fundamental constitutional right. Such errors have been declared reversible per se because, if they occur, reversal of the defendant's conviction is required regardless of actual prejudice to the defendant resulting from the error. An example of an error reversible per se would be the denial of a defendant's right to counsel.[4]

If the appellate court holds that the error committed by the trial court was harmless, it will **affirm** the judgment or order being reviewed. If the court holds that the error was prejudicial, it will **reverse** the judgment or order, and often will order further disposition of the case by the trial court (such as dismissal, retrial, or correction of the erroneous action of the trial judge). If the appellate court requires further action in the case by the trial court, it will *remand* the case to the trial court. A common statement at the end of appellate court decisions is "reversed and remanded for further proceedings consistent with this opinion," or words of a similar nature.

The decision of the appellate court is transmitted to the trial court by a process known as **remittitur.** Most decisions of the courts of appeal are reported in both official and unofficial reporters, which may be found in any law library and in many law offices.

PEOPLE v. PHILIP J. WATSON
46 Cal.2d 818 (July 3, 1956)

Defendant appeals from a judgment of conviction of second degree murder. His wife, Arlys Watson, was killed on February 15, 1953, in their San Francisco apartment. Defendant's conviction rests on circumstantial evidence. He does not challenge the sufficiency of the evidence to support the conviction, but he argues these points as grounds for reversal: (1) the restriction of the defense's cross-examination of one of the prosecution witnesses, Officer Mullen; (2) the giving of an instruction that neither the prosecution nor the defense was required to call as witnesses all persons present "at the events involved in the evidence"; (3) the refusal of an instruction requiring, in substance, that each essential fact in a chain of circumstantial evidence must be proved beyond a reasonable doubt; and (4) the overruling of the objection to certain cross-examination of defendant. Only points (3) and (4) raise any serious question, but a review of the records leads us to the conclusion that there was no prejudicial error resulting in a "miscarriage of justice," and the judgment of conviction should therefore be affirmed. (Cal. Const., art. VI, § 4½.)

* * *

[T]he court refused to instruct in language substantially embodying CALJIC No. 28: That "When the case which has been made out by the People against a defendant rests entirely or chiefly on circumstantial evidence, and in any case before the jury may find a defendant guilty basing its finding solely on such evidence, each fact which is essential to complete a chain of circumstances that will establish the defendant's guilt must be proved beyond a reasonable doubt."

Defendant argues that it was error for the court to refuse to give a requested instruction in language substantially embodying CALJIC No. 28.

* * *

Properly interpreted, CALJIC No. 28 applies the doctrine of reasonable doubt not to proof of miscellaneous collateral or incidental facts, but only to proof of "each fact which is essential to complete a chain of circumstances that will establish the defendant's guilt." Although the import of the opening phrase in CALJIC No. 28 may be somewhat confusing because of the reference to its applicability when the People's case rests "chiefly" on circumstantial evidence, it is clearly applicable to cases such as the present one, which rests entirely upon circumstantial evidence. Accordingly, the trial court erred in refusing to give defendant's instruction which substantially embodied CALJIC No 28. ... However, the jury here was correctly instructed on the doctrine of reasonable doubt (CALJIC No. 21; Penal Code, §§ 1096, 1096a), the law applicable where evidence is susceptible of different constructions (CALJIC No. 26), the principle that circumstantial evidence of defendant's guilt must be inconsistent with any other rational hypothesis (CALJIC No. 27), and other related matters as above noted. Under these circumstances, it does not appear here that the court's failure to give a further instruction substantially in the language of CALJIC No. 28 has "resulted in a miscarriage of justice" within the meaning of the constitutional provision as hereinafter discussed.

Defendant finally contends that the court erred in permitting the prosecution, over objection, to develop certain alleged collateral matters through his cross-examination, and which he claims could have had no purpose except to discredit and degrade him.

* * *

Defendant's second point of objection concerns his cross-examination as to his height and related facts. On direct examination, defendant stated that he was 6 feet 6 inches tall. On cross-examination, the prosecution asked defendant about certain marks on one of the door frames in his apartment, and defendant admitted that they were measurements of his height at various intervals. Then over objection, the prosecution was permitted to show that defendant had been attending gymnasium classes, the contention being that defendant did so to stretch his height beyond the 6 feet 6 inch limit fixed by the Army, and so he could be discharged from further Army service. The prosecution then made an offer of proof—that defendant had written a letter dated February 6, 1953, addressed to the Army authorities to the effect that he was above the maximum height of 78 inches acceptable to the Army and should be permitted to get out of the Army. The prosecution argued that defendant was wearing his Army uniform in court to gain sympathy and respect for his patriotic service, and the proffered evidence would serve to rebut this effect. Counsel for defendant responded that the proposed line of questioning was not only beyond the scope of the direct examination, but that defendant's motive in wearing the uniform was entirely collateral, for admittedly defendant was still in the Army and was entitled, in fact required, to wear the uniform. After considerable discussion with counsel, the trial court finally ruled that such evidence was admissible "for the limited purpose only ... of permitting the jury to determine in the last analysis the weight that it is to give to this line of testimony." The prosecution then proceeded to cross-examine defendant about his gymnasium exercises and about his letter to the Army authorities. He stated that in January, 1953, he attended these classes to improve his posture, not to stretch his height. He further stated that when he learned of the Army regulations as to height, he wrote the letter in question, not for the purpose of getting out of the Army earlier, for his discharge was due in March, 1953, and the letter would not be acted upon by that time, but he just wanted to see what would happen and to throw a "bombshell" into the Army administration.

* * *

The challenged but admitted evidence was undoubtedly collateral and irrelevant to any issue in the case. The casting of aspersions on defendant's reasons for wearing an Army uniform that he was entitled to wear, and offering evidence to show an attempt to get a discharge from the Army had no bearing on his motive or credibility in relation to the crime charged. Such questioning on collateral matters and having apparently no other purpose but to degrade defendant has been held reversible error under certain circumstances. The question now presented is whether the error here requires a reversal in view of the provisions of article VI, section $4\frac{1}{2}$ of the Constitution.

* * *

The controlling consideration in applying the section is whether the error has resulted in a "miscarriage of justice." ...

Somewhat different is the language used where the reviewing court has expressed doubt as to whether the error had affected the verdict. Such view has been stated in the form of a double negative, with a reversal required if the court is of the opinion that "a different verdict would not have been improbable had the error not occurred" or "if it cannot be said that, in the absence of the error

complained of, a different verdict would have been improbable, the erroneous ruling constitutes a miscarriage of justice within the meaning of the constitutional provision."

Giving due consideration to the varying language heretofore employed in relating the constitutional amendment to the particular situations involved, it appears that the test generally applicable may be stated as follows: That a "miscarriage of justice" should be declared only when the court, "after an examination of the entire cause, including the evidence," is of the "opinion" that it is reasonably probable that a result more favorable to the appealing party would have been reached in the absence of the error. Phrasing the test in this language avoids any complexity which may be said to result from the language employed in the double negative approach, and such phrasing seems to coincide with the affirmative language used in the constitutional provision. ...

Applying the test as above stated to the record before us, we are of the opinion that it is not reasonably probable that a result more favorable to defendant would have been reached in the absence of the error in permitting the cross-examination of defendant as to his gymnasium exercises and his letter to the Army authorities. He gave an explanation of both acts designed to remove any derogatory effect that otherwise might have resulted from the prosecution's inquiry. It does not appear reasonably probable that the jury was influenced by such evidence to defendant's prejudice, or that the admission of such evidence affected the verdict. Similarly, we are of the opinion, as heretofore indicated, that it is not reasonably probable that a result more favorable to defendant would have been reached in the absence of the error in refusing to give the additional instruction relating to circumstantial evidence. The uncontradicted evidence concerning the condition of the body of the deceased clearly showed that the deceased met her death during the hours that defendant admittedly was in the apartment; and this evidence, together with other evidence, unerringly pointed to defendant's guilt. In short, from an "examination of the entire cause, including the evidence," it is our "opinion" that "the error complained of has" not "resulted in a miscarriage of justice."

The judgment is affirmed.

The Right to Counsel on Appeal

There is no Sixth Amendment right to counsel on appeal. The Sixth Amendment right begins once a defendant is charged and continues, at all critical stages, through trial and sentencing. In some instances, it is in effect at probation revocation. It does not ever include appeals.

The right to counsel on appeal can be found, however, in the Equal Protection Clause of the Fourteenth Amendment. The United States Supreme Court said, in *Douglas v. California*, 372 U.S. 353 (1963), that indigent defendants convicted of a felony have a right to appointed counsel on appeal, provided that the appeal is an appeal of right. Recall that appeals from the superior courts to the courts of appeal and from the municipal courts to the appellate departments of the superior courts are appeals of right. So is the automatic appeal of a death sentence to the California Supreme Court. *Douglas v. California* involved a felony conviction and thus left open the question of whether appointed counsel is required on an appeal of right from a misdemeanor conviction.

The California courts that have dealt with this issue have developed the principle that appointed counsel is required if conviction of the misdemeanor may have serious consequences for the defendant. In one case, a defendant convicted of misdemeanor lewd conduct in public under Penal Code § 647 was held by an appellate court to be entitled to counsel on appeal because, in addition to the possible sentence, a person convicted of that offense was disqualified from teaching in the public schools and was required to register with law enforcement authorities.[5] Another court held that punishment for misdemeanor battery, which potentially includes imprisonment in the county jail for up to six months and a fine not exceeding $1,000, involved serious consequences to the defendant.[6] It has been held, however, that conviction of a misdemeanor traffic offense for which the potential sentence is limited to a fine does not involve serious consequences to the defendant. In such a case, the defendant is not entitled to appointed counsel on appeal.[7]

If an appeal is discretionary, the Equal Protection Clause of the Fourteenth Amendment does not compel the state to provide counsel.

As at trial, the defendant is entitled to effective counsel. The appointed attorney has an ethical obligation to zealously pursue the defendant's appeal. Because of the large number of frivolous appeals, the Supreme Court has stated that an appointed attorney may be allowed to withdraw. However, the following must be done: first, the attorney must request withdrawal from the appellate court; second, a brief must be filed explaining why the attorney believes the appeal to be wholly without merit. In that brief, all potential issues must be outlined for the court's review, including anything that might arguably support the appeal. If the appellate court agrees that there are no valid issues, the attorney may withdraw. If the court finds an issue that has some merit, the lawyer must continue to represent the defendant.[8]

Bail on Appeal

Under Penal Code § 1272, bail pending appeal is a matter of right if the defendant has been sentenced to imprisonment for a misdemeanor or has only been sentenced to a fine for either a felony or a misdemeanor. In other cases, bail pending appeal is a matter within the discretion of the court. (Refer to the discussion of bail in Chapter 16.)

§ 19.2 Habeas Corpus

There are a number of writs that may be sought by a criminal defendant. A **writ** is an order issued by a court to a public official ordering the official to do or refrain from doing a particular act. The writ most frequently sought by criminal defendants is the writ of habeas corpus. This writ is of ancient origin, dating back as far as the twelfth century in England. Habeas corpus relief is available under both the United States Constitution (article I, § 9) and the California Constitution (article I, § 11, and article VI, § 10).

Habeas corpus is a Latin term translating as "you have the body" or "let us have the body," (depending on which source you consult). The traditional function of the writ has been to afford a procedure to an incarcerated defendant to challenge the legality of his incarceration. The writ has provided a means for one illegally imprisoned to obtain an order from a court requiring that he be brought before the court for the purpose of inquiring into the lawfulness of the imprisonment. Thus the term *habeas corpus*—the court orders the public official holding the defendant to produce the defendant bodily before the court so that the lawfulness of the defendant's incarceration may be examined. If the court determines that the defendant's incarceration is illegal, it orders the defendant discharged from custody. Because of the significant power of this writ, it has come to be known as the "Great Writ of Liberty."

Modern judicial decisions have greatly expanded the circumstances in which a defendant may seek habeas corpus relief. It is no longer necessary that a defendant actually be imprisoned. Any restraint of liberty imposed as part of the criminal justice process is sufficient to support issuance of the writ. For example, a defendant serving a term of probation, released from custody on bail, or released from prison on parole is suffering a restraint of liberty and may seek habeas corpus relief. An illegal restraint of liberty may be the restraint itself or the conditions of that restraint. A prisoner may, for example, petition for habeas corpus to challenge not only her incarceration, but also the conditions in the prison in which she is incarcerated.

Modern judicial decisions have established that courts have wide discretion in fashioning remedies for persons who seek habeas corpus relief. Although courts may, as in the past, order discharge of a prisoner from custody, they may also order trial courts to take specific actions with respect to the case, such as reconsidering a denial of probation or granting a defendant a new trial. They may also order executive officials, particularly those having custody of a defendant, to remedy unlawful prison conditions, review a prisoner's application for parole, and to do or refrain from doing many other acts associated with the conditions of the defendant's imprisonment.

Required Grounds

Certain grounds must be established before a court will grant habeas corpus relief.

Custody or Other Restraint of Liberty   The defendant, who is referred to in this discussion as the *petitioner*, must be in actual custody or subjected to some other form of restraint of liberty, frequently called *constructive custody*. *Actual custody* means that the petitioner is in the custody of law enforcement or penal authorities (i.e., he or she is in jail or in prison). Actual custody may occur before, during, or after trial, and habeas corpus is available to challenge the legality of custody at any of those times. *Constructive custody* means that the petitioner is not in jail or prison, but his or her liberty is restrained in some way. Probation, parole, and bail are examples of constructive custody because, in each of those situations, the petitioner's liberty has been restrained. Habeas corpus is available to review the legality of constructive custody occurring before, during, or after trial.

Unlawful Restraint or Lawful Restraint under Unlawful Conditions   The restraint on the petitioner's liberty must be unlawful or, if lawful, must involve unlawful conditions. Restraint is unlawful when, as a matter of law, it should not have been imposed on the defendant. For example, a defendant denied bail may challenge the denial by writ of habeas corpus claiming that she is entitled to be released on bail. Similarly, a defendant imprisoned after trial may claim that the proceedings were legally defective for some reason, such as lack of jurisdiction of the court or a violation of the defendant's constitutional rights, and that his resulting imprisonment is therefore unlawful. A prisoner denied release on parole may challenge the denial by habeas corpus, claiming that the denial is wrongful and that further imprisonment is unlawful. If a petitioner's restraint is lawful, but the conditions of the restraint are unlawful, the restraint may still be challenged by habeas corpus. For example, violation of a prisoner's civil rights by prison authorities may be remedied by habeas corpus.

Exhaustion of Other Remedies   As a matter of policy, courts generally do not grant habeas corpus relief if relief is available through another procedure. This principle is most frequently applied when a petitioner has an adequate remedy through the normal appellate process. If appeal is available, and can adequately remedy the wrong asserted by the petitioner, the courts usually refrain from reviewing the situation through habeas corpus.

However, there are situations in which appeal is available but does not afford an adequate remedy to the petitioner. An example would be a petitioner being held in custody pending trial because of a denial of bail. Appeal is available after judgment at trial, but review by an appellate court at that time will not secure the pretrial release of the petitioner. Habeas corpus is the proper remedy in such a situation. Appeal may also be an inadequate remedy because of the time it takes to complete the appellate process. For example, a petitioner serving a sentence in a county jail after a misdemeanor conviction might very well complete his sentence before an appellate court can render a decision on an appeal.

Habeas corpus is the appropriate remedy in that situation because it affords more expeditious relief. Another attribute of the appellate process that may render appeal an inadequate remedy is the fact that an appellate court is limited to a review of the record of the proceedings in the lower court. If a petitioner's claim of unlawful restraint requires examination of factors not contained in the lower court's record, appeal is not an adequate remedy.

Finally, recall that the requirement of exhaustion of other remedies is a matter of policy, not law. Courts sometimes disregard the policy, particularly in situations involving violations of a petitioner's fundamental constitutional rights, and grant habeas corpus review despite the fact that appeal is available to the petitioner. As the *Stankewitz* case illustrates, a court may grant habeas corpus review in a case involving violation of a fundamental constitutional right even when the petitioner has an appeal pending in the same court.

In re LAIRD GENE STANKEWITZ
40 Cal.3d 391; 220 Cal.Rptr. 382; 708 P.2d 1260
(Nov. 25, 1985)

Petitioner Laird Gene Stankewitz seeks a writ of habeas corpus after he was convicted of first degree murder and robbery and sentenced to death. His automatic appeal from that judgment is pending in this court. (Pen. Code, § 1239, subd. (b).) In this proceeding he contends he was denied a fair trial because one of the jurors introduced erroneous "law" on a crucial issue into the guilt phase deliberations. We conclude the contention is meritorious and hence the judgment must be vacated.

* * *

While preparing the automatic appeal, petitioner's appellate counsel fortuitously received information that led him to obtain declarations of Marian Sparks and James F. Barbieri, who had served as jurors in the case. Each declaration stated in substance as follows: on several occasions during the guilt phase deliberations Juror Louis Knapp advised the other jurors that he had been a police officer for over 20 years; that as a police officer he knew the law; that the law provides a robbery takes place as soon as a person forcibly takes personal property from another person, whether or not he intends to keep it; and that as soon as petitioner took the wallets at gunpoint in this case he committed robbery, whether or not he intended to keep them.

Petitioner now seeks a writ of habeas corpus, contending that he was denied a fair trial by reason of such juror misconduct.

When extraneous law enters a jury room—i.e., a statement of law not given to the jury in the instructions of the court—the defendant is denied his constitutional right to a fair trial unless the People can prove that no actual prejudice resulted. This rule has special force in capital cases, in which "[i]t is vital ... that the jury should pass upon the case free from external causes tending to disturb the exercise of deliberate and unbiased judgment."

Although jury misconduct during deliberations is most often raised by motion for new trial and appeal, it may also be alleged as a ground of habeas corpus.

* * *

We must next decide whether the statement of Juror Knapp related in the declarations constituted misconduct.

In our system of justice it is the trial court that determines the law to be applied to the facts of the case, and the jury is "bound ... to receive as law what is laid down as such by the court." (Pen. Code, § 1126.) "Of course, it is a fundamental and historic precept of our judicial system that jurors are restricted solely to the determination of *factual* questions and are bound by the law as given them by the court. They are not allowed either to determine what the law *is* or what the law *should* be."

* * *

Here Knapp likewise violated the court's instructions and "consulted" his own outside experience as a police officer on a question of law. Worse, the legal advice he gave himself was totally wrong. Had he merely kept his erroneous advice to himself, his conduct might be the type of subjective reasoning that is immaterial for purposes of impeaching a verdict. But he did not keep his erroneous advice to himself; rather, vouching for its correctness on the strength of his long service as a police officer, he stated it again and again to his fellow jurors and thus committed overt misconduct.

* * *

The misconduct of Juror Knapp raises a presumption of prejudice. Such a presumption is even stronger when, as here, the misconduct goes to a key issue in the case: the resolution of the question whether a robbery took place was critical to the prosecution's felony-murder theory, to the separate robbery count, and to the robbery special-circumstance allegation. ...

It is settled that "unless the prosecution rebuts that presumption by proof that no prejudice actually resulted, the defendant is entitled to a new trial." The People's only attempt to carry that heavy burden in this case is the assertion that "the presumption of prejudice is fully rebutted because both of the jurors make it clear that their decisions fully included a determination concerning petitioner's intent to rob." The effort falls far short of the mark.

First, the argument is without evidentiary support. There is nothing in the second Barbieri declaration to support the claim. And what evidence there is in the second Sparks declaration—"I was not influenced by Juror Knapp in making my decision on how to vote in this matter"—is plainly inadmissible under Evidence Code section 1150, subdivision (a).

Second, even if each of the subsequent declarations could have established that Knapp's serious misconduct did not affect the deliberations of the declarant, no evidence has been offered, admissible or not, to rebut the presumption that it affected the deliberations of the *other* jurors. Such evidence is, of course, necessary: "it is settled that a conviction cannot stand if even a single juror has been improperly influenced."

The petition for writ of habeas corpus is granted. The judgment of conviction is vacated and petitioner is remanded to the Superior Court of Inyo County. Upon finality, the clerk shall remit a certified copy of this opinion and order to the superior court for filing, and respondent shall serve another copy thereof on the prosecuting attorney in conformity with Penal Code section 1382, subdivision 2.

Procedure

Habeas corpus procedures are prescribed in §§ 1473 through 1508 of the Penal Code. A habeas corpus proceeding is initiated by the filing of a petition for writ of habeas corpus. The petition must specify that the petitioner is imprisoned or restrained of his or her liberty; the officer by whom the petitioner is restrained; the place of restraint; and the identity of the parties involved, such as the petitioner, the Department of Corrections, the lower court, or the sheriff. The petition must state the basis for any allegation that the petitioner's restraint is illegal. Also, the petition must be verified by oath or affirmation.

A petition for writ of habeas corpus may lawfully be filed in the superior court, the court of appeal, or the California Supreme Court. As a matter of practice, however, habeas corpus petitions are generally filed in the lowest appropriate court. If unlawful restraint has been imposed by a municipal court, a habeas corpus petition challenging the restraint would normally be filed in the superior court. If unlawful restraint has been imposed by a superior court, a habeas corpus petition would normally be filed in the court of appeal. Challenges to unlawful prison conditions would normally be brought in the superior court. In a case such as *Stankewitz*, in which the petitioner has been sentenced to death, the petitioner would normally file a petition for habeas corpus in the

California Supreme Court, because that court has the lawful authority to grant relief to the petitioner, either through the automatic appeal process or through habeas corpus.

Upon receipt of a habeas corpus petition, the court may respond in a number of ways. First, the court may summarily deny the petition. A common ground for summary denial is a determination by the court that the claim made by the petitioner is frivolous. Another ground is failure of the petitioner to exhaust his or her other remedies, such as through the appellate process.

If the court does not summarily deny the petition, it may issue either an **order to show cause** or a writ of habeas corpus. California Rule of Court 260(a) provides:

> Unless a petition for a writ of habeas corpus is sooner denied ... , the court shall, within 30 days after the petition is filed ... , issue the writ or order the respondent to show cause why the relief sought in the petition should not be granted.

The respondent mentioned in Rule 260(a) is the authority having custody of the petitioner or otherwise responsible for the restraint of the petitioner's liberty. If the court grants a writ of habeas corpus, the petitioner must be bodily brought before the court. If the court issues an order to show cause, the issues raised by the petitioner will be reviewed by the court without the necessity of physically producing the petitioner before the court.

Whether the court grants a writ of habeas corpus or issues an order to show cause, the respondent is required to file a **return**, which is a response to the allegations in the petition. (*See* Penal Code § 1480.) In addition to being filed with the court, the return must be served on the other parties to the proceeding, including the petitioner.

Under California Rule of Court 260(b), within thirty days after the return is filed and served, the petitioner may file and serve a **denial** responding to the allegations made in the return. Any material allegation of the petition not controverted by the return, and any material allegation of the return not controverted by the denial, is deemed admitted.

Rule 260(c) provides that once the petition, return, and denial (if any) are filed, or if a denial is not filed, then upon expiration of the thirty days allowed for filing a denial, the court must either grant or deny the relief sought by the petitioner or order that an evidentiary hearing be held.[9] If an evidentiary hearing is held, it must be a full and fair hearing, and may include the testimony of witnesses. The petitioner has the burden of proof to establish his or her allegations by a preponderance of the evidence. If the proceedings are in the court of appeal or the California Supreme Court, the matter must be referred to a superior court for hearing, or a referee (usually a superior court judge) must be appointed to conduct the hearing, because the appellate courts are unable to take testimony.

After the hearing, the court in which the petition for habeas corpus was filed renders its decision on the petition. As previously mentioned, the courts, under modern judicial decisions defining the scope of habeas corpus relief, are not limited to discharge of the petitioner when granting a petition for a writ of habeas corpus. The courts have wide discretion to grant relief appropriate to the issues raised in the petition. For example, courts have annulled criminal convictions, modified sentences, required bail hearings, modified conditions of confinement in prison, and required the establishment of procedural safeguards for prison discipline.[10] Courts have commonly granted such relief even when denying the petition; that is, they have denied the petition by refusing to discharge the petitioner from custody or other restraint, but have issued orders requiring correction of the problem that was the basis for the petition. If, however, the court finds that there is no legal basis for the petitioner's custody or other restraint, or for continuation of the custody or other restraint, the court must discharge the petitioner.[11]

If a superior court grants part or all of the relief requested by the petitioner, the government may appeal to the court of appeal. In contrast, if the superior court denies part or all of the relief requested by the petitioner, the petitioner has no right to appeal, but may file a petition for writ of habeas corpus in the court of appeal. If the initial petition for writ of habeas corpus was filed in the court of appeal, and the requested relief is granted, denied, or granted in part and denied in part, the petitioner or the government, or both, may apply for a hearing in the California Supreme Court.[12] The California Supreme Court has discretion to either grant or deny the application for the hearing.

Right to Counsel

Under current law, an indigent petitioner does not have a right to appointed counsel to assist in preparing and presenting a petition for writ of habeas corpus. It is arguable that if an evidentiary hearing is held, a due process right to counsel exists to assure that the hearing is fair. This issue has not, however, been definitively resolved by the courts.

Federal Habeas Corpus

The federal legal system has its own habeas corpus procedures. The current federal habeas corpus statutes are found at 28 U.S.C. §§ 2241–2255. Federal habeas corpus is significant to persons in the California criminal justice system because federal habeas corpus relief is available to review alleged violations of federal law, particularly federal constitutional law, in state court proceedings. The grounds for federal habeas corpus relief and the procedures for obtaining such relief are similar, though not identical, to those in the California state system.

Federal habeas corpus relief may not be sought by a petitioner in the California criminal justice system unless all state remedies, including state habeas corpus, have been exhausted. Exceptions to this rule, provided in 28 U.S.C. § 2254(b), exist if "there is either an absence of available corrective process or the existence of circumstances rendering such process ineffective to protect the rights of the prisoner." As to the latter of the two exceptions, if a state remedy is available, but it would be futile to exhaust it, habeas corpus may be brought in the federal system without exhaustion. For example, if the California Supreme Court has previously addressed the legal issue raised by the petitioner, and has held contrary to the petitioner's position, there is no need for the petitioner to apply for a hearing in the California Supreme Court unless there is reason to believe that the California Supreme Court will reconsider its previous holding.

§ 19.3 Executive Clemency

The power of executive clemency resides in the governor. Article V, § 8, of the California Constitution provides:

> Subject to application procedures provided by statute, the Governor, on conditions the Governor deems proper, may grant a reprieve, pardon, and commutation, after sentence, except in case of impeachment ... . The Governor may not grant a pardon or commutation to a person twice convicted of a felony except on recommendation of the Supreme Court, four judges concurring.

As stated in the constitutional provision, executive clemency may take one of three forms: reprieve, commutation, or pardon. A **reprieve** is a stay—a postponement— of execution of a sentence. A **commutation** of a sentence is a reduction in the sentence, either in form or duration. For example, the governor may commute a sentence of death to a sentence of life with or without the possibility of parole, or may commute a sentence to imprisonment by reducing the number of years to which the defendant has been sentenced. A **pardon** is a complete cancellation of the punishment to which a defendant has been sentenced.

Use of the reprieve power is generally limited to execution of the death sentence, and very little is said of it in the Penal Code. Section 4800 recognizes the constitutional power of the governor to grant reprieves. Section 3700 recognizes the power of the governor to suspend the execution of a sentence of death. Section 1227.5 provides that when a death sentence has not been carried out because of a reprieve granted by the governor, it must be carried out the day following expiration of the reprieve.

General Procedural Rules for Commutations and Pardons

Commutations and pardons are addressed in Penal Code § 4800 *et seq.* Section 4801 provides that the Board of Prison Terms may report to the governor the names of persons imprisoned in the state prison "who, in its judgment, ought to have a commutation of sentence or be pardoned and set at liberty on account of good conduct, or unusual term of sentence, or any other cause, including evidence of battered woman syndrome." Alternatively, a person convicted of a crime may make direct application to the governor for commutation of sentence or a pardon. (*See* Penal Code §§ 4802, 4803.) In the latter situation, if the applicant has only one felony conviction, the governor may summarily grant or deny the application for clemency, or may refer the matter to the Board of Prison Terms for investigation and recommendation. If an applicant has two felony convictions, the governor must refer the application to the board for investigation.

If a person who has been recommended for commutation of sentence or pardon by the Board of Prison Terms, or who has applied for commutation of sentence or pardon directly to the governor, has two felony convictions, the governor, under article V, § 8, of the California Constitution, may not grant the requested clemency unless four justices of the California Supreme Court concur. As previously mentioned, if the applicant has two felony convictions, the governor will have referred the application to the Board of Prison Terms for investigation. If the board does not recommend in favor of the application, the application is not to be forwarded to the state supreme court unless the governor makes a special referral. When the Board of Prison Terms recommends that the application be granted, and when the board recommends denial but the governor decides to refer the application to the supreme court notwithstanding, the application (including prison records and recommendations of the Board of Prison Terms) is forwarded to the clerk of the supreme court for consideration by the justices. If at least four justices recommend that clemency be granted, the file is transmitted back to the governor. Otherwise, the file remains with the supreme court.[13] If the supreme court (at least four justices) recommends clemency, the governor may grant or deny the requested commutation or pardon. In doing so, the governor may impose conditions. For example, he or she may commute a death sentence to a sentence of life imprisonment and impose the condition that the defendant not be granted parole.[14]

Special Procedure: Rehabilitation Proceeding

Penal Code §§ 4852.01 through 4852.21 provide a special procedure whereby a person convicted of a felony may apply for and receive a **Certificate of Rehabilitation** and pardon for his or her offense. To qualify for issuance of a Certificate of Rehabilitation, the defendant must live an upright life during a "period of rehabilitation." The period of rehabilitation begins to run upon the discharge of the defendant from prison after completion of his or her sentence, or release on parole or probation, whichever is sooner. The period of rehabilitation is three years, plus an additional period of two years for most persons; the additional period is four years in the case of persons convicted of specified serious offenses. The person must reside in the state of California during the entire period of rehabilitation. Penal Code § 4852.05 provides that:

> During the period of rehabilitation the person shall live an honest and upright life, shall conduct himself or herself with sobriety and industry, shall exhibit a good moral character, and shall conform to and obey the laws of the land.

A person who has completed the rehabilitation period and has conducted himself or herself in accordance with the requirements of § 4852.05 may file a petition for ascertainment and declaration of the fact of rehabilitation and for a Certificate of Rehabilitation in the superior court of the county in which he or she resides. A date will be set by the court for a hearing on the petition. The petitioner must give notice of the petition to the district attorney of the county in which the petition has been filed, the district attorney of each county in which he or she has been convicted of a felony, and the governor.

The court may require production, at no expense to the petitioner, of all court records, prison records, and law enforcement records relating to the crime of which the petitioner was convicted and those relating to his or her conduct during the period of rehabilitation (such as police records of offenses committed during the period of rehabilitation). The court may also request that the district attorney conduct an investigation of the petitioner.[15]

At the hearing, the petitioner is entitled to be represented by counsel of his or her choice. If the petitioner does not have counsel, he or she is entitled to be represented by the public defender or, if there is no public defender in the county, by the adult probation officer of the county. If, in the opinion of the court, the petitioner needs counsel, the court must appoint counsel to represent him or her.[16]

At the hearing, the court determines, based on the evidence presented (which may include the testimony of witnesses), whether the petitioner has conformed to the standards of conduct required by § 4852.05 during the rehabilitation period. If the court determines that the petitioner has conformed his or her conduct to those standards, it issues an order declaring that the petitioner has been rehabilitated and recommending that the governor grant a full pardon to the petitioner. The order is filed with the clerk of the court and constitutes the Certificate of Rehabilitation.[17]

The clerk of the court transmits certified copies of the Certificate of Rehabilitation to the governor, the Board of Prison Terms, the Department of Justice, and, in the case of a person twice convicted of a felony, the California Supreme Court. Except in cases in which the petitioner has two or more felony convictions, the governor may grant the petitioner a full pardon without further investigation. In the case of a person having two or more felony convictions, the governor, under article V, § 8, of the California Constitution, may grant a pardon only if the supreme court, by a vote of at least four justices, concurs.[18]

Penal Code § 4852.01(d) states that the Certificate of Rehabilitation procedure is not available to persons serving a mandatory life parole (persons convicted of first- or second-degree murder), persons committed under death sentences, persons convicted of certain sex crimes, or persons in the military service. Also, the Penal Code provisions establishing the procedure do not mention persons convicted of misdemeanors and therefore are not available to persons convicted of misdemeanors.

Effect of Full Pardon

A full pardon granted by the governor restores to the convicted person "all the rights, privileges, and franchises of which he or she has been deprived in consequence of that conviction." There are certain exceptions to this principle; among them is that a pardon does not affect the power of certain agencies that license professional persons to take action with respect to the convicted person's professional license.[19] Also, a full pardon may not include the right to own, possess, and keep a firearm if the person was ever convicted of a felony involving the use of a dangerous weapon.[20]

Key Terms

affirm The decision of an appellate court upholding the decision of a lower court.

appellant The party appealing a decision of a lower court.

brief An argumentative document filed with an appellate court in which the filing party states the grounds for granting or denying the appeal and supporting legal arguments.

Certificate of Rehabilitation An order issued by a court after a rehabilitation proceeding declaring that the petitioner has been rehabilitated and recommending that the governor grant a full pardon to the petitioner.

clerk's transcript Part of the record on appeal, consisting of pertinent contents of the court's case file.

commutation A form of executive clemency consisting of reduction of a sentence, either in form or duration.

denial A term having several meanings in the field of criminal procedure. In the context of a habeas corpus proceeding, a *denial* is a response by the petitioner to the allegations made in the return filed by the official responsible for the petitioner's incarceration or other restraint of liberty.

habeas corpus A writ issued by a court commanding that a defendant who is incarcerated or otherwise suffering a restraint of his or her liberty be brought before the court for the purpose of examining the lawfulness of the incarceration or restraint or the conditions of the incarceration or restraint.

harmless error A trivial error committed by a trial court that is not likely to have changed the outcome of the case.

order to show cause An order of a court requiring a party to establish grounds why an action contemplated by the court should not be taken.

pardon A form of executive clemency consisting of a complete cancellation of the punishment to which a defendant has been sentenced.

prejudicial error An error committed by a trial court that is sufficiently serious to have been likely to have changed the outcome of the case.

record on appeal The record of proceedings in a lower court transmitted by the clerk of the court to an appellate court when the case has been appealed.

remand The requirement by an appellate court that a lower court take further action in a case.

remittitur The transmittal of the decision of an appellate court to the lower court from which the case was appealed.

reporter's transcript Part of the record on appeal, consisting of transcriptions of oral proceedings in the lower court that were stenographically recorded by the court reporter.

reprieve A form of executive clemency consisting of postponement of execution of a sentence.

respondent The party responding to an appeal or other court proceeding brought by another party.

return A term having several meanings in the field of criminal procedure. In the context of a habeas corpus proceeding, a *return* is a response by the official responsible for the incarceration or other restraint of the petitioner to the allegations made in the petition for writ of habeas corpus.

reverse The decision of an appellate court overturning the decision of a lower court.

writ An order issued by a court to a public official ordering the official to do or refrain from doing a particular act.

Review Questions

1. Distinguish between an appeal of right and a discretionary appeal.

2. Does the prosecution have a right to appeal in a criminal case? Briefly explain your answer.

3. When must notice of appeal be filed in a superior court case? In a municipal court case?

4. Does an indigent defendant have a right to appointed counsel on an appeal of right? If

so, what is the constitutional basis for the right to counsel?

5. Why is the writ of habeas corpus so named?

6. For purposes of habeas corpus, what is the difference between actual custody and constructive custody?

7. What are the three "pleadings" usually filed by the parties in a habeas corpus proceeding?

8. What are the three types of executive clemency?

Review Problems

1. Ellen is convicted of a misdemeanor in the municipal court. She appeals her conviction to the appellate department of the superior court. After considering Ellen's appeal, the appellate department of the superior court affirms Ellen's conviction. If Ellen wants to appeal further, what must she do?

2. George has been convicted of rape. Penal Code § 264 provides that rape is punishable by imprisonment in the state prison for three, six, or eight years. At the sentencing hearing, George's attorney makes an impassioned plea to the judge to have mercy on his client. Moved, the judge sentences George to eighteen months in the state prison. The prosecutor wants to appeal the sentence imposed by the judge. May he do so?

3. A defendant has been convicted of a felony in the superior court and her attorney has filed a timely notice of appeal. The record on appeal must now be prepared. List five documents that will be included in the clerk's transcript and three documents that will be included in the reporter's transcript. Also, the defendant believes that the prosecutor engaged in misconduct during the opening statement to the jury and wants to appeal on that ground in addition to her other grounds. What additional document should the defendant request be included in the reporter's transcript?

4. After conclusion of the evidence phase of the defendant's trial for grand theft (grand larceny) and the closing arguments of counsel, the judge instructs the jury on the elements of the offense. In his instruction on the specific intent element (intent to steal), the judge tells the jury that intent is presumed from the unlawful taking of the property and need not be proved by the prosecution. The defendant is convicted of the offense and then appeals, claiming that the judge's instruction on the intent element of the crime was erroneous. How will the appellate court evaluate the defendant's claim? What do you think the likely result of the defendant's appeal will be in this case?

5. Mark is a member of a church that uses cocaine as part of its religious services. He is arrested, tried, and imprisoned for possession and use of cocaine during several church services. He appeals, but his appeal is unsuccessful. While he is serving his sentence of imprisonment, the California Supreme Court reviews the conviction of another church member and holds that drug possession and use statutes, when applied against persons who possess and use drugs as part of their religious practices, violate the constitutional right of freedom of religion. Mark considers it extremely unfair that he must serve a prison sentence for an act that has been held to be constitutionally protected. Does Mark have a remedy?

6. Cathy has been convicted in the superior court of arson of a structure and has been sentenced to a four-year term of imprisonment. She is in custody while her appeal is pending in the court of appeal. Her appeal claims that the trial judge erroneously instructed the jury on the elements of the offense and that the misinstruction was prejudicial error. In an effort to expedite the resolution of her case, Cathy files a petition for writ of habeas corpus in the court of appeal in which her appeal is pending. Is it likely that the appellate court will proceed on the petition for writ of habeas corpus while Cathy's appeal is pending before it?

7. Steve is serving a sentence of imprisonment for carjacking. On several occasions, he has been subjected to corporal punishment by prison officials. Steve files a petition for writ of habeas corpus in the superior court, claiming that he should be discharged from

custody because of the unlawful conditions in the prison. His petition does not challenge the lawfulness of his conviction or his sentence. What ruling do you think the superior court will make on Steve's petition?

8. Chauncy is serving a sentence of imprisonment for mayhem. He has one prior felony conviction and received a sentence enhancement for that conviction. After serving a portion of his sentence, Chauncy applies to the governor for commutation of the remainder of his sentence. May the governor summarily grant Chauncy's application?

9. Ellen, an attorney, was convicted several years ago of embezzling money from the trust account she maintained for her clients' funds. The offense was a felony and Ellen was sentenced to prison. She was also disbarred by the California State Bar. Ellen served her sentence to imprisonment and, at the end of her term of imprisonment, was released on parole. She resided in California for five years after her release from prison and during that time committed no criminal offenses. At the end of the five years, Ellen petitioned the superior court in her county of residence for a Certificate of Rehabilitation. The court granted the petition and issued the certificate. Based on the Certificate of Rehabilitation, the governor granted Ellen a pardon. Ellen then applied to the California State Bar for reinstatement of her license to practice law and was surprised when the bar refused to reinstate her license. Ellen believes that her pardon from the governor entitles her to reinstatement of her law license. Is she correct?

Notes

[1] *See, e.g.,* Penal Code § 1235.

[2] For a listing of typical prejudgment orders that are reviewable only on appeal from final judgment, *see* 6 Witkin & Epstein, *California Criminal Law* § 3174 (2d ed., Bancroft-Whitney 1989).

[3] *See, e.g.,* California Rule of Court 33.

[4] *Gideon v. Wainwright,* 373 U.S. 335 (1963).

[5] *In re Henderson* (1964) 61 Cal.2d 541.

[6] *People v. Wilson* (1977) 72 Cal.App.3d Supp. 59.

[7] *People v. Batiste* (1980) 109 Cal.App.3d 328.

[8] *Anders v. California,* 386 U.S. 738 (1967).

[9] *See also* Penal Code § 1484.

[10] California Continuing Education of the Bar, *California Criminal Law Procedure and Practice* § 40.32 (3d ed. 1996).

[11] Penal Code § 1485.

[12] Penal Code § 1506.

[13] Penal Code § 4852.

[14] *See* 6 Witkin & Epstein, *supra* note 2, at § 1776.

[15] Penal Code §§ 4852.1, 4852.11, 4852.12.

[16] Penal Code § 4852.08.

[17] Penal Code § 4852.13.

[18] Penal Code §§ 4852.14, 4852.16.

[19] Penal Code §§ 4852.15, 4853.

[20] Penal Code § 4854.

APPENDIX A

THE BILL OF RIGHTS
Amendments I–XIV the United States Constitution

ARTICLES IN ADDITION TO, AND AMENDMENT OF, THE CONSTITUTION OF THE UNITED STATES OF AMERICA, PROPOSED BY CONGRESS, AND RATIFIED BY THE SEVERAL STATES, PURSUANT TO THE FIFTH ARTICLE OF THE ORIGINAL CONSTITUTION

AMENDMENT I (1791)

Congress shall make no law respecting an establishment of religion, or prohibiting the free exercise thereof; or abridging the freedom of speech, or of the press; or the right of the people peaceably to assemble, and to petition the Government for a redress of grievances.

AMENDMENT II (1791)

A well regulated Militia, being necessary to the security of a free state, the right of the people to keep and bear Arms, shall not be infringed.

AMENDMENT III (1791)

No Soldier shall, in time of peace be quartered in any house, without the consent of the Owner, nor in time of war, but in a manner to be prescribed by law.

AMENDMENT IV (1791)

The right of the people to be secure in their persons, houses, papers, and effects, against unreasonable searches and seizures, shall not be violated, and no Warrants shall issue, but upon probable cause, supported by Oath or affirmation, and particularly describing the place to be searched, and the persons or things to be seized.

AMENDMENT V (1791)

No person shall be held to answer for a capital, or otherwise infamous crime, unless on a presentment or indictment of a Grand Jury, except in cases arising in the land or naval forces, or in the Militia, when in actual service in time of War or public danger; nor shall any person be subject for the same offence to be twice put in jeopardy of life or limb; nor shall be compelled in any criminal case to be a witness against himself, nor be deprived of life, liberty, or property, without due process of law; nor shall private property be taken for public use, without just compensation.

AMENDMENT VI (1791)

In all criminal prosecutions, the accused shall enjoy the right to a speedy and public trial, by an impartial jury of the State and district wherein the crime shall have been committed, which district shall have been previously ascertained by law, and to be informed of the nature and cause of the accusation; to be confronted with the witnesses against him; to have compulsory process for obtaining witnesses in his favor, and to have the Assistance of Counsel for his defence.

AMENDMENT VII (1791)

In Suits at common law, where the value in controversy shall exceed twenty dollars, the right of trial by jury shall be preserved, and no fact tried by a jury, shall be otherwise re-examined in any Court of the United States, than according to the rules of the common law.

AMENDMENT VIII (1791)

Excessive bail shall not be required, nor excessive fines imposed, nor cruel and unusual punishments inflicted.

AMENDMENT IX (1791)

The enumeration in the Constitution, of certain rights, shall not be construed to deny or disparage others retained by the people.

AMENDMENT X (1791)

The powers not delegated to the United States by the Constitution, nor prohibited by it to the States, are reserved to the States respectively, or to the people.

AMENDMENT XI (1798)

The Judicial power of the United States shall not be construed to extend to any suit in law or equity, commenced or prosecuted against one of the United States by Citizens of another State, or by Citizens or Subjects of any Foreign State.

AMENDMENT XII (1804)

The Electors shall meet in their respective states and vote by ballot for President and Vice-President, one of whom, at least, shall not be an inhabitant of the same state with themselves; they shall name in their ballots the person voted for as President, and in distinct ballots the person voted for as Vice-President, and they shall make distinct lists of all persons voted for as President, and of all persons voted for as Vice-President, and of the number of votes for each, which lists they shall sign and certify, and transmit sealed to the seat of the government of the United States, directed to the President of the Senate;—The President of the Senate shall, in the presence of the Senate and House of Representatives, open all the certificates and the votes shall then be counted;—The person having the greatest number of votes for President, shall be the President, if such number be a majority of the whole number of Electors appointed; and if no person have such majority, then from the persons having the highest numbers not exceeding three on the list of those voted for as President, the House of Representatives shall choose immediately, by ballot, the President. But in choosing the President, the votes shall be taken by states, the representation from each state having one vote; a quorum for this purpose shall consist of a member or members from two-thirds of the states, and a majority of all the states shall be necessary to a choice. And if the House of Representatives shall not choose a President whenever the right of choice shall devolve upon them, before the fourth day of March next following, then the Vice-President shall act as President, as in the case of the death or other constitutional disability of the President—The person having the greatest number of votes as Vice-President, shall be the Vice-President, if such number be a majority of the whole number of Electors appointed, and if no person have a majority, then from the two highest numbers on the list, the Senate shall choose the Vice-President; A quorum for the purpose shall consist of two-thirds of the whole number of Senators, and a majority of the whole number shall be necessary to a choice. But no person constitutionally ineligible to the office of President shall be eligible to that of Vice-President of the United States.

AMENDMENT XIII (1865)

Section 1 Neither slavery nor involuntary servitude, except as a punishment for crime whereof the party shall have been duly convicted, shall exist within the United States, or any place subject to their jurisdiction.

Section 2 Congress shall have power to enforce this article by appropriate legislation.

AMENDMENT XIV (1868)

Section 1 All persons born or naturalized in the United States and subject to the jurisdiction thereof, are citizens of the United States and of the State wherein they reside. No State shall make or enforce any law which shall abridge the privileges or immunities of citizens of the United States; nor shall any State deprive any person of life, liberty, or property, without due process of law; nor deny to any person within its jurisdiction the equal protection of the laws.

Section 2 Representatives shall be apportioned among the several States according to their respective numbers, counting the whole number of persons in each State, excluding Indians not taxed. But when the right to vote at any election for the choice of electors for President and Vice-President of the United States, Representatives in Congress, the Executive and Judicial officers of a State, or the members of the Legislature thereof, is denied to any of the male inhabitants of such State, being twenty-one years of age, and citizens of the United States, or in any way abridged, except for participation in rebellion, or other crime, the basis of representation therein shall be reduced in the proportion which the number of such male citizens shall bear to the whole number of male citizens twenty-one years of age in such State.

Section 3 No person shall be a Senator or Representative in Congress, or elector of President and Vice-President, or hold any office, civil or military, under the United States, or under any State, who, having previously taken an oath, as a member of Congress, or as an officer of the United States, or as a member of any State legislature, or as an executive or judicial officer of any State, to support the Constitution of the United States, shall have engaged in insurrection or rebellion against the same, or given aid or comfort to the enemies thereof. But Congress may by a vote of two-thirds of each House, remove such disability.

Section 4 The validity of the public debt of the United States, authorized by law, including debts incurred for payment of pensions and bounties for services in suppressing insurrection or rebellion, shall not be questioned. But neither the United States nor any State shall assume or pay any debt or obligation incurred in aid of insurrection or rebellion against the United States, or any claim for the loss or emancipation of any slave; but all such debts, obligations and claims shall be held illegal and void.

Section 5 The Congress shall have power to enforce, by appropriate legislation, the provisions of this article.

APPENDIX B

CONSTITUTION OF THE STATE OF CALIFORNIA
Preamble and Article I

PREAMBLE

We, the People of the State of California, grateful to Almighty God for our freedom, in order to secure and perpetuate its blessings, do establish this Constitution.

ARTICLE I
DECLARATION OF RIGHTS

§1. All people are by nature free and independent and have inalienable rights. Among these are enjoying and defending life and liberty, acquiring, possessing, and protecting property, and pursuing and obtaining safety, happiness, and privacy.

§2. (a) Every person may freely speak, write and publish his or her sentiments on all subjects, being responsible for the abuse of this right. A law may not restrain or abridge liberty of speech or press.

(b) A publisher, editor, reporter, or other person connected with or employed upon a newspaper, magazine, or other periodical publication, or by a press association or wire service, or any person who has been so connected or employed, shall not be adjudged in contempt by a judicial, legislative, or administrative body, or any other body having the power to issue subpoenas, for refusing to disclose the source of any information procured while so connected or employed for publication in a newspaper, magazine or other periodical publication, or for refusing to disclose any unpublished information obtained or prepared in gathering, receiving or processing of information for communication to the public.

Nor shall a radio or television news reporter or other person connected with or employed by a radio or television station, or any person who has been so connected or employed, be so adjudged in contempt for refusing to disclose the source of any information procured while so connected or employed for news or news commentary purposes on radio or television, or for refusing to disclose any unpublished information obtained or prepared in gathering, receiving or processing of information for communication to the public.

As used in this subdivision, "unpublished information" includes information not disseminated to the public by the person from whom disclosure is sought, whether or not related information has been disseminated and includes, but is not limited to, all notes, outtakes, photographs, tapes or other data of whatever sort not itself disseminated to the public through a medium of communication, whether or not published information based upon or related to such material has been disseminated.

§3. The people have the right to instruct their representatives, petition government for redress of grievances, and assemble freely to consult for the common good.

§4. Free exercise and enjoyment of religion without discrimination or preference are guaranteed. This liberty of conscience does not excuse acts that are licentious or inconsistent with the peace or safety of the State. The Legislature shall make no law respecting an establishment of religion.

A person is not incompetent to be a witness or juror because of his or her opinions on religious beliefs.

§5. The military is subordinate to civil power. A standing army may not be maintained in peacetime. Soldiers may not be quartered in any house in wartime except as prescribed by law, or in peacetime without the owner's consent.

§6. Slavery is prohibited. Involuntary servitude is prohibited except to punish crime.

§7. (a) A person may not be deprived of life, liberty, or property without due process of law or denied equal protection of the laws; provided, that nothing contained herein or elsewhere in this Constitution imposes upon the State of California or any public entity, board, or official any obligations or responsibilities which exceed those imposed by the Equal Protection Clause of the 14th Amendment to the United States Constitution with respect to the use of pupil school assignment or pupil transportation. In enforcing this subdivision or any other provision of this Constitution, no court of this state may impose upon the State of California or any public entity, board, or official any obligation or responsibility with respect to the use of pupil school assignment or pupil transportation, (1) except to remedy a specific violation by such party that would also constitute a violation of the Equal Protection Clause of the 14th Amendment to the United States Constitution, and (2) unless a federal court would be permitted under federal decisional law to impose that obligation or responsibility upon such party to remedy the specific violation of the Equal Protection Clause of the 14th Amendment of the United States Constitution.

Except as may be precluded by the Constitution of the United States, every existing judgment, decree, writ, or other order of a court of this state, whenever rendered, which includes provisions regarding pupil school assignment or pupil transportation, or which requires a plan including any such provisions shall, upon application to a court having jurisdiction by any interested person, be modified to conform to the provisions of this subdivision as amended, as applied to the facts which exist at the time of such modification. In all actions or proceedings arising under or seeking application of the amendments to this subdivision proposed by the Legislature at its 1979–80 Regular Session, all courts, wherein such actions or proceedings are or may hereafter be pending, shall give such actions or proceedings first precedence over all other civil actions therein.

Nothing herein shall prohibit the governing board of a school district from voluntarily continuing or commencing a school integration plan after the effective date of this subdivision as amended.

In amending this subdivision, the Legislature and people of the State of California find and declare that this amendment is necessary to serve compelling public interests, including those of making the most effective use of the limited financial resources now and prospectively available to support public education, maximizing the educational opportunities and protecting the health and safety of all public school pupils, enhancing the ability of parents to participate in the educational process, preserving harmony and tranquility in this state and its public schools, preventing the waste of scarce fuel resources, and protecting the environment.

(b) A citizen or class of citizens may not be granted privileges or immunities not granted on the same terms to all citizens. Privileges or immunities granted by the Legislature may be altered or revoked.

§8. A person may not be disqualified from entering or pursuing a business, profession, vocation, or employment because of sex, race, creed, color, or national or ethnic origin.

§9. A bill of attainder, ex post facto law, or law impairing the obligation of contracts may not be passed.

§10. Witnesses may not be unreasonably detained. A person may not be imprisoned in a civil action for debt or tort, or in peacetime for a militia fine.

§11. Habeas corpus may not be suspended unless required by public safety in cases of rebellion or invasion.

§12. A person shall be released on bail by sufficient sureties, except for:

(a) Capital crimes when the facts are evident or the presumption great;

(b) Felony offenses involving acts of violence on another person, or felony sexual assault offenses on another person, when the facts are evident or the presumption great and the court finds based upon clear and convincing evidence that there is a substantial likelihood the person's release would result in great bodily harm to others; or

(c) Felony offenses when the facts are evident or the presumption great and the court finds based on clear and convincing evidence that the person has threatened another with great bodily harm and that there is a substantial likelihood that the person would carry out the threat if released.

Excessive bail may not be required. In fixing the amount of bail, the court shall take into consideration the seriousness of the offense charged, the previous criminal record of the defendant, and the probability of his or her appearing at the trial or hearing of the case.

A person may be released on his or her own recognizance in the court's discretion.

§13. The right of the people to be secure in their persons, houses, papers, and effects against unreasonable seizures and searches may not be violated; and a warrant may not issue except on probable cause, supported by oath or affirmation, particularly describing the place to be searched and the persons and things to be seized.

§14. Felonies shall be prosecuted as provided by law, either by indictment or, after examination and commitment by a magistrate, by information.

A person charged with a felony by complaint subscribed under penalty of perjury and on file in a court in the county where the felony is triable shall be taken without unnecessary delay before a magistrate of that court. The magistrate shall immediately give the defendant a copy of the complaint, inform the defendant of the defendant's right to counsel, allow the defendant a reasonable time to send for counsel, and on the defendant's request read the complaint to the defendant. On the defendant's request the magistrate shall require a peace officer to transmit within the county where the court is located a message to counsel named by defendant.

A person unable to understand English who is charged with a crime has a right to an interpreter throughout the proceedings.

§14.1. If a felony is prosecuted by indictment, there shall be no postindictment preliminary hearing.

§15. The defendant in a criminal cause has the right to a speedy public trial, to compel attendance of witnesses in the defendant's behalf, to have the assistance of counsel for the defendant's defense, to be personally present with counsel, and to be confronted with the witnesses against the defendant. The Legislature may provide for the deposition of a witness in the presence of the defendant and the defendant's counsel. Persons may not twice be put in jeopardy for the same offense, be compelled in a criminal cause to be a witness against themselves, or be deprived of life, liberty, or property without due process of law.

§16. Trial by jury is an inviolate right and shall be secured to all, but in a civil cause three-fourths of the jury may render a verdict. A jury may be waived in a criminal cause by the consent of both parties expressed in open court by the defendant and the defendant's counsel. In a civil cause a jury may be waived by the consent of the parties expressed as prescribed by statute.

In civil causes the jury shall consist of 12 persons or a lesser number agreed on by the parties in open court. In civil causes in municipal or justice court the Legislature may provide that the jury shall consist of eight persons or a lesser number agreed on by the parties in open court.

In criminal actions in which a felony is charged, the jury shall consist of 12 persons. In criminal actions in which a misdemeanor is charged, the jury shall consist of 12 persons or a lesser number agreed on by the parties in open court.

§17. Cruel or unusual punishment may not be inflicted or excessive fines imposed.

§18. Treason against the State consists only in levying war against it, adhering to its enemies, or giving them aid and comfort. A person may not be convicted of treason except on the evidence of two witnesses to the same overt act or by confession in open court.

§19. Private property may be taken or damaged for public use only when just compensation, ascertained by a jury unless waived, has first been paid to, or into court for, the owner. The Legislature may provide for possession by the condemnor following commencement of eminent domain proceedings upon deposit in court and prompt release to the owner of money determined by the court to be the probable amount of just compensation.

§20. Noncitizens have the same property rights as citizens.

§21. Property owned before marriage or acquired during marriage by gift, will, or inheritance is separate property.

§22. The right to vote or hold office may not be conditioned by a property qualification.

§23. One or more grand juries shall be drawn and summoned at least once a year in each county.

§24. Rights guaranteed by this Constitution are not dependent on those guaranteed by the United States Constitution.

In criminal cases the rights of a defendant to equal protection of the laws, to due process of law, to the assistance of counsel, to be personally present with counsel, to a speedy and public trial, to compel the attendance of witnesses, to confront the witnesses against him or her, to be free from unreasonable searches and seizures, to privacy, to not be compelled to be a witness against himself or herself, to not be placed twice in jeopardy for the same offense, and to not suffer the imposition of cruel or unusual punishment, shall be construed by the courts of this state in a manner consistent with the Constitution of the United States. This Constitution shall not be construed by the courts to afford greater rights to criminal defendants than those afforded by the Constitution of the United States, nor shall it be construed to afford greater rights to minors in juvenile proceedings on criminal causes than those afforded by the Constitution of the United States. This declaration of rights

may not be construed to impair or deny others retained by the people.

§25. The people shall have the right to fish upon and from the public lands of the state and in the waters thereof, excepting upon lands set aside for fish hatcheries, and no land owned by the state shall ever be sold or transferred without reserving in the people the absolute right to fish thereupon; and no law shall ever be passed making it a crime for the people to enter upon the public lands within this state for the purpose of fishing in any water containing fish that have been planted therein by the state; provided, that the legislature may by statute, provide for the season when and the conditions under which the different species of fish may be taken.

§26. The provisions of this Constitution are mandatory and prohibitory, unless by express words they are declared to be otherwise.

§27. All statutes of this state in effect on February 17, 1972, requiring, authorizing, imposing, or relating to the death penalty are in full force and effect, subject to legislative amendment or repeal by statute, initiative, or referendum. The death penalty provided for under those statutes shall not be deemed to be, or to constitute, the infliction of cruel or unusual punishments within the meaning of Article 1, Section 6 nor shall such punishment for such offenses be deemed to contravene any other provision of this constitution.

§28. (a) The People of the State of California find and declare that the enactment of comprehensive provisions and laws ensuring a bill of rights for victims of crime, including safeguards in the criminal justice system to fully protect those rights, is a matter of grave statewide concern.

The rights of victims pervade the criminal justice system, encompassing not only the right to restitution from the wrongdoers for financial osses suffered as a result of criminal acts, but also the more basic expectation that persons who commit felonious acts causing injury to innocent victims will be appropriately detained in custody, tried by the courts, and sufficiently punished so that the public safety is protected and encouraged as a goal of highest importance.

Such public safety extends to public primary, elementary, junior high, and senior high school campuses, where students and staff have the right to be safe and secure in their persons.

To accomplish these goals, broad reforms in the procedural treatment of accused persons and the disposition and sentencing of convicted persons are necessary and proper as deterrents to criminal behavior and to serious disruption of people's lives.

(b) Restitution. It is the unequivocal intention of the People of the State of California that all persons who suffer losses as a result of criminal activity shall have the right to restitution from the persons convicted of the crimes for losses they suffer.

Restitution shall be ordered from the convicted persons in every case, regardless of the sentence or disposition imposed, in which a crime victim suffers a loss, unless compelling and extraordinary reasons exist to the contrary. The Legislature shall adopt provisions to implement this section during the calendar year following adoption of this section.

(c) Right to Safe Schools. All students and staff of public primary, elementary, junior high and senior high schools have the inalienable right to attend campuses which are safe, secure and peaceful.

(d) Right to Truth-in-Evidence. Except as provided by statute hereafter enacted by a two-thirds vote of the membership in each house of the Legislature, relevant evidence shall not be excluded in any criminal proceeding, including pretrial and post conviction motions and hearings, or in any trial or hearing of a juvenile for a criminal offense, whether heard in juvenile or adult court. Nothing in this section shall affect any existing statutory rule of evidence relating to privilege or hearsay, or Evidence Code, Sections 352, 782 or 1103. Nothing in this section shall affect any existing statutory or constitutional right of the press.

(e) Public Safety Bail. A person may be released on bail by sufficient sureties, except for capital crimes when the facts are evident or the presumption great. Excessive bail may not be required. In setting, reducing or denying bail, the judge or magistrate shall take into consideration the protection of the public, the seriousness of the offense charged, the previous criminal record of the defendant, and the probability of his or her appearing at the trial or hearing of the case. Public safety shall be the primary consideration.

A person may be released on his or her own recognizance in the court's discretion, subject to the same factors considered in setting bail. However, no person charged with the commission of any serious felony shall be released on his or her own recognizance.

Before any person arrested for a serious felony may be released on bail, a hearing may be held before the magistrate or judge, and the prosecuting attorney shall be given notice and reasonable opportunity to be heard on the matter.

When a judge or magistrate grants or denies bail or release on a person's own recognizance, the reasons for that decision shall be stated in the record and included in the court's minutes.

(f) Use of Prior Convictions. Any prior felony conviction of any person in any criminal proceeding, whether adult or juvenile, shall subsequently be used without limitation for purposes of impeachment or enhancement of sentence in any criminal proceeding. When a prior felony conviction is an element of any felony offense, it shall be proven to the trier of fact in open court.

(g) As used in this article, the term "serious felony" is any crime defined in Penal Code, Section 1192.7(c).

§29. In a criminal case, the people of the State of California have the right to due process of law and to a speedy and public trial.

§30. (a) This Constitution shall not be construed by the courts to prohibit the joining of criminal cases as prescribed by the Legislature or by the people through the initiative process.

(b) In order to protect victims and witnesses in criminal cases, hearsay evidence shall be admissible at preliminary hearings, as prescribed by the Legislature or by the people through the initiative process.

(c) In order to provide for fair and speedy trials, discovery in criminal cases shall be reciprocal in nature, as prescribed by the Legislature or by the people through the initiative process.

§31. (a) The state shall not discriminate against, or grant preferential treatment to, any individual or group on the basis of race, sex, color, ethnicity, or national origin in the operation of public employment, public education, or public contracting.

(b) This section shall apply only to action taken after the section's effective date.

(c) Nothing in this section shall be interpreted as prohibiting bona fide qualifications based on sex which are reasonably necessary to the normal operation of public employment, public education, or public contracting.

(d) Nothing in this section shall be interpreted as invalidating any court order or consent decree which is in force as of the effective date of this section.

(e) Nothing in this section shall be interpreted as prohibiting action which must be taken to establish or maintain eligibility for any federal program, where ineligibility would result in a loss of federal funds to the state.

(f) For the purposes of this section, "state" shall include, but not necessarily be limited to, the state itself, any city, county, city and county, public university system, including the University of California, community college district, school district, special district, or any other political subdivision or governmental instrumentality of or within the state.

(g) The remedies available for violations of this section shall be the same, regardless of the injured party's race, sex, color, ethnicity, or national origin, as are otherwise available for violations of then-existing California antidiscrimination law.

(h) This section shall be self-executing. If any part or parts of this section are found to be in conflict with federal law or the United States Constitution, the section shall be implemented to the maximum extent that federal law and the United States Constitution permit. Any provision held invalid shall be severable from the remaining portions of this section.

GLOSSARY

accessory A person who, after a felony has been committed, harbors, conceals, or aids a principal in such felony, with the intent that said principal may avoid or escape from arrest, trial, conviction, or punishment, having knowledge that said principal has committed such felony or has been charged with such felony or convicted thereof. Formerly termed *accessory after the fact.*

accomplice A person called to testify in the trial of a defendant who himself or herself is a principal to the crime with which the defendant is charged. A defendant may not be convicted on accomplice testimony unless the testimony is independently corroborated.

accusatorial A type of legal system in which the government brings charges against a defendant and bears the burden of proving them.

accusatory pleading The formal charge that must be filed with the proper court before a defendant may be brought to trial. In misdemeanor cases, the accusatory pleading is the complaint filed in the municipal court. In felony cases, the accusatory pleading is the indictment or information filed in the superior court.

actual possession Actual physical possession of a thing, i.e., when it is on one's person.

actus reus An act or omission which, when joined with a criminal mental state, constitutes a crime.

admission A statement made by a person, other than at his or her trial, which does not by itself acknowledge guilt of a crime, but which tends to prove guilt when considered with other evidence.

admission to bail The order of a competent court or magistrate that a defendant be discharged from custody upon bail.

adversarial A method of conducting trials in which the opposing parties advocate their respective positions before a neutral trier of fact.

affirm The decision of an appellate court upholding the decision of a lower court.

affirmative defense A principle of law that completely or partially absolves the defendant of guilt when the defendant has committed the act with which he or she has been charged.

affray The offense committed by a person who unlawfully fights in a public place or challenges another person to fight in a public place.

aggravated arson Arson committed willfully, maliciously, deliberately, with premeditation, and with the intent to cause personal injury, property damage under circumstances likely to produce personal injury, or damage to one or more structures or inhabited dwellings, if the defendant has been convicted of arson within the past ten years, or the fire causes property damage in excess of $5,000,000, or the fire causes damage to or destruction of five or more inhabited structures.

aggravated kidnapping Kidnapping for ransom, reward, extortion, or robbery, and kidnapping during commission of a carjacking.

aggravated mayhem The malicious and intentional maiming or permanent disfiguring of another.

aggravated sexual assault of a child The commission upon a child under the age of fourteen, and at least ten years younger than the perpetrator, of rape, sodomy, oral copulation, or penetration of genital or anal openings, accomplished by means of force, violence, or fear.

aggravation Evidence regarding the circumstances of an offense or the criminal history of the defendant which supports imposition of a sentence at or near the maximum authorized by law.

agreeing to engage in prostitution The crime involving agreement to engage in an act of prostitution accompanied by an act in furtherance of an act of prostitution, such as the payment or receipt of money.

alibi A claim by the defendant that he or she was not present at the scene of the crime at the time the crime was committed.

apparent necessity A legal principle applicable to the law of self-defense which provides that a person is entitled to use deadly force in self-defense to repel an attack when the circumstances are such that he or she honestly and reasonably believes that he or she is being attacked with deadly force or that the attacker is attempting to perpetrate a "forcible and atrocious crime" upon him or her, even if such belief is mistaken.

appellant The party appealing a decision of a lower court.

appellate court A court to which a party to a civil lawsuit or criminal proceeding may appeal the decision of a lower court.

arraignment A procedure that consists of reading the accusatory pleading to the defendant, providing the defendant a true copy, and asking him or her how he or she pleads in response to the charge or charges in the accusatory pleading.

arraignment for judgment The initial procedure at the court proceeding at which judgment is pronounced and sentence imposed on a convicted defendant. Arraignment for judgment involves informing the defendant of the nature of the charge against him or her; his or her plea; and the verdict, if any; followed by a question to the defendant whether he or she has any legal cause to show why judgment should not be pronounced.

arrest Taking a person into custody, in a situation and in the manner authorized by law.

arrest warrant A written command issued by a magistrate to a peace officer to take the person identified therein into custody.

arson The offense committed by one who willfully and maliciously sets fire to, burns, or causes to be burned, or who aids, counsels, or procures the burning of, any structure, forest land, or property.

assault An unlawful attempt, coupled with a present ability, to commit a violent injury on the person of another.

attempt A direct but ineffectual act done toward the commission of a crime by one having the specific intent to commit the crime.

bail A deposit of money, property, or a bond with a court to assure the presence of the defendant at court proceedings.

bail bond A promise made by a surety, pursuant to a contract with the defendant, to pay the amount of the defendant's bail to the court if the defendant fails to appear at the proceeding to which the bail applies.

battery Any willful and unlawful use of force or violence upon the person of another.

bench trial A trial by the judge alone, without a jury; also referred to as a *court trial.*

bench warrant A warrant of arrest issued by a judge on the judge's own initiative, that is, without the filing of a complaint by the prosecutor.

beyond a reasonable doubt The highest standard of proof in the judicial system. *Reasonable doubt* is defined in Penal Code § 1096 as follows: "It is not a mere possible doubt; because everything relating to human affairs ... is open to some possible or imaginary doubt. It is that state of the case, which, after the entire comparison and consideration of all the evidence, leaves the minds of jurors in that condition that they ... cannot say they feel an abiding conviction ... of the truth of the charge."

bill of attainder An act by a legislature that imposes punishment on a person without the use of court proceedings.

Bill of Rights The first ten amendments to the United States Constitution; establishes certain fundamental rights of the citizenry.

booking   The recordation of an arrest in official police records, and the taking by police of fingerprints and photographs of the person arrested, or any of these acts following an arrest.

border search   A search of incoming persons and vehicles at the borders and other entry points to the United States. Border searches do not require a warrant and may be made without probable cause.

Brady doctrine   The rule developed by the United States Supreme Court that prosecutors must disclose exculpatory evidence to defendants.

bribery   The crime of giving, offering to give, requesting, receiving, or agreeing to receive anything of value or advantage, with a corrupt intent to influence the recipient in the discharge of his or her official or public duty.

brief   An argumentative document filed with an appellate court in which the filing party states the grounds for granting or denying the appeal and supporting legal arguments.

burden of persuasion   The duty to persuade the trier of fact of the existence or nonexistence of a fact.

burden of production   The duty to introduce evidence tending to show the existence or nonexistence of a particular fact. The burden of production does not require that the party having the burden actually persuade the trier of fact of the existence or nonexistence of the fact.

burden of proof   The duty to prove the existence or nonexistence of a fact or facts material to the outcome of a case.

burglary   Entry of a building or other enclosed place described in Penal Code § 459 with the specific intent to commit larceny or any felony.

California Courts of Appeal   The intermediate-level appellate courts in the California judicial system. California is divided geographically into six appellate districts, with one court of appeal sitting in each district.

California Supreme Court   The highest court in the California judicial system.

carjacking   The felonious taking of a motor vehicle in the possession of another, from his or her person or immediate presence, or from the person or immediate presence of a passenger of the motor vehicle, against his or her will and with the intent to either permanently or temporarily deprive the person in possession of the motor vehicle of his or her possession, accomplished by means of force or fear.

cause in fact   An occurrence (cause) that produces a result (effect). An act or omission by a defendant is the cause in fact of the criminal result if it can be said that, but for the act or omission, the criminal result would not have occurred, or if the act or omission was a substantial factor in producing the criminal result.

Certificate of Rehabilitation   An order issued by a court after a rehabilitation proceeding declaring that the petitioner has been rehabilitated and recommending that the governor grant a full pardon to the petitioner.

certiorari   An order issued by the United States Supreme Court to a lower court directing the lower court to transmit the record of a case so that it may be reviewed by the Supreme Court.

chain of custody   A method of maintaining accountability for evidence whereby a record is made of all persons having possession of the evidence from the time of seizure by law enforcement personnel to use of the evidence at trial. Maintenance of the chain of custody assures that the evidence presented at trial is the same evidence originally seized by law enforcement personnel.

challenge for cause   A challenge to a prospective juror on the ground that his or her answers to the voir dire questioning reveal that he or she is disqualified from serving on the jury or is biased.

child stealing   The malicious taking, detaining, concealing, or enticing away of a minor child by a person having no right to custody of the child, with the intent to detain or conceal the child from a person, guardian, or public agency having lawful charge of the child.

circumstantial evidence Evidence that does not directly establish the fact to be proved, but that is consistent with or supports the fact to be proved; facts and circumstances from which a jury or judge may reason and reach conclusions in a case.

civil liberties Freedoms granted to the people by the constitutions of the United States and the states.

clerk's transcript Part of the record on appeal, consisting of pertinent contents of the court's case file.

code A compilation of statutes, usually arranged by subject matter.

codification The process of organizing the enacted statutes of a government into one or more codes.

commercial bribery The crime involving bribery of an employee with the specific intent to injure or defraud the employee's employer, the employer of the person paying the bribe, or a competitor of any such employer.

commitment An order of a court directing that a defendant be delivered into the custody of a law enforcement agency.

common law The body of law created by judicial decisions and contained in the text of those decisions, rather than in statutes or other legislative enactments.

community service A modern sentencing alternative under which a convicted defendant may be ordered to perform work beneficial to the community.

commutation A form of executive clemency consisting of reduction of a sentence, either in form or duration.

compensatory damages A monetary sum, awarded to a plaintiff in a civil lawsuit, which is intended to compensate the plaintiff for monetary losses suffered because of the wrong complained of in the lawsuit.

complaint The initial document filed with the court in a criminal proceeding that accuses the defendant of a crime. The complaint is the document used to request an arrest warrant. It also serves as the accusatory pleading in a misdemeanor case.

concurrent jurisdiction Authority possessed by more than one government to legislate with respect to certain subjects, or the authority of more than one type of court to adjudicate certain types of cases.

concurrent sentences Multiple sentences that are served simultaneously.

conditional sentence Suspension of the imposition or execution of a sentence and an order of revocable release in the community, subject to conditions established by the court, without the supervision of a probation officer.

confession A statement made by a person, other than at his or her trial, in which he or she acknowledges guilt of a crime.

consecutive sentences Multiple sentences that are served one after the other.

consent Free and voluntary assent, based upon knowledge of the true nature of the act or transaction involved, by one possessing sufficient mental capacity to make an intelligent choice. Consent by the victim is a defense to a crime only if lack of consent is an element of the crime.

consent search A search authorized by the consent of a person having lawful authority to permit law enforcement officers to search the premises. A consent search is an exception to the usual requirement that a search must be pursuant to a warrant.

consolidated theft statute Penal Code § 484, which defines the crime of theft as any stealing involving the elements of larceny, embezzlement, or false pretenses.

conspiracy An agreement entered into between two or more persons with the specific intent to agree to commit a public offense and with the further specific intent to commit such offense, followed by an overt act committed in California by one or more of the parties for the purpose of accomplishing the object of the agreement.

constructive possession Possession deemed by the law to exist when one does not have actual physical possession of a thing, but exercises dominion and control over it.

contempt   Acts or omissions specified by statute that violate court orders or that undermine or disrupt the judicial process. Some contempts are crimes, whereas others are punished through civil proceedings.

continuous sexual abuse of a child   Three or more sex acts with a child under the age of fourteen committed by a person who resides with the child or who has recurring access to the child over a period of three months or more.

contract   An agreement between two or more persons which is enforceable in a court of law because it is supported by consideration and is not violative of law or public policy.

corporate liability   The liability of a corporation for criminal offenses committed by persons acting on its behalf.

corpus delicti   The "body of the crime," which consists of two factors: (1) injury, loss, or harm, and (2) a criminal act or omission as its cause. In a criminal trial, the prosecution must establish the corpus delicti—i.e., that a crime occurred—independently of any admissions or confessions of the defendant made prior to the trial.

court rules   Rules of procedure for the courts promulgated on both a statewide basis (California Rules of Court) and by individual courts (local rules).

court trial   A trial by the judge alone, without a jury; also referred to as a *bench trial*.

criminal law   The field of law that defines crimes, specifies the punishments for crimes, and specifies defenses to crimes.

criminal procedure   The field of law that establishes principles governing the procedures used in the investigation and prosecution of criminal offenses.

cross-examination   The questioning of a witness for one party by the attorney for the other party for the purpose of bringing out any weakness in the witness's testimony, such as faulty perception, bias, or lack of credibility.

curtilage   The area directly around one's home in which one has a reasonable expectation of privacy.

damages   The monetary recovery awarded to a successful plaintiff in a civil lawsuit.

deliberation   As an element of the crime of first-degree murder, means careful thought and weighing of considerations.

demurrer   A challenge by a defendant to an indictment or information based on a defect apparent on the face of the pleading.

denial   A term having several meanings in the field of criminal procedure. In the context of a habeas corpus proceeding, a *denial* is a response by the petitioner to the allegations made in the return filed by the official responsible for the petitioner's incarceration or other restraint of liberty.

detainer   A request made by one state to another state that the latter state retain custody of a prisoner so that the prisoner may be tried for an offense in the requesting state.

deter   To influence another to refrain from acting.

determinate sentence   A sentence to a specified term of imprisonment under the Determinate Sentencing Law. The full term specified must be served by the defendant.

dictum (pl. dicta)   Comments in the decision of an appellate court about principles of law which are not part of the legal basis of the court's opinion.

diminished capacity   A form of partial insanity defense under which a defendant claims that, although not sufficiently mentally impaired to be entitled to a defense of insanity, he or she may have been impaired to the point that he or she lacked the capacity to form the mental state necessary for commission of the crime. The diminished capacity defense is not recognized in California on the issue of guilt of the defendant.

direct evidence   Evidence (such as eyewitness testimony) that directly establishes the fact to be proved.

discovery The pretrial acquisition by one party to a criminal proceeding of evidence and information in the possession of the other party.

discretion The use of one's own judgment when making a decision, based on consideration of the circumstances pertinent to the decision.

disorderly conduct A general category of misdemeanor offenses involving: (1) offenses of sexual misconduct; (2) loitering, begging, and trespassing; (3) public intoxication; and (4) molesting or loitering about children.

district attorney The government official in each county having primary responsibility to prosecute persons accused of crimes.

disturbing the peace A description of a group of offenses involving: (1) unlawfully fighting in a public place or challenging another person to fight in a public place; (2) maliciously and willfully disturbing another person by loud and unreasonable noise; and (3) using offensive words in a public place which are inherently likely to provoke an immediate violent reaction.

double jeopardy A rule originating in the Fifth Amendment to the United States Constitution and Article I, § 15, of the California Constitution that prohibits a second punishment or a second trial for the same offense. It is sometimes referred to as *former jeopardy or prior jeopardy.*

driving under the influence The offense committed by driving a vehicle while under the influence of any alcoholic beverage or drug or the combined influence of any alcoholic beverage or drug. A person is under the influence when, as a result of ingestion of alcohol or drugs, his or her physical or mental abilities are impaired to such a degree that he or she no longer has the ability to drive a vehicle with the caution characteristic of a sober person of ordinary prudence, under the same or similar circumstances. This offense is to be contrasted with the offense of driving a vehicle with a blood alcohol level of 0.08 percent or more, which does not require evidence that the person's ability to operate the vehicle was actually impaired. The latter offense is committed by having the requisite blood alcohol level, without regard to actual impairment.

Due Process Clauses The provision appearing in the Fifth and Fourteenth Amendments to the United States Constitution and in the California constitution that a person may not be deprived of life, liberty, or property without due process of law.

duress A defense to a crime other than homicide, involving commission of an otherwise criminal act or omission under a threat to the defendant's life if he or she does not comply. The threat must be one that would cause a reasonable person to fear for his or her life, and the person threatened must have actually entertained such fear. There is some authority that a threat of serious bodily injury also constitutes duress.

Durham test A test for insanity of a defendant, which provides that the defendant will not be guilty of the crime charged, by reason of insanity, if his or her act was the product of mental disease. The Durham test is not recognized in California.

element An essential component of a crime.

embezzlement The fraudulent appropriation of property by a person to whom it has been entrusted.

employment of minor to perform sexual acts Employment of a minor in the preparation of visual media or a live performance involving sexual conduct by the minor.

equal protection The constitutional requirement that the government accord equal treatment to persons similarly situated.

Establishment Clause The provision of the First Amendment to the United States Constitution that prohibits the government from establishing, sponsoring, or giving preference to any religion.

ex post facto law A law that makes illegal past acts that were legal at the time they were committed.

exclusionary rule A principle of law which provides that evidence that has been illegally obtained by law enforcement authorities may not be used against a defendant at trial or other hearing in a criminal case.

exclusive jurisdiction The authority of a government to legislate with respect to certain subjects to the exclusion of other governments, or the authority of a court to adjudicate certain types of cases to the exclusion of other courts.

extortion The crime committed by the obtaining of property from another, with his or her involuntary consent, or the obtaining of an official act of a public officer, induced by a wrongful use of force or fear, or under color of official right.

extradition The surrender of a person from one jurisdiction to another where the person has been charged with or convicted of a crime.

factual impossibility As applied to the crime of attempt, means that the act intended by the defendant is a crime, but the circumstances are such that the crime cannot successfully be committed. Factual impossibility is not a defense to the crime of attempt. For example, if John points a replica of a gun at Sue, thinking it is a real gun, and tries to shoot Sue with it, John can be convicted of attempted murder despite the fact that shooting Sue with a replica of a gun is not possible.

false imprisonment The unlawful violation of the personal liberty of another.

false pretenses The use of false representations of fact for the purpose of inducing another to transfer ownership of money or property, with the result that the person defrauded transfers ownership of the money or property.

federalism The governmental structure established by the United States Constitution, consisting of a central or federal government possessing limited powers and state governments possessing all powers not reserved exclusively to the federal government.

felony In California, a crime punishable by death or by imprisonment in the state prison.

felony-misdemeanor A crime that may be charged either as a felony or as a misdemeanor, in the discretion of the district attorney.

felony-murder doctrine The legal doctrine that an unintended or accidental killing caused by the perpetrator of a felony during the commission of the felony is murder. Felony murder may be of the first or second degree.

fighting words Speech that is not protected by the First Amendment because it creates a clear and present danger of provoking others to immediate violence.

fine A monetary penalty imposed on a defendant as punishment for a crime, which is payable to the court.

first-degree felony-murder A killing that occurs during the commission of those felonies specified in Penal Code § 189.

forcible and atrocious crime A concept applicable to the use of deadly force in self-defense. A forcible and atrocious crime is a felony, the character and manner of commission of which threatens, or is reasonably believed by the person against whom it is directed to threaten, life or great bodily injury, so as to instill in the person a reasonable fear of death or great bodily injury. One is legally authorized to use deadly force to defend oneself against commission of a forcible and atrocious crime.

forfeiture The seizure, destruction, or other disposition of real or personal property used in the commission of certain offenses, particularly drug offenses.

forgery The falsification of a document having legal significance or the uttering (use) of such a falsified document with intent to defraud.

fraudulent check The crime of writing or transferring a check to another with knowledge that insufficient funds exist in the account to cover the check, accompanied by the intent to fraudulently cause a person to part with money or property in reliance on the check.

Free Exercise Clause The provision of the First Amendment to the United States Constitution that prohibits the government from interfering with the free exercise of religion by individual citizens.

gag order   An order by the court restricting participants in the criminal proceeding from discussing specified aspects of the case with news media representatives.

grand jury   A body of the required number of persons drawn from the citizens of a county, before a court of competent jurisdiction, and sworn to inquire of public offenses committed or triable within the county.

gross vehicular manslaughter while intoxicated   The killing of a human being as the result of operation of a motor vehicle or a vessel with gross negligence while intoxicated.

habeas corpus   A writ issued by a court commanding that a defendant who is incarcerated or otherwise suffering a restraint of his or her liberty be brought before the court for the purpose of examining the lawfulness of the incarceration or restraint or the conditions of the incarceration or restraint.

harmless error   A trivial error committed by a trial court that is not likely to have changed the outcome of the case.

hate crime   A crime motivated by the victim's race, color, religion, ancestry, national origin, disability, gender, or sexual orientation.

held to answer   A term describing the contents of an order issued by a magistrate after a preliminary examination, requiring the defendant to respond to a formal accusatory pleading.

home detention   A modern sentencing alternative under which eligible persons may voluntarily agree to be confined at home rather than in the county jail. The program is limited to minimum-security inmates and low-risk offenders committed to a county jail or other county correctional facility or granted probation, or inmates participating in a work-furlough program.

hot pursuit   The substantially continuous pursuit of a fleeing felon or other dangerous criminal. During hot pursuit, the pursuing officers may enter a house or other structure without a warrant to search for and arrest the fleeing

person if they have a reasonable belief that he or she is inside.

hung jury   A jury that is unable, after sufficient deliberation, to vote unanimously either for conviction or for acquittal.

imperfect self-defense   A killing resulting from an honest but unreasonable belief that use of deadly force in self-defense is necessitated by the circumstances. Imperfect self-defense is a form of voluntary manslaughter.

incest   Sexual intercourse between related persons who are prohibited by law from marrying.

incitement to riot   The offense committed by a person who, with intent to cause a riot, urges a riot, or urges others to commit acts of force or violence, or burning or destroying of property, if the time, place, and circumstances are such as to produce a clear and present and immediate danger that the acts urged will be committed.

indecent exposure   The willful and lewd exposure of one's person or private parts in the presence of other persons, or the procuring, counseling, or assisting of another person to do so.

independent grounds doctrine   The legal principle providing that the California Constitution constitutes a basis for individual rights independent of the United States Constitution. Under the independent grounds doctrine, the California courts and legislature may accord rights to individuals which exceed the rights granted by the United States Constitution.

indeterminate sentence   A sentence to imprisonment that does not specify the exact amount of time to be served by the defendant. An indeterminate sentence always specifies the maximum period of confinement authorized, and sometimes specifies the minimum amount of time that must be served. An example of an indeterminate sentence would be a sentence of from twenty-five years to life in a noncapital first-degree murder case.

indictment   An accusation in writing, presented by the grand jury to a competent court, charging a person with a public offense.

infancy   A defense to crime based on age. Under California law, a person under the age of fourteen is presumed incapable of forming the mental state required to commit a crime. The presumption may be rebutted by a showing of clear proof that, at the time of committing the act, the child knew its wrongfulness.

inference   A conclusion that may be drawn by the finder of fact from the evidence presented at trial.

inferior court   In jurisdictions having more than one level of trial court, the lower level trial court. Usually a court of limited subject matter jurisdiction. In California, the municipal court is an inferior court.

information   An accusation in writing, presented by the district attorney to a competent court, charging a person with a public offense.

infraction   The least serious form of criminal offense in California. Infractions are not punishable by imprisonment. They are usually punished by imposition of a fine or a sentence to community service.

initial appearance   The appearance of an in custody defendant before a magistrate without unnecessary delay, and in no case longer than forty-eight hours after arrest. The purpose of the initial appearance is protection of the defendant's rights, specifically: to prevent unwarranted police interrogation, to make it possible for the defendant to be promptly advised of his or her right to counsel, to enable the defendant to obtain bail, and to have the issue of probable cause for his or her arrest determined by a judicial officer.

initiative   A procedure in California whereby the electorate may directly enact laws and amend the California Constitution.

injunction   A court order that a person or entity refrain from a specified act or course of conduct.

intentional   Purposefully done.

interpret   To determine or explain the meaning of.

interrogation   Questioning of a person suspected of committing a crime by law enforcement officials, for the purpose of eliciting incriminating information.

intoxication   As a defense to crime, intoxication is categorized as voluntary or involuntary. *Voluntary intoxication* involves the voluntary ingestion, injection, or taking by any other means of any intoxicating liquor, drug, or other substance. Intoxication is involuntary when it is produced in a person without his or her willing and knowing use of intoxicating liquor, drugs, or other substance, and without his or her willing assumption of the risk of possible intoxication. Voluntary and involuntary intoxication have differing legal effects as defenses to crimes.

inventory search   A routine inventorying of the contents of an impounded vehicle by law enforcement personnel. An inventory search does not require a warrant or probable cause.

involuntary manslaughter   The unlawful killing of a human being without malice as a result of criminal negligence, or during the commission of certain misdemeanors.

irresistible impulse   A defense to a criminal charge, which asserts that the defendant is not guilty of the crime because, although he knew the act was wrong, he was unable to control his behavior because of a disease of the mind. The irresistible impulse defense is not recognized in California.

jeopardy   In a criminal case, the danger of conviction and punishment to which a defendant is exposed when he is brought to trial.

joint possession   Simultaneous possession of one thing by two or more persons.

judicial review   The power of the judiciary to review actions of the legislative and executive branches and to declare acts that are in violation of the constitution void.

jurisdiction   The power to act with respect to a particular subject. The jurisdiction of a legislature is the power to legislate with respect to particular subjects. The jurisdiction of a court is the power to adjudicate particular types of cases.

Kelly-Frye rule A rule of procedure in California pertaining to the admissibility of novel types of scientific evidence. Under the Kelly-Frye rule, new types of scientific evidence are admissible only if the techniques used are generally accepted in the applicable scientific community. This determination is usually made through the testimony of expert witnesses, who must be properly qualified to give an opinion on the subject. Also, the proponent of the evidence must demonstrate that correct scientific procedures were used in the particular case.

kidnapping The unlawful restraint of the liberty of another person, coupled with asportation, or a carrying away, of the person which is more than slight or trivial and which is not merely incidental to the commission of another offense.

knowingly In California criminal law, a mental state involving knowledge on the part of the actor of the facts surrounding his or her act or omission which make the act or omission a crime. The actor need only know the facts; he or she need not know that they constitute a crime.

larceny A taking of personal property of some value belonging to another, without the consent of the owner or person entitled to possession, with a specific intent to permanently deprive the owner, or person entitled to possession, of the property.

legal impossibility A defense to the crime of attempt; means that the act attempted is not a crime, despite the belief of the actor that it is a crime.

legislative history Records of legislative proceedings from which the intent of the legislature in enacting a statute may be determined that provide a basis for determining the legislative intent underlying a statute.

lewd or lascivious act with a child A touching of any part of the body of a child under the age of fourteen with the specific intent to sexually arouse either the perpetrator or the child.

lineup An investigative technique in which a suspect is included in a group of people that is viewed by the victim or witness. The victim or witness is asked whether the perpetrator of the crime is in the group and, if so, to identify the perpetrator.

looting Second-degree burglary committed during a state of emergency resulting from an earthquake, fire, flood, riot, or other natural or manmade disaster.

magistrate A judicial officer having power to issue a warrant for the arrest of a person charged with a public offense. This power is held by justices of the California Supreme Court, justices of the courts of appeal, and judges of the superior and municipal courts.

malice In California criminal law, other than for the crime of murder, means a mental state that imports a wish to vex, annoy, or injure another person, or an intent to do a wrongful act. (See definition of *malice aforethought* for the malice element of the crime of murder.)

malice aforethought The mens rea (mental state) required for the crime of murder. According to Penal Code § 188, malice aforethought may be express or implied. It is express when the killer manifests a deliberate intent to kill. It is implied when no considerable provocation appears or when the circumstances attending the killing show an abandoned and malignant heart.

malum in se A crime involving an act that is inherently evil, such as murder, rape, arson, or mayhem.

malum prohibitum A crime involving an act or omission that is not inherently evil but has been declared criminal by a legislative enactment. Malum prohibitum crimes frequently involve acts that are prohibited (or failures to perform acts that are required) for reasons of public health, welfare, or safety.

manslaughter The unlawful killing of a human being without malice aforethought.

mayhem The crime of maiming or permanently disfiguring another.

mens rea A criminal mental state; a state of mind which, when joined with an act or omission prohibited by law, results in the commission of a crime.

merger of offenses The doctrine that when a lesser offense is a component of a more serious offense, and the defendant is convicted of the more serious offense, the lesser is absorbed by the greater, and the defendant is not punished for both.

misdemeanor Any crime that is less serious than a felony and more serious than an infraction. Misdemeanors are usually punishable by imprisonment in the county jail and/or a fine.

misdemeanor-manslaughter The legal doctrine that an unintended or accidental killing caused by the perpetrator of a misdemeanor during commission of the misdemeanor is manslaughter if: the misdemeanor is one inherently dangerous to human life, it is committed with criminal intent, and there is a causal connection between the commission of the misdemeanor and the death.

mistake As a defense to crime, the law distinguishes between mistake of law and mistake of fact. Ignorance of the law is never a defense. A mistaken belief that the law authorizes the act for which the defendant has been charged may constitute a defense if the offense is more than a general-intent crime and the mistake negates the mental state required for the offense. Mistake of fact may be a defense if the factual circumstances, as believed by the defendant, would mean that the act did not constitute a crime.

mistrial Termination of a trial by the judge before the trial's conclusion for some legally recognized reason.

mitigation Evidence regarding the circumstances of an offense or the criminal history of the defendant which supports imposition of a minimal sentence.

M'Naghten test The test for insanity used in the California criminal justice system to determine whether a defendant is not guilty by reason of insanity. The defense may be established only when the defendant proves by a preponderance of the evidence that he or she was incapable of knowing or understanding the nature and quality of his or her act or of distinguishing right from wrong at the time of commission of the offense.

Model Penal Code One of the uniform and model acts developed by the American Law Institute; does not constitute law unless enacted by a state legislature. California has not adopted the Model Penal Code.

Model Penal Code test A test for insanity under the Model Penal Code, which provides that a person is not responsible for criminal conduct if, at the time of such conduct, as a result of mental disease or defect, he or she lacked substantial capacity either to appreciate the criminality of his or her conduct or to conform his or her conduct to the requirements of law. The Model Penal Code test is not recognized in California.

motion for change of venue A motion made to change the location of a trial on the grounds that the defendant cannot receive a fair and impartial trial in the originally scheduled location or that all the jury panels in the originally scheduled location have been exhausted.

motion for judgment of acquittal A motion made by the defendant in a criminal trial requesting the court to enter a judgment of acquittal before the normal termination of the trial, because of failure of the prosecution to prove its case.

motion for new trial A motion made by a defendant requesting a new trial because of judicial error or misconduct of the prosecutor or jury that is sufficiently serious to have prejudiced the defendant's right to a fair trial.

motion in arrest of judgment A posttrial motion in which the defendant claims that the accusatory pleading upon which he or she was prosecuted is defective.

motion in limine A motion requesting the court to rule, prior to trial, that opposing counsel and witnesses are to be instructed not to make reference during the trial to inadmissible evidence specified in the motion.

motion to set aside A motion made by a defendant prior to trial requesting the court to set aside an indictment or information charging the defendant with a crime. The motion challenges the proceedings that produced the indictment or information rather than the form of the indictment or information itself.

motion to sever A motion made by a defendant requesting the court to order that he or she be tried separately from other defendants, or that one or more multiple charges against him or her be tried separately from other offenses with which he or she has been charged.

motion to suppress Technically known as a *motion to return property or suppress evidence,* a motion, made pursuant to Penal Code § 1538.5, that requests the court to exclude from admissibility at trial evidence that was illegally obtained by the government.

motive The reason for a person's act.

motor vehicle search A search of a motor vehicle that may be made without a warrant if the searching officer has probable cause to believe that an item subject to seizure is located in the vehicle.

mug-shot files Files maintained by law enforcement agencies of photographs of persons who have been arrested and booked.

municipal court The inferior trial court in the California judicial system. The municipal court is a court of limited jurisdiction (it can hear only those types of cases specifically authorized by law). For example, the municipal court may hear civil cases involving amounts in controversy of not more than $25,000. In criminal cases, the jurisdiction of the municipal court is limited to misdemeanor and infraction cases.

necessity A defense of limited applicability in California to acts that would otherwise be criminal but which are necessary to avoid a threat to human life imposed by natural forces.

negligence In California criminal law, a mental state involving a want of such attention to the nature or probable consequences of an act or omission as a prudent person ordinarily bestows in acting in his or her own concerns. To constitute the basis for criminal liability, negligence must generally be aggravated, culpable, gross, or reckless, that is, the conduct of the actor must be such a departure from what would be the conduct of an ordinarily prudent or careful person under the same circumstances as to be incompatible with a proper regard for human life or to signal an indifference to consequences. Generally, it is the failure of a person to act with the same degree of care that a reasonable person would exercise in the same or similar circumstances.

nolle prosequi A legal document filed by a prosecutor with a court by means of which the prosecutor discontinues criminal proceedings against a defendant.

nolo contendere A plea to a criminal charge which informs the court that the defendant, though not admitting guilt, does not intend to defend against the charge or charges in the accusatory pleading.

notice to appear Frequently referred to as a *citation;* a written notice given to a person arrested for a misdemeanor that states the name and address of the person, the offense charged, and the time and place at which the person must appear in court.

objection An assertion made by a party in a trial that the conduct of the other party is improper, that evidence offered by the other party is inadmissible, or that some other occurrence in the trial is not in accordance with law.

obscene matter As defined in Penal Code § 311, matter, taken as a whole, which to the average person, applying contemporary statewide standards, appeals to the prurient interest, and is matter which, taken as a whole, depicts or describes in a patently offensive way sexual conduct; and which, taken as a whole, lacks serious literary, artistic, political, or scientific value.

omission A failure to act or to do what is required by law.

open fields Areas around the home that are outside the curtilage. One does not have a reasonable expectation of privacy in these areas, and they are not protected by the United States or California Constitutions from government searches.

oral copulation   As a criminal offense, the act of copulating the mouth of one person with the sexual organ or anus of another person.

order to show cause   An order of a court requiring a party to establish grounds why an action contemplated by the court should not be taken.

ordinances   Written laws of a political entity below the state level, such as a county or city.

overbreadth doctrine   A principle of constitutional law which provides that a statute is unconstitutional if, in addition to regulating conduct the government may constitutionally regulate, it attempts to regulate activity that the government may not constitutionally regulate.

overt act   A necessary element of the crime of conspiracy; an act committed by one of the conspirators within the state of California in furtherance of the conspirators' agreement. An agreement to commit a crime, if not followed by an overt act in furtherance of the agreement, does not amount to a conspiracy.

pandering   The crime of causing another person to become a prostitute.

pardon   A form of executive clemency consisting of a complete cancellation of the punishment to which a defendant has been sentenced.

parental kidnapping   The taking or concealing of a child by a parent with the malicious intent to deprive the other parent of the right to custody or visitation.

parole   The conditional release of a defendant from imprisonment.

peace officer   In California, a person having authority to enforce the law; a law enforcement officer.

peremptory challenge   A challenge to a prospective juror which requires no grounds.

perjury   The crime involving the willful making of a material statement under oath or penalty of perjury that the maker of the statement knows to be false, with the specific intent to make the false statement under oath or penalty of perjury.

petition for review   A petition filed by an appellant with the California Supreme Court requesting that the court review the decision of a lower appellate court. The California Supreme Court may grant or deny the petition as a matter of discretion.

pimping   The crime of knowingly deriving economic benefit from acts of prostitution committed by another person.

plain feel doctrine   The legal principle holding that an officer conducting a pat-down for weapons during a stop and frisk may seize contraband that he or she feels inside the detained person's clothing if the nature of the object as contraband is immediately apparent, that is, is apparent without further intrusion into the clothing of the detained person or manipulation of the object through the clothing of the detained person.

plain view doctrine   A principle of the law of search and seizure that permits a law enforcement officer to seize evidence without a search warrant if the evidence is in plain view from a place where the officer has a legal right to be.

plea   A defendant's formal answer to charges in an accusatory pleading.

plea bargain   An agreement between the defendant and the prosecutor, which is subject to approval by the court, that the prosecutor will dismiss a more serious charge if the defendant will plead guilty to a lesser charge, or that the defendant will receive a sentence no more severe than specified in the agreement if the defendant will plead guilty to the charged offense.

police power   The power of a government to enact laws to protect the health, safety, and welfare of its citizens.

polling the jury   Questioning of each individual juror after the verdict is announced to assure that the verdict is his or her verdict.

precedent   A legal principle developed or followed by an appellate court when deciding an issue that will be followed in future cases involving the same issue.

preemption   The doctrine that once Congress has enacted on a subject, a state may not enact a legislation on the same subject.

prejudicial error   An error committed by a trial court that is sufficiently serious to have been likely to have changed the outcome of the case.

preliminary examination   A hearing conducted before a magistrate in the municipal court in a felony case at which evidence is presented by the prosecution for the purpose of establishing probable cause to believe that an offense has been committed and that the defendant committed it. The defendant is entitled to be present and to present evidence on his or her behalf. A preliminary examination is required if the prosecution intends to formally charge the defendant by information.

premeditation   As an element of the crime of first-degree murder, means preexisting reflection.

presentence investigation report   A report prepared by a probation officer for use by the court in determining the sentence to impose on a defendant. The report considers the circumstances surrounding the crime and the prior history and record of the defendant.

presumption   A rule of law that accords probative value to certain facts in evidence or mandates a specific inference as to the existence of a fact; a conclusion that must be drawn. May be rebuttable or irrebuttable.

principal   A person involved in the commission of a crime. Such involvement may include: (1) directly committing the offense (formerly, a principal in the first degree); (2) aiding and abetting the person directly committing the offense while present at the scene of the crime (formerly, a principal in the second degree); or (3) advising or encouraging the commission of the crime, usually prior to actual commission of the crime (formerly, an accessory before the fact).

probable cause   In the law of search, seizure, and arrest, a basis for believing that seizable property will be found in a particular location or that a particular person committed a crime, which is founded upon facts that are sufficiently reliable that a person of ordinary caution would be justified in believing them.

probation   Suspension of the imposition or execution of a sentence and an order of conditional and revocable release of the defendant in the community under the supervision of a probation officer.

procedural due process   The constitutional requirement that any procedure used by the government to deprive a person of life, liberty, or property must be fair and reasonable and must, at a minimum, afford the affected person advance notice of the intended adverse action and a reasonable opportunity to be heard on the matter before a governmental decision is made.

promise to appear   A written promise to appear before a magistrate signed by a person arrested for an infraction.

prostitution   Any lewd act between persons for money or other consideration.

protective sweep   A limited search of the interior of a building for the purpose of discovering the presence of dangerous persons who might constitute a threat to law enforcement officers who are conducting the arrest of a person within the building.

proximate cause   The legal principle that limits the criminal liability of a person for remote or unforeseeable results of his or her acts or omissions, and holds the person accountable only for foreseeable results not produced by independent causes.

public defender   An attorney employed by a county to represent indigent defendants prosecuted in the courts situated in that county.

public intoxication   The offense committed by one who is found in any public place under the influence of intoxicating liquor, any drug, controlled substance, toluene, or any combination of the foregoing, in such a condition that he or she is unable to exercise care for his or her own safety or the safety of others, or who, by reason of his or her being under the influence of any of the foregoing substances, interferes with or obstructs or prevents the free use of any street, sidewalk, or other public way.

punitive damages A monetary sum awarded to a successful plaintiff in a civil lawsuit over and above compensatory damages; designed to punish the defendant for the wrong done. Punitive damages are usually awarded only in tort cases in which the defendant intentionally committed the wrong complained of by the plaintiff.

rape Sexual intercourse with a person not the spouse of the perpetrator committed without such person's legally effective consent.

rape shield laws Provisions of the California Evidence Code that limit the admissibility at a sex crime trial of evidence of the victim's past sexual conduct, or opinion or reputation evidence concerning the victim's sexual habits, for the purpose of attacking the victim's credibility or establishing that the victim consented to the sexual act constituting the offense.

receiving stolen property The crime committed by one who buys or receives stolen property, or conceals, sells, withholds, or aids in concealing, selling, or withholding stolen property, with actual knowledge that the property is stolen.

recklessly In California criminal law, a mental state in which a person is aware of and consciously disregards a substantial and unjustifiable risk that his or her act will cause harm to another person or property. The risk must be of such a nature and degree that disregard thereof constitutes a gross deviation from the standard of conduct that a reasonable person would observe in the situation.

record on appeal The record of proceedings in a lower court transmitted by the clerk of the court to an appellate court when the case has been appealed.

referendum A procedure in California whereby the electorate may annul or approve legislation enacted by the legislature.

registration The requirement that persons convicted of certain sex, drug, and arson crimes register with the police in their municipality or the sheriff of the county in which they reside.

regulations Legislative enactments of administrative agencies.

remand The requirement by an appellate court that a lower court take further action in a case.

remittitur The transmittal of the decision of an appellate court to the lower court from which the case was appealed.

reporter's transcript Part of the record on appeal, consisting of transcriptions of oral proceedings in the lower court that were stenographically recorded by the court reporter.

reprieve A form of executive clemency consisting of postponement of execution of a sentence.

resisting arrest The crime of resisting arrest by a peace officer under circumstances in which the arrested person knows or should know that the arresting person is a peace officer. In California, a person does not have the right to resist arrest by a peace officer, even if the person believes that the arrest is in error.

respondent The party responding to an appeal or other court proceeding brought by another party.

restitution Compensation a defendant is ordered to pay directly to the victim of his or her crime to compensate the victim for monetary loss sustained as a result of the crime.

restitution fine A monetary penalty imposed on a defendant as punishment for a crime, which is payable to the state Restitution Fund.

Restitution Fund A fund maintained by the state to compensate victims of crimes for unreimbursed economic losses caused by the crimes.

return A term having several meanings in the field of criminal procedure. In the context of a habeas corpus proceeding, a *return* is a response by the official responsible for the incarceration or other restraint of the petitioner to the allegations made in the petition for writ of habeas corpus.

reverse The decision of an appellate court overturning the decision of a lower court.

right of allocution The right of a defendant, before pronouncement of judgment, to show cause why judgment should not be pronounced against him or her.

right of privacy The constitutional right of the individual to be free from unwarranted governmental intrusion into his or her private life. The right to privacy is not specifically enumerated in the United States Constitution, but emanates from the penumbras of other specifically enumerated constitutional rights.

riot The crime involving any use of force or violence, disturbing the public peace, or any threat to use force or violence, if accompanied by immediate power of execution, by two or more persons acting together, and without authority of law.

robbery The felonious taking of personal property in the possession of another, from his or her person or immediate presence, and against his or her will, accomplished by means of force or fear.

rout The offense committed whenever two or more persons, assembled and acting together, make any attempt or advance toward the commission of an act which would be a riot if actually committed.

rules of court Rules promulgated both at the state level and by individual courts establishing court procedures.

scienter Knowledge that the act one is committing is legally or morally wrong.

search Governmental infringement of a person's reasonable expectation of privacy.

search incident to arrest A search of a person being arrested, and of the area within the person's immediate control, for weapons and destructible evidence. A search incident to arrest does not require probable cause.

search warrant An order in writing, in the name of the people, signed by a magistrate, directed to a peace officer, commanding him or her to search for personal property and bring it before the magistrate.

second-degree felony-murder A killing that occurs during the commission of a felony not enumerated in Penal Code § 189. The felony must be inherently dangerous to human life.

seduction of minor Distributing or exhibiting obscene matter to a minor with the dual intent of sexually arousing the perpetrator or the minor and of seducing the minor.

seizure A meaningful interference with an individual's possessory interest in property.

self-incrimination Testimony by a defendant or other witness constituting evidence that he or she committed a crime. Under the United States and California Constitutions, a person may not be compelled to give such testimony, with one exception: a witness may be compelled to give self-incriminating testimony if he or she has been granted immunity from prosecution.

sentence enhancement An additional term of imprisonment required or authorized by law under certain specified circumstances. Those circumstances generally involve an aggravating factor in the commission of the offense or the prior criminal history of the defendant.

separation of powers A division of power within a government and an allocation of specific powers to designated branches of the government. Thus, the legislative branch is given exclusive power to enact laws, the executive branch is given exclusive power to administer and enforce the law, and the judicial branch is given exclusive power to hear and determine cases and controversies.

sequestration order An order by the trial judge that the jury be kept in custody between court sessions.

sexual exploitation of a child The creation or exchanging of any photograph or other visual media depicting a child under the age of eighteen engaged in an act of sexual conduct.

showup An investigative technique in which the victim or witness is asked to observe the suspect alone and then to indicate whether the suspect is the person who committed the crime under investigation.

sidebar A discussion during a trial among the attorneys and judge, conducted outside the hearing of the jury.

simple kidnapping Kidnapping without the specific intent to commit enumerated crimes necessary to make the offense aggravated kidnapping.

simulated lineup A photograph of a lineup of individuals, which is shown to a victim or witness to determine whether the offender is among the persons photographed.

sodomy As a criminal offense, sexual conduct consisting of contact between the penis of one person and the anus of another person. Formerly referred to as "the infamous crime against nature" and "buggery."

solicitation The crime of encouraging, requesting, or commanding of another person to commit a crime.

solicitation of perjury The crime committed by one who, with intent that perjury be committed, solicits another to commit perjury. If the person solicited actually commits perjury, the solicitor becomes guilty of subornation of perjury, a more serious offense.

solicitation of prostitution The crime committed by one who offers to buy or sell sexual services.

special circumstances Circumstances enumerated in Penal Code § 190.2 which, if found by the jury to exist in a first-degree murder case, warrant imposition of the death penalty.

spousal rape Sexual intercourse with one's spouse committed without the spouse's legally effective consent.

stalking The willful, malicious, and repeated following or harassing of another accompanied by a credible threat with the intent to place the person in reasonable fear for his or her safety or the safety of his or her immediate family.

stare decisis An attribute of appellate court decisions in common-law legal systems which requires that the legal principles developed by an appellate court are to be followed by the same court and lower courts within its jurisdiction in later cases.

statutes Laws enacted by the United States Congress and state legislatures.

statutes of limitation Statutorily prescribed time limits within which prosecution for a crime must be commenced.

stop and frisk The police practice of temporarily detaining a person suspected of criminal activity (*stop*) accompanied by a pat-down of the person's outer clothing to detect the presence of weapons (*frisk*). To be lawful, the stop must be supported by a reasonable suspicion that the person has committed, is committing, or is about to commit a crime. The frisk is lawful only if the detaining officer has a reasonable belief that the person is armed and dangerous.

strict liability Liability imposed regardless of fault, intent, or negligence; absolute liability.

subornation of perjury The offense involving the willful procuring of another to commit perjury. The person procured must actually commit perjury for the procuring person to be guilty of subornation of perjury.

substantive due process The constitutional requirement that laws enacted by the government which may have the effect of depriving a person of life, liberty, or property must constitute a reasonable exercise of governmental power. If a person is deprived of life, liberty, or property on the basis of a law that is unreasonable or arbitrary, the deprivation constitutes a violation of substantive due process.

summons A command directed to an individual ordering him or her to appear before the magistrate. A summons may be used in lieu of an arrest warrant, subject to limitations specified in the Penal Code.

superior court The principal trial court in the California judicial system. The superior court is a court of general jurisdiction (it can hear all types of cases except as otherwise provided by law). There is one superior court in each California county. There may be several branches of the court within the county.

terrorizing A group of criminal offenses directed at persons because of race, religion, or other protected classification, which involve acts that would place reasonable persons in fear for their personal safety.

threat A criminal offense involving the making of a threat to commit a crime that will result in death or great bodily injury under circumstances that cause the person threatened to reasonably be in sustained fear for his or her safety or the safety of his or her immediate family.

tolling Exclusion of time from computation of a period prescribed by a statute of limitation.

tort A civil wrong involving a breach of duty imposed by law, in contrast to a breach of duty under a contract.

torture The crime of infliction of great bodily injury with the intent to cause cruel or extreme pain and suffering for the purpose of revenge, extortion, persuasion, or for any sadistic purpose.

totality of the circumstances test The test currently used by courts when determining whether information received from an informant by law enforcement officers is sufficient to support a determination that probable cause exists to issue a search warrant or arrest warrant.

transactional immunity Immunity that shields a witness from prosecution for the offense about which he or she is compelled to testify, even if the prosecution has independent evidence against the witness.

transferred intent A legal principle which holds that when one acts intending to harm a specific person, but instead harms another person, the actor will be deemed to have intended to harm the person actually injured.

trial court The level of court in which civil lawsuits and criminal cases are initially adjudicated based on the presentation of evidence and the determination of the case by a judge or jury.

"Truth in Evidence" The name given to a provision of Article I, § 28, of the California Constitution which provides that "relevant evidence is not to be excluded from criminal proceedings." The effect of this provision is to limit the application of the exclusionary rule in the California courts to evidence that is excludable under federal constitutional principles.

unlawful assembly The crime committed when two or more persons assemble together to do an unlawful act, or to do a lawful act in a violent, boisterous, or tumultuous manner.

unlawful sexual intercourse An act of sexual intercourse with a minor who is not the spouse of the perpetrator; called *statutory rape* in some jurisdictions.

unlawfully causing a fire The offense committed by one who recklessly sets fire to, burns, or causes to be burned any structure, forest land, or property. The offense is less serious than arson, which involves willful and malicious burning.

use immunity A form of immunity, more limited than transactional immunity, that prohibits the government from using a witness's testimony or any evidence derived from that testimony to prosecute the witness. However, all evidence that is independently obtained may be used against the witness.

vagueness doctrine A principle of constitutional law which provides that a statute is constitutionally invalid if it is so ambiguous that it fails to put citizens on notice of the act that it mandates or prohibits.

vandalism The crime committed by one who maliciously defaces, with graffiti or other inscribed material, damages, or destroys the property of another.

vehicular manslaughter The killing of a human being resulting from the operation of a motor vehicle in one of the following circumstances: (1) with gross negligence; (2) with simple negligence; (3) with simple negligence while under the influence of alcohol or drugs.

vicarious liability Criminal liability imposed on a person for an act or omission of another person.

voiceprint An analysis of the complex sound waves of a person's voice for the purpose of comparing the voice with a voice on a recording, such as an answering-machine tape. Presently, voiceprint evidence is inadmissible in a criminal trial because its reliability has not yet been sufficiently demonstrated.

voir dire The questioning of prospective jurors for the purpose of determining whether any are disqualified from serving or are biased in a manner that would deprive the defendant of a fair trial.

voluntary manslaughter The unlawful killing of a human being without malice, upon a sudden quarrel or heat of passion.

voluntary withdrawal As applied to the crime of attempt, means voluntary cessation of the criminal act by the defendant before the crime is completed. If the defendant's acts have reached the point at which they constitute an attempt, voluntary withdrawal thereafter is not a defense.

washout provision A provision stating that a sentence enhancement does not apply if a specified period of years has passed since the prior conviction or prison term which is the basis for the enhancement.

Wharton's Rule The legal principle applicable to the crime of conspiracy which provides that if an offense requires two persons for its commission, and only two defendants are involved, they cannot be charged with conspiracy to commit the offense, although they may be charged with commission of the offense itself.

willfully In California criminal law, a mental state that implies simply a purpose or willingness to commit the act or to make the omission referred to. It does not require any intent to violate the law, or to injure another, or to acquire any advantage.

work furlough An arrangement under which county jail prisoners reside in jail, but may leave to work or attend an educational program.

writ An order issued by a court to a public official ordering the official to do or refrain from doing a particular act.

INDEX

1538.5 motion. *See* motion to suppress

WELCOME

Welcome to the *1998 California Penal Code Compact Edition* on CD-ROM. This CD uses Adobe® Acrobat® Reader to display the text of the Penal Code and Accompanying Provisions. If you do not already have Acrobat Reader Version 3.0 or later installed on your system, then you need to follow the installation instructions below.

If you already have Acrobat Reader installed, then start Acrobat Reader and open the file CAPENAL.PDF on the CD-ROM. Insert the CD-ROM into your drive. Select **Open...** from the **File** menu in Reader. Navigate to your CD-ROM drive (typically, this is drive D:\). Select the file TOC.PDF. Click **Open.**

Installing Adobe Acrobat Reader

Windows 95 Users:

- Insert the *California Penal Code Compact Edition CD-ROM* into your CD drive.
- Select **Run...** from the **Start** menu.
- Type D:\ACROREAD\32BIT\SETUP.EXE, where D: is your CD-ROM drive letter.
- Click OK. Follow the on-screen instructions.
- After installation, start Acrobat Reader and open the file CAPENAL.PDF on the CD-ROM.

Windows 3.1 Users:

- Insert the *California Penal Code Compact Edition CD-ROM* into your CD drive.
- Select **Run...** from the **File** menu in the Program Manager.
- Type D:\ACROREAD\16BIT\SETUP.EXE, where D: is your CD-ROM drive letter.
- Click OK. Follow the on-screen instructions.
- After installation, start Acrobat Reader and open the file CAPENAL.PDF on the CD-ROM.